Anonymous

The Book of Praise

Or, hymns and tunes for public and social worship

Anonymous

The Book of Praise
Or, hymns and tunes for public and social worship

ISBN/EAN: 9783337290344

Printed in Europe, USA, Canada, Australia, Japan

Cover: Foto ©Thomas Meinert / pixelio.de

More available books at **www.hansebooks.com**

THE

BOOK OF PRAISE

OR

HYMNS AND TUNES

FOR PUBLIC AND SOCIAL WORSHIP.

PREPARED UNDER THE SANCTION AND AUTHORITY, AND IN BEHALF OF THE GENERAL
ASSOCIATION OF CONNECTICUT.

HARTFORD:
HAMERSLEY & CO.
PHILADELPHIA: J. B. LIPPINCOTT & CO.
1871.

Entered, according to Act of Congress, in the year 1868, by
W. T. EUSTIS, JR., EDWIN P. PARKER, M. M. G. DANA, H. N. DUNNING, and L. L. PAINE,
For the General Association of Connecticut,
In the Clerk's Office of the District Court of the District of Connecticut.

Manufactured by
CASE, LOCKWOOD & BRAINARD,
HARTFORD, CONN.

The General Association of Connecticut, constrained by a demand from many quarters for a more satisfactory book of praise, passed a resolution instructing and authorizing a committee of five pastors — namely, W. T. Eustis, Jr., E. P. Parker, M. M. G. Dana, H. N. Dunning, and L. L. Paine — to prepare and publish, in their behalf, a new Hymn and Tune Book.

Thus instructed and authorized, the Committee immediately set themselves to perform the work given into their hands, striving to fulfil both the letter and the spirit of the commission they had received, not in their own wisdom merely, but relying on the guidance of the Spirit of all wisdom and grace, and seeking, also, the suggestions and assistance of many of their brethren in the churches.

This "Book of Praise" they now offer to the General Association of Connecticut, and to all the churches of Christ in the land, as the fruit of their long and arduous labors.

In the selection of hymns from various sources, in the delicate work of deciding between different readings of well-known hymns, and in the adoption of a plan of arrangement, they have not proceeded without the most careful research and deliberation.

The division of the book into several distinct sections, each of which is prefaced by a summary statement of its contents, together with the index of sections which faces the first page of hymns, will, it is believed, greatly assist the readers in becoming speedily familiar with the entire book, and also in readily finding hymns suited to any given topic.

Here and there a hymn may be found which seems to be arbitrarily located. While a few such instances were unavoidable under the present plan of arrangement, they are quite unimportant as compared with its many and decided advantages.

In the selection of hymns, the chief aim has been to make the book, what its name imports, a Book of Praise. Hymns that throb with a warm spiritual life, — devotional rather than didactic, — that bear the soul upward toward God and Christ and heaven, "on devotion's lofty wing," and in which, as in the Psalms of David, the worshipping spirit delights to pour out and offer up the sacrifices of praise, have been chiefly sought. Watts and Charles Wesley are the principal contributors to this collection. While there are very few *new* hymns in this book (and these, for the most part, from the pen that wrote "My faith looks up to thee"), there are not a few of rare merit and beauty, which have never been published in any similar collection.

With respect to the "alterations" of hymns, suffice it to say that the hymns in this book have been faithfully compared with their original forms, so far as such comparisons were possible; and the original readings have been faithfully adhered to, except where hymns have been manifestly improved by alterations which usage has sanctioned. That this rule of criticism is indefinite, and leaves the door still open to errors and abuses, the editors are well aware. If in the application of the rule their judgments have been sometimes in fault, it will be to them less a matter of wonder than of regret. For some unusually sensible remarks upon this whole subject of hymn-mending, the reader is commended to a most delightful book by the Rev. S.

Preface.

W. Christophers (London: S. W. Partridge. New York: A. D. F. Randolph), entitled, "Hymn-Writers and their Hymns."

With regard to the music of this collection, the editors have endeavored to select tunes which would render congregational singing practicable, profitable, and pleasant, — avoiding the extremes of *commonplace* music on the one hand, and of too *difficult* music on the other.

To Dr. Ray Palmer, for permission to use many of his valuable hymns, and for his kindness in contributing several new and beautiful compositions for this work, thanks are most cordially rendered.

Many of the tunes in this book are the property of American authors or publishers, and are herein used by their permission. Among those from whom, by special arrangement, valuable tunes and hymns have been obtained, may be named, Messrs. Barnes & Burr, Messrs. Mason Bros., Mr. John Wiley, Mr. S. T. Gordon, Dr. Thomas Hastings, Mr. Asa Hull, Mr. George Kingsley, Mr. George F. Root, and Oliver Ditson & Co.

To those who have contributed either hymns or music to these pages, and to all who, in any way, have assisted in the preparation of this work, — and more particularly to Rev. T. J. Holmes, Mr. E. P. H. Thompson, and Dudley Buck, Jr., organist of the Park Church in Hartford, — the editors tender their grateful acknowledgments.

The rest of the Committee would express their own obligation to the Rev. E. P. Parker for the indefatigable zeal and energy which he has exhibited in the preparation and publication of this "Book of Praise." To him the churches are chiefly indebted for the completeness of this new aid to devotion.

The editors would present their completed task to the General Association of Connecticut, and to the churches of our common faith throughout the land, in the hope and prayer that it may prove a means of spiritual peace and comfort to many souls, a useful and profitable manual of devotion in the services of the sanctuary, and so an acceptable offering unto the Lord.

                W. T. EUSTIS, Jr.,
                EDWIN P. PARKER,
                M. M. G. DANA,
                H. N. DUNNING,
                L. L. PAINE.

HARTFORD, April, 1868.

TABLE OF CONTENTS.

SECTION I.   PAGE 1.
SELECTIONS FOR CHANTING OR READING, FROM THE PSALMS, THE PROPHETS, AND THE NEW TESTAMENT.
Also, the "Gloria in Excelsis," the "Te Deum Laudamus," and other Hymns, both Ancient and Modern, the Nicene and Apostles' Creeds, the Commandments, and Doxologies in Various Metres.

SECTION II.   PAGE 47.
PUBLIC WORSHIP.
The Lord's Day and House. — Opening and Closing of Worship.

SECTION III.   PAGE 78.
HOLY SCRIPTURES.

SECTION IV.   PAGE 85.
GOD THE FATHER, SON, AND HOLY GHOST.
Birth, Passion, Ressurection, etc., of Christ.

SECTION V.   PAGE 135.
SALVATION BY CHRIST.
Depravity. — Regeneration. — Atonement. — Gospel Call. — Repentance and Faith.

SECTION VI.   PAGE 183.
THE CHRISTIAN LIFE.
Hymns looking Godward. — Hymns looking unto Jesus. — Songs in the Night. — Songs by the Way. — Graces and Duties. — Prayer.

SECTION VII.   PAGE 289.
THE CHURCH OF CHRIST.
The Foundation, Glory, and Edification of the Church. — Lord's Supper. — Baptism. — The Ministry. — Ordination, Installation, Dedication Hymns. — The Spread of the Gospel.

SECTION VIII.   PAGE 325.
MORTALITY AND IMMORTALITY.
Brevity of Life. — Death. — Resurrection. — Judgment. — Eternity. — Heaven. — Funeral Hymns.

SECTION IX.   PAGE 361.
MISCELLANEOUS HYMNS.
New Year. — Fasts. — Thanksgivings. — Seamen. — Temperance. — National Blessings.

INDEXES.

SELECTIONS FOR CHANTING.

No. 1.

1.
       Matt. 6: 9.

1 { Our Father which art in heaven, hallowed | *be thy name;*
 { Thy kingdom come, thy will be done in | *earth as it is in heaven.*

2 { Give us this day our | *daily bread;*
 { And forgive us our debts as | *we forgive our debtors.*

3 { And lead us not into temptation, but deliver | *us from evil;*
 { For thine is the kingdom, and the power, and the | *glory, forever.* Amen.

1 { Oh, praise the Father, | *praise the Son,*
 { The | *Lamb for sinners given,*

2 { And Holy Ghost, through | *whom alone*
 { Our | *souls are raised to heaven.*

1 { Glory be to the Father, and | *to the Son,*
 { And | *to the Holy Ghost:*

2 { As it was in the beginning, is now, and | *ever shall be,*
 { World | *without end.* Amen.

No. 2.   *GLORIA TIBI.*

Glo - ry!   Glo - ry!   Glo - ry   be   to   thee,   O   Lord.

No. 3.   GREGORIAN.

2.   Psalm 1.
1. { Blessed is the man that walketh not in the counsel | *of the ungodly,*
   { Nor standeth in the way of sinners, nor sitteth in the | *seat - of the scornful.*
2. { But his delight is in the | *law of the Lord ;*
   { And in his law doth he | *meditate day and night.*
3. { And he shall be like a tree planted by the rivers of water that bringeth forth his | *fruit in his season ;*
   { His leaf also shall not wither, and whatsoever he | *do - eth shall prosper.*
4. { The ungodly | *are not so :*
   { But like the chaff which the | *wind -.driveth away.*
5. { Therefore the ungodly shall not | *stand in the judgment,*
   { Nor sinners in the congre | *gation of the righteous.*
6. { For the Lord knoweth the | *way of the righteous ;*
   { But the way of the un | *god - ly shall perish.*

3.   Psalm 8.
1. { O Lord our Lord, how excellent is thy name in | *all the earth !*
   { Who hast set thy | *glory above the heavens.*
2. { Out of the mouth of babes and sucklings hast thou ordained strength be | *cause of thine enemies,*
   { That thou mightest still the | *ene - my and the avenger.*
3. { When I consider thy heavens, the | *work of thy fingers ;*
   { The moon and the stars | *which thou hast ordained ;*
4. { What is man, that thou art | *mindful of him ?*
   { And the son of man | *that thou visitest him ?*
5. { For thou hast made him a little lower | *than the angels,*
   { And hast crowned | *him with glory and honor.*
6. { Thou madest him to have dominion over the | *works of thy hands :*
   { Thou hast put all | *things beneath his feet :*
7. { All | *sheep and oxen,*
   { Yea, and the | *beasts of the field :*
8. { The fowl of the air, and the | *fish of the sea,*
   { And whatsoever passeth | *through the paths of the seas.*

[9 O Lord our Lord, how excellent is thy name in all the earth !]

Note.—Omit last verse in chanting, and close with the "Gloria Patri."

Chants. 3

4.   Psalm 19.

1 { THE heavens declare the glory of God, and the firmament sheweth his | *handy work.*
    Day unto day uttereth speech, and night unto | *night - sheweth knowledge.*

2 { There is no speech nor language where their | *voice is not heard.*
    Their line is gone out through all the earth, and their | *words to the end of the world.*

3 { The law of the Lord is perfect, con | *verting the soul:*
    The testimony of the Lord is sure, | *making wise the simple.*

4 { The statutes of the Lord are right, re | *joicing the heart:*
    The commandment of the Lord is pure, en | *lightening the eyes.*

5 { The fear of the Lord is clean, en | *during forever:*
    The judgments of the Lord are true and | *righteous altogether.*

6 { More to be desired are they than gold, yea, than | *much fine gold;*
    Sweeter also than | *honey and the honey-comb.*

7 { Moreover, by them is thy | *servant warned;*
    And in keeping of | *them is great reward.*

8 { Who can under | *stand his errors;*
    Cleanse thou | *me from secret faults.*

9 { Keep back thy servant also from presumptuous sins: let them not have do | *minion over me;*
    Then shall I be upright, and I shall be innocent | *from the great transgression.*

10 { Let the words of my mouth, and the meditation | *of my heart,*
    Be acceptable in thy sight, O Lord, my | *strength and my redeemer.*

No. 4.

5.   Psalm 23.

1 { THE Lord is my Shepherd, I | *shall not want.*
    He maketh me to lie down in green pastures, he leadeth me beside the | *still - waters.*

2 { He restoreth my soul, he leadeth me in the paths of righteousness for his | *name's - sake.*
    Yea, though I walk through the valley of the shadow of death, I will fear no evil, for thou art with me, thy rod and thy | *staff they comfort me.*

3 { Thou preparest a table before me in the presence of mine enemies: thou anointest my head with oil: my | *cup runneth over.*
    Surely goodness and mercy shall follow me all the days of my life: and I will dwell in the house of the | *Lord forever.   Amen.*

Chants.

No. 5.   DR. HAYES.

6.   Psalm 24.

1 { The earth is the Lord's, and the | *fulness thereof;*
    The world, and | *they that dwell therein.*

2 { For he hath founded it up | *on the seas,*
    And established | *it upon the floods.*

3 { Who shall ascend into the | *hill of the Lord?*
    And who shall stand | *in his holy place?*

4 { He that hath clean hands and | *a pure heart;*
    Who hath not lifted up his soul unto vanity, nor | *sworn deceitfully.*

5 { He shall receive the blessing | *from the Lord;*
    And righteousness from the | *God of his salvation.*

6 { Lift up your heads, | *O ye gates;*
    And be ye lift up, ye everlasting doors; and the King of | *glory shall come in.*

7 { Who is this | *King of glory?*
    The Lord strong and mighty, the | *Lord mighty in battle.*

8 { Lift up your heads, | *O ye gates;*
    Even lift them up, ye everlasting doors; and the King of | *glory shall come in.*

9 { Who is this | *King of glory?*
    The Lord of hosts, he | *is the King of glory.*

7.   Psalm 25.

1 { Unto thee, O Lord, do I lift | *up my soul;*
    Shew me thy ways, O | *Lord, teach me thy paths.*

2 { Lead me in thy truth and | *teach - me;*
    For thou art the God of my salvation; on thee do | *I wait all the day.*

3 { Remember, O Lord, thy tender mercies, and | *loving kindnesses;*
    For they have been | *ever of - old.*

4 { Remember not the sins of my youth, nor | *my transgressions;*
    According to thy mercy remember thou me for thy | *goodness' sake, O Lord.*

5 { Good and upright | *is the Lord:*
    Therefore will he teach | *sinners in the way.*

6 { The meek will he | *guide in judgment;*
    And the | *meek will he teach his way.*

7 { All the paths of the Lord are | *mercy and truth*
    Unto such as keep his | *covenant and his testimonies.*

{ Glory be to the Father, and | *to the Son,*
  And | *to the Holy Ghost:*

{ As it was in the beginning, is now, and | *ever shall be,*
  World | *without end.   Amen.*

Chants. 5

No. 6.

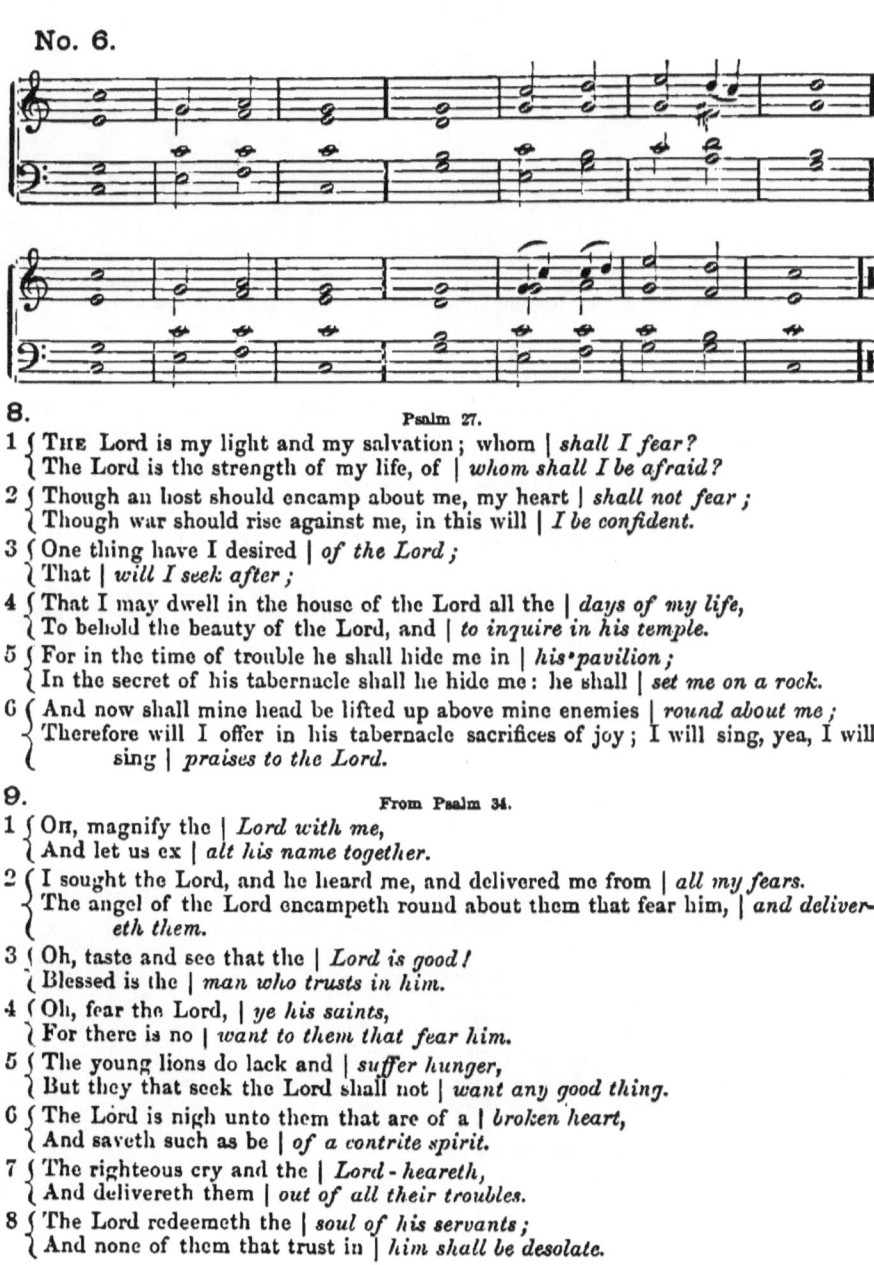

8.   Psalm 27.

1 { The Lord is my light and my salvation; whom | *shall I fear?*
    The Lord is the strength of my life, of | *whom shall I be afraid?*

2 { Though an host should encamp about me, my heart | *shall not fear;*
    Though war should rise against me, in this will | *I be confident.*

3 { One thing have I desired | *of the Lord;*
    That | *will I seek after;*

4 { That I may dwell in the house of the Lord all the | *days of my life,*
    To behold the beauty of the Lord, and | *to inquire in his temple.*

5 { For in the time of trouble he shall hide me in | *his pavilion;*
    In the secret of his tabernacle shall he hide me: he shall | *set me on a rock.*

6 { And now shall mine head be lifted up above mine enemies | *round about me;*
    Therefore will I offer in his tabernacle sacrifices of joy; I will sing, yea, I will sing | *praises to the Lord.*

9.   From Psalm 34.

1 { Oh, magnify the | *Lord with me,*
    And let us ex | *alt his name together.*

2 { I sought the Lord, and he heard me, and delivered me from | *all my fears.*
    The angel of the Lord encampeth round about them that fear him, | *and delivereth them.*

3 { Oh, taste and see that the | *Lord is good!*
    Blessed is the | *man who trusts in him.*

4 { Oh, fear the Lord, | *ye his saints,*
    For there is no | *want to them that fear him.*

5 { The young lions do lack and | *suffer hunger,*
    But they that seek the Lord shall not | *want any good thing.*

6 { The Lord is nigh unto them that are of a | *broken heart,*
    And saveth such as be | *of a contrite spirit.*

7 { The righteous cry and the | *Lord - heareth,*
    And delivereth them | *out of all their troubles.*

8 { The Lord redeemeth the | *soul of his servants;*
    And none of them that trust in | *him shall be desolate.*

No. 7.

10. *From Psalm 42.*

1 { As the hart panteth after the water-brooks, so panteth my soul after | *thee, O God;*
  { My soul thirsteth for God, for the living God: when shall I come and ap | *pear-*
  { *before God?*
2 { My tears have been my meat | *day and night,*
  { While they continually say unto | *me, where is thy God?*
3 { Why art thou cast down, O my soul? and why art thou disquiet | *ed within me?*
  { Hope thou in God! for I shall yet praise him for the | *help - of his countenance.*
4 { O my God, my soul is cast | *down within me,*
  { All thy waves and thy billows | *are gone over me.*
5 { Yet the Lord will command his loving-kindness | *in the day- time,*
  { And in the night his song shall be with me, and my prayer unto the | *God - of*
  { *my life.*
6 { Why art thou cast down, O my soul? and why art thou disquiet | *ed within me?*
  { Hope thou in God, for I shall yet praise him who is the health of my | *counte-*
  { *nance, and my God.*

11. *Psalm 48.*

1 { GREAT is the Lord, and greatly to be praised in the city | *of our God,*
  { In the | *mountain of his holiness.*
2 { Beautiful for | *situation,*
  { The joy of the whole | *earth is Mount- Zion.*
3 { We have thought of thy loving | *kindness, O God;*
  { In the | *midst - of thy temple.*
4 { According to thy name, O God, so is thy praise unto the | *ends of the earth;*
  { Thy right hand is | *full of righteousness.*
5 { Let Mount Zion rejoice, let the daughters of | *Judah be glad*
  { Be | *cause - of thy judgments.*
6 { Walk about Zion, and go | *round about her,*
  { ——— | *Tell the towers thereof.*
7 { Mark ye well her bulwarks, con | *sider her palaces,*
  { That ye may tell it to the gene | *ration following.*
8 { For this God is our God for | *ever and ever;*
  { He will be our guide | *even unto death.*

{ Glory be to the Father, and | *to the Son,*
{ And | *to the Holy Ghost;*
{ As it was in the beginning, is now, and | *ever shall be,*
{ World | *without end. Amen.*

No. 8.
DR. RANDALL.

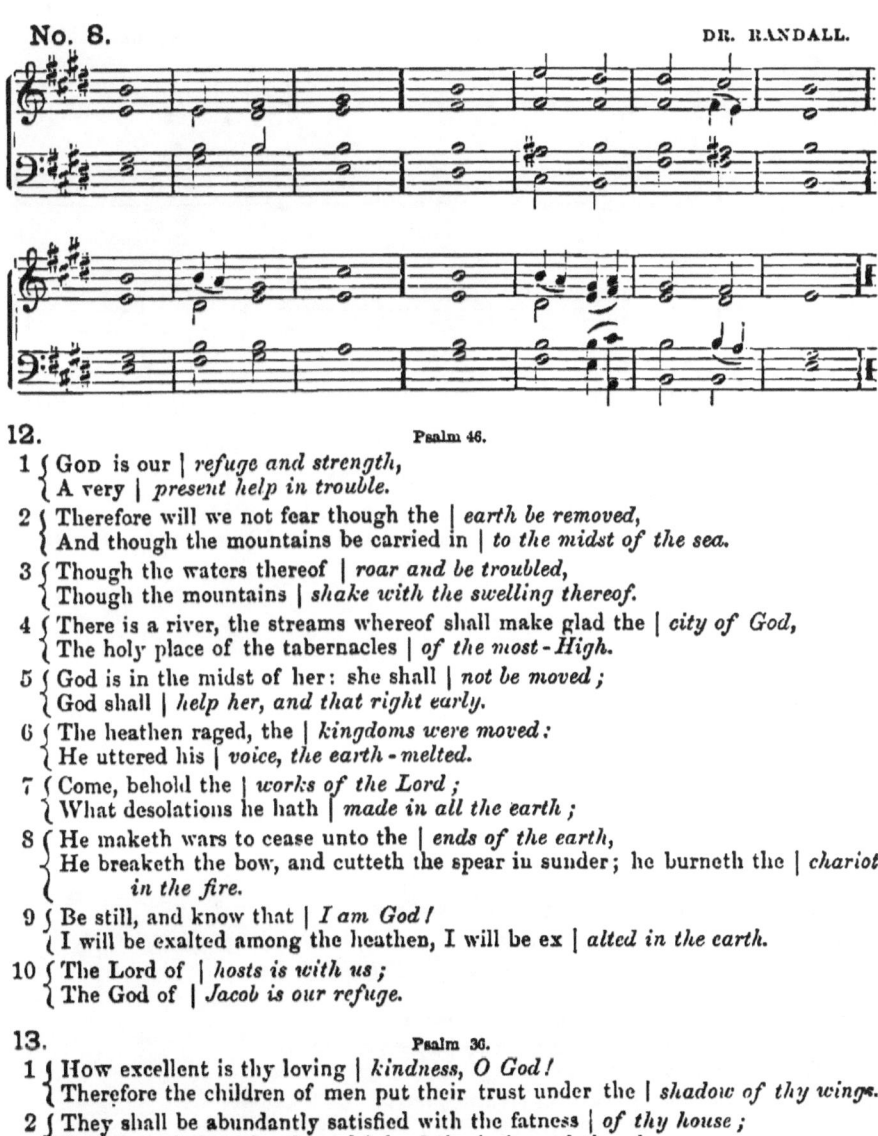

12.   Psalm 46.

1 { God is our | *refuge and strength,*
    A very | *present help in trouble.*

2 { Therefore will we not fear though the | *earth be removed,*
    And though the mountains be carried in | *to the midst of the sea.*

3 { Though the waters thereof | *roar and be troubled,*
    Though the mountains | *shake with the swelling thereof.*

4 { There is a river, the streams whereof shall make glad the | *city of God,*
    The holy place of the tabernacles | *of the most-High.*

5 { God is in the midst of her: she shall | *not be moved;*
    God shall | *help her, and that right early.*

6 { The heathen raged, the | *kingdoms were moved:*
    He uttered his | *voice, the earth-melted.*

7 { Come, behold the | *works of the Lord;*
    What desolations he hath | *made in all the earth;*

8 { He maketh wars to cease unto the | *ends of the earth,*
    He breaketh the bow, and cutteth the spear in sunder; he burneth the | *chariot in the fire.*

9 { Be still, and know that | *I am God!*
    I will be exalted among the heathen, I will be ex | *alted in the earth.*

10 { The Lord of | *hosts is with us;*
     The God of | *Jacob is our refuge.*

13.   Psalm 36.

1 { How excellent is thy loving | *kindness, O God!*
    Therefore the children of men put their trust under the | *shadow of thy wings.*

2 { They shall be abundantly satisfied with the fatness | *of thy house;*
    And thou shalt make them drink of the | *river of thy pleasure.*

3 { For with thee is the | *fountain of life;*
    In thy | *light shall we see light.*

4 { Oh, continue thy loving-kindness unto | *them that know thee,*
    And thy righteousness to the | *upright in heart.*   Amen.

No. 9.

GREGORIAN.

14.   Psalm 51.

1 { Have mercy upon me, O God, according to thy | *loving - kindness :*
    According unto the multitude of thy tender mercies | *blot out my transgressions*

2 { Wash me thoroughly from | *mine iniquity,*
    And | *cleanse me from my sin.*

3 { For I acknowledge | *my transgressions,*
    And my | *sin is ever before me.*

4 { Hide thy face | *from my sins,*
    And blot out | *all mine iniquities.*

5 { Create in me a clean | *heart, O God :*
    And renew a right | *spirit within me.*

6 { Cast me not away | *from thy presence,*
    And take not thy | *Holy Spirit from me.*

7 { Restore unto me the joy of | *thy salvation,*
    And uphold me | *with thy free - Spirit.*

8 { Then will I teach trans | *gressors thy ways,*
    And sinners shall be con | *verted unto thee.*

9 { Deliver me from blood-guiltiness, O God, thou God of | *my salvation :*
    And my tongue shall sing aloud | *of thy righteousness.*

10 { O Lord, open | *thou my lips;*
     And my mouth | *shall shew forth thy praise.*

11 { For thou desirest not sacrifice : else | *would I give it :*
     Thou delightest | *not in burnt - offering.*

12 { The sacrifices of God are a | *broken spirit ;*
     A broken and a contrite heart, O God, | *thou wilt not despise.*

{ Glory be to the Father, and | *to the Son,*
  And | *to the Holy Ghost ;*
{ As it was in the beginning, is now, and | *ever shall be,*
  World | *without end. Amen.*

Chants.

No. 10. WOODWARD.

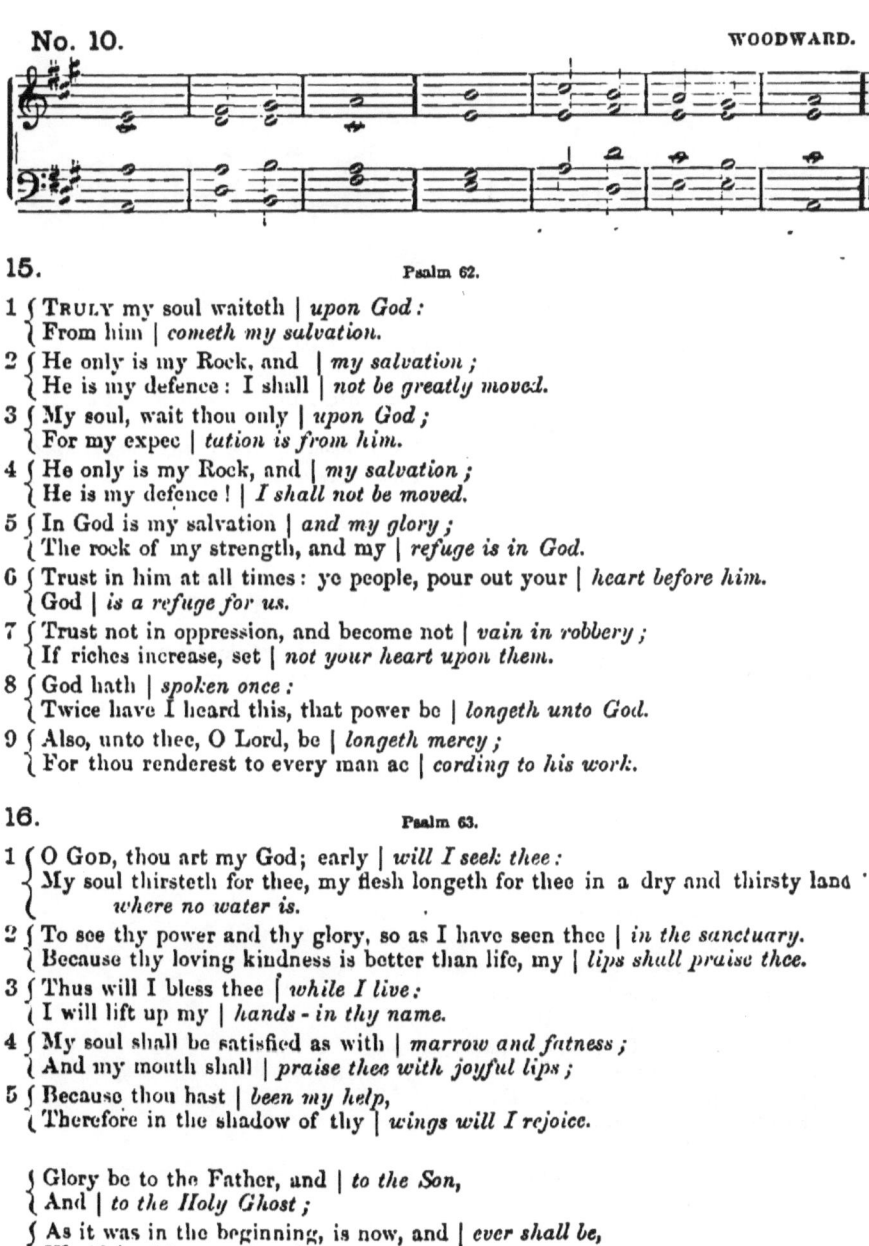

15. *Psalm 62.*

1 { TRULY my soul waiteth | *upon God:*
  { From him | *cometh my salvation.*
2 { He only is my Rock, and | *my salvation ;*
  { He is my defence : I shall | *not be greatly moved.*
3 { My soul, wait thou only | *upon God ;*
  { For my expec | *tation is from him.*
4 { He only is my Rock, and | *my salvation ;*
  { He is my defence ! | *I shall not be moved.*
5 { In God is my salvation | *and my glory ;*
  { The rock of my strength, and my | *refuge is in God.*
6 { Trust in him at all times : ye people, pour out your | *heart before him.*
  { God | *is a refuge for us.*
7 { Trust not in oppression, and become not | *vain in robbery ;*
  { If riches increase, set | *not your heart upon them.*
8 { God hath | *spoken once :*
  { Twice have I heard this, that power be | *longeth unto God.*
9 { Also, unto thee, O Lord, be | *longeth mercy ;*
  { For thou renderest to every man ac | *cording to his work.*

16. *Psalm 63.*

1 { O GOD, thou art my God; early | *will I seek thee :*
  { My soul thirsteth for thee, my flesh longeth for thee in a dry and thirsty land
  { *where no water is.*
2 { To see thy power and thy glory, so as I have seen thee | *in the sanctuary.*
  { Because thy loving kindness is better than life, my | *lips shall praise thee.*
3 { Thus will I bless thee | *while I live :*
  { I will lift up my | *hands - in thy name.*
4 { My soul shall be satisfied as with | *marrow and fatness ;*
  { And my mouth shall | *praise thee with joyful lips ;*
5 { Because thou hast | *been my help,*
  { Therefore in the shadow of thy | *wings will I rejoice.*

{ Glory be to the Father, and | *to the Son,*
{ And | *to the Holy Ghost ;*
{ As it was in the beginning, is now, and | *ever shall be,*
{ World | *without end.   Amen.*

Chants.

No. 11.

17.   Psalm 65.

1 { Praise waiteth for thee, O | *God in Zion ;*
    And unto thee | *shall the vow be performed.*
2 { O thou that hearest prayer, unto thee shall | *all flesh come ;*
    As for our transgressions, thou shalt | *purge - them away.*
3 { Blessed is the man whom thou choosest, and causest to approach unto thee, that
        he may | *dwell in thy courts :*
    We shall be satisfied with the goodness of thy house, even | *of thy holy temple.*
4 { By terrible things in righteousness wilt thou answer us, O God of | *our salva-
        tion ;*
    Who art the confidence of all the ends of the earth, and of them that are afar |
        off upon the sea :
5 { Which by his strength setteth fast the mountains : being | *girded with power ;*
    Which stilleth the noise of the seas, the noise of their waves, and the | *tumult of
        the people.*
6 { They also that dwell in the uttermost parts are afraid | *at thy tokens :*
    Thou makest the outgoings of the morning and | *evening to rejoice.*
7 { Thou visitest the earth and waterest it : thou greatly enrichest it with the river
        of God which is | *full of water :*
    Thou preparest them corn when thou hast | *so provided for it.*
8 { Thou waterest the ridges thereof abundantly ; thou settlest the | *furrows thereof :*
    Thou makest it soft with showers ; thou blessest the | *springing thereof.*

18.   Psalm 67.

1 { God be merciful unto | *us and bless us ;*
    And cause his | *face to shine upon us.*
2 { That thy way may be | *known on earth,*
    Thy saving | *health among all nations.*
3 { Let the people praise | *thee, O God,*
    Let | *all the people praise thee.*
4 { Oh, let the nations be glad, and | *sing for joy :*
    For thou shalt judge the people righteously, and govern the | *nations upon earth.*
5 { Let the people praise | *thee, O God,*
    Let | *all the people praise thee.*
6 { Then shall the earth | *yield her increase,*
    And God, even | *our own God shall bless us.*
7 { God shall | *bless - us ;*
    And all the ends of the | *earth shall fear - him.*

No. 12.
BOYCE.

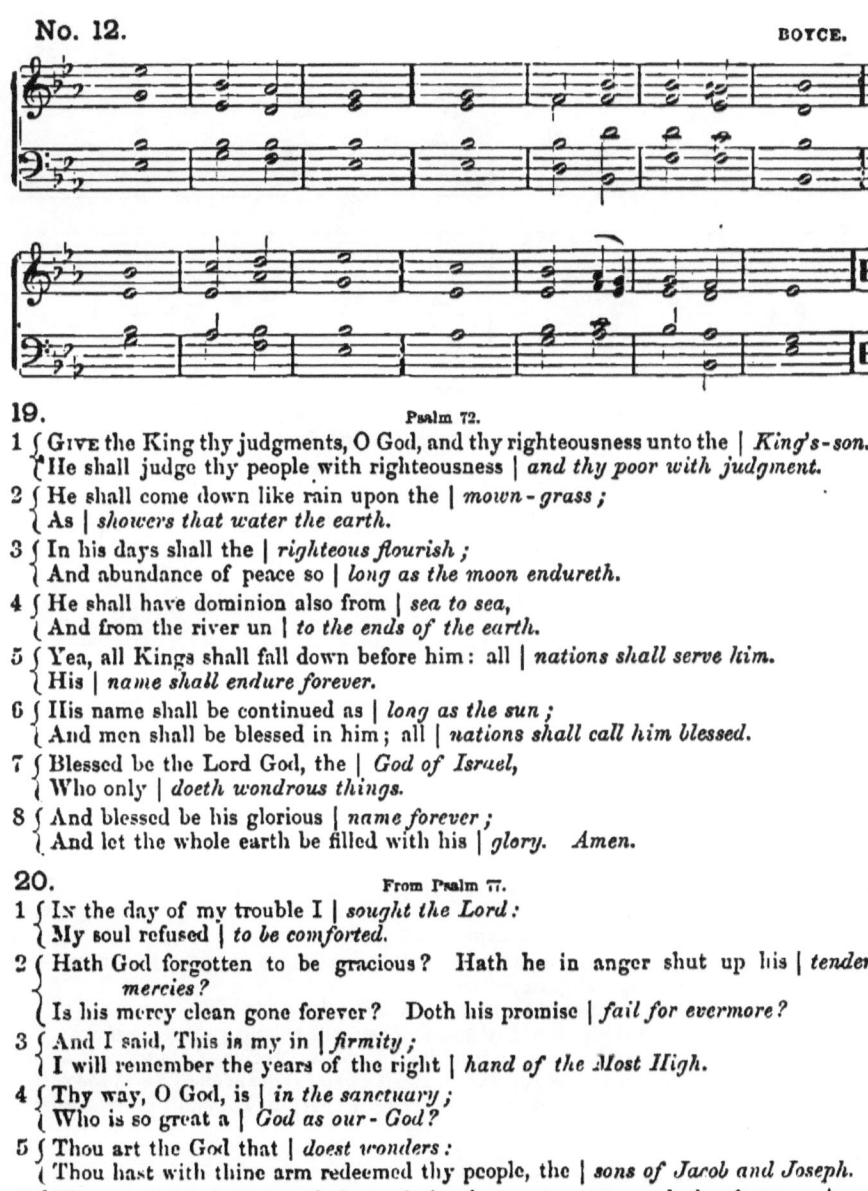

19.   Psalm 72.

1 { Give the King thy judgments, O God, and thy righteousness unto the | *King's-son.*
  { He shall judge thy people with righteousness | *and thy poor with judgment.*
2 { He shall come down like rain upon the | *mown-grass;*
  { As | *showers that water the earth.*
3 { In his days shall the | *righteous flourish;*
  { And abundance of peace so | *long as the moon endureth.*
4 { He shall have dominion also from | *sea to sea,*
  { And from the river un | *to the ends of the earth.*
5 { Yea, all Kings shall fall down before him: all | *nations shall serve him.*
  { His | *name shall endure forever.*
6 { His name shall be continued as | *long as the sun;*
  { And men shall be blessed in him; all | *nations shall call him blessed.*
7 { Blessed be the Lord God, the | *God of Israel,*
  { Who only | *doeth wondrous things.*
8 { And blessed be his glorious | *name forever;*
  { And let the whole earth be filled with his | *glory.* Amen.

20.   From Psalm 77.

1 { In the day of my trouble I | *sought the Lord:*
  { My soul refused | *to be comforted.*
2 { Hath God forgotten to be gracious? Hath he in anger shut up his | *tender mercies?*
  { Is his mercy clean gone forever? Doth his promise | *fail for evermore?*
3 { And I said, This is my in | *firmity;*
  { I will remember the years of the right | *hand of the Most High.*
4 { Thy way, O God, is | *in the sanctuary;*
  { Who is so great a | *God as our-God?*
5 { Thou art the God that | *doest wonders:*
  { Thou hast with thine arm redeemed thy people, the | *sons of Jacob and Joseph.*
6 { Thy way is in the sea, and thy path in the great waters, and thy footsteps | *are not known;*
  { Thou leddest thy people like a flock by the | *hand of Moses and Aaron.*

No. 13.

GREGORIAN.

21.   Psalm 80.

1 { Give ear, O Shepherd of Israel, thou that leadest Joseph | *like a flock;*
    Thou that dwellest between the | *cherubims, shine forth.*

2 { Turn us again, O God, and cause thy | *face to shine;*
    ——— | *And we shall be saved.*

3 { O Lord of hosts, how long wilt thou be angry against the | *prayer of thy people:*
    Thou feedest them with the bread of tears, and givest them | *tears to drink in*
       great measure.

4 { Turn us again, O Lord of hosts, and cause thy | *face to shine;*
    ——— | *And we shall be saved.*

5 { Return, we beseech thee, O | *Lord of hosts;*
    Look down from heaven, and be | *hold and visit this vine;*

6 { And the vineyard which thy right | *hand hath planted,*
    And the branch which thou | *madest strong for thyself.*

7 { So will we not go | *back from thee;*
    Quicken us, and we will | *call upon thy name.*

8 { Turn us again, O Lord God of hosts, cause thy | *face to shine;*
    ——— | *and we shall be saved.*

22.   Psalm 84.

1 { How amiable are thy tabernacles, O | *Lord of hosts!*
    My soul longeth, yea, even fainteth for the courts of the Lord: my heart and my
       flesh crieth | *out for the living God.*

2 { Yea, the sparrow hath found a house, and the swallow a nest for herself, where
       she may | *lay her young;*
    Even thine altars, O Lord of | *hosts, my King and my God.*

3 { Blessed are they that dwell in thy house: they will be still | *praising thee:*
    Blessed is the man whose strength is in thee; in whose | *heart are the ways of them,*

4 { Who passing through the vale of tears, make it a well; the rain also | *filleth the pools.*
    They go from strength to strength, every one of them in Zion ap | *peareth before*
       God.

5 { O Lord God of hosts, hear my prayer; give ear, O | *God of Jacob;*
    Behold, O God our Shield, and look upon the | *face of thine anointed.*

6 { For a day in thy courts is better | *than a thousand;*
    I had rather be a doorkeeper in the house of my God than to dwell in the | *tents*
       of wickedness.

23. From Psalm 89.

1 { God is greatly to be feared in the assembly | *of the saints,*
{ And to be had in reverence of all | *them that are about him.*
2 { O Lord God of hosts, who is a strong Lord like | *unto thee?*
{ Or to thy faithfulness | *round about - thee?*
3 { Thou hast a | *mighty arm;*
{ Strong is thy hand, and | *high is thy right hand.*
4 { Justice and judgment are the habitation | *of thy throne,*
{ Mercy and truth shall | *go before thy face.*
5 { Blessed is the people that know the | *joyful sound;*
{ They shall walk, O Lord, in the | *light - of thy countenance.*
6 { In thy name shall they rejoice | *all the day;*
{ And in thy righteousness | *shall they be exalted.*

24. Psalm 90.

1 { Lord, thou hast been our dwelling-place in | *all generations;*
{ Before the mountains were brought forth, or ever thou hadst formed the earth and the world, even from everlasting to ever | *lasting thou art God.*
2 { Thou turnest man | *to destruction,*
{ And sayest, Re | *turn, ye children of men.*
3 { For a thousand years in thy sight are but as yesterday | *when it is past,*
{ And | *as a watch in the night.*
4 { Thou carriest them away as with a flood; they are | *as a sleep;*
{ In the morning they are like | *grass which groweth up.*
5 { In the morning it flourisheth, and | *groweth up;*
{ In the evening it is cut | *down and withereth.*
6 { For we are consumed | *by thine anger,*
{ And by thy | *wrath are we troubled.*
7 { Thou hast set our iniqui | *ties before thee,*
{ Our secret sins in the light | *of thy countenance.*
8 { For all our days are passed away | *in thy wrath;*
{ We spend our | *years as a tale that is told.*
9 { The days of our years are threescore years and ten: and if by reason of strength they be fourscore years, yet is their strength | *labor and sorrow;*
{ For it is soon cut | *off and we fly away.*
10 { Who knoweth the power | *of thine anger?*
{ Even according to thy | *fear, so is thy wrath.*
11 { So teach us to number our days, that we may apply our | *hearts unto wisdom.*
{ Return, O Lord, how long? and let it repent thee con | *cer - ning thy servants.*
12 { Oh, satisfy us early with thy mercy; that we may rejoice and be glad | *all our days.*
{ Make us glad according to the days thou hast afflicted us, and the | *years we have seen evil.*
13 { Let thy work appear un | *to thy servants,*
{ And thy | *glory unto their children.*
14 { And let the beauty of the Lord our | *God be upon us;*
{ And establish thou the work of our hands upon us; yea, the work of our | *hands establish thou it.*

No. 14.
DR. RANDALL.

25.
Psalm 95.

1 { Oh, come, let us sing un | *to the Lord :*
  { Let us make a joyful noise to the | *Rock of our salvation.*
2 { Let us come before his presence | *with thanksgiving,*
  { And make a joyful | *noise unto him with psalms.*
3 { For the Lord is a | *great - God;*
  { And a great | *King above all gods.*
4 { In his hand are the deep places | *of the earth;*
  { The strength of the | *hills is his also.*
5 { The sea is his, | *and he made it;*
  { And his hand | *formed the dry land.*
6 { Oh, come, let us worship, | *and bow down;*
  { Let us kneel be | *fore the Lord our Maker.*
7 { For he is | *our - God;*
  { And we are the people of his pasture, and the | *sheep - of his hand.*
8 { So we thy people and sheep of thy pasture will give thee | *thanks forever;*
  { We will show forth thy | *praise to all generations.*

26.
From Psalm 96.

1 { Give unto the Lord, O ye kindreds of the people, give unto the Lord | *glory and strength;*
  { Give unto the Lord the glory | *due unto his name.*
2 { Oh, worship the Lord in the | *beauty of holiness;*
  { Fear be | *fore him, all the earth.*
3 { Say among the heathen, | *The Lord reigneth;*
  { He shall | *judge the people righteously.*
4 { Let the heavens rejoice, and let the | *earth be glad;*
  { Let the sea | *roar, and the fulness thereof.*
5 { Let the field be joyful, and all that | *is therein;*
  { Then shall all the trees of the wood re | *joice before the Lord.*
6 { For he cometh, for he cometh to | *judge the earth;*
  { With righteousness shall he judge the world, and the | *people with his truth.*

No. 15. HUMPHREYS.

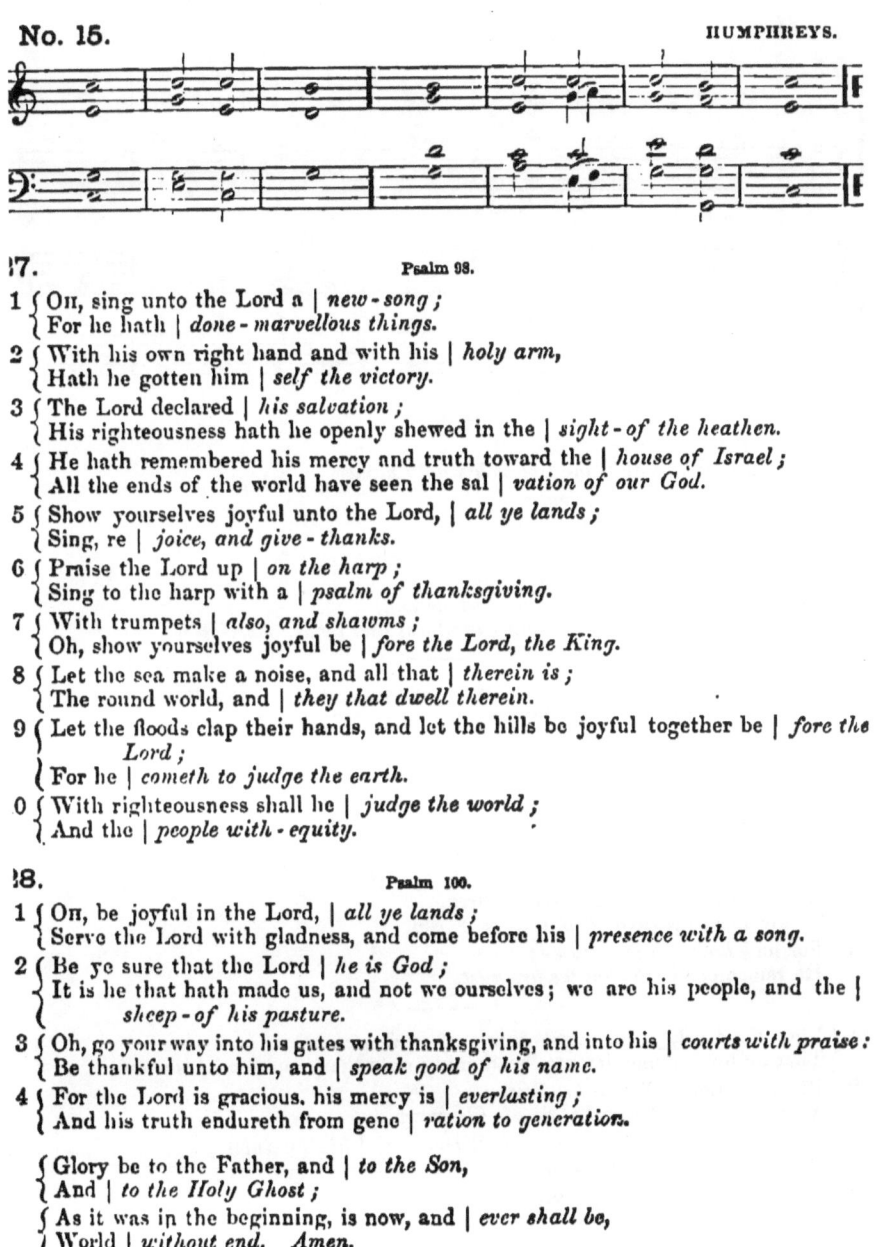

17. Psalm 98.

1 { Oh, sing unto the Lord a | *new - song ;*
{ For he hath | *done - marvellous things.*
2 { With his own right hand and with his | *holy arm,*
{ Hath he gotten him | *self the victory.*
3 { The Lord declared | *his salvation ;*
{ His righteousness hath he openly shewed in the | *sight - of the heathen.*
4 { He hath remembered his mercy and truth toward the | *house of Israel ;*
{ All the ends of the world have seen the sal | *vation of our God.*
5 { Show yourselves joyful unto the Lord, | *all ye lands ;*
{ Sing, re | *joice, and give - thanks.*
6 { Praise the Lord up | *on the harp ;*
{ Sing to the harp with a | *psalm of thanksgiving.*
7 { With trumpets | *also, and shawms ;*
{ Oh, show yourselves joyful be | *fore the Lord, the King.*
8 { Let the sea make a noise, and all that | *therein is ;*
{ The round world, and | *they that dwell therein.*
9 { Let the floods clap their hands, and let the hills be joyful together be | *fore the Lord ;*
{ For he | *cometh to judge the earth.*
0 { With righteousness shall he | *judge the world ;*
{ And the | *people with - equity.*

18. Psalm 100.

1 { Oh, be joyful in the Lord, | *all ye lands ;*
{ Serve the Lord with gladness, and come before his | *presence with a song.*
2 { Be ye sure that the Lord | *he is God ;*
{ It is he that hath made us, and not we ourselves ; we are his people, and the | *sheep - of his pasture.*
3 { Oh, go your way into his gates with thanksgiving, and into his | *courts with praise :*
{ Be thankful unto him, and | *speak good of his name.*
4 { For the Lord is gracious, his mercy is | *everlasting ;*
{ And his truth endureth from gene | *ration to generation.*

{ Glory be to the Father, and | *to the Son,*
{ And | *to the Holy Ghost ;*
{ As it was in the beginning, is now, and | *ever shall be,*
{ World | *without end. Amen.*

No. 16. TALLIS.

29. Psalm 103.

1 { Bless the Lord, | *O my soul:*
   { And all that is within me | *bless his holy name.*
2 { Bless the Lord, | *O my soul:*
   { And for | *get not all his benefits.*
3 { Who forgiveth | *all thy sin,*
   { And healeth | *all thine infirmities.*
4 { Who redeemeth thy life | *from destruction ;*
   { And crowneth thee with loving | *kindness and tender mercies.*

5 { The Lord is merciful and gracious ; slow to anger, and | *plenteous in mercy :*
   { He will not always chide, nor keep his | *an - ger forever.*
6 { He hath not dealt with us | *after our sins,*
   { Nor rewarded us ac | *cording to our iniquities.*
7 { For as the heaven is high a | *bove the earth,*
   { So great is his | *mercy toward them that fear him.*
8 { As far as the east is | *from the west,*
   { So far hath he removed | *our transgressions from us.*
9 { Like as a father | *pitieth his children,*
   { So the Lord | *pitieth them that fear him.*
10 { For he | *knoweth our frame ;*
    { He remember | *eth that we are dust.*

11 { Bless the Lord, ye his angels that ex | *cel in strength ;*
    { That do his commandments, hearkening unto the | *voice - of his word.*
12 { Bless the Lord, all | *ye his hosts ;*
    { Ye ministers of | *his that do his pleasure.*
13 { Bless the Lord, all his works, in all places of | *his dominion ;*
    { Bless the | *Lord, O my soul.*
14 { Bless the Lord, | *O my soul,*
    { And all that is within me | *bless his holy name.*

No. 17.

30. *Psalm 115.*

1 { Not unto | us, O Lord,
  { Not unto us, but | *unto thy name give glory;*
2 { For thy mercy, and for | *thy truth's sake.*
  { Wherefore should the heathen say, | *where is now their God?*
3 { O Israel, trust | *thou in the Lord;*
  { He | *is their help and their shield.*
4 { O house of Aaron, trust | *thou in the Lord;*
  { He | *is their help and their shield.*
5 { Ye that fear the Lord, trust | *in the Lord;*
  { He | *is their help and their shield.*
6 { The Lord hath been mindful of us; | *he will bless us;*
  { He will bless the house of Israel; he will | *bless the house of Aaron.*
7 { He will bless them that fear the Lord, both | *small and great.*
  { The Lord shall increase you more and | *more, you and your children.*
8 { The heaven, even the heavens | *are the Lord's;*
  { But the earth hath he given | *to the children of men.*
9 { The dead praise | *not the Lord,*
  { Neither any that go | *down - into silence.*
10 { But we will bless the Lord from this time forth and for | *evermore.*
   { Praise the | *Lord! Praise ye the Lord!*

31. *Isaiah 52: 7-11.*

1 { How beautiful upon the mountains are the feet of him that bringeth good tidings, that | *publisheth peace;*
  { That bringeth good tidings of good; that publisheth salvation; that saith unto | *Zion, Thy God reigneth!*
2 { Thy watchmen shall lift up the voice, with the voice together | *shall they sing:*
  { For they shall see eye to eye, when the | *Lord shall bring again Zion.*
3 { Break forth into joy, sing together, ye waste places | *of Jerusalem;*
  { For the Lord hath comforted his people, he | *hath redeemed Jerusalem.*
4 { The Lord hath made bare his holy arm in the eyes of | *all the nations:*
  { And all the ends of the earth shall see the sal | *vation of our God.*

No. 18.

32.   Psalm 121.

1 I WILL lift up mine eyes unto the hills, from whence | *cometh my help.*
2 My help cometh from the Lord, which made | *heaven and earth.*
3 He will not suffer thy foot to be moved: he that keepeth thee | *will not slumber.*
4 Behold, he that keepeth Israel shall not | *slumber nor sleep.*
5 The Lord is thy keeper, the Lord is thy shade upon thy | *right - hand.*
6 The sun shall not smite thee by day, nor the | *moon by night.*
7 The Lord shall preserve thee from all evil: he shall pre | *serve thy soul.*
8 The Lord shall preserve thy going out and thy coming in, from this time forth, and even for | *evermore.*

33.   Psalm 122.

1 I WAS glad when they said unto me, Let us go into the | *house of the Lord.*
2 Our feet shall stand within thy gates, | *O Jerusalem!*
3 Jerusalem is builded as a city that is com | *pact together ;*
4 Whither the tribes go up, the | *tribes of the Lord,*
5 Unto the testimony of Israel, to give thanks unto the | *name of the Lord.*
6 For there are set thrones of judgment, the thrones of the | *house of David.*
7 Pray for the peace of Jerusalem: they shall | *prosper that love thee !*
8 Peace be within thy walls, and prosperity with | *in thy palaces.*
9 For my brethren and companions' sakes, I will now say, | *Peace be within thee !*
10 Because of the house of the Lord our God, I will | *seek thy good.*

34.   Psalm 126.

1 WHEN the Lord turned again the captivity of Zion, we were like | *them that dream !*
2 Then was our mouth filled with laughter, and our | *tongue with singing.*
3 Then said they among the heathen, The Lord hath done great | *things for them !*
4 The Lord hath done great things for us; where | *of we are glad.*
5 Turn again our captivity, O Lord, as the | *streams in the south.*
6 They that sow in tears shall | *reap in joy.*
7 He that goeth forth and weepeth, bearing | *precious seed,*
8 Shall doubtless come again with rejoicing, bringing | *his sheaves with him.*

No. 19.   DR. WOODWARD.

35.   Psalm 130.

1 { Out of the depths have I cried unto | *thee, O Lord.*
    Lord, hear my voice; let thine ears be attentive to the | *voice of my supplications.*
2 { If thou, Lord, shouldest mark iniquities, O Lord, | *who shall stand?*
    But there is forgiveness with thee, | *that thou mayest be feared.*
3 { I wait for the Lord, my soul doth wait, and in his | *word do I hope;*
    My soul waiteth for the Lord more than | *they that watch for the morning.*
4 { Let Israel hope in the Lord: for with the Lord is mercy, and | *plenteous redemption.*
    And he shall redeem Israel from | *all his iniquities.*

36.   From Psalm 132.

1 { Arise, O Lord, into thy rest; thou, and the | *ark of thy strength;*
    Let thy priests be clothed with righteousness; and let thy | *saints - shout for joy.*
2 { For the Lord hath chosen Zion; he hath desired it for his | *habitation.*
    This is my rest forever; here will I dwell; for | *I have desired it.*
3 { I will abundantly bless her provision; I will satisfy her | *poor with bread:*
    I will also clothe her priests with salvation; and her saints shall | *shout aloud for joy.*

37.   Psalm 136.

1 { Oh, give thanks unto the Lord, for he is good; for his mercy en | *dureth forever.*
    Oh, give thanks unto the God of gods; for his | *mercy endureth forever.*
2 { Oh, give thanks to the Lord of lords; for his mercy en | *dureth forever.*
    To him who alone doeth great wonders; for his | *mercy endureth forever.*
3 { To him that by wisdom made the heavens; for his mercy en | *dureth forever.*
    To him that stretched out the earth above the waters; for his | *mercy endureth forever.*
4 { To him that made great lights; for his mercy en | *dureth forever.*
    The sun to rule by day; the moon and stars to rule by night; for his | *mercy endureth forever.*
5 { Who remembered us in our low estate; for his mercy en | *dureth forever.*
    And hath redeemed us from our enemies; for his | *mercy endureth forever.*
6 { Who giveth food to all flesh; for his mercy en | *dureth forever.*
    Oh, give thanks unto the God of heaven; for his | *mercy endureth forever.*

No. 20. FITZHERBERT.

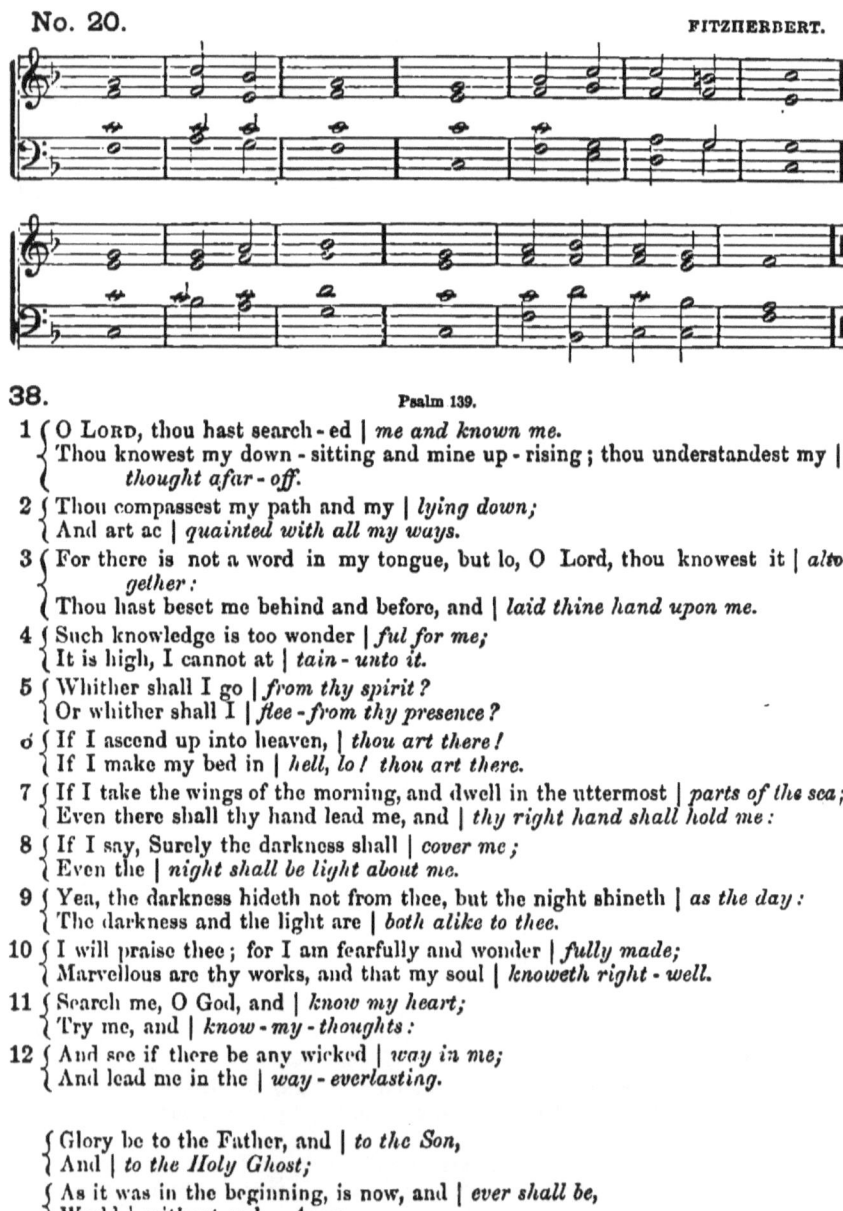

38. Psalm 139.

1. { O Lord, thou hast search-ed | *me and known me.*
   { Thou knowest my down-sitting and mine up-rising; thou understandest my | *thought afar-off.*
2. { Thou compassest my path and my | *lying down;*
   { And art ac | *quainted with all my ways.*
3. { For there is not a word in my tongue, but lo, O Lord, thou knowest it | *alto-gether:*
   { Thou hast beset me behind and before, and | *laid thine hand upon me.*
4. { Such knowledge is too wonder | *ful for me;*
   { It is high, I cannot at | *tain-unto it.*
5. { Whither shall I go | *from thy spirit?*
   { Or whither shall I | *flee-from thy presence?*
6. { If I ascend up into heaven, | *thou art there!*
   { If I make my bed in | *hell, lo! thou art there.*
7. { If I take the wings of the morning, and dwell in the uttermost | *parts of the sea;*
   { Even there shall thy hand lead me, and | *thy right hand shall hold me:*
8. { If I say, Surely the darkness shall | *cover me;*
   { Even the | *night shall be light about me.*
9. { Yea, the darkness hideth not from thee, but the night shineth | *as the day:*
   { The darkness and the light are | *both alike to thee.*
10. { I will praise thee; for I am fearfully and wonder | *fully made;*
    { Marvellous are thy works, and that my soul | *knoweth right-well.*
11. { Search me, O God, and | *know my heart;*
    { Try me, and | *know-my-thoughts:*
12. { And see if there be any wicked | *way in me;*
    { And lead me in the | *way-everlasting.*

{ Glory be to the Father, and | *to the Son,*
{ And | *to the Holy Ghost;*
{ As it was in the beginning, is now, and | *ever shall be,*
{ World | *without end. Amen.*

No. 21. DR. T. S. DUPUIS.

39. Psalm 145: 1-12.

1 { I WILL extol thee, my God, O King; and I will bless thy name for | *ever and ever,*
   { Every day will I bless thee, and I will praise thy | *name for ever and ever.*
2 { Great is the Lord, and greatly to be praised; and his greatness | *is unsearchable.*
   { One generation shall praise thy works to another, and shall de | *clare thy mighty acts.*
3 { I will speak of the glorious honor of thy majesty, and of thy | *wondrous works;*
   { And men shall speak of the might of thy terrible acts; and | *I will declare thy*
      greatness;
4 { They shall abundantly utter the memory of thy great goodness, and sing of thy |
      righteousness.
   { The Lord is gracious, and full of compassion, slow to anger | *and of great - mercy.*
5 { The Lord is good to all; and his tender mercies are over | *all his works;*
   { All thy works shall praise thee, O Lord; and thy | *saints shall bless - thee.*
6 { They shall speak of the glory of thy kingdom, and talk | *of thy power;*
   { To make known to the sons of men his mighty acts, and the glorious majesty |
      of his kingdom.

40. Psalm 145: 13-21.

1 { THY kingdom is an everlasting kingdom, and thy dominion throughout | *all gener-*
      ations.
   { The Lord upholdeth all that fall, and raiseth | *all that are bowed down.*
2 { The eyes of all wait upon thee; and thou givest them their meat | *in due season;*
   { Thou openest thine hand, and satisfiest the desire of | *every living thing.*
3 { The Lord is righteous in all his ways, and holy in | *all his works;*
   { The Lord is nigh unto all them that | *call on him in truth:*
4 { He will fulfil the desire of | *them that fear him;*
   { He will hear their | *cry and save them.*
5 { The Lord preserveth all | *them that love him;*
   { But all the | *wicked will he destroy.*
6 { My mouth shall speak the | *praise of the Lord;*
   { And let all flesh bless his holy | *name for ever and ever.*

No. 22.

HANDEL.

41. Psalm 146.

1 { Praise ye the Lord; praise the Lord, | *O my soul.*
  { While I | *live will I praise the Lord:*
2 { I will sing praises unto my God while | *I have being;*
  { Praise ye the Lord; praise the | *Lord - O my soul.*
3 { Happy is he that hath the God of Jacob | *for his help;*
  { Whose hope is | *in the Lord his God;*
4 { Which made heaven and earth and sea and all that | *therein is;*
  { Which keepeth | *truth forev - er.*
5 { Which executeth judgment | *for the oppressed;*
  { Which giveth | *food - to the hungry;*
6 { The Lord looseth the prisoners: the Lord openeth the | *eyes of the blind;*
  { The Lord raiseth them that are bowed down; the Lord | *lov - eth the righteous.*
7 { The Lord preserveth the strangers; he relieveth the fatherless | *and the widow;*
  { But the way of the wicked he | *turneth upside down.*
8 { The Lord shall reign forever, even thy God, O Zion, to | *all generations.*
  { Praise ye the Lord. Praise the | *Lord, O my soul.*

42. Psalm 147: 12-20.

1 { Praise the Lord, O Jerusalem; praise thy | *God, O Zion.*
  { For he hath strengthened the bars of thy gates; he hath blessed thy | *chil - dren within thee.*
2 { He maketh peace in thy borders; and filleth thee with the finest | *of the wheat.*
  { He sendeth forth his commandment; his word | *runneth very swiftly.*
3 { He giveth snow like wool; he scattereth the hoar | *frost like ashes.*
  { He casteth forth his ice like morsels: who can | *stand before his cold?*
4 { He sendeth out his word, and | *melteth them;*
  { He causeth his wind to | *blow, and melteth them.*
5 { He sheweth his word | *unto Jacob;*
  { His statutes and his | *judgments unto Israel.*
6 { He hath not dealt so with | *any nation;*
  { And as for his judgments, they have not known them. | *Praise - ye the Lord.*

Chants.

No. 23. BARROW.

43. Psalm 148.

1 { Praise | ye the Lord :
  { Praise ye the Lord from the heavens; | *praise him in the heights.*
2 { Praise ye him, all his angels; praise ye him, | *all his hosts.*
  { Praise ye him, sun and moon; praise him, | *all ye stars of light.*
3 { Praise him, ye heaven of heavens, and ye waters that be a | *bove the heavens.*
  { Let them praise the name of the Lord, for he commanded, | *and they were created.*
4 { He hath also established them for | *ever and ever;*
  { He hath made a de | *cree which shall not pass.*
5 { Praise the Lord from the earth, ye dragons, | *and all deeps :*
  { Fire and hail; snow and vapor; stormy | *wind fulfilling his word :*
6 { Mountains and all hills; fruitful trees, | *and all cedars;*
  { Beasts and all cattle; creeping | *things, and flying fowl :*
7 { Kings of the earth, and all people; princes, and all judges | *of the earth;*
  { Both young men and maidens; | *old-men and children:*
8 { Let them praise the name of the Lord; for his name a | *lone is excellent :*
  { His glory is a | *bove the heaven and earth.*

44. Psalm 150.

1 { Praise ye the Lord; praise God | *in his sanctuary;*
  { Praise him in the | *firmament of his power.*
2 { Praise him for his | *mighty acts;*
  { Praise him according to his | *excellent-greatness.*
3 { Praise him with the | *sound of the trumpet;*
  { Praise him with the | *psaltery and harp.*
4 { Praise him with the | *timbrel and dance;*
  { Praise him with stringed | *instruments and organs.*
5 { Praise him upon the | *loud-cymbals;*
  { Praise him upon the | *high-sounding cymbals.*
6 { Let everything that hath breath | *praise the Lord.*
  { Praise - | *ye the Lord.* Amen.

No. 24.
BOYCE.

45. 1 Chron. 29: 10-13.

1 { Blessed be thou, Lord God of Israel, for | ever and ever.
{ Thine, O Lord, is the | greatness and the power,
2 { And the glory and the victory | and the majesty;
{ For all that is in the heaven and | in the earth is thine.
3 { Thine is the | kingdom, O Lord:
{ And thou art exalted as | head - over all;
4 { Both riches and honor | come of thee;
{ And thou | reignest over all.
5 { And in thine hand is | power and might;
{ And in thine hand it is to make great, and to give | strength - unto all.
6 { Now, therefore, our | God, we thank thee,
{ And | praise thy glorious name.

46. Isaiah 12.

1 { O Lord, I will praise thee, though thou wast | angry with me.
{ Thine anger is turned away, and thou | comfortest - me.
2 { Behold, God is | my salvation;
{ I will | trust and not be afraid.
3 { For the Lord Jehovah is my | strength and song;
{ He also is be | come - my salvation.
4 { Therefore with joy shall ye draw water out of the | wells of salvation:
{ And in that day shall ye say, Praise the Lord, | call upon his name.
5 { Declare his doings among the people, make mention that his | name is exalted;
{ Sing unto the Lord, for he hath done excellent things; this is | known in all the
{   earth.
6 { Cry and shout, thou inhabi | tant of Zion;
{ For great is the Holy One of Israel | in the midst of thee.

{ Glory be to the Father, and | to the Son,
{ And | to the Holy Ghost;
{ As it was in the beginning, is now, and | ever shall be,
{ World | without end. Amen.

No. 25.

HIGGINS.

47. Isaiah 26.

1 { Thou wilt keep him in perfect peace, whose mind is | *stayed on thee;*
   { Be | *cause he trusteth in thee.*
2 { Trust ye in the | *Lord forever;*
   { For in the Lord Jehovah is | *everlasting strength.*
3 { The way of the just is | *uprightness;*
   { Thou, most upright, dost | *weigh the path of the just.*
4 { Yea, in the way of thy judgments, O Lord, have we | *waited for thee;*
   { The desire of our soul is to thy name, and | *to the remembrance of thee.*
5 { With my whole soul have I desired thee | *in the night;*
   { Yea, with my spirit within me, | *I will seek thee early:*
6 { For when thy judgments are | *in the earth,*
   { The inhabitants of the | *world will learn-righteousness.*
7 { Lord, thou wilt ordain | *peace for us,*
   { For thou hast wrought | *all our works in us.*
8 { O Lord our God, other lords beside thee have had dominion | *over us;*
   { But by thee only will we make | *mention of thy name.*

48. Isaiah 35.

1 { Say to them that are of a fearful heart, Be | *strong, fear not:*
   { Behold your God will come with vengeance, even God with a recompense, | *He will come and save you.*
2 { Then the eyes of the blind shall be opened, and the ears of the deaf shall | *be unstopped:*
   { Then shall the lame man leap as an hart, and the | *tongue of the dumb shall sing.*
3 { For in the wilderness shall waters break out, and | *streams in the desert:*
   { And an highway shall be there, and a way, and it shall be | *called the way of holiness:*
4 { And the ransomed of the Lord shall return, and come to Zion with songs and everlasting joy u | *pon their heads;*
   { They shall obtain joy and gladness, and sorrow and | *sighing shall flee away.*

Chants.

No. 26. GREGORIAN. From 7th Tone.

49. Isaiah 40

1. { Comfort ye, comfort ye my people | *saith your God;*
   { Speak ye comfortably | *to Jerusalem.*
2. { And cry unto her that her warfare is accomplished, her iniqui | *ty is pardoned;*
   { For she hath received of the Lord's hand | *double for all her sins.*
3. { The voice of him that crieth in the wilderness, Prepare the | *way of the Lord;*
   { Make straight in the desert a | *highway for our God.*
4. { Every valley shall be exalted, and every mountain and hill shall | *be made low;*
   { And the crooked shall be made straight, and the | *rough-places plain.*
5. { And the glory of the Lord shall be revealed, and all flesh shall | *see it together;*
   { For the mouth of the Lord, the mouth of the | *Lord hath spoken it.*
6. { Comfort ye, comfort ye my people, | *saith your God;*
   { Speak ye comfortably | *to Jerusalem.*

50. Isaiah 40.

1. { The voice said, Cry; and he said, | *What shall I cry?*
   { All flesh is grass, and all the goodliness thereof is as the | *flower-of the field:*
2. { The grass withereth, the | *flower fadeth;*
   { But the word of our | *God shall stand forever.*
3. { O Zion, that bringest good tidings, get thee up into the | *high-mountain:*
   { O Jerusalem, that bringest good tidings, lift | *up thy voice with strength;*
4. { Lift it up, be | *not afraid!*
   { Say unto the cities of | *Judah, behold your God!*
5. { Behold the Lord will come with strong hand, and his arm shall | *rule for him;*
   { Behold his reward is with him, | *and his work before him.*
6. { He shall feed his flock like a shepherd; he shall gather the | *lambs with his arm*
   { And carry them in his bosom, and shall gently lead | *those that are with young.*

{ Glory be to the Father, and | *to the Son,*
{ And | *to the Holy Ghost;*
{ As it was in the beginning, is now, and | *ever shall be;*
{ World | *without end. Amen.*

No. 27.

51.   Isaiah 40.

1 { THE everlasting | *God, the Lord,*
    The Creator of the ends of the earth, | *fainteth not, nor is weary.*
2 { He giveth | *power to the faint;*
    And to them that have no | *might, he increaseth strength.*
3 { Even the youths shall faint and be weary, and the young men shall | *utterly fall;*
    But they that wait upon the | *Lord shall renew their strength;*
4 { They shall mount | *up with wings as eagles:*
    They shall run and not be weary; they shall | *walk and not-faint.*

52.   Isaiah 41, 43, & 54.

1 { FEAR not, for | *I am with thee;*
    Be not dismayed, for | *I - am thy God.*
2 { I will strengthen thee: yea, | *I will help thee;*
    Yea, I will uphold thee with the right | *hand of my righteousness.*
3 { Fear not, for I have re | *deem - ed thee:*
    I have called thee by thy | *name, - thou art mine :*
4 { When thou passest through the waters, I | *will be with thee;*
    And through the rivers, they | *shall not overflow thee.*
5 { For a small moment have I for | *saken thee;*
    But with great mercies | *will I gather thee.*
6 (In a little wrath I hid my face from thee | *for a moment;*
    { But with everlasting kindness will I have mercy on thee, saith the | *Lord - thy*
    (*Redeemer.*
7 { For the mountains shall depart, and the | *hills be removed;*
    But my kindness shall | *not depart from thee.*
8 { Neither shall the covenant of my | *peace be removed;*
    Saith the | *Lord that hath mercy on thee.*
9 (O thou afflicted, tossed with tempest, not | *comforted;*
    { Behold I will lay thy stones with fair colors, and thy foun | *da - tions with sap-*
    (*phires;*
10 { And I will make thy | *windows of agates,*
     And thy gates of carbuncles, and all thy | *borders of pleasant stones.*

53.

Isaiah 53.

1 { He is despised and rejected of men; a man of sorrows, and ac | *quainted with grief.*
   And we hid as it were our faces from him; he was despised and we es | *teemed him not.*

2 { Surely he hath borne our griefs, and | *carried our sorrows;*
   Yet we did esteem him stricken, smitten of | *God, and afflicted.*

3 { But he was wounded for our transgressions; he was bruised for our in | *iquities:*
   The chastisement of our peace was upon him; and by his | *stripes we are healed.*

4 { All we like sheep have gone astray; we have turned every one to his | *own-way;*
   And the Lord hath laid on him the iniquity | *of us all.*

5 { He was oppressed, | *and afflicted;*
   Yet he opened | *not his mouth.*

6 { He is brought as a | *lamb to the slaughter,*
   And as a sheep before her shearers is dumb, so he openeth | *not his mouth.*

7 { He was taken from prison and from judgment; and who shall declare his | *generation?*
   For he was cut off out of the land of the living; for the transgression of my people | *was he stricken.*

8 { And he made his grave with the wicked, and with the | *rich in his death;*
   Because he hath done no violence, neither was any deceit | *in his mouth.*

9 { Yet it pleased the Lord to bruise him; yea, he hath | *put him to grief;*
   When thou shalt make his soul an offering for sin, he shall see his seed, he shall pro | *long his days.*

10 { And the pleasure of the Lord shall prosper | *in his hands.*
    He shall see of the travail of his soul and shall be | *satisfied.*

11 { By his knowledge shall my righteous servant | *justify many;*
    For he shall bear their in | *iquities;*

12 { Therefore will I divide him a portion | *with the great,*
    And he shall divide the | *spoil with the strong.*

13 { Because he hath poured out his | *soul unto death:*
    And he was numbered | *with the transgressors;*

14 { And he bare the | *sin of many,*
    And made intercession for | *the transgressors.*

No. 29. DR. T. S. DUPUIS.

54. Isaiah 60.

1 { Arise, shine, for thy | *light is come,*
    And the glory of the | *Lord is risen upon thee.*
2 { For behold the darkness shall | *cover the earth,*
    And | *gross darkness the people.*
3 { But the Lord shall a | *rise upon thee;*
    And his glory | *shall be seen upon thee;*
4 { And the Gentiles shall come | *to thy light,*
    And kings to the | *brightness of thy rising.*
5 { Violence shall no more be heard in thy land; wasting and destruction with | *in thy borders.*
    But thou shalt call thy walls salvation, | *and thy gates - praise.*
6 { The sun shall be no more thy | *light by day,*
    Neither for brightness shall the | *moon give light unto thee.*
7 { But the Lord God shall be unto thee an everlasting light, and thy | *God thy glory;*
    Thy sun shall no more go down, neither shall thy | *moon withdraw itself:*
8 { For the Lord shall be thine ever | *lasting light,*
    And the days of thy | *mourning shall be ended.*
9 { I will greatly rejoice in the Lord, my soul shall be joyful | *in my God;*
    For he hath clothed me with the garments of salvation, he hath covered me with the | *robe of righteousness:*
10 { For as the earth bringeth forth her bud, and as the garden causeth the things that are sown in it | *to spring forth;*
    So the Lord God will cause righteousness and praise to spring | *forth before all nations.*
11 { For Zion's sake I will not hold my peace, and for Jerusalem's sake I | *will not rest,*
    Until the righteousness thereof go forth as brightness, and her salvation | *as a lamp that burneth.*
12 { And the Gentiles shall see thy righteousness, and all | *kings thy glory;*
    And thou shalt be called by a new name which the | *mouth of the Lord shall name.*

No. 30.

55.   Luke 1: 68.

1 { Blessed be the Lord | *God of Israel;*
   For he hath visited | *and redeemed his people.*
2 { And hath raised up a horn of sal | *vation for us;*
   In the | *house of his servant David.*
3 { As he spake by the mouth of his | *holy prophets,*
   Which have been | *since the world began;*
4 { That we should be saved | *from our enemies;*
   And from the | *hand of all that hate us.*

{ Glory be to the Father, and | *to the Son,*
  And | *to the Holy Ghost;*
{ As it was in the beginning, is now, and | *ever shall be;*
  World | *without end. Amen.*

56.   Luke 1: 46.

1 { My soul doth magni | *fy the Lord,*
   And my spirit hath re | *joiced in God my Saviour;*
2 { For he hath regarded the low estate of | *his handmaiden;*
   For behold, from henceforth all gener | *ations shall call me blessed.*
3 { For he that is mighty hath done to | *me great things;*
   And | *holy is his name.*
4 { And his mercy is on | *them that fear him,*
   From gener | *ation to generation.*
5 { He hath shewed | *strength with his arm;*
   He hath scattered the proud in the imagi | *nation of their hearts.*
6 { He hath put down the mighty | *from their seats;*
   And exalted | *them of low degree.*
7 { He hath filled the hungry | *with good things;*
   And the rich he hath | *sent empty away.*
8 { He hath holpen his servant Israel in remembrance | *of his mercy;*
   As he spake to our fathers, to Abraham, and | *to his seed forever.*

No. 31.
GREGORIAN.

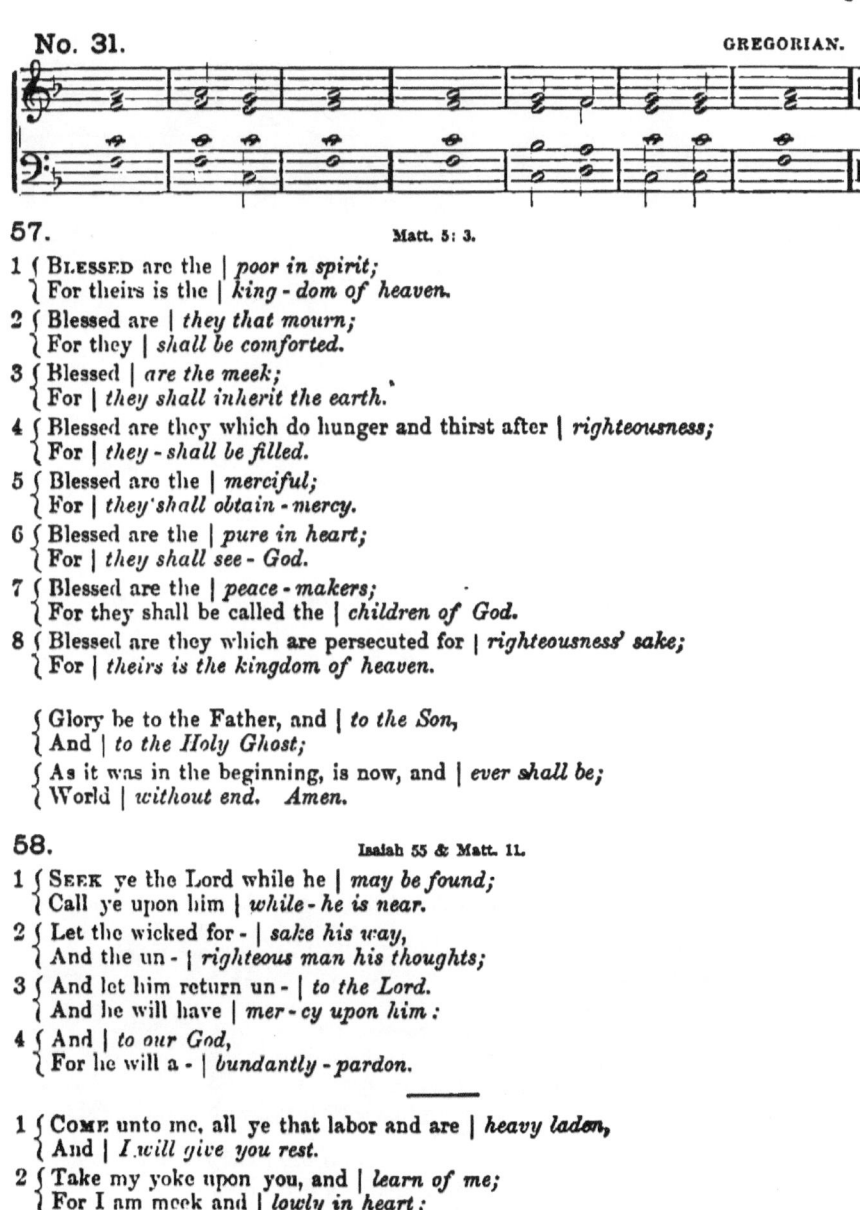

57. Matt. 5: 3.

1 { BLESSED are the | *poor in spirit;*
  { For theirs is the | *king - dom of heaven.*
2 { Blessed are | *they that mourn;*
  { For they | *shall be comforted.*
3 { Blessed | *are the meek;*
  { For | *they shall inherit the earth.*
4 { Blessed are they which do hunger and thirst after | *righteousness;*
  { For | *they - shall be filled.*
5 { Blessed are the | *merciful;*
  { For | *they shall obtain - mercy.*
6 { Blessed are the | *pure in heart;*
  { For | *they shall see - God.*
7 { Blessed are the | *peace - makers;*
  { For they shall be called the | *children of God.*
8 { Blessed are they which are persecuted for | *righteousness' sake;*
  { For | *theirs is the kingdom of heaven.*

{ Glory be to the Father, and | *to the Son,*
{ And | *to the Holy Ghost;*
{ As it was in the beginning, is now, and | *ever shall be;*
{ World | *without end. Amen.*

58. Isaiah 55 & Matt. 11.

1 { SEEK ye the Lord while he | *may be found;*
  { Call ye upon him | *while - he is near.*
2 { Let the wicked for - | *sake his way,*
  { And the un - | *righteous man his thoughts;*
3 { And let him return un - | *to the Lord.*
  { And he will have | *mer - cy upon him :*
4 { And | *to our God,*
  { For he will a - | *bundantly - pardon.*

---

1 { COME unto me, all ye that labor and are | *heavy laden,*
  { And | *I will give you rest.*
2 { Take my yoke upon you, and | *learn of me;*
  { For I am meek and | *lowly in heart :*
3 { And ye shall find rest un - | *to your souls;*
  { For my yoke is easy, and my | *bur - den is light.*

No. 32.

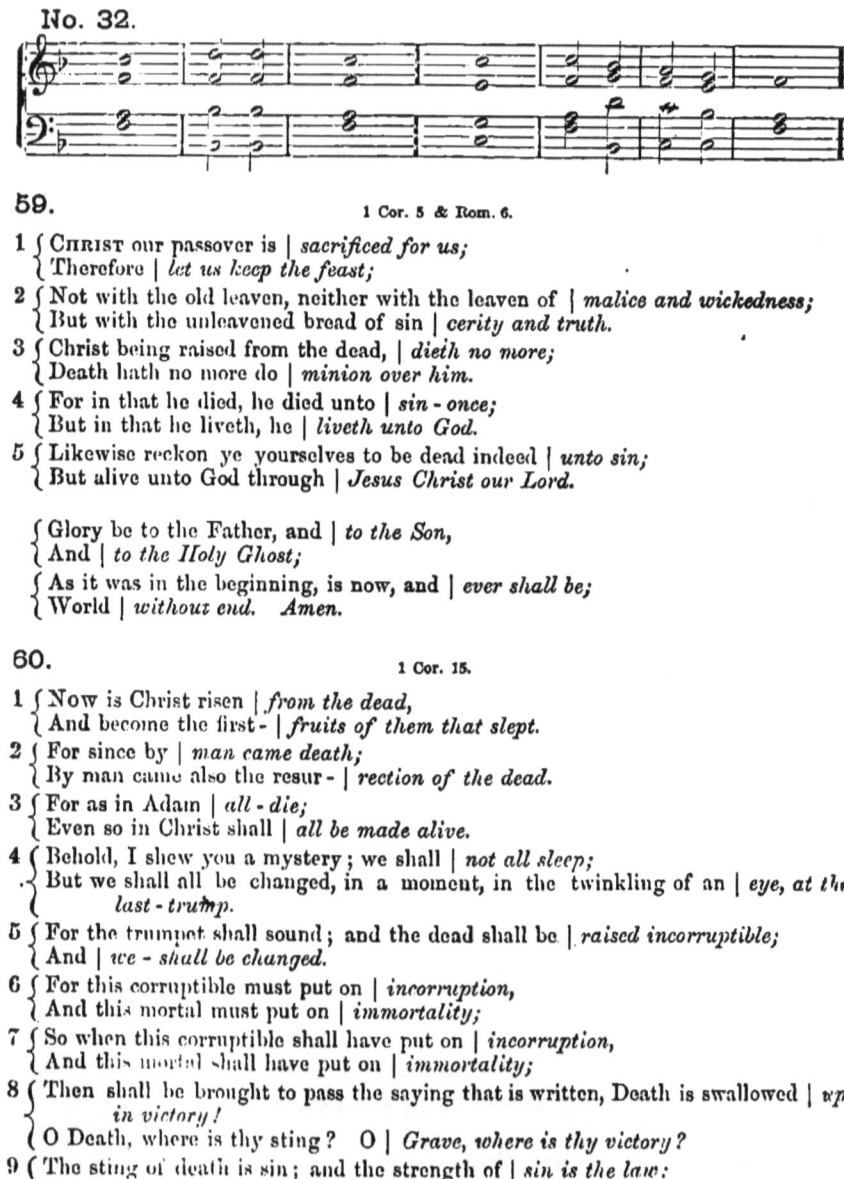

59. 1 Cor. 5 & Rom. 6.

1 { CHRIST our passover is | *sacrificed for us;*
  { Therefore | *let us keep the feast;*
2 { Not with the old leaven, neither with the leaven of | *malice and wickedness;*
  { But with the unleavened bread of sin | *cerity and truth.*
3 { Christ being raised from the dead, | *dieth no more;*
  { Death hath no more do | *minion over him.*
4 { For in that he died, he died unto | *sin - once;*
  { But in that he liveth, he | *liveth unto God.*
5 { Likewise reckon ye yourselves to be dead indeed | *unto sin;*
  { But alive unto God through | *Jesus Christ our Lord.*

{ Glory be to the Father, and | *to the Son,*
{ And | *to the Holy Ghost;*
{ As it was in the beginning, is now, and | *ever shall be;*
{ World | *without end. Amen.*

60. 1 Cor. 15.

1 { Now is Christ risen | *from the dead,*
  { And become the first - | *fruits of them that slept.*
2 { For since by | *man came death;*
  { By man came also the resur - | *rection of the dead.*
3 { For as in Adam | *all - die;*
  { Even so in Christ shall | *all be made alive.*
4 { Behold, I shew you a mystery; we shall | *not all sleep;*
  { But we shall all be changed, in a moment, in the twinkling of an | *eye, at the
        last - trump.*
5 { For the trumpet shall sound; and the dead shall be | *raised incorruptible;*
  { And | *we - shall be changed.*
6 { For this corruptible must put on | *incorruption,*
  { And this mortal must put on | *immortality;*
7 { So when this corruptible shall have put on | *incorruption,*
  { And this mortal shall have put on | *immortality;*
8 { Then shall be brought to pass the saying that is written, Death is swallowed | *up
        in victory!*
  { O Death, where is thy sting?   O | *Grave, where is thy victory?*
9 { The sting of death is sin; and the strength of | *sin is the law;*
  { But thanks be unto God, who giveth us the victory, through | *Jesus Christ our
        Lord.*

61. *Selections for Baptism.*

1 { And Jesus said, Suffer little children, and forbid them not, to | *come unto me,*
  { For of | *such is the kingdom of heaven.*

2 { Verily I say unto you, Except ye be converted, and become as | *little children,*
  { Ye shall not enter in | *to the kingdom of heaven.*

3 { Whosoever therefore shall humble himself as this | *little child;*
  { The same is greatest | *in the kingdom of heaven.*

4 { Take heed that ye despise not one of these | *little ones;*
  { For I say unto you, that in heaven their angels do always behold the face of my |
     Father which is in heaven.

62.

1 { And Jesus came, and spake | *unto them, saying,*
  { All power is given unto | *me in heaven and in earth.*

2 { Go ye therefore and | *teach all nations,*
  { Baptizing them in the name of the Father, and of the Son, and | *of the Holy
     Ghost.*

63.

1 { The mercy of the Lord is from everlasting to everlasting upon | *them that fear
     him;*
  { And his righteousness | *unto children's children.*

2 { To such as | *keep his covenant;*
  { And to those that remember his com | *mandments to do them.*

3 } The promise is unto you, and | *unto your children;*
  { And to all that are afar off, even as many as the | *Lord our God shall call.*

4 { He shall feed his flock | *like a shepherd;*
  { He shall gather the lambs with his arm, and | *carry them in his bosom.*

{ Glory be to the Father, and | *to the Son,*
{ And | *to the Holy Ghost;*

{ As it was in the beginning, is now, and | *ever shall be,*
{ World | *without end.   Amen.*

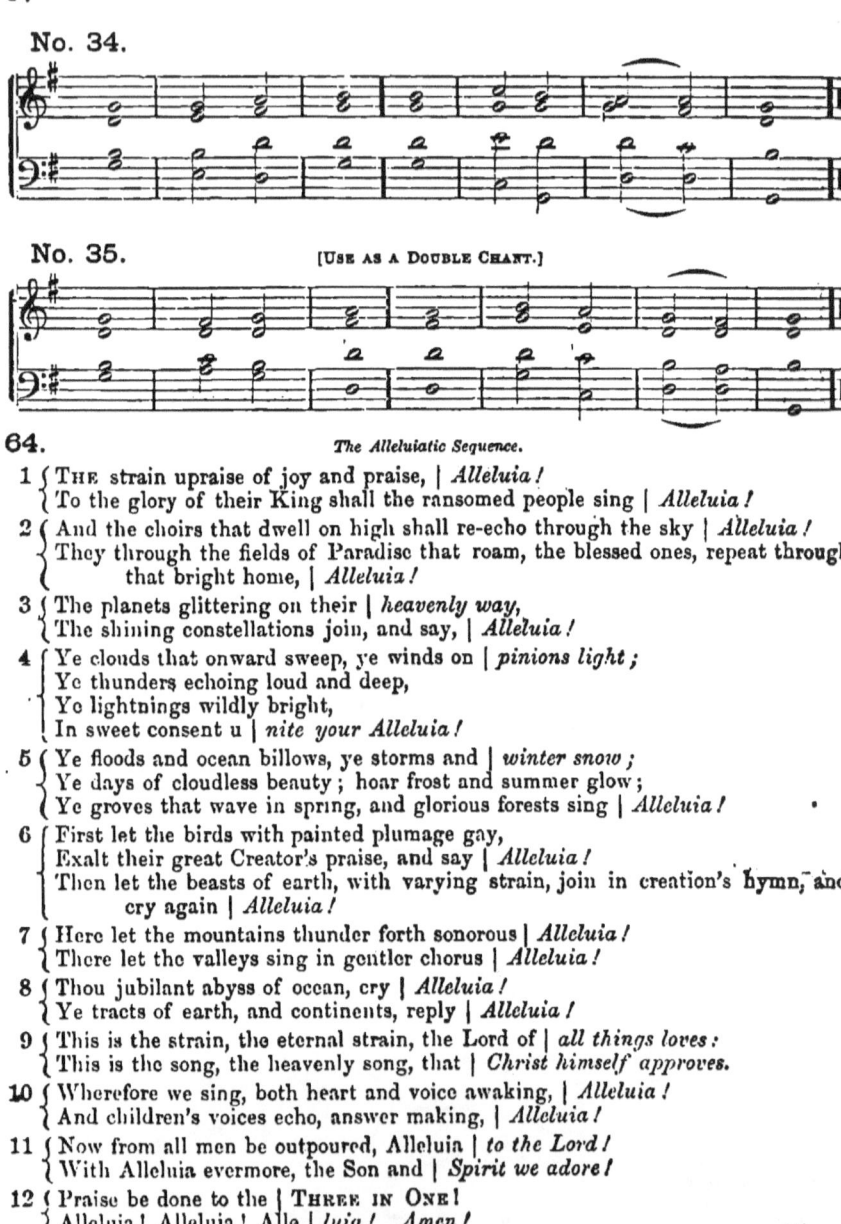

64. *The Alleluiatic Sequence.*

1. { The strain upraise of joy and praise, | *Alleluia!*
   { To the glory of their King shall the ransomed people sing | *Alleluia!*
2. { And the choirs that dwell on high shall re-echo through the sky | *Alleluia!*
   { They through the fields of Paradise that roam, the blessed ones, repeat through that bright home, | *Alleluia!*
3. { The planets glittering on their | *heavenly way,*
   { The shining constellations join, and say, | *Alleluia!*
4. { Ye clouds that onward sweep, ye winds on | *pinions light ;*
   { Ye thunders echoing loud and deep,
   { Ye lightnings wildly bright,
   { In sweet consent u | *nite your Alleluia!*
5. { Ye floods and ocean billows, ye storms and | *winter snow ;*
   { Ye days of cloudless beauty ; hoar frost and summer glow ;
   { Ye groves that wave in spring, and glorious forests sing | *Alleluia!*
6. { First let the birds with painted plumage gay,
   { Exalt their great Creator's praise, and say | *Alleluia!*
   { Then let the beasts of earth, with varying strain, join in creation's hymn, and cry again | *Alleluia!*
7. { Here let the mountains thunder forth sonorous | *Alleluia!*
   { There let the valleys sing in gentler chorus | *Alleluia!*
8. { Thou jubilant abyss of ocean, cry | *Alleluia!*
   { Ye tracts of earth, and continents, reply | *Alleluia!*
9. { This is the strain, the eternal strain, the Lord of | *all things loves :*
   { This is the song, the heavenly song, that | *Christ himself approves.*
10. { Wherefore we sing, both heart and voice awaking, | *Alleluia!*
    { And children's voices echo, answer making, | *Alleluia!*
11. { Now from all men be outpoured, Alleluia | *to the Lord!*
    { With Alleluia evermore, the Son and | *Spirit we adore!*
12. { Praise be done to the | THREE IN ONE!
    { Alleluia! Alleluia! Alle | *luia! Amen!*

NEALE'S MEDIEVAL HYMNS.

No. 36.

65. *Doxologies.*

1 { Worthy | *is the Lamb,*
  { The | *Lamb that once was slain,*

2 { To receive power and riches and | *wisdom and strength*
  { And honor and | *glory and - blessing.*

3 { Blessing and honor and | *glory and power*
  { Be unto him that sitteth upon the throne, and unto the | *Lamb, for ever and ever.*

4 { Unto him that | *loved us,*
  { And washed us from our | *sins in his own blood,*

5 { And hath made us kings and priests unto | *God and his Father;*
  { To him be glory and dominion for ever and | *ever. A - men.*

6 { Behold he | *cometh with clouds;*
  { And | *every eye shall see him.*

7 { And they | *also that pierced him;*
  { And all kindreds of the earth shall | *wail because of him.*

No. 37. REQUIEM.

66.

1 { Blessed are the dead who | *die in the Lord,*
  { From hence - | *forth; Yea, saith the Spirit;*

2 { For they | *rest from their labors,*
  { And their | *works do follow them.*

3 { And God shall wipe away all | *tears from their eyes:*
  { And there shall | *be - no more death,*

4 { Neither sorrow nor crying nor | *any more pain;*
  { For the former | *things are passed away.*

Chants.

No. 38. SANCTUS.

Holy, Holy, Ho - ly Lord God Al-mignt - y, who was, and is, and is to come.

LITANY.

No. 39.
E. P. PARKER.

A - men.

67.

1. { O Saviour of the world, the | *Son, Lord Jesus;*
   Stir up thy strength and help us, we | *hum-bly beseech thee.*

2. { By thy cross and precious blood thou | *hast redeemed us;*
   Save us and help us, we | *hum-bly beseech thee.*

3. { Thou didst save thy disciples when | *ready to perish;*
   Hear us and save us, we | *hum-bly beseech thee.*

4. { Let the pitifulness of | *thy great mercy*
   Loose us from our sins, we | *hum-bly beseech thee.*

5. { Make it appear that thou art our Saviour and | *mighty Deliverer;*
   Oh, save us, that we may praise thee, we | *hum - bly beseech thee.*

6. { Draw near, according to thy promise, from the | *throne of thy glory;*
   Look down, and hear our crying, we | *hum-bly beseech thee.*

7. { Come again, and dwell with us, O | *Lord, Christ Jesus;*
   Abide with us forever, we | *hum-bly beseech thee.*

8. { And when thou shalt appear with | *power and glory;*
   May we be made like unto thee | *in thy glorious kingdom.*

{ Glory be to the Father, and | *to the Son,*
And | *to the Holy Ghost;*

{ As it was in the beginning, is now, and | *ever shall be;*
World | *without end. Amen.*

Chants.   37

No. 40.   GREGORIAN.

No. 41.

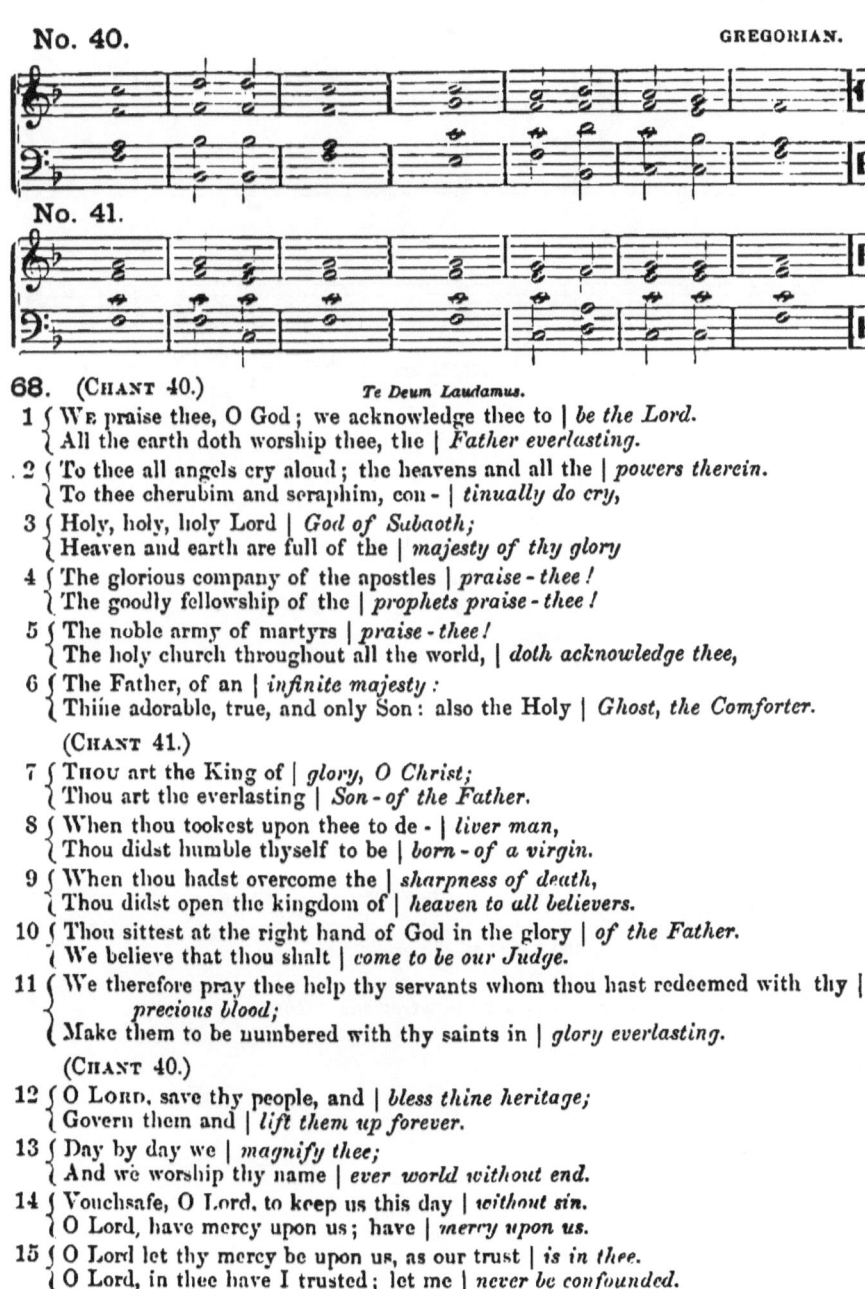

68. (CHANT 40.)   *Te Deum Laudamus.*
1 { WE praise thee, O God; we acknowledge thee to | *be the Lord.*
   { All the earth doth worship thee, the | *Father everlasting.*
2 { To thee all angels cry aloud; the heavens and all the | *powers therein.*
   { To thee cherubim and seraphim, con - | *tinually do cry,*
3 { Holy, holy, holy Lord | *God of Sabaoth;*
   { Heaven and earth are full of the | *majesty of thy glory*
4 { The glorious company of the apostles | *praise - thee!*
   { The goodly fellowship of the | *prophets praise - thee!*
5 { The noble - army of martyrs | *praise - thee!*
   { The holy church throughout all the world, | *doth acknowledge thee,*
6 { The Father, of an | *infinite majesty :*
   { Thine adorable, true, and only Son : also the Holy | *Ghost, the Comforter.*

(CHANT 41.)
7 { THOU art the King of | *glory, O Christ;*
   { Thou art the everlasting | *Son - of the Father.*
8 { When thou tookest upon thee to de - | *liver man,*
   { Thou didst humble thyself to be | *born - of a virgin.*
9 { When thou hadst overcome the | *sharpness of death,*
   { Thou didst open the kingdom of | *heaven to all believers.*
10 { Thou sittest at the right hand of God in the glory | *of the Father.*
    { We believe that thou shalt | *come to be our Judge.*
11 { We therefore pray thee help thy servants whom thou hast redeemed with thy |
    {   *precious blood;*
    { Make them to be numbered with thy saints in | *glory everlasting.*

(CHANT 40.)
12 { O LORD, save thy people, and | *bless thine heritage;*
    { Govern them and | *lift them up forever.*
13 { Day by day we | *magnify thee;*
    { And we worship thy name | *ever world without end.*
14 { Vouchsafe, O Lord, to keep us this day | *without sin.*
    { O Lord, have mercy upon us; have | *mercy upon us.*
15 { O Lord let thy mercy be upon us, as our trust | *is in thee.*
    { O Lord, in thee have I trusted; let me | *never be confounded.*

No. 42.

No. 43.

69. (CHANT 42.) *Gloria in Excelsis.*

1 { GLORY be to | *God on high;*
   { And on earth, | *peace, good will towards men.*

2 { We praise thee, we bless thee, we | *worship thee,*
   { We glorify thee, we give thanks to | *thee for thy great glory.*

3 { O Lord God, | *heavenly King;*
   { God the | *Father Al-mighty.*

(CHANT 43.)

4 { O LORD, the only begotten Son, | *Jesus Christ;*
   { O Lord God, Lamb of God, | *Son - of the Father.*

5 { That takest away the | *sins of the world,*
   { Have | *mercy upon us.*

6 { Thou that takest away the | *sins of the world,*
   { Have | *mercy upon us.*

7 { Thou that takest away the | *sins of the world,*
   { Re - | *ceive, receive our prayer.*

8 { Thou that sittest at the right hand of | *God the Father,*
   { Have | *mercy upon us.*

(CHANT 42.)

9 { FOR thou | *only art holy;*
   { Thou | *only art the Lord.*

10 { Thou only, O Christ, with the | *Holy Ghost,*
    { Art most high in the | *glory of God the Father.*

Chants.

No. 44.

70.

1. { Holy, holy, holy Lord | *God Almighty!*
   { Early in the morning shall our | *song arise to thee.*

2. { Holy, holy, holy! All the | *saints adore thee,*
   { Casting down their golden crowns a - | *round the glassy sea.*

3. { Cherubim and seraphim fall | *down before thee,*
   { Who wast, and art, and | *evermore shalt be.*

4. { Holy, holy, holy! Though the | *darkness hide thee,*
   { Though the eye of sinful man thy | *glory may not see;*

5. { Only thou art holy, there is | *none beside thee,*
   { Perfect in power, in | *love, and purity.*

6. { Holy, holy, holy Lord | *God Almighty!*
   { All thy works shall praise thy name, in | *earth and sky and sea.*

71. (Chant 45.)

1. { Thou Maker of my vital frame, unveil thy face, pro - | *nounce thy name;*
   { Shine to my sight, and let the ear which thou hast | *formed, thy language hear:*
   (Divide, ye clouds, and let me see the Power that | *gives me leave to be.*

2. { Where is thy residence? Oh, why dost thou avoid my | *searching eye?*
   { Mysterious Being! Great Unknown! say, do the | *clouds conceal thy throne?*
   (Or art thou all diffused abroad, through boundless | *space, a present God?*

3. { Is there not some delightful art, to feel thy presence | *in my heart?*
   { To hear thy whispers, soft and kind, in holy | *silence of the mind!*
   (Then rest, my thoughts; no longer roam in quest of | *joy, for heaven's at home!*

WATTS.

No. 45.

72.

1 From the recesses of a lowly spirit
My humble prayer ascends, — O | *Father, hear it!*
Borne on the trembling wings of fear and meekness;
For - | *give its weakness.*

2 I know, I feel how mean, and how unworthy
The lowly sacrifice I | *pour before thee:*
What can I offer thee, O thou most holy,
But | *sin and folly?*

3 Lord, in thy sight, who every bosom viewest,
Cold in our warmest vows, and | *vain our truest;*
Thoughts of a hurrying hour — our lips repeat them —
Our | *hearts forget them.*

4 We see thy hand; it leads us; it supports us;
We hear thy voice; it | *counsels, and it courts us;*
And then we turn away! and still thy kindness
For - | *gives our blindness.*

5 Who can resist thy gentle call, appealing
To every generous thought and | *grateful feeling?*
Oh, who can hear the accents of thy mercy,
And | *never love thee?*

6 Kind Benefactor! plant within this bosom
The | *seeds of holiness;* and let them blossom
In fragrance, and in beauty bright and vernal,
And | *spring eternal.*

7 Then place them in those everlasting gardens,
Where angels walk, and | *seraphs are the wardens;*
Where every flower, brought safe through death's dark portal,
Be | *comes immortal!*

Downing

No. 47.

73.

1 LEAD, kindly Light, amid th' encircling gloom, lead | *thou me on!*
The night is dark, and I am far from | *home; lead thou me on!*
Keep thou my feet; I do not | *ask to see*
The distant scene; one | *step's enough for me.*

2 I was not ever thus, nor prayed that thou shouldst | *lead me on;*
I loved to choose and see my path; but | *now, lead thou me on!*
I loved the garish day, and | *spite of fears,*
Pride ruled my will: re - | *member not past years!*

3 So long thy power hath blessed me, sure it still will | *lead me on*
O'er moor and fen, o'er crag and torrent, | *till the night is gone,*
And with the morn those angel | *faces smile,*
Which I have loved long | *since, and lost awhile.*

NEWMAN.

74.

1 " *Thy will be done!* " In devious way
The hurrying stream of | *life may run;*
Yet still our grateful hearts shall say,
" *Thy will be done* "!

2 " *Thy will be done* "! If o'er us shine
A gladdening and a | *prosperous sun;*
This prayer will make it more divine, —
" *Thy will be done* "!

3 " *Thy will be done* "! Though shrouded o'er
Our | *path with gloom;* one comfort, one
Is ours, — to breathe, while we adore, " *Thy will be done* "!
" *Thy will be done* "! *

BOWRING.

No. 48.

* Close by repeating the first two measures — " Thy will be done "!

No. 49.   C. W. HUNTINGTON.

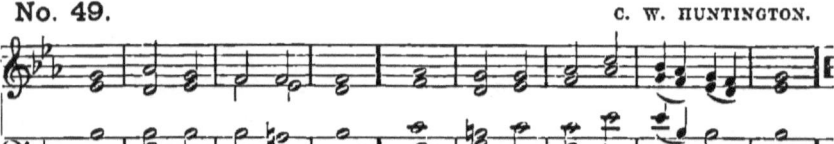

75.

1 { My God, is any hour so sweet, from blush of | *morn till evening star,*
  { As that which calls me to thy feet, — the | *hour of prayer — the hour of prayer.*

2 { Then is my strength by thee renewed, then are my | *sins by thee forgiven;*
  { Then thou dost cheer my solitude with | *hopes of heaven — with hopes of heaven.*

3 { No words can tell what sweet relief, there for my | *every want I find;*
  { What strength for warfare, balm for grief, what | *peace of mind — what peace of mind.*

4 { Hushed is each doubt, gone every fear; my spirit | *seems in heaven to stay;*
  { And ev'n the penitential tear is | *wiped away — is wiped away.*

5 { Lord! till I reach that blissful shore, no privi- | *lege so dear shall be,*
  { As thus my inmost soul to pour in | *prayer to thee — in prayer to thee.*

76.

1 When winds are raging o'er the upper ocean,
   And billows wild con - | *tend with angry roar,*
   'Tis said, far down beneath the wild commotion,
   That peaceful | *stillness reigneth evermore.*

2 Far, far beneath, the noise of tempests dieth,
   And silver waves chime | *ever peacefully;*
   And no rude storm, how fierce soe'er it flieth,
   Disturbs the | *Sabbath of that deeper sea.*

3 So to the heart that knows thy love, O Purest!
   There is a temple, | *sacred evermore,*
   And all the babble of life's angry voices
   Dies in hushed | *stillness, at its peaceful door.*

4 Far, far away, the roar of passion dieth,
   And loving thoughts rise | *calm and peacefully,*
   And no rude storm, how fierce soe'er it flieth,
   Disturbs the | *soul that dwells, O Lord, in thee.*

5 O rest of rests! O peace serene, eternal!
   Thou ever livest | *and thou changest never;*
   And in the secret of thy presence dwelleth
   Fulness of | *joy, forever and forever.*

                                                    MRS. STOWE.

I AM THE LORD THY GOD, WHICH HAVE BROUGHT THEE OUT OF THE LAND OF EGYPT, AND OUT OF THE HOUSE OF BONDAGE.

I.

Thou shalt have no other gods before me.

II.

Thou shalt not make unto thee any graven image, or any likeness of anything that is in heaven above, or that is in the earth beneath, or that is in the water under the earth: thou shalt not bow down thyself to them, nor serve them: for I the Lord thy God am a jealous God, visiting the iniquity of the fathers upon the children, unto the third and fourth generation of them that hate me; and showing mercy unto thousands of them that love me, and keep my commandments.

III.

Thou shalt not take the name of the Lord thy God in vain, for the Lord will not hold him guiltless that taketh his name in vain.

IV.

Remember the Sabbath day to keep it holy: six days shalt thou labor and do all thy work; but the seventh day is the Sabbath of the Lord thy God: in it thou shalt not do any work, thou, nor thy son, nor thy daughter, thy man-servant, nor thy maid-servant, nor thy cattle, nor the stranger that is within thy gates: for in six days the Lord made heaven and earth, the sea, and all that in them is, and rested on the seventh day; wherefore the Lord blessed the Sabbath day and hallowed it.

V.

Honor thy father and thy mother, that thy days may be long in the land which the Lord thy God giveth thee.

VI.

Thou shalt not kill.

VII.

Thou shalt not commit adultery.

VIII.

Thou shalt not steal.

IX.

Thou shalt not bear false witness against thy neighbor.

X.

Thou shalt not covet thy neighbor's house, thou shalt not covet thy neighbor's wife, nor his man-servant, nor his maid-servant, nor his ox, nor his ass, nor anything that is thy neighbor's.

" For this, — Thou shalt not commit adultery, thou shalt not kill, thou shalt not steal, thou shalt not bear false witness, thou shalt not covet: and if there be any other commandment, it is briefly comprehended in this saying; namely, Thou shalt love thy neighbor as thyself. Love worketh no ill to his neighbor, therefore love is the fulfilling of the law."

THE APOSTLES' CREED.

I believe in God, the Father Almighty, Maker of heaven and earth; and in Jesus Christ, his only Son, our Lord, who was conceived by the Holy Ghost. born of the Virgin Mary, suffered under Pontius Pilate, was crucified, dead, and buried. He descended into hell [Hades]; the third day he arose again from the dead, he ascended into heaven, and sitteth on the right hand of God, the Father Almighty: from thence he shall come to judge the quick and the dead.

I believe in the Holy Ghost; the holy catholic church; the communion of saints; the forgiveness of sins; the resurrection of the body, and the life everlasting. Amen.

THE NICENE CREED.

I believe in one God the Father Almighty, Maker of heaven and earth, and of all things visible and invisible:

And in one Lord Jesus Christ, the only begotten Son of God, begotten of his Father before all worlds; God of God, Light of Light, very God of very God, begotten, not made, being of one substance with the Father; by whom all things were made; who, for us men, and for our salvation, came down from heaven, and was incarnate by the Holy Ghost of the Virgin Mary, and was made man, and was crucified for us under Pontius Pilate. He suffered and was buried; and the third day he rose again, according to the Scriptures; and ascended into heaven, and sitteth on the right hand of the Father. And he shall come again with glory to judge both the quick and the dead; whose kingdom shall have no end.

And I believe in the Holy Ghost, the Lord and Giver of life, who proceedeth from the Father and the Son; who, with the Father and the Son, is worshipped and glorified; who spake by the prophets.

And I believe one Catholic and Apostolic Church.

I acknowledge one baptism for the remission of sins; and I look for the resurrection of the dead, and the life of the world to come. Amen.

THE LORD'S PRAYER.

Our Father which art in heaven, hallowed be thy name; thy kingdom come; thy will be done in earth as it is in heaven. Give us this day our daily bread. And forgive us our debts as we forgive our debtors. And lead us not into temptation, but deliver us from evil. For thine is the kingdom, and the power, and the glory forever. Amen.

THE APOSTOLIC BENEDICTION.

The grace of the Lord Jesus Christ, and the love of God, and the communion of the Holy Ghost, be with you all. Amen.

Doxologies.

1. L. M.

PRAISE God, from whom all blessings flow,
Praise him, all creatures here below;
Praise him above, ye heavenly host!
Praise Father, Son, and Holy Ghost!

2. L. M.

To God the Father, God the Son,
And God the Spirit, Three in One,
Be honor, praise, and glory given,
By all on earth, and all in heaven!

3. L. M.

To Father, Son, and Holy Ghost,
  The God whom earth and heaven adore,
Be glory as it was of old,
  Is now, and shall be evermore!

4. C. M.

To Father, Son, and Holy Ghost,
  One God, whom we adore,
Be glory as it was, is now,
  And shall be evermore!

5. C. M.

Let God the Father, and the Son,
  And Spirit be adored,
Where there are works to make him known,
  Or saints to love the Lord.

6. C. M.

The grace of Jesus Christ our Lord,
  God's love in boundless store,
The Holy Spirit's fellowship,
  Be with us evermore!

7. S. M.

The Father and the Son
  And Spirit we adore;
We praise, we bless, we worship thee,
  Both now and evermore!

8. S. M.

To God, the Father, Son,
  And Spirit, glory be,
As was, is now, and shall remain
  Through all eternity.

9. S. M.

The grace of Christ our Lord,
  God's love in boundless store,
The Holy Spirit's fellowship,
  Be with us evermore!

10. 7s.

Sing we to our God above
Praise eternal as his love;
Praise him, all ye heavenly host,
Father, Son, and Holy Ghost!

11. 7s.

Praise the name of God most high;
Praise him, all below the sky;
Praise him, all ye heavenly host,—
Father, Son, and Holy Ghost!
As through countless ages past,
Evermore his praise shall last.

12. 8s. & 7s.

Praise the God of our salvation,
  Praise the Father's boundless love;
Praise the Lamb, our expiation;
  Praise the Spirit from above;
Praise the Fountain of salvation,
  Him by whom our spirits live;
Undivided adoration
  To the one Jehovah give!

13. 6s. & 4s.

To God, the Father, Son,
And Spirit, Three in One,
  All praise be given!
Crown him in every song;
To him all hearts belong;
Let all his praise prolong,
  On earth, in heaven!

Section II.

PUBLIC WORSHIP.

(*a*.) *The Lord's Day and House.*

(*b*.) *Opening and Closing of Worship.*

(*c*.) *Morning and Evening Hymns.*

"PRAISE THE LORD IN THE SANCTUARY."

PUBLIC WORSHIP.

WEBB. 7s. & 6s.   GEO. JAMES WEBB.

The Sabbath.

1. O DAY of rest and gladness,
  O day of joy and light,
O balm of care and sadness,
  Most beautiful, most bright!
On thee, the high and lowly,
  Bending before the throne,
Sing, Holy, Holy, Holy,
  To the Great Three in One!

2. On thee, at the creation,
  The light first had its birth;
On thee, for our salvation,
  Christ rose from depths of earth;
On thee, our Lord, victorious,
  The Spirit sent from Heaven,
And thus on thee, most glorious
  A triple light was given.

3. To-day on weary nations
  The heavenly manna falls;
To holy convocations
  The silver trumpet calls,
Where gospel light is glowing
  With pure and radiant beams,
And living water flowing
  With soul-refreshing streams.

4. New graces ever gaining
  From this our day of rest,
We reach the rest remaining
  To spirits of the blest:
To Holy Ghost be praises,
  To Father and to Son;
The Church her voice upraises
  To thee, blest Three in One.
                    WORDSWORTH.

UXBRIDGE. L. M.
DR. MASON.

2. *Psalm 92.*

1 Sweet is the work, my God, my King,
  To praise thy name, give thanks, and sing;
  To show thy love by morning light,
  And talk of all thy truth at night.

2 Sweet is the day of sacred rest;
  No mortal care shall seize my breast;
  Oh, may my heart in tune be found,
  Like David's harp of solemn sound!

3 My heart shall triumph in my Lord,
  And bless his works and bless his word;
  Thy works of grace, how bright they shine!
  How deep thy counsels! how divine!

4 Lord, I shall share a glorious part,
  When grace hath well refined my heart,
  And fresh supplies of joy are shed,
  Like holy oil to cheer my head.

5 Then shall I see and hear and know
  All I desired or wished below,
  And every power find sweet employ
  In that eternal world of joy.
  WATTS.

3. *Psalm 84.*

1 How pleasant, how divinely fair,
  O Lord of hosts, thy dwellings are!
  With long desire my spirit faints
  To meet th' assemblies of thy saints.

2 My flesh would rest in thine abode;
  My panting heart cries out for God.
  My God, my King, why should I be
  So far from all my joys and thee!

3 Blest are the souls that find a place
  Within the temple of thy grace;
  There they behold thy gentler rays,
  And seek thy face, and learn thy praise.

4 Blest are the men whose hearts are set
  To find the way to Zion's gate;
  God is their strength, and thro' the road
  They lean upon their helper, God.

5 Cheerful they walk with growing strength,
  Till all shall meet in heaven at length;
  Till all before thy face appear,
  And join in nobler worship there.
  WATTS.

4. *Joy in Worship.*

1 Lord, how delightful 'tis to see
  A whole assembly worship thee!
  At once they sing, at once they pray;
  They hear of heaven, and learn the way.

2 I have been there, and still would go;
  'Tis like a little heaven below:
  Not all that careless sinners say
  Shall tempt me to forget this day.

3 Oh, write upon my memory, Lord,
  The texts and doctrines of thy word!
  That I may break thy laws no more,
  But love thee better than before.

4 With thoughts of Christ, and things divine,
  Fill up this foolish heart of mine;
  That, finding pardon through his blood,
  I may lie down, and wake with God.
  WATTS.

Public Worship.

ALSACE. L. M. — BEETHOVEN.

1. Thine earthly Sabbaths, Lord, we love, But there's a nobler rest above; To that our longing souls aspire, With cheerful hope and strong desire.

5.

2 No more fatigue, no more distress,
Nor sin nor death shall reach the place;
No groans shall mingle with the songs
Which warble from immortal tongues.

3 No rude alarms of raging foes;
No cares to break the long repose;
No midnight shade, no clouded sun,—
But sacred, high, eternal noon!

4 O long-expected day, begin!
Dawn on these realms of woe and sin;
Fain would we leave this weary road,
And sleep in death, to rest with God.
DODDRIDGE.

6.

1 FAR from my thoughts, vain world, begone!
Let my religious hours alone:
Fain would mine eyes my Saviour see:
I wait a visit, Lord, from thee.

2 My heart grows warm with holy fire,
And kindles with a pure desire:
Come, my dear Jesus! from above,
And feed my soul with heavenly love.

3 Blest Saviour! what delicious fare,
How sweet thine entertainments are!
Never did angels taste, above,
Redeeming grace and dying love.

4 Hail, great Immanuel, all-divine!
In thee thy Father's glories shine:
Thou brightest, sweetest, fairest One
That eyes have seen, or angels known!
WATTS.

7. Gen. 28: 17.

1 How sweet to leave the world awhile,
And seek the presence of our Lord!
Dear Saviour! on thy people smile,
And come, according to thy word.

2 From busy scenes we now retreat,
That we may here converse with thee:
Ah! Lord, behold us at thy feet;—
Let this the "gate of heaven" be.

3 "Chief of ten thousand!" now appear,
That we by faith may see thy face:
Oh! speak, that we thy voice may hear,
And let thy presence fill this place.
KELLY.

8. Psalm 118.

1 Lo! what a glorious corner-stone
The Jewish builders did refuse;
But God hath built his Church thereon,
In spite of envy and the Jews.

2 Great God! the work is all divine,
The joy and wonder of our eyes;
This is the day that proves it thine,
The day that saw our Saviour rise.

3 Sinners, rejoice, and saints be glad;
Hosanna, let his name be blest;
A thousand honors on his head,
With peace and light and glory rest!

4 In God's own name he comes to bring
Salvation to our dying race;
Let the whole Church address their King
With hearts of joy, and songs of praise.
WATTS.

Public Worship.

NEWTON. 7s.   DR. MASON.

1. Safe-ly through an-oth-er week God has brought us on our way; Wait-ing
Let us now a bless-ing seek, in his courts to-day; Day of all the week the best, Emblem of e-ter-nal rest. Day of all the week the best, Em-blem of e-ter-nal rest.

9.   *The Lord's Day.*

2 While we pray for pard'ning grace,
    Through the dear Redeemer's name,
Show thy reconciling face;
    Take away our sin and shame:
From our worldly cares set free,
May we rest this day in thee.

3 Here we come, thy name to praise;
    Let us feel thy presence near;
May thy glories meet our eyes,
    While we in thy house appear:
Here afford us, Lord, a taste
Of our everlasting feast.

4 May the gospel's joyful sound
    Conquer sinners, comfort saints;
Make the fruits of grace abound;
    Bring relief for all complaints:
Thus let all our Sabbaths prove.
Till we rest in thee above.
                      NEWTON.

10.   *Psalm 84.*

1 PLEASANT are thy courts above,
    In the land of light and love;
Pleasant are thy courts below,
    In this land of sin and woe.
Oh, my spirit longs and faints
    For the converse of thy saints;
For the brightness of thy face,
King of glory, King of grace!

2 Happy birds that sing and fly
    Round thy altars, O Most High!
Happier souls that find a rest
    In a heavenly Father's breast!
Happy souls! their praises flow
Even in this world of woe;
Waters in the desert rise,
Manna feeds them from the skies.

3 On they go from strength to strength,
    Till they reach thy throne at length;
At thy feet adoring fall,
    Who hast led them safe through all.
Lord, be mine this prize to win!
Guide me through a world of sin,
Keep me by thy saving grace,
Give me, at thy side, a place!
                      LYTE.

Opening of Worship.

WARWICK. C. M.   STANLEY.

11.   Psalm 5.

1 LORD, in the morning thou shalt hear
    My voice ascending high;
To thee will I direct my prayer,
    To thee lift up mine eye: —

2 Up to the hills where Christ is gone,
    To plead for all his saints,
Presenting at his Father's throne
    Our songs and our complaints.

3 Thou art a God before whose sight
    The wicked shall not stand;
Sinners shall ne'er be thy delight,
    Nor dwell at thy right hand.

4 But to thy house will I resort,
    To taste thy mercies there;
I will frequent thy holy court,
    And worship in thy fear.

5 Oh, may thy Spirit guide my feet
    In ways of righteousness!
Make every path of duty straight
    And plain before my face.
                  WATTS.

12.   Psalm 118.

1 THIS is the day the Lord hath made;
    He calls the hours his own:
Let heaven rejoice, let earth be glad,
    And praise surround the throne.

2 To-day he rose, and left the dead,
    And Satan's empire fell;
To-day the saints his triumph spread,
    And all his wonders tell.

3 Hosanna to th' anointed King,
    To David's holy Son:
Help us, O Lord! descend, and bring
    Salvation from thy throne.

4 Blest be the Lord who comes to men
    With messages of grace;
Who comes, in God his Father's name,
    To save our sinful race.

5 Hosanna in the highest strains
    The Church on earth can raise;
The highest heavens, in which he reigns,
    Shall give him nobler praise.
                  WATTS.

13.   Psalm 63.

1 EARLY, my God! without delay,
    I haste to seek thy face;
My thirsty spirit faints away,
    Without thy cheering grace.

2 So pilgrims on the scorching sand,
    Beneath a burning sky,
Long for a cooling stream at hand,
    And they must drink or die.

3 I've seen thy glory and thy power
    Through all thy temple shine:
My God! repeat that heavenly hour,
    That vision so divine.

4 Not life itself, with all its joys,
    Can my best passions move,
Or raise so high my cheerful voice,
    As thy forgiving love.

5 Thus, till my last expiring day,
    I'll bless my God and King;
Thus will I lift my hands to pray,
    And tune my lips to sing.
                  WATTS.

BRATTLE STREET. C. M. Double.
PLEYEL.

14. *Providence.*

1 While thee I seek, protecting Power!
    Be my vain wishes stilled;
  And may this consecrated hour
    With better hopes be filled!

2 Thy love the power of thought bestowed;
    To thee my thoughts would soar;
  Thy mercy o'er my life has flowed;
    That mercy I adore.

3 In each event of life, how clear
    Thy ruling hand I see!
  Each blessing to my soul more dear,
    Because conferred by thee.

4 In every joy that crowns my days,
    In every pain I bear,
  My heart shall find delight in praise,
    Or seek relief in prayer.

5 When gladness wings my favored hour,
    Thy love my thoughts shall fill;
  Resigned, when storms of sorrow lower,
    My soul shall meet thy will.

6 My lifted eye, without a tear,
    The gathering storm shall see;
  My steadfast heart shall know no fear;
    That heart will rest on thee.
                                    MISS WILLIAMS.

15. *Psalm 84.*

1 My soul, how lovely is the place,
    To which thy God resorts!
  'Tis heaven to see his smiling face,
    Though in his earthly courts.

2 There the great Monarch of the skies
    His saving power displays;
  And light breaks in upon our eyes,
    With kind and quickening rays.

3 With his rich gifts, the heavenly Dove
    Descends and fills the place;
  While Christ reveals his wondrous love,
    And sheds abroad his grace.

4 There, mighty God, thy words declare
    The secrets of thy will;
  And still we seek thy mercy there,
    And sing thy praises still.
                                    WATTS.

MICHAEL. H. M.   HAYDN.

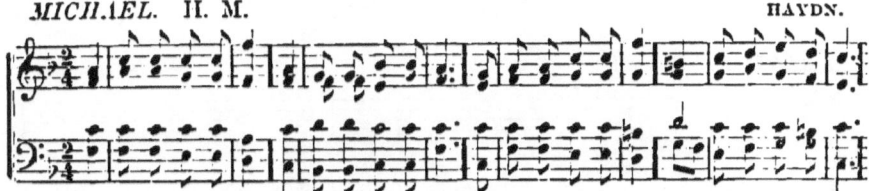

16.   Psalm 84.

1 LORD of the worlds above,
   How pleasant and how fair
The dwellings of thy love,
   Thine earthly temples are!
To thine abode my heart aspires,
With warm desires, (with warm desires)
   To see my God.

2 The sparrow for her young
   With pleasure seeks a nest;
And wandering swallows long
   To find their wonted rest:
My spirit faints with equal zeal,
To rise and dwell (to rise and dwell)
   Among thy saints.

3 Oh, happy souls that pray
   Where God appoints to hear;
Oh, happy men that pay
   Their constant service there!
They praise thee still; and happy they
That love the way (that love the way)
   To Zion's hill!

4 They go from strength to strength,
   Through this dark vale of tears,
Till each arrives at length,
   Till each in heaven appears:

Oh, glorious seat, when God our King
Shall thither bring (shall thither bring)
   Our willing feet!
                         WATTS.

17.   The Lord's Day.

1 WELCOME, delightful morn,
   Thou day of sacred rest!
I hail thy kind return;—
   Lord, make these moments blest:
From the low train of mortal toys,
I soar to reach (I soar to reach)
   Immortal joys.

2 Now may the King descend
   And fill his throne of grace;
Thy sceptre, Lord, extend,
   While saints address thy face:
Let sinners feel thy quickening word,
And learn to know (and learn to know)
   And fear the Lord.

3 Descend, celestial Dove,
   With all thy quickening powers;
Disclose a Saviour's love,
   And bless these sacred hours:
Then shall my soul new life obtain,
Nor Sabbaths be (nor Sabbaths be)
   Enjoyed in vain.
                         HAYWARD.

DALSTON. S. P. M.   WILLIAMS.

18.   Psalm 122.

1 How pleased and blest was I
  To hear the people cry,
    "Come, let us seek our God to-day!"
  Yes, with a cheerful zeal,
  We haste to Zion's hill,
    And there our vows and honors pay.

2 Zion, thrice happy place,
  Adorned with wondrous grace, [round!
    And walls of strength embrace thee
  In thee our tribes appear
  To pray and praise, and hear
    The sacred gospel's joyful sound.

3 May peace attend thy gate,
  And joy within thee wait
    To bless the soul of every guest:
  The man who seeks thy peace,
  And wishes thine increase,
    A thousand blessings on him rest!

4 My tongue repeats her vows,
  "Peace to this sacred house!" [dwell;
    For here my friends and kindred
  And since my glorious God
  Makes thee his blest abode,
    My soul shall ever love thee well.
                       WATTS.

19.   God's Government.

1 The Lord Jehovah reigns,
  And royal state maintains,
    His head with awful glories crowned;
  Arrayed in robes of light,
  Begirt with sovereign might,
    And rays of majesty around.

2 Upheld by thy commands,
  The world securely stands,
    And skies and stars obey thy word;
  Thy throne was fixed on high
  Before the starry sky:
    Eternal is thy kingdom, Lord!

3 Let floods and nations rage,
  And all their powers engage;
    Let swelling tides assault the sky:
  The terrors of thy frown
  Shall beat their madness down:
    Thy throne forever stands on high.

4 Thy promises are true;
  Thy grace is ever new;   [remove:
    There fixed, thy church shall ne'er
  Thy saints, with holy fear,
  Shall in thy courts appear,
    And sing thine everlasting love.
                       WATTS.

The Lord's Day.

ARIEL. C. P. M.   DR. MASON.

20.   *Psalm 122.*

1 The festal morn, my God, is come,
That calls me to thy sacred dome,
  Thy presence to adore :
My feet the summons shall attend,
With willing steps thy courts ascend,
  And tread the hallowed floor.

2 With holy joy I hail the day
That warns my thirsting soul away
  To dwell among the blest!
For, lo! my great Redeemer's power
Unfolds the everlasting door,
  And leads me to his rest!

3 Hither, from earth's remotest end,
Lo! the redeemed of God ascend,
  Their tribute hither bring:
Here, crowned with everlasting joy,
In hymns of praise their tongues employ,
  And hail th' immortal King.
                          Merrick.

21.   *The Glorious Works of God.*

1 Thy mighty working, mighty God!
Wakes all my powers; I look abroad,
  And can no longer rest;
I, too, must sing when all things sing,
And from my heart the praises ring
  The Highest loveth best.

2 If thou, in thy great love to us,
Wilt scatter joy and beauty thus
  O'er this poor earth of ours;
What nobler glories shall be given
Hereafter in thy shining heaven,
  Set round with golden towers!

3 What thrilling joy, when on our sight
Christ's garden beams in cloudless light,
  Where all the air is sweet;
Still laden with th' unwearied hymn
From all the thousand seraphim
  Who God's high praise repeat!

4 Oh, were I there! oh that I now
Before thy throne, my God, could bow,
  And bear my heavenly palm!
Then, like the angels, would I raise
My voice, and sing thine endless praise
  In many a sweet-toned psalm.

Public Worship.

LEIGHTON. S. M. — GREATOREX.

22. *The Sanctuary.*

1 How charming is the place
  Where my Redeemer, God,
Unveils the beauties of his face,
  And sheds his love abroad!

2 Not the fair palaces
  To which the great resort,
Are once to be compared with this,
  Where Jesus holds his court.

3 Here on the mercy-seat,
  With radiant glory crowned,
Our joyful eyes behold him sit,
  And smile on all around.

4 To him their prayers and cries
  Each humble soul presents;
He listens to their broken sighs,
  And grants them all their wants.

5 Give me, O Lord, a place
  Within thy bless'd abode,
Among the children of thy grace,
  The servants of my God.
  STENNETT.

23. Psalm 92.

1 SWEET is the work, O Lord,
  Thy glorious acts to sing,
To praise thy name, and hear thy word,
  And grateful offerings bring.

2 Sweet, at the dawning light,
  Thy boundless love to tell:
And when approach the shades of night,
  Still on the theme to dwell.

3 Sweet, on this day of rest,
  To join in heart and voice
With those who love and serve thee best,
  And in thy name rejoice.

4 To songs of praise and joy,
  Be every Sabbath given,
That such may be our blest employ
  Eternally in heaven.
  LYTE.

24. *Call to Praise.*

1 STAND up, and bless the Lord,
  Ye people of his choice;
Stand up and bless the Lord your God,
  With heart and soul and voice.

2 Though high above all praise,
  Above all blessing high,
Who would not fear his holy name,
  And laud, and magnify?

3 Oh, for the living flame
  From his own altar brought,
To touch our lips, our souls inspire,
  And wing to heaven our thought!

4 God is our strength and song,
  And his salvation ours:
Then be his love in Christ proclaimed,
  With all our ransomed powers.

5 Stand up and bless the Lord;
  The Lord your God adore;
Stand up, and bless his glorious name,
  Henceforth, for evermore.
  MONTGOMERY.

The Lord's Day and House.

LISBON. S. M. READ.

25. *Psalm 118.*

1 SEE what a living stone
  The builders did refuse!
Yet God hath built his church thereon,
  In spite of envious Jews.

2 The scribe and angry priest
  Reject thine only Son;
Yet on this rock shall Zion rest,
  As the chief corner-stone.

3 The work, O Lord, is thine,
  And wondrous in our eyes:
This day declares it all divine;
  This day did Jesus rise.

4 This is the glorious day
  That our Redeemer made:
Let us rejoice and sing and pray;
  Let all the church be glad.

5 Hosanna to the King,
  Of David's royal blood!
Bless him, ye saints! he comes to bring
  Salvation from your God.
                              WATTS.

26. *Psalm 48.*

1 GREAT is the Lord our God,
  And let his praise be great;
He makes his churches his abode,
  His most delightful seat.

2 These temples of his grace,
  How beautiful they stand!
The honors of our native place,
  And bulwarks of our land.

3 In Zion God is known
  A refuge in distress;
How bright has his salvation shone
  Through all her palaces!

4 Oft have our fathers told,
  Our eyes have often seen,
How well our God secures the fold
  Where his own sheep have been.

5 In every new distress
  We'll to his house repair,
We'll think upon his wondrous grace,
  And seek deliverance there.
                              WATTS.

27. *Day of Rest.*

1 WELCOME, sweet day of rest,
  That saw the Lord arise,
Welcome to this reviving breast,
  And these rejoicing eyes.

2 The King himself comes near,
  And feasts his saints to-day;
Here we may sit, and see him here,
  And love and praise and pray.

3 One day, amid the place
  Where God, my God, hath been,
Is sweeter than ten thousand days
  Within the tents of sin.

4 My willing soul would stay
  In such a frame as this,
And sit and sing herself away
  To everlasting bliss.
                              WATTS.

SHELDON. C. M.   From the "PSALTERY."

.28.   *Invocation.*

1 Again our earthly cares we leave,
    And to thy courts repair;
  Again with joyful feet we come,
    To meet our Saviour here.

2 Great Shepherd of thy people, hear!
    Thy presence now display;
  We bow within thy house of prayer;
    Oh! give us hearts to pray.

3 The clouds which veil thee from our sight,
    In pity, Lord, remove;
  Dispose our minds to hear aright
    The message of thy love.

4 The feeling heart, the melting eye,
    The humble mind, bestow;
  And shine upon us from on high,
    To make our graces grow.

5 Show us some token of thy love,
    Our fainting hopes to raise;
  And pour thy blessing from on high,
    To aid our feeble praise.

29.   Psalm 65.

1 Praise waits in Zion, Lord, for thee,
    There shall our vows be paid;
  Thou hast an ear when sinners pray;
    All flesh shall seek thine aid.

2 Lord, our iniquities prevail,
    But pardoning grace is thine;
  And thou wilt grant us power and skill
    To conquer every sin.

3 Blest are the men whom thou wilt choose
    To bring them near thy face,
  Give them a dwelling in thy house,
    To feast upon thy grace.

4 In answering what thy church requests,
    Thy truth and terror shine;
  And works of dreadful righteousness
    Fulfil thy kind design.

5 Thus shall the wondering nations see
    The Lord is good and just;
  And distant islands fly to thee,
    And make thy name their trust.
                        Watts.

30.   Psalm 84.

1 How lovely are thy dwellings, Lord,
    From noise and trouble free!
  How beautiful the sweet accord
    Of souls that pray to thee!

2 Lord God of hosts, that reign'st on high!
    They are the truly blest,
  Who only will on thee rely,
    In thee alone will rest.

3 They pass refreshed the thirsty vale,
    The dry and barren ground,
  As through a fruitful, watery dale,
    Where springs and showers abound.

4 They journey on from strength to strength,
    With joy and gladsome cheer,
  Till all before our God at length
    In Zion's courts appear.
                        Milton.

HOLMES. L. M.

1. Great God, attend, while Zion sings
The joy that from thy presence springs;
To spend one day with thee on earth,
Exceeds a thousand days of mirth.

31. *Psalm 84.*

2 Might I enjoy the meanest place
Within thy house, O God of grace,
Not tents of ease, nor thrones of power,
Should tempt my feet to leave thy door.

3 God is our sun — he makes our day;
God is our shield — he guards our way
From all th' assaults of hell and sin,
From foes without and foes within.

4 O God, our King, whose sovereign sway
The glorious host of heaven obey,
Display thy grace, exert thy power,
Till all on earth thy name adore!
WATTS.

32. *John 4: 21-23.*

1 O Thou to whom, in ancient time,
The psalmist's sacred harp was strung,
Whom kings adored in song sublime,
And prophets praised with glowing tongue;

2 Not now on Zion's height alone,
The favored worshipper may dwell;
Nor where, at sultry noon, thy Son
Sat, weary, by the patriarch's well.

3 From every place below the skies,
The grateful song, the fervent prayer,
The incense of the heart may rise
To heaven, and find acceptance there.

4 O Thou to whom, in ancient time,
The holy prophet's harp was strung,
To thee at last, in every clime,
Shall temples rise, and praise be sung.
WARE.

33. *Daily Mercies.*

1 NEW every morning is the love
Our wakening and uprising prove:
Through sleep and darkness safely brought,
Restored to life and power and thought.

2 New mercies, each returning day,
Hover around us while we pray;
New perils past, new sins forgiven, [en.
New thoughts of God, new hopes of heav-

3 Old friends, old scenes will lovelier be
As more of heaven in each we see;
Some softening gleam of love and prayer
Shall dawn on every cross and care.

4 Only, O Lord, in thy dear love,
Fit us for perfect rest above,
And keep us this, and every day,
To live more nearly as we pray.
KEBLE.

34. *"God is in this place."*

1 Lo, God is here! — let us adore,
And own how dreadful is this place!
Let all within us feel his power,
And silent bow before his face!

2 Lo, God is here! — him day and night,
United choirs of angels sing:
To him, enthroned above all height,
Let saints their humble worship bring.

3 Lord God of hosts! oh, may our praise
Thy courts with grateful incense fill!
Still may we stand before thy face,
Still hear and do thy sovereign will!
J. WESLEY.

Public Worship.

ST. ANN'S. C. M.   DR. CROFT.

35. *Sabbath Morning.*

1 BLEST morning, whose young dawning
   Beheld our rising God,   [rays
That saw him triumph o'er the dust,
   And leave his dark abode.

2 In the cold prison of the tomb
   The dead Redeemer lay,
Till the revolving skies had brought
   The third, th' appointed day.

3 Hell and the grave unite their force
   To hold our Lord, in vain;
The sleeping Conqueror arose,
   And burst their feeble chain.

4 To thy great name, almighty Lord,
   These sacred hours we pay,
And loud hosannas shall proclaim
   The triumph of the day.
                    WATTS.

36.

1 FREQUENT the day of God returns,
   To shed its quickening beams;
And yet how slow devotion burns!
   How languid are its flames!

2 Accept our faint attempts to love;
   Our follies, Lord, forgive;
We would be like thy saints above,
   And praise thee while we live.

3 Increase, O Lord, our faith and hope,
   And fit us to ascend
Where th' assembly ne'er breaks up,
   And Sabbaths never end.
                    BROWNE.

37.

1 SPIRIT of truth! on this thy day,
   To thee for help we cry,
To guide us through the dreary way
   Of dark mortality.

2 We ask not, Lord, the cloven flame,
   Or tongues of various tone;
But long thy praises to proclaim
   With fervor in our own.

3 No heavenly harpings soothe our ear,
   No mystic dreams we share;
Yet hope to feel thy comfort near,
   And bless thee in our prayer.

4 When tongues shall cease, and power
   And knowledge empty prove, [decay,
Do thou thy trembling servants stay,
   With faith and hope and love.
                    HEBER.

38. *Closing Hymn.*

1 THOU Holy Spirit, Lord of grace,
   Eternal fount of love,
Inflame, we pray, our inmost hearts
   With fire from heaven above.

2 As thou in bond of love dost join
   The Father and the Son,
So fill us all with mutual love,
   And knit our hearts in one.

3 All glory to the Father be,
   All glory to the Son,
All glory to the Holy Ghost,
   While endless ages run.

Opening and Closing of Worship.

PLEYEL'S HYMN. 7s. — PLEYEL.

39. *Opening of Worship.*

1 Lord, we come before thee now,
 At thy feet we humbly bow;
 Oh, do not our suit disdain!
 Shall we seek thee, Lord, in vain?

2 Lord, on thee our souls depend,
 In compassion now descend;
 Fill our hearts with thy rich grace,
 Tune our lips to sing thy praise.

3 In thine own appointed way,
 Now we seek thee; here we stay;
 Lord, we know not how to go,
 Till a blessing thou bestow.

4 Comfort those who weep and mourn;
 Let the time of joy return;
 Those that are cast down lift up;
 Make them strong in faith and hope.

5 Grant that all may seek and find
 Thee a God supremely kind;
 Heal the sick, the captive free;
 Let us all rejoice in thee.
 HAMMOND.

40. *Opening of Worship.*

1 To thy temple we repair —
 Lord, we love to worship there,
 When within the veil we meet
 Thee upon the mercy-seat.

2 While thy glorious name is sung,
 Tune our lips — unloose our tongue;
 Then our joyful souls shall bless
 Thee, the Lord our Righteousness.

3 While to thee our prayers ascend,
 Let thine ear in love attend;
 Hear us, for thy Spirit pleads, —
 Hear, for Jesus intercedes.

4 While thy word is heard with awe,
 While we tremble at thy law,
 Let thy gospel's wondrous love
 Every doubt and fear remove.

5 From thy house when we return,
 Let our hearts within us burn;
 That at evening we may say,
 "We have walked with God to-day."
 MONTGOMERY.

41. *Close of Worship.*

1 For the mercies of the day,
 For this rest upon our way,
 Thanks to thee alone be given,
 Lord of earth and King of heaven!

2 Cold our services have been,
 Mingled every prayer with sin;
 But thou canst and wilt forgive;
 By thy grace alone we live.

3 While this thorny path we tread,
 May thy love our footsteps lead;
 When our journey here is past,
 May we rest with thee at last.

4 Let these earthly Sabbaths prove
 Foretastes of our joys above;
 While their steps thy children bend
 To the rest which knows no end.
 MONTGOMERY.

Public Worship.

ELPARAN. L. M. — SHULTZ.

42. *Sabbath-Day.*

1 Another six days' work is done;
Another Sabbath is begun:
Return, my soul, unto thy rest;
Enjoy the day thy God hath blest.

2 Oh, that our thoughts and thanks may rise,
As grateful incense to the skies!
And draw from heaven that calm repose,
Which none but he who feels it knows.

3 That heavenly calm within the breast!
It is the pledge of that dear rest
Which for the church of God remains,—
The end of cares, the end of pains.

4 In holy duties let the day,
In holy pleasures, pass away.
How sweet a Sabbath thus to spend,
In hope of one that ne'er shall end!
STENNETT.

43. *"Return, O God of Hosts."*

1 Lord, in the temples of thy grace
Thy saints behold thy smiling face;
And oft have seen thy glory shine,
With power and majesty divine.

2 Come, dearest Lord, thy children cry,
Our graces droop, our comforts die;
Return, and let thy glories rise
Again to our admiring eyes:

3 Till, filled with light and joy and love,
Thy courts below, like those above,
Triumphant hallelujahs raise, [praise.
And heaven and earth resound thy

44. *Morning Psalm.*

1 O Christ! with each returning morn
Thine image to our hearts be borne;
And may we ever clearly see
Our God and Saviour, Lord, in thee!

2 All hallowed be our walk this day;
May meekness form our early ray,
And faithful love our noontide light,
And hope our sunset, calm and bright.

3 May grace each idle thought control,
And sanctify our wayward soul;
May guile depart, and malice cease,
And all within be joy and peace.

4 Our daily course, O Jesus, bless;
Make plain the way of holiness:
From sudden falls our feet defend,
And cheer at last our journey's end.

45. *John 4: 21.*

1 Jesus, where'er thy people meet,
There they behold thy mercy-seat;
Where'er they seek thee, thou art found;
And every place is hallowed ground.

2 For thou, within no walls confined,
Inhabitest the humble mind;
Such ever bring thee where they come,
And, going, take thee to their home.

3 Dear Shepherd of thy chosen few,
Thy former mercies here renew:
Here to our waiting hearts proclaim
The sweetness of thy saving name.
COWPER.

Sabbath Morning. 65

HYMN. C. M.   From "MODERN HARP."

1. Come, thou desire of all thy saints, Our humble strains attend, While, with our praises and complaints, Low at thy feet we bend.

46.   *Invocation.*

2 How should our songs, like those above,
   With warm devotion rise!
 How should our souls, on wings of love,
   Mount upward to the skies!

3 Come, Lord! thy love alone can raise
   In us the heavenly flame;
 Then shall our lips resound thy praise,
   Our hearts adore thy name.

4 Dear Saviour, let thy glory shine,
   And fill thy dwellings here,
 Till life and love and joy divine
   A heaven on earth appear.

5 Then shall our hearts enraptured say,
   Come, great Redeemer! come,
 And bring the bright, the glorious day
   That calls thy children home.
                              STEELE.

47.   *Sabbath Morning.*

1 How sweet, how calm, this Sabbath morn!
   How pure the air that breathes,
 And soft the sounds upon it borne,
   And light its vapor wreaths!

2 It seems as if the Christian's prayer,
   For peace and joy and love,
 Were answered by the very air
   That wafts its strain above.

3 Let each unholy passion cease,
   Each evil thought be crushed,
 Each anxious care that mars thy peace
   In Faith and Love be hushed.

48.   Psalm 122.

1 WITH joy we hail the sacred day
   Which God has called his own;
 With joy the summons we obey
   To worship at his throne.

2 Thy chosen temple, Lord, how fair!
   Where willing votaries throng
 To breathe the humble, fervent prayer,
   And pour the choral song.

3 Spirit of grace! oh, deign to dwell
   Within thy church below;
 Make her in holiness excel,
   With pure devotion glow.

4 Let peace within her walls be found;
   Let all her sons unite
 To spread with grateful zeal around
   Her clear and shining light.
                              LYTE.

49.   Luke 8: 5-15.

1 O GOD! by whom the seed is given,
   By whom the harvest blest;
 Whose word, like manna showered from
   Is planted in our breast,— [heaven,

2 Preserve it from the passing feet,
   And plunderers of the air,
 The sultry sun's intenser heat,
   And thorns of worldly care.

3 Though buried deep, or thinly strown,
   Do thou thy grace supply;
 The hope in earthly furrows sown
   Shall ripen in the sky.
                              HEBER.

UNDERWOOD. S. M.
D. E. JONES.

50. *Evening Hymn.*

1 The day is past and gone,
 The evening shades appear;
Oh, may we all remember well,
 The night of death draws near.

2 Lord! keep us safe this night,
 Secure from all our fears;
May angels guard us while we sleep,
 Till morning light appears.

3 And when we early rise,
 And view th' unwearied sun,
May we set out to win the prize,
 And after glory run.

4 And when our days are past,
 And we from time remove,
Oh, may we in thy bosom rest,
 The bosom of thy love.
  LELAND.

51. *Psalm 48.*

1 Far as thy name is known,
 The world declares thy praise;
Thy saints, O Lord, before thy throne,
 Their songs of honor raise.

2 With joy thy people stand
 On Zion's chosen hill,
Proclaim the wonders of thy hand,
 And counsels of thy will.

3 Let strangers walk around
 The city where we dwell,
Compass and view thine holy ground,
 And mark the building well —

4 The order of thy house,
 The worship of thy court,
The cheerful songs, the solemn vows;
 And make a fair report.

5 How decent and how wise!
 How glorious to behold!
Beyond the pomp that charms the eyes,
 And rites adorned with gold.

6 The God we worship now
 Will guide us till we die;
Will be our God, while here below,
 And ours above the sky.
  WATTS.

52. *Closing Hymn.*

1 We love the place, O God,
 Wherein thine honor dwells;
The pleasures of thy blest abode,
 All earthly joy excels.

2 We love the house of prayer,
 Wherein thy servants meet,
For thou, O Lord, art ever there,
 Thy chosen flock to greet.

3 We love the word of life, —
 The word that tells of peace,
Of comfort in our daily strife,
 Of joys that never cease.

4 Lord Jesus! give us grace
 On earth to love thee more,
In heaven to see thy glorious face,
 And with thy saints adore.

Evening Worship: Parting Hymn.

HOLLEY. 7s. GEO. HEWS.

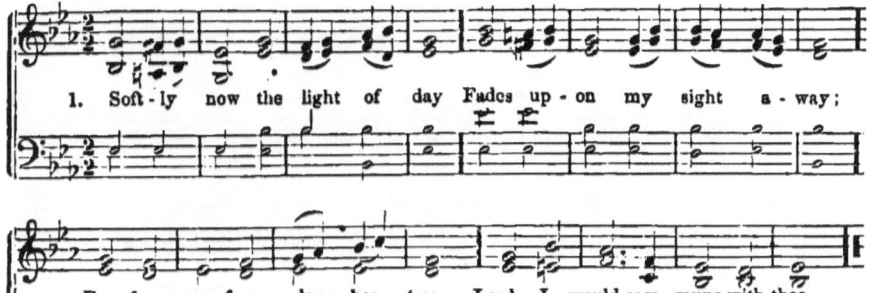

1. Soft-ly now the light of day Fades up-on my sight a-way;
Free from care, from la-bor free, Lord, I would com-mune with thee.

53.
2 Soon for me the light of day
 Shall forever pass away;
 Then, from sin and sorrow free,
 Take me, Lord! to dwell with thee.
  DOANE.

54.
1 O MY Saviour, Guardian true,
  All my life is thine to keep;
 At thy feet my work I do,
  In thine arms I fall asleep.

2 Leaning on thy tender care,
  Thou hast led my soul aright;
 Fervent was my morning prayer;
  Joyful is my song to-night.

3 Tender mercies on my way
  Falling softly like the dew,
 Sent me freshly every day —
  I will bless the Lord for you.

4 Source of all that comforts me,
  Well of joy for which I long;
 Let the song I sing to thee
  Be an everlasting song!

55. *Parting Hymn.*
1 CHRISTIAN brethren, ere we part,
  Every voice and every heart
 Join, and to our Father raise
  One last hymn of grateful praise.

2 Though we here should meet no more,
  Yet there is a brighter shore;
 There, released from toil and pain,
  There we all may meet again.

56. *Evening Worship.*
1 SOFTLY fades the twilight ray
  Of the holy Sabbath-day;
 Gently as life's setting sun,
  When the Christian's course is run.

2 Peace is on the world abroad;
  'Tis the holy peace of God, —
 Symbol of the peace within,
  When his people rest from sin.

3 Still the Spirit lingers near,
  Where the evening worshipper
 Seeks communion with the skies,
  Pressing onward to the prize.

4 Saviour, may our Sabbaths be
  Days of peace and joy in thee,
 Till in heaven our souls repose,
  Where the Sabbath ne'er shall close.
   S. F. SMITH.

57. Heb. 13: 20, 21.
1 Now may He who from the dead
  Brought the Shepherd of the sheep,
 Jesus Christ, our King and Head,
  All our souls in safety keep.

2 May he teach us to fulfil
  What is pleasing in his sight;
 Make us perfect in his will,
  And preserve us day and night!

3 To that great Redeemer's praise,
  Who the cov'nant sealed with blood,
 Let our hearts and voices raise
  Loud thanksgivings to our God.
   NEWTON.

Public Worship.

INVITATION. C. M.   By permission of WM. HALL & SON.
Arranged from WALLACE.

58. *Evening Twilight.*

1 I LOVE to steal awhile away
From every cumbering care,
And spend the hours of setting day
In humble, grateful prayer.

2 I love, in solitude, to shed
The penitential tear;
And all his promises to plead,
Where none but God can hear.

3 I love to think on mercies past,
And future good implore;
And all my cares and sorrows cast
On Him whom I adore.

4 I love, by faith, to take a view
Of brighter scenes in heaven;
The prospect doth my strength renew,
While here by tempests driven.

5 Thus, when life's toilsome day is o'er,
May its departing ray
Be calm as this impressive hour,
And lead to endless day!
MRS. BROWN.

59. Psalm 139: 12.

1 GOD of the sunlight hours, how sad
Would evening's shadows be;
Or night, in deeper shadows clad,
If aught were dark to thee!

2 How mournfully that golden gleam
Would touch the thoughtful heart,
If, with its soft, retiring beam,
We saw thy light depart!

3 Enough, while these dull heavens may
If here thy presence be; [lower,
Then midnight shall be morning hour,
And darkness light to me.

4 Through the deep gloom of mortal
Thy light of love can throw [things,
That ray which gilds an angel's wings,
To soothe a pilgrim's woe.

60. *Sabbath Rest.*

1 WHEN the worn spirit wants repose,
And sighs her God to seek;
How sweet to hail the evening's close
That ends the weary week.

2 How sweet to hail the early dawn
That opens on the sight,
When first that soul-reviving morn
Beams its new rays of light.

3 Sweet day, thine hours too soon will
cease;
Yet, while they gently roll,
Breathe, heavenly Spirit, source of
A Sabbath o'er my soul. [peace,

4 When will my pilgrimage be done,
The world's long week be o'er,
That Sabbath dawn which needs no sun,
That day which fades no more?
EDMESTON.

Evening Hymns.

HUNTINGTON. C. M.   C. W. HUNTINGTON.

61. *Vesper Hymn.*

1 The sun is sinking in the west,
  The daylight swiftly flies;
Arise, my soul, and haste to pay
  Thine evening sacrifice.

2 O Lord, into thy sacred charge,
  In whom all spirits live,
My helpless soul, in humble faith,
  Herself would wholly give.

3 Beneath thine ever-watchful eye,
  My soul would calmly rest,
Without a wish, without a thought
  Abiding in the breast, —

4 Save that thy blessed will be done,
  Whatever may betide;
Dead to herself, and also dead,
  In thee, to all beside.

5 Lord, on the cross thine arms were stretched
  To draw thy people nigh;
Oh, grant us then, that cross to love,
  And in those arms to die.

62. *1 Peter 5: 7.*

1 The twilight falls, the night is near;
  I fold my work away;
And kneel to Him who bends to hear
  The story of the day.

2 The old, old story! yet I kneel
  To tell it at His call;
And cares grow lighter as I feel
  That Jesus knows them all.

3 Yes, all! the morning and the night,
  The joy, the grief, the loss,
The roughened path, the sunbeam bright,
  The hourly thorn and cross.

4 And Jesus loves me! all my heart
  With answering love is stirred;
And every anguish, every smart,
  Finds healing in the Word.

5 So then I lay me down to rest,
  As nightly shadows fall;
And lean, confiding, on His breast
  Who knows and pities all.

63. *Psalm 4.*

1 Lord, thou wilt hear me when I pray;
  I am forever thine;
I fear before thee all the day,
  Nor would I dare to sin.

2 And while I rest my weary head,
  From cares and business free,
'Tis sweet conversing on my bed
  With my own heart and thee.

3 I pay this evening sacrifice;
  And when my work is done,
Great God! my faith and hope relies
  Upon thy grace alone.

4 Thus, with my thoughts composed to peace,
  I give mine eyes to sleep;
Thy hand in safety keeps my days,
  And will my slumbers keep.

                         WATTS.

Public Worship.

KEBLE.   L. M.

64. *Luke 24: 29.*

1 Sun of my soul! thou Saviour dear,
  It is not night if thou be near:
  Oh, may no earth-born cloud arise
  To hide thee from thy servant's eyes!

2 When soft the dews of kindly sleep
  My weary eyelids gently steep,
  Be my last thought,— how sweet to rest
  Forever on my Saviour's breast!

3 Abide with me from morn till eve,
  For without thee I cannot live;
  Abide with me when night is nigh,
  For without thee I dare not die.

4 Be near to bless me when I wake,
  Ere through the world my way I take;
  Till in the ocean of thy love
  I lose myself in Heaven above.
                             KEBLE.

65.   *Lam. 3: 23. Isa. 45: 7.*

1 My God, how endless is thy love!
  Thy gifts are every evening new;
  And morning mercies from above
  Gently distil like early dew.

2 Thou spread'st the curtains of the night,
  Great Guardian of my sleeping hours;
  Thy sovereign word restores the light,
  And quickens all my drowsy powers.

3 I yield my powers to thy command;
  To thee I consecrate my days;
  Perpetual blessings from thine hand
  Demand perpetual songs of praise.
                             WATTS.

66.   *Sabbath Evening.*

1 Sweet is the light of Sabbath eve,
  And soft the sunbeams ling'ring there;
  For these blest hours the world I leave,
  Wafted on wings of faith and prayer.

2 Season of rest! the tranquil soul [love;
  Feels the sweet calm, and melts in
  And while these sacred moments roll,
  Faith sees a smiling heaven above.

3 Nor will our days of toil be long:
  Our pilgrimage will soon be trod;
  And we shall join the ceaseless song,
  The endless Sabbath of our God.
                             EDMESTON.

67.   *Psalm 35: 18.*

1 Millions within thy courts have met;
  Millions, this day, before thee bowed;
  Their faces Zionward were set, [vowed.
  Vows with their lips to thee they

2 From east to west, the sun surveyed,
  From north to south, adoring throngs;
  And still, when evening stretched her shade,
  The stars came out to hear their songs.

3 And not a prayer, a tear, a sigh,
  Hath failed this day some suit to gain;
  To those in trouble thou wert nigh:
  Not one hath sought thy face in vain.

4 Yet one prayer more!— and be it one
  In which both heaven and earth accord,
  Fulfil thy promise to thy Son;
  Let all that breathe call Jesus LORD!
                             MONTGOMERY.

Close of Worship.

PARTING SONG. L. M. 61.

Chorus: Through the day, through the night, O gentle Jesus, be our Light.

68. *"The Lord is my Light."*

1 SWEET Saviour, bless us ere we go;
  Thy word into our minds instil;
And make our lukewarm hearts to glow
  With lowly love and fervent will.
Thro' life's long day and death's dark
O gentle Jesus, be our Light. [night,
  Through the day, through the night,
  O gentle Jesus, be our Light.

2 The day is gone, its hours have run,
  And thou hast taken count of all,
The scanty triumphs grace hath won,
  The broken vow, the frequent fall.
Thro' life's long day and death's dark
O gentle Jesus, be our Light. [night,
  Chorus:

3 Grant us, dear Lord, from evil ways
  True absolution and release;
And bless us, more than in past days,
  With purity and inward peace.
Thro' life's long day and death's dark
O gentle Jesus, be our Light. [night,
  Chorus:

4 Do more than pardon; give us joy,
  Sweet fear, and sober liberty,
And simple hearts without alloy
  That only long to be like thee.
Thro' life's long day and death's dark
O gentle Jesus, be our Light. [night,
  Chorus:

5 Labor is sweet, for thou hast toiled;
  And care is light, for thou hast cared;
Ah! never let our works be soiled
  With strife, or by deceit ensnared.
Thro' life's long day and death's dark
O gentle Jesus, be our Light. [night,
  Chorus:

6 For all we love, the poor, the sad,
  The sinful, unto thee we call;
Oh, let thy mercy make us glad:
  Thou art our Jesus, and our All.
Thro' life's long day and death's dark
O gentle Jesus, be our Light. [night,
  Chorus:
                              MONK'S COLL.

Public Worship.

HEBRON. L. M. — DR. MASON.

69. *Evening Hymn.*

1 Thus far the Lord has led me on;
  Thus far his power prolongs my days;
  And every evening shall make known
  Some fresh memorial of his grace.

2 Much of my time has run to waste,
  And I, perhaps, am near my home;
  But he forgives my follies past,
  He gives me strength for days to come.

3 I lay my body down to sleep;
  Peace is the pillow for my head,
  While well-appointed angels keep
  Their watchful stations round my bed.

4 Thus, when the night of death shall come,
  My flesh shall rest beneath the ground,
  And wait thy voice to rouse my tomb,
  With sweet salvation in the sound.
  WATTS.

70. *Close of Worship.*

1 Ere to the world again we go,
  Its pleasures, cares, and idle show,
  Thy grace, once more, O God, we crave,
  From folly and from sin to save.

2 May the great truths we here have heard,
  The lessons of thy holy word,
  Dwell in our inmost bosoms deep,
  And all our souls from error keep.

3 Oh, may the influence of this day
  Long as our memory with us stay,
  And as an angel guardian prove,
  To guide us to our home above.

71. *Psalm 17: 8.*

1 Glory to thee, my God! this night,
  For all the blessings of the light;
  Keep me, oh, keep me, King of kings!
  Beneath thine own almighty wings.

2 Forgive me, Lord, for thy dear Son,
  The ill that I this day have done;
  That with the world, myself, and thee,
  I, ere I sleep, at peace may be.

3 Teach me to live, that I may dread
  The grave as little as my bed;
  Teach me to die, that so I may
  Rise glorious at the awful day.

4 Oh, let my soul on thee repose;
  And may sweet sleep my eyelids close,—
  Sleep that shall me more vigorous make
  To serve my God, when I awake.

5 Praise God, from whom all blessings flow;
  Praise him, all creatures here below;
  Praise him above, ye heavenly host!
  Praise Father, Son, and Holy Ghost.
  KENN.

72. *Close of Worship.*

1 Dismiss us with thy blessing, Lord!
  Help us to feed upon thy word;
  All that has been amiss, forgive,
  And let thy truth within us live.

2 Though we are guilty, thou art good;
  Wash all our works in Jesus' blood;
  Give every burdened soul release,
  And bid us all depart in peace.
  HART.

Evening Hymns.

VESPER. 8s. & 7s. Arranged from **FLOTOW.**

73. *"Abide with us; for it is toward evening."*

1 TARRY with me, O my Saviour!
  For the day is passing by;
  See! the shades of evening gather,
  And the night is drawing nigh.

2 Deeper, deeper grow the shadows,
  Paler now the glowing west,
  Swift the night of death advances;
  Shall it be the night of rest?

3 Feeble, trembling, fainting, dying,
  Lord, I cast myself on thee;
  Tarry with me through the darkness;
  While I sleep, still watch by me.

4 Tarry with me, O my Saviour!
  Lay my head upon thy breast
  Till the morning; then awake me, —
  Morning of eternal rest!

74. *The Evening Blessing.*

1 SAVIOUR, breathe an evening blessing,
  Ere repose our spirits seal:
  Sin and want we come confessing;
  Thou canst save and thou canst heal.

2 Though destruction walk around us,
  Though the arrow near us fly,
  Angel guards from thee surround us;
  We are safe, if thou art nigh.

3 Though the night be dark and dreary,
  Darkness cannot hide from thee:
  Thou art he, who, never weary,
  Watcheth where thy people be.

4 Should swift death this night o'ertake us,
  And our couch become our tomb,
  May the morn in heaven awake us,
  Clad in light and deathless bloom!
  EDMESTON.

75. *Holy Memories.*

1 SILENTLY the shades of evening
  Gather round my lowly door;
  Silently they bring before me
  Faces I shall see no more.

2 Oh! the lost, the unforgotten,
  Though the world be oft forgot;
  Oh! the shrouded and the lonely,
  In our hearts they perish not.

3 Living in the silent hours,
  Where our spirits only blend,
  They, unlinked with earthly trouble,
  We, still hoping for its end.

4 How such holy memories cluster,
  Like the stars when storms are past;
  Pointing up to that far heaven
  We may hope to gain at last.

76. *Parting Hymn.*

1 Lo, the day of rest declineth,
  Gather fast the shades of night;
  May the Sun which ever shineth
  Fill our souls with heavenly light!

2 While, thine ear of love addressing,
  Thus our parting hymn we sing,
  Father, grant thine evening blessing,
  Fold us safe beneath thy wing!
  ROBBINS.

Public Worship.

EVENTIDE. 10s.

77. Luke 24: 29.

1 ABIDE with me! Fast falls the eventide,
The darkness deepens; Lord, with me abide!
When other helpers fail, and comforts flee,
Help of the helpless, oh, abide with me!

2 Swift to its close ebbs out life's little day;
Earth's joys grow dim, its glories pass away;
Change and decay in all around I see;
O Thou, who changest not, abide with me!

3 I need thy presence every passing hour:
What but thy grace can foil the tempter's power?
Who, like thyself, my guide and stay can be?
Through cloud and sunshine, Lord, abide with me!

4 I fear no foe with thee at hand to bless:
Ills have no weight, and tears no bitterness:
Where is death's sting; where, grave, thy victory?
I triumph still, if thou abide with me!

5 Hold thou thy cross before my closing eyes;
Shine through the gloom and point me to the skies;
Heaven's morning breaks, and earth's vain shadows flee!
In life, in death, O Lord, abide with me!

LYTE.

Parting Hymns: Benediction.

SICILY. 8s. & 7s.

78. *Closing Hymn.*

1 Lord, dismiss us with thy blessing,
  Fill our hearts with joy and peace;
  Let us each, thy love possessing,
    Triumph in redeeming grace:
      Oh, refresh us,
  Travelling through this wilderness.

2 Thanks we give, and adoration,
  For thy gospel's joyful sound;
  May the fruits of thy salvation
    In our hearts and lives abound;
      May thy presence
  With us evermore be found.

3 Then, whene'er the signal's given,
  Us from earth to call away,
  Borne on angel's wings to heaven,
    Glad the summons to obey,
      May we ever
  Reign with Christ in endless day.
                                BURDER.

79. *Opening Hymn.*

1 In thy name, O Lord! assembling,
  We thy people now draw near:
  Teach us to rejoice with trembling;
    Speak, and let thy servants hear;
      Hear with meekness,—
  Hear thy word with godly fear.

2 While our days on earth are lengthened,
  May we give them, Lord, to thee;
  Cheered by hope, and daily strengthened,
    May we run, nor weary be;
      Till thy glory
  Without cloud in heaven we see.

3 There, in worship purer, sweeter,
  All thy people shall adore;
  Tasting of enjoyment greater
    Than they could conceive before;
      Full enjoyment,—
  Full, and pure, for evermore.
                                KELLY.

80. *Parting Hymn.*

1 God of our salvation, hear us;
  Bless, oh, bless us, ere we go;
  When we join the world, be near us,
    Lest we cold and careless grow.
      Saviour, keep us;
  Keep us safe from every foe.

2 May we live in view of heaven,
  Where we hope to see thy face;
  Save us from unhallowed leaven,
    All that might obscure thy grace;
      Keep us walking
  Each in his appointed place.

3 As our steps are drawing nearer
  To the place we call our home,
  May our view of heaven grow clearer,
    Hope more bright of joys to come;
      And, when dying,
  May thy presence cheer the gloom.

81. *Benediction.*

1 May the grace of Christ our Saviour,
  And the Father's boundless love,
  With the Holy Spirit's favor,
    Rest upon us from above!
  Thus may we abide in union
    With each other and the Lord,
  And possess, in sweet communion,
    Joys which earth cannot afford.
                                NEWTON.

SECTION III.

THE HOLY SCRIPTURES.

(a.) Delight in the Word of God.

(b.) The Word a Lamp and Guide.

(c.) The Gospel Glorious and Everlasting.

"*THY STATUTES HAVE BEEN MY SONGS IN THE HOUSE OF MY PILGRIMAGE.*" — Psalm 119: 54.

The Holy Scriptures.

NAZARETH. L. M.   S. WEBBE.

82.   Psalm 19.

1 The heavens declare thy glory, Lord;
   In every star thy wisdom shines;
   But when our eyes behold thy word,
   We read thy name in fairer lines.

2 The rolling sun, the changing light,
   And night and day thy power confess;
   But the blest volume thou hast writ,
   Reveals thy justice and thy grace.

3 Sun, moon, and stars convey thy praise
   Round the whole earth, and never stand;
   So when thy truth began its race,
   It touched and glanced on every land.

4 Nor shall thy spreading gospel rest,
   Till through the world thy truth hath run;
   Till Christ hath all the nations blest
   That see the light, or feel the sun.
                         WATTS.

83.

1 Great Sun of Righteousness, arise!
   Bless the dark world with heavenly light,
   Thy gospel makes the simple wise,
   Thy laws are pure, thy judgments right.

2 Thy noblest wonders here we view
   In souls renewed, and sins forgiven;
   Lord, cleanse my sins, my soul renew,
   And make thy word my guide to heaven.
                         WATTS.

84.   The Gospel.

1 God, in the gospel of his Son,
   Makes his eternal counsels known:
   Here love in all its glory shines,
   And truth is drawn in fairest lines.

2 Here sinners, of an humble frame,
   May taste his grace and learn his name;
   May read, in characters of blood,
   The wisdom, power, and grace of God.

3 Here faith reveals to mortal eyes
   A brighter world beyond the skies;
   Here shines the light which guides our way
   From earth to realms of endless day.

4 Oh, grant us grace, almighty Lord!
   To read, and mark thy holy word:
   Its truths with meekness to receive,
   And by its holy precepts live.
                         BEDDOME.

The Holy Scriptures.

MIGDOL. L. M.   DR. MASON.

85.   *The Bible Precious.*

1 I LOVE the sacred book of God!
    No other can its place supply;
    It points me to his own abode,
    It gives me wings, and bids me fly.

2 Sweet book! in thee my eyes discern
    The very image of my Lord;
    From thine instructive page I learn
    The joys his presence will afford.

3 In thee I read my title clear
    To mansions that will ne'er decay; —
    Dear Lord, oh, when wilt thou appear,
    And bear thy prisoner away!

4 While I am here, these leaves supply
    His place, and tell me of his love;
    I read with faith's discerning eye,
    And gain a glimpse of joys above.

5 I know in them the Spirit breathes
    To animate his people here;
    Oh, may these truths prove life to all,
    Till in his presence we appear!
                     KELLY.

86.   *The Gospel Glorious.*

1 UPON the gospel's sacred page
    The gathered beams of ages shine;
    And, as it hastens, every age
    But makes its brightness more divine.

2 On mightier wing, in loftier flight,
    From year to year does knowledge
    And, as it soars, the gospel light [soar;
    Becomes effulgent more and more.

3 More glorious still, as centuries roll,
    New regions blest, new powers unfurled,
    Expanding with the expanding soul,
    Its radiance shall o'erflow the world, —

4 Flow to restore, but not destroy;
    As when the cloudless lamp of day
    Pours out its floods of light and joy,
    And sweeps the lingering mist away.
                     BOWRING.

87.   *Praise for the Gospel.*

1 LET everlasting glories crown
    Thy head, my Saviour and my Lord!
    Thy hands have brought salvation down,
    And writ the blessings in thy Word.

2 In vain the trembling conscience seeks
    Some solid ground to rest upon;
    With long despair the spirit breaks,
    Till we apply to Christ alone.

3 How well thy blessed truths agree!
    How wise and holy thy commands!
    Thy promises, how firm they be!
    How firm our hope and comfort stands!

4 Should all the forms that men devise
    Assault my faith with treacherous art,
    I'd call them vanity and lies,
    And bind the gospel to my heart.
                     WATTS.

Doxology.

PRAISE God, from whom all blessings flow,
Praise him, all creatures here below;
Praise him above, ye heavenly host,
Praise Father, Son, and Holy Ghost.

The Holy Scriptures: Hymn of Praise.

NASHVILLE. L. P. M.   OLD MELODY.

88.   Psalm 19.

1 I LOVE the volume of thy word.
What light and joy those leaves afford
To souls benighted and distressed!
Thy precepts guide my doubtful way,
Thy fear forbids my feet to stray,
Thy promise leads my heart to rest.

2 Thy threatenings wake my slumbering eyes,
And warn me where my danger lies;
But 'tis thy blessed gospel, Lord,
That makes my guilty conscience clean,
Converts my soul, subdues my sin,
And gives a free, but large reward.

3 Who knows the errors of his thoughts?
My God! forgive my secret faults,
And from presumptuous sins restrain:
Accept my poor attempts of praise,
That I have read thy book of grace,
And book of nature not in vain.
                    WATTS.

89.   Psalm 146.

1 I'LL praise my Maker with my breath;
And when my voice is lost in death,
Praise shall employ my nobler powers:
My days of praise shall ne'er be past,
While life and thought and being last,
Or immortality endures.

2 Happy the man whose hopes rely
On Israel's God; he made the sky
And earth and seas, with all their train:
His truth forever stands secure;
He saves th' oppressed, he feeds the poor,
And none shall find his promise vain.

3 The Lord hath eyes to give the blind;
The Lord supports the sinking mind;
He sends the lab'ring conscience peace;
He helps the stranger in distress,
The widow and the fatherless,
And grants the pris'ner sweet release.

4 He loves his saints, he knows them well,
But turns the wicked down to hell:
Thy God, O Zion, ever reigns!
Let every tongue, let every age,
In this exalted work engage:
Praise him in everlasting strains.

5 I'll praise him while he lends me breath;
And when my voice is lost in death,
Praise shall employ my nobler powers:
My days of praise shall ne'er be past,
While life and thought and being last,
Or immortality endures.
                    WATTS.

The Holy Scriptures.

DARWIN. C. M.

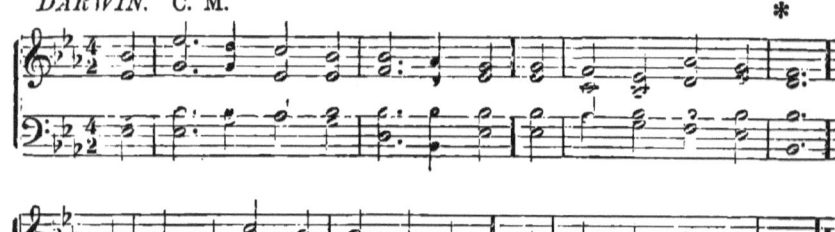

90. *The Bible.*

1 LAMP of our feet! whereby we trace
  Our path when wont to stray;
Stream from the fount of heavenly grace!
  Brook by the traveller's way!

2 Bread of our souls! whereon we feed;
  True manna from on high!
Our guide and chart! wherein we read
  Of realms beyond the sky.

3 Pillar of fire through watches dark,
  And radiant cloud by day! [bark,
When waves would whelm our tossing
  Our anchor and our stay!

4 Word of the everlasting God!
  Will of his glorious Son!
Without thee how could earth be trod,
  Or heaven itself be won?

5 Lord! grant us all aright to learn
  The wisdom it imparts,
And to its heavenly teaching turn
  With simple, childlike hearts.

91. *Psalm 119.*

1 How shall the young secure their hearts,
  And guard their lives from sin?
Thy word the choicest rules imparts,
  To keep the conscience clean.

2 'Tis like the sun, a heavenly light,
  That guides us all the day;
And, through the dangers of the night,
  A lamp to lead our way.

3 Thy precepts make me truly wise:
  I hate the sinner's road:
I hate my own vain thoughts that rise,
  But love thy law, my God.

4 Thy word is everlasting truth,
  How pure is every page!
That holy book shall guide our youth,
  And well support our age.
    WATTS.

92. *Psalm 119.*

1 OH, how I love thy holy law!
  'Tis daily my delight;
And thence my meditations draw
  Divine advice by night.

2 My waking eyes prevent the day,
  To meditate thy word;
My soul with longing melts away
  To hear thy gospel, Lord.

3 How doth thy word my heart engage!
  How well employ my tongue!
And, in my tiresome pilgrimage,
  Yields me a heavenly song.

4 When nature sinks, and spirits droop,
  Thy promises of grace
Are pillars to support my hope;
  And there I write thy praise.
    WATTS.

Doxology.

LET God the Father, and the Son,
  And Spirit, be adored,
Where there are works to make him
Or saints to love the Lord. [known,

The Gospel Glorious and Precious.

STEPHENS. C. M.   W. JONES.

93.   *The Glorious Gospel.*

1 A GLORY gilds the sacred page,
   Majestic, like the sun ;
It gives a light to every age ;
   It gives, but borrows none.

2 The hand that gave it still supplies
   The gracious light and heat ;
Its truths upon the nations rise, —
   They rise, but never set.

3 Let everlasting thanks be thine,
   For such a bright display
As makes a world of darkness shine
   With beams of heavenly day.

4 My soul rejoices to pursue
   The steps of Him I love,
Till glory breaks upon my view,
   In brighter worlds above.
                            COWPER.

94.   Psalm 89.

1 BLEST are the souls that hear and know
   The gospel's joyful sound ;
Peace shall attend the path they go,
   And light their steps surround.

2 Their joy shall bear their spirits up
   Through their Redeemer's name ;
His righteousness exalts their hope,
   Nor Satan dares condemn.

3 The Lord, our glory and defence,
   Strength and salvation gives ;
Israel, thy King forever reigns,
   Thy God forever lives.
                            WATTS.

95.   Psalm 119.

1 LORD, I have made thy word my choice,
   My lasting heritage ;
There shall my noblest powers rejoice,
   My warmest thoughts engage.

2 I'll read the hist'ries of thy love,
   And keep thy laws in sight ;
While through the promises I rove,
   With ever fresh delight.

3 'Tis a broad land of wealth unknown,
   Where springs of life arise,
Seeds of immortal bliss are sown,
   And hidden glory lies.

4 The best relief that mourners have ;
   It makes our sorrows blest ;
Our fairest hope beyond the grave,
   And our eternal rest.
                            WATTS.

96.   Psalm 119: 105.

1 How precious is the book divine,
   By inspiration given !
Bright as a lamp its doctrines shine
   To guide our souls to heaven.

2 It sweetly cheers our drooping hearts,
   In this dark vale of tears ;
Life, light, and joy it still imparts,
   And quells our rising fears.

3 This lamp, through all the tedious night
   Of life, shall guide our way ;
Till we behold the clearer light
   Of an eternal day.
                            FAWCETT.

The Holy Scriptures.

MARLOW. C. M.   ENGLISH.

97.   Matt. 13: 8.

1 ALMIGHTY God! thy word is cast
    Like seed into the ground;
Let now the dew of heaven descend,
    And righteous fruits abound.

2 Let not the foe of Christ and man
    This holy seed remove;
But give it root in every heart,
    To bring forth fruits of love.

3 Let not the world's deceitful cares
    The rising plant destroy;
But let it yield, a hundred-fold,
    The fruits of peace and joy.

4 Oft as the precious seed is sown,
    Thy quickening grace bestow,
That all, whose souls the truth receive,
    Its saving power may know.

98.   *Praise for the Gospel.*

1 FATHER of mercies, in thy word
    What endless glory shines!
Forever be thy name adored
    For these celestial lines.

2 Here my Redeemer's welcome voice
    Spreads heavenly peace around;
And life and everlasting joys
    Attend the blissful sound.

3 Oh, may these heavenly pages be
    My ever dear delight;

And still new beauties may I see,
    And still increasing light!

4 Divine Instructor, gracious Lord,
    Be thou forever near;
Teach me to love thy sacred word,
    And view my Saviour there.
                        STEELE.

99.   Psalm 119.

1 OH that the Lord would guide my ways
    To keep his statutes still!
Oh that my God would grant me grace
    To know and do his will!

2 Oh, send thy Spirit down, to write
    Thy law upon my heart;
Nor let my tongue indulge deceit,
    Nor act the liar's part.

3 Order my footsteps by thy word,
    And make my heart sincere;
Let sin have no dominion, Lord,
    But keep my conscience clear.

4 Make me to walk in thy commands,
    'Tis a delightful road;
Nor let my head nor heart nor hands
    Offend against my God.
                        WATTS.

Doxology.

LET God the Father, and the Son,
    And Spirit, be adored,
Where there are works to make him known,
    Or saints to love the Lord.

Section IV.

GOD:

THE FATHER, THE SON, AND THE HOLY GHOST.

(*a.*) *The Being, Attributes, Works, Providence, Government, and Glory of God. Adoration.*

(*b.*) *The Incarnation: The Birth, Life, Works, Passion, Resurrection, Ascension, and Exaltation of Jesus Christ.*

(*c.*) *The Holy Ghost and the Ever-Blessed Trinity.*

"*SERVE THE LORD WITH GLADNESS; COME BEFORE HIS PRESENCE WITH SINGING.*"—*Psalm* 100.

GOD:
THE FATHER, THE SON, AND THE HOLY GHOST.

OLD HUNDREDTH. L. M.

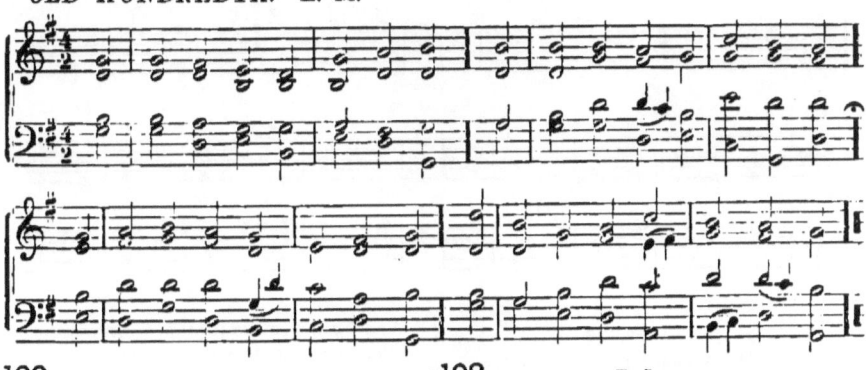

100.   *Psalm 57.*
1 Be thou exalted, O my God!
   Above the heavens where angels dwell;
   Thy power on earth be known abroad,
   And land to land thy wonders tell.

2 My heart is fixed: my song shall raise
   Immortal honors to thy name;
   Awake my tongue to sound his praise,
   My tongue, the glory of my frame.

3 High o'er the earth his mercy reigns,
   And reaches to the utmost sky;
   His truth to endless years remains,
   When lower worlds dissolve and die.

4 Be thou exalted, O my God!
   Above the heavens where angels dwell;
   Thy power on earth be known abroad,
   And land to land thy wonders tell.
                              WATTS.

101.   *Psalm 68.*
1 Kingdoms and thrones to God belong;
   Crown him, ye nations, in your song;
   His wondrous names and powers rehearse;
   His honors shall enrich your verse.

2 Proclaim him King, pronounce him blest;
   He's your defence, your joy, your rest;
   When terrors rise, and nations faint,
   God is the strength of every saint.
                              WATTS.

102.   *Te Deum.*
1 To Thee all angels cry aloud,
   And ceaseless raise their songs on high;
   Both cherubim and seraphim,
   The heavens and all the powers therein.

2 The apostles join the glorious throng;
   The prophets swell the immortal song;
   The martyrs' noble army raise
   Eternal anthems to thy praise.

3 Thee, holy, holy, holy King,
   Thee, O Lord God of Hosts! they sing;
   Thus earth below, and heaven above,
   Resound thy glory and thy love.

4 Thee we adore, Eternal Lord;
   We praise thy name with one accord;
   Thy saints who here thy goodness see
   Through all the world do worship thee.

103.   *Psalm 117.*
1 From all that dwell below the skies,
   Let the Creator's praise arise;
   Let the Redeemer's name be sung,
   Through every land, by every tongue.

2 Eternal are thy mercies, Lord;
   Eternal truth attends thy word: [shore,
   Thy praise shall sound from shore to
   Till suns shall rise and set no more!
                              WATTS.

LUTON. L. M.
G. BURDER.

104. *The Glory of God.*

1 Come, O my soul! in sacred lays,
Attempt thy great Creator's praise:
But, oh, what tongue can speak his fame!
What mortal verse can reach the theme!

2 Enthroned amid the radiant spheres,
He, glory, like a garment, wears;
To form a robe of light divine,
Ten thousand suns around him shine.

3 In all our Maker's grand designs,
Almighty power, with wisdom, shines;
His works through all this wondrous frame
Declare the glory of his name.

4 Raised on devotion's lofty wing,
Do thou, my soul, his glories sing;
And let his praise employ thy tongue,
Till listening worlds shall join the song!
BLACKLOCK.

105. Psalm 46: 10.

1 Wait, O my soul, thy Maker's will!
Tumultuous passions, all be still!
Nor let a murmuring thought arise;
His ways are just, his counsels wise.

2 He in the thickest darkness dwells,
Performs his work, the cause conceals;
But, though his methods are unknown,
Judgment and truth support his throne.

3 In heaven and earth and air and seas,
He executes his firm decrees;
And by his saints it stands confessed,
That what he does is ever best.

4 Wait, then, my soul, submissive wait,
Prostrate before his awful seat;
And, 'mid the terrors of his rod,
Trust in a wise and gracious God.
BEDDOME.

106. Job 11: 7.

1 Great God! in vain man's narrow view
Attempts to look thy nature through;
Our laboring powers with reverence own
Thy glories never can be known.

2 Not the high seraph's mighty thought,
Who countless years his God has sought,
Such wondrous height or depth can find,
Or fully trace thy boundless mind.

3 Yet, Lord, thy kindness deigns to show
Enough for mortal minds to know;
While wisdom, goodness, power divine,
Through all thy works and conduct shine.

4 Oh, may our souls with rapture trace
Thy works of nature and of grace;
Explore thy sacred name, and still
Press on to know and do thy will!
KIPPIS.

Doxology.

Praise God, from whom all blessings flow,
Praise him, all creatures here below;
Praise him above, ye heavenly host,
Praise Father, Son, and Holy Ghost.

107. Psalm 100.

1 Ye nations round the earth, rejoice
   Before the Lord, your sovereign King;
   Serve him with cheerful heart and voice,
     With all your tongues his glory sing.

2 The Lord is God; 'tis he alone
   Doth life and breath and being give:
   We are his work, and not our own,
     The sheep that on his pastures live.

3 Enter his gates with songs of joy,
   With praises to his courts repair;
   And make it your divine employ,
     To pay your thanks and honors there.

4 The Lord is good; the Lord is kind;
   Great is his grace, his mercy sure;
   And all the race of man shall find
     His truth from age to age endure.
                  WATTS.

108. Psalm 146.

1 Praise ye the Lord! my heart shall join
   In work so pleasant, so divine:
   My days of praise shall ne'er be passed,
     While life and thought and being last.

2 Happy the man whose hopes rely
   On Israel's God: he made the sky
   And earth and seas, with all their train;
     And none shall find his promise vain.

3 His truth forever stands secure; [poor,
   He saves th' oppressed, he feeds the
   He helps the stranger in distress,
     The widow and the fatherless.

4 He loves his saints, he knows them well,
   But turns the wicked down to hell:
   Thy God, O Zion, ever reigns;
     Praise him in everlasting strains!
                  WATTS.

109. Psalm 113: 5, 6.

1 Up to the Lord, who reigns on high,
   And views the nations from afar,
   Let everlasting praises fly,
     And tell how large his bounties are.

2 God, who must stoop to view the skies,
   And bow to see what angels do, —
   Down to our earth he casts his eyes,
     And bends his footsteps downward too.

3 He overrules all mortal things,
   And manages our mean affairs;
   On humble souls, the King of kings
     Bestows his counsels and his cares.

4 Our sorrows and our tears we pour
   Into the bosom of our God;
   He hears us in the mournful hour,
     And helps to bear the heavy load.

5 Oh! could our thankful hearts devise
   A tribute equal to thy grace,
   To the third heaven our song should rise,
     And teach the golden harps thy praise.
                  WATTS.

110. Psalm 97.

1 Th' Almighty reigns, exalted high
   O'er all the earth, o'er all the sky;
   Though clouds and darkness veil his feet,
     His dwelling is the mercy-seat.

2 O ye that love his holy name,
   Hate every work of sin and shame;
   He guards the souls of all his friends,
     And from the snares of hell defends.

3 Immortal light and joys unknown,
   Are for the saints in darkness sown;
   Those glorious seeds shall spring and rise,
     And the bright harvest bless our eyes.

4 Rejoice, ye righteous, and record
   The sacred honors of the Lord;
   None but the soul that feels his grace
     Can triumph in his holiness.
                  WATTS.

111. Psalm 97.

1 Jehovah reigns; his throne is high,
   His robes are light and majesty:
   His glory shines with beams so bright,
     No mortal can sustain the sight.

2 His terrors keep the world in awe;
   His justice guards his holy law;
   His love reveals a smiling face;
     His truth and promise seal the grace.

3 Through all his works what wisdom
   He baffles Satan's deep designs; [shines!
   His power is sovereign to fulfil
     The noblest counsels of his will.

4 And will this glorious Lord descend
   To be my Father and my Friend?
   Then let my songs with angels join;
     Heaven is secure, if God is mine.
                  WATTS.

God in Nature: His Sovereign Wisdom.

LOUVAN. L. M. — V. C. TAYLOR.

112. *Rom. 1: 20.*

1 There's nothing bright, above, below,
From flowers that bloom to stars that
But in its light my soul can see [glow,
Some features of the Deity.

2 There's nothing dark, below, above,
But in its gloom I trace thy love,
And meekly wait the moment when
Thy touch shall make all bright again.

3 The light, the dark, where'er I look,
Shall be one pure and shining book,
Where I may read, in words of flame,
The glories of thy wondrous name.
  MOORE.

113. *God our Source and End.*

1 Thou, Lord, of all the parent art,
Of all things thou alone the end :
On thee still fix our wavering heart;
To thee let all our actions tend.

2 Thou, Lord, art light; thy native ray
No change nor shadow ever knows;
To our dark souls thy light display,
The glory of thy face disclose.

3 Thou, Lord, art love ; the fountain thou
Whence mercy unexhausted flows;
On barren hearts, oh, shed it now,
And make the desert bear the rose!

4 So shall our every power to thee
In love and holy service rise;
And body, soul, and spirit be
Thy ever-living sacrifice.
  MARTINEAU'S COLL.

114. *Rom. 11: 33.*

1 Lord, my weak thought in vain would
  climb
To search the starry vault profound :
In vain would wing her flight sublime,
To find creation's outmost bound.

2 But weaker yet that thought must prove
To search thy great eternal plan, —
Thy sovereign counsels, born of love
Long ages ere the world began.

3 When my dim reason would demand
Why that or this thou dost ordain,
By some vast deep I seem to stand,
Whose secrets I must ask in vain.

4 When doubts disturb my troubled breast,
And all is dark as night to me,
Here, as on solid rock, I rest ;
That so it seemeth good to thee.
  RAY PALMER.

115. *Psalm 93.*

1 The floods, O Lord, lift up their voice,
The mighty floods lift up their roar;
The floods in tumult loud rejoice,
And climb in foam the sounding shore.

2 But mightier than the mighty sea,
The Lord of glory reigns on high :
Far o'er its waves we look to thee,
And see their fury break and die.

3 Thy word is true, thy promise sure,
That ancient promise, sealed in love;
Here be thy temple ever pure
As thy pure mansions shine above.
  G. BURGESS.

Sovereignty, Spirituality, and Love.

DELIVERANCE. C. M. JULIUS MULLER.

116. *God's Sovereignty.*

1 KEEP silence, all created things,
   And wait your Maker's nod!
   My soul stands trembling while she sings
   The honors of her God.

2 Life, death, and hell, and worlds un-
   Hang on his firm decree; [known,
   He sits on no precarious throne,
   Nor borrows leave to be.

3 Before his throne a volume lies,
   With all the fates of men,
   With every angel's form and size,
   Drawn by th' eternal pen.

4 His providence unfolds the book,
   And makes his counsels shine;
   Each opening leaf, and every stroke,
   Fulfils some deep design.

5 My God, I would not long to see
   My fate with curious eyes,—
   What gloomy lines are writ for me,
   Or what bright scenes may rise.

6 In thy fair book of life and grace,
   May I but find my name
   Recorded in some humble place,
   Beneath my Lord, the Lamb!
                        WATTS.

117. John 4: 24.

1 GOD is a Spirit, just and wise;
   He sees our inmost mind:
   In vain to Heaven we raise our cries,
   And leave our hearts behind.

2 Nothing but truth before his throne
   With honor can appear;
   The painted hypocrites are known
   Through the disguise they wear.

3 Their lifted eyes salute the skies;
   Their bending knees the ground;
   But God abhors the sacrifice,
   Where not the heart is found.

4 Lord, search my thoughts, and try my
   And make my soul sincere; [ways,
   Then shall I stand before thy face,
   And find acceptance there.
                        WATTS.

118. 1 John 4: 8.

1 AMID the splendors of thy state,
   O God! thy love appears,
   Soft as the radiance of the moon
   Among a thousand stars.

2 In all thy doctrines and commands,
   Thy counsels and designs,
   In every work thy hands have framed,
   Thy love supremely shines.

3 Sinai, in clouds and smoke and fire,
   Thunders thine awful name!
   But Zion sings, in melting notes,
   The honors of the Lamb.

4 Angels and men the news proclaim
   Through earth and heaven above;
   And all, with holy transport, sing
   That God, the Lord, is love.
                        PRATT'S COLL.

Omnipresence and Gracious Power.

WILLIAMS. C. M.   WILLIAMS.

119.   Psalm 139.

1 Lord, where shall guilty souls retire,
   Forgotten and unknown?
In hell they meet thy dreadful fire,
   In heaven thy glorious throne.

2 Should I suppress my vital breath,
   T' escape the wrath divine,
Thy voice would break the bars of death,
   And make the grave resign.

3 If, winged with beams of morning light,
   I fly beyond the west,
Thy hand, which must support my flight,
   Would soon betray my rest.

4 If o'er my sins I think to draw
   The curtains of the night,
Those flaming eyes that guard thy law
   Would turn the shades to light.

5 The beams of noon, the midnight hour,
   Are both alike to thee:
Oh, may I ne'er provoke that power
   From which I cannot flee!
                  WATTS.

120.   Psalm 139.

1 In all my vast concerns with thee,
   In vain my soul would try
To shun thy presence, Lord, or flee
   The notice of thine eye.

2 Thine all-surrounding sight surveys
   My rising and my rest;
My public walks, my private ways,
   The secrets of my breast.

3 My thoughts lie open to the Lord,
   Before they're formed within;
And ere my lips pronounce the word,
   He knows the sense I mean.

4 Oh, wondrous knowledge, deep and high!
   Where can a creature hide?
Within thy circling arms I lie,
   Beset on every side.

5 So let thy grace surround me still,
   And like a bulwark prove,
To guard my soul from every ill,
   Secured by sovereign love.
                  WATTS.

121.   Psalm 139.

1 Jehovah, God! thy gracious power
   On every hand we see;
Oh, may the blessings of each hour
   Lead all our thoughts to thee!

2 If, on the wings of morn, we speed
   To earth's remotest bound,
Thy hand will there our footsteps lead,
   Thy love our path surround.

3 Thy power is in the ocean deeps,
   And reaches to the skies;
Thine eye of mercy never sleeps,
   Thy goodness never dies.

4 From morn till noon, till latest eve,
   Thy hand, O God, we see;
And all the blessings we receive
   Proceed alone from thee.

5 In all the varying scenes of time,
   On thee our hopes depend;
Through every age, in every clime,
   Our Father, and our Friend.
                  THOMSON.

God our Refuge: His "Various Praise."

WARD. L. M.   SCOTTISH.

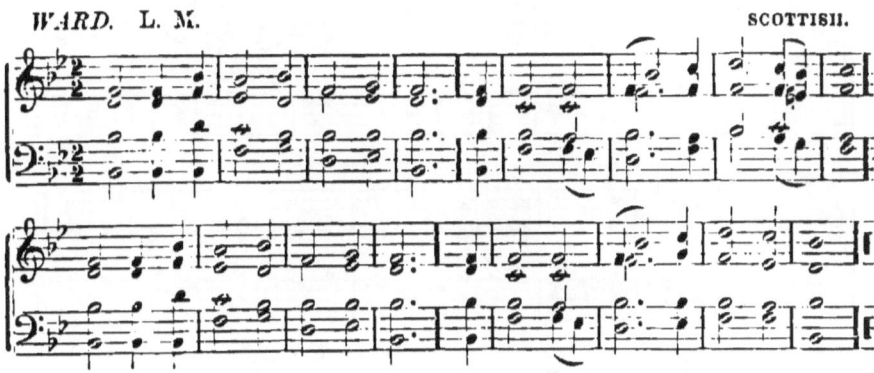

122.   *Psalm 46.*

1 GOD is the refuge of his saints,
   When storms of sharp distress invade;
Ere we can offer our complaints,
   Behold him present with his aid.

2 Let mountains from their seats be hurled
   Down to the deep and buried there,
Convulsions shake the solid world;
   Our faith shall never yield to fear.

3 Loud may the troubled ocean roar;
   In sacred peace our souls abide;
While every nation, every shore,
   Trembles and dreads the swelling tide.

4 There is a stream, whose gentle flow
   Supplies the city of our God,
Life, love, and joy, still gliding through,
   And watering our divine abode.

5 That sacred stream, thine holy word,
   Our grief allays, our fear controls;
Sweet peace thy promises afford, [souls.
   And give new strength to fainting

6 Zion enjoys her Monarch's love,
   Secure against a threatening hour;
Nor can her firm foundations move,
   Built on his truth and armed with
      power.
                     WATTS.

123.   *Psalm 145.*

1 MY God, my King, thy various praise
   Shall fill the remnant of my days;
Thy grace employ my humble tongue,
   Till death and glory raise the song.

2 The wings of every hour shall bear
   Some thankful tribute to thine ear;
And every setting sun shall see
   New works of duty done for thee.

3 Let distant times and nations raise
   The long succession of thy praise;
And unborn ages make my song
   The joy and triumph of their tongue.

4 But who can speak thy wondrous deeds?
   Thy greatness all our thoughts exceeds;
Vast and unsearchable thy ways!
   Vast and immortal be thy praise!
                     WATTS.

124.   *Psalm 36.*

1 HIGH in the heavens, eternal God!
   Thy goodness in full glory shines:
Thy truth shall break through every
      cloud
   That veils and darkens thy designs.

2 Forever firm thy justice stands,
   As mountains their foundations keep:
Wise are the wonders of thy hands;
   Thy judgments are a mighty deep.

3 My God, how excellent thy grace!
   Whence all our hope and comfort
      springs;
The sons of Adam, in distress,
   Fly to the shadow of thy wings.

4 From the provisions of thy house
   We shall be fed with sweet repast;
There, mercy like a river flows,
   And brings salvation to our taste.

5 Life, like a fountain rich and free,
   Springs from the presence of my Lord;
And in thy light our souls shall see
   The glories promised in thy word.
                     WATTS.

PARK STREET. L. M.   VENUA.

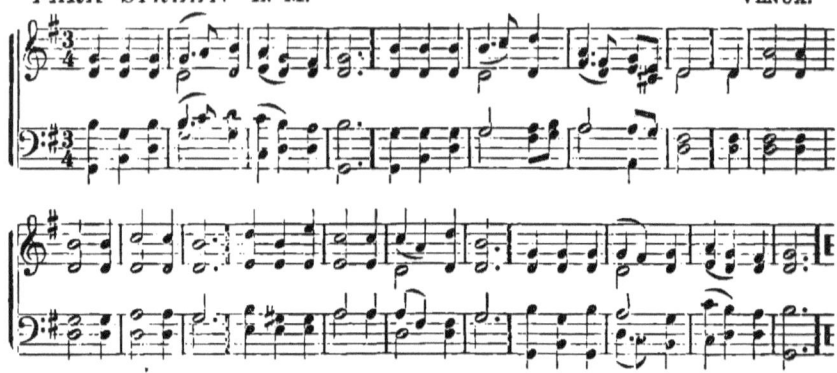

125.   Psalm 19.

1 The spacious firmament on high,
   With all the blue ethereal sky,
   And spangled heavens, a shining frame,
   Their great Original proclaim.

2 Th' unwearied sun, from day to day,
   Does his Creator's power display;
   And publishes to every land
   The work of an almighty hand.

3 Soon as the evening shades prevail,
   The moon takes up the wondrous tale;
   And nightly, to the listening earth,
   Repeats the story of her birth;

4 While all the stars that round her burn,
   And all the planets in their turn,
   Confirm the tidings as they roll,
   And spread the truth from pole to pole.

5 What though in solemn silence all
   Move round the dark terrestrial ball;
   What though no real voice nor sound
   Amid their radiant orbs are found;

6 In reason's ear they all rejoice,
   And utter forth a glorious voice,
   Forever singing as they shine—
   "The hand that made us is divine."
                             ADDISON.

126.   Psalm 7.

1 The Lord is Judge: before his throne
   All nations shall his justice own:
   Oh, may my soul be found sincere,
   And stand approved, with courage there.

2 The Lord, in righteousness arrayed,
   Surveys the world his hands have made;
   Pierces the heart, and tries the reins,
   And judgment from on high ordains.

3 My God, my shield! around me place
   The shelter of the Saviour's grace:
   Then, when thine arm the just shall save,
   My life shall triumph o'er the grave.
                            W. GOODE.

127.   Psalm 100.

1 Before Jehovah's awful throne,
   Ye nations bow with sacred joy;
   Know that the Lord is God alone,
   He can create, and he destroy.

2 His sovereign power, without our aid,
   Made us of clay, and formed us men;
   And when, like wandering sheep, we strayed,
   He brought us to his fold again.

3 We are his people, we his care,
   Our souls, and all our mortal frame;
   What lasting honors shall we rear,
   Almighty Maker, to thy name!

4 We'll crowd thy gates with thankful songs;
   High as the heavens our voices raise:
   And earth, with her ten thousand tongues,   [praise.
   Shall fill thy courts with sounding

5 Wide as the world is thy command,
   Vast as eternity thy love;
   Firm as a rock thy truth must stand,
   When rolling years shall cease to move.
                             WATTS.

The Compassions of God.

PENTONVILLE. S. M.

128. *Psalm 103.*

1 The pity of the Lord
  To those that fear his name,
Is such as tender parents feel:
  He knows our feeble frame.

2 He knows we are but dust,
  Scattered with every breath;
His anger, like a rising wind,
  Can send us swift to death.

3 Our days are as the grass,
  Or like the morning flower;
If one sharp blast sweep o'er the field,
  It withers in an hour.

4 But thy compassions, Lord,
  To endless years endure;
And children's children ever find
  Thy words of promise sure.
                              WATTS.

129. *Psalm 103.*

1 Oh, bless the Lord, my soul!
  His grace to thee proclaim;
And all that is within me join
  To bless his holy name.

2 Oh, bless the Lord, my soul!
  His mercies bear in mind;
Forget not all his benefits:
  The Lord to thee is kind.

3 He will not always chide;
  He will with patience wait;
His wrath is ever slow to rise,
  And ready to abate.

4 He pardons all thy sins,
  Prolongs thy feeble breath;
He healeth thy infirmities,
  And ransoms thee from death.

5 He clothes thee with his love,
  Upholds thee with his truth;
Then, like the eagle, he renews
  The vigor of thy youth.

6 Then bless His holy name,
  Whose grace hath made thee whole;
Whose loving kindness crowns thy days:
  Oh, bless the Lord, my soul!
                              MONTGOMERY.

130. *Psalm 103.*

1 Oh, bless the Lord, my soul!
  Let all within me join,
And aid my tongue to bless his name,
  Whose favors are divine.

2 Oh, bless the Lord, my soul!
  Nor let his mercies lie
Forgotten in unthankfulness,
  And without praises die.

3 'Tis he forgives thy sins;
  'Tis he relieves thy pain;
'Tis he that heals thy sicknesses,
  And makes thee young again.

4 He crowns thy life with love,
  When ransomed from the grave:
He that redeemed my soul from hell
  Hath sovereign power to save.
                              WATTS.

96 God: Creator and Benefactor.

SILVER STREET. S. M.   I. SMITH.

131.   Psalm 95.
1 Come, sound his praise abroad,
   And hymns of glory sing:
Jehovah is the sovereign God,
   The universal King.

2 He formed the deeps unknown;
   He gave the seas their bound;
The watery worlds are all his own,
   And all the solid ground.

3 Come, worship at his throne,
   Come, bow before the Lord:
We are his work and not our own;
   He formed us by his word.

4 To-day attend his voice,
   Nor dare provoke his rod;
Come, like the people of his choice,
   And own your gracious God.
                   WATTS.

132.   Psalm 8.
1 O Lord, our heavenly King,
   Thy name is all divine;
Thy glories round the earth are spread,
   And o'er the heavens they shine.

2 When to thy works on high
   I raise my wondering eyes,
And see the moon, complete in light,
   Adorn the darksome skies;

3 When I survey the stars.
   And all their shining forms,
Lord, what is man, that worthless thing,
   Akin to dust and worms?

4 Lord, what is worthless man,
   That thou shouldst love him so?
Next to thine angels is he placed,
   And lord of all below.

5 How rich thy bounties are!
   How wondrous are thy ways!
Of meanest things thy power can frame
   A monument of praise.

6 O Lord, our heavenly King,
   Thy name is all divine;
Thy glories round the earth are spread.
   And o'er the heavens they shine.
                   WATTS.

133.   *God our Creator and Benefactor.*
1 My Maker and my King!
   To thee my all I owe;
Thy sovereign bounty is the spring,
   Whence all my blessings flow.

2 The creature of thy hand,
   On thee alone I live;
My God, thy benefits demand
   More praise than life can give.

3 Lord, what can I impart,
   When all is thine before?
Thy love demands a thankful heart;
   The gift, alas, how poor!

4 Shall I withhold thy due?
   And shall my passions rove?
Lord, form this wretched heart anew,
   And fill it with thy love.
                   MRS. STEELE.

Our Shepherd. God in Nature.

BROWNELL. L. M. 6 LINES.   HAYDN.

134. *Psalm 23.*

1 The Lord my pasture shall prepare,
And feed me with a shepherd's care;
His presence shall my wants supply,
And guard me with a watchful eye;
My noonday walks he shall attend,
And all my midnight hours defend.

2 When in the sultry glebe I faint,
Or on the thirsty mountain pant,
To fertile vales and dewy meads,
My weary, wandering steps he leads,
Where peaceful rivers, soft and slow,
Amid the verdant landscape flow.

3 Though in the paths of death I tread,
With gloomy horrors overspread,
My steadfast heart shall fear no ill,
For thou, O Lord, art with me still:
Thy friendly rod shall give me aid,
And guide me through the dreadful shade.

4 Though in a bare and rugged way,
Through devious lonely wilds I stray;
Thy bounty shall my wants beguile,
The barren wilderness shall smile,
With sudden greens and herbage crowned,
And streams shall murmur all around.
ADDISON.

135. *Psalm 74: 16, 17.*

1 Thou art, O God, the life and light
Of all this wondrous world we see;
Its glow by day, its smile by night,
Are but reflections caught from thee;
Where'er we turn, thy glories shine,
And all things fair and bright are thine.

2 When day, with farewell beam, delays
Among the opening clouds of even,
And we can almost think we gaze
Through opening vistas into heaven,
Those hues that mark the sun's decline,
So soft, so radiant, Lord, are thine.

3 When night, with wings of starry gloom,
O'ershadows all the earth and skies,
Like some dark, beauteous bird, whose plume
Is sparkling with unnumbered eyes,
That sacred gloom, those fires divine,
So grand, so countless, Lord, are thine.

4 When youthful spring around us breathes,
Thy spirit warms her fragrant sigh;
And every flower that summer wreathes
Is born beneath thy kindling eye;
Where'er we turn, thy glories shine,
And all things fair and bright are thine.
MOORE.

CHRISTMAS. C. M. HANDEL.

136. *Psalm 89.*

1 WITH reverence let the saints appear,
  And bow before the Lord ;
  His high commands with reverence hear,
  And tremble at his word.

2 Great God! how high thy glories rise ;
  How bright thine armies shine !
  Where is the power with thee that vies,
  Or truth compared to thine !

3 The northern pole, and southern, rest
  On thy supporting hand ;
  Darkness and day, from east to west,
  Move round at thy command.

4 Thy words the raging winds control,
  And rule the boisterous deep ;
  Thou mak'st the sleeping billows roll,
  The rolling billows sleep.
                                    WATTS.

137. *Psalm 77: 11-14.*

1 I SING th' almighty power of God,
  That made the mountains rise,
  That spread the flowing seas abroad,
  And built the lofty skies.

2 I sing the wisdom that ordained
  The sun to rule the day ;
  The moon shines full at his command,
  And all the stars obey.

3 I sing the goodness of the Lord,
  That filled the earth with food ;
  He formed the creatures with his word,
  And then pronounced them good.

4 Lord, how thy wonders are displayed,
  Where'er I turn mine eye ;
  If I survey the ground I tread,
  Or gaze upon the sky !

5 There's not a plant or flower below
  But makes thy glories known ;
  And clouds arise and tempests blow
  By order from thy throne.

6 Creatures that borrow life from thee
  Are subject to thy care :
  There's not a place where we can flee,
  But God is present there.
                                    WATTS.

138. *The Power of God.*

1 THE Lord, our God, is full of might,
  The winds obey his will ;
  He speaks, and in his heavenly height,
  The rolling sun stands still.

2 Rebel, ye waves, and o'er the land
  With threatening aspect roar ;
  The Lord uplifts his awful hand,
  And chains you to the shore.

3 Howl, winds of night, your force combine ;
  Without his high behest,
  Ye shall not, in the mountain-pine,
  Disturb the sparrow's nest.

4 His voice sublime is heard afar,
  In distant peals it dies ;
  He yokes the whirlwind to his car,
  And sweeps the howling skies.

5 Ye nations, bend, — in reverence bend ;
  Ye monarchs, wait his nod,
  And bid the choral song ascend
  To celebrate your God.
                                    H. K. WHITE.

Calls to Worship God.

LYONS. 10s. & 11s.　　　　　　　　　　　　　HAYDN.

139.　*Call to Worship.*

1 YE servants of God, your Master proclaim,
And publish abroad his wonderful name;
The name all victorious of Jesus extol;
His kingdom is glorious, he rules over all.

2 God ruleth on high, almighty to save;
And still he is nigh, — his presence we have;
The great congregation his triumph shall sing,
Ascribing salvation to Jesus our King.

3 Salvation to God, who sits on the throne,
Let all cry aloud, and honor the Son;
The praises of Jesus the angels proclaim,
Fall down on their faces and worship the Lamb.

4 Then let us adore, and give him his right,
All glory and power, and wisdom and might;
All honor and blessing, with angels above,
And thanks never ceasing, and infinite love.
　　　　　　　　　　PRATT'S COLL.

140.　*Call to Worship.*

1 OH, worship the King, all-glorious above;
Oh, gratefully sing his power and his love!
Our Shield and Defender, the Ancient of Days,　　[praise.
Pavilioned in splendor, and girded with

2 Oh, tell of his might, oh, sing of his grace,
Whose robe is the light, whose canopy, space!　　[clouds form,
His chariots of wrath the deep thunder-
And dark is his path on the wings of the storm.

3 Thy bountiful care what tongue can recite?
It breathes in the air, it shines in the light,
It streams from the hills, it descends to the plains,
And sweetly distils in the dew and the rains.

4 Frail children of dust, and feeble as frail,
In thee do we trust, nor find thee to fail;
Thy mercies how tender! how firm to the end!　　[Friend.
Our Maker, Defender, Redeemer, and
　　　　　　　　　　R. GRANT.

God: His Wisdom and Love.

GARDNER. 8s. & 7s.   From MORNINGTON.

141. *Praise to Jehovah.*

1 Praise to thee, thou great Creator!
   Praise to thee from every tongue:
Join, my soul, with every creature,
   Join the universal song.

2 Father, Source of all compassion,
   Pure, unbounded grace is thine:
Hail the God of our salvation!
   Praise him for his love divine.

3 For ten thousand blessings given,
   For the hope of future joy,
Sound his praise through earth and heaven,
   Sound Jehovah's praise on high.

4 Joyfully on earth adore him,
   Till in heaven our song we raise;
There, enraptured, fall before him,
   Lost in wonder, love, and praise.
                    FAWCETT.

142. *The Grace of God.*

1 Lord, with glowing heart I'd praise thee
   For the bliss thy love bestows;
For the pardoning grace that saves me,
   And the peace that from it flows.

2 Help, O God, my weak endeavor;
   This dull soul to rapture raise;
Thou must light the flame, or never
   Can my love be warmed to praise.

3 Praise, my soul, the God that sought thee,
   Wretched wanderer, far astray;
Found thee lost, and kindly brought thee
   From the paths of death away.

4 Praise, with love's devoutest feeling,
   Him, who saw thy guilt-born fear,
And, the light of hope revealing,
   Bade the blood-stained cross appear.

5 Lord, this bosom's ardent feeling
   Vainly would my lips express;
Low before thy footstool kneeling,
   Deign thy suppliant's prayer to bless;

6 Let thy grace, my soul's chief treasure,
   Love's pure flame within me raise;
And, since words can never measure,
   Let my life show forth thy praise.
                    S. F. KEY.

143. *1 John 4: 8.*

1 God is love; his mercy brightens
   All the path in which we rove;
Bliss he wakes, and woe he lightens
   God is wisdom, God is love.

2 Chance and change are busy ever;
   Man decays, and ages move:
But his mercy waneth never;
   God is wisdom, God is love.

3 E'en the hour that darkest seemeth
   Will his changeless goodness prove;
From the gloom his brightness streameth;
   God is wisdom, God is love.

4 He with earthly cares entwineth
   Hope and comfort from above:
Everywhere his glory shineth;
   God is wisdom, God is love.
                    BOWRING.

Mercies of God. Our All in All. 101

MILTON. 7s. In part from MENDELSSOHN.

144. Psalm 136.

1 Let us with a joyful mind
Praise the Lord, for he is kind,
For his mercies shall endure,
Ever faithful, ever sure.
Let us sound his name abroad,
For of gods he is the God
Who by wisdom did create
Heaven's expanse and all its state;

2 Did the solid earth ordain
How to rise above the main;
Who, by his commanding might,
Filled the new-made world with light;
Caused the golden-tressèd sun
All the day his course to run;
And the moon to shine by night,
'Mid her spangled sisters bright.

3 All his creatures God doth feed,
His full hand supplies their need;
Let us therefore warble forth
His high majesty and worth.
He his mansion hath on high,
'Bove the reach of mortal eye;
And his mercies shall endure,
Ever faithful, ever sure.
                             MILTON.

145. Psalm 73: 25.

1 Lord of earth! thy forming hand
Well this beauteous frame hath planned,
Woods that wave, and hills that tower,
Ocean rolling in his power.
Lord of heaven! beyond our sight
Rolls a world of purer light;
There in love's unclouded reign
Parted hands shall clasp again.

2 Oh, that world is passing fair,
Yet if thou wert absent there,
What were all its joys to me?
Whom have I in heaven but thee?
Lord of earth and heaven! my breast
Seeks in thee its only rest;
I was lost; thy accents mild
Homeward lured thy wandering child.

3 I was blind; thy healing ray
Charmed the long eclipse away;
Source of every joy I know,
Solace of my every woe!
Oh, if once thy smile divine
Ceased upon my soul to shine,
What were earth or heaven to me?
Whom have I in *each* but thee?
                             GRANT.

GOODMAN. 7s.

146. *Hymn of Praise.*

1 Sweet the time, exceeding sweet!
 When the saints together meet,
 When the Saviour is the theme,
 When they joy to sing of him.

2 Sing we, then, eternal love,
 Such as did the Father move:
 He beheld the world undone,
 Loved the world, and gave his Son.

3 Sing the Son's amazing love;
 How he left the realms above,
 Took our nature and our place,
 Lived and died to save our race.

4 Sing we, too, the Spirit's love;
 With our stubborn hearts he strove,
 Filled our minds with grief and fear,
 Brought the precious Saviour near.

5 Sweet the place, exceeding sweet,
 Where the saints in glory meet;
 Where the Saviour's still the theme,
 Where they see and sing of him.
 BURDER.

147. 1 Cor. 3: 16.

1 Come, divine and peaceful Guest,
 Enter each devoted breast;
 Holy Ghost, our hearts inspire,
 Kindle there the gospel fire.

2 Bid our sin and sorrow cease;
 Fill us with thy heavenly peace;
 Joy divine we then shall prove,
 Light of truth, and fire of love.

148. *Blessing Invoked.*

1 Mighty One, before whose face
 Wisdom had her glorious seat,
 When the orbs that people space
 Sprang to birth beneath thy feet!

2 Source of truth, whose rays alone
 Light the mighty world of mind!
 God of love, who from thy throne
 Kindly watchest all mankind!

3 Shed on those who in thy name
 Teach the way of truth and right,
 Shed that love's undying flame,
 Shed that wisdom's guiding light.
 BRYANT.

149. 1 Cor. 2: 4.

1 Father, bless thy word to all,
 Quick and powerful let it prove;
 Oh, may sinners hear thy call,
 Let thy people grow in love.

2 Thine own gracious message bless.
 Follow it with power divine:
 Give the gospel great success,
 Thine the work, the glory thine.

3 Father, bid the world rejoice,
 Send, oh, send thy truth abroad
 Let the nations hear thy voice,
 Hear it and return to God.

4 Sing we to our God above
 Praise eternal as his love:
 Praise him, all ye heavenly host,
 Father, Son, and Holy Ghost.
 KELLY.

Omnipresence and Omniscience.

STONEFIELD. L. M.   STANLEY.

150.   *Omnipresence.*—Psalm 84: 11.

1 LORD of all being, throned afar,
Thy glory flames from sun and star;
Centre and soul of every sphere,
Yet to each loving heart how near!

2 Sun of our life, thy quickening ray
Sheds on our path the glow of day;
Star of our hope, thy softened light
Cheers the long watches of the night.

3 Our midnight is thy smile withdrawn;
Our noontide is thy gracious dawn;
Our rainbow arch thy mercy's sign;
All, save the clouds of sin, are thine!

4 Lord of all life, below, above,
Whose light is truth, whose warmth is
Before thy ever-blazing throne [love,
We ask no lustre of our own.

5 Grant us thy truth, to make us free,
And kindling hearts that burn for thee,
Till all thy living altars claim
One holy light, one heavenly flame!
                       HOLMES.

151.   Psalm 103.

1 BLESS, O my soul! the living God;
Call home thy thoughts that rove
  abroad:
Let all the powers within me join
In work and worship so divine.

2 Bless, O my soul! the God of grace:
His favors claim thy highest praise;
Why should the wonders he hath
Be lost in silence, and forgot? [wrought

3 'Tis he, my soul, that sent his Son
To die for crimes which thou hast done;
He owns the ransom, and forgives
The hourly follies of our lives.

4 Let every land his power confess;
Let all the earth adore his grace:
My heart and tongue with rapture join,
In work and worship so divine.
                       WATTS.

152.   *The all-seeing God.*—Psalm 139.

1 LORD, thou hast searched and seen me
  through:
Thine eye commands, with piercing view,
My rising and my resting hours,
My heart and flesh with all their powers.

2 My thoughts, before they are my own,
Are to my God distinctly known;
He knows the words I mean to speak,
Ere from my opening lips they break.

3 Within thy circling power I stand;
On every side I find thy hand:
Awake, asleep, at home, abroad,
I am surrounded still with God.

4 How awful is thy searching eye!
Thy knowledge, oh, how deep! how high!
My soul, with all the powers I boast,
Is in the boundless prospect lost.

5 Oh, may these thoughts possess my
  breast,
Where'er I rove, where'er I rest!
Nor let my weaker passions dare
Consent to sin, for God is there.
                       WATTS.

Providence of God.

HARTFORD. C. M.

153. *The Mystery of Providence.*

1 God moves in a mysterious way
 His wonders to perform ;
 He plants his footsteps in the sea,
 And rides upon the storm.

2 Deep in unfathomable mines
 Of never-failing skill,
 He treasures up his bright designs,
 And works his sovereign will.

3 Ye fearful saints, fresh courage take ;
 The clouds ye so much dread
 Are big with mercy, and shall break
 In blessings on your head.

4 Judge not the Lord by feeble sense,
 But trust him for his grace ;
 Behind a frowning providence,
 He hides a smiling face.

5 His purposes will ripen fast,
 Unfolding every hour ;
 The bud may have a bitter taste,
 But sweet will be the flower.

6 Blind unbelief is sure to err,
 And scan his work in vain ;
 God is his own interpreter,
 And he will make it plain.
 COWPER.

154. *Psalm 121.*

1 To heaven I lift my waiting eyes :
 There all my hopes are laid ;
 The Lord that built the earth and skies
 Is my perpetual aid.

2 Their steadfast feet shall never fall
 Whom he designs to keep ;
 His ear attends the softest call,
 His eyes can never sleep.

3 Israel, rejoice, and rest secure ;
 Thy keeper is the Lord :
 His wakeful eyes employ his power
 For thine eternal guard.

4 He guards thy soul, he keeps thy breath,
 Where thickest dangers come :
 Go and return, secure from death,
 Till God commands thee home.
 WATTS.

155. *God's Eternity.*

1 Great God ! how infinite art thou !
 What worthless worms are we !
 Let the whole race of creatures bow,
 And pay their praise to thee.

2 Thy throne eternal ages stood,
 Ere seas or stars were made ;
 Thou art the ever-living God,
 Were all the nations dead.

3 Eternity, with all its years,
 Stands present in thy view ;
 To thee there's nothing old appears ;
 Great God ! there's nothing new.

4 Our lives through various scenes are drawn,
 And vexed with trifling cares ;
 While thine eternal thought moves on
 Thine undisturbed affairs.

5 Great God ! how infinite art thou !
 What worthless worms are we !
 Let the whole race of creatures bow,
 And pay their praise to thee.
 WATTS.

ALFORD. L. M.   WHITTAKER.

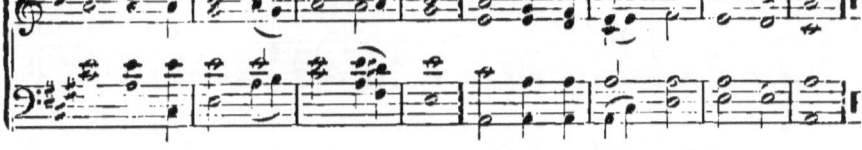

156.   *Birth of Christ.*

1 ALL praise to Thee, eternal Lord!
  Clothed in a garb of flesh and blood;
  Choosing a manger for thy throne,
  While worlds on worlds are thine alone.

2 Once did the skies before thee bow;
  A virgin's arms contain thee now;
  Angels, who did in thee rejoice,
  Now listen for thine infant voice.

3 A little child, thou art our guest,
  That weary ones in thee may rest;
  Forlorn and lowly is thy birth,
  That we may rise to heaven from earth.

4 Thou comest in the darksome night
  To make us children of the light, —
  To make us, in the realms divine,
  Like thine own angels round thee shine;

5 All this for us thy love hath done;
  By this to thee our love is won:
  For this we tune our cheerful lays,
  And shout our thanks in ceaseless praise.
                      MARTIN LUTHER.

157.   Luke 2: 11.

1 WHEN Jordan hushed his waters still,
  And silence slept on Zion's hill;
  When Bethlehem's shepherds through
    the night
  Watched o'er their flocks by starry light:

2 Hark! from the midnight hills around,
  A voice of more than mortal sound,
  In distant hallelujahs stole
  Wild murmuring o'er the raptured soul.

3 On wheels of light, on wings of flame,
  The glorious hosts of angels came;
  And while they struck their harps and
    sung,   [rung:—
  High heaven with songs of triumph

4 "O Zion! lift thy raptured eye,
  The long-expected hour is nigh;
  Renewed, creation smiles again,
  The Prince of Salem comes to reign.

5 "He comes to cheer the trembling heart,
  Bid Satan and his host depart;
  Again the Day-star gilds the gloom,
  Again the bowers of Eden bloom."
                      T. CAMPBELL.

158.   *Praise to Christ.*

1 Now for a tune of lofty praise,
  To great Jehovah's equal Son!
  Awake, my voice, in heavenly lays,
  Tell the loud wonders he hath done.

2 Sing how he left the worlds of light,
  And the bright robes he wore above;
  How swift and joyful was the flight,
  On wings of everlasting love.

3 Deep in the shades of gloomy death,
  Th' almighty Captive prisoner lay;
  Th' almighty Captive left the earth,
  And rose to everlasting day.

4 Lift up your eyes, ye sons of light,
  Up to his throne of shining grace;
  See what immortal glories sit
  Round the sweet beauties of his face.
                      WATTS.

Song of the Angels

ATWATER. C. M.

159.   Luke 2: 13.

1 It came upon the midnight clear,
   That glorious song of old,
From angels bending near the earth
   To touch their harps of gold;
"Peace to the earth, good-will to man,
   From heaven's all-gracious King:"
The earth in solemn stillness lay,
   To hear the angels sing.

2 Still through the cloven skies they come,
   With peaceful wings unfurled;
And still celestial music floats
   O'er all the weary world;
Above its sad and lowly plains
   They bend on heavenly wing,
And ever, o'er its Babel sounds,
   The blessed angels sing.

3 O ye, beneath life's crushing load,
   Whose forms are bending low,
Who toil along the climbing way,
   With painful steps and slow,
Look up! for glad and golden hours
   Come swiftly on the wing;
Oh, rest beside the weary road,
   And hear the angels sing!

4 For lo! the days are hastening on,
   By prophet-bards foretold,
When with the ever-circling years
   Comes round the age of gold!
When peace shall over all the earth
   Its final splendors fling,

And the whole world send back the song
   Which now the angels sing!
                   E. H. SEARS.

160.   Luke 2.

1 Calm, on the listening ear of night,
   Come heaven's melodious strains,
Where wild Judea stretches far
   Her silver-mantled plains.

2 Celestial choirs, from courts above,
   'Mid sacred glories there;
And angels, with their sparkling lyres,
   Make music on the air.

3 The answering hills of Palestine
   Send back the glad reply;
And greet from all their holy heights,
   The dayspring from on high.

4 O'er the blue depths of Galilee
   There comes a holier calm;
And Sharon waves, in solemn praise,
   Her silent groves of palm.

5 "Glory to God!" the sounding skies
   Loud with their anthems ring;
"Peace to the earth — good-will to men,
   From heaven's eternal King."

6 Light on thy hills, Jerusalem!
   The Saviour now is born!
And bright on Bethlehem's joyous plains
   Breaks the first Christmas morn.
                   E. H. SEARS.

ST. MARTIN'S. C. M.   TANSUR.

161.   Luke 2.

1 HARK, the glad sound! the Saviour
    The Saviour promised long; [comes,
    Let every heart prepare a throne,
    And every voice a song.

2 He comes, the prisoner to release,
    In Satan's bondage held;
    The gates of brass before him burst,
    The iron fetters yield.

3 He comes, from thickest films of vice
    To clear the mental ray,
    And, on the eyes long closed in night,
    To pour celestial day.

4 He comes, the broken heart to bind,
    The bleeding soul to cure,
    And, with the treasures of his grace,
    Enrich the humble poor.

5 Our glad hosannas, Prince of peace,
    Thy welcome shall proclaim,
    And heaven's eternal arches ring
    With thy belovèd name.
                       DODDRIDGE.

162.   Eph. 4: 8.

1 HOSANNA to the Prince of light,
    That clothed himself in clay;
    Entered the iron gates of death,
    And tore the bars away.

2 See how the Conqueror mounts aloft,
    And to his Father flies,
    With scars of honor in his flesh,
    And triumph in his eyes.

3 There our exalted Saviour reigns,
    And scatters blessings down;
    Our Jesus fills the middle seat
    Of the celestial throne.

4 Raise your devotion, mortal tongues,
    To reach his bless'd abode;
    Sweet be the accents of your songs
    To our incarnate God.

5 Bright angels, strike your loudest strings,
    Your sweetest voices raise;
    Let heaven, and all created things,
    Sound our Immanuel's praise.
                       WATTS.

163.   Psalm 98.

1 Joy to the world! the Lord is come;
    Let earth receive her King;
    Let every heart prepare him room,
    And heaven and nature sing.

2 Joy to the earth! the Saviour reigns:
    Let men their songs employ; [plains
    While fields and floods, rocks, hills, and
    Repeat the sounding joy.

3 No more, let sins and sorrows grow,
    Nor thorns infest the ground;
    He comes to make his blessings flow
    Far as the curse is found.

4 He rules the world with truth and grace,
    And makes the nations prove
    The glories of his righteousness,
    And wonders of his love.
                       WATTS.

Christ: the Star in the East.

RODMAN. 11s. & 10s.   PSALTERY.

164.   *The Star in the East.*

1 Brightest and best of the sons of the morning!
   Dawn on our darkness, and lend us thine aid;
Star of the East, the horizon adorning,
   Guide where our infant Redeemer is laid.

2 Cold on his cradle the dew-drops are shining;
   Low lies his head with the beasts of the stall:
Angels adore him, in slumber reclining,
   Maker and Monarch and Saviour of all!

3 Say, shall we yield him, in costly devotion,
   Odors of Edom, and offerings divine?
Gems of the mountain, and pearls of the ocean,
   Myrrh from the forest, or gold from the mine?

4 Vainly we offer each ample oblation,
   Vainly with gold would his favors secure:
Richer, by far, is the heart's adoration;
   Dearer to God are the prayers of the poor.

5 Brightest and best of the sons of the morning!
   Dawn on our darkness, and lend us thine aid;
Star of the East, the horizon adorning,
   Guide where our infant Redeemer is laid.
                        HEBER.

MICHAEL. H. M.   HAYDN.

165.   Luke 2.

1 HARK! what celestial sounds,
    What music fills the air!
Soft warbling to the morn,
    It strikes the ravished ear:
Now all is still; now wild it floats
: | In tuneful notes, | :
    Loud, sweet, and shrill.

2 Th' angelic hosts descend
    With harmony divine;
See how from heaven they bend,
    And in full chorus join:
"Fear not," they say; "great joy we bring;
: | Jesus your King | :
    Is born to-day!"

3 He comes, your souls to save
    From death's eternal gloom;
To realms of bliss and light
    He lifts you from the tomb:
Your voices raise, with sons of light;
: | Your songs unite | :
    Of endless praise.

4 "Glory to God on high!"
    Ye mortals, spread the sound,
And let your raptures fly
    To earth's remotest bound;
For peace on earth, from God in heaven,
: | To man is given | :
    At Jesus' birth.
                SALISBURY COLL.

166.   Psalm 121.

1 UPWARD I lift mine eyes;
    From God is all my aid,
The God that built the skies,
    And earth and nature made:
God is the tower to which I fly;
: | His grace is nigh | :
    In every hour.

2 My feet shall never slide,
    Nor fall in fatal snares,
Since God, my guard and guide,
    Defends me from my fears:
Those wakeful eyes that never sleep,
: | Shall Israel keep | :
    When dangers rise.

3 No burning heats by day,
    Nor blasts of evening air,
Shall take my health away,
    If God be with me there:
Thou art my sun, and thou my **shade**,
: | To guard my head | :
    By night or noon.

4 Hast thou not given thy word
    To save my soul from death?
And I can trust my Lord
    To keep my mortal breath:
I'll go and come, nor fear to die,
: | Till from on high | :
    Thou call me home.
                WATTS.

Jesus Christ: Born in Bethlehem.

MILTON. 7s.   In part from MENDELSSOHN.

167. *Luke 2.*

1 HARK! the herald angels sing,
 "Glory to the new-born King!
 :| Peace on earth, and mercy mild;
 God and sinners reconciled." |:

2 Joyful, all ye nations, rise;
 Join the triumphs of the skies;
 :| With the angelic hosts proclaim,
 "Christ is born in Bethlehem."

3 Mild he lays his glory by;
 Born that man no more may die;
 :| Born to raise the sons of earth;
 Born to give them second birth. |:

4 Hail, the heaven-born Prince of peace!
 Hail, the Sun of righteousness!
 :| Light and life to all he brings,
 Risen with healing in his wings. |:

5 Let us then with angels sing,
 "Glory to the new-born King!—
 :| Peace on earth and mercy mild;
 God and sinners reconciled!"
  C. WESLEY.

168. *Example of the "Wise Men from the East."*

1 As with gladness, men of old
 Did the guiding star behold;
 As with joy they hailed its light,
 Leading onward, beaming bright;
 So, most gracious Lord, may we
 Evermore be led by thee.

2 As with joyful steps they sped
 To that lowly manger-bed;
 There to bend the knee before
 Him whom earth and heaven adore;
 So may we, with willing feet,
 Ever seek thy mercy-seat.

3 As they offered gifts most rare,
 At that manger rude and bare;
 So may we, with holy joy,
 Pure and free from sin's alloy,
 All our costliest treasures bring
 Unto Thee, O Christ our King!

4 Holy Jesus, every day
 Keep us in the narrow way;
 And when earthly things are past,
 Bring our ransomed souls at last,
 Where they need no star to guide,
 Where no clouds thy glory hide.

The Birth of Christ.

WILMOT 8s. & 7s.   WEBER.

169.   *Luke 2: 14.*
1 Hark! what mean those holy voices,
   Sweetly sounding through the skies?
   Lo, th' angelic host rejoices;
   Heavenly hallelujahs rise.

2 Hear them tell the wondrous story,
   Hear them chant in hymns of joy;
   Glory in the highest, glory!
   Glory be to God most high!

3 Peace on earth, good-will from heaven,
   Reaching far as man is found;
   Souls redeemed, and sins forgiven;
   Loud our golden harps shall sound.

4 Christ is born, the Great Anointed;
   Heaven and earth his praises sing;
   Oh, receive whom God appointed,
   For your Prophet, Priest, and King.

5 Haste, ye mortals, to adore him;
   Learn his name, and taste his joy;
   Till in heaven ye sing before him,
   "Glory be to God most high."
                      CAWOOD.

170.   *Praise for a Saviour.*
1 Let our songs of praise ascending,
   Rise to thee, O God most high;
   While before thee, humbly bending,
   Glory to thy name we cry.

2 With the shepherds in the story,
   Let our hearts to Bethlehem go,
   Where the Lord of life and glory,
   In a manger lieth low.

3 With the angels, filled with wonder,
   Let us praise him in the height!
   With the blessed Virgin ponder
   All love's mystery and might.

4 Age to age thy glory beareth
   On the stream of time abroad;
   Race to race thy name declareth,
   Son of Mary! Son of God!

5 Heaven exults and earth rejoices
   In the work that thou hast wrought;
   Lord, attune our trembling voices,
   Let us praise thee as we ought.

171.   *Luke 2.*
1 Hail the night, all hail the morn,
   When the Prince of peace was born!
   When, amid the wakeful fold,
   Tidings good the angels told.

2 Now our solemn chant we raise
   Duly to the Saviour's praise;
   Now with carol hymns we bless
   Christ the Lord, our Righteousness.

3 While resounds the joyful cry,
   "Glory be to God on high,
   Peace on earth, good-will to men!"
   Gladly we respond, "Amen!"

4 Thus we greet this holy day,
   Pouring forth our festive lay;
   Thus we tell, with saintly mirth,
   Of Immanuel's wondrous birth.

Christ our Pattern: His Glory and Goodness.

MENDON. L. M.

172. *Our Example.*

1 My dear Redeemer, and my Lord,
I read my duty in thy word;
But in thy life the law appears,
Drawn out in living characters.

2 Such was thy truth, and such thy zeal,
Such deference to thy Father's will,
Such love, and meekness so divine,
I would transcribe and make them mine.

3 Cold mountains and the midnight air
Witnessed the fervor of thy prayer;
The desert thy temptations knew,
Thy conflict and thy victory too.

4 Be thou my pattern; make me bear
More of thy gracious image here;
Then God, the Judge, shall own my name
Among the followers of the Lamb.
WATTS.

173. Psalm 45.

1 Now be my heart inspired to sing
The glories of my Saviour King:
Jesus, the Lord, how heavenly fair
His form! how bright his beauties are!

2 O'er all the sons of human race
He shines with a superior grace;
Love from his lips divinely flows,
And blessings all his state compose.

3 Thy throne, O God, forever stands!
Grace is the sceptre in thy hands:
Thy laws and works are just and right;
Justice and grace are thy delight.

4 God, thine own God, has richly shed
His oil of gladness on thy head;
And with his sacred Spirit blest
His first-born Son above the rest.
WATTS.

174. *The Beneficence of Christ.*

1 When, like a stranger on our sphere,
The lowly Jesus wandered here,
Where'er he went, affliction fled,
And sickness reared her fainting head.

2 The eye that rolled in irksome night
Beheld his face, — for God is light!
The opening ear, the loosened tongue,
His precepts heard, his praises sung.

3 With bounding steps the halt and lame,
To hail their great Deliverer came;
O'er the cold grave he bowed his head,
He spake the word, and raised the dead.

4 Despairing madness, dark and wild,
In his inspiring presence smiled;
The storm of horror ceased to roll,
And reason lightened through the soul.

5 Through paths of loving-kindness led,
Where Jesus triumphed we would tread;
To all, with willing hands, dispense
The gifts of our benevolence.
MONTGOMERY.

Praise of Christ: His Zeal, Agony, and Victory.

MEDFIELD. C. M. — WM. MATHER.

175. *Praise of Christ.*

1 Oh! for a shout of sacred joy
  To God, the sovereign King;
Let every land their tongues employ,
  And hymns of triumph sing.

2 Jesus, our God, ascends on high;
  His heavenly guards around
Attend him rising through the sky,
  With trumpets' joyful sound.

3 While angels shout and praise their King,
  Let mortals learn their strains;
Let all the earth his honor sing; —
  O'er all the earth he reigns.

4 Rehearse his praise with awe profound;
  Let knowledge lead the song;
Nor mock him with a solemn sound
  Upon a thoughtless tongue.

5 In Israel stood his ancient throne: —
  He loved that chosen race;
But now he calls the world his own;
  The heathen taste his grace.
                             WATTS.

176. *Mark 10: 32.*

1 The Saviour! — what a noble flame
  Was kindled in his breast,
When, hasting to Jerusalem,
  He marched before the rest!

2 Good-will to men, and zeal for God,
  His every thought engross;
He longs to be baptized with blood;
  He pants to reach the cross.

3 With all his sufferings full in view,
  And woes to us unknown,
Forth to the task his spirit flew:
  'Twas love that urged him on.

4 Lord, we return thee what we can;
  Our hearts shall sound abroad
Salvation to the dying Man,
  And to the rising God!

5 And while thy bleeding glories here
  Engage our wondering eyes,
We learn our lighter cross to bear,
  And hasten to the skies.
                             COWPER.

177. *Psalm 22.*

1 In deep distress our Saviour prayed
  With mighty cries and tears;
God heard him in that hour of dread,
  And chased away his fears.

2 Great was the victory of his death,
  His throne exalted high:
And all the kindreds of the earth
  Shall worship, or shall die.

3 A numerous offspring must arise
  From his expiring groans;
They shall be reckoned in his eyes
  For daughters and for sons.

4 The meek and humble souls shall see
  His table richly spread;
And all that seek the Lord shall be
  With joys immortal fed.
                             WATTS.

The Lamb of God.

BEHOLD THE LAMB OF GOD. P. M. E. P. PARKER.

178.

1 BEHOLD the Lamb of God!
  O thou for sinners slain,
  Let it not be in vain
    That thou hast died:
  Thee for my Saviour let me take,
  My only refuge let me make
    Thy piercèd side.

2 Behold the Lamb of God!
  Into the sacred flood
  Of thy most precious blood
    My soul I cast:
  Wash me, and make me clean within,
  And keep me pure from every sin,
    Till life be past.

3 Behold the Lamb of God!
  All hail, incarnate Word,
  Thou everlasting Lord,
    Saviour most blest!
  Fill us with love that never faints,
  Grant us, with all thy blessed saints,
    Eternal rest.

4 Behold the Lamb of God!
  Now at the Father's side
  Is he, the Crucified,
    Who bore our pains.
  The glory of adoring throngs,
  The theme of all their ceaseless songs,
    The Saviour reigns!

5 Behold the Lamb of God!
  Worthy is he alone,
  That sitteth on the throne
    Of God above;
  One with the Ancient of all days,
  One with the Comforter in praise,
    All light and love!

Christ Crucified. Our Sacrifice.

ST. DENYS. 8s. & 7s. 61.

179. *"Wounded for our Transgressions."*

1 Now, my soul, thy voice upraising,
   Tell in sweet and mournful strain,
How the Crucified, enduring
   Grief and wounds and dying pain,
Freely of his love was offered,
   Sinless, was for sinners slain.

2 See! his hands and feet are fastened;
   So he makes his people free!
Not a wound whence blood is flowing
   But a fount of grace shall be:
Yea, the very nails which nail him
   Nail us, also, to the tree!

3 Through his heart the spear is piercing,
   Though his foes have seen him die;
Blood and water thence are streaming
   In a tide of mystery;
Water from our guilt to cleanse us,
   Blood to win us crowns on high.

4 Jesus, may those precious fountains
   Life to thirsting souls afford:
Let them be our present healing,
   And at length our great reward:
So a ransomed world shall ever
   Praise thee, its redeeming Lord.
          MONK'S COLL.

180. *"Redeemed by his Blood."*

1 He, who once in righteous vengeance
   Whelmed the world beneath the flood,
Once again in mercy cleansed it
   With his own most precious blood;
Coming from his throne on high
   On the painful cross to die.

2 Oh, the wisdom of th' Eternal!
   Oh, the depth of love divine!
Oh, the sweetness of that mercy
   Which in Jesus Christ did shine!
We were sinners doomed to die;
   Jesus paid the penalty.

3 When before the Judge we tremble,
   Conscious of his broken laws,
May the blood of his atonement
   Cry aloud, and plead our cause,
Bid our guilty terrors cease,
   Be our pardon and our peace.

4 Prince and Author of salvation,
   Lord of majesty supreme,
Jesus, praise to thee be given
   By the world thou didst redeem;
Glory to the Father be,
   And the Spirit, One with thee!
          MONK'S COLL.

Christ's Agony and Sacrifice.

MARY. L. M.   CHERUBINI.

181.   *Gal. 6: 14.*

1 When I survey the wondrous cross
   On which the Prince of glory died,
My richest gain I count but loss,
   And pour contempt on all my pride.

2 Forbid it, Lord, that I should boast,
   Save in the death of Christ my God;
All the vain things that charm me most,
   I sacrifice them to his blood.

3 See, from his head, his hands, his feet,
   Sorrow and love flow mingled down:
Did e'er such love and sorrow meet,
   Or thorns compose so rich a crown?

4 Were the whole realm of nature mine,
   That were a present far too small;
Love so amazing, so divine,
   Demands my soul, my life, my all.
                        WATTS.

182.   *Luke 22: 43.*

1 'Tis midnight; and on Olive's brow
   The star is dimmed that lately shone:
'Tis midnight; in the garden now
   The suffering Saviour prays alone.

2 'Tis midnight, and from all removed,
   The Saviour wrestles lone with fears;
E'en that disciple whom he loved
   Heeds not his Master's grief and tears.

3 'Tis midnight; and for others' guilt
   The Man of sorrows weeps in blood;
Yet he that hath in anguish knelt
   Is not forsaken by his God.

4 'Tis midnight; and from ether-plains
   Is borne the song that angels know;
Unheard by mortals are the strains
   That sweetly soothe the Saviour's woe.
                        TAPPAN.

183.   *Isaiah 53: 4–6.*

1 Jesus, whom angel hosts adore,
   Became a man of griefs for me;
In love, though rich, becoming poor,
   That I through him enriched might be.

2 Though Lord of all, above, below,
   He went to Olivet for me;
There drank my cup of wrath and woe,
   When bleeding in Gethsemane.

3 The ever-blessed Son of God
   Went up to Calvary for me;
There paid my debt, there bore my load,
   In his own body on the tree.

4 Jesus, whose dwelling is the skies,
   Went down into the grave for me;
There overcame my enemies,
   There won the glorious victory.

5 'Tis finished all: the veil is rent,
   The welcome sure, the access free;
Now then we leave our banishment,
   O Father, to return to thee!
                        BONAR.

Contemplation of Christ's Sacrifice.

ROCKINGHAM. L. M.   DR. MASON.

184.   *John 19: 30.*
1 'Tis finished! so the Saviour cried,
 And meekly bowed his head and died.
 'Tis finished! yes, the race is run,
 The battle fought, the victory won.

2 'Tis finished! this thy dying groan
 Shall sins of every kind atone;
 Millions shall be redeemed from death
 By this thy last expiring breath.

3 'Tis finished! Heaven is reconciled,
 And all the powers of darkness spoiled;
 Peace, love, and happiness again
 Return, and dwell with sinful men.

4 'Tis finished! let the joyful sound
 Be heard through all the nations round;
 'Tis finished! let the echo fly
 Through heaven and hell, through earth
  and sky.
                     STENNETT.

185.   *Christ's Dying Love.*
1 Lord, when my thoughts delighted rove
 Amid the wonders of thy love,
 Sweet hope revives my drooping heart,
 And bids intruding fears depart.

2 The Lord of life, the Saviour, dies
 For mortal crimes a sacrifice:
 What love, what mercy, how divine!
 Jesus, and can I call thee mine?

3 Be all my heart and all my days
 Devoted to my Saviour's praise:
 And let my glad obedience prove
 How much I owe, how much I love.
                     MRS. STEELE.

186.   *1 John 2: 1.*
1 He lives! the great Redeemer lives!
 What joy the blest assurance gives!
 And now before his Father, God,
 Pleads the full merit of his blood.

2 Repeated crimes awake our fears,
 And justice armed with frowns appears;
 But in the Saviour's lovely face
 Sweet mercy smiles, and all is peace.

3 In every dark, distressful hour,
 When sin and Satan join their power,
 Let this dear hope repel the dart,
 That Jesus bears us on his heart.

4 Great Advocate, Almighty Friend!
 On him our humble hopes depend;
 Our cause can never, never fail,
 For Jesus pleads, and must prevail.
                     MRS. STEELE.

187.   *The Cross.*
1 Oh, the sweet wonders of that cross
 Where my Redeemer loved and died!
 Her noblest life my spirit draws [side.
 From his dear wounds and bleeding

2 I would forever speak his name
 In sounds to mortal ears unknown;
 With angels join to praise the Lamb,
 And worship at his Father's throne.
                     WATTS.

Doxology.
Praise God, from whom all blessings flow,
Praise him, all creatures here below;
Praise him above, ye heavenly host,
Praise Father, Son, and Holy Ghost.

Christ Risen and Victorious.

DUKE ST.   HATTON.

188.   Psalm 24.

1 Our Lord is risen from the dead;
    Our Jesus is gone up on high;
    The powers of hell are captive led,
    Dragged to the portals of the sky.

2 There his triumphal chariot waits,
    And angels chant the solemn lay: —
    "Lift up your heads, ye heavenly gates,
    Ye everlasting doors, give way!"

3 Loose all your bars of massy light,
    And wide unfold th' ethereal scene;
    He claims these mansions as his right;
    Receive the King of glory in.

4 Who is the King of glory, who?
    The Lord that all his foes o'ercame;
    That sin and death and hell o'erthrew;
    And Jesus is the conqueror's name.

5 Lo! his triumphal chariot waits,
    And angels chant the solemn lay: —
    "Lift up your heads, ye heavenly gates,
    Ye everlasting doors, give way!"
                                       C. Wesley.

189.   Christ Victorious.

1 Hail to the Prince of life and peace,
    Who holds the keys of death and hell!
    The spacious world unseen is his,
    And sovereign power becomes him well.

2*In shame and anguish once he died;
    But now he lives for evermore:
    Bow down, ye saints around his seat,
    And, all ye angel-bands, adore.

3 So live forever, glorious Lord, [friends;
    To crush thy foes, and guard thy
    While all thy chosen tribes rejoice
    That thy dominion never ends.

4 Forever reign, victorious King! [known,
    Wide through the earth thy name be
    And call my longing soul to sing
    Sublimer anthems near thy throne.
                                   Doddridge.

190.   Luke 24: 26.

1 He dies! the Friend of sinners dies!
    Lo! Salem's daughters weep around:
    A solemn darkness veils the skies;
    A sudden trembling shakes the ground.

2 Here's love and grief beyond degree:
    The Lord of glory dies for men!
    But, lo! what sudden joys we see, —
    Jesus the dead revives again!

3 The rising God forsakes the tomb;
    Up to his Father's court he flies;
    Cherubic legions guard him home,
    And shout him welcome to the skies.

4 Break off your tears, ye saints, and tell
    How high our great Deliverer reigns;
    Sing how he spoiled the hosts of hell,
    And led the tyrant death in chains.

5 Say, "Live forever, glorious King,
    Born to redeem, and strong to save!
    Where now, O death, where is thy sting?
    And where thy vict'ry, boasting
    Grave?"
                                       Watts.

The Resurrection of Christ.

NUREMBURG. 7s. Arranged by DR. MASON.

191.   1 Cor. 15: 20.
1 Christ, the Lord, is risen to-day,
 Our triumphant holy day:
 He endured the cross and grave,
 Sinners to redeem and save.

2 Lo! he rises, mighty King!
 Where, O Death! is now thy sting?
 Lo! he claims his native sky!
 Grave! where is thy victory?.

3 Sinners, see your ransom paid,
 Peace with God forever made:
 With your risen Saviour rise;
 Claim with him the purchased skies.

4 Christ, the Lord, is risen to-day,
 Our triumphant holy day;
 Loud the song of victory raise;
 Shout the great Redeemer's praise.
                CUDWORTH.

192.   Matt. 28: 6.
1 Morning breaks upon the tomb;
 Jesus scatters all its gloom:
 Day of triumph through the skies,
 See the glorious Saviour rise!

2 Now, disciples, dry your tears,
 Banish unbelieving fears:
 Look on his deserted grave,
 Doubt no more his power to save.

3 Ye who are of death afraid,
 Triumph in the scattered shade:
 Drive your anxious cares away,
 See the place where Jesus lay.
                COLLYER.

193.   Job 38: 7.
1 Songs of praise the angels sang,
 Heaven with hallelujahs rang,
 When Jehovah's work begun,
 When he spake, and it was done.

2 Songs of praise awoke the morn,
 When the Prince of peace was born:
 Songs of praise arose, when he
 Captive led captivity.

3 Heaven and earth must pass away;
 Songs of praise shall crown that day:
 God will make new heavens and earth;
 Songs of praise shall hail their birth.

4 Saints below, with heart and voice,
 Still in songs of praise rejoice;
 Learning here, by faith and love,
 Songs of praise to sing above.

5 Borne upon their latest breath
 Songs of praise shall conquer death;
 Then, amid eternal joy,
 Songs of praise their powers employ.
                MONTGOMERY.

194.   *Hymn of the Resurrection.*
1 Jesus Christ is risen to-day,—
 Our triumphant holy day,—
 Who did once, upon the cross,
 Suffer to redeem our loss.

2 Hymns of praise then let us sing
 Unto Christ, our heavenly King;
 Who endured the cross and grave,
 Sinners to redeem and save.

Christ glorified, but present with us.

WILLIAMS C. M. — WILLIAMS.

195. *John 14: 3.*

1 THE golden gates are lifted up,
  The doors are opened wide,
The King of glory is gone in
  Unto his Father's side.

2 Thou art gone up before us, Lord,
  To make for us a place,
That we may be where now thou art,
  And look upon God's face.

3 And ever on thine earthly path
  A gleam of glory lies;
A light still breaks behind the cloud
  That veils thee from our eyes.

4 Lift up our hearts, lift up our minds,
  Let thy dear grace be given,
That while we tarry here below,
  Our treasure be in heaven!

5 That where thou art, at God's right hand,
  Our hope, our love may be;
Dwell thou in us, that we may dwell
  For evermore in thee!

196. *A present Christ.*

1 OH, say to all men, far and near,
  That Christ is risen again!
That Christ is with us, now and here,
  And ever shall remain.

2 Now let the mourner grieve no more,
  Though his beloved sleep;
A happier meeting shall restore
  Their light to eyes that weep.

3 The way of darkness that he trod,
  To heaven, at last, shall come;
And he who hearkens to Christ's word,
  Shall reach his Father's home.

4 Now every heart each noble deed
  With new resolve may dare;
A glorious harvest shall the seed,
  In happier regions, bear.
  NOVALIS.

197. *Christ Risen and Reigning.*

1 YE humble souls that seek the Lord,
  Chase all your fears away;
And bow with reverence down, to see
  The place where Jesus lay.

2 Thus low the Lord of life was brought,
  Such wonders love can do!
Thus cold in death that bosom lay,
  Which throbbed and bled for you.

3 If ye have wept at yonder cross,
  And still your sorrows rise, [grave,
Stoop down and view the vanquished
  Then wipe your weeping eyes.

4 Then dry your tears, and tune your songs,
  The Saviour lives again;
Not all the bolts and bars of death
  The Conqueror could detain.

5 High o'er th' angelic band he rears
  His once dishonored head; [reigns
And through unnumbered years he
  Who dwelt among the dead.
  DODDRIDGE.

200. The Suffering Saviour exalted.

1 HE, who on earth as man was known,
  And bore our sins and pains,
Now, seated on th' eternal throne,
  The God of glory reigns.

2 His hands the wheels of nature guide
  With an unerring skill;
And countless worlds, extended wide,
  Obey his sovereign will.

3 While harps unnumbered sound his praise
  In yonder world above,
His saints on earth admire his ways,
  And glory in his love.

4 When troubles, like a burning sun,
  Beat heavy on their head;
To this almighty rock they run,
  And find a pleasing shade.

5 How glorious he, how happy they,
  In such a glorious friend!
Whose love secures them all the way,
  And crowns them at the end.
                              NEWTON.

201.   Rev. 5: 6-10.

1 BEHOLD the glories of the Lamb
  Amid his Father's throne:
Prepare new honors for his name,
  And songs before unknown.

2 Let elders worship at his feet,
  The Church adore around,
With vials full of odors sweet,
  And harps of sweeter sound.

3 Now to the Lamb that once was slain
  Be endless blessings paid;
Salvation, glory, joy remain
  Forever on thy head.

4 Thou hast redeemed our souls with blood,
  Hast set the prisoners free,
Hast made us kings and priests to God,
  And we shall reign with thee.

5 The worlds of nature and of grace
  Are put beneath thy power;
Then shorten these delaying days,
  And bring the promised hour.
                              WATTS.

Christ Risen: our Advocate and Saviour.

THATCHER. S. M.   HANDEL.

202. *"The Lord is risen indeed."* — Luke 24: 34.

1 "The Lord is risen indeed:"
  Now is his work performed;
  Now is the mighty Captive freed,
  And death our foe disarmed.

2 "The Lord is risen indeed:"
  The grave has lost its prey;
  With him is risen the ransomed seed
  To reign in endless day.

3 "The Lord is risen indeed:"
  He lives, to die no more;
  He lives, the sinner's cause to plead,
  Whose curse and shame he bore.

4 "The Lord is risen indeed:"
  Attending angels hear;
  Up to the courts of heaven with speed,
  The joyful tidings bear.

5 Then take your golden lyres,
  And strike each cheerful chord;
  Join all the bright celestial choirs,
  To sing our risen Lord!
                KELLY.

203.   Rev. 15: 3, 4.

1 Awake, and sing the song
  Of Moses and the Lamb;
  Wake, every heart and every tongue
  To praise the Saviour's name.

2 Sing of his dying love;
  Sing of his rising power;
  Sing how he intercedes above
  For those whose sins he bore.

3 Ye pilgrims on the road
  To Zion's city, sing!
  Rejoice ye in the Lamb of God, —
  In Christ, th' eternal King.

4 Soon shall we hear him say, —
  "Ye blessèd children, come;"
  Soon will he call us hence away,
  And take his wand'rers home.

5 Then shall each raptured tongue
  His endless praise proclaim,
  And sweeter voices tune the song
  Of Moses and the Lamb.
                HAMMOND.

204.   John 3 : 17.

1 Raise your triumphant songs
  To an immortal tune;
  Wide let the earth resound the deeds
  Celestial grace has done.

2 Sing how eternal love
  Its chief Belovèd chose,
  And bade him raise our wretched race
  From their abyss of woes.

3 'Twas mercy filled the throne,
  And wrath stood silent by,   [down
  When Christ was sent with pardons
  To rebels doomed to die.

4 Now, sinners, dry your tears;
  Let hopeless sorrow cease:
  Bow to the sceptre of his love,
  And take the offered peace.
                WATTS.

Christ in Gethsemane: Christ Risen.

HOW CALM AND BEAUTIFUL! C. L. M.   DR. HASTINGS.

1. How calm and beau-ti-ful the morn
That gilds the sa-cred tomb,
Where once the Cru-ci-fied was borne,
And veiled in mid-night gloom!
Oh, weep no more the Sav-iour slain;
The Lord is risen, He lives again.

---

205.   Luke 24: 5.

1 Ye mourning saints, dry every tear
  For your departed Lord,
"Behold the place, he is not here!"
  The tomb is all unbarred:
The gates of death were closed in vain,
The Lord is risen, he lives again.

3 Now cheerful to the house of prayer,
  Your early footsteps bend;
The Saviour will himself be there,
  Your Advocate and Friend:
Once by the law your hopes were slain,
But now, in Christ, ye live again.

4 How tranquil now the rising day!
  'Tis Jesus still appears,
A risen Lord, to chase away
  Your unbelieving fears:
Oh, weep no more your comforts slain,
The Lord is risen, he lives again.

5 And when the shades of evening fall,
  When life's last hour draws nigh,
If Jesus shines upon the soul,
  How blissful then to die!
Since he hath risen that once was slain,
Ye die in Christ to live again.
                       HASTINGS.

206.   Matt. 26: 36–46.

1 HE knelt: the Saviour knelt and prayed,
  When but his Father's eye
Looked thro' the lonely garden's shade,
  On that dread agony;
The Lord of all above, beneath,
Was bowed with sorrow unto death.

2 He knew them all; the doubt, the strife,
  The faint, perplexing dread;
The mists that hang o'er parting life,
  All darkened round his head;
And the Deliverer knelt to pray;—
Yet passed it not, that cup, away.

3 It passed not, though the stormy wave
  Had sunk beneath his tread;
It passed not, though to him the grave
  Had yielded up its dead:
But there was sent him from on high,
A gift of strength for man to die.

4 And was his mortal hour beset
  With anguish and dismay?
How may we meet our conflict yet
  In the dark, narrow way?
How but thro' him, that path who trod?
Save or we perish, Son of God!
                       MRS. HEMANS.

Jesus Christ Crowned and Worshipped.

CORONATION. C. M.   HOLDEN.

207.   *The Coronation.*

1 ALL hail! the power of Jesus' name!
Let angels prostrate fall,
Bring forth the royal diadem,
And crown him Lord of all.

2 Crown him, ye martyrs of our God,
Who from his altar call;
Extol the stem of Jesse's rod,
And crown him Lord of all.

3 Ye chosen seed of Israel's race,
Ye ransomed from the fall,
Hail Him who saves you by his grace,
And crown him Lord of all.

4 Sinners, whose love can ne'er forget
The wormwood and the gall:
Go, spread your trophies at his feet,
And crown him Lord of all.

5 Let every kindred, every tribe,
On this terrestrial ball,
To him all majesty ascribe,
And crown him Lord of all.
                              DUNCAN.

208.   Heb. 2: 9.

1 THE head that once was crowned with
Is crowned with glory now; [thorns
A royal diadem adorns
The mighty Victor's brow.

2 The highest place that heaven affords
Is his by sovereign right;
The King of kings, and Lord of lords,
He reigns in glory bright.

3 Jesus, the joy of all above!
The joy of all below,
To whom he manifests his love,
And grants his name to know.

4 To them the cross, with all its shame,
With all its grace is given;
Their name — an everlasting name,
Their joy — the joy of heaven.

5 To them the cross is life and health,
Though shame and death to him:
His people's hope, his people's wealth,
Their everlasting theme.
                                KELLY.

209.   Rev. 5: 9.

1 COME let us join our cheerful songs
With angels round the throne;
Ten thousand thousand are their tongues,
But all their joys are one.

2 Worthy the Lamb that died, they cry,
To be exalted thus;
Worthy the Lamb, our lips reply,
For he was slain for us.

3 Jesus is worthy to receive
Honor and power divine;
And blessings more than we can give,
Be, Lord, forever thine.

4 The whole creation join in one
To bless the sacred name
Of him who sits upon the throne,
And to adore the Lamb.
                                WATTS.

Adoration of Christ.

SICILY. 8s. & 7s.

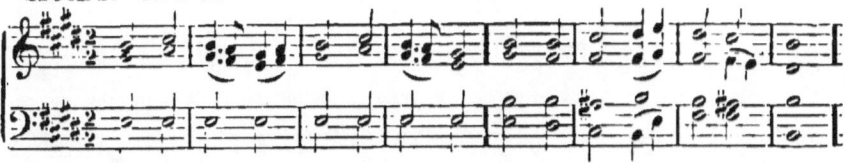

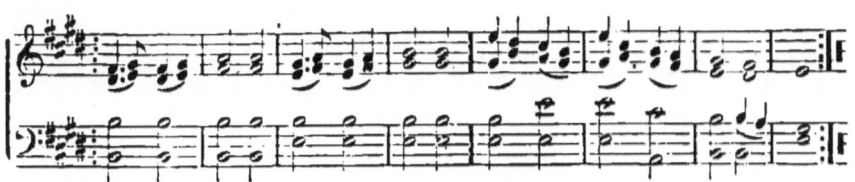

210. *The Voice from Calvary.* — John 19: 30.

1 HARK! the voice of love and mercy
  Sounds aloud from Calvary;
  See! it rends the rocks asunder,
  Shakes the earth and veils the sky:
    "It is finished!"
  Hear the dying Saviour cry.

2 "It is finished!" — Oh, what pleasure
  Do these charming words afford!
  Heavenly blessings, without measure,
  Flow to us from Christ, the Lord:
    "It is finished!"
  Saints, the dying words record.

3 Tune your harps anew, ye seraphs;
  Join to sing the pleasing theme:
  All on earth and all in heaven,
  Join to praise Immanuel's name:
    Hallelujah!
  Glory to the bleeding Lamb!
                              FRANCIS.

211.   *Adoration of Christ.*

1 CROWN his head with endless blessing,
  Who, in God the Father's name,
  With compassion never ceasing,
  Comes, salvation to proclaim.

2 Lo, Jehovah, we adore thee!
  Thee, our Saviour — thee our God!
  From thy throne let beams of glory
  Shine through all the world abroad.

3 Jesus! thee our Saviour hailing,
  Thee our God in praise we own;
  Highest honors, never failing,
  Rise eternal round thy throne.

4 Now, ye saints, his power confessing,
  In your grateful strains adore;
  For his mercy never ceasing,
  Flows and flows for evermore.

212.   Heb. 1: 6.

1 HARK! ten thousand harps and voices
  Sound the note of praise above:
  Jesus reigns, and heaven rejoices;
  Jesus reigns, the God of love;
  See, he sits on yonder throne;
  Jesus rules the world alone.

2 King of glory, reign forever!
  Thine an everlasting crown;
  Nothing from thy love shall sever
  Those whom thou hast made thine
  Happy objects of thy grace,   [own:
  Destined to behold thy face.

3 Saviour, hasten thine appearing;
  Bring, oh, bring the glorious day,
  When, the awful summons hearing,
  Heaven and earth shall pass away!
  Then, with golden harps, we'll sing,
  "Glory, glory to our King!"
                              KELLY.

126 *Christ: Going to Die, Coming to Judge, Equal with God.*

JUDGMENT HYMN. L. M.   M. LUTHER.

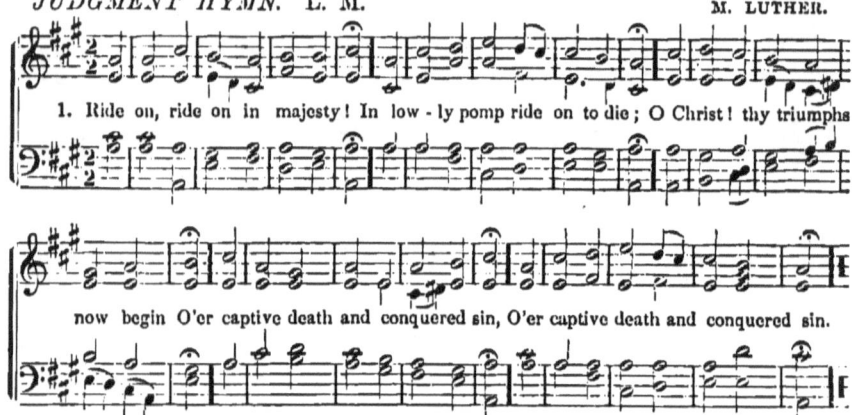

1. Ride on, ride on in majesty! In low-ly pomp ride on to die; O Christ! thy triumphs now begin O'er captive death and conquered sin, O'er captive death and conquered sin.

213. John 12: 12-15.

2 Ride on, ride on in majesty!
  The wingèd squadrons of the sky [eyes,
  Look down, with sad and wondering
  To see th' approaching sacrifice.

3 Ride on, ride on in majesty!
  Thy last and fiercest strife is nigh:
  The Father, on his sapphire throne,
  Expects his own anointed Son.

4 Ride on, ride on in majesty!
  In lowly pomp ride on to die:
  Bow thy meek head to mortal pain;
  Then take, O God, thy power, and reign.
          MILMAN.

214. Psalm 97.

1 HE reigns; the Lord, the Saviour, reigns;
  Praise him in evangelic strains:
  Let the whole earth in songs rejoice,
  And distant islands join their voice.

2 Deep are his counsels and unknown,
  But grace and truth support his throne,
  Though gloomy clouds his way surround,
  Justice is their eternal ground.

3 In robes of judgment, lo, he comes!
  Shakes the wide earth, and cleaves the tombs;
  Before him burns devouring fire;
  The mountains melt, the seas retire.

4 His enemies, with sore dismay,
  Fly from the sight, and shun the day:
  Then lift your heads, ye saints, on high,
  And sing, for your redemption's nigh.
          WATTS.

215. *"Unto the Lamb forever."*—Rev. 5.

1 WHAT equal honors shall we bring
  To thee, O Lord our God, the Lamb,
  When all the notes that angels sing
  Are far inferior to thy name?

2 Worthy is he who once was slain,
  The Prince of peace, who groaned and died;
  Worthy to rise and live and reign
  At his almighty Father's side.

3 Blessings forever on the Lamb,
  Who bore the curse for wretched men!
  Let angels sound his sacred name,
  And every creature say, Amen!
          WATTS.

216. Phil. 2: 6-8.

1 BRIGHT King of glory, dreadful God!
  Our spirits bow before thy feet:
  To thee we lift an humble thought,
  And worship at thine awful seat.

2 A thousand seraphs strong and bright
  Stand round the glorious Deity;
  But who, among the sons of light,
  Pretends comparison with thee?

3 Yet there is one of human frame;
  Jesus, arrayed in flesh and blood,
  Thinks it no robbery to claim
  A full equality with God.

4 Their glory shines with equal beams:
  Their essence is forever one, [names,
  Though they are known by different
  The Father God, and God the Son.
          WATTS.

Worship of Christ. Offices of Christ.

MISSIONARY CHANT. L. M.   CHAS. ZEUNER.

217.   *Worship of Christ.*

1 Around the Saviour's lofty throne,
   Ten thousand times ten thousand sing;
   They worship him as God alone,
   And crown him everlasting King.

2 Approach, ye saints! this God is yours!
   'Tis Jesus fills the throne above:
   Ye cannot want while God endures;
   Ye cannot fail while God is love.

3 Jesus, thou everlasting King!
   To thee the praise of heaven belongs;
   Yet smile on us, who fain would bring
   The tribute of our humble songs.

4 Though sin defile our worship here,
   We hope ere long thy face to view;
   And when our souls in heaven appear,
   We'll praise thy name as angels do.
                              KELLY.

218.   *"Worthy the Lamb."*—Rev. 5.

1 Come, let us sing the song of songs,
   The saints in heaven began the strain,
   The homage which to Christ belongs:
   "Worthy the Lamb, for he was slain!"

2 Slain to redeem us by his blood,
   To cleanse from every sinful stain,
   And make us kings and priests to God,
   "Worthy the Lamb, for he was slain!"

3 To him, enthroned by filial right,
   All power in heaven and earth proclaim,
   Honor and majesty and might;
   "Worthy the Lamb, for he was slain!"

4 Long as we live, and when we die,
   And while in heaven with him we reign;
   This song, our song of songs shall be:
   "Worthy the Lamb, for he was slain!"
                              MONTGOMERY.

219.   *Worship of Christ.*

1 Worthy the Lamb of boundless sway,
   In earth and heaven the Lord of all:
   Let all the powers of earth obey,
   And low before his footstool fall.

2 Higher, still higher, swell the strain;
   Creation's voice the note prolong!
   Jesus, the Lamb, shall ever reign!
   Let hallelujahs crown the song!
                              SHIRLEY.

220.   *The Offices of Christ.*

1 Now to the Lord who makes us know
   The wonders of his dying love,
   Be humble honors paid below,
   And strains of nobler praise above.

2 To Jesus, our atoning Priest,
   To Jesus, our exalted King,
   Be everlasting power confessed,
   And every tongue his glory sing.

3 Behold! on flying clouds he comes,
   And every eye shall see him move:
   Though with our sins we pierced him once,
   Then he displays his pardoning love.

4 The unbelieving world shall wail,
   While we rejoice to see the day:
   Come, Lord! nor let thy promise fail,
   Nor let thy chariot long delay.
                              WATTS.

The Holy Ghost

MANOAH. C. M. — ROSSINI.

221. *Rom. 5: 5.*

1 Come, Holy Spirit, heavenly Dove!
　With all thy quickening powers;
　Kindle a flame of sacred love
　　In these cold hearts of ours.

2 Look, how we grovel here below,
　Fond of these trifling toys;
　Our souls can neither fly nor go
　　To reach eternal joys.

3 In vain we tune our formal songs,
　In vain we strive to rise;
　Hosannas languish on our tongues,
　　And our devotion dies.

4 Dear Lord! and shall we ever live
　At this poor dying rate?
　Our love so faint, so cold to thee,
　　And thine to us so great?

5 Come, Holy Spirit, heavenly Dove,
　With all thy quickening powers;
　Come, shed abroad a Saviour's love,
　　And that shall kindle ours.
　　　　　　　　　　　WATTS.

222. *John 16: 7.*

1 Our blest Redeemer, ere he breathed
　His tender, last farewell,
　A Guide, a Comforter bequeathed,
　　With us on earth to dwell.

2 He came in tongues of living flame,
　To teach, convince, subdue;
　All-powerful as the wind he came,
　　And all as viewless too.

3 And his that gentle voice we hear,
　Soft as the breath of even, [fear,
　That checks each fault, that calms each
　　And whispers us of heaven.

4 And every virtue we possess,
　And every virtue won,
　And every thought of holiness
　　Are his and his alone.

5 Spirit of purity and grace,
　Our weakness pitying see;
　Oh, make our hearts thy dwelling-place,
　　Purer and worthier thee.
　　　　　　　　　　　LYTE.

223. *Rom. 8: 14-16. Eph. 1: 13.*

1 Why should the children of a King
　Go mourning all their days?
　Great Comforter, descend, and bring
　　Some tokens of thy grace.

2 Dost thou not dwell in all the saints,
　And seal the heirs of heaven?
　When wilt thou banish my complaints,
　　And show my sins forgiven?

3 Assure my conscience of her part
　In the Redeemer's blood;
　And bear thy witness with my heart,
　　That I am born of God.

4 Thou art the earnest of his love,
　The pledge of joys to come;
　And thy soft wings, celestial Dove,
　　Will safe convey me home.
　　　　　　　　　　　WATTS.

Invocation of the Spirit.

ERNAN. L. M.   DR. MASON.

224.   *Rom. 8: 14.*

1 Come, gracious Spirit, heavenly Dove,
With light and comfort from above;
Be thou our guardian, thou our guide,
O'er every thought and step preside.

2 The light of truth to us display,
And make us know and choose thy way;
Plant holy fear in every heart,
That we from God may ne'er depart.

3 Lead us to holiness, the road
That we must take to dwell with God;
Lead us to Christ, the living way,
Nor let us from his precepts stray.
BROWNE.

225.   *Work of the Spirit.*

1 Eternal Spirit! we confess
And sing the wonders of thy grace;
Thy power conveys our blessings down
From God the Father and the Son.

2 Enlightened by thy heavenly ray,
Our shades and darkness turn to day;
Thine inward teachings make us know
Our danger and our refuge too.

3 Thy power and glory work within,
And break the chains of reigning sin;
Do our imperious lusts subdue,
And form our wretched hearts anew.

4 The troubled conscience knows thy voice;
Thy cheering words awake our joys;
Thy words allay the stormy wind,
And calm the surges of the mind.
WATTS.

226.   *Invocation of the Spirit.*

1 Creator Spirit! by whose aid
The world's foundations first were laid,
Come, visit every waiting mind,
Come, pour thy joys on human-kind.

2 Thrice holy Fount, thrice holy Fire,
Our hearts with heavenly love inspire;
Come, and thy sacred unction bring
To sanctify us, while we sing.

3 Our frailties help, our wills control,
Subdue the senses to the soul;
And when rebellious they are grown,
Then lay thy hand, and hold them down..

4 Make us eternal truths receive,
And practise all that we believe;
Give us thyself, that we may see
The Father and the Son, by thee.
DRYDEN'S TRANS.

227.   *Invocation of the Spirit.*

1 Come, Holy Spirit! calm my mind,
And fit me to approach my God;
Remove each vain, each worldly thought,
And lead me to thy blest abode.

2 Hast thou imparted to my soul
A living spark of holy fire?
Oh! kindle now the sacred flame;
Make me to burn with pure desire.

3 A brighter faith and hope impart,
And let me now my Saviour see:
Oh! soothe and cheer my burdened heart,
And bid my spirit rest in thee.
BURDER.

The Holy Ghost.

VENI, SANCTE SPIRITUS. 7s. H. KNECHT, 1793.

228.

Ancient Hymn to the Holy Ghost.

1 Holy Spirit! Lord of light!
From thy clear celestial height,
  Thy pure beaming radiance give.
Come, thou Father of the poor!
Come, with treasures which endure!
  Come, thou Light of all that live!

2 Thou of all consolers best,
Visiting the troubled breast,
  Dost refreshing peace bestow;
Thou in toil art comfort sweet,
Pleasant coolness in the heat,
  Solace in the midst of woe.

3 Light immortal! Light divine!
Visit thou these hearts of thine,
  And our inmost being fill:
If thou take thy grace away,
Nothing pure in man will stay;
  All his good is turned to ill.

4 Heal our wounds, our strength renew;
On our dryness pour thy dew;
  Wash the stains of guilt away:
Bend the stubborn heart and will;
Melt the frozen, warm the chill;
  Guide the steps that go astray.

5 Thou, on those who evermore
Thee confess, and thee adore,
  In thy sevenfold gifts, descend;
Give them comfort when they die;
Give them life with thee on high;
  Give them joys which never end.

KING ROBERT OF FRANCE.

The Gifts of the Spirit besought.

ELYRIA. 7s.   CHERUBINI.

229. *2 Cor. 1: 22.*

1 GRACIOUS Spirit, Love divine!
  Let thy light within me shine;
  All my guilty fears remove,
  Fill me with thy heavenly love.

2 Speak thy pardoning grace to me,
  Set the burdened sinner free;
  Lead me to the Lamb of God,
  Wash me in his precious blood.

3 Life and peace to me impart,
  Seal salvation on my heart;
  Breathe thyself into my breast, —
  Earnest of immortal rest.

4 Let me never from thee stray,
  Keep me in the narrow way;
  Fill my soul with joy divine,
  Keep me, Lord! forever thine.
                        STOCKER.

230. *The Spirit invoked.*

1 HOLY GHOST, thou Source of light!
  We invoke thy kindling ray:
  Dawn upon our spirits' night,
  Turn our darkness into day.

2 To the anxious soul impart
  Hope, all other hopes above;
  Stir the dull and hardened heart
  With a longing and a love.

3 Give the struggling, peace for strife;
  Give the doubting, light for gloom;
  Speed the living into life,
  Warn the dying of their doom.

4 Work in all, in all renew,
  Day by day, the life divine;
  All our wills to thee subdue,
  All our hearts to thee incline.

231. *2 Cor. 1: 22.*

1 HOLY GHOST, with light divine,
  Shine upon this heart of mine;
  Chase the shades of night away,
  Turn my darkness into day.

2 Holy Ghost, with power divine,
  Cleanse this guilty heart of mine;
  Long hath sin, without control,
  Held dominion o'er my soul.

3 Holy Ghost, with joy divine,
  Cheer this saddened heart of mine;
  Bid my many woes depart,
  Heal my wounded, bleeding heart!

4 Holy Spirit, all divine,
  Dwell within this heart of mine;
  Cast down every idol-throne;
  Reign supreme, and reign alone!
                        REED.

The Holy Spirit's Presence and Power.

ASPIRATION. S. M.   E. P. PARKER.

1. Blest Comforter divine, Let rays of heavenly love Amid our gloom and darkness shine, And guide our souls above

232.   *"Blest Comforter."*

2 Draw, with thy still, small voice,
From every sinful way;
And bid the mourning saint rejoice,
Though earthly joys decay.

3 By thine inspiring breath
Make every cloud of care,
And e'en the gloomy vale of death,
A smile of glory wear.

233.   *Presence of the Spirit.*

1 The Comforter has come;
We feel his presence here;
Our hearts would now no longer roam,
But bow in filial fear.

2 This tenderness of love,
This hush of solemn power,—
'Tis heaven descending from above,
To fill this favored hour.

3 Earth's darkness all has fled,
Heaven's light serenely shines,
And every heart divinely led,
To holy thought inclines.

4 No more let sin deceive,
Nor earthly cares betray,
Oh, let us never, never grieve
The Comforter away!

234.   *Invocation.*

1 Come, Holy Spirit! come;
Let thy bright beams arise;
Dispel the sorrow from our minds,
The darkness from our eyes.

2 Convince us of our sin;
Then lead to Jesus' blood:
And to our wondering view reveal
The secret love of God.

3 Revive our drooping faith,
Our doubts and fears remove,
And kindle in our breasts the flame
Of never-dying love.

4 'Tis thine to cleanse the heart,
To sanctify the soul,
To pour fresh life in every part,
And new create the whole.

5 Dwell, Spirit! in our hearts;
Our minds from bondage free;
Then shall we know and praise and love
The Father, Son, and Thee.
                Hart.

235.   Phil. 2: 13.

1 'Tis God the Spirit leads
In paths before unknown;
The work to be performed is ours,
The strength is all his own.

2 Supported by his grace,
We still pursue our way;
And hope at last to reach the prize,
Secure in endless day.

3 'Tis he that works to will,
'Tis he that works to do;
His is the power by which we act,
His be the glory too.

Prayer for the Spirit. The Trinity.

NEWMAN. H. M.   CARMINA SACRA.

236.   *Prayer for the Holy Spirit.*

1 O THOU that hearest prayer!
    Attend our humble cry,
    And let thy servants share
      Thy blessing from on high:
We plead the promise of thy word,
Grant us thy Holy Spirit, Lord!

2 If earthly parents hear
    Their children when they cry;
    If they, with love sincere,
      Their children's wants supply;
Much more wilt thou thy love display,
And answer when thy children pray.

3 Our heavenly Father thou,—
    We, children of thy grace,—
    Oh, let thy Spirit now
      Descend and fill the place;
That all may feel the heavenly flame,
And all unite to praise thy name.

237.   *Trinity.*

1 To Him that chose us first,
    Before the world began;
    To Him that bore the curse
      To save rebellious man;
To Him that formed | Is endless praise
Our hearts anew, | And glory due.

2 The Father's love shall run
    Through our immortal songs:
    We bring to God the Son
      Hosannas on our tongues;
Our lips address | With equal praise,
The Spirit's name | And zeal the same.

3 Let every saint above,
    And angel round the throne,
    Forever bless and love
      The sacred Three in One;
Thus, heaven shall | When earth and time
  raise | Grow old and die.
His honors high, | WATTS.

238.   *The Divine Perfections.*

1 THE Lord Jehovah reigns:
    His throne is built on high;
    The garments he assumes
      Are light and majesty.
His glories shine | No mortal eye
With beams so bright, | Can bear the sight.

2 The thunders of his hand
    Keep the wide world in awe;
    His wrath and justice stand
      To guard his holy law;
And where his love | His truth confirms
Resolves to bless, | And seals the grace.

3 Through all his ancient works
    Surprising wisdom shines,
    Confounds the powers of hell,
      And breaks their fell designs.
Strong is his arm, | His great decrees,
And shall fulfil | His sovereign will.
                            WATTS.

The Trinity. Praise of Christ.

ITALIAN HYMN. 6s. & 4s.   GIARDINI.

239.   *The Trinity.*

1 COME, thou Almighty King!
  Help us thy name to sing,
    Help us to praise.
  Father all glorious,
  O'er all victorious,
  Come and reign over us,
    Ancient of days.

2 Come, thou Incarnate Word!
  Gird on thy mighty sword,
    Our prayer attend.
  Come, and thy people bless,
  And give thy word success;
  Spirit of holiness,
    On us descend.

3 Come, Holy Comforter!
  Thy sacred witness bear,
    In this glad hour.
  Thou, who almighty art,
  Now rule in every heart,
  And ne'er from us depart,
    Spirit of power.

4 To the great ONE in THREE
  The highest praises be,
    Hence evermore!
  His sovereign majesty
  May we in glory see,
  And to eternity,
    Love and adore!
                    MADAN.

240.   Rev. 5: 12.

1 GLORY to God on high!
  Let heaven and earth reply,
    Praise ye his name;
  His love and grace adore,
  Who all our sorrows bore;
  And sing for evermore,
    "Worthy the Lamb!"

2 Ye who surround the throne,
  Join cheerfully in one,
    Praising his name;
  Ye who have felt his blood
  Sealing your peace with God,
  Sound his dear name abroad:
    "Worthy the Lamb!"

3 Join, all ye ransomed race,
  Our Lord and God to bless;
    Praise ye his name;
  In him we will rejoice,
  And make a joyful noise,
  Shouting with heart and voice,
    "Worthy the Lamb!"

4 Soon must we change our place;
  Yet will we never cease
    Praising his name;
  To him our songs we'll bring,
  Hail him our gracious King,
  And through all ages sing,
    "Worthy the Lamb!"

Section V.

SALVATION BY CHRIST.

(*a.*) *Depravity, Regeneration, Atonement.*

(*b.*) *Invitations, Warnings, and Expostulations of the Gospel.*

(*c.*) *Repentance and Faith.*

"*BLESSED BE THE LORD GOD OF ISRAEL; FOR HE HATH VISITED AND REDEEMED HIS PEOPLE, AND HATH RAISED UP AN HORN OF SALVATION FOR US, IN THE HOUSE OF HIS SERVANT DAVID.*"
— *Zacharias' Hymn.* Luke 1 : 68, 69.

i

SALVATION BY CHRIST.

BOND. C. M.   G. F. ROOT.

241.   Zech. 9: 12.
1 How sad our state by nature is!
   Our sin, how deep it stains!
  And Satan holds our captive minds
   Fast in his slavish chains.

2 But there's a voice of sovereign grace
   Sounds from the sacred word:
  "Ho! ye despairing sinners, come,
   And trust upon the Lord."

3 My soul obeys th' almighty call,
   And runs to this relief:
  I would believe thy promise, Lord:
   Oh, help my unbelief!

4 A guilty, weak, and helpless worm,
   On thy kind arms I fall:
  Be thou my strength and righteousness,
   My Saviour and my All.
                     WATTS.

242.   *God revealed in the Atonement.*
1 FATHER, how wide thy glory shines!
   How high thy wonders rise! [signs,
  Known through the earth by thousand
   By thousand through the skies.

2 Those mighty orbs proclaim thy power,
   Their motions speak thy skill;
  And on the wings of every hour
   We read thy patience still.

3 But when we view thy strange design
   To save rebellious worms,
  Where vengeance and compassion join
   In their divinest forms,—

4 Here the whole Deity is known;
   Nor dares a creature guess
  Which of the glories brightest shine,
   The justice or the grace.

5 Now the full glories of the Lamb
   Adorn the heavenly plains;
  Bright seraphs learn Immanuel's name,
   And try their choicest strains.

6 Oh, may I bear some humble part
   In that immortal song!
  Wonder and joy shall tune my heart,
   And love command my tongue.
                     WATTS.

243.   Gal. 2: 16.
1 IN vain we seek for peace with God
   By methods of our own:
  Nothing, O Saviour! but thy blood,
   Can bring us near the throne.

2 But thine illustrious sacrifice
   Hath answered all demands;
  And peace and pardon from the skies
   Are offered by thy hands.

3 'Tis by thy death we live, O Lord!
   'Tis on thy cross we rest:
  Forever be thy love adored,
   Thy name forever blessed.
                     WATTS.

Depravity. End of the Wicked.

HAMBURG. L. M.   DR. MASON.

244.   Psalm 51.

1 LORD, I am vile, conceived in sin,
   And born unholy and unclean;
   Sprung from the man, whose guilty fall
   Corrupts the race, and taints us all.

2 Soon as we draw our infant breath,
   The seeds of sin grow up for death:
   Thy law demands a perfect heart;
   But we're defiled in every part.

3 Great God! create my heart anew,
   And form my spirit pure and true;
   No outward rites can make me clean,
   The leprosy lies deep within.

4 No bleeding bird, nor bleeding beast,
   Nor hyssop branch, nor sprinkling priest,
   Nor running brook, nor flood, nor sea,
   Can wash the dismal stain away.

5 Jesus, my God, thy blood alone
   Hath power sufficient to atone:
   Thy blood can make me white as snow;
   No Jewish types could cleanse me so.
                        WATTS.

245.   Matt. 7: 13, 14.

1 BROAD is the road that leads to death,
   And thousands walk together there;
   But wisdom shows a narrow path,
   With here and there a traveller.

2 "Deny thyself, and take thy cross,"
   Is the Redeemer's great command:
   Nature must count her gold but dross,
   If she would gain this heavenly land.

3 The fearful soul that tires and faints,
   And walks the ways of God no more,
   Is but esteemed almost a saint,
   And makes his own destruction sure.

4 Lord! let not all my hopes be vain;
   Create my heart entirely new:
   Which hypocrites could ne'er attain;
   Which false apostates never knew.
                        WATTS.

246.   Psalm 73.

1 LORD, what a thoughtless wretch was I
   To mourn and murmur and repine,
   To see the wicked, placed on high,
   In pride and robes of honor shine!

2 But oh, their end, their dreadful end!
   Thy sanctuary taught me so:
   On slippery rocks, I see them stand,
   And fiery billows roll below.

3 Their fancied joys, how fast they flee!
   Just like a dream when man awakes;
   Their songs of softest harmony
   Are but a prelude to their plagues.

4 Now I esteem their mirth and wine
   Too dear to purchase with my blood·
   Lord, 'tis enough that thou art mine,
   My life, my portion, and my God!
                        WATTS.

Doxology.

PRAISE God, from whom all blessings flow,
Praise him, all creatures here below;
Praise him above, ye heavenly host,
Praise Father, Son, and Holy Ghost.

Salvation in Christ alone.

HARMONY. L. M.   HERZ.

247.   Jer. 8: 22.
1 Deep are the wounds which sin has made;
    Where shall the sinner find a cure?
    In vain, alas, is nature's aid;
    The work exceeds all nature's power.

2 And can no sovereign balm be found?
    And is no kind physician nigh,
    To ease the pain and heal the wound,
    Ere life and hope forever fly?

3 There is a great physician near,
    Look up, O fainting soul, and live;
    See, in his heavenly smiles appear
    Such ease as nature cannot give!

4 See, in the Saviour's dying blood,
    Life, health, and bliss abundant flow!
    'Tis only this dear sacred flood
    Can ease thy pain, and heal thy woe.
              MRS. STEELE.

248.   *Hope in Christ.*
1 Look up, my soul, with cheerful eye,
    See where the great Redeemer stands,
    The glorious Advocate on high,
    With precious incense in his hands!

2 He sweetens every humble groan,
    He recommends each broken prayer;
    Recline thy hope on him alone
    Whose power and love forbid despair.

3 Teach my weak heart, O gracious Lord!
    With stronger faith to call thee mine;
    Bid me pronounce the blissful word,
    My Father, God, with joy divine.

249.   Rom. 1: 16.
1 What shall the dying sinner do,
    That seeks relief for all his woe?
    Where shall the guilty conscience find
    Ease for the torment of the mind?

2 In vain we search, in vain we try,
    Till Jesus brings his gospel nigh!
    'Tis there the power and glory dwell,
    That save rebellious souls from hell.

3 This is the pillar of our hope,
    That bears our fainting spirits up;
    We read the grace, we trust the word,
    And find salvation in the Lord.
              WATTS.

250.   Phil. 2: 9.
1 There is none other name than thine,
    Jehovah Jesus! Name divine!
    On which to rest for sins forgiven, —
    For peace with God, for hope of heaven.

2 There is none other name than thine,
    When cares and fears and griefs are mine,
    That, with a gracious power, can heal
    Each care and fear and grief I feel.

3 There is no other name than thine,
    When called my spirit to resign,
    To bear me through that latest strife,
    And ev'n in death to be my life.

4 Name above every name! thy praise
    Shall fill the remnant of my days:
    Jehovah Jesus! Name divine!
    Rock of salvation! thou art mine.

Salvation by Grace.

HAYDN. S. M.   Arranged from HAYDN.

251.   1 Cor. 1: 30.

1 How heavy is the night
   That hangs upon our eyes,
Till Christ, with his reviving light,
   Upon our souls arise!

2 Our guilty spirits dread
   To meet the wrath of Heaven;
But in his righteousness arrayed,
   We see our sins forgiven.

3 Unholy and impure
   Are all our thoughts and ways:
His hands infected nature cure,
   With sanctifying grace.

4 The powers of hell agree
   To hold our souls in vain:
He sets the sons of bondage free,
   And breaks th' accursed chain.

5 Lord, we adore thy ways,
   To bring us near to God, —
Thy sovereign power, thy healing grace,
   And thine atoning blood.
                      WATTS.

252.   *Necessity of Pardon.*

1 Can sinners hope for heaven,
   Who love this world so well?
Or dream of future happiness,
   While on the road to hell?

2 Shall they hosannas sing,
   With an unhallowed tongue?
Shall palms adorn the guilty hand
   Which does its neighbor wrong?

3 Can sin's deceitful way
   Conduct to Zion's hill?
Or those expect with God to reign
   Who disregard his will?

4 Thy grace, O God, alone,
   Good hope can e'er afford!
The pardoned and the pure shall see
   The glory of the Lord.

253.   Eph. 2: 5.

1 Grace! 'tis a charming sound,
   Harmonious to the ear;
Heaven with the echo shall resound,
   And all the earth shall hear.

2 Grace first contrived a way
   To save rebellious man;
And all the steps that grace display,
   Which drew the wondrous plan.

3 Grace led my wandering feet
   To tread the heavenly road;
And new supplies each hour I meet,
   While pressing on to God.

4 Grace all the work shall crown,
   Through everlasting days;
It lays in heaven the topmost stone,
   And well deserves the praise.
                     DODDRIDGE.

Doxology.

Ye angels round the throne,
   And saints that dwell below,
Worship the Father, praise the Son,
   And bless the Spirit too.

The Blood of Christ.

THOMPSON. S. M.

254. *John 1: 29.*

1 Not all the blood of beasts,
   On Jewish altars slain,
Could give the guilty conscience peace,
   Or wash away the stain.

2 But Christ, the heavenly Lamb,
   Takes all our sins away,—
A sacrifice of nobler name,
   And richer blood than they.

3 My faith would lay her hand
   On that dear head of thine,
While like a penitent I stand,
   And there confess my sin.

4 My soul looks back to see
   The burdens thou didst bear,
When hanging on th' accursèd tree,
   And hopes her guilt was there.

5 Believing, we rejoice
   To see the curse remove;
We bless the Lamb with cheerful voice,
   And sing his bleeding love.
                              WATTS.

255. *John 10: 11.*

1 Like sheep we went astray,
   And broke the fold of God;
Each wandering in a different way,
   But all the downward road.

2 How dreadful was the hour,
   When God our wanderings laid,
And did at once his vengeance pour
   Upon the Shepherd's head!

3 How glorious was the grace,
   When Christ sustained the stroke!
His life and blood the Shepherd pays,
   A ransom for the flock.

4 But God shall raise his head
   O'er all the sons of men,
And make him see a numerous seed,
   To recompense his pain.
                              WATTS.

256. *Job 9: 2.*

1 Ah, how shall fallen man
   Be just before his God?
If he contend in righteousness,
   We fall beneath his rod.

2 If he our ways should mark,
   With strict inquiring eyes,
Could we for one of thousand faults,
   A just excuse devise?

3 All-seeing, powerful God!
   Who can with thee contend?
Or who that tries th' unequal strife,
   Shall prosper in the end?

4 The mountains, in thy wrath,
   Their ancient seats forsake;
The trembling earth deserts her place,
   Her rooted pillars shake.

5 Ah, how shall guilty man
   Contend with such a God?
None, none can meet him and escape,
   But through the Saviour's blood.
                              WATTS.

Necessity of Regeneration.

DUNDEE. C. M.   SCOTCH.

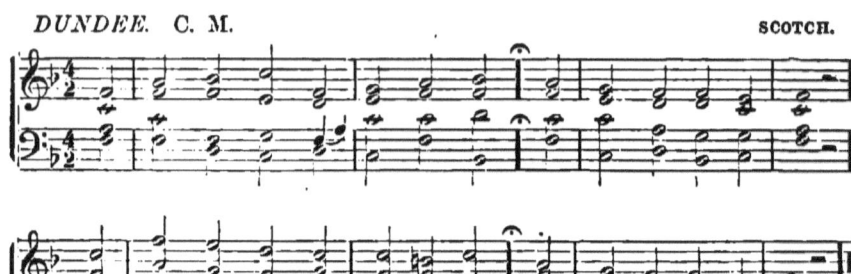

257.   Rom. 7: 9.

1 LORD, how secure my conscience was,
   And felt no inward dread!
  I was alive without the law,
   And thought my sins were dead.

2 My hopes of heaven were firm and
   But since the precept came [bright;
  With such convincing power and light,
   I find how vile I am.

3 My guilt appeared but small before,
   Till I with terror saw
  How perfect, holy, just, and pure
   Is thine eternal law.

4 Then felt my soul the heavy load;
   My sins revived again:
  I had provoked a dreadful God,
   And all my hopes were slain.

5 My God! I cry with every breath,
   For some kind power to save;
  Oh, break the yoke of sin and death,
   And thus redeem the slave.
                    WATTS.

258.   Rom. 8: 8.

1 How helpless guilty nature lies,
   Unconscious of its load!
  The heart, unchanged, can never rise
   To happiness and God.

2 Can aught, beneath a power divine,
   The stubborn will subdue?
  'Tis thine, almighty Spirit! thine,
   To form the heart anew.

3 'Tis thine the passions to recall,
   And upward bid them rise;
  To make the scales of error fall,
   From reason's darkened eyes;—

4 To chase the shades of death away,
   And bid the sinner live;
  A beam of heaven, a vital ray,
   'Tis thine alone to give.

5 Oh, change these wretched hearts of
   And give them life divine;   [ours,
  Then shall our passions and our powers,
   Almighty Lord, be thine.
                  MRS. STEELE.

259.   John 1: 12, 13.

1 NOT all the outward forms on earth,
   Nor rites that God has given,
  Nor will of man, nor blood, nor birth,
   Can raise a soul to heaven.

2 The sovereign will of God alone
   Creates us heirs of grace;
  Born in the image of his Son,
   A new, peculiar race.

3 The Spirit, like some heavenly wind,
   Breathes on the sons of flesh,
  New-models all the carnal mind,
   And forms the man afresh.

4 Our quickened souls awake and rise
   From the long sleep of death;
  On heavenly things we fix our eyes,
   And praise employs our breath.
                    WATTS.

Salvation by Christ. Deceitfulness of Sin.

EASTLAND. C. M.   GEORGE SMART.

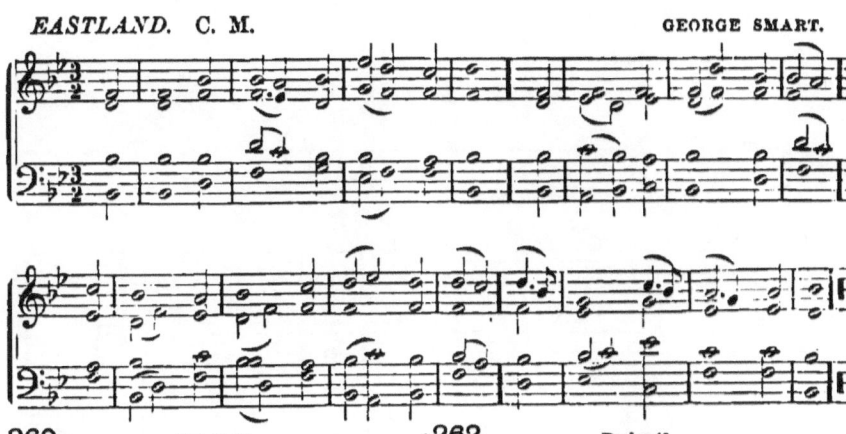

260.   Gal. 2: 20.

1 GREAT God, when I approach thy throne,
    And all thy glory see;
  This is my stay, and this alone,
    That Jesus died for me.

2 How can a soul condemned to die
    Escape the just decree?
  Helpless and full of sin am I,
    But Jesus died for me.

3 Burdened with sin's oppressive chain,
    Oh, how can I get free?
  No peace can all my efforts gain,
    But Jesus died for me.

4 And, Lord, when I behold thy face,
    This must be all my plea;
  Save me by thy almighty grace,
    For Jesus died for me.

261.   *Salvation.*

1 SALVATION!—oh, the joyful sound!
    'Tis pleasure to our ears;
  A sovereign balm for every wound,
    A cordial for our fears.

2 Buried in sorrow and in sin,
    At hell's dark door we lay;—
  But we arise by grace divine,
    To see a heavenly day.

3 Salvation!—let the echo fly
    The spacious earth around;
  While all the armies of the sky
    Conspire to raise the sound.
                     WATTS.

262.   Psalm 40.

1 O LORD, how infinite thy love!
    How wondrous are thy ways!
  Let earth beneath, and heaven above,
    Combine to sing thy praise.

2 Man in immortal beauty shone,
    Thy noblest work below;
  Too soon by sin made heir alone
    To death and endless woe.

3 Then, "Lo! I come," the Saviour said:
    Oh, be his name adored,
  Who, with his blood, our ransom paid,
    And life and bliss restored!
                     LYTE.

263.   *The Throne of Love.*

1 COME, let us lift our joyful eyes
    Up to the courts above,
  And smile to see our Father there,
    Upon a throne of love.

2 Come, let us bow before his feet,
    And venture near the Lord:
  No fiery cherubs guard his seat,
    Nor double-flaming sword.

3 The peaceful gates of heavenly bliss
    Are opened by the Son;
  High let us raise our notes of praise,
    And reach th' almighty Throne.

4 To thee ten thousand thanks we bring,
    Great Advocate on high,
  And glory to the eternal King,
    Who lays his anger by.
                     WATTS.

ARLINGTON. C. M.   DR. ARNE.

264.   *Zech. 13: 1.*

1 THERE is a fountain filled with blood,
    Drawn from Immanuel's veins;
And sinners, plunged beneath that flood,
    Lose all their guilty stains.

2 The dying thief rejoiced to see
    That fountain in his day;
And there may I, though vile as he,
    Wash all my sins away.

3 Dear dying Lamb, thy precious blood
    Shall never lose its power,
Till all the ransomed church of God
    Be saved, to sin no more.

4 E'er since, by faith, I saw the stream
    Thy flowing wounds supply,
Redeeming love has been my theme,
    And shall be till I die.

5 Then in a nobler, sweeter song,
    I'll sing thy power to save, [tongue
When this poor lisping, stammering
    Lies silent in the grave.
                          COWPER.

265.   *The Love of Christ.*

1 THE Saviour! Oh, what endless charms
    Dwell in the blissful sound!
Its influence every fear disarms,
    And spreads sweet comfort round.

2 Wrapped in the gloom of dark despair,
    We helpless, hopeless lay;
But sovereign mercy reached us there,
    And smiled despair away.

3 Th' almighty Former of the skies
    Stooped to our vile abode;   [eyes,
While angels viewed with wondering
    And hailed th' incarnate God.

4 Here pardon, life, and joys divine,
    In rich effusion flow,
For guilty rebels lost in sin,
    And doomed to endless woe.

5 Come, heavenly love, inspire my song
    With thy immortal flame, [tongue,
And teach my heart, and teach my
    The Saviour's lovely name.
                          MRS. STEELE.

266.   *Calvary.*

1 O CHRIST, our ever blessèd Lord,
    For man's transgression slain,
We thy redeeming love record
    In songs of thankful strain.

2 We upward lift our longing eyes,
    And muse on Calvary;
On thy mysterious sacrifice,
    Thy shame and agony.

3 We all like erring sheep had strayed
    From God the Father's care;
The guilt of all on thee was laid;
    Our burden thou didst bear.

4 O Christ, be thou our present joy,
    Our future great reward;
Our only glory may it be,
    To glory in the Lord!

267. *Christ's Pity and Love.*

1 Plunged in a gulf of dark despair,
  We wretched sinners lay,
Without one cheerful beam of hope,
  Or spark of glimmering day.

2 With pitying eyes the Prince of grace
  Beheld our helpless grief;
He saw, and — oh, amazing love! —
  He ran to our relief.

3 Down from the shining seats above,
  With joyful haste he fled,
Entered the grave in mortal flesh,
  And dwelt among the dead.

4 Oh, for this love let rocks and hills
  Their lasting silence break;
And all harmonious human tongues
  The Saviour's praises speak.

5 Angels, assist our mighty joys;
  Strike all your harps of gold;
But when you raise your highest notes,
  His love can ne'er be told.
                              WATTS.

268.   John 14: 6.

1 Thou art the Way: to thee alone
  From sin and death we flee;
And he who would the Father seek,
  Must seek him, Lord, by thee.

2 Thou art the Truth: thy word alone
  True wisdom can impart;
Thou only canst instruct the mind,
  And purify the heart.

3 Thou art the Life: the rending tomb
  Proclaims thy conqu'ring arm;
And those who put their trust in thee
  Nor death nor hell shall harm.

4 Thou art the Way, the Truth, the Life;
  Grant us to know that Way;
That Truth to keep, that Life to win,
  Which leads to endless day.
                              DOANE.

269.   Eph. 2: 8.

1 Amazing grace! how sweet the sound
  That saved a wretch like me!
I once was lost, but now am found, —
  Was blind, but now I see.

2 'Twas grace that taught my heart to fear,
  And grace my fears relieved;
How precious did that grace appear,
  The hour I first believed!

3 Through many dangers, toils, and snares,
  I have already come;
'Tis grace hath brought me safe thus far,
  And grace will lead me home.

4 Yea, when this flesh and heart shall fail,
  And mortal life shall cease,
I shall possess, within the veil,
  A life of joy and peace.
                              NEWTON.

270.   Rom. 5: 8.

1 Jesus, — and didst thou leave the sky,
  To bear our griefs and woes?
And didst thou bleed and groan and die
  For thy rebellious foes?

2 Well might the heavens with wonder view
  A love so strange as thine!
No thought of angels ever knew
  Compassion so divine!

3 Is there a heart that will not bend
  To thy divine control?
Descend, O sovereign Love, descend,
  And melt that stubborn soul!

4 Oh! may our willing hearts confess
  Thy sweet, thy gentle sway;
Glad captives of thy matchless grace,
  Thy righteous rule obey.
                              MRS. STEELE.

271.   1 Cor. 1: 23; 3: 6–7.

1 Christ and his cross are all our theme;
  The mysteries that we speak
Are scandal in the Jews' esteem,
  And folly to the Greek.

2 But souls enlightened from above,
  With joy receive the word;
They see what wisdom, power, and love
  Shine in their dying Lord.

3 The vital savor of his name
  Restores their fainting breath;
But unbelief perverts the same
  To guilt, despair, and death.

4 Till God diffuse his graces down,
  Like showers of heavenly rain,
In vain Apollos sows the ground,
  And Paul may plant in vain.
                              WATTS.

The Sin-atoning Saviour.

WARSAW. H. M.   T. CLARK.

272.   Acts I: 11.

1 COME, every pious heart,
  That loves the Saviour's name,
  Your noblest powers exert
    To celebrate his fame:
Tell all above, | The debt of love
And all below, | To him you owe.

2 He left his starry crown,
  And laid his robes aside;
  On wings of love came down,
    And wept and bled and died:
What he endured, | To save our souls
No tongue can tell, | From death and hell.

3 From the dark grave he rose, —
  The mansion of the dead, —
  And thence his mighty foes
    In glorious triumph led;
Up through the sky | And reigns on high,
The conqueror rode, | The Saviour-God.

4 From thence he'll quickly come, —
  His chariot will not stay, —
  And bear our spirits home
    To realms of endless day:
There shall we see | And ever be
His lovely face, | In his embrace.
              STENNETT.

273.   *The Sin-atoning Saviour.*

1 THY works, not mine, O Christ!
  Speak gladness to this heart;
  They tell me all is done;
    They bid my fear depart:
To whom, save thee, | For sin atone.
Who canst alone | Lord, shall I flee?

2 Thy tears, not mine, O Christ,
  Have wept my guilt away;
  And turned this night of mine
    Into a blessèd day:
To whom, save thee, | For sin atone,
Who canst alone | Lord, shall I flee?

3 Thy wounds, not mine, O Christ,
  Can heal my bruisèd soul;
  Thy stripes, not mine, contain
    The balm that makes me whole:
To whom, save thee, | For sin atone,
Who canst alone | Lord, shall I flee?

4 Thy righteousness alone
  Can clothe and beautify;
  I wrap it round my soul;
    In this I'll live and die:
To whom, save thee, | For sin atone,
Who canst alone | Lord! shall I flee?
              BONAR.

274.   *Luke 4: 19.*
1 Blow ye the trumpet, blow!
    The gladly solemn sound,
Let all the nations know,
    To earth's remotest bound:
The year of jubilee is come;
Return, ye ransomed sinners, home.

2 Exalt the Lamb of God,
    The sin-atoning Lamb!
Redemption by his blood,
    Through every land, proclaim:
The year of jubilee is come;
Return, ye ransomed sinners, home.

3 The gospel trumpet hear,
    The news of pardoning grace:
Ye happy souls, draw near;
    Behold your Saviour's face:
The year of jubilee is come;
Return, ye ransomed sinners, home.

4 Jesus, our great High Priest,
    Has full atonement made;
Ye weary spirits, rest;
    Ye mourning souls, be glad:
The year of jubilee is come;
Return, ye ransomed sinners, home.
                              Toplady.

275.   *Prophet, Priest, and King.*
1 Join all the glorious names
    Of wisdom, love, and power,
That ever mortals knew,
    That angels ever bore:
All are too mean to speak his worth,
Too mean to set my Saviour forth.

2 Great Prophet of our God!
    Our tongues would bless thy name:
By thee the joyful news
    Of our salvation came;
The joyful news of sins forgiven,
Of hell subdued, and peace with heaven.

3 Jesus, our great High Priest,
    Offered his blood and died;
My guilty conscience needs
    No sacrifice beside;
His powerful blood did once atone,
And now it pleads before the throne.
                              Watts.

276.   *In Christ.* — *Heb. 7: 22.*
1 Arise, my soul, arise,
    Shake off thy guilty fears;
The bleeding Sacrifice
    In my behalf appears;
Before the throne my Surety stands:
My name is written on his hands.

2 He ever lives above,
    For me to intercede,
His all-redeeming love,
    His precious blood to plead;
His blood atoned for all our race,
And sprinkles now the throne of grace.

3 My God is reconciled;
    His pardoning voice I hear;
He owns me for his child;
    I can no longer fear;
His Spirit answers to the blood,
And tells me "Thou art born of God."
                              C. Wesley.

277.   *Col. 1: 20.*
1 Ye saints, your music bring,
    Attuned to sweetest sound;
Strike every trembling string,
    Till earth and heaven resound:
The triumphs of the cross we sing;
Awake, ye saints, each joyful string!

2 The cross hath power to save
    From all the foes that rise;
The cross hath made the grave
    A passage to the skies:
The triumphs of the cross we sing;
Awake, ye saints, each joyful string!
                              Reed.

278.   *The Glad Tidings.*
1 Hark, hark! — the notes of joy
    Roll o'er the heavenly plains,
And seraphs find employ
    For their sublimest strains;
Some new delight in heaven is known:
Loud sound the harps around the throne.

2 Hark, hark! — the sound draws nigh,
    The joyful hosts descend;
Jesus forsakes the sky,
    To earth his footsteps bend;
He comes to bless our fallen race;
He comes with messages of grace.

3 Bear, bear the tidings round;
    Let every mortal know
What love in God is found,
    What pity he can show;
Ye winds that blow! ye waves that roll!
Bear the glad news from pole to pole.

FEDERAL STREET. L. M.
H. K. OLIVER.

279. *Matt. 11: 28-30.*

1 With tearful eyes I look around,
Life seems a dark and stormy sea;
Yet, 'midst the gloom, I hear a sound,
A heavenly whisper, "Come to Me."

2 It tells me of a place of rest —
It tells me where my soul may flee;
Oh, to the weary, faint, oppressed,
How sweet the bidding, "Come to Me."

3 When nature shudders, loath to part
From all I love, enjoy, and see;
When a faint chill steals o'er my heart,
A sweet voice utters, "Come to Me."

4 Come, for all else must fail and die;
Earth is no resting-place for thee;
Heavenward direct thy weeping eye;
I am thy portion, "Come to Me."

5 Oh, voice of mercy! voice of love!
In conflict, grief, and agony,
Support me, cheer me from above!
And gently whisper, "Come to Me."

280. *The Love of Christ.*

1 Have we no tears to shed for Him,
While soldiers scoff, and Jews deride?
Ah! look, how patiently he hangs,—
Jesus, our Love, is crucified!

2 What was thy crime, my dearest Lord?
By earth, by heaven, thou hast been tried,
And guilty found of too much love;
Jesus, our Love, is crucified!

3 Found guilty of excess of love!
It was thine own sweet will that tied
Thee tighter far than helpless nails;
Jesus, our Love, is crucified!

4 Oh, break, oh, break, hard heart of mine!
Thy weak self-love and guilty pride
His Pilate and his Judas were;
Jesus, our Love, is crucified!

5 A broken heart, a fount of tears,—
Ask, and they will not be denied;
A broken heart love's cradle is;
Jesus, our Love, is crucified!
Lyra Cath.

281. *Invitation.*

1 Come, weary souls, with sin distressed,
Come, and accept the promised rest;
The Saviour's gracious call obey,
And cast your gloomy fears away.

2 Oppressed with guilt,— a painful load,—
Oh, come and bow before your God!
Divine compassion, mighty love
Will all the painful load remove.

3 Here mercy's boundless ocean flows,
To cleanse your guilt and heal your woes;
Pardon and life and endless peace,—
How rich the gift, how free the grace!

4 Dear Saviour! let thy powerful love
Confirm our faith, our fears remove;
Oh, sweetly reign in every breast,
And guide us to eternal rest.
Mrs. Steele.

282. Psalm 88.

1 WHILE life prolongs its precious light,
  Mercy is found and peace is given;
  But soon, ah! soon, approaching night
  Shall blot out every hope of heaven.

2 Soon, borne on time's most rapid wing,
  Shall death command you to the grave,
  Before his bar your spirits bring,
  And none be found to hear or save.

3 In that lone land of deep despair,
  No Sabbath's heavenly light shall rise;
  No God regard your bitter prayer,
  Nor Saviour call you to the skies.

4 Now God invites — how blest the day!
  How sweet the gospel's charming sound!
  Come, sinners, haste, oh, haste away,
  While yet a pardoning God is found.
  DWIGHT.

283. Rev. 3: 20.

1 BEHOLD a Stranger at the door!
  He gently knocks, has knocked before;
  Has waited long, is waiting still:
  You treat no other friend so ill.

2 Oh, lovely attitude! he stands
  With melting heart and open hands:
  Oh, matchless kindness! — and he shows
  This matchless kindness to his foes!

3 Rise, touched with gratitude divine,
  Turn out his enemy and thine;
  Turn out thy soul-enslaving sin,
  And let the heavenly Stranger in.

4 Oh, welcome him, the Prince of peace!
  Now may his gentle reign increase!
  Throw wide the door, each willing mind,
  And be his empire all mankind.
  GREGG.

284. Matt. 11: 28.

1 COME hither, all ye weary souls,
  Ye heavy-laden sinners come;
  I'll give you rest from all your toils,
  And raise you to my heavenly home.

2 They shall find rest who learn of me;
  I'm of a meek and lowly mind;
  But passion rages like the sea,
  And pride is restless as the wind.

3 Blest is the man whose shoulders take
  My yoke, and bear it with delight;
  My yoke is easy to his neck,
  My grace shall make the burden light.

4 Jesus! we come at thy command,
  With faith and hope and humble zeal;
  Resign our spirits to thy hand,
  To mould and guide us at thy will.
  WATTS.

285. Gen. 6: 3.

1 SAY, sinner! hath a voice within
  Oft whispered to thy secret soul,
  Urged thee to leave the ways of sin,
  And yield thy heart to God's control?

2 Sinner, it was a heavenly voice,
  It was the Spirit's gracious call;
  It bade thee make the better choice,
  And haste to seek in Christ thine all.

3 Spurn not the call to life and light;
  Regard, in time, the warning kind;
  That call thou mayst not always slight,
  And yet the gate of mercy find.

4 God's Spirit will not always strive
  With hardened, self-destroying man;
  Ye who persist his love to grieve
  May never hear his voice again.
  HYDE.

286. Luke 10: 42.

1 WHY will ye waste on trifling cares
  That life which God's compassion spares?
  While, in the various range of thought,
  The one thing needful is forgot.

2 Shall God invite you from above?
  Shall Jesus urge his dying love?
  Shall troubled conscience give you pain,
  And all these pleas unite in vain?

3 Not so your eyes will always view
  Those objects which you now pursue:
  Not so will heaven and hell appear,
  When death's decisive hour is near.

4 Almighty God! thy grace impart;
  Fix deep conviction on each heart;
  Nor let us waste on trifling cares
  That life which thy compassion spares.
  DODDRIDGE.

Invitations. Living Water.

DEDHAM. C. M. — WM. GARDINER.

287. *John 3: 17.*

1 Come, happy souls, approach your God
With new, melodious songs;
Come, render to almighty Grace,
The tribute of your tongues.

2 So strange, so boundless was the love
That pitied dying men,
The Father sent his equal Son
To give them life again.

3 Here, sinners, come and heal your wounds;
Come, wipe your sorrows dry;
Come, trust the mighty Saviour's name,
And you shall never die.

4 See, dearest Lord, our willing souls
Accept thine offered grace;
We bless the great Redeemer's love,
And give the Father praise.
WATTS.

288. *Psalm 34.*

1 O sinners, come and taste his love,
Come, learn his pleasant ways,
And let your own experience prove
The sweetness of his grace.

2 He bids his angels pitch their tents
Where'er his children dwell;
What ills their heavenly care prevents,
No earthly tongue can tell.

3 Oh, love the Lord, ye saints of his;
His eye regards the just:
How richly blest their portion is
Who make the Lord their trust!
WATTS.

289. *The Living Water.*

1 Oh! what amazing words of grace
Are in the gospel found,
Suited to every sinner's case
Who hears the joyful sound!

2 Come, then, with all your wants and
Your every burden bring; [wounds,
Here love, unchanging love, abounds,—
A deep, celestial spring.

3 This spring with living water flows,
And heavenly joy imparts;
Come, thirsty souls! your wants disclose,
And drink, with thankful hearts.

4 Millions of sinners, vile as you,
Have here found life, and peace;
Come then, and prove its virtues too,
And drink, adore, and bless.
MEDLEY.

290. *Luke 15: 18.*

1 Return, O wanderer, to thy home,
Thy Father calls for thee:
No longer now an exile roam,
In guilt and misery.

2 Return, O wanderer, to thy home,
Thy Saviour calls for thee:
"The Spirit and the Bride say, Come;"
Oh, now for refuge flee!

3 Return, O wanderer, to thy home,
'Tis madness to delay:
There are no pardons in the tomb,
And brief is mercy's day!
HASTINGS.

Invitations.

291.   *Est. 4: 16.*

1 Come, trembling sinner, in whose breast
    A thousand thoughts revolve;
Come, with your guilt and fear oppressed,
    And make this last resolve: —

2 "I'll go to Jesus, though my sins
    Like mountains round me close;
I know his courts; I'll enter in,
    Whatever may oppose.

3 "Prostrate I'll lie before his throne,
    And there my guilt confess;
I'll tell him I'm a wretch undone,
    Without his sovereign grace.

4 "I can but perish if I go;
    I am resolved to try;
For if I stay away, I know
    I must forever die."
                                  JONES.

292.   *Eccl. 12: 1.*

1 Remember thy Creator now,
    In these thy youthful days;
He will accept thine earliest vow,
    And listen to thy praise.

2 Remember thy Creator now,
    And seek him while he's near;
For evil days will come, when thou
    Shalt find no comfort near.

3 Remember thy Creator now;
    His willing servant be:
Then, when thy head in death shall bow,
    He will remember thee.

4 Almighty God! our hearts incline
    Thy heavenly voice to hear;
Let all our future days be thine,
    Devoted to thy fear.

293.   *Luke 14: 22.*

1 Ye wretched, hungry, starving poor,
    Behold a royal feast!
Where mercy spreads her bounteous store
    For every humble guest.

2 See, Jesus stands with open arms;
    He calls, he bids you come;
Guilt holds you back, and fear alarms;
    But see, there yet is room! —

3 Room in the Saviour's bleeding heart;
    There love and pity meet;
Nor will he bid the soul depart
    That trembles at his feet.

4 Oh, come, and with his children taste
    The blessings of his love;
While hope attends the sweet repast
    Of nobler joys above.
                              Mrs. STEELE.

294.   *Luke 14: 22.*

1 The King of heaven his table spreads,
    And dainties crown the board;
Not paradise, with all its joys,
    Could such delight afford.

2 Pardon and peace to dying men,
    And endless life are given,
And the rich blood that Jesus shed,
    To raise the soul to heaven.

3 Millions of souls in glory now
    Were fed and feasted here;
And millions more still on the way,
    Around the board appear.

4 Yet is his house and heart so large,
    That millions more may come,
Nor could the wide assembling world
    O'erfill the spacious room.
                              DODDRIDGE.

295.   *Prov. 8: 17.*

1 Ye hearts with youthful vigor warm,
    In smiling crowds draw near,
And turn from every mortal charm
    A Saviour's voice to hear.

2 He, Lord of all the worlds on high,
    Stoops to converse with you,
And lays his radiant glories by,
    Your friendship to pursue.

3 "The soul that longs to see my face
    Is sure my love to gain;
And those that early seek my grace
    Shall never seek in vain."

4 What object, Lord, my soul should move,
    If once compared with thee?
What beauty should command my love,
    Like what in Christ I see?

5 Away, ye false, delusive toys,
    Vain tempters of the mind!
'Tis here I fix my lasting choice,
    For here true bliss I find.
                              DODDRIDGE.

Invitations.

INVITATION. C. M.

By permission of WM. HALL & SON.
Arranged from WALLACE.

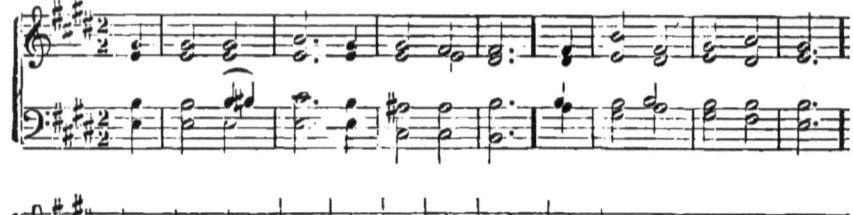

296.   *Luke 14: 22.*
1 Come, sinner, to the gospel feast;
  Oh, come without delay;
For there is room in Jesus' breast
  For all who will obey.

2 There's room in God's eternal love
  To save thy precious soul;
Room in the Spirit's grace above
  To heal and make thee whole.

3 There's room within the church, redeemed
  With blood of Christ divine;
Room in the white-robed throng convened,
  For that dear soul of thine.

4 There's room in heaven among the choir,
  And harps and crowns of gold,
And glorious palms of victory there,
  And joys that ne'er were told.

5 There's room around thy Father's board
  For thee and thousands more:
Oh, come and welcome to the Lord;
  Yea, come this very hour.
                    HUNTINGDON.

297.   *"Return, O Wanderer."*
1 Return, O wanderer, now return,
  And seek thy Father's face!
Those new desires, which in thee burn,
  Were kindled by his grace.

2 Return, O wanderer, now return;
  He hears thy humble sigh;
He sees thy softened spirit mourn,
  When no one else is nigh.

3 Return, O wanderer, now return;
  Thy Saviour bids thee live:
Go to his bleeding feet, and learn
  How freely he'll forgive.

4 Return, O wanderer, now return,
  And wipe the falling tear;
Thy Father calls, no longer mourn;
  His love invites thee near.
                    COLLYER.

298.   *Voice of Mercy.*
1 The Saviour calls; let every ear
  Attend the heavenly sound;
Ye doubting souls, dismiss your fear;
  Hope smiles reviving round.

2 For every thirsty, longing heart,
  Here streams of bounty flow,
And life and health and bliss impart,
  To banish mortal woe.

3 Ye sinners, come; 'tis mercy's voice;
  That gracious voice obey;
'Tis Jesus calls to heavenly joys;
  And can you yet delay?

4 Dear Saviour, draw reluctant hearts;
  To thee let sinners fly,
And take the bliss thy love imparts,
  And drink, and never die.
                    MRS. STEELE.

Doxology.
Let God the Father, and the Son,
  And Spirit, be adored,
Where there are works to make him known,
  Or saints to love the Lord.

Invitation and Exhortation.

ROSEFIELD. 7s. 6l.   DR. MALAN.

299. *Invitation.*

1 FROM the cross uplifted high,
Where the Saviour deigns to die,
What melodious sounds we hear,
Bursting on the ravished ear!—
"Love's redeeming work is done;
Come and welcome, sinner, come.

2 "Sprinkled now with blood the throne,
Why beneath thy burdens groan?
On my piercèd body laid,
Justice owns the ransom paid;
Bow the knee, and kiss the Son;
Come and welcome, sinner, come.

3 "Spread for thee, the festal board
See with richest dainties stored;
To thy Father's bosom pressed,
Yet again a child confessed,
Never from his house to roam,
Come and welcome, sinner, come.

4 "Soon the days of life shall end;
Lo, I come, your Saviour, Friend,
Safe your spirits to convey
To the realms of endless day,
Up to my eternal home;
Come and welcome, sinner, come."
HAWES.

300. *Exhortation.*

1 WEARY souls, that wander wide
From the central point of bliss,
Turn to Jesus crucified;
Fly to those dear wounds of his;
Sanctified by Jesus' blood,
Rise into the life of God.

2 Find in Christ the way of peace,—
Peace unspeakable, unknown;
By his pain, he gives you ease,
Life by his expiring groan;
Rise, exalted by his fall;
Find in Christ your all in all.

3 Oh, believe the record true!
God to you his Son hath given!
Ye may now be happy too;
Find on earth the life of heaven;
Live the life of heaven above,
All the life of glorious love.
C. WESLEY.

301. *Exhortation.*

1 YE who in these courts are found,
Listening to the joyful sound,—
Lost and helpless, as ye are,
Sons of sorrow, sin, and care,—
Glorify the King of kings,
Take the peace the gospel brings.

2 Turn to Christ your longing eyes,
View his bleeding sacrifice;
See, in him, your sins forgiven,
Pardon, holiness, and heaven:
Glorify the King of kings,
Take the peace the gospel brings.

Invitations. The Accepted Time.

DAWN. S. M.   E. P. PARKER.

1. How gentle God's commands! How kind his precepts are!
Come, cast your burdens on the Lord, And trust his constant care.

302.   *Psalm 55.*
2 Beneath his watchful eye,
His saints securely dwell;
That hand which bears all nature up
Shall guard his children well.

3 Why should this anxious load
Press down your weary mind?
Haste to your heavenly Father's throne,
And sweet refreshment find.

4 His goodness stands approved,
Unchanged from day to day;
I'll drop my burden at his feet,
And bear a song away.
                      DODDRIDGE.

303.   *Rev. 22: 17.*
1 THE Spirit, in our hearts,
Is whispering, "Sinner, come;"
The Bride, the Church of Christ, pro-
To all his children, "Come!" [claims

2 Let him that heareth say
To all about him, "Come!"
Let him that thirsts for righteousness,
To Christ, the fountain, come!

3 Yes, whosoever will,
Oh, let him freely come,
And freely drink the stream of life;
'Tis Jesus bids him come.

4 Lo! Jesus, who invites,
Declares, "I quickly come:"
Lord, even so! we wait thine hour;
O blest Redeemer, come!
                      EPIS. COLL.

304.   *Gen. 8: 9.*
1 OH, cease, my wand'ring soul,
On restless wing to roam;
All this wide world, to either pole,
Hath not for thee a home.

2 Behold the ark of God!
Behold the open door!
Oh, haste to gain that dear abode,
And rove, my soul, no more.

3 There, safe thou shalt abide,
There sweet shall be thy rest,
And every longing satisfied,
With full salvation blest.
                      MUHLENBURG.

305.   *2 Cor. 6: 2.*
1 Now is th' accepted time,
Now is the day of grace;
O sinners! come, without delay,
And seek the Saviour's face.

2 Now is th' accepted time,
The Saviour calls to-day;
To-morrow it may be too late; —
Then why should you delay?

3 Now is th' accepted time,
The gospel bids you come;
And every promise in his word
Declares there yet is room.

4 Lord, draw reluctant souls,
And feast them with thy love;
Then will the angels spread their wings,
And bear the news above.
                      DOBELL.

Invitations. No Rest in the World.

SERENE. S. M.   J. E. GOULD, from "Flora Sacra."

306.   *Land of Peace.*

1 Come to the land of peace;
   From shadows come away;
Where all the sounds of weeping cease,
   And storms no more have sway.

2 Fear hath no dwelling here;
   But pure repose and love
Breathe through the bright, celestial air,
   The spirit of the dove.

3 Come to the bright and blest,
   Gathered from every land;
For here thy soul shall find its rest,
   Amid the shining band.

4 In this divine abode,
   Change leaves no saddening trace;
Come, trusting spirit, to thy God,
   Thy holy resting-place.

307.   1 John 1:3.

1 Our heavenly Father calls,
   And Christ invites us near;
With both, our friendship shall be sweet,
   And our communion dear.

2 God pities all our griefs;
   He pardons every day;
Almighty to protect our souls,
   And wise to guide our way.

3 How large his bounties are!
   What various stores of good,
Diffused from our Redeemer's hand,
   And purchased with his blood!

4 Jesus, our living Head,
   We bless thy faithful care;
Our Advocate before the throne,
   And our Forerunner there.

5 Here fix, my roving heart!
   Here wait, my warmest love!
Till the communion be complete,
   In nobler scenes above.
               DODDRIDGE.

308.   *Rest not to be found in the World.*

1 Oh! where shall rest be found,—
   Rest for the weary soul?
'Twere vain the ocean depths to sound,
   Or pierce to either pole.

2 The world can never give
   The bliss for which we sigh:
'Tis not the whole of life to live,
   Nor all of death to die.

3 Beyond this vale of tears,
   There is a life above,
Unmeasured by the flight of years;
   And all that life is love.

4 There is a death whose pang
   Outlasts the fleeting breath:
Oh, what eternal horrors hang
   Around the second death!

5 Lord God of truth and grace!
   Teach us that death to shun;
Lest we be banished from thy face,
   And evermore undone.
               MONTGOMERY.

The Saviour's Gracious Call.

HORTON. 7s. GERMAN.

309. *Matt. 11: 28–30.*

1 Come, said Jesus' sacred voice,
Come, and make my paths your choice;
I will guide you to your home,
Weary wanderer, hither come!

2 Thou who, homeless and forlorn,
Long hast borne the proud world's scorn,
Long hast roamed the barren waste,
Weary wanderer, hither haste.

3 Ye who, tossed on beds of pain,
Seek for ease, but seek in vain;
Ye, by fiercer anguish torn,
In remorse for guilt who mourn:—

4 Hither come! for here is found
Balm that flows for every wound,
Peace that ever shall endure,
Rest eternal, sacred, sure.
BARBAULD.

310. *Matt. 11: 28.*

1 Come, ye weary souls, oppressed,
Answer to the Saviour's call;
"Come, and I will give you rest;
Come, and I will save you all."

2 Jesus, full of truth and love,
We thy kindest call obey,
Faithful let thy mercies prove,
Take our load of guilt away.

3 Weary of this war within,
Weary of this endless strife,
Weary of ourselves and sin,
Weary of a wretched life;—

4 Burdened with a world of grief,
Burdened with our sinful load,
Burdened with this unbelief,
Burdened with the wrath of God;—

5 Lo, we come to thee for ease,
True and gracious as thou art;
Now our weary souls release,
Write forgiveness on our heart.

311. *Isaiah 53: 4.*

1 Weary sinner! keep thine eyes
On th' atoning Sacrifice;
View him bleeding on the tree,
Pouring out his life for thee.

2 Surely, Christ thy griefs hath borne;
Weeping soul, no longer mourn:
Now by faith the Son embrace,
Plead his promise, trust his grace.

3 Cast thy guilty soul on him;
Find him mighty to redeem:
At his feet thy burden lay;
Look thy doubts and care away.

4 Lord, come thou with power to heal;
Now thy mighty arm reveal:
At thy feet myself I lay;
Take, oh, take my sins away!

2.   Ezek. 33: 11.

Sinners, turn, why will ye die?
God, your Saviour, asks you, Why?
He who did your souls retrieve
Died himself, that ye might live.

Sinners, turn, why will ye die?
God, the Spirit, asks you, Why?
He who all your lives hath strove
Urged you to embrace his love:
Will ye not his grace receive?
Will ye still refuse to live?
O ye dying sinners! why,
Why will ye forever die?
                      C. WESLEY.

3.   Eph. 5: 14.

Sinner, rouse thee from thy sleep;
Wake, and o'er thy folly weep;
Raise thy spirit dark and dead;
Jesus waits his light to shed.

Wake from sleep, arise from death;
See the bright and living path:
Watchful tread that path — be wise;
Leave thy folly, seek the skies.

Leave thy folly, cease from crime,
From this hour redeem the time;
Life secure, without delay;
Evil is thy mortal day.

Rouse thee, sinner, from thy sleep;
Wake, and o'er thy folly weep;
Jesus calls from death and night,
Wake, and he shall give thee light.
                      EPIS. COLL.

314.   1 Pet. 4: 18.

1 When thy mortal life is fled,
   When the death-shades o'er thee spread,
   When is finished thy career,
   Sinner, where wilt thou appear?

2 When the Judge descends in light,
   Clothed in majesty and might,
   When the wicked quail with fear,
   Where, oh, where wilt thou appear?

3 What shall soothe thy bursting heart,
   When the saints and thou must part?
   When the good with joy are crowned,
   Sinner, where wilt thou be found?

4 While the Holy Ghost is nigh,
   Quickly to the Saviour fly;
   Then shall peace thy spirit cheer;
   Then in heaven shalt thou appear.
                      S. F. SMITH.

315.   *Danger of Delay.*

1 Hasten, sinner! to be wise,
    Stay not for the morrow's sun;
   Wisdom, if you still despise,
    Harder is it to be won.

2 Hasten mercy to implore,
    Stay not for the morrow's sun,
   Lest thy season should be o'er,
    Ere this evening's stage be run.

3 Hasten, sinner! to be blest,
    Stay not for the morrow's sun,
   Lest perdition thee arrest,
    Ere the morrow is begun.
                      T. SCOTT.

Friend of Sinners. Self-Surrender. Jesus' Call.

STOCKWELL. 8s. & 7s.   D. E. JONES.

316.   Prov. 18: 24.

1 ONE there is, above all others,
 Well deserves the name of Friend;
 His is love beyond a brother's,
  Costly, free, and knows no end.

2 Which of all our friends, to save us,
 Could or would have shed his blood?
 But our Jesus died to have us
  Reconciled in him to God.

3 When he lived on earth abasèd,
 Friend of sinners was his name;
 Now above all glory raisèd,
  He rejoices in the same.

4 Oh, for grace our hearts to soften,
 Teach us, Lord, at length to love;
 We, alas! forget too often
  What a Friend we have above.
      NEWTON.

317.   Self-Surrender.

1 TAKE me, O my Father, take me!
 Take me, save me through thy Son;
 That which thou wouldst have me, make [me,
  Let thy will in me be done.

2 Long from thee my footsteps straying,
 Thorny proved the way I trod;
 Weary come I now, and praying —
  Take me to thy love, my God!

3 Fruitless years with grief recalling,
 Humbly I confess my sin;
 At thy feet, O Father, falling,
  To thy household take me in.

4 Freely to thee now I proffer
 This relenting heart of mine;
 Freely life and soul I offer, —
  Gift unworthy love like thine.

5 Father, take me! all forgiving,
 Fold me to thy loving breast;
 In thy love forever living,
  I must be forever blest.
      RAY PALMER.

318.   Matt. 4: 19.

1 JESUS calls us! o'er the tumult
 Of our life's wild, restless sea,
 Day by day his sweet voice soundeth,
  Saying, Christian, follow me!

2 Jesus calls us, from the worship
 Of the vain world's golden store;
 From each idol that would keep us,
  Saying, Christian, love me more!

3 In our joys and in our sorrows,
 Days of toil and hours of ease,
 Still he calls, in cares and pleasures,
  Christian, love me more than these!

4 Jesus calls us! by thy mercies,
 Saviour, may we hear thy call;
 Give our hearts to thy obedience,
  Serve and love thee best of all.

Benediction.

MAY the grace of Christ our Saviour,
 And the Father's boundless love,
 With the Holy Spirit's favor,
  Rest upon us from above.

Invitations and Expostulations.

GREENVILLE. 8s., 7s., & 4s.

319. *Hasten to the Saviour.*

HEAR, O sinner! mercy hails you;
Now with sweetest voice she calls;
Bids you haste to seek the Saviour,
Ere the hand of justice falls:
Hear, O sinner!
'Tis the voice of mercy calls.

Haste, O sinner, to the Saviour!
Seek his mercy while you may;
Soon the day of grace is over;
Soon your life will pass away:
Haste, O sinner!
You must perish if you stay.
REED.

320. *Look to Jesus.*

COME, ye souls by sin afflicted,
Bowed with fruitless sorrow down,
By the perfect law convicted,
Through the cross behold the crown;
Look to Jesus;
Mercy flows through him alone.

Take his easy yoke, and wear it;
Love will make obedience sweet;
Christ will give you strength to bear it,
While his wisdom guides your feet
Safe to glory,
Where his ransomed captives meet.

Sweet as home to pilgrims weary,
Light to newly-opened eyes,
Or full springs in deserts dreary,
Is the rest the cross supplies;
All who taste it
Shall to rest immortal rise.
SWAIN.

321. *The Message of Mercy.*

1 HEAR the heralds of the gospel
News from Zion's King proclaim:—
"To each rebel sinner pardon;
Free forgiveness in his name:"
Oh, what mercy!
"Free forgiveness in his name."

2 Sinners, will you scorn the message
Sent in mercy from above?
Every sentence, oh, how tender!
Every line is full of love:
Listen to it;
Every line is full of love.

3 O ye angels, hovering round us,
Waiting spirits, speed your way;
Hasten to the court of heaven,
Tidings bear without delay;
Rebel sinners
Glad the message will obey.
ALLEN'S COLL.

322. *Jesus received.*

1 WELCOME, welcome, dear Redeemer,—
Welcome to this heart of mine;
Lord, I make a full surrender,
Every power and thought be thine,—
Thine entirely,
Through eternal ages thine.

2 Known to all to be thy mansion,
Earth and hell will disappear,
Or in vain attempt possession,
When they find the Lord is near:
Shout, O Zion!
Shout, ye saints! the Lord is here.

Invitation. Clinging to Christ. Christ's Intercession.

BRASTOW. 8s. & 6. Arranged.

323. *John 7: 37.*

1 BURDENED with guilt, wouldst thou be blest?
Trust not the world; it gives no rest:
I bring relief to hearts oppressed;
O weary sinner, come!

2 Come, leave thy burden at the cross;
Count all thy gains but empty dross;
My grace repays all earthly loss:
O needy sinner, come!

3 Come, hither bring thy boding fears,
Thy aching heart, thy bursting tears;
'Tis mercy's voice salutes thine ears:
O trembling sinner, come!

4 " The Spirit and the Bride say, Come!"
Rejoicing saints re-echo, Come!
Who faints, who thirsts, who will, may come;
Thy Saviour bids thee come.

324. *The Unseen Friend.*

1 O HOLY Saviour! Friend unseen!
Since on thine arm thou bid'st me lean,
Help me, throughout life's changing scene,
By faith to cling to thee!

2 Blest with this fellowship divine,
Take what thou wilt, I'll not repine;
For, as the branches to the vine,
My soul would cling to thee.

3 What though the world deceitful prove,
And earthly friends and hopes remove;
With patient, uncomplaining love,
Still would I cling to thee.

4 Though oft I seem to tread alone
Life's dreary waste, with thorns o'grown,
Thy voice of love, in gentlest tone,
Still whispers, "Cling to me!"

5 Though faith and hope are often tri
I ask not, need not, aught beside;
So safe, so calm, so satisfied,
The soul that clings to thee!

325. *Christ's Intercession.*

1 O THOU, the contrite sinner's Friend
Who, loving, lov'st them to the end,
On this alone my hopes depend,
That thou wilt plead for me.

2 When weary in the Christian race,
Far off appears my resting-place,
And, fainting, I mistrust thy grace,
Then, Saviour, plead for me.

3 When I have erred and gone astray,
Afar from thine and wisdom's way,
And see no glimmering, guiding ray
Still, Saviour, plead for me.

4 When Satan, by my sins made bold,
Strives from thy cross to loose my ho
Then with thy pitying arms enfold,
And plead, oh, plead for me!

5 And when my dying hour draws nea
Darkened with anguish, guilt, and fe
Then to my fainting sight appear,
Pleading in heaven for me.

COME, YE DISCONSOLATE. 11s. & 10s.
WEBBE.

326.

1 Come, ye disconsolate, where'er ye languish:
Come to the mercy-seat, fervently kneel;
Here bring your wounded hearts, here tell your anguish;
Earth has no sorrow that heaven cannot heal.

2 Joy of the desolate, light of the straying,
Hope when all others die, fadeless and pure;
Here speaks the Comforter, in God's name saying,
Earth has no sorrow that heaven cannot cure.

MOORE.

NOTE.—The first two lines of this tune may be sung with the best effect as a Soprano Solo.

THE SAVIOUR'S CALL. 6s. & 4s.

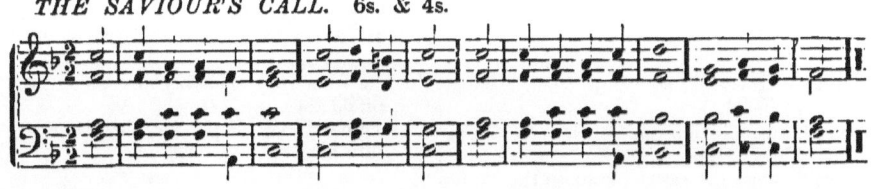

327. Heb. 3: 15.

1 To-day the Saviour calls:
Ye wanderers, come;
O ye benighted souls,
Why longer roam?

2 To-day the Saviour calls;
Oh, hear him now;
Within these sacred walls
To Jesus bow.

3 To-day the Saviour calls;
For refuge fly;
The storm of justice falls,
And death is nigh.

4 The Spirit calls to-day;
Yield to his power;
Oh, grieve him not away:
'Tis mercy's hour.

SCOTLAND. 12s. DR. JOHN CLARKE.

328. Gen. 19:7.

2 Ye souls that are wounded, oh, flee to
    the Saviour!
He calls you in mercy; 'tis infinite favor;
Your sins are increasing; escape to the
    mountain;
His blood can remove them; it flows from
    the fountain.
    Hallelujah to the Lamb, etc.

3 With joy shall we stand, when escaped
    to the shore;
With harps in our hands, we will praise
    him the more;
We'll range the sweet plains on the banks
    of the river,
And sing of salvation for ever and ever!
    Halellujah to the Lamb, etc.
                        THORNDY.

329. John 11:25.

1 THOU art gone to the grave; but we
    will not deplore thee,
Though sorrows and darkness encompass
    the tomb;
The Saviour hath passed through its por-
    tals before thee;
And the lamp of his love is thy guide
    through the gloom.

2 Thou art gone to the grave; we no
    longer behold thee,
Nor tread the rough paths of the world
    by thy side;
But the wide arms of mercy are spread to
    enfold thee,
And sinners may hope, for the Sinless
    hath died.

3 Thou art gone to the grave; and, its
    mansion forsaking,
Perchance thy weak spirit in doubt lin-
    gered long;
But the sunshine of heaven beamed
    bright on thy waking,
And the sound thou didst hear was the
    seraphim's song.
                        HEBER.

Jesus' Gentle Call.

AVA. 6s. & 4. DR. HASTINGS.

1. Child of sin and sorrow! Filled with dismay,
   Wait not for to-morrow, Yield thee to-day.
   Heav'n bids thee come While yet there's room;
   D.C. Child of sin and sorrow! Hear and obey.

330. Heb. 3: 13-15.

2 Child of sin and sorrow,
   Why wilt thou die?
   Come while thou canst borrow
   Help from on high:
   Grieve not that love
   Which from above,
   Child of sin and sorrow,
   Would bring thee nigh.

3 Child of sin and sorrow,
   Thy moments glide,
   Like the flitting arrow,
   Or the rushing tide;
   Ere time is o'er,
   Heaven's grace implore ;
   Child of sin and sorrow,
   In Christ confide.

331. GENTLE CALL.

1. Jesus gently calls, Weary sinner, come! Leave the land of sin and want, Hasten to thy happy home! God thy Father comes to meet thee; Saints and angels wait to greet thee; To thy Father and thy home, Weary sinner, come!

2 Jesus gently calls!
   We would fain obey:
   Low before thy feet we fall;
   Cast us not from thee away.
   By thy blood for sinners spilt,
   Cleanse us from our sin and guilt,
   Be our advocate and friend,
     Save us to the end.

3 Jesus, thy sweet call
   Falls like evening dew
   On our weary, thirsty souls,
   Shedding life and strength anew.
   Though to-day be full of sorrow,
   Thy sweet smile can make to-morrow
   Bright and clear; O Saviour dear,
     Let thy smile appear!

Repentance.

HAMBURG. L. M.   Arranged by DR. MASON.

332.   Luke 18: 13.
1 WITH broken heart and contrite sigh,
   A trembling sinner, Lord, I cry;
   Thy pardoning grace is rich and free:
   O God, be merciful to me!

2 I smite upon my troubled breast,
   With deep and conscious guilt oppressed;
   Christ and his cross my only plea:
   O God, be merciful to me!

3 Far off I stand with tearful eyes,
   Nor dare uplift them to the skies;
   But thou dost all my anguish see:
   O God, be merciful to me!

4 Nor alms, nor deeds that I have done,
   Can for a single sin atone;
   To Calvary alone I flee:
   O God, be merciful to me!

333.   John 1: 29.
1 JUST as I am, without one plea,
   But that thy blood was shed for me,
   And that thou bid'st me come to thee,
   O Lamb of God, I come! I come!

2 Just as I am, and waiting not
   To rid my soul of one dark blot, [spot.
   To thee, whose blood can cleanse each
   O Lamb of God, I come! I come!

3 Just as I am, though tossed about
   With many a conflict, many a doubt,
   Fightings within, and fears without,
   O Lamb of God, I come! I come!

4 Just as I am,— poor, wretched, blind;
   Sight, riches, healing of the mind,
   Yea, all I need, in thee to find,
   O Lamb of God, I come! I come!

5 Just as I am, thou wilt receive,
   Wilt welcome, pardon, cleanse, relieve;
   Because thy promise I believe,
   O Lamb of God, I come! I come!

6 Just as I am, thy love unknown
   Hath broken every barrier down;
   Now, to be thine, yea, thine alone,
   O Lamb of God, I come! I come!
              CHARLOTTE ELLIOTT.

334.   Psalm 51.
1 A BROKEN heart, my God, my King,
   Is all the sacrifice I bring;
   The God of grace will ne'er despise
   A broken heart for sacrifice.

2 My soul lies humbled in the dust,
   And owns thy dreadful sentence just;
   Look down, O Lord, with pitying eye,
   And save the soul condemned to die.

3 Then will I teach the world thy ways;
   Sinners shall learn thy sovereign grace;
   I'll lead them to my Saviour's blood,
   And they shall praise a pardoning God.

4 Oh, may thy love inspire my tongue!
   Salvation shall be all my song;
   And all my powers shall join to bless
   The Lord, my Strength and Righteousness.
              WATTS.

335. *Prayer for Pardon.*

1 Oh that my load of sin were gone!
    Oh that I could at last submit
 At Jesus' feet to lay it down, —
    To lay my soul at Jesus' feet!

2 Rest for my soul I long to find:
    Saviour of all, if mine thou art,
 Give me thy meek and lowly mind,
    And stamp thine image on my heart.

3 Break off the yoke of inbred sin,
    And fully set my spirit free:
 I cannot rest till pure within,
    Till I am wholly lost in thee.

4 Fain would I learn of thee, my God;
    Thy light and easy burden prove;
 The cross all stained with hallowed blood,
    The labor of thy dying love.

5 I would, but thou must give the power;
    My heart from every sin release;
 Bring near, bring near the joyful hour,
    And fill me with thy perfect peace!
            C. WESLEY.

336. *Psalm 51.*

1 Show pity, Lord! O Lord, forgive!
  Let a repenting rebel live;
  Are not thy mercies large and free?
  May not a sinner trust in thee?

2 My crimes are great, but ne'er surpass
  The power and glory of thy grace:
  Great God! thy nature hath no bound,
  So let thy pardoning love be found.

3 Oh, wash my soul from every sin,
  And make my guilty conscience clean!
  Here on my heart the burden lies,
  And past offences pain mine eyes.

4 My lips with shame my sins confess,
  Against thy law, against thy grace;
  Lord, should thy judgment grow severe,
  I am condemned, but thou art clear.

5 Yet save a trembling sinner, Lord!
    Whose hope, still hovering round thy word,
  Would light on some sweet promise there,
  Some sure support against despair.
            WATTS.

337. Rom. 5: 1.

1 Thou Prince of glory, slain for me,
    Breathing forgiveness in thy prayer;
  That loving, melting look I see,
    That bursting sigh, that tender tear.

2 Can I behold that closing eye,
    Still fixed on me, still beaming love?
  And can I see my Saviour die,
    Nor feel one holy passion move?

3 Let me but hear thy dying voice
    Pronounce forgiveness in my breast;
  My trembling spirit shall rejoice,
    And feel the calm of heavenly rest.

4 Lord, thine atoning blood apply,
    And life or death is sweet to me;
  In life's last hour, thy presence, nigh,
    From fear shall set my spirit free.
            COLLYER.

338. *The Sinner reconciled to God.*

1 Trembling before thine awful throne,
  O Lord! in dust my sins I own;
  Justice and Mercy for my life
  Contend; oh, smile and heal the strife.

2 The Saviour smiles! upon my soul
  New tides of hope tumultuous roll;
  His voice proclaims my pardon found,
  Seraphic transport wings the sound.

3 Earth has a joy unknown in heaven, —
  The new-born peace of sin forgiven!
  Tears of such pure and deep delight,
  Ye angels, never dimmed your sight.

4 Ye saw of old, on chaos rise
  The beauteous pillars of the skies:
  Ye know where morn, exulting springs,
  And evening folds her drooping wings.

5 Bright heralds of th' eternal Will,
  Abroad his errands ye fulfil;
  Or, throned in floods of beamy day,
  Symphonious, in his presence play.

6 But I amid your choirs shall shine,
  And all your knowledge will be mine:
  Ye on your harps must lean to hear
  A secret chord that mine will bear.
            HILLHOUSE.

Justification by Faith. Choosing Christ.

HERBERT. L. M.

1. No more, my God, I boast no more Of all the du-ties I have done;
I quit the hopes I held be-fore, To trust the mer-its of thy Son.

339. Phil. 3: 7–9.

2 Now, for the love I bear his name,
   What was my gain, I count my loss;
My former pride I call my shame,
   And nail my glory to his cross.

3 Yes, and I must and will esteem
   All things but loss for Jesus' sake;
Oh, may my soul be found in him,
   And of his righteousness partake!

4 The best obedience of my hands
   Dares not appear before thy throne;
But faith can answer thy demands,
   By pleading what my Lord has done.
         WATTS.

340. Isaiah 61: 10.

1 JESUS! thy blood and righteousness
   My beauty are, my glorious dress;
'Mid flaming worlds, in these arrayed,
   With joy shall I lift up my head.

2 When from the dust of earth I rise
   To claim my mansion in the skies;
E'en then shall this be all my plea:
   "Jesus hath lived and died for me."

3 This spotless robe the same appears,
   When ruined nature sinks in years;
No age can change its glorious hue;
   The robe of Christ is ever new.

4 Oh, let the dead now hear thy voice;
   Now bid thy banished ones rejoice;
Their beauty this, their glorious dress,—
   Jesus! thy blood and righteousness!
         TRANS. BY C. WESLEY.

341. Rom. 1: 16.

1 THOUGH all the world my choice deride,
   Yet Jesus shall my portion be;
For I am pleased with none beside;
   The fairest of the fair is he.

2 Sweet is the vision of thy face,
   And kindness o'er thy lips is shed;
Lovely art thou, and full of grace,
   And glory beams around thy head.

3 Thy sufferings I embrace with thee,
   Thy poverty and shameful cross;
The pleasures of the world I flee,
   And deem its treasures only dross.

4 Be daily dearer to my heart,
   And ever let me feel thee near;
Then willingly with all I'd part,
   Nor count it worthy of a tear.
         G. TERSTEEGAN.

342. Psalm 51: 11.

1 STAY, thou insulted Spirit, stay!
   Though I have done thee such despite,
Cast not a sinner quite away,
   Nor take thine everlasting flight.

2 Though I have most unfaithful been
   Of all who e'er thy grace received;
Ten thousand times thy goodness seen,
   Ten thousand times thy goodness grieved;

3 Yet, oh, the chief of sinners spare,
   In honor of my great High Priest!
Nor, in thy righteous anger, swear
   I shall not see thy people's rest.
         C. WESLEY.

Repentance.

ARDEN. C. M.   E. P. PARKER.

343.   *The Blood of Christ.*
1 FOREVER here my rest shall be,
   Close to thy bleeding side;
  This all my hope and all my plea, —
   For me the Saviour died.

2 My dying Saviour, and my God,
   Fountain for guilt and sin,
  Sprinkle me ever with thy blood,
   And cleanse and keep me clean.

3 Wash me, and make me thus thine own:
   Wash me, and mine thou art;
  Wash me, but not my feet alone, —
   My hands, my head, my heart.

4 Th' atonement of thy blood apply,
   Till faith to sight improve;
  Till hope in full fruition die,
   And all my soul be love.
                C. WESLEY.

344.   Jer. 3: 22.
1 How oft, alas! this wretched heart
   Has wandered from the Lord!
  How oft my roving thoughts depart,
   Forgetful of his word!

2 Yet sovereign mercy calls, "Return!"
   Dear Lord, and may I come?
  My vile ingratitude I mourn:
   Oh, take the wanderer home!

3 And canst thou, wilt thou yet forgive,
   And bid my crimes remove?
  And shall a pardoned rebel live,
   To speak thy wondrous love?

4 Almighty grace, thy healing power,
   How glorious, how divine!
  That can to life and bliss restore
   A heart so vile as mine.

5 Thy pard'ning love, so free, so sweet,
   Dear Saviour, I adore;
  Oh, keep me at thy sacred feet,
   And let me rove no more!
                MRS. STEELE.

345.   Luke 15: 17–21.
1 A STRANGER in a barren land,
   Weary and faint I roam;
  Why did I scorn a Father's yoke,
   Or leave my happy home?

2 I will arise, I will return
   And seek my Father's face;
  Tell him my sorrow, sin, and shame,
   And plead his pardoning grace.

3 O Father, thy poor, sinful child
   Returns, at length, to thee!
  Unworthy to be called thy son,
   Let me thy servant be!

4 He meets me yet a great way off,
   And clasps me to his breast;
  He takes me to his home again,
   And gives the wanderer rest.
                E. P. PARKER.
      Doxology.
LET God the Father, and the Son,
   And Spirit be adored,
Where there are works to make him known,
   Or saints to love the Lord.

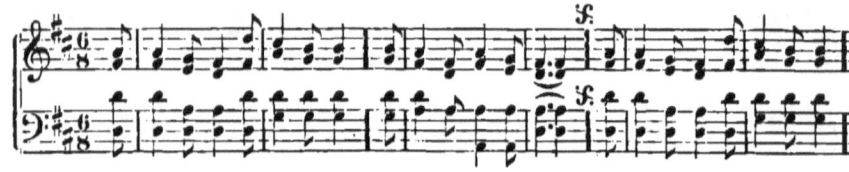

346
The Voice of Jesus.

1 I HEARD the voice of Jesus say,
  "Come unto me and rest;
 Lay down, thou weary one, lay down
  Thy head upon my breast."
 I came to Jesus as I was,
  Weary and worn and sad;
 I found in him a resting-place,
  And he has made me glad.

2 I heard the voice of Jesus say,
  "Behold, I freely give
 The living water! thirsty one,
  Stoop down, and drink, and live."
 I came to Jesus, and I drank
  Of that life-giving stream; [vived,
 My thirst was quenched, my soul re-
  And now I live in him.

3 I heard the voice of Jesus say,
  "I am this dark world's light:
 Look unto me; thy morn shall rise,
  And all thy day be bright."
 I looked to Jesus and I found
  In him my Star, my Sun;
 And in that light of life I'll walk
  Till all my journey's done.
            BONAR.

347
Psalm 51.

1 TURN not thy face away, O Lord!
  From them that lowly lie,
 Lamenting sore their sinful life
  With tears and bitter cry.
 Thy mercy-gate stands open wide
  To them that mourn their sin;
 Shut not that gate against us, Lord!
  But let us enter in.

2 Thou knowest, Lord, what things be past,
  And all the things that be;
 Thou knowest well what is to come;
  There's nothing hid from thee.
 So press we to thy mercy-gate,
  Where mercy doth abound,
 Imploring pardon for our sin,
  To heal our deadly wound.

3 O Lord! we need not to repeat
  What we do beg and crave;
 For thou dost know, before we ask,
  The blessing we would have.
 Mercy, O Lord! we mercy seek;
  This is the height and sum;
 For mercy, Lord, is all our prayer,
  Oh, let thy mercy come!

Faith in God. Joys of the Penitent.

BOWDOIN SQUARE. C. M.   VOGLER.

348.   Psalm 27
1 Soon as I heard my Father say,
   "Ye children, seek my grace,"
My heart replied without delay,
   "I'll seek my Father's face."

2 Let not thy face be hid from me,
   Nor frown my soul away;
God of my life, I fly to thee,
   In each distressing day.

3 My fainting flesh had died with grief,
   Had not my soul believed
Thy grace would soon provide relief;
   Nor was my hope deceived.

4 Wait on the Lord, ye trembling saints,
   And keep your courage up;
He'll raise your spirit when it faints,
   And far exceed your hope.
                 WATTS.

349.   Prov. 23: 26.
1 My God, accept my heart this day,
   And make it always thine;
That I from thee no more may stray,
   No more from thee decline.

2 Before the cross of Him who died,
   Behold, I prostrate fall;
Let every sin be crucified,
   Let Christ be all in all.
                 LYRA CATH.

350.   Hosea 14: 1.
1 O Thou, whose tender mercy hears
   Contrition's humble sigh;
Whose hand indulgent wipes the tears
   From sorrow's weeping eye; —

2 See, Lord, before thy throne of grace,
   A wretched wanderer mourn:
Hast thou not bid me seek thy face?
   Hast thou not said, "Return"?

3 And shall my guilty fears prevail
   To drive me from thy feet?
Oh, let not this dear refuge fail,
   This only safe retreat!

4 Oh, shine on this benighted heart,
   With beams of mercy shine!
And let thy healing voice impart
   The sense of joy divine.
                 MRS. STEELE.

351.   Luke 15: 7.
1 Oh, how divine, how sweet the joy,
   When but one sinner turns,
And with an humble, broken heart,
   His sins and errors mourns!

2 Pleased with the news, the saints below
   In songs their tongues employ;
Beyond the skies the tidings go,
   And heaven is filled with joy.

3 Well pleased the Father sees and hears
   The conscious sinner's moan;
Jesus receives him in his arms,
   And claims him for his own.

4 Nor angels can their joys contain,
   But kindle with new fire; —
"The sinner lost is found," they sing,
   And strike the sounding lyre.
                 NEEDHAM.

Repentance and Self-Devotion.

ECKARDTSHEIM. C. M.   ANCIENT LYRE.

352.   *Penitence.*
1 WE sinners, Lord, with earnest heart,
   With sighs and prayers and tears,
To thee our inmost cares impart,
   Our burdens and our fears.

2 Thy sovereign grace can give relief,
   Thou Source of peace and light!
Dispel the gloomy cloud of grief,
   And make our darkness bright.

3 Around thy Father's throne on high,
   All heaven thy glory sings;
And earth, for which thou cam'st to die,
   Loud with thy praises rings.

4 Dear Lord! to thee our prayers ascend;
   Our eyes thy face would see:
Oh! let our weary wanderings end,
   Our spirits rest in thee!
                     BERNARD.

353.   *Matt. 27: 45.*
1 ALAS! and did my Saviour bleed?
   And did my Sovereign die?
Would he devote that sacred head
   For such a worm as I?

2 Was it for crimes that I had done
   He groaned upon the tree?
Amazing pity! grace unknown!
   And love beyond degree!

3 Well might the sun in darkness hide,
   And shut his glories in,
When God, the mighty Maker, died
   For man the creature's sin.

4 Thus might I hide my blushing face,
   While his dear cross appears;
Dissolve my heart in thankfulness,
   And melt mine eyes to tears.

5 But drops of grief can ne'er repay
   The debt of love I owe:
Here, Lord, I give myself away;
   'Tis all that I can do.
                     WATTS.

354.   *Repentance.*
1 DEAR Saviour, when my thoughts recall
   The wonders of thy grace,
Low at thy feet, ashamed, I fall,
   And hide this wretched face.

2 Shall love like thine be thus repaid?
   Ah, vile, ungrateful heart!
By earth's low cares so oft betrayed
   From Jesus to depart.

3 But he, for his own mercy's sake,
   My wandering soul restores;
He bids the mourning heart partake
   The pardon it implores.

4 Oh, while I breathe to thee, my Lord,
   The deep, repentant sigh,
Confirm the kind, forgiving word,
   With pity in thine eye!

5 Then shall the mourner at thy feet
   Rejoice to seek thy face;
And grateful, own how kind, how sweet
   Thy condescending grace!
                     MRS. STEELE.

Prayer for Grace. The Lost Sheep Found. 171

SEBASTIAN. S. M. Double.   J. S. BACH.

355.   *" Grace to Help."*
1 THOU art gone up on high,
   To realms beyond the skies;
And round thy throne unceasingly
   The songs of praise arise.
But we are lingering here,
   With sin and care oppressed;
Lord, send thy promised Comforter,
   And lead us to thy rest.

2 Thou art gone up on high;
   But thou didst first come down,
Through earth's most bitter misery,
   To pass unto thy crown;
And girt with griefs and fears,
   Our onward course must be;
But only let this path of tears
   Lead us at last to thee.

3 Thou art gone up on high;
   But thou shalt come again,
With all the bright ones of the sky
   Attendant in thy train.
Lord, by thy saving power,
   So make us live and die,
That we may stand, in that dread hour,
   At thy right hand on high.

356.   1 Pet. 2: 25.
1 I WAS a wandering sheep;
   I did not love the fold;
I did not love my Shepherd's voice;
   I would not be controlled.

2 I was a wayward child;
   I did not love my home;
I did not love my Father's voice;
   I loved afar to roam.

3 The Shepherd sought his sheep;
   The Father sought his child;
They followed me o'er vale and hill,
   O'er deserts waste and wild.

4 They found me nigh to death,
   Famished and faint and lone;
They bound me with the bands of love;
   They saved the wandering one.

5 Jesus my Shepherd is;
   'Twas he that loved my soul;
'Twas he that washed me in his blood;
   'Twas he that made me whole.

6 'Twas he that sought the lost
   That found the wandering sheep;
'Twas he that brought me to the fold;
   'Tis he that still doth keep.
                             BONAR.

Repentance. Prayer for Mercy.

BURTON. S. M.   Arranged from DONIZETTI.

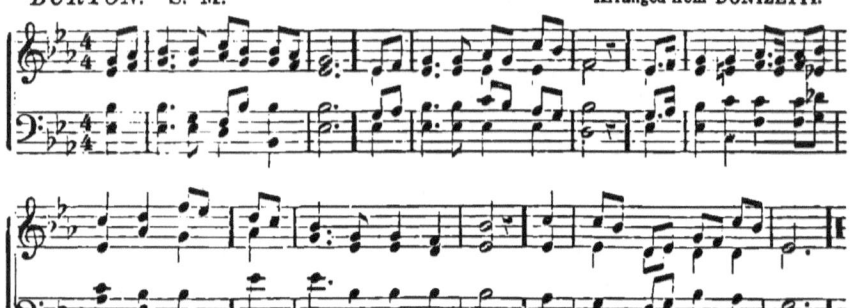

357. *The Hidden Snare.*
1 My Saviour bids me come;
    Ah! why do I delay?
    He calls the weary sinner home,
    And yet from him I stay!

2 What worldly tie must break?
    What idol yet depart,
    Which will not let the Saviour take
    Possession of my heart?

3 Jesus, the hind'rance show
    Which I have feared to see;
    And let me now consent to know
    What keeps me back from thee.

4 Oh! break the fatal chain,
    And all my bonds remove;
    Nor let one bosom-sin remain,
    To keep me from thy love.
                      C. WESLEY.

358. *Psalm 32.*
1 Oh, blessèd souls are they
    Whose sins are covered o'er!
    Divinely blest to whom the Lord
    Imputes their guilt no more.

2 They mourn their follies past,
    And keep their hearts with care;
    Their lips and lives without deceit
    Shall prove their faith sincere.

3 While I concealed my guilt,
    I felt the festering wound;
    Till I confessed my sins to thee,
    And ready pardon found.

4 Let sinners learn to pray,
    Let saints keep near the throne;
    Our help in times of deep distress
    Is found in God alone.
                      WATTS.

359. *Rom. 2: 4.*
1 Is this the kind return?
    Are these the thanks we owe?
    Thus to abuse eternal Love,
    Whence all our blessings flow?

2 To what a stubborn frame
    Hath sin reduced our mind!
    What strange rebellious wretches we!
    And God as strangely kind!

3 Turn, turn us, mighty God,
    And mould our souls afresh;
    Break, sovereign Grace, these hearts of stone,
    And give us hearts of flesh.

4 Let past ingratitude
    Provoke our weeping eyes,
    And hourly, as new mercies fall,
    Let hourly thanks arise.
                      WATTS.

360. *Prayer for Mercy.*
1 Thou gracious God and kind,
    Oh, cast our sins away;
    Nor call our former guilt to mind,
    Thy justice to display.

2 Thy tenderest mercies show,
    Thy richest grace prepare,
    Ere yet, with guilty fears laid low,
    We perish in despair.

3 Save us from guilt and shame,
    Thy glory to display;
    And, for the great Redeemer's name,
    Wash all our sins away.
                      PRATT'S COLL.

Repentance and Faith.

PENITENCE. 7s., 6s., & 8s.   OAKLEY.

361.   Matt. 26: 75.

Jesus, let thy pitying eye
  Call back a wandering sheep;
False to thee, like Peter, I
  Would fain like Peter weep.
Let me be by grace restored,
On me be all long-suffering shown,
Turn, and look upon me, Lord,
  And break my heart of stone.

2 Saviour, Prince, enthroned above,
  Repentance to impart,
Give me, through thy dying love,
  The humble, contrite heart.
Give what I have long implored,
A portion of thy grief unknown;
Turn, and look upon me, Lord,
  And break my heart of stone.

3 See me, Saviour, from above,
  Nor suffer me to die;
Life and happiness and love
  Beam from thy gracious eye.
If thy mercies now are stirred,
If now I do myself bemoan,
Turn, and look upon me, Lord,
  And break my heart of stone.
                        C. WESLEY.

362.   Matt. 11: 19.

1 God of my salvation, hear,
  And help me to believe;
Simply do I now draw near
  Thy blessing to receive:
Full of guilt, alas! I am,
But to thy wounds for refuge flee:
Friend of sinners, spotless Lamb,
  Thy blood was shed for me.

2 Standing now as newly slain,
  To thee I lift mine eye;
Balm of all my grief and pain,
  Thy blood is always nigh.
Now as yesterday the same
Thou art, and wilt forever be:
Friend of sinners, spotless Lamb,
  Thy blood was shed for me.

3 Saviour, from thy wounded side
  I never will depart;
Here will I my spirit hide,
  When I am pure in heart:
Till my place above I claim,
This only shall be all my plea;
Friend of sinners, spotless Lamb,
  Thy blood was shed for me.
                        C. WESLEY.

Repentance and Faith.

MERCY. 7s.

From Gottschalk's "Last Hope,"
by permission of Wm. Hall & Son.

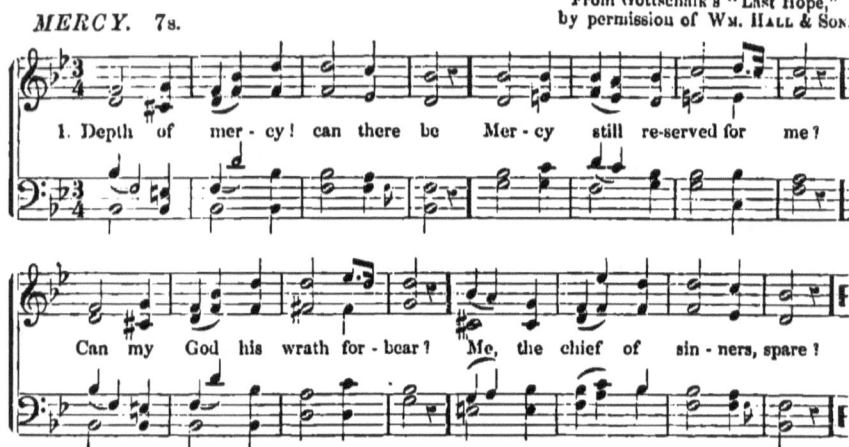

1. Depth of mer-cy! can there be Mer-cy still re-served for me?
Can my God his wrath for-bear? Me, the chief of sin-ners, spare!

363. *Repentance.*

2 I have long withstood his grace,
Long provoked him to his face,
Would not hearken to his calls,
Grieved him by a thousand falls.

3 Lord, incline me to repent;
Let me now my fall lament,
Deeply my revolt deplore,
Weep, believe, and sin no more.

4 Still for me the Saviour stands,
Shows his wounds, and spreads his hands:
God is love! I know, I feel;
Jesus weeps, and loves me still.
C. WESLEY.

364. *Prayer for Pardon.*

1 JESUS, save my dying soul;
Make the broken spirit whole:
Humble in the dust I lie:
Saviour, leave me not to die.

2 Jesus, full of every grace,
Now reveal thy smiling face;
Grant the joy of sin forgiven,
Foretaste of the bliss of heaven.

3 All my guilt to thee is known;
Thou art righteous, thou alone:
All my help is from thy cross,
All beside I count but loss.

4 Lord, in thee I now believe;
Wilt thou, wilt thou not forgive?
Helpless at thy feet I lie;
Saviour, leave me not to die.
HASTINGS.

365. Luke 23: 33.

1 WHEN on Sinai's top I see
God descend, in majesty,
To proclaim his holy law,
All my spirit sinks with awe.

2 When in ecstasy sublime,
Tabor's glorious steep I climb,
At the too transporting light,
Darkness rushes o'er my sight.

3 When on Calvary I rest,
God, in flesh made manifest,
Shines in my Redeemer's face,
Full of beauty, truth, and grace.

4 Here I would forever stay,
Weep and gaze my soul away;
Thou art heaven on earth to me,
Lovely, mournful Calvary.
MONTGOMERY.

366. Psalm 6: 1, 2.

1 GENTLY, gently, lay the rod
On my sinful head, O God!
Stay thy wrath, in mercy stay,
Lest I sink beneath its sway.

2 Heal me, for my flesh is weak;
Heal me, for thy grace I seek;
This my only plea I make,—
Heal me for thy mercy's sake.

3 Lo! he comes — he heeds my plea;
Lo! he comes — the shadows flee;
Glory round me dawns once more;
Rise, my spirit, and adore.
LYTE.

Prayer for Mercy. Leaving all for Christ. 175

SOUTH CHURCH. 8s. & 7s.   E. P. PARKER.

367.   *Prayer for Blessing.*
1 Lord, I hear that showers of blessing
    Thou art scattering, full and free, —
Showers the thirsty land refreshing ;
    Let thy blessing fall on me.

2 Long have I in sin been straying,
    Long been grieving, slighting thee ;
Slight me not as I stand praying ;
    Oh, forgive and comfort me !

3 Pass me not, O gracious Saviour,
    Sinful though my heart may be ;
Give me tokens of thy favor,
    Speak some word of grace to me.

4 Love of God, so pure and changeless,
    Blood of Christ, so rich and free,
Grace of God, so strong and boundless, —
    Magnify it all to me !

5 Pass me not ; thy lost one bringing,
    Bind my heart, O Lord, to thee :
While the streams of life are springing,
    Blessing others, oh, bless me !
               Dublin Hymn Book.

368.   Luke 9: 23.
1 Jesus, I my cross have taken,
    All to leave and follow thee ;
Naked, poor, despised, forsaken,
    Thou, from hence, my all shalt be.

2 Perish every fond ambition,
    All I've sought, or hoped, or known,
Yet how rich is my condition,
    God and heaven are still my own !

3 Man may trouble and distress me ;
    'Twill but drive me to thy breast ;
Life with trials hard may press me ;
    Heaven will bring me sweeter rest.

4 Oh ! 'tis not in grief to harm me,
    While thy love is left to me ;
Oh ! 'twere not in joy to charm me,
    Were that joy unmixed with thee.
               Lyte.

369.   Luke 9: 23.
1 Soul, then know thy full salvation,
    Rise o'er sin, and fear, and care ;
Joy to find in every station,
    Something still to do or bear.

2 Think what Spirit dwells within thee ;
    Think what Father's smiles are thine ;
Think that Jesus died to win thee ;
    Child of heaven, canst thou repine ?

3 Haste thee on from grace to glory,
    Armed by faith, and winged by prayer ;
Heaven's eternal day's before thee,
    God's own hand shall guide thee there.

4 Soon shall close thy earthly mission,
    Soon shall pass thy pilgrim days,
Hope shall change to glad fruition,
    Faith to sight, and prayer to praise.
               Lyte.

WILSON. 8s. & 7s.   MENDELSSOHN.

1. Take my heart, O Father, take it! Make and keep it all thine own:
Let thy Spirit melt and break it,— This proud heart of sin and stone.

370.   *"Take my Heart."*

2 Father, make it pure and lowly,
   Fond of peace and far from strife;
Turning from the paths unholy
   Of this vain and sinful life.

3 Ever let thy grace surround it;
   Strengthen it with power divine,
Till thy cords of love have bound it:
   Make it to be wholly thine.

4 May the blood of Jesus heal it,
   And its sins be all forgiven;
Holy Spirit, take and seal it,
   Guide it in the path to heaven.

371.   Matt. 11: 28-30.

1 LABORING and heavy laden
   With my sins, O Lord, I roam,
While I know thou hast invited
   All such wanderers to their home.

2 Make my stubborn spirit willing
   To obey thy gracious voice,
At the cross to leave its burden,
   And departing to rejoice.

3 Thy sweet yoke I'd take upon me,
   And would learn, O Lord, of thee;
Thou art meek in heart, and lowly;
   Teach me like thyself to be.

4 Laboring and heavy laden,
   Lord, no longer will I roam:
Here I fix my habitation,
   In thy sheltering love at home.
                          RANKIN.

372.   *Repentance.*

1 JESUS! who on Calv'ry's mountain
   Poured thy precious blood for me,
Wash me in its flowing fountain,
   That my soul may spotless be.

2 I have sinned, but, oh, restore me;
   For unless thou smile on me,
Dark is all the world before me,
   Darker yet eternity!

3 In thy word I hear thee saying,
   "Come, and I will give you rest;"
Glad the gracious call obeying,
   See, I hasten to thy breast.

4 Grant, oh, grant thy Spirit's teaching,
   That I may not go astray,
Till, the gate of heaven reaching,
   Earth and sin are passed away!

373.   Matt. 17: 8.

1 JESUS only, when the morning
   Beams upon the path I tread;
Jesus only, when the darkness
   Gathers round my weary head.

2 Jesus only, when the billows
   Cold and sullen o'er me roll;
Jesus only, when the trumpet
   Rends the tomb and wakes the soul.

3 Jesus only, when, adoring,
   Saints their crowns before him bring;
Jesus only, I will, joyous,
   Through eternal ages sing.
                          NASON.

LITANY. 7s.   HEROLD.

374. *Litany.*

1 Saviour, when in dust to thee
Low we bow th' adoring knee;
When repentant, to the skies
Scarce we lift our streaming eyes;
Oh, by all thy pains and woe,
Suffered once for man below,
Bending from thy throne on high,
Hear our solemn litany.

2 By thy birth and early years,
By thy human griefs and fears,
By thy fasting and distress
In the lonely wilderness,
By thy vict'ry in the hour
Of the subtle tempter's power;
Jesus, look with pitying eye,
Hear our solemn litany.

3 By thine hour of dark despair,
By thine agony of prayer,
By the purple robe of scorn,
By thy wounds, thy crown of thorn,
By thy cross, thy pangs and cries,
By thy perfect sacrifice;
Jesus, look with pitying eye,
Hear our solemn litany.

4 By thy deep expiring groan,
By the sealed sepulchral stone,
By thy triumph o'er the grave,
By thy power from death to save;
Mighty God, ascended Lord,
To thy throne in heaven restored,
Prince and Saviour, hear our cry,
Hear our solemn litany.
                            GRANT.

375. *Trinity invoked.*

1 Holy Father, hear my cry;
   Holy Saviour, bend thine ear;
  Holy Spirit, come thou nigh:
   Father, Saviour, Spirit, hear!

2 Father, save me from my sin;
   Saviour, I thy mercy crave;
  Gracious Spirit, make me clean:
   Father, Son, and Spirit, save!

3 Father, let me taste thy love;
   Saviour, fill my soul with peace;
  Spirit, come my heart to move:
   Father, Son, and Spirit, bless!

4 Father, Son, and Spirit — Thou
   One Jehovah, shed abroad
  All thy grace within me now;
   Be my Father and my God!
                            BONAR.

Repentance and Faith.

ALTAR. 7s. & 6s.   From the "CASKET" by permission.

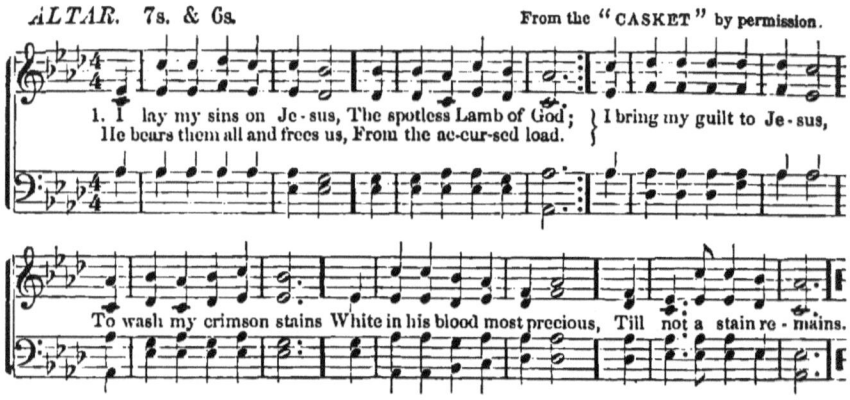

1. I lay my sins on Jesus, The spotless Lamb of God; I bring my guilt to Jesus, He bears them all and frees us, From the accursed load. To wash my crimson stains White in his blood most precious, Till not a stain remains.

376.   *Isaiah 53: 3.*

2 I lay my wants on Jesus,
  All fulness dwells in him;
 He heals all my diseases,
  He doth my soul redeem:
 I lay my griefs on Jesus,
  My burdens and my cares;
 He from them all releases,
  He all my sorrow shares.

3 I rest my soul on Jesus,
  This weary soul of mine;
 His right hand me embraces,
  I on his breast recline.
 I love the name of Jesus,
  Immanuel, Christ, the Lord;
 Like fragrance on the breezes,
  His name abroad is poured.

4 I long to be like Jesus,
  Meek, loving, lowly, mild;
 I long to be like Jesus,
  The Father's holy Child:
 I long to be with Jesus
  Amid the heavenly throng,
 To sing with saints his praises,
  To learn the angels' song.
                        BONAR.

377.   *John 6: 68.*

1 WE stand in deep repentance
  Before thy throne of love;
 O God of grace, forgive us,
  The stain of guilt remove;
 Behold us while with weeping
  We lift our eyes to thee;
 And all our sins subduing,
  Our Father, set us free.

2 Oh! shouldst thou from us fallen
  Withhold thy grace to guide,
 Forever we should wander
  From thee, and peace, aside;
 But thou to spirits contrite
  Dost light and life impart,
 That man may learn to serve thee
  With thankful, joyous heart.

3 Our souls, on thee we cast them,
  Our only refuge thou!
 Thy cheering words revive us,
  When pressed with grief we bow:
 Thou bear'st the trusting spirit
  Upon thy loving breast,
 And givest all thy ransomed
  A sweet, unending rest.
                        RAY PALMER.

378.   *Psalm 20.*

1 THE Lord in trouble hear thee,
  And help from Zion send;
 The God of grace be near thee
  To comfort and befriend!
 Thy human weakness strengthen,
  Thy earthly wants supply,
 Thy span of nature lengthen
  To endless life on high!

2 Above his own anointed
  His banner bright shall wave:
 Their times are all appointed;
  The Lord his flock will save:
 Through life's deceitful mazes,
  Their steps will safely bear;
 Accept their feeble praises,
  And hear their every prayer.
                        LYTE.

Justification by Faith. Redeeming Love.

MERIBAH. C. P. M.   DR. MASON.

379. *Justification by Faith.*

1 O THOU who hear'st the prayer of faith,
  Wilt thou not save a soul from death,
    That casts itself on thee?
  I have no refuge of my own,
  But fly to what my Lord hath done,
    And suffered once for me.

2 Slain in the guilty sinner's stead,
  His spotless righteousness I plead,
    And his availing blood:
  That righteousness my robe shall be,
  That merit shall atone for me,
    And bring me near to God.

3 Then save me from eternal death,
  The Spirit of adoption breathe,
    His consolations send:
  By him some word of life impart,
  And sweetly whisper to my heart,
    "Thy Maker is thy friend."

4 The King of terrors then would be
  A welcome messenger to me,
    To bid me come away:
  Unclogged by earth, or earthly things,
  I'd mount upon his sable wings
    To everlasting day.
                                TOPLADY.

380.   John 3: 3.

1 AWAKED by Sinai's awful sound,
  My soul in bonds of guilt I found,
    And knew not where to go;
  One solemn truth increased my pain,
  "The sinner must be born again,"
    Or sink to endless woe.

2 I heard the law its thunders roll,
  While guilt lay heavy on my soul,
    A vast oppressive load;
  All creature-aid I saw was vain;
  "The sinner must be born again,"
    Or drink the wrath of God.

3 The saints I heard with rapture tell,
  How Jesus conquered death and hell
    To bring salvation near;
  Yet still I found this truth remain,
  "The sinner must be born again,"
    Or sink in deep despair.

4 But while I thus in anguish lay,
  The bleeding Saviour passed that way,
    My bondage to remove;
  The sinner, once by justice slain,
  Now by his grace is born again,
    And sings redeeming love.
                                OCCUM.

Repentance. Prayer for Mercy.

381. JESUS, MOST HOLY.
E. P. PARKER.

1. Jesus, most holy, Pray I to thee; My sinful fetters, Lord, break from me; Take this sad spirit, Mourning for sin, Back to thy bosom,—Lord, take me in!

2 Over the mountains,
   Long have I strayed;
Cold winds of sorrow
   Round me have played;
None to bring comfort,
   None have I found;
While tears of anguish
   Watered the ground.

3 To this dear refuge,
   Now have I fled;
Jesus, thy kind heart
   For me hath bled;
Take now the wanderer
   Home to thy rest,
Under thy kind wings,
   Sheltered and blest.

382. LENT. 7s.
*

1. Lord, in this thy mercy's day, Ere it pass for aye away, On our knees we fall and pray.

2 Lord, on us thy Spirit pour,
Kneeling lowly at the door
Ere it close for evermore.

3 By thy night of agony,
By thy supplicating cry,
By thy willingness to die;

4 By thy tears of bitter woe
For Jerusalem below,
Let us not thy love forego.

5 Grant us 'neath thy wings a place,
Lest we lose this day of grace,
Ere we shall behold thy face.

Warning and Entreaty.

WHEN THE HARVEST IS PAST. 12s. & 8s.

383. Jer. 8: 20; 12: 5.

1 WHEN the harvest is past, and the summer is gone,
 And sermons and prayers shall be o'er;
 When the beams cease to break of the blest Sabbath morn,
 And Jesus invites thee no more;

2 When the rich gales of mercy no longer shall blow,
 The gospel no message declare, —
 Sinner, how canst thou bear the deep wailing of woe,
 How suffer the night of despair?

3 When the holy have gone to the regions of peace,
 To dwell in the mansion above;
 When their harmony wakes, in the fulness of bliss,
 Their song to the Saviour of love, —

4 Say, O sinner, that livest at rest and secure,
 Who fearest no trouble to come,
 Can thy spirit the swellings of sorrow endure,
 Or bear the impenitent's doom?

S. F. SMITH.

SHEPHERD-CALL.

384.

1 COME, wand'ring sheep, oh, come!
 I'll bind thee to my breast;
 I'll bear thee to thy home,
 And lay thee down to rest.

2 I saw thee stray forlorn;
 I heard thee faintly cry;
 And on the tree of scorn,
 For thee I deigned to die.

3 I shield thee from alarms,
 And wilt thou not be blest?
 I bear thee in my arms,
 Thou, bear me in thy breast.

CALVARY. P. M.   OLD CHORAL.

385.   *Behold the Man!*

1 O SINNER, lift the eye of faith,
   To true repentance turning;
Bethink thee of the curse of sin,
   Its awful guilt discerning:
Upon the crucified One look,
And thou shalt read, as in a book,
   What well is worth thy learning.

2 Look on his head, that bleeding head,
   With crown of thorns surrounded;
Look on his sacred hands and feet
   Which piercing nails have wounded:
See every limb with scourges rent!
On him, the Just, the Innocent,
   What malice hath abounded!

3 'Tis not alone those limbs are racked,
   But friends, too, are forsaking;
And more than all, for thankless man
   That tender heart is aching.
Oh, fearful was the pain and scorn
By Jesus, Son of Mary, borne,
   Their peace for sinners making!

4 None ever knew such pain before,
   Such infinite affliction;
None ever felt a grief like his
   In that dread crucifixion.
For us he bare those bitter throes,
For us those agonizing woes,
   In oft-renewed infliction.

5 O sinner, mark and ponder well
   Sin's awful condemnation;
Think what a sacrifice it cost
   To purchase thy salvation:
Had Jesus never bled and died,
Then what could thee and all betide,
   But uttermost damnation!

6 Lord, give us grace to flee from sin,
   And Satan's wiles ensnaring,
And from those everlasting flames
   For evil ones preparing:
Jesus, we thank thee, and entreat
To rest forever at thy feet,
   Thy heavenly glory sharing.

Section VI.

THE CHRISTIAN LIFE.

(*a.*) *God our Refuge, Portion, Strength, and Joy. His Grace, Mercies, Counsels, Care, and Love. Trusting, Resting, and Rejoicing in God.*

(*b.*) *Looking unto Jesus. Friend of Sinners. Fount of Blessings. Glorying in Christ's Cross. His Blood and Righteousness. His Sympathy and Intercession. The Good Shepherd. Trusting and Resting in Christ. Love Divine. Light in Darkness. Always with us. Sweet Moments at his Cross. Longing to be with Jesus. Not ashamed of Jesus. Lamb of Calvary. Lover of my Soul. Rock of Ages.*

(*c.*) *Songs in the Night. Trials, Sorrows, Afflictions.*

(*d.*) *Songs by the Way. Christian Pilgrimage. Prayers for Guidance. Encouragements. Rejoicings.*

(*e.*) *Graces and Duties. Purity, Steadfastness, Faith, Meekness, Love, Christian Fellowship, Zeal, etc.*

(*f.*) *Prayer. What Prayer is. The Mercy-Seat. Lord's Prayer. Power of Prayer. Calls to Prayer. Importunity.*

"BY THE GRACE OF GOD I AM WHAT I AM."—1 Cor. 15: 10.

Repentance. Lesson of the Cross.

CALVARY. P. M.   OLD CHORAL.

385.   *Behold the Man!*

1 O SINNER, lift the eye of faith,
    To true repentance turning;
Bethink thee of the curse of sin,
    Its awful guilt discerning:
Upon the crucified One look,
And thou shalt read, as in a book,
    What well is worth thy learning.

2 Look on his head, that bleeding head,
    With crown of thorns surrounded;
Look on his sacred hands and feet
    Which piercing nails have wounded:
See every limb with scourges rent!
On him, the Just, the Innocent,
    What malice hath abounded!

3 'Tis not alone those limbs are racked,
    But friends, too, are forsaking;
And more than all, for thankless man
    That tender heart is aching.
Oh, fearful was the pain and scorn
By Jesus, Son of Mary, borne,
    Their peace for sinners making!

4 None ever knew such pain before,
    Such infinite affliction;
None ever felt a grief like his
    In that dread crucifixion.
For us he bare those bitter throes,
For us those agonizing woes,
    In oft-renewed infliction.

5 O sinner, mark and ponder well
    Sin's awful condemnation;
Think what a sacrifice it cost
    To purchase thy salvation:
Had Jesus never bled and died,
Then what could thee and all betide,
    But uttermost damnation!

6 Lord, give us grace to flee from sin,
    And Satan's wiles ensnaring,
And from those everlasting flames
    For evil ones preparing:
Jesus, we thank thee, and entreat
To rest forever at thy feet,
    Thy heavenly glory sharing.

Section VI.

THE CHRISTIAN LIFE.

(*a.*) *God our Refuge, Portion, Strength, and Joy. His Grace, Mercies, Counsels, Care, and Love. Trusting, Resting, and Rejoicing in God.*

(*b.*) *Looking unto Jesus. Friend of Sinners. Fount of Blessings. Glorying in Christ's Cross. His Blood and Righteousness. His Sympathy and Intercession. The Good Shepherd. Trusting and Resting in Christ. Love Divine. Light in Darkness. Always with us. Sweet Moments at his Cross. Longing to be with Jesus. Not ashamed of Jesus. Lamb of Calvary. Lover of my Soul. Rock of Ages.*

(*c.*) *Songs in the Night. Trials, Sorrows, Afflictions.*

(*d.*) *Songs by the Way. Christian Pilgrimage. Prayers for Guidance. Encouragements. Rejoicings.*

(*e.*) *Graces and Duties. Purity, Steadfastness, Faith, Meekness, Love, Christian Fellowship, Zeal, etc.*

(*f.*) *Prayer. What Prayer is. The Mercy-Seat. Lord's Prayer. Power of Prayer. Calls to Prayer. Importunity.*

"*BY THE GRACE OF GOD I AM WHAT I AM.*"—1 Cor. 15: 10.

THE CHRISTIAN LIFE.

HERSCHEL. L. M.   Arranged.

386.   Psalm 146.

1 GOD of my life! through all my days
My grateful powers shall sound thy praise;
The song shall wake with opening light,
And warble to the silent night.

2 When anxious care would break my rest,
And grief would tear my throbbing breast,
Thy tuneful praises raised on high
Shall check the murmur and the sigh.

3 When death o'er nature shall prevail,
And all my powers of language fail,
Joy through my swimming eyes shall break,
And mean the thanks I cannot speak.

4 But, oh! when that last conflict's o'er,
And I am chained to flesh no more,
With what glad accents shall I rise
To join the music of the skies!
                 DODDRIDGE.

387.   Psalm 121.

1 UP to the hills I lift mine eyes,
Th' eternal hills beyond the skies;
Thence all her help my soul derives;
There my almighty Refuge lives.

2 He lives — the everlasting God [flood;
That built the world, that spread the
The heavens with all their hosts he made,
And the dark regions of the dead.

3 He guides our feet, he guards our way;
His morning smiles bless all the day;
He spreads the evening veil, and keeps
The silent hours, while Israel sleeps.
                 WATTS.

388.   Psalm 31.

1 LORD, in thy great, thy glorious name,
I place my hope, my only trust;
Save me from sorrow, guilt, and shame,
Thou ever gracious, ever just.

2 Thou art my rock! thy name alone
The fortress where my hopes retreat;
Oh, make thy power and mercy known;
To safety guide my wandering feet.

3 Blest be the Lord, forever blest,
Whose mercy bids my fears remove;
The sacred walls which guard my rest
Are his almighty power and love.
                 MRS. STEELE.

The Christian Life.

BRANDT. L. M.   Arranged from HAYDN.

389.   *Psalm 138.*

1 WITH all my powers of heart and tongue,
   I'll praise my Maker in my song;
   Angels shall hear the notes I raise,
     Approve the song, and join the praise.

2 To God I cried when troubles rose;
   He heard me, and subdued my foes;
   He did my rising fears control, [soul.
     And strength diffused through all my

3 Amid a thousand snares, I stand
   Upheld and guarded by thy hand;
   Thy words my fainting soul revive,
     And keep my dying faith alive.

4 I'll sing thy truth and mercy, Lord;
   I'll sing the wonders of thy word;
   Not all thy works and names below
     So much thy power and glory show.
                  WATTS.

390.   *Renunciation of the World.*

1 I send the joys of earth away;
   Away, ye tempters of the mind,
   False as the smooth, deceitful sea,
     And empty as the whistling wind!

2 Your streams were floating me along,
   Down to the gulf of black despair;
   And while I listened to your song, [there.
     Your streams had e'en conveyed me

3 Lord! I adore thy matchless grace,
   Which warned me of that dark abyss,
   Which drew me from those treacherous
     And bade me seek superior bliss. [seas,

4 Now to the shining realms above
   I stretch my hands and glance my eyes;
   Oh for the pinions of a dove,
     To bear me to the upper skies!

5 There, from the bosom of my God,
   Oceans of endless pleasure roll;
   There would I fix my last abode,
     And drown the sorrows of my soul!
                  WATTS.

391.   *John 6: 68.*

1 THOU only Sovereign of my heart,
   My Refuge, my almighty Friend,
   And can my soul from thee depart,
     On whom alone my hopes depend?

2 Whither, ah! whither shall I go,
   A wretched wanderer from my Lord?
   Can this dark world of sin and woe
     One glimpse of happiness afford?

3 Eternal life thy words impart;
   On these my fainting spirit lives;
   Here sweeter comforts cheer my heart
     Than all the round of nature gives.

4 Let earth's alluring joys combine;
   While Thou art near, in vain they call!
   One smile, one blissful smile of thine,
     My dearest Lord, outweighs them all.

5 Low at thy feet my soul would lie;
   Here safety dwells, and peace divine;
   Still let me live beneath thine eye,
     For life, eternal life, is thine.
                 MRS. STEELE.

God our Refuge and Strength.

EIN' FESTE BURG. DR. MARTIN LUTHER, 1529.

392. Rom. 8: 35-39.

1 A MIGHTY fortress is our God,
  A bulwark never failing:
Our Helper he, amid the flood
  Of mortal ills prevailing.
For still our ancient foe
Doth seek to work us woe;
His craft and power are great,
And armed with cruel hate,
  On earth is not his equal.

2 Did we in our own strength confide,
  Our striving would be losing;
Were not the right man on our side,
  The man of God's own choosing.
Dost ask who that may be?
Christ Jesus, it is he;
Lord Sabaoth is his name,
From age to age the same,
  And he must win the battle.

3 And though this world, with devils filled,
  Should threaten to undo us;
We will not fear, for God hath willed
  His truth to triumph through us.
The Prince of darkness grim, —
We tremble not for him;
His rage we can endure,
For lo! his doom is sure, —
  One little word shall fell him!

4 That word above all earthly powers —
  No thanks to them — abideth;
The Spirit and the gifts are ours
  Through him who with us sideth.
Let goods and kindred go,
This mortal life also:
The body they may kill:
God's truth abideth still,
  His kingdom is forever.
        LUTHER BY DR. HEDGE.

393.

1 REJOICE to-day with one accord,
  Sing out with exultation.
Rejoice and praise our mighty Lord,
  Whose arm hath brought salvation.
His works of love proclaim
The greatness of his name;
For he is God alone,
Who hath his mercy shown; —
  Let all his saints adore him!

2 When in distress to him we cried,
  He heard our sad complaining;
Oh, trust in him, whate'er betide,
  His love is all-sustaining.
Triumphant songs of praise
To him our hearts shall raise:
Now every voice shall say,
"Oh, praise our God alway!"
  Let all his saints adore him!

NOTE.—This choral should be sung *in unison*, the organ supplying the harmony.

The Christian Life.

OLMUTZ. S. M.

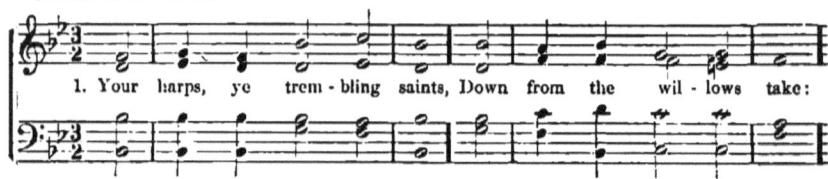

1. Your harps, ye trembling saints, Down from the willows take: Loud to the praise of love divine. Bid ev-'ry string a-wake.

394. Rom. 13: 11.

2 Though in a foreign land,
   We are not far from home;
   And nearer to our house above
   We every moment come.

3 His grace will to the end
   Stronger and brighter shine;
   Nor present things, nor things to come,
   Shall quench the spark divine.

4 When we in darkness walk,
   Nor feel the heavenly flame,
   Then is the time to trust our God,
   And rest upon his name.

5 Soon shall our doubts and fears
   Subside at his control;
   His loving-kindness shall break through
   The midnight of the soul.

6 Blest is the man, O Lord,
   Who stays himself on thee;
   Who waits for thy salvation, Lord,
   Shall thy salvation see.
                  TOPLADY.

395. 1 Cor. 10: 31.

1 TEACH me, my God and King,
   In all things thee to see;
   And what I do in anything,
   To do it as for thee!

2 To scorn the senses' sway,
   While still to thee I tend;
   In all I do, be thou the way,
   In all, be thou the end.

3 All may of thee partake;
   Nothing so small can be
   But draws, when acted for thy sake,
   Greatness and worth from thee.

4 If done beneath thy laws,
   E'en servile labors shine;
   Hallowed is toil, if this the cause;
   The meanest work, divine.
                  G. HERBERT.

396. Psalm 23.

1 THE Lord my Shepherd is;
   I shall be well supplied;
   Since he is mine, and I am his,
   What can I want beside?

2 He leads me to the place
   Where heavenly pasture grows;
   Where living waters gently pass,
   And full salvation flows.

3 If e'er I go astray,
   He doth my soul reclaim;
   And guides me, in his own right way,
   For his most holy name.

4 While he affords his aid,
   I cannot yield to fear;
   Though I should walk through death's dark shade,
   My Shepherd's with me there.

5 The bounties of thy love
   Shall crown my following days;
   Nor from thy house will I remove,
   Nor cease to speak thy praise.
                  WATTS.

Confidence in God's Love and Wisdom.

WATCHMAN. S. M.   LEACH.

397.   1 John 3: 1, 2.
1   BEHOLD, what wondrous grace
      The Father has bestowed
    On sinners of a mortal race,
      To call them sons of God!

2   Nor doth it yet appear
      How great we must be made;
    But when we see our Saviour here,
      We shall be like our Head.

3   A hope so much divine
      May trials well endure;
    May purify our souls from sin,
      As Christ, the Lord, is pure.

4   If in my Father's love
      I share a filial part,
    Send down thy Spirit, like a dove,
      To rest upon my heart.

5   We would no longer lie
      Like slaves beneath the throne;
    Our faith shall "Abba, Father," cry,
      And thou the kindred own.
                                 WATTS.

398.   Psalm 27: 14.
1   GIVE to the winds thy fears,
      Hope, and be undismayed;
    God hears thy sighs, and counts thy tears,
      God shall lift up thy head.

2   Through waves, through clouds and storms,
      He gently clears thy way;
    Wait thou his time; so shall this night
      Soon end in joyous day.

3   Far, far above thy thought
      His counsel shall appear,
    When fully he the work hath wrought
      That caused thy needless fear.

4   What though thou rulest not!
      Yet heaven and earth and hell
    Proclaim, God sitteth on the throne,
      And ruleth all things well!
                                 GERHARDT.

399.   Psalm 55.
1   LET sinners take their course,
      And choose the road to death,
    But in the worship of my God
      I'll spend my daily breath.

2   My thoughts address his throne,
      When morning brings the light;
    I seek his blessing every noon,
      And pay my vows at night.

3   Thou wilt regard my cries,
      O my eternal God!
    While sinners perish in surprise,
      Beneath thine angry rod.

4   Because they dwell at ease,
      And no sad changes feel,
    They neither fear, nor trust thy name,
      Nor learn to do thy will.

5   But I, with all my cares,
      Will lean upon the Lord;
    I'll cast my burdens on his arm,
      And rest upon his word.
                                 WATTS.

GALENA. C. M.   Arranged from COOKE.

400. *"The Eternal God is thy Refuge."*

1 IMMORTAL Power, Eternal One,
   With thee what can compare?
Thy glory shines in heaven and earth,
   And fills the ambient air.
All time, all space, by thee illumed,
   Grows bright and brighter still,
Obedient to thy high behest,
   And to thy sovereign will.

2 To thee dominion sole belongs,
   And 'tis to thee alone,
My Father, Saviour, living God,
   I make my sorrows known:
Thy love, celestial and divine,
   Descends upon my heart,
Inspiring courage, hope, and joy,
   And bidding grief depart.

3 Protected by thy power and love,
   My body sinks to rest;
My soul, within thy heavenly arms,
   Reposes, calm and blest.
Lord of my life, in darkest night
   I sleep and have no fear,
And in the early dawn of day
   I wake and find thee near.

401. *Following Christ.*

1 THE Son of God goes forth to war,
   A kingly crown to gain;
His blood-red banner streams afar;—
   Who follows in his train?
Who best can drink his cup of woe,
   Triumphant over pain;
Who patient bears his cross below,—
   He follows in his train.

2 The martyr first, whose eagle eye
   Could pierce beyond the grave;
Who saw his Master in the sky,
   And called on him to save.
Like him, with pardon on his tongue
   In midst of mortal pain,
He prayed for them that did the wrong;—
   Who follows in his train?

3 A glorious band, the chosen few
   On whom the Spirit came; [knew,
Twelve valiant saints, their hope they
   And mocked the cross and flame.
They met the tyrant's brandished steel,
   The lion's gory mane, [feel;—
They bowed their necks, the death to
   Who follows in their train?

4 A noble army, men and boys,
   The matron and the maid,
Around the Saviour's throne rejoice,
   In robes of light arrayed.
They climbed the steep ascent of heaven,
   Through peril, toil, and pain;
O God, to us may grace be given
   To follow in their train.
                      MONK'S COLL.

DENFIELD. C. M.   GLASER.

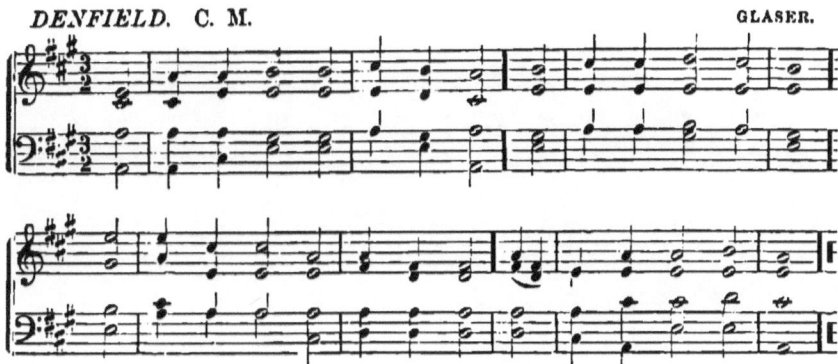

402. *Divine Mercies.*

1 WHEN all thy mercies, O my God,
   My rising soul surveys,
Transported with the view, I'm lost
   In wonder, love, and praise!

2 Unnumbered comforts on my soul
   Thy tender care bestowed,
Before my infant heart conceived
   From whom those comforts flowed.

3 When, in the slippery paths of youth,
   With heedless step I ran,
Thine arm, unseen, conveyed me safe,
   And led me up to man.

4 Ten thousand thousand precious gifts
   My daily thanks employ;
Nor is the least a cheerful heart,
   That tastes those gifts with joy.

5 Through every period of my life
   Thy goodness I'll pursue;
And, after death, in distant worlds,
   The glorious theme renew.
                        ADDISON.

403. Col. 3: 1-4.

1 OH, happy soul, that lives on high,
   While men lie grovelling here!
His hopes are fixed above the sky,
   And faith forbids his fear.

2 His conscience knows no secret stings,
   While peace and joy combine
To form a life, whose holy springs
   Are hidden and divine.

3 He waits in secret on his God;
   His God in secret sees:
Let earth be all in arms abroad;
   He dwells in heavenly peace.

4 His pleasures rise from things unseen,
   Beyond this world of time,
Where neither eyes nor ears have been,
   Nor thoughts of mortals climb.

5 He wants no pomp nor royal throne,
   To raise his honor here:
Content and pleased to live unknown,
   Till Christ his life appear.
                        WATTS.

404. Psalm 116.

1 I LOVE the Lord; he heard my cries,
   And pitied every groan:
Long as I live, when troubles rise,
   I'll hasten to his throne.

2 I love the Lord; he bowed his ear,
   And chased my grief away;
Oh, let my heart no more despair,
   While I have breath to pray!

3 The Lord beheld me sore distressed,
   He bade my pains remove:
Return, my soul, to God, thy rest,
   For thou hast known his love!

4 My God hath saved my soul from death,
   And dried my falling tears;
Now to his praise I'll spend my breath
   And my remaining years.
                        WATTS.

192 The Christian Life. God our Portion and Strength.

HEBER. C. M.   GEO. KINGSLEY.

405.   Psalm 73.
1 God, my supporter and my hope,
   My help forever near,
Thine arm of mercy held me up,
   When sinking in despair.

2 Thy counsels, Lord, shall guide my feet
   Through this dark wilderness;
Thy hand conduct me near thy seat,
   To dwell before thy face.

3 Were I in heaven without my God,
   'Twould be no joy to me;
And while this earth is my abode,
   I long for none but thee.

4 What if the springs of life were broke,
   And flesh and heart should faint?
God is my soul's eternal rock,
   The strength of every saint.

5 Then, to draw near to thee, my God,
   Shall be my sweet employ:
My tongue shall sound thy works abroad,
   And tell the world my joy.   WATTS.

406.   Psalm 126.
1 When God revealed his gracious name,
   And changed my mournful state,
My rapture seemed a pleasing dream,
   The grace appeared so great.

2 The world beheld the glorious change,
   And did thy hand confess;
My tongue broke out in unknown strains,
   And sung surprising grace.

3 The Lord can clear the darkest skies,
   Can give us day for night;
Make drops of sacred sorrow rise
   To rivers of delight.

4 Let those that sow in sadness wait
   Till the fair harvest come: [great
They shall confess their sheaves are
   And shout the blessings home.
                           WATTS.

407.   Psalm 145.
1 Sweet is the memory of thy grace,
   My God, my heavenly King;
Let age to age thy righteousness
   In sounds of glory sing.

2 God reigns on high; but ne'er confines
   His goodness to the skies:
Thro' the whole earth his bounty shines,
   And every want supplies.

3 With longing eyes thy creatures wait
   On thee for daily food;
Thy liberal hand provides their meat,
   And fills their mouth with good.

4 How kind are thy compassions, Lord!
   How slow thine anger moves!
But soon he sends his pardoning word
   To cheer the souls he loves.

5 Sweet is the memory of thy grace,
   My God, my heavenly King;
Let age to age thy righteousness
   In sounds of glory sing.
                           WATTS.

408. *"His tender mercies are over all his works."*

1 Thy goodness, Lord, our souls confess;
Thy goodness we adore:
A spring, whose blessings never fail;
A sea without a shore.

2 Sun, moon, and stars, thy love attest
In every golden ray;
Love draws the curtains of the night,
And love brings back the day.

3 Thy bounty every season crowns,
With all the bliss it yields;
With joyful clusters loads the vines,
With strengthening grain, the fields.

4 But chiefly thy compassion, Lord,
Is in the gospel seen;
There, like a sun, thy mercy shines,
Without a cloud between.

5 There pardon, peace, and holy joy,
Through Jesus' name are given;
He on the cross was lifted high,
That we might reign in heaven.
GIBBONS.

409. *God's Covenant sure.*

1 I know thy thoughts are peace toward
Safe am I in thy hands;   [me;
Firmly I build my hope on thee,
For sure thy counsel stands.

2 Whate'er thy word hath promised, all
Wilt thou full surely give!
Wherefore, from thee I will not fall;
Thy word doth make me live.

3 Though mountains crumble into dust,
Thy cov'nant standeth fast;
Who follows thee in pious trust,
Shall reach the goal at last.

4 Though strange and winding seems the
While yet on earth I dwell,   [way,
In heaven my heart shall gladly say,
Thou, God, dost all things well.
GERMAN.

410. 1 Cor. 3: 21-23.

1 If God is mine, then present things
And things to come are mine;
Yea, Christ, his Word, and Spirit, too,
And glory all divine.

2 If he is mine, then from his love
He every trouble sends;
All things are working for my good,
And bliss his rod attends.

3 If he is mine, let friends forsake,
Let wealth and honor flee;
Sure he who giveth me himself
Is more than these to me.

4 Oh, tell me, Lord, that thou art mine!
What can I wish beside?
My soul shall at the fountain live,
When all the streams are dried.

411. Gen. 28: 19-22.

1 O God of Bethel! by whose hand
Thy people still are fed;
Who through this weary pilgrimage
Hast all our fathers led, —

2 Our vows, our prayers, we now present
Before thy throne of grace;
God of our fathers, be the God
Of their succeeding race.

3 Through each perplexing path of life
Our wand'ring footsteps guide;
Give us, each day, our daily bread,
And raiment fit provide.

4 Oh, spread thy covering wings around,
Till all our wand'rings cease,
And at our Father's loved abode,
Our souls arrive in peace.
DODDRIDGE.

412. *Benevolence of God's Decrees.*

1 Since all the varying scenes of time
God's watchful eye surveys,
Oh, who so wise to choose our lot,
Or to appoint our ways?

2 Good, when he gives, supremely good;
Nor less when he denies:
E'en crosses, from his sovereign hand,
Are blessings in disguise.

3 Why should we doubt a Father's love,
So constant and so kind?
To his unerring, gracious will,
Be every wish resigned.

4 In thy fair book of life divine,
My God, inscribe my name;
There let it fill some humble place
Beneath my Lord the Lamb.
HERVEY.

The Christian Life. Trust in God.

BALERMA. C. M.

413. Psalm 125.
1 Unshaken as the sacred hill,
  And fixed as mountains be,
  Firm as a rock the soul shall rest,
  That leans, O Lord, on thee!

2 Not walls, nor hills, could guard so well
  Old Salem's happy ground,
  As those eternal arms of love,
  That every saint surround.

3 Deal gently, Lord, with souls sincere,
  And lead them safely on
  To the bright gates of paradise,
  Where Christ, their Lord, is gone.
                                WATTS.

414. Gal. 6: 14.
1 Let worldly minds the world pursue;
  It has no charms for me;
  Once I admired its trifles, too,
  But grace has set me free.

2 Its pleasures now no longer please,
  No more content afford;
  Far from my heart be joys like these,
  Now I have seen the Lord.

3 As by the light of opening day
  The stars are all concealed;
  So earthly pleasures fade away
  When Jesus is revealed.

4 Creatures no more divide my choice,
  I bid them all depart;
  His name and love and gracious voice
  Have fixed my roving heart.
                                NEWTON.

415. Rom. 8: 15.
1 My Father, God! how sweet the sound,
  How tender and how dear!
  Not all the melody of heaven
  Could so delight the ear.

2 Come, sacred Spirit, seal the name
  On my expanding heart;
  And show, that in Jehovah's grace
  I share a filial part.

3 Cheered by a signal so divine,
  Unwavering I believe;
  'My spirit Abba, Father! cries,
  Nor can the sign deceive.
                                DODDRIDGE.

416. 2 Pet. 1: 10.
1 When I can read my title clear
  To mansions in the skies,
  I bid farewell to every fear,
  And wipe my weeping eyes.

2 Should earth against my soul engage,
  And fiery darts be hurled,
  Then I can smile at Satan's rage,
  And face a frowning world.

3 Let cares like a wild deluge come,
  And storms of sorrow fall;
  May I but safely reach my home,
  My God, my heaven, my all!—

4 There shall I bathe my weary soul
  In seas of heavenly rest,
  And not a wave of trouble roll
  Across my peaceful breast.
                                WATTS.

God our Portion. Self-Consecration.

HAGAR. C. M.   OLD CHORAL.

417.   Psalm 73: 25.
1 My God, my portion, and my love,
   My everlasting All!
I've none but thee in heaven above,
   Or on this earthly ball.

2 To thee we owe our wealth and friends,
   And health and safe abode;
Thanks to thy name for meaner things,
   But they are not my God.

3 How vain a toy is glittering wealth,
   If once compared with thee!
Or what's my safety or my health,
   Or all my friends to me?

4 Were I possessor of the earth,
   And called the stars my own,
Without thy graces and thyself,
   I were a wretch undone.

5 Let others stretch their arms like seas,
   And grasp in all the shore;
Grant me the visits of thy face,
   And I desire no more.   WATTS.

418.   *The Grace of God.*
1 ARISE, my soul! my joyful powers,
   And triumph in my God;
Awake, my voice! and loud proclaim
   His glorious grace abroad.

2 The arms of everlasting love
   Beneath my soul he placed,
And on the Rock of Ages set
   My slippery footsteps fast.

3 The city of my blest abode
   Is walled around with grace;
Salvation for a bulwark stands,
   To shield the sacred place.

4 Arise, my soul! awake, my voice!
   And tunes of pleasure sing;
Loud hallelujahs shall address
   My Saviour and my King.   WATTS.

419.   Psalm 116.
1 WHAT shall I render to my God,
   For all his kindness shown?
My feet shall visit thine abode,
   My songs address thy throne.

2 Among the saints that fill thy house,
   My offerings shall be paid;
There shall my zeal perform the vows
   My soul in anguish made.

3 Now I am thine, forever thine,
   Nor shall my purpose move;
Thy hand hath loosed my bonds of pain,
   And bound me with thy love.

4 Here in thy courts I leave my vow,
   And thy rich grace record;
Witness, ye saints, who hear me now,
   If I forsake the Lord.   WATTS.

196   The Christian Life. God's Love and Care.

LUCY. C. M.

420.   *"Herein is Love."*

1 My God, how wonderful thou art!
    Thy majesty how bright!
  How glorious is thy mercy seat,
    In depths of burning light!

2 Yet I may love thee too, O Lord,
    Almighty as thou art;
  For thou hast stooped to ask of me
    The love of my poor heart.

3 No earthly father loves like thee,
    No mother half so mild
  Bears and forbears, as thou hast done
    With me, thy sinful child.

4 My God, how wonderful thou art,
    Thou everlasting Friend!
  On thee I stay my trusting heart,
    Till faith in vision end.

421.   *God our Guide.*

1 Oh, what a lonely path were ours,
    Could we, O Father, see
  No home of rest beyond it all,
    No guide, no help in thee!

2 But thou art near and with us still,
    To guide us in the way
  That leads along this vale of tears
    To the bright realms of day.

3 There shall thy glory, O our God,
    Break fully on our view,
  And we, thy saints, rejoice to find
    That all thy word was true.
                    MRS. WARING.

422.   *Adoption.* — Heb. 12: 7.

1 My God, my Father, blissful name!
    Oh, may I call thee mine?
  May I with sweet assurance claim
    A portion so divine?

2 Whate'er thy providence denies,
    I calmly would resign,
  For thou art good and just and wise:
    Oh, bend my will to thine!

3 Whate'er thy sacred will ordains,
    Oh, give me strength to bear!
  And let me know my Father reigns,
    And trust his tender care.

4 Thy sovereign ways are all unknown
    To my weak, erring sight;
  Yet let my soul adoring own
    That all thy ways are right.
                    MRS. STEELE.

423.   Mark 9: 24.

1 Lord, I believe; thy power I own,
    Thy word I would obey;
  I wander comfortless and lone,
    When from thy truth I stray.

2 Lord, I believe; but gloomy fears
    Sometimes bedim my sight;
  I look to thee with prayers and tears,
    And cry for strength and light.

3 Yes! I believe; and only thou
    Canst give my soul relief:
  Lord! to thy truth my spirit bow;
    "Help thou mine unbelief!"
                    WREFORD.

Resting in God's Mercy and Providence.

GERMANY. L. M. — BEETHOVEN.

424. *God's Great Mercies.*

1 How do thy mercies close me round!
   Forever be thy name adored!
   I blush in all things to abound;
   The servant is above his Lord.

2 Inured to poverty and pain,
   A suffering life my Master led;
   The Son of God, the Son of man,
   He had not where to lay his head.

3 But lo! a place he hath prepared
   For me, whom watchful angels keep;
   Yea, he himself becomes my guard;
   He smooths my bed, and gives me sleep.

4 Jesus protects! My fears begone!
   What can the Rock of Ages move?
   Safe in thine arms I lay me down,—
   Thine everlasting arms of love.
              C. WESLEY.

425. Psalm 116.

1 RETURN, my soul, and sweetly rest
   On thy almighty Father's breast;
   The bounties of his grace adore,
   And count his wondrous mercies o'er.

2 Thy mercy, Lord, preserved my breath,
   And snatched my fainting soul from death;
   Removed my sorrows, dried my tears,
   And saved me from surrounding snares.

3 What shall I render to the Lord?
   Or how his wondrous grace record?
   To him my grateful voice I'll raise,
   With just thanksgiving to his praise.

4 O Zion! in thy sacred courts,
   Where glory dwells and joy resorts,
   To notes divine I'll tune the song,
   And praise shall flow from every tongue.
              LATROBE.

426. Jer. 10: 23.

1 WHITHER, oh, whither should I fly,
   But to my loving Father's breast?
   Secure within thine arms to lie,
   And safe beneath thy wings to rest.

2 In all my ways thy hand I own,
   Thy ruling providence I see;
   Assist me still my course to run,
   And still direct my paths to thee.

3 I have no skill the snare to shun;
   But thou, O God, my wisdom art;
   I ever into ruin run;
   But thou art greater than my heart.

4 Foolish and impotent and blind,
   Lead me a way I have not known,
   Bring me where I my heaven may find,
   The heaven of loving thee alone.
              C. WESLEY.

427. Psalm 62.

1 My spirit looks to God alone;
   My rock and refuge is his throne;
   In all my fears, in all my straits,
   My soul on his salvation waits.

2 Trust him, ye saints, in all your ways
   Pour out your hearts before his face;
   When helpers fail, and foes invade,
   God is our all-sufficient aid.

BARBY. C. M.   TANSUR.

428.   Psalm 73: 26.

1 O Lord! I would delight in thee,
   And on thy care depend;
  To thee in every trouble flee,
   My best, my only Friend.

2 When all created streams are dried,
   Thy fulness is the same;
  May I with this be satisfied,
   And glory in thy name!

3 No good in creatures can be found,
   But may be found in thee;
  I must have all things, and abound,
   While God is God to me.

4 O Lord! I cast my care on thee;
   I triumph and adore;
  Henceforth my great concern shall be
   To love and please thee more.
                              RYLAND.

429.   Psalm 34.

1 Through all the changing scenes of life,
   In trouble and in joy,
  The praises of my God shall still
   My heart and tongue employ.

2 Of his deliverance I will boast,
   Till all who are distressed
  From my example comfort take,
   And charm their griefs to rest.

3 Oh, magnify the Lord with me,
   With me exalt his name!
  When in distress to him I called,
   He to my rescue came.

4 The hosts of God encamp around
   The dwellings of the just;
  Deliverance he affords to all
   Who on his succor trust.

5 Oh, make but trial of his love:
   Experience will decide
  How blest are they, and only they,
   Who in his truth confide.

6 Fear him, ye saints, and ye will then
   Have nothing else to fear;
  Make ye his service your delight,
   He'll make your wants his care.

430.   Psalm 36: 9.

1 Eternal Sun of righteousness,
   Display thy beams divine,
  And cause the glory of thy face
   Upon my heart to shine.

2 Light, in thy light, oh, may I see,
   Thy grace and mercy prove,
  Revived and cheered and blest by thee,
   The God of pardoning love.

3 Lift up thy countenance serene,
   And let thy happy child
  Behold, without a cloud between,
   The Father reconciled.

4 On me thy promised peace bestow,
   The peace by Jesus given; —
  The joys of holiness below,
   And then the joys of heaven.
                              C. WESLEY.

431. *Things Visible and Invisible.* — Rom. 1: 20.

1 THERE is a book who runs may read,
  Which heavenly truth imparts,
And all the lore its scholars need,
  Pure eyes and Christian hearts.

2 The works of God above, below,
  Within us and around,
Are pages in that book to show
  How God himself is found.

3 Two worlds are ours; 'tis only sin
  Forbids us to descry
The mystic heaven and earth within,
  Plain as the sea and sky.

4 Thou who hast given me eyes to see
  And love this sight so fair,
Give me a heart to find out thee,
  And read thee everywhere.
                                KEBLE.

432.   Titus 3: 5-7.

1 LORD, we confess our numerous faults,
  How great our guilt has been;
Foolish and vain were all our thoughts,
  And all our lives were sin.

2 But, O my soul! forever praise,
  Forever love his name,
Who turns thy feet from dangerous ways
  Of folly, sin, and shame.

3 'Tis not by works of righteousness,
  Which our own hands have done;
But we are saved by sovereign grace,
  Abounding through his Son.

4 'Tis from the mercy of our God
  That all our hopes begin;
'Tis by the water and the blood
  Our souls are washed from sin.
                                WATTS.

433.   Rom. 5: 3.

1 Is not the way to heavenly gain
  Through earthly grief and loss?
Rest must be won by toil and pain, —
  The crown repays the cross.

2 In tears and trials thou must sow
  To reap in joy and love;
We cannot find our home below,
  And hope for one above.

3 As woods, when shaken by the breeze,
  Take deeper, firmer root;
As winter's frosts but make the trees
  Abound in summer fruit;

4 So every heaven-sent pang and throe
  That Christian firmness tries,
But nerves us for our work below,
  And forms us for the skies.
                                LYTE.

434.   *The Covenant.* — Heb. 13: 20.

1 MY God, the covenant of thy love
  Abides forever sure;
And in its matchless grace I feel
  My happiness secure.

2 Since thou, the everlasting God,
  My Father art become,
Jesus my Guardian and my Friend,
  And heaven my final home; —

3 I welcome all thy sovereign will,
  For all that will is love;
And when I know not what thou dost,
  I wait the light above.

4 Thy covenant in the darkest gloom
  Shall heavenly rays impart,
And when my eyelids close in death,
  Sustain my fainting heart.
                                DODDRIDGE.

435.   Psalm 136.

1 OH, praise the Lord! for he is good;
  In him we rest obtain,
His mercy has through ages stood,
  And ever shall remain.

2 Let all the people of the Lord
  His praises spread around;
Let them his grace and love record,
  Who have salvation found.

3 Now let the east in him rejoice,
  The west its tribute bring,
The north and south lift up their voice
  In honor of their King.

4 Oh, praise the Lord! for he is good;
  In him we rest obtain:
His mercy has through ages stood,
  And ever shall remain.
                                WRANGHAM.

The Christian Life. Seeking and Resting in God.

WEBERTON. L. M.   WEBER, by DUDLEY BUCK, JR.

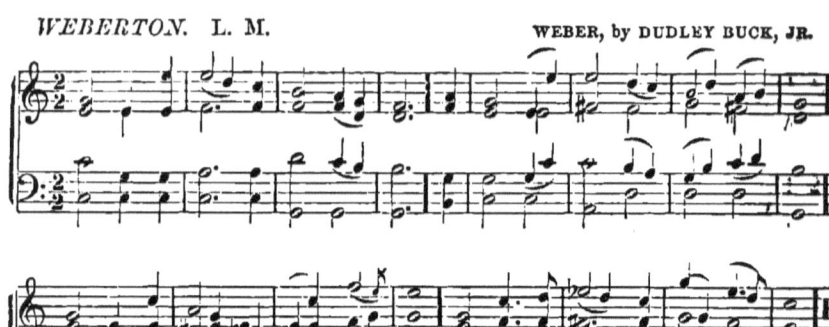

436.   *Psalm 4: 4.*

1 RETURN, my roving heart, return,
   And life's vain shadows chase no more;
   Seek out some solitude to mourn,
   And thy forsaken God implore.

2 O thou great God! whose piercing eye
   Distinctly marks each deep retreat,
   In these sequestered hours draw nigh,
   And let me here thy presence meet.

3 Through all the windings of my heart,
   My search let heavenly wisdom guide,
   And still its beams unerring dart,
   Till all be known and purified.

4 Then let the visits of thy love,
   My inmost soul be made to share,
   Till every grace combine to prove
   That God has fixed his dwelling there.
                       DODDRIDGE.

437.   *" Rest in God."*

1 FATHER, beneath thy sheltering wing,
   In sweet security we rest;
   And fear no evil earth can bring;
   In life, in death, supremely blest.

2 For life is good whose tidal flow
   The motions of thy will obeys;
   And death is good, that makes us know
   The Love Divine that all things sways.

3 And good it is to bear the cross,
   And so thy perfect peace to win;
   And naught is ill, nor brings us loss,
   Nor works us harm, save only sin!

4 Redeemed from sin we ask no more,
   But trust the love that saves, to guide;
   The grace that yields so rich a store
   Will grant us all we need beside.

438.   *Isaiah 7: 14.*

1 OH, sweetly breathe the lyres above,
   When angels touch the quivering string,
   And wake, to chant Immanuel's love,
   Such strains as angel-lips can sing!

2 And sweet, on earth, the choral swell,
   From mortal tongues, of gladsome lays;
   When pardoned souls their raptures tell,
   And, grateful, hymn Immanuel's praise.

3 Jesus, thy name our souls adore;
   We own the bond that makes us thine;
   And carnal joys that charmed before,
   For thy dear sake we now resign.

4 Our hearts, by dying love subdued,
   Accept thine offered grace to-day;
   Beneath the cross, with blood bedewed,
   We bow, and give ourselves away.

5 In thee we trust, — on thee rely;
   Though we are feeble, thou art strong;
   Oh, keep us till our spirits fly
   To join the bright, immortal throng!
                       RAY PALMER.

Doxology.

PRAISE God, from whom all blessings flow!
Praise him, all creatures here below!
Praise him above, ye heavenly host!
Praise Father, Son, and Holy Ghost!

Comfort in the Love of God.

FEDERAL STREET. L. M.   H. K. OLIVER.

439.   Psalm 119: 151.

1 O LOVE divine! that stooped to share
   Our sharpest pang, our bitterest tear,
   On thee we cast each earth-born care,
   We smile at pain while thou art near.

2 Though long the weary way we tread,
   And sorrow crown each lingering year,
   No path we shun, no darkness dread,
   Our hearts still whispering thou art
     near.

3 When drooping pleasure turns to grief,
   And trembling faith is changed to fear,
   The murmuring wind, the quivering leaf,
   Shall softly tell us thou art near.

4 On thee we fling our burdening woe,
   O Love divine, forever dear;
   Content to suffer while we know,
   Living or dying, thou art near!
                O. W. HOLMES.

440.   Matt. 6: 10.

1 MY God, my Father, while I stray
   Far from my home, on life's rough way,
   Oh, teach me from my heart to say,
   :| "Thy will be done!" |:

2 What though in lonely grief I sigh
   For friends beloved no longer nigh;
   Submissive still would I reply,
     "Thy will be done!"

3 If thou shouldst call me to resign
   What most I prize, — it ne'er was mine;
   I only yield thee what was thine:
     "Thy will be done!"

4 If but my fainting heart be blest
   With thy sweet Spirit for its guest,
   My God, to thee I leave the rest;
     "Thy will be done!"

5 Renew my will from day to day;
   Blend it with thine, and take away
   Whate'er now makes it hard to say,
     "Thy will be done!"

6 Then when on earth I breathe no more
   The prayer oft mixed with tears before,
   I'll sing upon a happier shore,
     "Thy will be done!"
                CHARLOTTE ELLIOTT.

441.   1 John 4: 8.

1 I CANNOT always trace the way
   Where thou, Almighty One, dost
     move;
   But I can always, always say,
   :| That God is love. |:

2 When fear her chilling mantle throws
   O'er earth, my soul to heaven above,
   As to her native home, upsprings,
     For God is love.

3 When mystery clouds my darkened path,
   I'll check my dread, my doubts reprove,
   In this my soul sweet comfort hath,
     That God is love.

4 Yes, God is love; — a thought like this
   Can every gloomy thought remove,
   And turn all tears, all woes, to bliss,
     For God is love.

HOLLAND. L. M. CHORAL, from Mendelssohn.

442. *John 14: 19.*

1 WHEN sins and fears prevailing rise,
  And fainting hope almost expires,
  Jesus, to thee I lift my eyes,
  To thee I breathe my soul's desires.

2 If my immortal Saviour lives,
  Then my immortal life is sure;
  His word a firm foundation gives;
  Here let me build and rest secure.

3 Here let my faith unshaken dwell;
  Immovable the promise stands;
  Not all the powers of earth or hell
  Can e'er dissolve the sacred bands.

4 Here, O my soul! thy trust repose:
  If Jesus is forever mine,
  Not death itself, that last of foes,
  Shall break a union so divine.
                             MRS. STEELE.

443. *A Good Conscience.* — 1 Peter 3: 16.

1 SWEET peace of conscience, heavenly guest,
  Come, fix thy mansion in my breast;
  Dispel my doubts, my fears control,
  And heal the anguish of my soul.

2 Come, smiling hope, and joy sincere,
  Come, make your constant dwelling here;
  Still let your presence cheer my heart,
  Nor sin compel you to depart.

3 O God of hope and peace divine!
  Make thou these secret pleasures mine;
  Forgive my sins, my fears remove,
  And fill my heart with joy and love.
                             HEGINBOTHAM.

444. *Contentment.* — Phil. 4: 11.

1 O LORD, how full of sweet content
  Our years of pilgrimage are spent!
  Where'er we dwell, we dwell with thee,
  In heaven, in earth, or on the sea.

2 To us remains nor place nor time;
  Our country is in every clime:
  We can be calm and free from care
  On any shore, since God is there.

3 While place we seek, or place we shun,
  The soul finds happiness in none;
  But with our God to guide our way,
  'Tis equal joy to go or stay.
                             MADAME GUION.

445. *Psalm 63.*

1 O GOD, thou art my God alone:
  Early to thee my soul shall cry, —
  A pilgrim in a land unknown,
  A thirsty land where springs are dry.

2 Yet through this rough and thorny maze,
  I follow hard on thee. my God;
  Thy hand unseen upholds my ways;
  I safely tread where thou hast trod.

3 Thee, in the watches of the night,
  When I remember on my bed,
  Thy presence makes the darkness light;
  Thy guardian wings are round my head.

4 Better than life itself thy love,
  Dearer than all beside to me;
  For whom have I in heaven above,
  Or what on earth compared with thee?
                             MONTGOMERY.

Longing for God in Sorrow and Trial.

BEMERTON. C. M. — GREATOREX'S COLL.

446. *"Oh, that I knew where I might find Him!"*
Job 23: 3, 4.

1 OH that I knew the secret place
  Where I might find my God!
  I'd spread my wants before his face,
  And pour my woes abroad.

2 I'd tell him how my sins arise,
  What sorrows I sustain;
  How grace decays, and comfort dies,
  And leaves my heart in pain.

3 He knows what arguments I'd take
  To wrestle with my God:
  I'd plead for his own mercy's sake, —
  I'd plead my Saviour's blood.

4 My God will pity my complaints,
  And drive my foes away;
  He knows the meaning of his saints,
  When they in sorrow pray.

5 Arise, my soul! from deep distress,
  And banish every fear;
  He calls thee to his throne of grace,
  To spread thy sorrows there.
            WATTS.

447. *"Lord, remember me."* — Luke 23: 42.

1 O THOU from whom all goodness flows,
  I lift my soul to thee;
  In all my sorrows, conflicts, woes,
  O Lord, remember me!

2 When on my aching, burdened heart
  My sins lie heavily,
  Thy pardon grant, new peace impart;
  Then, Lord, remember me!

3 When trials sore obstruct my way,
  And ills I cannot flee,
  Oh, let my strength be as my day;
  Dear Lord, remember me!

4 When in the solemn hour of death
  I wait thy just decree;
  Be this the prayer of my last breath:
  Now, Lord, remember me!

5 And when before thy throne I stand,
  And lift my soul to thee,
  Then with the saints at thy right hand,
  O Lord, remember me!

448. *The Comforter.*

1 O THOU who driest the mourner's tear!
  How dark this world would be,
  If, when deceived and wounded here,
  We could not fly to thee!

2 When joy no longer soothes or cheers,
  And e'en the hope that threw
  A moment's sparkle o'er our tears
  Is dimmed and vanished too; —

3 Oh, who would bear life's stormy doom,
  Did not thy wing of love [gloom
  Come brightly wafting through the
  Our peace-branch from above?

4 Then sorrow touched by thee grows bright,
  With more than rapture's ray;
  As darkness shows us worlds of light
  We never saw by day.
            MOORE.

The Christian Life. Thirsting for God.

WOODSTOCK. C. M.   R. DUTTON.

449.   Gen. 5: 24.
1 Oh for a closer walk with God,
   A calm and heavenly frame,
   A light to shine upon the road
   That leads me to the Lamb!

[2 Where is the blessedness I knew
   When first I saw the Lord?
   Where is the soul-refreshing view
   Of Jesus and his word?

3 What peaceful hours I once enjoyed!
   How sweet their memory still!
   But they have left an aching void
   The world can never fill.]

4 Return, O holy Dove, return,
   Sweet messenger of rest;
   I hate the sins that made thee mourn,
   And drove thee from my breast.

5 The dearest idol I have known,
   Whate'er that idol be,
   Help me to tear it from thy throne,
   And worship only thee.

6 So shall my walk be close with God,
   Calm and serene my frame;
   So purer light shall mark the road
   That leads me to the Lamb.
                    COWPER.

450.   Psalm 22.
1 Oh, help us, Lord!—each hour of need
   Thy heavenly succor give;
   Help us in thought and word and deed,
   Each hour on earth we live.

2 Oh, help us when our spirits bleed,
   With contrite anguish sore;
   And when our hearts are cold and de
   Oh, help us, Lord, the more!

3 Oh, help us, through the prayer of fai
   More firmly to believe!
   For still the more the servant hath,
   The more shall he receive.

4 Oh, help us, Jesus! from on high;
   We know no help but thee;
   Oh, help us so to live and die,
   As thine in heaven to be!
                    MILMAN

451.   Psalm 42.
1 As pants the hart for cooling streams
   When heated in the chase,
   So longs my soul, O God, for thee,
   And thy refreshing grace.

2 For thee, my God—the living God,
   My thirsty soul doth pine;
   Oh, when shall I behold thy face,
   Thou Majesty divine!

3 I sigh to think of happier days,
   When thou, O Lord! wast nigh;
   When every heart was tuned to prais
   And none more blest than I.

4 Why restless, why cast down, my sou
   Hope still; and thou shalt sing
   The praise of him who is thy God,
   Thy health's eternal spring.

Communion with God. Joy in Sorrow.

ROSE HILL. L. M.   ROOT & SWEETSER'S COLL.

152.   *Communion with God.*

My God, permit me not to be
  A stranger to myself and thee;
Amid a thousand thoughts I rove,
  Forgetful of my highest love.

Why should my passions mix with earth,
  And thus debase my heavenly birth?
Why should I cleave to things below,
  And let my God, my Saviour, go?

Call me away from flesh and sense;
  One sovereign word can draw me thence;
I would obey the voice divine,
  And all inferior joys resign.

Be earth, with all her scenes, withdrawn;
  Let noise and vanity be gone;
In secret silence of the mind
  My heaven, and there my God, I find.
                    WATTS.

453.   Luke 6: 21.

Oh, deem not they are blest alone,
  Whose lives a peaceful tenor keep;
For God, who pities man, hath shown
  A blessing for the eyes that weep.

The light of smiles shall fill again
  The lids that overflow with tears;
And weary hours of woe and pain
  Are promises of happier years.

There is a day of sunny rest
  For every dark and troubled night;
And grief may bide an evening guest,
  But joy shall come with early light.

4 Nor let the good man's trust depart,
  Though life its common gifts deny;
Though with a pierced and broken heart,
  And spurned of men, he goes to die.

5 For God has marked each sorrowing day,
  And numbered every secret tear,
And heaven's long age of bliss shall pay
  For all his children suffer here.
                    BRYANT.

454.   Psalm 42: 1.

1 I THIRST, but not as once I did,
  The vain delights of earth to share;
Thy wounds, Immanuel, all forbid
  That I should seek my pleasures there.

2 It was the sight of thy dear cross
  First weaned my heart from earthly things,
And taught me to esteem as dross
  The mirth of fools and pomp of kings.

3 Oh for that grace which springs from thee,
  And quickens all things where it flows;
Which makes a wretched thorn like me
  Bloom as the myrtle or the rose!

4 For sure of all the plants that share
  The notice of thy Father's eye,
None proves less grateful to his care,
  Or yields him meaner fruit than I.
                    COWPER.

Doxology.

PRAISE God, from whom all blessings flow,
Praise him, all creatures here below;
Praise him above, ye heavenly host,
Praise Father, Son, and Holy Ghost.

The Christian Life. Nearness to God.

HEBER. C. M. — GEO. KINGSLEY.

455. *Psalm 51: 10.*

1 Oh for a heart to praise my God,
  A heart from sin set free,
  A heart that always feels thy blood
  So freely shed for me.

2 A heart resigned, submissive, meek,
  My dear Redeemer's throne,
  Where only Christ is heard to speak,
  Where Jesus reigns alone.

3 Oh for a lowly, contrite heart,
  Believing, true, and clean;
  Which neither life nor death can part
  From him that dwells within!

4 Thy nature, gracious Lord, impart;
  Come quickly from above;
  Write thy new name upon my heart,
  Thy new, best name of Love.
  C. WESLEY.

456. *Trusting in Darkness.*

1 My God! — oh, could I make the claim —
  My Father and my Friend —
  And call thee mine by every name
  On which thy saints depend.

2 By every name of power and love,
  I would thy grace entreat;
  Nor should my humble hopes remove,
  Nor leave thy sacred seat.

3 Speak, Lord! and bid celestial peace
  Relieve my aching heart;
  Oh, smile and bid my sorrows cease,
  And all the gloom depart.
  MRS. STEELE.

457. *1 Cor. 13: 12.*

1 I love the windows of thy grace,
  Through which my Lord is seen;
  And long to meet my Saviour's face,
  Without a cloud between.

2 Oh that the happy hour were come,
  To change my faith to sight;
  I shall behold my Lord at home,
  In a diviner light.

3 Haste, my Beloved, and remove
  These interposing days;
  Then shall my passions all be love,
  And all my powers be praise.
  WATTS.

458. *Nearness to God.*

1 Oh, could I find, from day to day,
  A nearness to my God,
  Then would my hours glide sweet away
  While leaning on his word.

2 Lord, I desire with thee to live
  Anew from day to day,
  In joys the world can never give,
  Nor ever take away.

3 Blest Jesus, come, and rule my heart,
  And make me wholly thine,
  That I may never more depart,
  Nor grieve thy love divine.

4 Thus, till my last expiring breath,
  Thy goodness I'll adore;
  And when my frame dissolves in death,
  My soul shall love thee more.

459.
Job 29: 2.

1 Sweet was the time when first I felt
The Saviour's pard'ning blood
Applied to cleanse my soul from guilt,
And bring me home to God.

2 Soon as the morn the light revealed,
His praises tuned my tongue;
And, when the evening shade prevailed,
His love was all my song.

3 In prayer, my soul drew near the Lord,
And saw his glory shine;
And when I read his holy word,
I called each promise mine.

4 But now, when evening shade prevails,
My soul in darkness mourns;
And when the morn the light reveals,
No light to me returns.

5 Rise, Saviour! help me to prevail,
And make my soul thy care;
I know thy mercy cannot fail;
Let me that mercy share.
NEWTON.

460.
Watchfulness and Prayer.

1 Alas, what hourly dangers rise!
What snares beset my way!
To heaven, oh, let me lift mine eyes,
And hourly watch and pray.

2 How oft my mournful thoughts complain,
And melt in flowing tears!
My weak resistance!—ah, how vain!
How strong my foes and fears!

3 O gracious God! in whom I live,
My feeble efforts aid;
Help me to watch and pray and strive,
Though trembling and afraid.

4 Increase my faith, increase my hope,
When foes and fears prevail,
And bear my fainting spirit up,
Or soon my strength will fail.

5 Oh, keep me in thy heavenly way,
And bid the tempter flee;
And let me never, never stray
From happiness and thee.
MRS. STEELE.

461.
"Casting all your Care upon Him."

1 Lord, it belongs not to my care
Whether I die or live;
To love and serve thee is my share,
And this thy grace must give.

2 Christ leads me through no darker rooms
Than he went through before;
No one into his kingdom comes,
But through his opened door.

3 Come, Lord, when grace has made me meet
Thy blessed face to see;
For if thy work on earth be sweet,
What will thy glory be?

4 Then shall I end my sad complaints,
And weary, sinful days,
And join with all triumphant saints
Who sing Jehovah's praise.

5 My knowledge of that life is small;
The eye of faith is dim;
But 'tis enough that Christ knows all,
And I shall be with him.
BAXTER.

462.
Psalm 38.

1 Amidst thy wrath remember love;
Restore thy servant, Lord;
Nor let a Father's chastening prove
Like an avenger's sword.

2 My sins a heavy load appear,
And o'er my head are gone;
Too heavy they for me to bear,
Too hard for me t' atone.

3 My thoughts are like a troubled sea,
My head still bending down;
And I go mourning all the day,
Beneath my Father's frown.

4 All my desire to thee is known;
Thine eye counts every tear;
And every sigh and every groan
Is noticed by thine ear.

5 My God, forgive my follies past,
And be forever nigh;
O Lord of my salvation, haste,
Before thy servant die.
WATTS.

The Christian Life. Clinging to Christ. Solitude.

GEER. C. M.   GREATOREX'S COLL.

463.   *John 6: 68.*

1 To whom, my Saviour, shall I go,
   If I depart from thee?
My guide through all this vale of woe,
   And more than all to me.

2 The world reject thy gentle reign,
   And pay thy death with scorn;
Oh! they could plait thy crown again,
   And sharpen every thorn.

3 But I have felt thy dying love
   Breathe gently through my heart,
To whisper hope of joys above, —
   And can we ever part?

4 Ah! no, with thee I'll walk below,
   My journey to the grave:
To whom, my Saviour, shall I go,
   When only thou canst save?

464.   *Retirement.*

1 Far from the world, O Lord, I flee,
   From strife and tumult far;
From scenes where Satan wages still
   His most successful war.

2 The calm retreat, the silent shade,
   With prayer and praise agree;
And seem by thy sweet bounty made
   For those who follow thee.

3 There, if thy Spirit touch the soul,
   And grace her mean abode,
Oh, with what peace and joy and love
   Does she commune with God!

4 There, like the nightingale, she pours
   Her solitary lays;
Nor asks a witness of her song,
   Nor thirsts for human praise.

5 Author and Guardian of my life,
   Sweet Source of light divine,
And — all harmonious names in one —
   My Saviour, thou art mine!
                    COWPER.

465.   *Alone with God.*

1 How deep and tranquil is the joy
   Which thou hast kindly given
To those who seek thy presence, Lord,
   And tread the path to heaven!

2 'Tis in the silence of the shade
   My sober thoughts begin,
And earth's illusive charms appear
   But vanity and sin.

3 'Tis here the troubled springs of life
   Are calmed to sweetest rest;
The stillness of this hour expels
   The tumult of my breast.

4 Far, far above all mortal things
   I walk with God alone;
And while he names celestial joys,
   I call them all my own.

5 Then let the noisy world pursue
   The trifles of a day, —
Mine be the silent, secret joys
   That never fade away.
                    REED.

HUNTINGTON. C. M.   C. W. HUNTINGTON.

466. *God's Goodness.*

1 I BOW my forehead to the dust,
   I veil my eyes for shame,
And urge, in trembling self-distrust,
   A prayer without a claim.

2 I see the wrong that round me lies,
   I feel the guilt within,
I hear with groans and travail-cries
   The world confess its sin.

3 Yet, in the maddening maze of things,
   And tossed by storm and flood,
To one fixed star my spirit clings; —
   I know that God is good!

4 I know not where his islands lift
   Their fronded palms in air;
I only know I cannot drift
   Beyond his love and care.

5 And so, beside the silent sea,
   I wait the muffled oar;
No harm from him can come to me,
   On ocean or on shore!
                    WHITTIER.

467. *God's Peace.*

1 WE bless thee for thy peace, O God!
   Deep as the soundless sea,
Which falls like sunshine on the road
   Of those who trust in thee.

2 That peace which suffers and is strong,
   Trusts where it cannot see,
Deems not the trial way too long,
   But leaves the end with thee; —

3 That peace which flows serene and deep, —
   A river in the soul,
Whose banks a living verdure keep
   God's sunshine o'er the whole! —

4 Such, Father, give our hearts such peace,
   Whate'er the outward be,
Till all life's discipline shall cease,
   And we go home to thee.

468. *God's Glory.*

1 GOD's glory is a wondrous thing,
   Most strange in all its ways,
And, of all things on earth, least like
   What men agree to praise.

2 Oh, blest is he to whom is given
   The instinct that can tell
That God is on the field, when he
   Is most invisible!

3 And blest is he who can divine
   Where real right doth lie,
And dares to take the side that seems
   Wrong to man's blindfold eye!

4 Oh, learn to scorn the praise of men!
   Oh, learn to lose with God!
For Jesus won the world through shame,
   And beckons thee his road.

5 And right is right, since God is God;
   And right the day must win;
To doubt would be disloyalty,
   To falter would be sin!
                    FABER.

210 The Christian Life. Faith in God's Will and Word.

GALENA. C. M.   Arranged from COOKE.

469. *For the Spirit of a Child.*

1 FATHER, I know that all my life
  Is portioned out for me ;
  The changes that will surely come
  I do not fear to see :
  I ask thee for a present mind,
  Intent on pleasing thee.

2 I ask thee for a thoughtful love,
  Through constant watching wise,
  To meet the glad with joyful smiles,
  And wipe the weeping eyes, —
  A heart at leisure from itself,
  To soothe and sympathize.

3 I would not have the restless will
  That hurries to and fro,
  That seeks for some great thing to do,
  Or secret thing to know :
  I would be treated as a child,
  And guided where I go.

4 Wherever in the world I am,
  In whatsoe'er estate,
  I have a fellowship with hearts,
  To keep and cultivate ;
  A work of lowly love to do
  For Him on whom I wait.

5 I ask thee for the daily strength,
  To none that ask denied,
  A mind to blend with outward life,
  While keeping at thy side ;
  Content to fill a little space,
  If thou be glorified.
                              MRS. WARING.

470. *Not Forsaken.*

1 AND wilt thou now forsake me, Lord ?
  I feel it cannot be ;
  No earthly tongue can ever tell
  What thou hast been to me.

2 Through all the changing scenes of life
  Thy love hath sheltered me ;
  And wilt thou now forget thy child ?
  I feel it cannot be.

3 Thy love hath been my heritage
  Through many a weary year ;
  I've trusted in thy promises,
  And thou hast dried each tear.

4 In life or death, I take my stand
  Where I have ever stood,
  Beneath the shelter of thy cross,
  And trusting in thy blood.

5 And then, when youth and health and
    And energy have fled,   [strength
  The shades of evening peacefully
  Shall close around my head.

6 And when in all the helplessness
  Of death I turn to thee,
  Thou wilt not then forsake me, Lord !
  I feel it cannot be.

NOTE. — In singing hymn 470, repeat the first two lines of the tune, making of it a double tune.

Joy in Christ. God's Grace in Christ.

GROSTETE. L. M.   GREATOREX'S COLL.

471.   *"The Rock of our Salvation."*

1 REJOICE, ye saints, rejoice and praise
    The blessings of redeeming grace!
    Jesus, your everlasting tower,
    Stands firm against the tempest's power.

2 He is a refuge ever nigh;
    His love endures as mountains high;
    His name's a rock, which winds above,
    And waves below, can never move.

3 While all things change, he changes not;
    He ne'er forgets, though oft forgot;
    His love will ever be the same;
    His word, enduring as his name.

4 Rejoice, ye saints, rejoice and praise
    The blessings of this wondrous grace!
    Jesus, your everlasting tower,
    Can bear, unmoved, the tempest's power.

472.   *The Star of Bethlehem.*

1 WHEN marshalled on the nightly plain,
    The glittering host bestud the sky,
    One star alone, of all the train,
    Can fix the sinner's wandering eye.

2 Hark, hark! to God the chorus breaks,
    From every host, from every gem;
    But one alone, the Saviour, speaks:
    It is the Star of Bethlehem.

3 Once on the raging seas I rode: [dark;
    The storm was loud, the night was
    The ocean yawned, and rudely blowed
    The wind that tossed my foundering bark.

4 Deep horror then my vitals froze; [stem;
    Death-struck, I ceased the tide to
    When suddenly a star arose!
    It was the Star of Bethlehem.

5 It was my guide, my light, my all;
    It bade my dark forebodings cease;
    And through the storm, and danger's thrall,
    It led me to the port of peace.

6 Now safely moored, my perils o'er,
    I'll sing, first in night's diadem,
    Forever and for evermore,
    The Star — the Star of Bethlehem!
                      H. K. WHITE.

473.   *The Grace of God.*

1 Now to the Lord a noble song:
    Awake, my soul! awake my tongue!
    Hosanna to th' eternal Name,
    And all his boundless love proclaim!

2 See where it shines in Jesus' face,
    The brightest image of his grace:
    God, in the person of his Son,
    Has all his mightiest works outdone.

3 Grace! —'tis a sweet, a charming theme;
    My thoughts rejoice at Jesus' name:
    Ye angels, dwell upon the sound;
    Ye heavens, reflect it to the ground!

4 Oh, may I live to reach the place
    Where he unveils his lovely face!
    Where I his beauties shall behold,
    And sing his name to harps of gold!
                            WATTS.

The Christian Life. Christ our Joy and Hope.

HYMN. C. M. From "MODERN HARP."

474. *"One Lord."*

1 O LORD and Master of us all,
  Whate'er our name or sign ;
 We own thy sway, we hear thy call,
  We test our lives by thine.

2 We faintly hear, we dimly see,
  In differing phrase we pray ;
 But, dim or clear, we own in thee,
  The Light, the Truth, the Way !

3 Apart from thee all gain is loss,
  And labor vainly done ;
 The solemn shadow of thy cross
  Is better than the sun.

4 Alone, O Love ineffable !
  Thy saving name is given ;
 To turn aside from thee is hell,
  To walk with thee is heaven.

5 Deep strike thy roots, O heavenly Vine,
  Within our earthly sod ;
 Most human and yet most divine,
  The flower of man and God !
              WHITTIER.

475. *Preciousness of Christ.*

1 THOU dear Redeemer, dying Lamb,
  I love to hear of thee ;
 No music's like thy charming name,
  Nor half so sweet can be.

2 Oh, may I ever hear thy voice
  In mercy to me speak ;
 In thee, my Priest, will I rejoice,
  And thy salvation seek.

3 My Jesus shall be still my theme,
  While on this earth I stay ;
 I'll sing my Jesus' lovely name,
  When all things else decay.

4 When I appear in yonder cloud,
  With all his favored throng,
 Then will I sing more sweet, more loud,
  And Christ shall be my song.
              CENNICK.

476. Luke 23: 42.

1 JESUS ! thou art the sinner's Friend ;
  As such I look to thee ;
 Now in the fulness of thy love,
  O Lord ! remember me.

2 Remember thy pure word of grace,
  Remember Calvary,
 Remember all thy dying groans,
  And, then, remember me.

3 Thou wondrous Advocate with God !
  I yield myself to thee ;
 While thou art sitting on thy throne,
  Dear Lord ! remember me.

4 Lord ! I am guilty, I am vile,
  But thy salvation's free ;
 Then, in thine all-abounding grace,
  Dear Lord ! remember me.

5 And, when I close my eyes in death,
  When creature-helps all flee,
 Then, O my dear Redeemer-God !
  I pray, remember me.
              PARKINSON.

The Praise of Christ's Love and Grace.

477. Matt. 10: 24.

1 Didst thou, dear Jesus! suffer shame,
    And bear the cross for me?
And shall I fear to own thy name,
    Or thy disciple be?

2 Inspire my soul with life divine,
    And make me truly bold; [shine,
Let knowledge, faith, and meekness
    Nor love, nor zeal, grow cold.

3 Let mockers scoff, the world defame,
    And treat me with disdain;
Still may I glory in thy name,
    And count reproach my gain.

4 To thee I cheerfully submit,
    And all my powers resign;
Let wisdom point out what is fit,
    And I'll no more repine.
                        KIRKHAM.

478. *The King of Saints.*

1 Come, ye that love the Saviour's name,
    And joy to make it known;
The sovereign of your hearts proclaim,
    And bow before his throne.

2 Behold your King, your Saviour, crowned
    With glories all divine;
And tell the wondering nations round
    How bright those glories shine.

3 When in his earthly courts we view
    The beauties of our King,
We long to love as angels do,
    And with their voice to sing.

4 Oh for the day, the glorious day!
    When heaven and earth shall raise,
With all their powers, the raptured lay,
    To celebrate thy praise.
                        MRS. STEELE.

479. John 21: 15.

1 Do not I love thee, O my Lord?
    Behold my heart, and see;
And turn the dearest idol out
    That dares to rival thee.

2 Is not thy name melodious still
    To mine attentive ear?
Doth not each pulse with pleasure bound,
    My Saviour's voice to hear?

3 Hast thou a lamb in all thy flock
    I would disdain to feed?
Hast thou a foe, before whose face
    I fear thy cause to plead?

4 Would not my heart pour forth its blood
    In honor of thy name?
And challenge the cold hand of death
    To damp th' immortal flame?

5 Thou knowest that I love thee, Lord;
    But oh! I long to soar
Far from the sphere of mortal joys,
    And learn to love thee more.
                        DODDRIDGE.

480. Rom. 5: 8.

1 To our Redeemer's glorious name
    Awake the sacred song;
Oh, may his love — immortal flame! —
    Tune every heart and tongue.

2 His love, what mortal thought can reach!
    What mortal tongue display!
Imagination's utmost stretch
    In wonder dies away.

3 Dear Lord, while we, adoring, pay
    Our humble thanks to thee,
May every heart with rapture say,
    "The Saviour died for me!"

4 Oh, may the sweet, the blissful theme,
    Fill every heart and tongue!
Till strangers love thy charming name,
    And join the sacred song.
                        MRS. STEELE.

481. Psalm 71.

1 My Saviour! my almighty Friend!
    When I begin thy praise,
Where will the growing numbers end,
    The numbers of thy grace?

2 Thou art my everlasting trust;
    Thy goodness I adore:
And since I knew thy graces first,
    I speak thy glories more.

3 My feet shall travel all the length
    Of the celestial road; [strength,
And march, with courage in thy
    To see my Father, God.
                        WATTS.

HAYDN. S. M.   Arranged from HAYDN.

482.   Psalm 77: 19. 1 Cor. 13: 12.
1   Thy way is in the sea;
     Thy paths we cannot trace;
     Nor solve, O Lord! the mystery
     Of thy unbounded grace.

2   As through a glass we see
     The wonders of thy love;
     How little do we know of thee,
     Or of the joys above!

3   In part we know thy will,
     And bless thee for the sight;
     Soon will thy love the rest reveal
     In glory's clearer light.

4   With joy shall we survey
     Thy providence and grace;
     And spend an everlasting day
     In wonder, love, and praise.
                              FAWCETT.

483.   1 Peter 1: 8.
1   Not with our mortal eyes
     Have we beheld the Lord;
     Yet we rejoice to hear his name,
     And love him in his word.

2   On earth we want the sight
     Of our Redeemer's face;
     Yet, Lord, our inmost thoughts delight
     To dwell upon thy grace.

3   And when we taste thy love,
     Our joys divinely grow
     Unspeakable, like those above,
     And heaven begins below.
                                WATTS.

484.   Phil. 4: 4.
1   Rejoice! the Lord is King!
     Your Lord and King adore;
     Ye ransomed saints, give thank
     And triumph evermore.

2   The mighty Saviour reigns,
     The God of truth and love;
     When he himself had purged our stain,
     He took his seat above.

3   He sits at God's right hand,
     Till all his foes submit,
     And humbly bow at his command,
     And fall beneath his feet.

4   Rejoice in glorious hope!
     Jesus, the Judge, shall come,
     And take his waiting servants up
     To their eternal home.

485.   Luke 19: 41.
1   Did Christ o'er sinners weep,
     And shall our cheeks be dry?
     Let floods of penitential grief
     Burst forth from every eye.

2   The Son of God in tears,
     Angels with wonder see!
     Be thou astonished, O my soul;
     He shed those tears for thee.

3   He wept that we might weep;
     Each sin demands a tear;
     In heaven alone no sin is found,
     And there's no weeping there.
                                BEDDOME.

Preciousness and Beauty of Christ.

ATWATER. C. M.

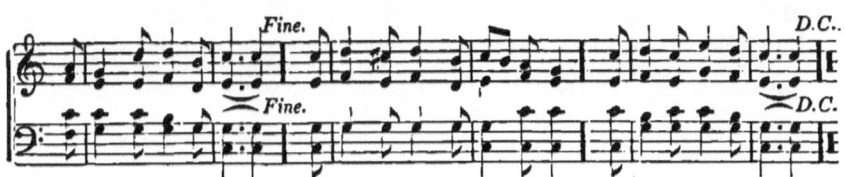

486. Matt. 17: 8.

1 JESUS! the very thought of thee
  With sweetness fills my breast;
But sweeter far thy face to see,
  And in thy presence rest.
No voice can sing, nor heart can frame,
  Nor can the memory find,
A sweeter sound than thy blest name,
  O Saviour of mankind!

2 Oh, hope of every contrite heart,
  Oh, joy of all the meek;
To those who fall, how kind thou art,
  How good to those who seek!
But what to those who find? ah! this
  Nor tongue nor pen can show:
The love of Jesus, what it is,
  None but his loved ones know.

---

3 Thy lovely presence shines so clear
  Through every sense and way, [near,
That souls which once have seen thee
  See all things else decay.
Come then, dear Lord, possess my heart,
  Chase thence the shades of night;
Bid all but perfect love depart
  Before thy shining light.

4 Jesus, our hope, when we repent,
  Sweet source of all our grace;
Sole comfort in our banishment;
  Oh! what, when face to face!

Jesus! our only joy be thou,
  As thou our prize wilt be;
Jesus! be thou our glory now,
  And in eternity.
                         BERNARD.

487. Cant. 5: 10-16.

1 MAJESTIC sweetness sits enthroned
  Upon the Saviour's brow;
His head with radiant glories crowned,
  His lips with grace o'erflow.
No mortal can with him compare,
  Among the sons of men;
Fairer is he than all the fair
  That fill the heavenly train.

2 He saw me plunged in deep distress,
  He flew to my relief;
For me he bore the shameful cross,
  And carried all my grief.
To him I owe my life and breath,
  And all the joys I have;
He makes me triumph over death,
  He saves me from the grave.

3 To heaven the place of his abode,
  He brings my weary feet;
Shows me the glories of my God,
  And makes my joy complete.
Since from his bounty I receive
  Such proofs of love divine,
Had I a thousand hearts to give,
  Lord! they should all be thine.
                         STENNETT.

216 *The Christian Life. Jesus only. Blessedness of Believers.*

SPANISH HYMN. 7s.

488.   *"Only Thee."*

1 Blessed Saviour! thee I love,
All my other joys above;
All my hopes in thee abide;
Thou my hope, and naught beside:
Ever let my glory be
Only, only, only thee.

2 Once again beside the cross,
All my gain I count but loss;
Earthly pleasures fade away,
Clouds they are that hide my day:
Hence, vain shadows! let me see
Jesus crucified for me.

3 Blessed Saviour! thine am I,
Thine to live, and thine to die;
Height or depth or earthly power
Ne'er shall hide my Saviour more:
Ever shall my glory be
Only, only, only thee!
                      DUFFIELD.

489.   2 Pet. 1: 19.

1 Christ, whose glory fills the skies,
Christ, the true, the only light,
Sun of righteousness! arise,
Triumph o'er the shades of night:
Day-spring from on high, be near;
Day-star, in my heart appear!

2 Dark and cheerless is the morn,
If thy light is hid from me;
Joyless is the day's return,
Till thy mercy's beams I see,—
Till they inward light impart,
Glad my eyes, and warm my heart.

3 Visit, then, this soul of mine;
Pierce the gloom of sin and grief;
Fill me, radiant Sun divine!
Scatter all my unbelief:
More and more thyself display,
Shining to the perfect day.
                      TOPLADY.

490.   1 John 3: 14.

1 Blessed are the sons of God!
They are bought with Jesus' blood;
They are ransomed from the grave;
Life eternal they shall have:
With them numbered may we be,
Here, and in eternity!

2 God did love them in his Son
Long before the world begun;
All their sins are washed away;
They shall stand in God's great day:
With them numbered may we be,
Here, and in eternity!

3 They are harmless, meek, and mild,
Holy, humble, undefiled;
They are by the Spirit sealed,
They with love and peace are filled:
With them numbered may we be,
Here, and in eternity!

4 They are lights upon the earth,
Children of a heavenly birth;
One with God, with Jesus one,
Glory is in them begun:
With them numbered may we be,
Here, and in eternity!
                      HUMPHRIES.

491.   Psalm 42.

1 Hearken, Lord, to my complaints,
For my soul within me faints;
Thee, far off, I call to mind,
In the land I left behind.
Where the streams of Jordan flow,
Where the heights of Hermon glow.

2 Once the morning's earliest light
Brought thy mercy to my sight,
And my wakeful song was heard
Later than the evening bird;
Hast thou all my prayers forgot?
Dost thou scorn, or hear them not?

Abiding in Christ. God's Preserving Grace.

ST. THOMAS. S. M.   A. WILLIAMS.

492.   1 Cor. 12: 27.
1 Dear Saviour! we are thine,
    By everlasting bands;
    Our hearts, our souls, we would resign
    Entirely to thy hands.
2 To thee we still would cleave
    With ever growing zeal;
    If millions tempt us Christ to leave,
    Oh, let them ne'er prevail!
3 Thy Spirit shall unite
    Our souls to thee, our Head;
    Shall form in us thine image bright,
    And teach thy paths to tread.
4 Death may our souls divide
    From these abodes of clay;
    But love shall keep us near thy side,
    Through all the gloomy way.
5 Since Christ and we are one,
    Why should we doubt or fear?
    If he in heaven has fixed his throne,
    He'll fix his members there.
                           DODDRIDGE.

493.   Jude 24 25.
1 To God, the only wise,
    Our Saviour and our King;
    Let all the saints below the skies
    Their humble praises bring.
2 'Tis his almighty love,
    His counsel and his care,
    Preserves us safe from sin and death,
    And every hurtful snare.
3 He will present our souls,
    Unblemished and complete,
    Before the glory of his face,
    With joys divinely great.
4 Then all the chosen seed
    Shall meet around the throne,
    Shall bless the conduct of his grace,
    And make his wonders known.
5 To our Redeemer, God,
    Wisdom and power belong,
    Immortal crowns of majesty,
    And everlasting song.
                           WATTS.

494.   *"Singing in the Ways of the Lord."*
1 Come, ye that love the Lord,
    And let your joys be known;
    Join in a song of sweet accord,
    And thus surround the throne.
2 Let those refuse to sing
    Who never knew our God;
    But children of the heavenly King
    May speak their joys abroad.
3 The men of grace have found
    Glory begun below;
    Celestial fruits on earthly ground
    From faith and hope may grow.
4 The hill of Zion yields
    A thousand sacred sweets
    Before we reach the heavenly fields,
    Or walk the golden streets.
5 Then let our songs abound,
    And every tear be dry;   [ground
    We're marching through Immanuel's
    To fairer worlds on high.
                           WATTS.

The Christian Life. Jesus Precious.

DEDHAM. C. M.   WM. GARDINER.

495.   Cant. 2: 16.
1 My God! the spring of all my joys,
    The life of my delights,
The glory of my brightest days,
    And comfort of my nights!

2 In darkest shades, if he appear,
    My dawning is begun:
He is my soul's sweet morning star,
    And he my rising sun.

3 The opening heavens around me shine
    With beams of sacred bliss,
While Jesus shows his heart is mine,
    And whispers, I am his!

4 My soul would leave this heavy clay
    At that transporting word,
Run up with joy the shining way,
    T' embrace my dearest Lord.

5 Fearless of hell and ghastly death,
    I'd break through every foe;
The wings of love and arms of faith
    Should bear me conqu'ror through.
                             WATTS.

496.   Matt. 1: 21.
1 Jesus! I love thy charming name,
    'Tis music to mine ear;
Fain would I sound it out so loud
    That earth and heaven should hear.

2 Yes, thou art precious to my soul,
    My transport and my trust;
Jewels, to thee, are gaudy toys,
    And gold is sordid dust.

3 All my capacious powers can wish,
    In thee doth richly meet;
Not to mine eyes is light so dear,
    Nor friendship half so sweet.

4 Thy grace still dwells upon my heart,
    And sheds its fragrance there; —
The noblest balm of all its wounds,
    The cordial of its care.

5 I'll speak the honors of thy name,
    With my last lab'ring breath; [arms,
Then, speechless, clasp thee in mine
    The antidote of death.
                           DODDRIDGE.

497.   Psalm 73.
1 Whom have we, Lord, in heaven, but
    And whom on earth beside? [thee,
Where else for succor can we flee,
    Or in whose strength confide?

2 Thou art our portion here below,
    Our promised bliss above;
Ne'er may our souls an object know
    So precious as thy love.

3 When heart and flesh, O Lord, shall
    Thou wilt our spirit cheer, [fail,
Support us through life's thorny vale,
    And calm each anxious fear.

4 Yes, thou shalt be our guide through life,
    And help and strength supply,
Sustain us in death's fearful strife,
    And welcome us on high.
                             LYTE.

498. *Joy of Forgiveness.*

1 My Saviour, let me hear thy voice
  Pronounce the word of peace,
And all my warmest powers shall join
  To celebrate thy grace.

2 With gentle smiles call me thy child,
  And speak my sins forgiven;
The accents mild shall charm my ear
  Like the sweet harps of heaven.

3 Cheerful, where'er thy hand shall lead,
  The darkest path I'll tread;
Cheerful I'll quit these mortal shores,
  And mingle with the dead.

4 When dreadful guilt is done away,
  No other fears we know;
That hand which scatters pardons down
  Shall crowns of life bestow.
                              DODDRIDGE.

499. 2 Tim. 1: 12.

1 I'm not ashamed to own my Lord,
  Or to defend his cause;
Maintain the honor of his word,
  The glory of his cross.

2 Jesus, my God! — I know his name;
  His name is all my trust;
Nor will he put my soul to shame,
  Nor let my hope be lost.

3 Firm as his throne his promise stands,
  And he can well secure
What I've committed to his hands
  Till the decisive hour.

4 Then will he own my worthless name
  Before his Father's face,
And in the New Jerusalem
  Appoint my soul a place.
                              WATTS.

500. *Joy and Comfort in Christ.*

1 Thou lovely Source of true delight,
  Whom I unseen adore,
Unveil thy beauties to my sight,
  That I may love thee more.

2 Thy glory o'er creation shines,
  But in thy sacred word
I read, in fairer, brighter lines,
  My bleeding, dying Lord.

3 'Tis here, whene'er my comforts droop,
  And sins and sorrows rise,
Thy love, with cheerful beams of hope,
  My fainting heart supplies.

4 Jesus! my Lord, my life, my light,
  Oh, come with blissful ray,
Break radiant through the shades of [night,
  And chase my fears away.

501. *Jesus' Praise.*

1 Oh for a thousand tongues to sing
  My dear Redeemer's praise, —
The glories of my God and King,
  The triumphs of his grace!

2 My gracious Master and my God,
  Assist me to proclaim,
To spread through all the earth abroad
  The honors of thy name.

3 Jesus! the name that calms our fears,
  That bids our sorrows cease;
'Tis music in the sinner's ears;
  'Tis life and health and peace.

4 He breaks the power of reigning sin;
  He sets the pris'ner free;
His blood can make the foulest clean;
  His blood availed for me.
                              C. WESLEY.

502. Isaiah 54: 8.

1 Children of God, who, faint and slow,
  Your pilgrim-path pursue,
In strength and weakness, joy and woe,
  To God's high calling true! —

2 Why move ye thus, with lingering tread,
  A doubting, mournful band?
Why faintly hangs the drooping head?
  Why fails the feeble hand?

3 Oh! weak to know a Saviour's power,
  To feel a Father's care;
A moment's toil, a passing shower,
  Is all the grief ye share.

4 Then, Christian, dry the falling tear,
  The faithless doubt remove;
Redeemed at last from guilt and fear,
  Oh, wake thy heart to love.
                              BOWDLER.

Self-Consecration to Christ.

EVER THINE, ONLY THINE.

503.

Ever Thine, Only Thine!

1 O Love! who, ere life's earliest dawn,
  On me thy choice hast gently laid;
  O Love! who here as man wast born,
  And wholly like to us wast made;
  O Love! I give myself to thee,
  Thine ever, only thine to be.

  Chorus: { Ever thine, only thine!
             { O Love, I give myself to thee!

2 O Love! who once in time wast slain,
  Pierced through and through with bitter woe;
  O Love! who wrestling thus didst gain
  That we eternal joy might know;
  O Love! I give myself to thee,
  Thine ever, only thine to be.
  Chorus:

3 O Love! who lovest me for aye,
  Who for my soul dost ever plead;
  O Love! who didst my ransom pay,
  Whose power sufficeth in my stead;
  O Love! I give myself to thee,
  Thine ever, only thine to be.
  Chorus:

4 O Love! who once shalt bid me rise
  From out this dying life of ours;
  O Love! who once o'er yonder skies
  Shalt set me in the fadeless bowers;
  O Love! I give myself to thee,
  Thine ever, only thine to be.
  Chorus:

MONK'S COLL.

Christ's Matchless Worth. Thirsting for Christ.

ARIEL. C. P. M.   DR. MASON.

504.   1 Peter 2: 7.

1 OH, could I speak the matchless worth,
Oh, could I sound the glories forth,
   Which in my Saviour shine!
I'd soar, and touch the heavenly strings,
And vie with Gabriel while he sings
   In notes almost divine.

2 I'd sing the precious blood he spilt,
My ransom from the dreadful guilt
   Of sin and wrath divine!
I'd sing his glorious righteousness,
In which all-perfect heavenly dress
   My soul shall ever shine.

3 I'd sing the characters he bears,
And all the forms of love he wears,
   Exalted on his throne:
In loftiest songs of sweetest praise,
I would to everlasting days
   Make all his glories known.

4 Well, the delightful day will come,
When my dear Lord will bring me home,
   And I shall see his face:

Then with my Saviour, Brother, Friend,
A blest eternity I'll spend,
   Triumphant in his grace.
                        MEDLEY.

505.   Luke 10: 42.

1 O LOVE divine, how sweet thou art!
When shall I find my willing heart
   All taken up by thee?
I thirst, I faint, I die to prove
The greatness of redeeming love,—
   The love of Christ to me.

2 God only knows the love of God;
Oh that it now were shed abroad
   In this poor stony heart!
For love I sigh, for love I pine;
This only portion, Lord, be mine,
   Be mine the better part!

3 Oh that I could, with favored John,
Recline my weary head upon
   The dear Redeemer's breast;
From care and sin and sorrow free,
Give me! O Lord, to find in thee
   My everlasting rest?
                        C. WESLEY.

The Christian Life. Glorying in the Cross.

RATHBUN. 8s. & 7s.   GREATOREX'S COLL.

506.   Gal. 6: 14.

1 In the cross of Christ I glory,
   Towering o'er the wrecks of time;
  All the light of sacred story
   Gathers round its head sublime.

2 When the woes of life o'ertake me,
   Hopes deceive, and fears annoy,
  Never shall the cross forsake me:
   Lo! it glows with peace and joy.

3 When the sun of bliss is beaming
   Light and love upon my way,
  From the cross the radiance streaming,
   Adds new lustre to the day.

4 Bane and blessing, pain and pleasure,
   By the cross are sanctified;
  Peace is there, that knows no measure,
   Joys that through all time abide.

5 In the cross of Christ I glory,
   Towering o'er the wrecks of time;
  All the light of sacred story
   Gathers round its head sublime.
                 BOWRING.

507.   1 Cor. 15: 10.

1 Come, thou Fount of every blessing,
   Tune my heart to sing thy grace;
  Streams of mercy, never ceasing,
   Call for songs of loudest praise.

2 Jesus sought me when a stranger,
   Wandering from the fold of God;
  He, to save my soul from danger,
   Interposed his precious blood.

3 Oh! to grace how great a debtor
   Daily I'm constrained to be!
  Let that grace, Lord, like a fetter,
   Bind my wandering heart to thee.

4 Prone to wander, Lord, I feel it;
   Prone to leave the God I love;
  Here's my heart —oh, take and seal it,—
   Seal it from thy courts above.
                 ROBINSON.

508.   Psalm 91.

1 Call Jehovah thy salvation,
   Rest beneath th' Almighty's shade;
  In his secret habitation
   Dwell, and never be dismayed!

2 There no tumult can alarm thee,
   Thou shalt dread no hidden snare;
  Guile nor violence can harm thee,
   In eternal safeguard there.

3 He shall charge his angel legions
   Watch and ward o'er thee to keep,
  Though thou walk through hostile regions,
   Though in desert wilds thou sleep.

4 Since, with firm and pure affection,
   Thou on God hast set thy love,
  With the wings of his protection
   He shall shield thee from above.

5 Thou shalt call on him in trouble,
   He will hearken, he will save;
  Here, for grief reward thee double,
   Crown with life beyond the grave.
                 MONTGOMERY.

Christ unseen but precious. His great Love.

BEMERTON. C. M.   GREATOREX'S COLL.

509.   *1 Peter 1: 8.*

1 Jesus, these eyes have never seen
    That radiant form of thine!
The veil of sense hangs dark between
    Thy blessed face and mine!

2 I see thee not, I hear thee not,
    Yet art thou oft with me;
And earth hath ne'er so dear a spot,
    As where I meet with thee.

3 Like some bright dream that comes un-
    When slumbers o'er me roll, [sought,
Thine image ever fills my thought,
    And charms my ravished soul.

4 Yet though I have not seen, and still
    Must rest in faith alone;
I love thee, dearest Lord! — and will,
    Unseen, but not unknown.

5 When death these mortal eyes shall seal,
    And still this throbbing heart,
The rending veil shall thee reveal,
    All glorious as thou art!
                             Ray Palmer.

510.   *1 Peter 2: 7.*

1 How sweet the name of Jesus sounds
    In a believer's ear!
It soothes his sorrows, heals his wounds,
    And drives away his fear.

2 It makes the wounded spirit whole,
    And calms the troubled breast;
'Tis manna to the hungry soul,
    And to the weary, rest.

3 By thee, my prayers acceptance gain,
    Although with sin defiled;
Satan accuses me in vain,
    And I am owned a child.

4 Weak is the effort of my heart,
    And cold my warmest thought;
But when I see thee as thou art,
    I'll praise thee as I ought.

5 Till then I would thy love proclaim,
    With every fleeting breath;
And may the music of thy name
    Refresh my soul in death.
                             Newton.

511.   *"Can we Forget?"*

1 Jesus! thy love shall we forget,
    And never bring to mind
The grace that paid our hopeless debt,
    And bade us pardon find?

2 Shall we thy life of grief forget,
    Thy fasting and thy prayer,
Thy locks with mountain vapors wet,
    To save us from despair?

3 Gethsemane can we forget,
    Thy struggling agony,
When night lay dark on Olivet,
    And none to watch with thee?

4 Our sorrows and our sins were laid
    On thee, alone on thee:
Thy precious blood our ransom paid, —
    Thine all the glory be!

The Christian Life. Trusting and Rejoicing in Jesus.

CORNER-STONE. L. M. 6l. OLD CHORAL.

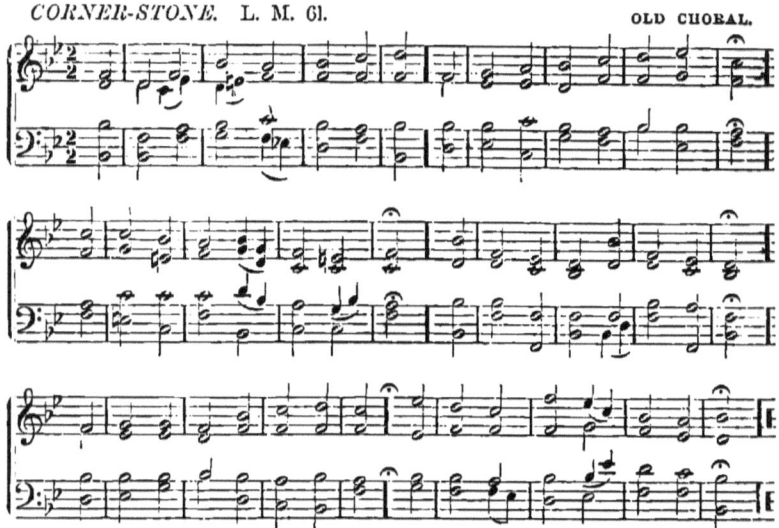

512. *The Solid Rock.*

1 My hope is built on nothing less
  Than Jesus' blood and righteousness;
  I dare not trust the sweetest frame,
  But wholly lean on Jesus' name.
  On Christ, the solid rock, I stand;
  All other ground is sinking sand.

2 When darkness seems to veil his face,
  I rest on his unchanging grace;
  In every high and stormy gale,
  My anchor holds within the veil.
  On Christ, the solid rock, I stand;
  All other ground is sinking sand.

3 His oath, his covenant, and his blood,
  Support me in the whelming flood;
  When all around my soul gives way,
  He then is all my hope and stay.
  On Christ, the solid rock, I stand;
  All other ground is sinking sand.

513. Gen. 32: 24.

1 Come, O thou traveller unknown,
    Whom still I hold but cannot see,
  My company before is gone,
    And I am left alone with thee:
  With thee all night I mean to stay,
  And wrestle till the break of day.

2 I need not tell thee who I am;
    My sin and misery declare;
  Thyself hast called me by my name,
    Look on thy hands and read it there;
  But who, I ask thee, who art thou?
  Tell me thy name, and tell me now.

3 'Tis Love! 'tis Love! thou died'st for
    I hear thy whisper in my heart; [me;
  The morning breaks, the shadows flee;
    Pure, universal Love thou art:
  To me, to all, thy mercies move;
  Thy nature and thy name is Love.

4 My prayer hath power with God; the
    Unspeakable I now receive: [grace
  Through faith I see thee face to face;
    I see thee face to face and live!
  In vain I have not wept and strove;
  Thy nature and thy name is Love.

5 I know thee, Saviour, who thou art,—
    Jesus, the feeble sinner's Friend;
  Nor wilt thou with the night depart,
    But stay and love me to the end;
  Thy mercies never shall remove;
  Thy nature and thy name is Love.
                              WESLEY.

Our High Priest. Christ's Sympathy and Saving Grace. 225

REO. C. M.   DR. MASON.

514.   *Sympathy of Christ.*—Heb. 2: 17.
1 WITH joy we meditate the grace
    Of our High Priest above;
His heart is made of tenderness,
    His bosom glows with love.

2 Touched with a sympathy within,
    He knows our feeble frame;
He knows what sore temptations mean,
    For he hath felt the same.

3 He in the days of feeble flesh
    Poured out his cries and tears;
And in his measure feels afresh
    What every member bears.

4 Then let our humble faith address
    His mercy and his power;
We shall obtain delivering grace,
    In each distressing hour.
                        WATTS.

515.   *Our High Priest.*—Isaiah 49: 16.
1 Now let our cheerful eyes survey
    Our great High Priest above,
And celebrate his constant care
    And sympathetic love.

2 Though raised to a superior throne,
    Where angels bow around,
And high o'er all the shining train,
    With matchless honors crowned;—

3 The names of all his saints he bears
    Engraven on his heart;
Nor shall a name once treasured there
    E'er from his care depart.

4 Those characters shall fair abide,
    Our everlasting trust,
When gems and monuments and crowns
    Are mouldered down to dust.

5 So, gracious Saviour! on my breast,
    May thy dear name be worn,
A sacred ornament and guard,
    To endless ages borne.
                        DODDRIDGE.

516.   1 Cor. 1: 22-24.
1 DEAREST of all the names above,
    My Jesus and my God,
Who can resist thy heavenly love,
    Or trifle with thy blood?

2 'Tis by the merits of thy death
    Thy Father smiles again;
'Tis by thine interceding breath
    The Spirit dwells with men.

3 Till God in human flesh I see,
    My thoughts no comfort find:
The holy, just, and sacred Three
    Are terrors to my mind.

4 But if Immanuel's face appear,
    My hope, my joy, begin:
His name forbids my slavish fear,
    His grace removes my sin.

5 While Jews on their own law rely,
    And Greeks of wisdom boast,
I love th' incarnate Mystery,
    And there I fix my trust.
                        WATTS.

The Christian Life. Christ's Sympathy and Love.

HULLAH. L. M. 6l. Arranged from DONIZETTI.

1. When gath'-ring clouds a-round I view, And days are dark and friends are few,
On Him I lean, who, not in vain, Ex-pe-rienced ev-'ry hu-man pain;
He sees my wants, al-lays my fears, And counts and trea-sures up my tears.

517. *Heb. 4: 15.*

2 If aught should tempt my soul to stray
From heavenly wisdom's narrow way,
To fly the good I would pursue,
Or do the ill I would not do;
Still He who felt temptation's power
Will guard me in that dangerous hour.

3 When sorrowing o'er some stone I bend,
Which covers all that was a friend,
And from his hand, his voice, his smile,
Divides me for a little while;
Thou, Saviour, seest the tears I shed,
For thou didst weep o'er Lazarus dead.

4 And, oh! when I have safely passed
Through every conflict but the last,
Still, still unchanging, watch beside
My painful bed, for thou hast died;
Then point to realms of cloudless day,
And wipe the latest tear away!
GRANT.

518. *The Returning Wanderer.*

1 WEARY of wandering from my God,
  And now made willing to return,
I hear, and bow beneath the rod;

For thee, not without hope, I mourn:
I have an Advocate above,
A Friend before the throne of love.

2 O Jesus, full of truth and grace!
  More full of grace than I of sin;
Yet once again I seek thy face,
Open thine arms and take me in;
And freely my backslidings heal,
And love the faithless sinner still.
WESLEY.

519. *Complete in Christ.*

1 JESUS! thy boundless love to me
  No thought can reach, no tongue declare;
Oh, knit my thankful heart to thee,
  And reign without a rival there!
Thine wholly, thine alone, I live:
Thyself to me, my Saviour, give!

2 What in thy love possess I not?
  My star by night, my sun by day,
My spring of life when parched with drought,
  My wine to cheer, my bread to stay;
My strength, my shield, my safe abode,
My robe before the throne of God.

Praise of Christ's Grace. Prayer for Guidance.

WALDO. 7s.   Arranged from MOZART.

520.   Isaiah 7: 14.

1 SWEETER sounds than music knows
    Charm me in Immanuel's name;
  All her hopes my spirit owes
    To his birth and cross and shame.

2 When he came, the angels sung,
    "Glory be to God on high!"
  Lord! unloose my stammering tongue;
    Who should louder sing than I?

3 Did the Lord a man become
    That he might the law fulfil,
  Bleed and suffer in my room,
    And canst thou, my tongue, be still?

4 No, I must my praises bring,
    Though they worthless are and weak;
  For should I refuse to sing,
    Sure the very stones would speak.

5 O my Saviour, Shield, and Sun,
    Shepherd, Brother, Lord, and Friend,
  Every precious name in one!
    I will love thee without end.
                      NEWTON.

521.   1 Cor. 15: 10.

1 BLESSED fountain, full of grace!
    Grace for sinners, grace for me;
  To this source alone I trace
    What I am and hope to be.

2 What I am, as one redeemed,
    Saved and rescued by the Lord;
  Hating what I once esteemed,
    Loving what I once abhorred.

3 What I hope to be ere long,
    When I take my place above,
  When I join the heavenly throng,
    When I see the God of love.

4 Then I hope like him to be,
    Who redeemed his saints from sin,
  Whom I now obscurely see,
    Through a veil that stands between.

5 Blessed fountain, full of grace!
    Grace for sinners, grace for me;
  To this source alone I trace
    What I am and hope to be.
                      KELLY.

522.   *The Good Shepherd.*

1 JESUS, Shepherd of the sheep;
  Powerful is thine arm to keep
  All thy flocks with safest care,
  Fed in pastures large and fair.

2 Thee their guide and guard they own;
  Thee they love, and thee alone;
  Thee they follow day by day,
  Fearful lest their feet should stray.

3 Lord, thy helpless sheep behold;
  Gather all unto thy fold;
  Gently lead the wanderers home;
  Watch them, lest again they roam.

4 Bring thy sheep, now far astray,
  Lost in Satan's evil way;
  Then, the fold and Shepherd one,
  We shall praise thee round the throne.

The Christian Life. Guidance and Grace besought.

GRACE. 7s.   Arranged from S. X. CHWATAL.

1. Shepherd, with thy tenderest love, Guide me to thy fold above; Let me hear thy gentle voice; More and more in thee rejoice; From thy fulness grace receive, Ever in thy Spirit live.

523.   John 4: 16.

2 Filled by thee my cup o'erflows,
  For thy love no limit knows:
  Guardian angels, ever nigh,
  Lead and draw my soul on high;
  Constant to my latest end,
  Thou my footsteps wilt attend.

3 Jesus, with thy presence blest,
  Death is life, and labor rest;
  Guide me while I draw my breath,
  Guide me through the gate of death,
  And at last, oh, let me stand,
  With the sheep at thy right hand.

524.   Psalm 42.

1 As the hart, with eager looks,
  Panteth for the water-brooks,
  So my soul, athirst for thee,
  Pants the living God to see;
  When, oh, when with filial fear,
  Lord, shall I to thee draw near?

2 Why art thou cast down, my soul?
  God, thy God, shall make thee whole;
  Why art thou disquieted?
  God shall lift thy fallen head,
  And his countenance benign
  Be the saving health of thine.
                    MONTGOMERY.

525.   The Childlike Heart.

1 Quiet, Lord, my froward heart;
  Make me teachable and mild,
  Upright, simple, free from art:
  Make me as a weanèd child,
  From distrust and envy free,
  Pleased with all that pleases thee.

2 What thou shalt to-day provide,
  Let me as a child receive;
  What to-morrow may betide,
  Calmly to thy wisdom leave:
  'Tis enough that thou wilt care;
  Why should I the burden bear?

3 As a little child relies
  On a care beyond his own,
  Knows he's neither strong nor wise,
  Fears to stir a step alone;
  Let me thus with thee abide,
  As my Father, Guard, and Guide.
                    NEWTON.

Prayers for Grace. Looking to Jesus.

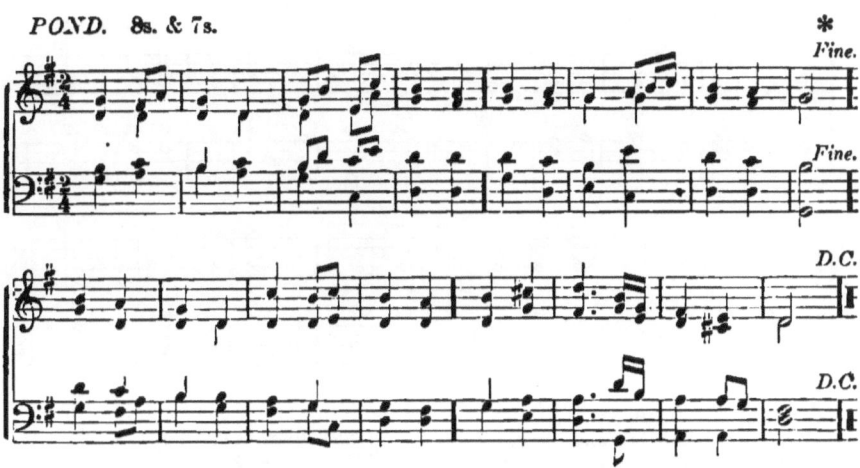

POND. 8s. & 7s.

526. *Isaiah 40: 11.*
1 SAVIOUR, like a shepherd lead us,
　　Much we need thy tender care;
　In thy pleasant pastures feed us;
　　For our use thy folds prepare:
　　　:| Blessed Jesus! |:
　　Thou hast bought us, thine we are.

2 Thou hast promised to receive us,
　　Poor and sinful though we be;
　Thou hast mercy to relieve us,
　　Grace to cleanse and power to free:
　　　Blessed Jesus!
　　Let us early turn to thee.

3 Early let us seek thy favor;
　　Early let us learn thy will;
　Do thou, Lord, our only Saviour,
　　With thy love our bosoms fill:
　　　Blessed Jesus!
　　Thou hast loved us, — love us still!

527. *"Rejoice Always."*
1 O MY soul! what means this sadness?
　　Wherefore art thou thus cast down?
　Let thy griefs be turned to gladness,
　　Bid thy restless fears begone;
　　　:| Look to Jesus, |:
　　And rejoice in his dear name.

2 Though distresses now attend thee,
　　And thou tread'st the thorny road;
　His right hand shall still defend thee;
　　Soon he'll bring thee home to God.

　Therefore praise him,
　Praise the great Redeemer's name.

3 Oh that I could now adore him
　　Like the heavenly host above,
　Who forever bow before him,
　　And unceasing sing his love!
　　　Happy songsters!
　　When shall I your chorus join?
　　　　　　　　　　FAWCETT.

528. *Prayer for Guidance, Pardon, and Joy.*
1 LEAD us, heavenly Father! lead us
　　O'er the world's tempestuous sea;
　Guard us, guide us, keep us, feed us,
　　For we have no help but thee.
　　　Yet possessing
　　　Every blessing,
　　If our God our Father be.

2 Saviour! breathe forgiveness o'er us;
　　All our weakness thou dost know;
　Thou didst tread this earth before us,
　　Thou didst feel its keenest woe.
　　　Lone and dreary,
　　　Faint and weary,
　　Through the desert thou didst go.

3 Spirit of our God descending!
　　Fill our hearts with heavenly joy;
　Love with every passion blending,
　　Pleasure that can never cloy.
　　　Thus provided,
　　　Pardoned, guided,
　　Nothing can our peace destroy.

STILL-WATERS. 7s. DR. MALAN.

529. *Psalm 23.*

1 To thy pastures fair and large,
Heavenly Shepherd, lead thy charge,
And my couch, with tenderest care,
'Mid the springing grass prepare.

2 When I faint with summer's heat,
Thou shalt guide my weary feet
To the streams that, still and slow,
Through the verdant meadows flow.

3 Safe the dreary vale I tread,
By the shades of death o'erspread,
With thy rod and staff supplied,
This my guard, and that my guide.

4 Constant to my latest end,
Thou my footsteps shalt attend;
And shalt bid thy hallowed dome
Yield me an eternal home.
MERRICK.

530. *1 John 4: 19.*

1 Saviour! teach me day by day,
Love's sweet lesson to obey;
Sweeter lesson cannot be,
Loving him who first loved me.

2 With a childlike heart of love,
At thy bidding may I move;
Prompt to serve and follow thee,
Loving him who first loved me.

3 Teach me all thy steps to trace,
Strong to follow in thy grace;
Learning how to love from thee,
Loving him who first loved me.

4 Love in loving finds employ,
In obedience all her joy;
Ever new that joy will be,
Loving him who first loved me.

5 Thus may I rejoice to show
That I feel the love I owe;
Singing, till thy face I see,
Of his love who first loved me.

531. *"Glorify thyself in me."*

1 Father of eternal grace,
Glorify thyself in me:
Meekly beaming in my face,
May the world thine image see.

2 Happy only in thy love,
Poor, unfriended, or unknown,
Fix my thoughts on things above,
Stay my heart on thee alone.

3 Humble, holy, all resigned
To thy will; thy will be done!
Give me, Lord, the perfect mind
Of thy well-beloved Son.

4 Counting gain and glory loss,
May I tread the path he trod, —
Die with Jesus on the cross,
Rise with him to thee, my God.
MONTGOMERY.

Doxology.

Praise the name of God most high,
Praise him, all below the sky;
Praise him, all ye heavenly host,
Father, Son, and Holy Ghost.

Jesus, Love Divine and Light of Men.

AUTUMN. 8s. & 7s.   LUDOVICK NICHOLSON.

532.   *Love Divine.*
1 Love divine, all love excelling,
   Joy of heaven to earth come down,
   Fix in us thy humble dwelling,
   All thy faithful mercies crown.
Jesus, thou art all compassion,
   Pure, unbounded love thou art;
Visit us with thy salvation,
   Enter every trembling heart.

2 Breathe, oh, breathe thy loving spirit
   Into every troubled breast;
Let us all in thee inherit,
   Let us find that Second Rest:
Come, almighty to deliver,
   Let us all thy life receive;
Speedily return, and never,
   Never more thy temples leave.

3 Finish then thy new creation,
   Pure, unspotted may we be;
Let us see thy great salvation
   Perfectly restored in thee:
Changed from glory into glory,
   Till in heaven we take our place,
Till we cast our crowns before thee,
   Lost in wonder, love, and praise.
                       C. WESLEY.

533.   John 1: 9.
1 Light of those whose dreary dwelling
   Borders on the shades of death,
Rise on us, thyself revealing, —
   Rise, and chase the clouds beneath.

2 Thou of heaven and earth Creator,
   In our deepest darkness rise;
Scatter all the night of nature;
   Pour the day upon our eyes.

3 Still we wait for thine appearing;
   Life and joy thy beams impart,
Chasing all our fears, and cheering
   Every poor, benighted heart.

4 By thine all-sufficient merit,
   Every burdened soul release;
Every weary, wandering spirit
   Guide into thy perfect peace.
                       C. WESLEY.

534.   Isaiah 60: 18.
1 Hear what God the Lord hath spoken;
   O my people, faint and few,
Comfortless, afflicted, broken,
   Fair abodes I build for you;
Scenes of heartfelt tribulation
   Shall no more perplex your ways;
You shall name your walls "Salvation,"
   And your gates shall all be "Praise."

2 Ye, no more your suns descending,
   Waning moons no more shall see,
But, your griefs forever ending,
   Find eternal noon in me.
God shall rise, and shining o'er you,
   Change to day the gloom of night;
He, the Lord, shall be your Glory,
   God your everlasting Light.
                       COWPER.

232 *The Christian Life. A Present Saviour. At the Cross.*

STOCKWELL. 8s. & 7s.   D. E. JONES.

535. *"I am with you alway."*—Matt. 28: 20.

1 ALWAYS with us, always with us,—
 Words of cheer and words of love;
Thus the risen Saviour whispers,
 From his dwelling-place above.

2 With us when we toil in sadness,
 Sowing much and reaping none;
Telling us that in the future
 Golden harvests shall be won.

3 With us when the storm is sweeping
 O'er our pathway dark and drear;
Waking hope within our bosoms,
 Stilling every anxious fear.

4 With us in the lonely valley,
 When we cross the chilling stream;
Lighting up the steps to glory
 With salvation's radiant beam.
      NEVIN.

536.   Matt. 27: 36.

1 SWEET the moments, rich in blessing,
 Which before the cross we spend;
Life and health and peace possessing,
 From the sinner's dying Friend.

2 Truly blessed is this station,
 Low before his cross to lie,
While we see divine compassion
 Beaming in his gracious eye.

3 Love and grief our hearts dividing,
 With our tears his feet we bathe;
Constant still, in faith abiding,
 Life deriving from his death.

4 For thy sorrows we adore thee,
 For the pains that wrought our peace;
Gracious Saviour! we implore thee
 In our souls thy love increase.

5 Still in ceaseless contemplation,
 Fix our hearts and eyes on thee,
Till we taste thy full salvation,
 And, unveiled, thy glories see.

537.   Psalm 18: 35.

1 GENTLY, Lord, oh, gently lead us
 Through this lonely vale of tears;
Through the changes thou'st decreed us,
 Till our last, great change appears.

2 When temptation's darts assail us,
 When in devious paths we stray,
Let thy goodness never fail us,
 Lead us in thy perfect way.

3 In the hour of pain and anguish,
 In the hour when death draws near,
Suffer not our hearts to languish,
 Suffer not our souls to fear.

4 And, when mortal life is ended,
 Bid us on thy bosom rest,
Till, by angel-bands attended,
 We awake among the blest.
      HASTINGS.

Doxology.

PRAISE the Father, earth and heaven,
 Praise the Son, the Spirit praise,
As it was, and is, be given
 Glory through eternal days.

Consolation, Blessedness, and Rest in Christ.

BERA. L. M.   ROOT & SWEETSER'S COLL.

538. *Heb. 13: 8.*

1 Sweeter to Jesus when on earth,
  Than angel's praise, the prayers of men;
  And still thou art the same, O Lord,
    The same dear Christ that thou wert then.

2 We have no tears thou wilt not dry;
  We have no wounds thou wilt not heal;
  No sorrows pierce our human hearts,
    That thou, dear Saviour, dost not feel.

3 Thy pity like the dew distils,
  And thy compassion, like the light,
  Our every morning overfills,
    And crowns with stars our every night.

4 Let not the world's rude conflict drown
  The charmèd music of thy voice,
  That calls all weary souls to rest,
    And bids all mourning souls rejoice.
                  HARRIET KIMBALL.

539. *John 19: 25.*

1 Dear Lord, amid the throng that pressed
  Around thee on the cursèd tree,
  Some loyal, loving hearts were there,
    Some pitying eyes that wept for thee.

2 Like them, may we rejoice to own
  Our dying Lord, though crowned with thorn;
  Like thee, thy blessed self, endure
    The cross with all its joy or scorn.

3 Thy cross, thy lonely path below,
  Show what thy brethren all should be,
  Pilgrims on earth, disowned by those
    Who see no beauty, Lord, in thee.

540. *John 17: 24.*

1 Let me be with thee where thou art,
  My Saviour, my eternal Rest;
  Then only will this longing heart
    Be fully and forever blest.

2 Let me be with thee where thou art,
  Thine unveiled glory to behold;
  Then only will this wandering heart
    Cease to be false to thee and cold.

3 Let me be with thee where thou art,
  Where spotless saints thy name adore;
  Then only will this sinful heart
    Be evil and defiled no more.

4 Let me be with thee where thou art,
  Where none can die, where none remove;
  There neither death nor life will part
    Me from thy presence and thy love.

541. *Rest in Christ.*

1 My only Saviour! when I feel
  O'erwhelmed in spirit, faint, oppressed,
  'Tis sweet to tell thee, while I kneel
    Low at thy feet, thou art my rest.

2 I'm weary of the strife within; [test;
  Strong powers against my soul con-
  Oh, let me turn from self and sin
    To thy dear cross, for there is rest!

3 Oh, sweet will be the welcome day,
  When from her toils and woes released,
  My parting soul in death shall say,
    "Now, Lord, I come to thee for rest."

The Christian Life. Christ our Glory and Joy.

ERNAN. L. M.   DR. MASON.

542.   Mark 8: 38.

1 Jesus! and shall it ever be,
   A mortal man ashamed of thee? —
   Ashamed of thee whom angels praise,
   Whose glories shine through endless
      days.

2 Ashamed of Jesus! sooner far
   Let evening blush to own a star;
   He sheds the beams of light divine
   O'er this benighted soul of mine.

3 Ashamed of Jesus! that dear Friend
   On whom my hopes of heaven depend!
   No; — when I blush, be this my shame,
   That I no more revere his name.

4 Ashamed of Jesus! yes, I may,
   When I've no guilt to wash away;
   No tear to wipe, no good to crave,
   No fears to quell, no soul to save.

5 Till then — nor is my boasting vain —
   Till then I boast a Saviour slain!
   And oh, may this my glory be,
   That Christ is not ashamed of me!
                          GREGG.

543.   Delight in Christ.

1 Jesus, thou joy of loving hearts!
     Thou Fount of life! thou Light of
       men!
   From the best bliss that earth imparts,
   We turn unfilled to thee again.

2 Thy truth unchanged hath ever stood;
    Thou savest those that on thee call;
   To them that seek thee thou art good,
    To them that find thee, All in all!

3 We taste thee, O thou Living Bread,
   And long to feast upon thee still;
   We drink of thee, the Fountain Head,
   And thirst our souls from thee to fill.

4 Our restless spirits yearn for thee,
   Where'er our changeful lot is cast;
   Glad, when thy gracious smile we see,
   Blest, when our faith can hold thee
      fast.

5 O Jesus, ever with us stay,
   Make all our moments calm and bright;
   Chase the dark night of sin away, —
   Shed o'er the world thy holy light!
                    BERNARD BY PALMER.

544.   Col. 1: 19.

1 Fountain of grace, rich, full, and free,
   What need I that is not in thee?
   Full pardon, strength to meet the day,
   And peace which none can take away.

2 Doth sickness fill the heart with fear?
   'Tis sweet to know that thou art near;
   Am I with dread of justice tried?
   'Tis sweet to feel that Christ hath died.

3 In life, thy promises of aid
   Forbid my heart to be afraid;
   In death, peace gently veils the eyes;
   Christ rose, and I shall surely rise.

4 O all sufficient Saviour! be
   This all-sufficiency to me;
   Nor pain, nor sin, nor death can harm
   The weakest, shielded by thine arm.

Looking to Jesus, our Leader and Saviour.

JESUS STILL LEAD ON. 8s. & 5s. — ADAM DRESE, 1680.

545. Luke 5: 11.

1 Jesus, still lead on
  Till our rest be won;
  And although the way be cheerless,
  We will follow, calm and fearless:
  Guide us by thy hand
  To our Fatherland!

2 If the way be drear,
  If the foe be near,
  Let not faithless fears o'ertake us,
  Let not faith and hope forsake us;
  For, through many a foe,
  To our home we go!

3 When we seek relief
  From a long-felt grief;
  When temptations come alluring,
  Make us patient and enduring:
  Show us that bright shore
  Where we weep no more!

4 Jesus, still lead on,
  Till our rest be won;
  Heavenly Leader, still direct us,
  Still support, console, protect us,
  Till we safely stand
  In our Fatherland!

  ZINZENDORF.

OLIVET. 6s. & 4s. — DR. MASON.

1. My faith looks up to thee, Thou Lamb of Calvary, Saviour divine! Now hear me while I pray; Take all my guilt away; Oh, let me, from this day, Be wholly thine!
2. May thy rich grace impart Strength to my fainting heart; My zeal inspire; As thou hast died for me, Oh! may my love to thee Pure, warm, and changeless be — A living fire.

546.

3 While life's dark maze I tread,
  And griefs around me spread, Be thou my guide;
  Bid darkness turn to day, Wipe sorrow's tears away,
  Nor let me ever stray From thee aside.

4 When ends life's transient dream,
  When death's cold, sullen stream Shall o'er me roll;
  Blest Saviour, then, in love, Fear and distrust remove;
  Oh, bear me safe above — A ransomed soul.

  RAY PALMER.

The Christian Life. Jesus' Dying Sorrow and Love.

O SACRED HEAD. 7s. & 6s.   OLD GERMAN CHORAL.

547.   *"O Sacred Head."*

1 O SACRED Head, now wounded,
   With grief and shame weighed down;
Now scornfully surrounded
   With thorns, thy only crown;
O sacred Head, what glory,
   What bliss till now was thine!
Yet though despised and gory,
   I joy to call thee mine.

2 O noblest brow and dearest,
   In other days the world
All feared when thou appearedst;
   What shame on thee is hurled;
How art thou pale with anguish,
   With sore abuse and scorn!
How does that visage languish
   Which once was bright as morn!

3 What language shall I borrow,
   To thank thee, dearest Friend,
For this thy dying sorrow,
   Thy pity without end?
Oh, make me thine forever,
   And should I fainting be,
Lord, let me never, never
   Outlive my love to thee.

4 If I, a wretch, should leave thee,
   O Jesus, leave not me;
In faith may I receive thee,
   When death shall set me free.
When strength and comfort languish
   And I must hence depart,
Release me then from anguish,
   By thine own wounded heart.

5 Be near when I am dying,
   Oh, show thy cross to me!
And for my succor flying,
   Come, Lord, to set me free.
These eyes new faith receiving,
   From Jesus shall not move;
For he who dies believing
   Dies safely — through thy love.

                     PAUL GERHARDT 1656

Longing to know Christ fully. Abiding in Christ.

GERMANIA. 7s. & 6s.

1. O Christ, I long to know thee, As thou art known above; Long, face to face, to show thee, In faultless praise my love. But thou thyself now hidest Beyond my feeble sense; Though all my steps thou guidest, Thine arm my sure defence.

548. *Longing to see Christ.*

2 O'erpowering is the splendor
  Of thy pure unveiled throne,
Where bright archangels render
  A service all their own ;
That glory, sight-confounding,
  Those wonders rich and rare,
The anthems high-resounding,
  This mortal could not bear.

3 Yet, Lord, to see thee, pining,
  In thought I oft ascend,
And where thy hosts are shining,
  I, too, before thee bend.
As one all sweetly dreaming,
  Celestial bliss I feel;
And in that moment's seeming,
  Glow with a seraph's zeal.

4 When from this dream awaking,
  A weary pilgrim still,
Sloth from my spirit shaking,
  With fixed, unfaltering will,
My soul, in courage stronger,
  Holds on her toilsome way,
Content to watch yet longer,
  Till dawns the wished-for day.

549. *Abiding in Christ.*

1 O LAMB of God! still keep me
  Near to thy wounded side;
'Tis only there in safety
  And peace I can abide !
What foes and snares surround me!
  What doubts and fears within!
The grace that sought and found me
  Alone can keep me clean.

2 'Tis only in thee hiding,
  I feel my life secure, —
Only in thee abiding,
  The conflict can endure ;
Thine arm the victory gaineth
  O'er every hateful foe;
Thy love my heart sustaineth
  In all its care and woe.

3 Soon shall my eyes behold thee,
  With rapture, face to face ;
One half hath not been told me
  Of all thy power and grace ;
Thy beauty, Lord, and glory,
  The wonders of thy love,
Shall be the endless story
  Of all thy saints above.

238 The Christian Life. Christ our Refuge and Trust.

LITANY. 7s. HEROLD.

550. *Christ a Refuge.*

1 JESUS, Lover of my soul,
　Let me to thy bosom fly,
While the nearer waters roll,
　While the tempest still is high.
Hide me, O my Saviour, hide,
　Till the storm of life is past;
Safe into the haven guide;
　Oh, receive my soul at last.

2 Other refuge have I none;
　Hangs my helpless soul on thee;
Leave, ah, leave me not alone;
　Still support and comfort me:
All my trust on thee is stayed,
　All my help from thee I bring;
Cover my defenceless head
　With the shadow of thy wing.

3 Thou, O Christ, art all I want;
　More than all in thee I find:
Raise the fallen, cheer the faint,
　Heal the sick, and lead the blind.
Just and holy is thy name;
　I am all unrighteousness;
False and full of sin I am;
　Thou art full of truth and grace.

4 Plenteous grace with thee is found,—
　Grace to cover all my sin;
Let the healing streams abound;
　Make and keep me pure within.
Thou of life the fountain art;
　Freely let me take of thee;
Spring thou up within my heart:
　Rise to all eternity.
　　　　　　　　　C. WESLEY.

551. *Phil. 1: 21.*

1 CHRIST, of all my hopes the ground,
　Christ, the spring of all my joy,
Still in thee let me be found,
　Still for thee my powers employ.

2 Fountain of o'erflowing grace,
　Freely from thy fulness give:
Till I close my earthly race,
　Be it "Christ for me to live."

3 When I touch the blessed shore,
　Back the closing waves shall roll;
Death's dark stream shall never more
　Part from thee my ravished soul.

4 Thus, oh, thus an entrance give
　To the land of cloudless sky!
Having known it "Christ to live,"
　Let me know it "gain to die."
　　　　　　　　　WINDHAM.

ROCK OF AGES.

DR. HASTINGS.

552.   1 Cor. 10: 4.

1 Rock of Ages! cleft for me;
Let me hide myself in thee!
Let the water and the blood,
From thy riven side that flowed,
Be of sin the double cure, —
Cleanse me from its guilt and power.

2 Could my zeal no respite know,
Could my tears forever flow,
All for sin could not atone:
Thou must save, and thou alone!
Nothing in my hand I bring;
Simply to thy cross I cling.

3 While I draw this fleeting breath,
When my eyelids close in death,
When I soar to worlds unknown,
See thee on thy judgment throne, —
Rock of Ages! cleft for me,
Let me hide myself in thee!
TOPLADY.

553.   *"Have Pity on me!"*

1 Pity, Lord! the child of clay,
Who can only weep and pray, —
Only on thy love depend:
Thou who art the sinner's Friend, —
Thou the sinner's only plea, —
Jesus, Saviour, pity me!

2 From thy flock, a straying lamb,
Tender Shepherd, though I am,
Now upon the mountain cold,
Lost, I long to gain the fold,
And within thine arms to be:
Jesus, Saviour, pity me!

3 Oh, where stillest streams are poured,
In green pastures lead me, Lord!
Bring me back, where angels sound
Joy to the poor wanderer found;
Evermore my Shepherd be:
Jesus, Saviour, pity me!

554.   *Conflict with Sin.*

1 Once I thought my mountain strong,
   Firmly fixed, no more to move;
Then my Saviour was my song,
   Then my soul was filled with love:
Those were happy, golden days,
Sweetly spent in prayer and praise.

2 Little then myself I knew,
   Little thought of Satan's power;
Now I feel my sins anew,
   Now I feel the stormy hour:
Sin has put my joys to flight,
Sin has turned my day to night.

3 Saviour! shine and cheer my soul,
   Bid my dying hopes revive;
Make my wounded spirit whole;
   Far away the tempter drive:
Speak the word, and set me free:
Let me live alone to thee.
NEWTON.

BETHANY. 6s. & 4s.   DR. MASON.

555.   Gen. 28: 10-22.

1 NEARER, my God, to thee,
   Nearer to thee:
Ev'n though it be a cross
   That raiseth me,
Still all my song shall be,
Nearer, my God, to thee,
   Nearer to thee.

2 Though like a wanderer,
   Daylight all gone,
Darkness be over me,
   My rest a stone,
Yet in my dreams I'd be
Nearer, my God, to thee,
   Nearer to thee.

3 There let the way appear
   Steps up to heaven;
All that thou sendest me
   In mercy given,
Angels to beckon me
Nearer, my God, to thee,
   Nearer to thee.

4 Then with my waking thoughts,
   Bright with thy praise,
Out of my stony griefs,
   Bethel I'll raise;
So by my woes to be
Nearer, my God, to thee,
   Nearer to thee.

5 Or if on joyful wing,
   Cleaving the sky,
Sun, moon, and stars forgot,
   Upward I fly,
Still all my song shall be,
Nearer, my God, to thee,
   Nearer to thee.
                S. F. ADAMS.

556.   Psalm 39: 12.

1 I'M but a stranger here,
   Heaven is my home;
Earth is a desert drear,
   Heaven is my home:
Danger and sorrow stand
Round me on every hand;
Heaven is my fatherland, —
   Heaven is my home.

2 What though the tempest rage,
   Heaven is my home;
Short is my pilgrimage,
   Heaven is my home:
Time's cold and wintry blast
Soon will be overpast;
I shall reach home at last;
   Heaven is my home.

3 There, at my Saviour's side,
   Heaven is my home;
I shall be glorified,
   Heaven is my home:
There are the good and blest,
Those I loved most and best,
And there I, too, shall rest;
   Heaven is my home!
                T. R. TAYLOR.

CALM. S. M. HANDEL POND.

557. Psalm 31.

1 My spirit on thy care,
   Blest Saviour, I recline;
   Thou wilt not leave me to despair,
   For thou art love divine.

2 In thee I place my trust;
   On thee I calmly rest:
   I know thee good, I know thee just,
   And count thy choice the best.

3 Whate'er events betide,
   Thy will they all perform;
   Safe in thy breast my head I hide,
   Nor fear the coming storm.

4 Let good or ill befall,
   It must be good for me,—
   Secure of having thee in all,
   Of having all in thee.
                                    LYTE.

558. Psalm 23.

1 While my Redeemer's near,
   My Shepherd and my Guide,
   I bid farewell to anxious fear:
   My wants are all supplied.

2 To ever fragrant meads,
   Where rich abundance grows,
   His gracious hand indulgent leads,
   And guards my sweet repose.

3 Dear Shepherd, if I stray,
   My wand'ring feet restore;
   And guard me with thy watchful eye,
   And let me rove no more.
                                    MRS. STEELE.

559. 2 Cor. 5: 7.

1 If through unruffled seas
   Toward heav'n we calmly sail,
   With grateful hearts, O God, to thee,
   We'll own the fost'ring gale.

2 But should the surges rise,
   And rest delay to come,
   Blest be the sorrow, kind the storm,
   Which drives us nearer home.

3 Soon shall our doubts and fears
   All yield to thy control;
   Thy tender mercies shall illume
   The midnight of the soul.

4 Teach us, in every state,
   To make thy will our own;
   And when the joys of sense depart,
   To live by faith alone.

560. Phil. 4: 13.

1 O Saviour, who didst come
   By water and by blood;
   Confessed on earth, adored in heaven,
   Eternal Son of God!

2 By faith in thee we live,
   By faith in thee we stand;
   By thee we vanquish sin and death,
   And gain the heavenly land.

3 O Lord, increase our faith,
   Our fearful spirits calm;
   Sustain us through this mortal strife,
   Then give the victor's palm!

The Christian Life. Waiting on God.

ST. BRIDE'S. S. M. — DR. HOWARD, 1782.

561. Psalm 25.

1 MINE eyes and my desire
  Are ever to the Lord;
  I love to plead his promises,
  And rest upon his word.

2 Lord, turn thee to my soul;
  Bring thy salvation near:
  When will thy hand release my feet
  From sin's destructive snare?

3 When shall the sovereign grace
  Of my forgiving God
  Restore me from those dangerous ways
  My wandering feet have trod?

4 Oh, keep my soul from death,
  Nor put my hope to shame!
  For I have placed my only trust
  In my Redeemer's name.

5 With humble faith I wait
  To see thy face again;
  Of Israel it shall ne'er be said,
  He sought the Lord in vain.
                              WATTS.

562. John 13: 7.

1 ALONG my earthly way,
  How many clouds are spread!
  Darkness, with scarce one cheerful ray,
  Seems gathering o'er my head.

2 Yet, Father, thou art Love;
  Oh, hide not from my view!
  But when I look, in prayer, above,
  Appear in mercy through!

3 My pathway is not hid;
  Thou knowest all my need;
  And I would do as Israel did,—
  Follow where thou wilt lead.

4 Lead me, and then my feet
  Shall never, never stray;
  But safely I shall reach the seat
  Of happiness and day.

5 And oh, from that bright throne
  I shall look back, and see,—
  The path I went, and that alone,
  Was the right path for me.
                              EDMESTON.

563. Psalm 61.

1 WHEN overwhelmed with grief,
  My heart within me dies;
  Helpless, and far from all relief,
  To heaven I lift mine eyes.

2 Oh, lead me to the Rock
  That's high above my head,
  And make the covert of thy wings
  My shelter and my shade!

3 Within thy presence, Lord,
  Forever I'll abide;
  Thou art the tower of my defence,
  The refuge where I hide.

4 Thou givest me the lot
  Of those that fear thy name;
  If endless life be their reward,
  I shall possess the same.
                              WATTS.

Pressing Homeward. Watchfulness. Purity.

DANA. S. M.   E. P. PARKER.

564.   *Psalm 137.*
1. FAR from my heavenly home,
 Far from my Father's breast,
 Fainting, I cry, "Blest Spirit, come,
 And speed me to my rest!"

2. Upon the willows long
 My harp has silent hung;
 How should I sing a cheerful song,
 Till thou inspire my tongue?

3. My spirit homeward turns,
 And fain would thither flee;
 My heart, O Zion, droops and yearns,
 When I remember thee.

4. To thee, to thee I press,—
 A dark and toilsome road:
 When shall I pass the wilderness,
 And reach the saint's abode?

5. God of my life, be near;
 On thee my hopes I cast:
 Oh, guide me through the desert here,
 And bring me home at last!
                        LYTE.

565.   *Psalm 126.*
1. THE harvest dawn is near,
 The year delays not long;
 And he who sows with many a tear
 Shall reap with many a song.

2. Sad to his toil he goes,
 His seed with weeping leaves;
 But he shall come at twilight's close,
 And bring his golden sheaves.
                        BURGESS.

566.   *Keeping Guard.*
1. LET us keep steadfast guard
 With lighted hearts all night,
 That when Christ comes, we stand prepared,
 And meet him with delight.

2. At midnight's season chill
 Lay Paul and Silas bound,—
 Bound, and in prison sang they still,
 And, singing, freedom found.

3. Our prison is this earth,
 And yet we sing to thee:
 Break sin's strong fetters, lead us forth,
 Set us, believing, free!

4. Meet for thy realm in heaven,
 Make us, O holy King!
 That through the ages it be given
 To us thy praise to sing.
                        BREVIARY.

567.   *Matt. 5 : 8.*
1. BLEST are the pure in heart,
 For they shall see their God;
 The secret of the Lord is theirs,
 Their soul is Christ's abode.

2. He to the lowly soul
 Doth still himself impart;
 And for his dwelling and his throne,
 Chooseth the pure in heart.

3. Lord, we thy presence seek:
 May ours this blessing be;
 Oh, give the pure and lowly heart
 A temple meet for thee!

The Christian Life. Songs in the Night.

ZAMORA. 8s. & 7s.

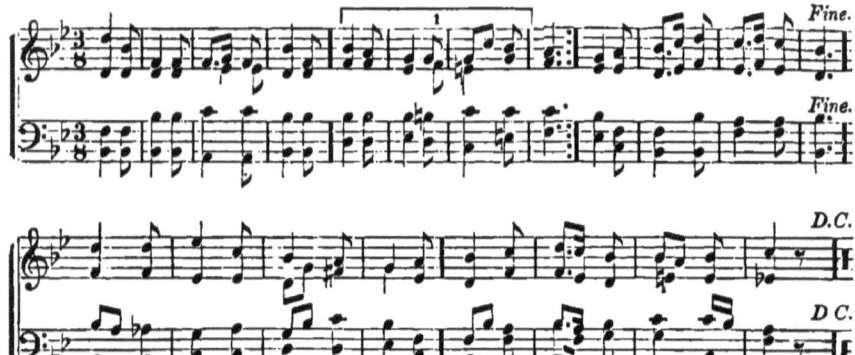

568. *Pressing Forward.*

1 PILGRIMS in this vale of sorrow
Pressing onward toward the prize,
Strength and comfort here we borrow
From the Hand that rules the skies.

2 'Mid these scenes of self-denial,
We are called the race to run;
We must meet full many a trial
Ere the victor's crown is won.

3 Love shall every conflict lighten,
Hope shall urge us swifter on,
Faith shall every prospect brighten,
Till the morn of heaven shall dawn.

4 On the eternal arm reclining,
We, at length, shall win the day;
All the powers of earth combining
Shall not snatch our crown away.
HASTINGS.

569. *Zeal Rewarded.* —Psalm 126: 6.

1 HE that goeth forth with weeping,
Bearing precious seed in love,
Never tiring, never sleeping,
Findeth mercy from above.

2 Soft descend the dews of heaven,
Bright the rays celestial shine;
Precious fruits will thus be given,
Through an influence all divine.

3 Sow thy seed, be never weary,
Let no fears thy soul annoy;
Be the prospect ne'er so dreary,
Thou shalt reap the fruits of joy.

4 Lo, the scene of verdure brightening!
See the rising grain appear;
Look again! the fields are whitening,
For the harvest time is near.
HASTINGS.

570. John 15: 4.

1 ALL is dying; hearts are breaking,
Which to ours were closely bound;
And the lips have ceased from speaking
Which once uttered such sweet sound;

2 And the arms are powerless lying,
Which were our support and stay;
And the eyes are dim and dying, [day.
Which once watched us night and

3 Everything we love and cherish
Hastens onward to the grave;
Earthly joys and pleasures perish,
And whate'er the world e'er gave.

4 All is fading, all is fleeing;
Earthly flames must cease to glow,
Earthly beings cease from being,
Earthly blossoms cease to blow.

5 Yet unchanged, while all decayeth
Jesus stands upon the dust;
Lean on me alone, he sayeth;
Hope and love and firmly trust.

6 Oh, abide, abide with Jesus,
Who himself forever lives,
Who from death eternal frees us,
Yea, who life eternal gives!

The Peace of Christ. Activity. Watchfulness.

INVERNESS. S. M.   DR. MASON.

571. *Sincerity and Watchfulness.*—Psalm 19.

1 I HEAR thy word with love,
   And I would fain obey;
Send thy good Spirit from above,
   To guide me lest I stray.

2 Warn me of every sin,
   Forgive my secret faults,
And cleanse this guilty soul of mine,
   Whose crimes exceed my thoughts.

3 While with my heart and tongue
   I spread thy praise abroad,
Accept the worship and the song,
   My Saviour and my God.
                              WATTS.

572.   John 14: 27.

1 LET not your heart be faint,
   My peace I give to you,—
Such peace as reason never planned,
   Nor sinners ever knew.

2 It tells of joys to come;
   It soothes the troubled breast;
It shines, a star amid the storm,—
   The harbinger of rest.

3 Then murmur not, nor mourn,
   My people faint and few;
Though earth to its foundation shake,
   My peace I leave with you.

573. *Trustful Activity.*—Eccl. 11: 6.

1 Sow in the morn thy seed,
   At eve hold not thy hand;
To doubt and fear give thou no heed;
   Broadcast it o'er the land.

2 Then duly shall appear,
   In verdure, beauty, strength,
The tender blade, the stalk, the ear,
   And the full corn at length.

3 Thou canst not toil in vain;
   Cold, heat, and moist, and dry,
Shall foster and mature the grain
   For garners in the sky.

4 Then, when the glorious end,
   The day of God shall come,
The angel-reapers shall descend,
   And heaven sing, "Harvest home!"
                            MONTGOMERY.

574.   *Watchfulness.*

1 A CHARGE to keep I have,
   A God to glorify,
A never-dying soul to save,
   And fit it for the sky.

2 To serve the present age,
   My calling to fulfil;
Oh, may it all my powers engage
   To do my Master's will.

3 Arm me with jealous care,
   As in thy sight to live;
And oh, thy servant, Lord, prepare
   A strict account to give.

4 Help me to watch and pray,
   And on thyself rely;
Assured, if I my trust betray,
   I shall forever die.
                            C. WESLEY.

The Christian Life. Comfort and Rest in Christ.

SEYMOUR. 7s.   WEBER.

575.   *Psalm 55.*

1 Cast thy burden on the Lord;
Lean thou only on his word:
Ever will he be thy stay,
Though the heavens shall melt away.

2 Ever in the raging storm,
Thou shalt see his cheering form,
Hear his pledge of coming aid:
"It is I, be not afraid."

3 Cast thy burden at his feet;
Linger near his mercy-seat:
He will lead thee by the hand
Gently to the better land.

4 He will gird thee by his power,
In thy weary, fainting hour;
Lean, then, loving, on his word;
Cast thy burden on the Lord.

576.   *Rest in Christ.*

1 Does the gospel word proclaim
Rest for those that weary be?
Then, my soul, advance thy claim,—
Sure that promise speaks to thee!

2 Marks of grace I cannot show,
All polluted is my best;
But I weary am, I know,
And the weary long for rest.

3 Burdened with a load of sin,
Harassed with tormenting doubt,
Hourly conflicts from within,
Hourly crosses from without;—

4 All my little strength is gone,
Sink I must without supply;
Sure upon the earth is none
Can more weary be than I.

5 In the ark the weary dove
Found a welcome resting-place;
Thus my spirit longs to prove
Rest in Christ, the Ark of grace.

6 Tempest-tossed I long have been,
And the flood increases fast;
Open, Lord, and take me in,
Till the storm be overpast!
                        Newton.

577.   *John 21: 16.*

1 Hark, my soul! it is the Lord;
'Tis thy Saviour; hear his word;
Jesus speaks, and speaks to thee;
"Say, poor sinner, lov'st thou me?

2 "Mine is an unchanging love,
Higher than the heights above,
Deeper than the depths beneath,
Free and faithful, strong as death.

3 "Thou shalt see my glory soon,
When the work of grace is done;
Partner of my throne shalt be:
Say, poor sinner, lov'st thou me?"

4 Lord! it is my chief complaint
That my love is cold and faint;
Yet I love thee, and adore:
Oh for grace to love thee more!
                        Cowper.

HORTON. 7s.   GERMAN.

578.   *The Arm of Strength.*
1 EVERLASTING arms of love
  Are beneath, around, above:
  He who left his throne of light,
  And unnumbered angels bright;

2 He who on th' accursèd tree
  Gave his precious life for me, —
  He it is that bears me on,
  His the arm I lean upon.

3 He who now enthroned above,
  Still retains his heart of love,
  Marking still each falling tear
  Of his burdened pilgrims here;

4 He who wields creation's rod,
  He my Brother, yet my God;
  Faithful he, whate'er betide,
  Is my everlasting Guide!

5 Scenes will vary, friends grow strange,
  But the changeless cannot change:
  Gladly will I journey on,
  With his arm to lean upon.
                        MACDUFF.

579.   *Heb. 12: 6–11.*
1 'TIS my happiness below,
  Not to live without the cross,
  But the Saviour's power to know,
  Sanctifying every loss.

2 Trials must and will befall;
  But, with humble faith to see
  Love inscribed upon them all, —
  This is happiness to me.

3 Trials make the promise sweet;
  Trials give new life to prayer;
  Trials bring me to his feet,
  Lay me low, and keep me there.
                        COWPER.

580.   *Jesus our Refuge.*
1 WHEN along life's thorny road,
  Faints the soul beneath the load,
  By its cares and sins oppressed,
  Finds on earth no peace or rest;

2 When the wily tempter's near,
  Filling us with doubts and fear:
  Jesus, to thy feet we flee,
  Jesus, we will look to thee.

3 Thou, our Saviour, from the throne
  List'nest to thy people's moan;
  Thou, the living Head, dost share
  Every pang thy members bear.

4 Full of tenderness thou art,
  Thou wilt heal the broken heart;
  Full of power, thine arm shall quell
  All the rage and might of hell.

5 Mighty to redeem and save,
  Thou hast overcome the grave;
  Thou the bars of death hast riven,
  Opened wide the gate of heaven.

6 Soon in glory thou shalt come,
  Taking thy poor pilgrims home:
  Jesus, then we all shall be,
  Ever, ever, Lord, with thee!

HATTON. 7s.

581. *Son of Mary.*

1 When our heads are bowed with woe,
When our bitter tears o'erflow;
When we mourn the lost, the dear,
Jesus, Son of Mary, hear!

2 Thou our throbbing flesh hast worn,
Thou our mortal griefs hast borne;
Thou hast shed the human tear;
Jesus, Son of Mary, hear!

3 When the heart is sad within,
With the thought of all its sin:
When the spirit shrinks with fear,
Jesus, Son of Mary, hear!

4 Thou the shame, the grief hast known,
Though the sins were not thine own;
Thou hast deigned their load to bear;
Jesus, Son of Mary, hear!

5 When the solemn death-bell tolls
For our own departing souls;
When our final doom is near,
Jesus, Son of Mary, hear!

6 Thou hast bowed the dying head,
Thou the blood of life hast shed;
Thou hast filled a mortal bier;
Jesus, Son of Mary, hear!
                          HEBER.

582. 2 Cor. 1: 5.

1 In the dark and cloudy day,
When earth's riches flee away,
And the last hope will not stay,
O my Saviour, comfort me!

2 When the secret idol's gone,
That my poor heart yearned upon,—
Desolate, bereft, alone,
O my Saviour, comfort me!

3 Thou who wast so sorely tried,
In the darkness crucified,
Bid me in thy love confide;
O my Saviour, comfort me!

4 Comfort me! I am cast down;
'Tis my heavenly Father's frown;
I deserve it all, I own;
O my Saviour, comfort me!

5 So, it shall be good for me
Much afflicted now to be,
If thou wilt but tenderly,
O my Saviour, comfort me!

583. John 14: 27.

1 Prince of peace! control my will;
Bid this struggling heart be still;
Bid my fears and doubtings cease;
Hush my spirit into peace.

2 Thou hast bought me with thy blood,
Opened wide the gate to God;
Peace I ask,— but peace must be,
Lord, in being one with thee.

3 May thy will, not mine, be done;
May thy will and mine be one:
Chase these doubtings from my heart;
Now thy perfect peace impart.

Rest in Christ. Prayer for Strength.

COMFORT. 11s. & 10s.

584. Matt. 11: 28.

1 COME unto me, when shadows darkly gather,
  When the sad heart is weary and distressed;
  Seeking for comfort from your heavenly Father,
  Come unto me, and I will give you rest.

2 Large are the mansions in our Father's dwelling,
  Glad are those homes that sorrows never dim;
  Sweet are the harps in holy music swelling,
  Soft are the tones that raise the heavenly hymn.

3 There, like an Eden blossoming in gladness,
  Bloom the fair flowers by earth so rudely pressed;
  Come unto him, all ye who droop in sadness,
  "Come unto me, and I will give you rest."

585. *Prayer for Strength, etc.*

1 LORD, we have wandered forth through doubt and sorrow,
  And thou hast made each step an onward one;
  And we will ever trust each unknown morrow, —
  Thou wilt sustain us till its work is done.

2 O Father, now in thy dear presence kneeling,
  Our spirits yearn to feel thy kindling love;
  Now make us strong through thine own deep revealing
  Of trust and strength and calmness from above.

586. John 12: 21.

1 WE would see Jesus, for the shadows lengthen
  Across this little landscape of our life;
  We would see Jesus our weak faith to strengthen,
  For the last weariness, the final strife.

2 We would see Jesus, the great Rock Foundation,
  Whereon our feet were set by sovereign grace;
  Not life, nor death, with all their agitation,
  Can thence remove us, if we see his face.

3 We would see Jesus; other lights are fading,
  Which for long years we have rejoiced to see;
  The blessings of our pilgrimage are failing,
  We would not mourn them, for we go to thee.

4 We would see Jesus; this is all we're needing,
  Strength, joy, and willingness come with the sight;
  We would see Jesus, dying, risen, pleading,
  Then welcome day, and farewell mortal night.

GREENFIELD. L. M.   WM. MASON.
Quartette.

587. *The Assaults of Temptation.*

1 The billows swell, the winds are high,
   Clouds overcast my wintry sky;
   Out of the depths to thee I call;
   My fears are great, my strength is small.

2 O Lord, the pilot's part perform,
   And guide and guard me through the storm;
   Defend me from each threatening ill,
   Control the waves; say, "Peace be still!"

3 Amid the roaring of the sea,
   My soul still hangs her hope on thee;
   Thy constant love, thy faithful care,
   Is all that saves me from despair.

4 Though tempest-tossed, and half a wreck,
   My Saviour through the floods I seek;
   Let neither winds nor stormy main,
   Force back my shattered bark again.
                              COWPER.

588.   Luke 10: 39.

1 Oh that I could forever dwell,
   Delighted at the Saviour's feet;
   Behold the form I love so well,
   And all his tender words repeat!

2 The world shut out from all my soul,
   And heaven brought in with all its bliss,
   Oh, is there aught, from pole to pole,
   One moment to compare with this?

3 This is the hidden life I prize,
   A life of penitential love;
   When most my follies I despise,
   And raise my highest thoughts above;

4 When all I am I clearly see,
   And freely own, with deepest shame;
   When the Redeemer's love to me
   Kindles within a deathless flame.

5 Thus would I live till nature fail,
   And all my former sins forsake;
   Then rise to God within the veil,
   And of eternal joys partake.
                              REED.

589.   James 5: 13.

1 God of my life, to thee I call!
   Afflicted, at thy feet I fall;
   When the great water-floods prevail,
   Leave not my trembling heart to fail.

2 Friend of the friendless and the faint,
   Where should I lodge my deep complaint?
   Where, but with thee, whose open door
   Invites the helpless and the poor?

3 Did ever mourner plead with thee,
   And thou refuse that mourner's plea?
   Does not the word still fixed remain,
   That none shall seek thy face in vain?

4 That were a grief I could not bear,
   Didst thou not hear and answer prayer;
   But a prayer-hearing, answering God
   Supports me under every load.
                              COWPER.

Submission to the Lord's Leadings and Dealings.

WEBSTER. 6s. Arranged from WEBER.

590. *Submission.*

1 My Jesus, as thou wilt!
  Oh, may thy will be mine!
  Into thy hand of love
  I would my all resign.
  Through sorrow or through joy,
  Conduct me as thine own,
  And help me still to say,
  My Lord, thy will be done!

2 My Jesus, as thou wilt!
  Though seen through many a tear,
  Let not my star of hope
  Grow dim or disappear.
  Thou, Lord, on earth along
  The thorny path hast gone;
  Then lead me after thee;—
  My Lord, thy will be done!

3 My Jesus, as thou wilt!
  When death itself draws nigh,
  To thy dear wounded side
  I would for refuge fly.
  Leaning on thee, to go
  Where thou before hast gone;
  The rest as thou shalt please;—
  My Lord, thy will be done!

4 My Jesus, as thou wilt!
  All shall be well with me:
  Each changing future scene
  I gladly trust with thee.
  Straight to my home above
  I travel calmly on;
  And sing, in life and death,
  My Lord, thy will be done!
  SCHMOLK.

591. Prov. 3: 6.

1 Thy way, not mine, O Lord,
  However dark it be;
  Lead me by thine own hand,
  Choose out the path for me.
  The kingdom that I seek
  Is thine: so let the way
  That leads to it be thine,
  Else surely I must stray.

2 Take thou my cup, and it
  With joy or sorrow fill,
  As best to thee may seem;
  Choose thou my good and ill.
  Not mine, not mine the choice
  In things or great or small;
  Be thou my guide, my strength,
  My wisdom, and my all.
  BONAR.

The Christian Life. Sickness and Affliction.

NAOMI. C. M.   DR. MASON.

592.   *The Request.*

1 FATHER! whate'er of earthly bliss
    Thy sovereign will denies,
Accepted at thy throne of grace,
    Let this petition rise : —

2 "Give me a calm, a thankful heart,
    From every murmur free!
The blessings of thy grace impart,
    And make me live to thee.

3 "Let the sweet hope that thou art mine,
    My life and death attend;   [shine,
Thy presence through my journey
    And crown my journey's end."
                           MRS. STEELE.

593.   *"My Times are in thy Hand."*

1 WHEN languor and disease invade
    This trembling house of clay,
'Tis sweet to look beyond our cage,
    And long to fly away;

2 Sweet to look inward and attend
    The whispers of his love;
Sweet to look upward to the place
    Where Jesus pleads above;

3 Sweet to reflect how grace divine
    My sins on Jesus laid;
Sweet to remember that his blood
    My debt of sufferings paid;

4 Sweet on his faithfulness to rest,
    Whose love can never end;
Sweet on his covenant of grace
    For all things to depend;

5 Sweet in the confidence of faith
    To trust his firm decrees;
Sweet to lie passive in his hands,
    And know no will but his;

6 Sweet to rejoice in lively hope,
    That when my change shall come,
Angels will hover round my bed,
    To waft my spirit home.

7 If such the sweetness of the stream,
    What must the fountain be,   [bliss
Where saints and angels draw their
    Immediately from thee?
                           TOPLADY.

594.   Hos. 5 : 15.

1 I CANNOT call affliction sweet,
    And yet 'twas good to bear;
Affliction brought me to thy feet,
    And I found comfort there.

2 My weaned soul was all resigned
    To thy most gracious will;
Oh, had I kept that better mind,
    Or been afflicted still!

3 Where are the vows which then I vowed,
    The joys which then I knew?
Those vanished like the morning cloud,
    These like the early dew.

4 Lord, grant me grace for every day,
    Whate'er my state may be,
Through life, in death, with truth to say,
    My God is all to me!
                           MONTGOMERY.

Trusting at all Times in the Lord.

GREENPORT. C. M.   Arranged from THALBERG.

595.   *"Thy Will be done."*

1 Thy holy will, my God, be mine;
   I yield my all to thee;
No more shall thought or wish repine,
   Whate'er my lot shall be.
Thy wisdom is a mighty deep,
   Beyond my thought thy grace,
My soul shall lay her fears asleep,
   Secure in thine embrace.

2 When clouds and darkness rule the hour,
   Thy bow on high I see;
And e'en the rending tempest's power
   Shall work but good for me.
At every step mine eyes shall turn
   To watch thy guiding hand;
My dearest wish shall be to learn
   And do thy good command.

3 On thee I rest my trusting soul;
   Thou wilt not let me fall;
Though surging billows o'er me roll,
   I shall be safe through all.
Grant me, my God, at last to hear,
   Well pleased, the call to die;
And 'mid the shades, with vision clear,
   To see my Saviour nigh.
                     Ray Palmer.

596.   Heb. 12: 11.

1 We praise thee oft for hours of bliss,
   For days of quiet rest;
But, ah, how seldom do we feel
   That pain and tears are best!
We praise thee for the shining sun,
   For kind and gladsome ways;
How shall we learn, O Lord, to sing
   Through weary nights and days?

2 Teach thou our weak and wandering
     hearts
   Aright to read thy way;
That thou, with loving hand, dost trace
   Our history every day.
Then every thorny crown of care,
   Worn well in patience now,
Shall grow a glorious diadem
   Upon the faithful brow.

3 Then every word of grief shall change,
   And wave a beauteous flower,
And lift its face beneath our feet,
   To bless us every hour.
Then sorrow's face shall be unveiled,
   And we, at last, shall see
Her eyes are eyes of tenderness,
   Her speech but echoes thee!
                  John Page Hopps.

The Christian Life. Looking to Jesus.

LOOKING OFF. 11s. (OLDENBURG.)   T. SELLE, 1500.

597.   Heb. 12 : 2.

1 O EYES that are weary, and hearts that are sore,
Look off unto Jesus, now sorrow no more;
The light of his countenance shineth so bright,
That here, as in heaven, there need be no night.

2 Looking off unto Jesus, my spirit is blest;
In the world I have turmoil, in him I have rest!
The sea of this life all about me may roar, [more.
While looking to Jesus, I hear it no

3 While looking to Jesus, my heart cannot fear;
I tremble no more when I see Jesus near;
I know that his presence my safeguard will be, [saith unto me.
For, "Why are you troubled?" he

4 Still looking to Jesus, oh, may I be found,
When Jordan's dark waters encompass me round;
They bear me away in his presence to be; [see.
I see him still nearer whom always I

5 Then, then shall I know the full beauty and grace
Of Jesus, my Lord, when I stand face to face;
Shall know how his love went before me each day,
And wonder that ever my eyes turned away.

598.   Mark 4: 37-41.

1 O ZION, afflicted with wave upon wave!
Whom no man can comfort, whom no man can save;
With darkness surrounded, by terrors dismayed,
In toiling and rowing thy strength is decayed.

2 Loud roaring, the billows now nigh overwhelm,
But skilful's the Pilot who sits at the helm;
His wisdom conducts thee, his power defends;
In safety and quiet thy warfare he ends.

3 "O fearful! O faithless!" in mercy he cries;
"My promise, my truth, are they light in thine eyes?
Still, still I am with thee, my promise shall stand; [thee to land."
Through tempest and tossing I'll bring

NOTE.— Beware of singing this fine old choral, and all other chorals as well, too slowly.

The Lord's Word a Firm Foundation.

PORTUGUESE HYMN. 11s.   JOHN READING, 1700.

599.   Heb. 13: 5.

1 How firm a foundation, ye saints of the Lord!
Is laid for your faith in his excellent word!
What more can he say than to you he hath said,—
To you, who for refuge to Jesus have fled?

2 "Fear not, I am with thee; oh, be not dismayed,
For I am thy God, I will still give thee aid:
I'll strengthen thee, help thee, and cause thee to stand,
Upheld by my gracious, omnipotent hand.

3 "When through the deep waters I call thee to go,
The rivers of sorrow shall not overflow;
For I will be with thee thy trials to bless,
And sanctify to thee thy deepest distress.

4 "When through fiery trials thy pathway shall lie,
My grace, all-sufficient, shall be thy supply,
The flame shall not hurt thee; I only design
Thy dross to consume, and thy gold to refine.

5 "E'en down to old age all my people shall prove
My sovereign, eternal, unchangeable love;
And then, when gray hairs shall their temples adorn,
Like lambs they shall still in my bosom be borne.

6 "The soul that on Jesus hath leaned for repose,
I will not — I will not desert to his foes;
That soul, though all hell should endeavor to shake,
I'll never — no, never — no, never forsake!"

KIRKHAM.

ROBINSON. 11s.

600. *John 14: 18.*

1 Come, Jesus, Redeemer, abide thou
    with me; [thee;
  Come, gladden my spirit that waiteth for
  Thy smile every shadow shall chase
    from my heart,
  And soothe every sorrow, though keen
    be the smart.

2 Without thee but weakness, with thee I
    am strong;
  By day thou shalt lead me, by night be
    my song;
  Though dangers surround me, I still
    every fear,
  Since thou, the Most Mighty, my Help-
    er, art near.

3 Thy love, oh, how faithful! so tender,
    so pure!
  Thy promise, faith's anchor, how stead-
    fast and sure!
  That love, like sweet sunshine, my cold
    heart can warm,
  That promise make steady my soul in
    the storm.

4 Breathe, breathe on my spirit, oft ruffled,
    thy peace;
  From restless, vain wishes, bid thou my
    heart cease;
  In thee all its longings henceforward
    shall end,
  Till, glad, to thy presence my soul shall
    ascend.

5 Oh, then, blessed Jesus, who once for
    me died,
  Made clean in the fountain that gushed
    from thy side,
  I shall see thy full glory, thy face shall
    behold,
  And praise thee with raptures forever
    untold!
                                RAY PALMER.

601. *Psalm 23.*

1 The Lord is my shepherd, no want
    shall I know;
  I feed in green pastures, safe folded I
    rest;
  He leadeth my soul where the still wa-
    ters flow,
  Restores me when wandering, re-
    deems when oppressed.

2 Through the valley and shadow of death
    though I stray,
  Since thou art my guardian, no evil
    I fear;
  Thy rod shall defend me, thy staff be
    my stay; [forter near
  No harm can befall, with my Com-

3 Let goodness and mercy, my bountiful
    God!
  Still follow my steps till I meet thee
    above;
  I seek — by the path which my forefa-
    thers trod,
  Through the land of their sojourn —
    thy kingdom of love.
                                MONTGOMERY.

Perseverance. Adoration of Christ.

THOUGH FAINT, YET PURSUING. 11s. Arranged from MENDELSSOHN.

602. Judges 8: 4.

1 Though faint, yet pursuing, we go on our way;
The Lord is our Leader, his word is our stay;
Though suffering and sorrow and trial be near,
The Lord is our refuge, and whom can we fear?

2 He raiseth the fallen, he cheereth the faint;
The weak, and oppressed — he will hear their complaint;
The way may be weary, and thorny the road,
But how can we falter? our help is in God!

3 Though clouds may surround us, our God is our light;
Though storms rage around us, our God is our might;
So faint, yet pursuing, still onward we come;
The Lord is our Leader, and heaven is our home!

603. Psalm 46.

1 The Lord is our refuge, the Lord is our guide;
We smile upon danger with him at our side;
The billows may blacken, the tempest increase,
Though earth may be shaken, his saints shall have peace.

2 A voice still and small by his people is heard,
A whisper of peace from his life-giving word;
A stream in the desert, a river of love,
Flows down to their hearts from the fountain above.

3 The Lord is our helper! ye scorners, be awed!
Ye earthlings, be still, and acknowledge your God:
The proud he will humble, the lowly defend;
Oh, happy the people with God for a friend!

LYTE.

The Christian Life. A Pilgrimage.

PILGRIM SONG. S. M. — MENDELSSOHN.

604. *The Pilgrim's Song.*

1 A FEW more years shall roll,
  A few more seasons come,
And we shall be with those that rest,
  Asleep within the tomb:
    Then, O my Lord, prepare
    My soul for that great day;
  Oh, wash me in thy precious blood,
    And take my sins away!

2 A few more storms shall beat
  On this wild rocky shore;
And we shall be where tempests cease,
  And surges swell no more:
    Then, O my Lord, prepare
    My soul for that calm day;
  Oh, wash me in thy precious blood,
    And take my sins away!

3 A few more struggles here,
  A few more partings o'er,
A few more toils, a few more tears,
  And we shall weep no more.
    Then, O my' Lord, prepare
    My soul for that blest day;
  Oh, wash me in thy precious blood,
    And take my sins away!

4 A few more Sabbaths here
  Shall cheer us on our way;
And we shall reach the endless rest,
  Th' eternal Sabbath-day:
    Then, O my Lord, prepare
    My soul for that sweet day;
  Oh, wash me in thy precious blood,
    And take my sins away!
        BONAR.

605. Phil. 1: 21.

1 FOR me to live is Christ,
  To die is endless gain,
For him I gladly bear the cross,
  And welcome grief and pain.
    Faithful may I endure,
    And hear my Saviour say,
  Thrice welcome home, beloved child,
    Inherit endless day!

2 A pilgrimage my lot,
  My home is in the skies,
I nightly pitch my tent below,
  And daily higher rise.
    My journey soon will end,
    My scrip and staff laid down;
  Oh, tempt me not with earthly toys!
    I go to wear a crown.

HAMDEN. 8s., 7s., & 4s.
DR. MASON.

606. *Pilgrim's Song.*

1 GUIDE me, O thou great Jehovah,
   Pilgrim through this barren land;
  I am weak, but thou art mighty;
   Hold me with thy powerful hand;
    Bread of heaven,
  Feed me till I want no more.

2 Open thou the crystal fountain
   Whence the healing streams do flow;
  Let the fiery, cloudy pillar
   Lead me all my journey through;
    Strong Deliverer,
  Be thou still my strength and shield.

3 When I tread the verge of Jordan,
   Bid my anxious fears subside;
  Bear me through the swelling current,
   Land me safe on Canaan's side;
    Songs of praises
  I will ever give to thee.
                OLIVER.

607. *Psalm 91: 11.*

1 KEEP us, Lord, oh, keep us ever!
   Vain our hope, if left by thee;
  We are thine; oh, leave us never,
   Till thy glorious face we see!
    Then to praise thee
  Through a bright eternity.

2 Precious is thy word of promise,—
   Precious to thy people here;
  Never take thy presence from us.
   Jesus, Saviour, still be near:
    Living, dying,
  May thy name our spirits cheer.

608. *Rev. 19: 3.*

1 HALLELUJAH! best and sweetest
   Of the hymns of praise above!
  Hallelujah! thou repeatest,
   Angel-host, these notes of love;
    This ye utter,
  While your golden harps ye move.

2 Hallelujah! church victorious,
   Join the concert of the sky!
  Hallelujah! bright and glorious,
   Lift, ye saints, this strain on high!
    We, poor exiles,
  Join not yet your melody.

3 Hallelujah! strains of gladness
   Comfort not the faint and worn;
  Hallelujah! sounds of sadness
   Best become the heart forlorn;
    Our offences
  We with bitter tears must mourn.

4 But our earnest supplication,
   Holy God! we raise to thee;
  Visit us with thy salvation,
   Make us all thy peace to see!
    Hallelujah!
  Ours at length this strain shall be.
                BREVIARY.

Doxology.

GREAT Jehovah! we adore thee,
  God the Father, God the Son
God the Spirit, joined in glory
  On the same eternal throne;
    Endless praises
  To Jehovah, Three in One.

The Christian Life. Encouragements.

SOJOURNER'S SONG. 7s. & 6s.   Arranged from F. GUMBERT.

609.   *Pilgrim's Song.*

1 From every earthly pleasure,
    From every transient joy,
From every mortal treasure,
    That soon will fade and die;
No longer these desiring,
    Upward our wishes tend,
To nobler bliss aspiring,
    And joys that never end.

2 From every piercing sorrow
    That heaves our breast to-day,
Or threatens us to-morrow,
    Hope turns our eyes away;
On wings of faith ascending,
    We see the land of light,
And feel our sorrows ending
    In infinite delight.

3 What though we are but strangers
    And sojourners below,
And countless snares and dangers
    Surround the path we go;
Though painful and distressing,
    Yet there's a rest above;
And onward still we're pressing,
    To reach that land of love.
                  DAVIS.

610.   *"He Leadeth me."*

1 In heavenly love abiding,
    No change my heart shall fear,
And safe is such confiding,
    For nothing changes here.
The storm may roar without me,
    My heart may low be laid,
But God is round about me,
    And can I be dismayed?

2 Wherever he may guide me,
    No want shall turn me back;
My Shepherd is beside me,
    And nothing can I lack.
His wisdom ever waketh;
    His sight is never dim;
He knows the way he taketh,
    And I will walk with him.

3 Green pastures are before me,
    Which yet I have not seen;
Bright skies will soon be o'er me,
    Where the dark clouds have been.
My hope I cannot measure,
    My path to life is free,
My Saviour has my treasure,
    And he will walk with me.
                  WARING.

Encouragements. Songs by the Way.

CARVER STREET. 7s. OLD MELODY.

611. *Isaiah 35: 8-10.*

1 Children of the heavenly King,
As ye journey, sweetly sing;
Sing your Saviour's worthy praise,
Glorious in his works and ways.

2 Ye are travelling home to God,
In the way the fathers trod;
They are happy now, and ye
Soon their happiness shall see.

3 Shout, ye little flock, and blest!
You on Jesus' throne shall rest;
There your seat is now prepared;
There your kingdom and reward.

4 Fear not, brethren; joyful stand
On the borders of your land;
Jesus Christ, your Father's Son,
Bids you undismayed go on.

5 Lord, submissive make us go,
Gladly leaving all below;
Only thou our Leader be,
And we still will follow thee.
CENNICK.

612. *Pressing Onward.*

1 Oft in sorrow, oft in woe,
Onward, Christian, onward go!
Fight the fight, maintain the strife,
Strengthened with the bread of life.

2 Onward, Christian, onward go!
Join the war, and face the foe:
Will you flee in danger's hour?
Know you not your Captain's power?

3 Let your drooping hearts be glad;
March, in heavenly armor clad;
Fight, nor think the battle long;
Soon shall vict'ry tune your song.

4 Let not sorrow dim your eye;
Soon shall every tear be dry:
Let not fears your course impede;
Great your strength, if great your need.

5 Onward, then, to battle move!
More than conqu'ror you shall prove;
Though opposed by many a foe,
Christian soldier, onward go!
H. K. WHITE.

613. *Rejoicing in the Ways of God.*

1 Now begin the heavenly theme,
Sing aloud in Jesus' name!
Ye, who his salvation prove,
Triumph in redeeming love.

2 Ye, who see the Father's grace
Beaming in the Saviour's face,
As to Canaan on ye move,
Praise and bless redeeming love.

3 Mourning souls! dry up your tears,
Banish all your guilty fears:
See your guilt and curse remove,
Cancelled by redeeming love.

4 Hither, then, your tribute bring,
Strike aloud each joyful string:
Saints below and saints above,
Join to praise redeeming love.
LANGFORD.

The Christian Life. "The Joy set before us."

WILL NOT THAT JOYFUL BE? 6s. & 7s.

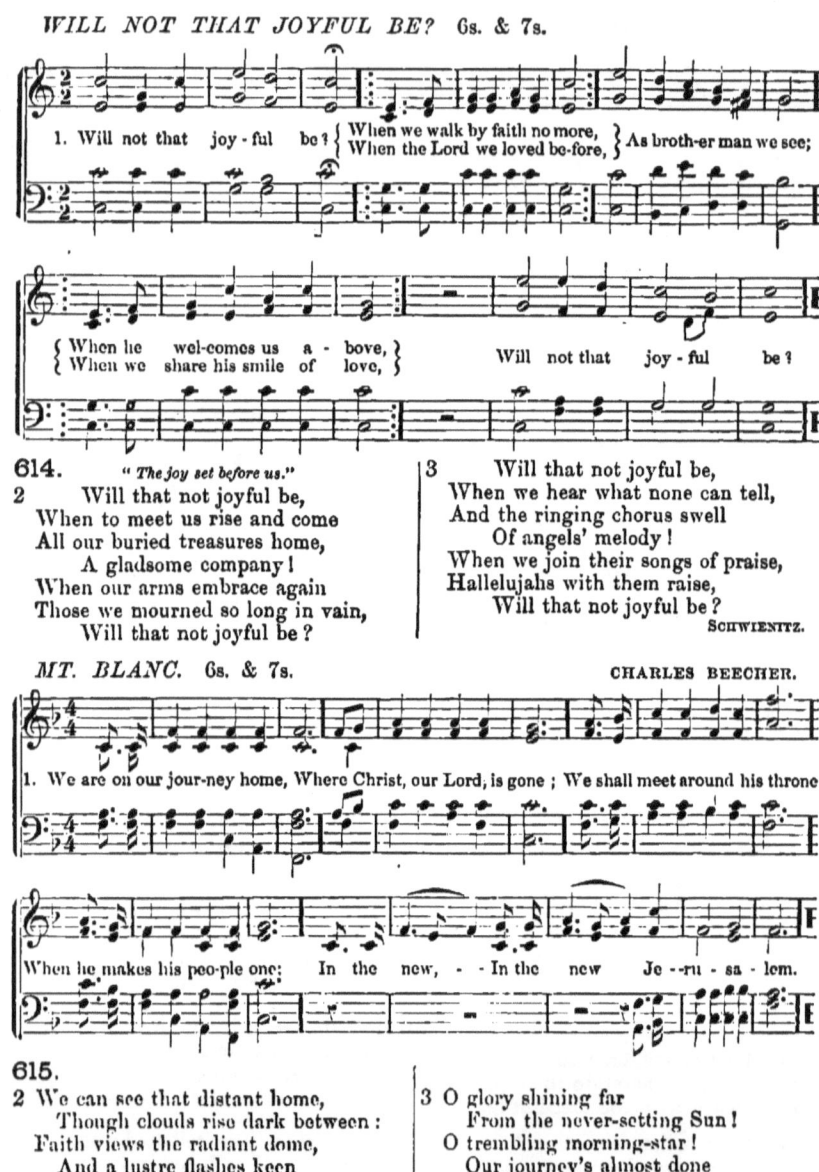

1. Will not that joyful be? When we walk by faith no more, When the Lord we loved before, As brother man we see; When he welcomes us above, When we share his smile of love, Will not that joyful be?

614. *"The joy set before us."*

2 Will that not joyful be,
When to meet us rise and come
All our buried treasures home,
   A gladsome company!
When our arms embrace again
Those we mourned so long in vain,
   Will that not joyful be?

3 Will that not joyful be,
When we hear what none can tell,
And the ringing chorus swell
   Of angels' melody!
When we join their songs of praise,
Hallelujahs with them raise,
   Will that not joyful be?

SCHWIENITZ.

MT. BLANC. 6s. & 7s.

CHARLES BEECHER.

1. We are on our journey home, Where Christ, our Lord, is gone; We shall meet around his throne When he makes his people one: In the new, — In the new Jerusalem.

615.

2 We can see that distant home,
   Though clouds rise dark between:
Faith views the radiant dome,
   And a lustre flashes keen
    |: From the new :| Jerusalem.

3 O glory shining far
   From the never-setting Sun!
O trembling morning-star!
   Our journey's almost done
    |: To the new :| Jerusalem.

Christian Watchfulness, Activity, and Enthusiasm.

GREENWOOD. S. M.   ROOT & SWEETSER'S COLL.

616.   Psalm 60: 4.
1 ARISE, ye saints, arise!
    The Lord our Leader is;
The foe before his banner flies,
    And victory is his.

2 We follow thee, our Guide,
    Our Saviour, and our King!
We follow thee, through grace supplied
    From heaven's eternal spring.

3 We soon shall see the day
    When all our toils shall cease;
When we shall cast our arms away,
    And dwell in endless peace.

4 This hope supports us here;
    It makes our burdens light;
'Twill serve our drooping hearts to cheer,
    Till faith shall end in sight.

5 Till, of the prize possessed,
    We hear of war no more;
And ever with our Leader rest,
    On yonder peaceful shore.

617.   Eph. 6: 11-14.
1 SOLDIERS of Christ! arise,
    And put your armor on, —
Strong in the strength which God sup-
    Through his eternal Son, — [plies

2 Strong in the Lord of hosts,
    And in his mighty power:
Who in the strength of Jesus trusts
    Is more than conqueror.

3 Stand, then, in his great might,
    With all his strength endued;
But take, to arm you for the fight,
    The panoply of God:

4 That, having all things done,
    And all your conflicts past,
Ye may o'ercome, through Christ alone,
    And stand entire at last.
                      C. WESLEY.

618.   "*Watch ye therefore.*"—Matt. 25: 13.
1 YE servants of the Lord,
    Each in his office wait,
Observant of his heavenly word, —
    And watchful at his gate.

2 Let all your lamps be bright,
    And trim the golden flame;
Gird up your loins as in his sight,
    For awful is his name.

3 Watch! 'tis your Lord's command;
    And while we speak, he's near:
Mark the first signal of his hand,
    And ready all appear.

4 Oh, happy servant he
    In such a posture found!
He shall his Lord with rapture see,
    And be with honor crowned.
                      DODDRIDGE.
        Doxology.
YE angels round the throne,
    And saints that dwell below,
Worship the Father, praise the Son,
    And bless the Spirit, too.

264   The Christian Life. Watchfulness and Cheerfulness.

LABAN. S. M.   DR. MASON.

619. *Watchfulness.*—Matt. 26: 41.
1 My soul, be on thy guard,
   Ten thousand foes arise ;
And hosts of sin are pressing hard
   To draw thee from the skies.

2 Oh, watch and fight and pray !
   The battle ne'er give o'er ;
Renew it boldly every day,
   And help divine implore.

3 Ne'er think the victory won,
   Nor once at ease sit down ;
Thy arduous work will not be done
   Till thou obtain thy crown.

4 Fight on, my soul, till death
   Shall bring thee to thy God !
He'll take thee at thy parting breath,
   Up to his blest abode.
                              HEATH.

620.   *Joy.*—Phil. 4: 4.
1 REJOICE in God alway ;
   When earth looks heavenly bright,
When joy makes glad the livelong day,
   And peace shuts in the night.

2 Rejoice when care and woe
   The fainting soul oppress ;
When tears at wakeful midnight flow,
   And morn brings heaviness.

3 Rejoice in hope and fear ;
   Rejoice in life and death ;
Rejoice when threatening storms are
   And comfort languisheth.   [near,

4 When should not they rejoice,
   Whom Christ his brethren calls ;
Who hear and know his guiding voice,
   When on their hearts it falls ?

5 So, though our path is steep,
   And many a tempest lowers,
Shall his own peace our spirits keep,
   And Christ's dear love be ours.
                              MOULTRIE.

621.   Psalm 138: 5.
1 Now let our voices join
   To form a sacred song ;
Ye pilgrims, in Jehovah's ways,
   With music pass along.

2 How straight the path appears,
   How open and how fair !
No lurking gins t' entrap our feet ;
   No fierce destroyer there.

3 But flowers of paradise
   In rich profusion spring ;
The sun of glory gilds the path,
   And dear companions sing.

4 See Salem's golden spires
   In beauteous prospect rise ;
And brighter crowns than mortals wear,
   Which sparkle through the skies.

5 All honor to his name,
   Who marks the shining way ;
To him who leads the wanderers on
   To realms of endless day.
                              DODDRIDGE.

Activity, Energy, Enthusiasm.

GILEAD. L. M.   MEHUL.

622.   *Zeal.* — John 9: 4.

1 Go, labor on, while it is day; [on;
   The world's dark night is hastening
Speed, speed thy work, cast sloth away!
   It is not thus that souls are won.

2 Men die in darkness at your side,
   Without a hope to cheer the tomb:
Take up the torch and wave it wide, —
   The torch that lights time's thickest gloom.

3 Toil on; faint not; keep watch and pray!
   Be wise the erring soul to win;
Go forth into the world's highway;
   Compel the wanderer to come in.

4 Go, labor on; your hands are weak;
   Your knees are faint, your soul cast down;
Yet falter not; the prize you seek
   Is near, — a kingdom and a crown!

5 Toil on, and in thy toil rejoice;
   For toil comes rest, for exile, home;
Soon shalt thou hear the Bridegroom's voice,   [come!"
   The midnight peal, "Behold I
                                    BONAR.

623.   Eph. 6: 14.

1 STAND up, my soul! shake off thy fears,
   And gird the gospel armor on!
March to the gates of endless joy,
   Where Jesus thy great Captain's gone.

2 Hell and thy sins resist thy course;
   But hell and sin are vanquished foes,
Thy Jesus nailed them to the cross,
   And sung the triumph when he rose.

3 Then let my soul march boldly on;
   Press forward to the heavenly gate;
There peace and joy eternal reign,
   And glittering robes for conquerors wait.

4 Then shall I wear a starry crown,
   And triumph in almighty grace;
While all the armies of the skies
   Join in my glorious Leader's praise.
                                    WATTS.

624.   Isaiah 40: 28-31.

1 AWAKE our souls, away our fears,
   Let every trembling thought be gone;
Awake and run the heavenly race,
   And put a cheerful courage on.

2 True, 'tis a straight and thorny road,
   And mortal spirits tire and faint;
But they forget the mighty God
   That feeds the strength of every saint: — .

3 The mighty God whose matchless power
   Is ever new and ever young,
And firm endures while endless years
   Their everlasting circles run.

4 From thee, the overflowing spring,
   Our souls shall drink a fresh supply,
While such as trust their native strength
   Shall melt away, and droop and die.

5 Swift as an eagle cuts the air,
   We'll mount aloft to thine abode;
On wings of love our souls shall fly,
   Nor tire amid the heavenly road.
                                    WATTS.

The Christian Life. Zeal and Activity.

HUMMEL. C. M.   ZEUNER.

625.   *Phil. 3: 14.*

1 AWAKE, my soul! stretch every nerve,
    And press with vigor on;
A heavenly race demands thy zeal,
    And an immortal crown.

2 A cloud of witnesses around
    Hold thee in full survey;
Forget the steps already trod,
    And onward urge thy way.

3 'Tis God's all-animating voice
    That calls thee from on high;
'Tis his own hand presents the prize
    To thine aspiring eye.

4 Blest Saviour! introduced by thee,
    Have I my race begun;
And, crowned with victory, at thy feet
    I'll lay my honors down.
                    DODDRIDGE.

626.   *Activity.*

1 AM I a soldier of the cross,
    A follower of the Lamb,
And shall I fear to own his cause,
    Or blush to speak his name?

2 Must I be carried to the skies
    On flowery beds of ease,
While others fought to win the prize,
    And sailed through bloody seas?

3 Are there no foes for me to face?
    Must I not stem the flood?
Is this vile world a friend to grace,
    To help me on to God?

4 Sure I must fight, if I would reign;
    Increase my courage, Lord!
I'll bear the toil, endure the pain,
    Supported by thy word.

5 Thy saints, in all this glorious war,
    Shall conquer, though they die;
They view the triumph from afar,
    And seize it with their eye.

6 When that illustrious day shall rise,
    And all thine armies shine
In robes of victory through the skies,
    The glory shall be thine.
                    WATTS.

627.   *Isaiah 35: 8-10.*

1 SING, ye redeemed of the Lord,
    Your great Deliverer sing;
Pilgrims for Zion's city bound,
    Be joyful in your King.

2 A hand divine shall lead you on
    Through all the blissful road,
Till to the sacred mount you rise,
    And see your smiling God.

3 There garlands of immortal joy
    Shall bloom on every head;
While sorrow, sighing, and distress
    Like shadows all are fled.

4 March on in your Redeemer's strength
    Pursue his footsteps still;
And let the prospect cheer your eye,
    While laboring up the hill.
                    DODDRIDGE.

Graces and Duties.

ROME. L. M. (QUARTETTE.)

1. Who shall ascend thy heav'nly place, Great God, and dwell before thy face? The man who minds religion now, And humbly walks with God below.

628. Psalm 15.

2 Whose hands are pure, whose heart is clean; [mean;
Whose lips still speak the thing they
No slanders dwell upon his tongue;
He hates to do his neighbor wrong.

3 He loves his enemies, and prays
For those who curse him to his face;
And does to all men still the same
That he would hope or wish from them.

4 Yet when his holiest works are done,
His soul depends on grace alone:
This is the man thy face shall see,
And dwell forever, Lord, with thee.
WATTS.

629. Tit. 2: 10–13.

1 So let our lips and lives express
The holy gospel we profess;
So let our works and virtues shine,
To prove the doctrine all divine.

2 Thus shall we best proclaim abroad
The honors of our Saviour God;
When his salvation reigns within,
And grace subdues the power of sin.

3 Our flesh and sense must be denied,
Passion and envy, lust and pride;
While justice, temperance, truth, and love,
Our inward piety approve.

4 Religion bears our spirits up,
While we expect that blessed hope,
The bright appearance of the Lord,—
And faith stands leaning on his word.
WATTS.

630. Deut. 34: 1.

1 As when the weary traveller gains
The height of some o'erlooking hill,
His heart revives, if, o'er the plains,
He eyes his home, though distant still.

2 So when the Christian pilgrim views,
By faith, his mansion in the skies;
The sight his fainting strength renews,
And wings his speed to reach the prize.

3 'Tis there, he says, I am to dwell
With Jesus in the realms of day;
Then I shall bid my cares farewell,
And he will wipe my tears away.
NEWTON.

631. Psalm 1.

1 HAPPY the man whose cautious feet
Shun the broad way that sinners go;
Who hates the place where atheists meet,
And fears to talk as scoffers do.

2 He loves t' employ the morning light
Among the statutes of the Lord,
And spends the wakeful hours of night,
With pleasure pondering o'er his word.

3 He, like a plant by gentle streams,
Shall flourish in immortal green;
And heaven will shine, with kindest beams,
On every work his hands begin.
WATTS.

DALLAS. 7s.   CHERUBINI.

632.   *Consecration.*
1 Jesus, take me for thine own;
   To thy will my spirit frame;
  Thou shalt reign, and thou alone,
   Over all I have and am.

2 Making thus the Lord my choice,
   I have nothing more to choose,
  But to listen to thy voice,
   And my will in thine to lose.

3 Then, whatever may betide,
   I shall safe and happy be;
  Still content and satisfied; —
   Having all in having thee.

633.   *Psalm 15.*
1 Who, O Lord, when life is o'er,
   Shall to heaven's blest mansions soar?
  Who, an ever-welcome guest,
   In thy holy place shall rest?

2 He whose heart thy love has warmed;
   He whose will to thine conformed,
  Bids his life unsullied run;
   He whose words and thoughts are one;

3 He who shuns the sinner's road,
   Loving those who love their God;
  Who, with hope and faith unfeigned,
   Treads the path by thee ordained; —

4 He who trusts in Christ alone,
   Not in aught himself hath done; —
  He, great God, shall be thy care,
   And thy choicest blessings share.
                                  LYTE.

634.   *Consecration. — Luke 10: 42.*
1 Jesus, all-atoning Lamb,
   Thine, and only thine I am:
  Take my body, spirit, soul;
   Only thou possess the whole.

2 Thou my one thing needful be;
   Let me ever cleave to thee;
  Let me choose the better part;
   Let me give thee all my heart.

3 Whom have I on earth below?
   Thee, and only thee I know:
  Whom have I in heaven but thee?
   Thou art all in all to me.
                                  C. WESLEY.

635.   *Simplicity.*
1 Jesus, cast a look on me!
   Give me true simplicity;
  Make me poor, and keep me low,
   Seeking only thee to know.

2 All that feeds my busy pride,
   Cast it evermore aside:
  Bid my will to thine submit;
   Lay me humbly at thy feet!

3 Make me like a little child,
   Simple, teachable, and mild;
  Seeing only in thy light;
   Walking only in thy might!

4 Leaning on thy loving breast,
   Where a weary soul may rest;
  Feeling well the peace of God
   Flowing from thy precious blood!
                                  BERRIDGE.

Steadfastness, Cross-bearing, Faith.

MANOAH. C. M. ROSSINI.

636. *"Pressing towards the Mark."*

1 THE bird let loose in Eastern skies,
  Returning fondly home,
Ne'er stoops to earth her wing, nor flies
  Where idle warblers roam.

2 But high she shoots through air and light,
  Above all low delay,
Where nothing earthly bounds her flight,
  Nor shadow dims her way.

3 So grant me, Lord, from every snare
  Of sinful passion free,
Aloft through faith's serener air,
  To hold my course to thee.

4 No sin to cloud, no lure to stay
  My soul, as home she springs;
Thy sunshine on her joyful way,
  Thy freedom in her wings.
                              MOORE.

637. Luke 9: 23.

1 MUST Jesus bear the cross alone,
  And all the world go free?
No, there's a cross for every one,
  And there's a cross for me.

2 This consecrated cross I'll bear,
  Till death shall set me free,
And then go home my crown to wear,
  For there's a crown for me.

3 Upon the crystal pavement, down
  At Jesus' piercèd feet,
Joyful I'll cast my golden crown,
  And his dear name repeat.

4 And palms shall wave, and harps shall
    Beneath heaven's arches high; [ring,
  The Lord that lives, the ransomed sing,
    That lives no more to die.

5 Oh, precious cross! oh, glorious crown!
    Oh, resurrection day!
  Ye angels, from the stars come down,
    And bear my soul away.
                              ALLEN.

638. *Faith.*

1 FAITH adds new charms to earthly bliss,
    And saves me from its snares;
  Its aid, in every duty, brings,
    And softens all my cares.

2 The wounded conscience knows its power
    The healing balm to give;
  That balm the saddest heart can cheer,
    And make the dying live.

3 Wide it unveils celestial worlds,
    Where deathless pleasures reign;
  And bids me seek my portion there,
    Nor bids me seek in vain.

4 It shows the precious promise sealed
    With the Redeemer's blood;
  And helps my feeble hope to rest
    Upon a faithful God.

5 There, there unshaken would I rest,
    Till this frail body dies:
  And then, on faith's triumphant wings,
    To endless glory rise.
                              WATTS.

The Christian Life. Faith, Self-Sacrifice, Meekness.

UXBRIDGE. L. M. — DR. MASON.

639. *Faith.*

1 FAITH is a living power from heaven,
That grasps the promise God hath given;
A trust that cannot be o'erthrown,
Fixed heartily on God alone.

2 Faith finds in Christ whate'er we need
To save, or strengthen us indeed;
Receives the grace he sendeth down,
And makes us share his cross and crown.

3 Faith feels the Spirit's kindling breath,
In love and hope that conquer death;
Faith worketh hourly joy in God,
And trusts and blesses e'en his rod.

4 Faith in the conscience worketh peace,
And bids the mourner's weeping cease;
By faith the children's place we claim,
And give all honor to One Name.

640. *Faith.* — Heb. 11: 8.

1 'Tis by the faith of joys to come,
We walk through deserts dark as night;
Till we arrive at heaven, our home,
Faith is our guide, and faith our light.

2 The want of sight she well supplies;
She makes the pearly gates appear;
Far into distant worlds she pries,
And brings eternal glories near.

3 Cheerful we tread the desert through,
While faith inspires a heavenly ray;
Though lions roar, and tempests blow,
And rocks and dangers fill the way.
WATTS.

641. *Self-Sacrifice in the Daily Life.*

1 NOT by the martyrs' death alone, [won;
The saints in heaven their crowns have
There is a triumph robe on high,
For bloodless fields of victory.

2 What though they were not called to feel
The cross, the flame, the torturing wheel?
Yet daily to the world they died,
And sinful passions crucified.

3 What though nor chains, nor scourges sore,
Nor bloody beasts their members tore?
Enough if faith and love arise
To Christ, a daily sacrifice.

4 Lord, grant us so to thee to turn,
That we to die through life may learn;
And when our earthly toils are o'er,
Rejoice with thee for evermore.

642. *Meekness.* — Matt. 5: 5.

1 HAPPY the meek, whose gentle breast,
Clear as the summer's evening ray,
Calm as the regions of the blest,
Enjoys on earth celestial day.

2 His heart no broken friendships sting,
No storms his peaceful tent invade;
He rests beneath th' Almighty's wing,
Hostile to none, of none afraid.

3 Spirit of grace, all meek and mild!
Inspire our breasts, our souls possess:
Repel each passion rude and wild,
And bless us as we aim to bless.
J. SCOTT.

Christian Conflict. Thanks for all Saints.

CALM. S. M.   HANDEL POND.

643. *Jesus All in All.*
1 THOU very present aid
   In suffering and distress;
The mind which still on thee is stayed,
   Is kept in perfect peace.

2 The soul by faith reclined
   On the Redeemer's breast,
'Mid raging storms, exults to find
   An everlasting rest.

3 Sorrow and fear are gone
   Whene'er thy face appears;
It stills the sighing orphan's moan,
   And dries the widow's tears.

4 It hallows every cross;
   It sweetly comforts me;
Makes me forget my every loss,
   And find my all in thee.

5 Jesus, to whom I fly,
   Doth all my wishes fill;
What though created streams are dry?
   I have the fountain still.
                      C. WESLEY.

644.   Rev. 21: 3, 4.
1 THE people of the Lord
   Are on their way to heaven;
There they obtain their great reward;
   The prize will there be given.

2 'Tis conflict here below;
   'Tis triumph there, and peace:
On earth we wrestle with the foe;
   In heaven our conflicts cease.

3 'Tis gloom and darkness here;
   'Tis light and joy above;
There all is pure, and all is clear;
   There all is peace and love.

4 There rest shall follow toil,
   And ease succeed to care:
The victors there divide the spoil:
   They sing and triumph there.

5 Then let us joyful sing;
   The conflict is not long:
We hope in heaven to praise our king
   In one eternal song.

645.   *Thanks for all Saints.*
1 FOR all thy saints, O God,
   Who strove in Christ to live,
Who followed him, obeyed, adored,
   Our grateful hymn receive.

2 For all thy saints, O God,
   Accept our thankful cry,
Who counted Christ their great reward
   And yearned for him to die.

3 They all, in life and death,
   With him, their Lord, in view,
Learned from thy Holy Spirit's breath
   To suffer and to do.

4 For this thy name we bless,
   And humbly pray that we
May follow them in holiness,
   And live and die in thee.

BOND. C. M.   G. F. ROOT.

646.   *Prayer for Submission.*

1 I ASK not now for gold to gild
    An aching, weary frame;
The yearning of the mind is stilled, —
    I ask not now for fame.

2 But, bowed in lowliness of mind,
    I make my wishes known;
I only ask a will resigned,
    O Father, to thine own.

3 In vain I task my aching brain,
    The sage's thoughts to scan;
I only feel how weak I am,
    How poor and blind is man.

4 And now my spirit sighs for home,
    And longs for light to see,
And, like a weary child, would come,
    O Father! unto thee.
                WHITTIER.

647.   *Prayer for Purity.*

1 O LORD, our carnal mind control,
    And make us pure within;
Purge more and more our inmost soul
    From wilful thoughts of sin.

2 Let not the world with spot or soil
    Our secret heart defile;
Nor Satan round our spirit coil
    His chain of fraud and guile.

3 Be ours the blessed lot of those
    Who every evil flee;
Whose holy converse clearly shows
    Communion full with thee.

648.   Heb. 11: 13.

1 GLORY to God! whose witness-train —
    Those heroes bold in faith —
Could smile on poverty and pain,
    And triumph e'en in death.

2 Oh, may that faith our hearts sustain,
    Wherein they fearless stood,
When, in the power of cruel men
    They poured their willing blood.

3 God, whom we serve, our God can save,
    Can damp the scorching flame,
Can build an ark, can smooth a wave,
    For such as love his name.

4 Lord! if thine arm support us still
    With its eternal strength,
We shall o'ercome the mightiest ill,
    And conquerors prove at length.
                MORAVIAN.

649.   *The Pilgrimage.*

1 OUR country is Immanuel's ground;
    We seek that promised soil;
The songs of Zion cheer our hearts,
    While strangers here we toil.

2 Oft do our eyes with joy o'erflow,
    And oft are bathed in tears; [raise,
Yet naught but heaven our hopes can
    And naught but sin our fears.

3 The flowers that spring along the road
    We scarcely stoop to pluck;
We walk o'er beds of shining ore,
    Nor waste one wishful look.
                BARBAULD.

Love, Watchfulness, and Christian Communion.

HEBRON. L. M.   DR. MASON.

650.   *Love.* — 1 Cor. 13: 1.

1 Had I the tongues of Greeks and Jews,
And nobler speech than angels use,
If love be absent, I am found
Like tinkling brass, an empty sound.

2 Were I inspired to preach and tell
All that is done in heaven and hell,
Or could my faith the world remove,
Still I am nothing without love.

3 Should I distribute all my store
To feed the hungry, clothe the poor;
Or give my body to the flame,
To gain a martyr's glorious name:

4 If love to God, and love to men
Be absent, all my hopes are vain;
Nor tongues, nor gifts, nor fiery zeal,
The work of love can e'er fulfil.
         WATTS.

651. *Watchfulness and Prayer.* — Psalm 141.

1 My God, accept my early vows,
Like morning incense in thy house;
And let my nightly worship rise
Sweet as the evening sacrifice.

2 Watch o'er my lips, and guard them, Lord,
From every rash and heedless word;
Nor let my feet incline to tread
The guilty path where sinners lead.

3 Oh, may the righteous, when I stray,
Smite and reprove my wandering way!
Their gentle words, like ointment shed,
Shall never bruise, but cheer my head.

4 When I behold them pressed with grief,
I'll cry to heaven for their relief;
And by my warm petitions prove
How much I prize their faithful love.
         WATTS.

652.   *Social Worship.*

1 May He by whose kind care we meet
   Send his good Spirit from above,
Make our communications sweet,
   And cause our hearts to burn with love.

2 Forgotten be each worldly theme,
   When Christians see each other thus;
We only wish to speak of him
   Who lived and died and reigns for us.

3 We'll talk of all he did and said,
   And suffered for us here below;
The path he marked for us to tread,
   And what he's doing for us now.

4 Thus, as the moments pass away,
   We'll love and wonder and adore,
And hasten on the glorious day,
   When we shall meet to part no more.
         NEWTON.

653.   Eph. 4 : 30–32.

1 The Spirit, like a peaceful Dove,
   Flies from the realms of noise and strife:
Why should we vex and grieve his love
   Who seals our souls to heavenly life!

2 Tender and kind be all our thoughts;
   Through all our lives let mercy run:
So God forgives our numerous faults,
   For the dear sake of Christ his Son.
         WATTS.

BURLINGTON. C. M.   J. F. BURROWES.

654.   *Love.* — 1 Cor. 13 : 13.

1 HAPPY the heart where graces reign,
   Where love inspires the breast;
  Love is the brightest of the train,
   And strengthens all the rest.

2 Knowledge — alas! 'tis all in vain,
   And all in vain our fear;
  Our stubborn sins will fight and reign,
   If love be absent there.

3 This is the grace that lives and sings,
   When faith and hope shall cease;
  'Tis this shall strike our joyful strings,
   In the sweet realms of bliss.

4 Before we quite forsake our clay,
   Or leave this dark abode,
  The wings of love bear us away,
   To see our smiling God.   WATTS.

655.   *Eph.* 3: 15.

1 LET saints below in concert sing
   With those to glory gone;
  For all the servants of our King
   In earth and heaven are one.

2 One family — we dwell in him, —
   One church above, beneath,
  Though now divided by the stream,
   The narrow stream of death.

3 One army of the living God,
   To his command we bow;
  Part of the host have crossed the flood,
   And part are crossing now.

4 E'en now to their eternal home
   Some happy spirits fly;
  And we are to the margin come,
   And soon expect to die.

5 E'en now, by faith, we join our hands
   With those that went before,
  And greet the ransomed blessed bands
   Upon th' eternal shore.

6 Lord Jesus! be our constant guide;
   And, when the word is given,
  Bid death's cold flood its waves divide,
   And land us safe in heaven.
                              C. WESLEY.

656.   *Blessedness of the Communion of Saints.*

1 HAPPY the souls to Jesus joined,
   And saved by grace alone;
  Walking in all his ways, they find
   Their heaven on earth begun.

2 The church triumphant in thy love, —
   Their mighty joys we know:
  They sing the Lamb in hymns above,
   And we in hymns below.

3 Thee, in thy glorious realm, they praise
   And bow before thy throne:
  We in the kingdom of thy grace; —
   The kingdoms are but one.

4 The holy to the holiest leads;
   From thence our spirits rise;
  And he that in thy statutes treads
   Shall meet thee in the skies.
                              C. WESLEY.

GOODMAN. 7s.

657. *Fellowship.* —Eph. 4: 5.

1 FATHER, hear our humble claim;
We are met in thy great name;
In the midst do thou appear,
Manifest thy presence here.

2 Lord, our fellowship increase;
Knit us in the bond of peace;
Join our hearts, O Father! join
Each to each, and all to thine.

3 Build us in one spirit up,
Called in one high calling's hope,
One the spirit, one the aim,
One the pure baptismal flame; —

4 One the faith, and one the Lord,
Whom by heaven and earth adored,
We our God and Father call;
O'er all, through all, with us all.
WESLEYAN.

658. *Fellowship.*

1 JESUS, Lord, we look to thee;
Let us in thy name agree;
Show thyself the Prince of peace;
Bid our jars forever cease.

2 By thy reconciling love,
Every stumbling-block remove:
Each to each unite, endear,
Come and spread thy banner here.

3 Make us of one heart and mind, —
Courteous, pitiful, and kind;
Lowly, meek, in thought and word, —
Altogether like our Lord.

4 Let us for each other care;
Each the other's burden bear;
To thy church the pattern give;
Show how true believers live.

5 Free from anger and from pride,
Let us thus in God abide:
All the depths of love express, —
All the heights of holiness.

6 Let us, then, with joy remove
To the family above;
On the wings of angels fly;
Show how true believers die.
C. WESLEY.

659. *Parting Hymn.*

1 FOR a season called to part,
Let us now ourselves commend
To the gracious eye and heart
Of our ever-present Friend.

2 Jesus, hear our humble prayer:
Tender Shepherd of thy sheep,
Let thy mercy and thy care
All our souls in safety keep.

3 In thy strength may we be strong;
Sweeten every cross and pain;
Spare us, that we may, ere long,
Meet and worship thee again.
NEWTON.

Doxology.

SING we to our God above
Praise eternal as his love;
Praise him, all ye heavenly host,—
Father, Son, and Holy Ghost.

276   The Christian Life. Unity and Fellowship.

DENTON. S. M.   TAYLOR.

660. *Blessings of Christian Unity.—Psalm 133.*

1 BLEST are the sons of peace
   Whose hearts and hopes are one;
Whose kind designs to serve and please
   Through all their actions run.

2 Blest is the pious house
   Where zeal and friendship meet:
Their songs of praise, their mingled vows
   Make their communion sweet.

3 From those celestial springs
   Such streams of pleasure flow,
As no increase of riches brings,
   Nor honors can bestow.

4 Thus on the heavenly hills
   The saints are blest above,
Where joy, like morning dew distils,
   And all the air is love!
                        WATTS.

661. *Christian Fellowship.*

1 BLEST be the tie that binds
   Our hearts in Christian love;
The fellowship of kindred minds
   Is like to that above.

2 Before our Father's throne
   We pour our ardent prayers;
Our fears, our hopes, our aims are one,
   Our comforts and our cares.

3 We share our mutual woes,
   Our mutual burdens bear;
And often for each other flows
   The sympathizing tear.

4 When we asunder part,
   It gives us inward pain;
But we shall still be joined in heart,
   And hope to meet again.

5 This glorious hope revives
   Our courage by the way;
While each in expectation lives,
   And longs to see the day.

6 From sorrow, toil, and pain,
   And sin, we shall be free,
And perfect love and friendship reign
   Through all eternity.
                        FAWCETT.

662.   Luke 4: 18.

1 SAVIOUR! what gracious words
   Are ever, ever thine!
Thy voice is music to the soul,
   And life and peace divine.

2 Good, everlasting good —
   Glad tidings full of joy,
Flow from thy lips, the lips of truth
   And flow without alloy.

3 The broken heart, the poor
   The bruised, the deaf, the blind,
The dumb, the dead, the captive wretch,
   In thee compassion find.

4 Lord Jesus! speed the day, —
   The promised day of grace, —
To all the poor, the dumb, the deaf,
   The dead of Adam's race.

Kindness to the Distressed. Brotherly Love.

ELIJAH. C. M.   MENDELSSOHN.

663. *Kindness to the Afflicted.*

1 Bright Source of everlasting love!
   To thee our souls we raise;
And to thy sovereign bounty rear
   A monument of praise.

2 Thy mercy gilds the paths of life
   With every cheering ray;
Kindly restrains the rising tear,
   Or wipes that tear away.

3 What shall we render, bounteous Lord!
   For all the grace we see?
Alas! the goodness we can yield
   Extendeth not to thee.

4 To tents of woe, to beds of pain,
   We cheerfully repair;
And, with the gifts thy hand bestows,
   Relieve the mourners there.

5 Thus passing through the vale of tears,
   Our useful light shall shine;
And others learn to glorify
   Our Father's name divine.

664.   1 John 4: 21.

1 How sweet, how heavenly is the sight,
   When those who love the Lord
In one another's peace delight,
   And so fulfil his word!

2 When each can feel his brother's sigh,
   And with him bear a part!
When sorrow flows from eye to eye,
   And joy from heart to heart!

3 When free from envy, scorn, and pride,
   Our wishes all above,
Each can his brother's failings hide,
   And show a brother's love!

4 Let love, in one delightful stream,
   Through every bosom flow,
And union sweet, and dear esteem,
   In every action glow.

5 Love is the golden chain that binds
   The happy souls above;
And he's an heir of heaven who finds
   His bosom glow with love.
                    SWAIN.

665. *"For ye have the Poor always with you."*

1 Lord, lead the way the Saviour went,
   By lane and cell obscure,
And let our treasures still be spent,
   Like his, upon the poor.

2 Like him, through scenes of deep distress,
   Who bore the world's sad weight,
We, in their gloomy loneliness,
   Would seek the desolate.

3 For thou hast placed us side by side
   In this wide world of ill;
And that thy followers may be tried,
   The poor are with us still.

4 Small are the offerings we can make;
   Yet thou hast taught us, Lord,
If given for the Saviour's sake,
   They lose not their reward.
                    CROSWELL.

STEPHENS. C. M.   W. JONES.

666.   *"Blessed are the Merciful."*

1 BLEST is the man whose softening heart
   Feels all another's pain;
  To whom the supplicating eye
   Was never raised in vain; —

2 Whose breast expands with generous warmth,
   A stranger's woe to feel;
  And bleeds in pity o'er the wound
   He wants the power to heal.

3 He spreads his kind, supporting arms
   To every child of grief;
  His secret bounty largely flows,
   And brings unasked relief.

4 To gentle offices of love,
   His feet are never slow;
  He views, through mercy's melting eye,
   A brother in a foe.

5 He hears the Saviour's cheering word,
   " My peace to him I give;"
  And when he kneels before the throne,
   His trembling soul shall live.
                          BARBAULD.

667.   *Likeness to Christ.*

1 LORD, as to thy dear cross we flee,
   And pray to be forgiven,
  Oh, let thy life our pattern be,
   And form our souls for heaven.

2 Help us, through good report and ill,
   Our daily cross to bear;
  Like thee, to do our Father's will,
   Our brother's griefs to share.

3 Let grace our selfishness expel,
   Our earthliness refine;
  And kindness in our bosoms dwell
   As free and true as thine.

4 Kept peaceful in the midst of strife,
   Forgiving and forgiven,
  Oh, may we lead the pilgrim's life,
   And follow thee to heaven!

668.   Luke 10: 29–37.

1 FATHER of mercies! send thy grace,
   All powerful, from above,
  To form in our obedient souls
   The image of thy love.

2 Oh, may our sympathizing breasts
   The generous pleasure know,
  Kindly to share in others' joy,
   And weep for others' woe.

3 When the most helpless sons of grief,
   In low distress are laid,
  Soft be our hearts their pains to feel,
   And swift our hands to aid.

4 So Jesus looked on dying man,
   When throned above the skies;
  And mid th' embraces of his God,
   He felt compassion rise.

5 On wings of love the Saviour flew,
   To raise us from the ground,
  And shed the richest of his blood,
   A balm for every wound.
                           DODDRIDGE.

669.   *1 Peter 2: 21-23.*

1 WHAT grace, O Lord, and beauty shone
    Around thy steps below;
What patient love was seen in all
    Thy life and death of woe.

2 For, ever on thy burdened heart
    A weight of sorrow hung;
Yet no ungentle, murmuring word
    Escaped thy silent tongue.

3 Thy foes might hate, despise, revile;
    Thy friends unfaithful prove;
Unwearied in forgiveness still,
    Thy heart could only love.

4 Oh, give us hearts to love like thee!
    Like thee, O Lord, to grieve
Far more for others' sins than all
    The wrongs that we receive.

5 One with thyself, may every eye,
    In us, thy brethren see
The gentleness and grace that spring
    From union, Lord! with thee.

670.   *Charitableness.* — Gal. 6: 1.

1 THINK gently of the erring one!
    And let us not forget,
However darkly stained by sin,
    He is our brother yet.

2 Heir of the same inheritance,
    Child of the self-same God;
He hath but stumbled in the path
    We have in weakness trod.

3 Forget not thou hast often sinned,
    And sinful yet must be:
Deal gently with the erring one,
    As God has dealt with thee.
                  FLETCHER.

671.   *John 13: 1.*

1 LORD, thou on earth didst love thine own;
    Didst love them to the end;
Oh, still from thy celestial throne
    Let gifts of love descend.

2 The love the Father bears to thee,
    His own eternal Son,
Fill all thy saints, till all shall be
    In pure affection one.

3 As thou for us didst stoop so low,
    Warmed by love's holy flame,
So let our deeds of kindness flow
    To all that bear thy name.

4 One blessed fellowship of love,
    Thy living church should stand,
Till, faultless, she at last above
    Shall shine at thy right hand.
                  RAY PALMER.

672.   *Matt. 25: 40.*

1 JESUS, our Lord, how rich thy grace!
    Thy bounties how complete!
How shall we count the matchless sum!
    How pay the mighty debt!

2 High on a throne of radiant light
    Dost thou exalted shine;
What can our poverty bestow,
    When all the worlds are thine?

3 But thou hast brethren here below,
    The partners of thy grace;
And wilt confess their humble names,
    Before thy Father's face.

4 In them thou mayst be clothed and fed,
    And visited and cheered;
And in their accents of distress,
    Our Saviour's voice is heard.
                  DODDRIDGE.

673.   *" Perfect us in Love."*

1 TRY us, O God, and search the ground
    Of every sinful heart;
Whate'er of sin in us is found,
    Oh, bid it all depart!

2 Help us to help each other, Lord,
    Each other's cross to bear;
Let each his friendly aid afford,
    And feel his brother's care.

3 Help us to build each other up,
    Our heart and life improve;
Increase our faith, confirm our hope,
    And perfect us in love.

4 Up into thee, our living Head,
    Let us in all things grow,
Till thou hast made us free indeed,
    And spotless here below.
                  C. WESLEY.

The Christian Life. Prayer.

HARDY. C. M.   "SABBATH TUNE BOOK."

674. *"Dear Refuge of my Weary Soul."*

1 Dear Refuge of my weary soul,
   On thee, when sorrows rise,—
: | On thee when waves of trouble roll, |:
   My fainting hope relies.

2 To thee I tell each rising grief,
   For thou alone canst heal;
Thy word can bring a sweet relief
   For every pain I feel.

3 Hast thou not bid me seek thy face?
   And shall I seek in vain?
And can the ear of sovereign grace
   Be deaf when I complain?

4 No: still the ear of sovereign grace
   Attends the mourner's prayer;
Oh, may I ever find access
   To breathe my sorrows there!

5 Thy mercy-seat is open still;
   Here let my soul retreat,
With humble hope attend thy will,
   And wait beneath thy feet.
             Mrs. Steele.

675.   Psalm 65: 2.

1 Prayer is the soul's sincere desire,
   Uttered or unexpressed;
: | The motion of a hidden fire | :
   That trembles in the breast.

2 Prayer is the burden of a sigh,
   The falling of a tear,
The upward glancing of an eye,
   When none but God is near.

3 Prayer is the simplest form of speech
   That infant lips can try;
Prayer the sublimest strains that reach
   The Majesty on high.

4 Prayer is the contrite sinner's voice,
   Returning from his ways;
While angels in their songs rejoice,
   And cry, "Behold he prays!"

5 Prayer is the Christian's vital breath,
   The Christian's native air,
His watchword at the gates of death;
   He enters heaven with prayer.

6 O thou by whom we come to God,
   The Life, the Truth, the Way!
The path of prayer thyself hast trod;
   Lord! teach us how to pray.
             Montgomery.

676.   Matt. 6. Luke 11.

1 Our Father, God, who art in heaven,
   All hallowed be thy name!
: | Thy kingdom come; thy will be done, |:
   In earth and heaven the same!

2 Give us this day our daily bread;
   And, as we those forgive
Who sin against us, so may we
   Forgiving grace receive.

3 Into temptation lead us not;
   From evil set us free;
And thine the kingdom, thine the power
   And glory ever be.
             Judson.

Note.—This tune requires the repetition of the *third line* of each verse.

677. 1 Sam. 1: 12-13.

1 Prayer is the breath of God in man,
  Returning whence it came;
  Love is the sacred fire within,
  And prayer the rising flame.

2 It gives the burdened spirit ease,
  And soothes the troubled breast;
  Yields comfort to the mourning soul,
  And to the weary rest.

3 When God inclines the heart to pray,
  He hath an ear to hear;
  To him there's music in a sigh,
  And beauty in a tear.

4 The humble suppliant cannot fail
  To have his wants supplied,
  Since He for sinners intercedes
  Who once for sinners died.

678. *The Safe Retreat.*

1 Dear Father, to thy mercy-seat
  My soul for shelter flies;
  'Tis here I find a safe retreat
  When storms and tempests rise.

2 My cheerful hope can never die,
  If thou, my God, art near;
  Thy grace can raise my comforts high,
  And banish every fear.

3 My great Protector and my Lord,
  Thy constant aid impart;
  Oh, let thy kind, thy gracious word
  Sustain my trembling heart!

4 Oh, never let my soul remove
  From this divine retreat!
  Still let me trust thy power and love,
  And dwell beneath thy feet.
  Mrs. Steele.

679. *Blessedness of Prayer.*

1 No, never shall my heart despond,
  Long as my lips can pray;
  My latest breath, with effort fond,
  Shall pass in prayer away.

2 There is a heavenly mercy-seat
  To calm the sinner's fears;
  There is a Saviour at whose feet
  The mourner dries his tears.

3 When friends depart, and hopes are riven,
  And gathering storms I see,
  My soul is but the sooner driven,
  Eternal Rock! to thee.

4 Oh for a voice of sweeter sound,
  For every wind to bear,
  To teach the listening world around
  The blessedness of prayer!

680. *Secret Prayer.*

1 Sweet is the prayer whose holy stream
  In earnest pleading flows;
  Devotion dwells upon the theme,
  And warm and warmer glows.

2 Faith grasps the blessing she desires,
  Hope points the upward gaze,
  And love, untrembling love inspires
  The eloquence of praise.

3 But sweeter far the still small voice,
  Heard by no human ear,
  When God hath made the heart rejoice,
  And dried the bitter tear.

4 Nor accents flow, nor words ascend;
  All utterance faileth there;
  But listening spirits comprehend,
  And God accepts the prayer.
  H. Martineau.

681. *"Teach us to pray."*

1 Lord, teach us how to pray aright,
  With reverence and with fear:
  Though dust and ashes in thy sight,
  We may, we must draw near.

2 God of all grace, we come to thee,
  With broken, contrite hearts;
  Give what thine eye delights to see,—
  Truth in the inward parts.

3 Give deep humility; the sense
  Of godly sorrow give;
  A strong desiring confidence
  To see thy face and live.

4 Patience to watch and wait and weep,
  Though mercy long delay;
  Courage, our fainting souls to keep,
  And trust thee, though thou slay.

5 Give these, and then thy will be done;
  Thus strengthened with all might,
  We, by thy Spirit and thy Son,
  Shall pray, and pray aright.
  Montgomery.

The Christian Life.

EASTON. L. M. — MOZART.

682. *Luke 21: 37.*

1 Thou Saviour, from thy throne on high,
  Enrobed in light and girt with power,
Dost note the thought, the prayer, the sigh,
  Of hearts that love the tranquil hour.

2 Oft thou thyself didst steal away
  At eventide, from labor done,
In some still peaceful shade to pray
  Till morning watches were begun.

3 Thou hast not, dearest Lord, forgot
  Thy wrestlings on Judea's hills;
And still thou lov'st the quiet spot
  Where praise the lowly spirit fills.

4 Now to our souls, withdrawn awhile
  From earth's rude noise, thy face reveal;
And as we worship, kindly smile,
  And for thine own our spirits seal.

5 To thee we bring each grief and care,
  To thee we fly while tempests lower;
Thou wilt the weary burdens bear
  Of hearts that love the tranquil hour.
  RAY PALMER.

683. *The Power of Prayer.*

1 What various hindrances we meet
  In coming to a mercy-seat!
Yet who that knows the worth of [prayer
  But wishes to be often there?

2 Prayer makes the darkened clouds withdraw;
  Prayer climbs the ladder Jacob saw,
Gives exercise to faith and love,
  Brings every blessing from above.

3 Restraining prayer, we cease to fight;
  Prayer makes the Christian's armor bright;
And Satan trembles when he sees
  The weakest saint upon his knees.

4 Have you no words? ah! think again;
  Words flow apace when you complain,
And fill a fellow-creature's ear
  With the sad tale of all your care.

5 Were half the breath thus vainly spent,
  To heaven in supplication sent,
Our cheerful song would oftener be,
  "Hear what the Lord hath done for me!"
  COWPER.

684. *Matt. 21: 22.*

1 And dost thou say, "Ask what thou wilt"?
  Lord, I would seize the golden hour:
I pray to be released from guilt,
  And freed from sin and Satan's power.

2 More of thy presence, Lord, impart;
  More of thine image let me bear;
Erect thy throne within my heart,
  And reign without a rival there.

3 Give me to read my pardon sealed,
  And from thy joy to draw my strength:
Oh, be thy boundless love revealed
  In all its height and breadth and length.

4 Grant these requests, — I ask no more,
  But to thy care the rest resign:
Sick, or in health, or rich, or poor,
  All shall be well, if thou art mine.

Prayer.

RETREAT. L. M.   DR. HASTINGS.

685.   Heb. 4: 16. Ex. 25: 22.

1 From every stormy wind that blows,
From every swelling tide of woes,
There is a calm, a sure retreat;
'Tis found beneath the mercy-seat.

2 There is a place where Jesus sheds
The oil of gladness on our heads, —
A place than all besides more sweet;
It is the blood-bought mercy-seat.

3 There is a scene where spirits blend,
Where friend holds fellowship with friend;
Though sundered far, by faith they meet
Around one common mercy-seat!

4 There, there on eagle wings we soar,
And sense and sin molest no more,
And heaven comes down our souls to greet,
And glory crowns the mercy-seat.
                         STOWELL.

686.   *Hour of Prayer.*

1 Blest hour when mortal man retires
To hold communion with his God,
To send to heaven his warm desires,
And listen to the sacred word.

2 Blest hour when God himself draws nigh,
Well pleased his people's voice to hear,
To hush the penitential sigh,
And wipe away the mourner's tear.

3 Blest hour, for where the Lord resorts,
Foretastes of future bliss are given,
And mortals find his earthly courts
The house of God, the gate of heaven.
                         RAFFLES.

687.   *The Mercy-Seat.*

1 Approach, my soul, the mercy-seat,
Where Jesus sits to answer prayer;
Thus humbly fall before his feet;
For none have ever perished there.

2 Thy promise is my only plea;
With this I humbly venture nigh;
Thou callest burdened souls to thee,
And surely such, O Lord, am I.

3 Bowed down beneath a load of sin,
By Satan tempted, sorely pressed,
By war without and fear within,
I come to thee, my Lord, for rest.

4 Be thou my shield and hiding-place,
That, safely sheltered near thy side,
I may the fierce accuser face,
And tell him, Jesus, thou hast died.
                         NEWTON.

688.   Matt. 11: 28.

1 How sweetly flowed the gospel sound,
From lips of gentleness and grace,
When listening thousands gathered round,
And joy and gladness filled the place.

2 From heaven he came, of heaven he spoke,
To heaven he led his followers' way;
Dark clouds of gloomy night he broke,
Unveiling an immortal day.

3 "Come, wanderers, to my Father's home;
Come, all ye weary ones, and rest;"
Yes, sacred Teacher, we will come,
Obey thee, love thee, and be blest!
                         BOWRING.

The Christian Life.

ADRIAN. S. M. J. E. GOULD, from "Modern Harp."

689. *The Call to Prayer.*

1 Come at the morning hour,
 Come, let us kneel and pray;
Prayer is the Christian pilgrim's staff
 To walk with God all day.

2 At noon, beneath the Rock
 Of Ages, rest and pray;
Sweet is that shelter from the sun
 In the weary heat of day.

3 At evening, in thy home,
 Around its altar, pray;
And finding there the house of God,
 With heaven then close the day.
 BRIGGS' COLL.

690. *Delight in Worship.*

1 How sweet to bless the Lord,
 And in his praises join,
With saints his goodness to record,
 And sing his power divine!

2 Thus may our joys increase,
 Our love more ardent grow,
While rich supplies of Jesus' grace
 Refresh our souls below.

3 But, oh, the bliss sublime,
 When joy shall be complete,
In that unclouded, glorious clime
 Where all thy servants meet!

4 Then shall the ransomed throng
 The Saviour's love record,
And shout in everlasting song,—
 "Salvation to the Lord!"
 URWICK'S COLL.

691. *Call to Prayer.*

1 Come to the house of prayer,
 O thou afflicted, come;
The God of peace shall meet thee there;
 He makes that house his home.

2 Come to the house of praise,
 Ye who are happy now;
In sweet accord your voices raise,
 In kindred homage bow.

3 Ye aged, hither come!
 For ye have felt his love; [dumb,
Soon shall your trembling tongues be
 Your lips forget to move.

4 Ye young! before his throne,
 Come, bow; your voices raise;
Let not your hearts his praise disown,
 Who gives the power to praise.
 TAYLOR.

692. *God our Strength.*

1 Man's wisdom is to seek
 His strength in God alone;
And e'en an angel would be weak
 Who trusted in his own.

2 Retreat beneath his wings,
 And in his grace confide;
This more exalts the King of kings
 Than all your works beside.

3 In Jesus is our store;
 Grace issues from his throne;
Whoever says, "I want no more,"
 Confesses he has none.
 COWPER.

Prayer.

BOYLSTON. S. M.   DR. MASON.

693.   Luke 18 : 1.
1 JESUS, who knows full well
    The heart of every saint,
  Invites us all our griefs to tell,
    To pray, and never faint.

2 He bows his gracious ear;
    We never plead in vain;
  Yet we must wait till he appear,
    And pray, and pray again.

3 Jesus, the Lord, will hear
    His chosen when they cry;
  Yes, though he may a while forbear,
    He'll help them from on high.

4 Then let us earnest be,
    And never faint in prayer;
  He loves our importunity,
    And makes our cause his care.
                          NEWTON.

694.   Heb. 4 : 16.
1 BEHOLD the throne of grace!
    The promise calls me near;
  There Jesus shows a smiling face,
    And waits to answer prayer.

2 That rich, atoning blood,
    Which sprinkled round I see,
  Provides for those who come to God
    An all-prevailing plea.

3 My soul! ask what thou wilt;
    Thou canst not be too bold;
  Since his own blood for thee he spilt,
    What else can he withhold?

4 Thine image, Lord, bestow,
    Thy presence and thy love;
  I ask to serve thee here below,
    And reign with thee above.

5 Teach me to live by faith;
    Conform my will to thine;
  Let me victorious be in death,
    And then in glory shine.
                          NEWTON.

695.   Matt. 18: 20.
1 JESUS, we look to thee,
    Thy promised presence claim;
  Thou in the midst of us shalt be,
    Assembled in thy name.

2 Not in the name of pride
    Or selfishness we meet;
  From nature's paths we turn aside,
    And worldly thoughts forget.

3 We meet, the grace to take
    Which thou hast freely given;
  We meet on earth for thy dear sake,
    That we may meet in heaven.

4 Present we know thou art,
    But, oh, thyself reveal!
  Now, Lord, let every bounding heart
    Thy mighty comfort feel.

5 Oh, may thy quickening voice
    The death of sin remove;
  And bid our inmost souls rejoice
    In hope of perfect love.
                          C. WESLEY.

WEBER. 7s.

696. Col. 4 : 2.
1 Heavenly Father, sovereign Lord,
 Be thy glorious name adored!
 Lord, thy mercies never fail;
 Hail, celestial goodness, hail!

2 Though unworthy, Lord, thine ear,
 Deign our humble songs to hear;
 Purer praise we hope to bring,
 When around thy throne we sing.

3 While on earth ordained to stay,
 Guide our footsteps in thy way,
 Till we come to dwell with thee,
 Till we all thy glory see.

4 Then, with angel-harps again,
 We will wake a nobler strain;
 There, in joyful songs of praise,
 Our triumphant voices raise.
 MONTGOMERY.

697. Isaiah 56: 7.
1 Soft and holy is the place,
  Where the light that beams from heaven
  Shows the Saviour's smiling face,
  With the joy of sin forgiven.

2 There, with one accord we meet,
  All the words of life to hear;
  Bending low at Jesus' feet,
  Worshipping with godly fear.

3 Let the world and all its cares
  Now retire from every breast;
  Let the tempter and his snares
  Cease to hinder or molest.
  HASTINGS.

698. Acts 10: 33.
1 Stealing from the world away,
  We are come to seek thy face;
  Kindly meet us, Lord, we pray,
  Grant us thy reviving grace.

2 Yonder stars that gild the sky
  Shine but with a borrowed light;
  We, unless thy light be nigh,
  Wander, wrapt in gloomy night.

3 Sun of righteousness! dispel
  All our darkness, doubts, and fears;
  May thy light within us dwell,
  Till eternal day appears.

4 Warm our hearts in prayer and praise,
  Lift our every thought above;
  Hear the grateful songs we raise,
  Fill us with thy perfect love.
  RAY PALMER.

699. *Invocation.*
1 Holy Lord, our hearts prepare
  For the solemn work of prayer;
  Grant that while we bend the knee,
  All our thoughts may turn to thee.

2 While we come around thy throne,
  Make thy power and glory known;
  As thy children may we call
  On our Father, Lord of all.

3 Teach us, while we breathe our woes,
  On thy promise to repose;
  All thy tender love to trace
  In the Saviour's work of grace.

Prayer.

PLEYEL'S HYMN. 7s.

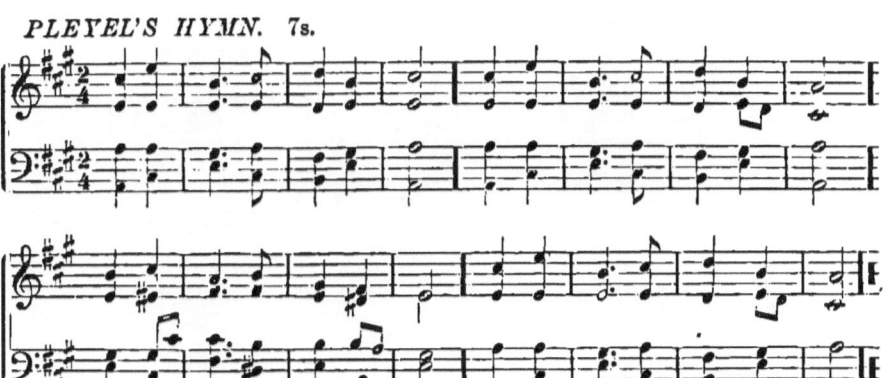

700. Eph. 6 : 18.
1 They who seek the throne of grace
Find that throne in every place;
If we live a life of prayer,
God is present everywhere.

2 In our sickness and our health,
In our want, or in our wealth,
If we look to God in prayer,
God is present everywhere.

3 When our earthly comforts fail,
When the foes of life prevail,
'Tis the time for earnest prayer;
God is present everywhere.

4 Then, my soul, in every strait,
To thy Father come and wait;
He will answer every prayer;
God is present everywhere.

701. Matt. 7: 7.
1 Come, my soul, thy suit prepare,
Jesus loves to answer prayer;
He himself has bid thee pray,
Therefore will not say thee nay.

2 With my burden I begin; —
Lord, remove this load of sin;
Let thy blood, for sinners spilt,
Set my conscience free from guilt.

3 Lord! I come to thee for rest,
Take possession of my breast;
There thy sovereign right maintain,
And, without a rival, reign.

4 While I am a pilgrim here,
Let thy love my spirit cheer;
Be my Guide, my Guard, my Friend,
Lead me to my journey's end.
NEWTON.

702. Acts 16: 13.
1 Heavenly Spirit! may each heart
Through these sacred hours be thine;
May we from the world depart,
Breathing after things divine.

2 Lead us forth with joy and peace,
To thy temple, in thy ways;
And when this sweet day shall cease,
May its sun go down with praise.
EDMESTON.

703. John 17: 9.
1 Thine forever! God of love,
Hear us from thy throne above!
Thine forever may we be,
Here, and in eternity!

2 Thine forever! oh, how blest
They who find in thee their rest!
Saviour, Guardian, heavenly Friend,
Oh, defend us to the end!

3 Thine forever! Saviour, keep
These thy frail and trembling sheep;
Safe alone beneath thy care,
Let us all thy goodness share.

4 Thine forever! thou our Guide, —
All our wants by thee supplied, —
All our sins by thee forgiven, —
Lead us, Lord, from earth to heaven!

SWEETLAND. C. M. Arranged from KUCKEN.

704. *Matt. 6: 10; 26:42.*

1 How sweet to be allowed to pray
   To God, the Holy One;
 With filial love and trust to say,
   "O God, thy will be done."

2 We in these sacred words can find
   A cure for every ill;
 They calm and soothe the troubled mind,
   And bid all care be still.

3 Oh, let that will which gave me breath,
   And an immortal soul,
 In joy, in grief, in life or death,
   My every wish control.

4 Oh, could my heart thus ever pray,
   Thus imitate thy Son!
 Teach me, O God, with truth to say,
   "Thy will, not mine, be done."
                                FOLLETT.

705. *Coming to God.*

1 I come to thee, once more, my God,
   No longer will I roam,   [through,
 For I have sought the wide world
   And never found a home.

2 Oh, bright and many are the spots
   Where I have built a nest,
 Yet in the brightest still I pined
   For more abiding rest.

3 Thou, Lord, hast made this wondrous
     soul
   All for thyself alone;
 Oh, send thy sweet, transforming grace
   To make it all thine own.
                                FABER.

706. *Job 1: 21.*

1 One prayer I have — all prayers in one.
   When I am wholly thine;
 Thy will, my God, thy will be done,
   And let that will be mine.

2 All-wise, almighty, and all-good,
   In thee I firmly trust;
 Thy ways, unknown or understood,
   Are merciful and just.

3 And though thy wisdom takes away,
   Shall I arraign thy will?
 No, let me bless thy name, and say,
   "The Lord is gracious still."

4 A pilgrim through the earth I roam,
   Of nothing long possessed;
 And all must fail when I go home,
   For this is not my rest.
                                MONTGOMERY.

707. *Psalm 133.*

1 Spirit of peace, celestial Dove,
   How excellent thy praise!
 How rich the gift of Christian love
   Thy gracious power displays!

2 Sweet as the dew on hill and flower,
   That silently distils,
 At evening's soft and balmy hour,
   On Zion's fruitful hills.

3 So, with mild influence from above,
   Shall promised grace descend;
 Till universal peace and love
   O'er all the earth extend.
                                LYTE.

Section VII.

THE CHURCH OF CHRIST.

(*a.*) *Church divinely founded. God's Dwelling-Place and Peculiar Care. Catholic and True. Christ its Corner-Stone. Kingdom that cannot be shaken. Church's Pilgrimage. Love of the Church. Glorious Things spoken of her.*

(*b.*) *The Lord's Supper. Hymns of Consecration, of Covenant Love, of Christian Fellowship and Greeting.*

(*c.*) *Baptism. Offering of Children. Pleading the Covenant Promises.*

(*d.*) *The Christian Ministry. Hymns for Ordination and Installation. Prayers for Pastors. The Death of Pastors. Dedication Hymns.*

(*e.*) *Spread of the Gospel. Missionary Hymns.*

"AS CHRIST ALSO LOVED THE CHURCH, AND GAVE HIMSELF FOR IT, THAT HE MIGHT SANCTIFY AND CLEANSE IT WITH THE WASHING OF WATER BY THE WORD, THAT HE MIGHT PRESENT IT TO HIMSELF A GLORIOUS CHURCH, NOT HAVING SPOT OR WRINKLE, OR ANY SUCH THING; BUT THAT IT SHOULD BE HOLY AND WITHOUT BLEMISH." — *Eph.* 5: 25-27.

The Church of Christ.

SALEM. 8s. & 7s.   "URBS BEATA."

708. *"Behold I Lay in Sion a Chief Corner-Stone."*

1 Christ is made the sure Foundation,
    Christ the Head and Corner-Stone,
Chosen of the Lord, and precious,
    Binding all the Church in one;
Holy Sion's help forever,
    And her confidence alone.

2 All that dedicated City,
    Dearly loved of God on high,
In exultant jubilation
    Pours perpetual melody;
God the One in Three adoring
    In glad hymns eternally.

3 To this Temple, where we call thee,
    Come, O Lord of Hosts, to-day;
With thy wonted loving-kindness,
    Hear thy servants as they pray;
And thy fullest benediction
    Shed within its walls alway.

709.   *New Jerusalem.*

1 Glorious city, heavenly Salem,
    Vision dear of peace and love,
Who of living stones art builded
    In the height of heaven above,
And with angel hosts encircled,
    As a bride to earth dost move;

2 From celestial realms descending,
    Bridal glory round thee shed,
Meet for Him whose love espoused thee,
    To thy Lord shalt thou be led:
All thy streets and all thy bulwarks
    Of pure gold are fashionèd.

3 Bright thy gates of pearl are shining;
    They are open evermore;
And by virtue of his merits
    Thither faithful souls do soar,
Who for Christ's dear name in this
    world
Pain and tribulation bore.

The Church: Repenting, Encouraged.

DORMAN. L. M.

710. *Psalm 80.*

1 Great Shepherd of thine Israel,
Who didst between the cherubs dwell,
And lead the tribes, thy chosen sheep,
Safe through the desert and the deep:

2 Thy Church is in the desert now:
Shine from on high and guide us through;
Turn us to thee, thy love restore;
We shall be saved, and sigh no more.

3 Hast thou not planted with thy hand
A lovely vine in this our land?
Did not thy power defend it round,
And heavenly dew enrich the ground?

4 Return, Almighty God, return!
Nor let thy bleeding vineyard mourn:
Turn us to thee, thy love restore;
We shall be saved, and sigh no more.
WATTS.

711. *Christ's Indwelling Besought.*

1 Come, dearest Lord, descend and dwell
By faith and love in every breast;
Then shall we know and taste and feel
The joys that cannot be expressed.

2 Come, fill our hearts with inward strength,
Make our enlargèd souls possess,
And learn the height and breadth and length
Of thine immeasurable grace.

3 Now to the God whose power can do
More than our thoughts and wishes know,
Be everlasting honors done
By all the church, through Christ his Son!
WATTS.

712. *Isaiah 52: 1.*

1 Triumphant Zion, lift thy head
From dust and darkness and the dead;
Though humbled long, awake at length,
And gird thee with thy Saviour's strength.

2 Put all thy beauteous garments on,
And let thy various charms be known;
The world thy glories shall confess,
Decked in the robes of righteousness.

3 No more shall foes unclean invade,
And fill thy hallowed walls with dread;
No more shall hell's insulting host
Their victory and thy sorrows boast.

4 God, from on high, thy groans will hear;
His hand thy ruins shall repair;
Nor will thy watchful Monarch cease
To guard thee in eternal peace.
DODDRIDGE.

713. *"Brethren, pray for us."*

1 Father of mercies, bow thine ear,
Attentive to our earnest prayer;
We plead for those who plead for thee:
Successful pleaders may they be.

2 Clothe thou with energy divine [thine;
Their words, and let those words be
Teach them immortal souls to gain,
Nor let them labor, Lord, in vain.

3 Let thronging multitudes around
Hear from their lips the joyful sound;
And light through distant realms be spread,
Till Zion rears her drooping head.
BEDDOME.

The Church of Christ.

WARWICK. C. M.   STANLEY.

714.   *Psalm 27.*

1 THE Lord of glory is my light,
    And my salvation, too:
God is my strength, nor will I fear
    What all my foes can do.

2 One privilege my heart desires,
    Oh, grant me an abode
Among the churches of thy saints,
    The temples of my God.

3 There shall I offer my requests,
    And see thy beauty still;
Shall hear thy messages of love,
    And there inquire thy will.

4 When troubles rise, and storms appear,
    There may his children hide;
God has a strong pavilion, where
    He makes my soul abide.

5 Now shall my head be lifted high
    Above my foes around;
And songs of joy and victory
    Within thy temple sound.
                  WATTS.

715.   *Christ the Head of the Church.*

1 OUR Christ hath reached his heavenly
      seat,
    Through sorrows and through scars;
The golden lamps are at his feet,
    And in his hand the stars.

2 O Lord of life and truth and grace,
    Ere nature was begun!
Make welcome to our erring race
    Thy Spirit and thy Son.

3 We hail the Church, built high o'er all
    The heathen's rage and scoff;
Thy Providence its fencèd wall,
    "The Lamb the light thereof."

4 Oh, may he walk among us here,
    With his rebuke and love,
A brightness o'er this lower sphere,
    A ray from worlds above!
                  FROTHINGHAM.

716.   *Psalm 132.*

1 ARISE, O King of grace, arise!
    And enter to thy rest;
Lo! thy church waits with longing eyes,
    Thus to be owned and blest.

2 Enter with all thy glorious train,
    Thy Spirit and thy word;
All that the ark did once contain
    Could no such grace afford.

3 Here, mighty God, accept our vows;
    Here let thy praise be spread;
Bless the provisions of thy house,
    And fill thy poor with bread.

4 Here let the Son of David reign,
    Let God's Anointed shine;
Justice and truth his court maintain,
    With love and power divine.

5 Here let him hold a lasting throne,
    And as his kingdom grows,
Fresh honors shall adorn his crown,
    And shame confound his foes.
                  WATTS.

GEER. C. M.   GREATOREX'S COLL.

717.   *Ye are God's Building.*

1 THE lovely form of God's own Church,
    It riseth in all lands;
On mountain sides, in wooded vales,
    And by the desert sands.

2 Though sects and factions rule the world,
    Peace is its heritage;
Unchanged, though empires by it pass,
    The same from age to age.

3 The hallowed form our fathers built,
    That hallowed form build we;
Let not one stone from its own place
    Removèd ever be!

4 Clear voices from above sound out
    Their blessing on the pile;
The dead beneath support our hands,
    And succor us the while.

5 Yea, when we climb the rising walls,
    Is peace and comfort given;
Because the work is not of earth,
    But hath its end in heaven.
                      ALFORD.

718.   Dan. 2: 44.

1 OH, where are kings and empires now,
    Of old that went and came?
But, Lord, thy church is praying yet,
    A thousand years the same.

2 We mark her goodly battlements,
    And her foundations strong;
We hear within the solemn voice
    Of her unending song.

3 For not like kingdoms of the world,
    Thy holy church, O God!   [ing her,
Though earthquake shocks are threaten-
    And tempests are abroad;—

4 Unshaken as eternal hills,
    Immovable she stands,—
A mountain that shall fill the earth,
    A house not made by hands.
                      A. C. COXE.

719.   *The House of God.*

1 WE love the venerable house
    Our fathers built to God;
In heaven are kept their grateful vows,
    Their dust endears the sod.

2 Here holy thoughts a light have shed
    From many a radiant face;
And prayers of tender hope have spread
    A perfume through the place.

3 From humble tenements around
    Came up the pensive train;
And in the church a blessing found,
    Which filled their homes again.

4 They live with God, their homes are dust,
    But here their children pray,
And in this fleeting lifetime trust
    To find the narrow way.

5 On him who by the altar stands,
    Lord, let thy blessing fall!   [mands,
Speak through his lips thy pure com-
    Thou Heart that lovest all!
                      EMERSON.

OLMUTZ. S. M.

720. *Psalm 137.*

1 I LOVE thy kingdom, Lord, —
  The house of thine abode,
 The Church our blest Redeemer saved
  With his own precious blood.

2 I love thy Church, O God!
  Her walls before thee stand,
 Dear as the apple of thine eye,
  And graven on thy hand.

3 For her my tears shall fall,
  For her my prayers ascend;
 To her my cares and toils be given,
  Till toils and cares shall end.

4 Beyond my highest joy
  I prize her heavenly ways,
 Her sweet communion, solemn vows,
  Her hymns of love and praise.

5 Jesus, thou Friend divine,
  Our Saviour and our King,
 Thy hand from every snare and foe
  Shall great deliverance bring.

6 Sure as thy truth shall last,
  To Zion shall be given
 The brightest glories earth can yield,
  And brighter bliss of heaven.
   DWIGHT.

721. *The Pilgrim Church.*

1 FAR down the ages now,
  Much of her journey done,
 The pilgrim Church pursues her way,
  Until her crown be won.

2 No wider is the gate,
  No broader is the way,
 No smoother is the ancient path,
  That leads to life and day.

3 No slacker grows the fight,
  No feebler is the foe,
 Nor less the need of armor tried,
  Of shield and spear and bow.

4 Still faithful to our God,
  And to our Captain true,
 We follow where he leads the way,
  The kingdom in our view.
   BONAR.

722. *Safety of the Church.*

1 How honored is the place
  Where we adoring stand!
 Zion, the glory of the earth,
  And beauty of the land.

2 Bulwarks of grace defend
  The city where we dwell;
 While walls of strong salvation made
  Defy th' assaults of hell.

3 Here taste unmingled joys,
  And live in perfect peace;
 You that have known Jehovah's name,
  And ventured on his grace.

4 Trust in the Lord, ye saints,
  And banish all your fears;
 Strength in the Lord Jehovah dwells,
  Eternal as his years.
   WATTS.

The Church of Christ.

RATHBUN. 8s. & 7s. — GREATOREX'S COLL.

723. *"Zion, City of our God."* — Psalm 87.

1 GLORIOUS things of thee are spoken,
  Zion, city of our God ;
He whose word can ne'er be broken
  Chose thee for his own abode.

2 Lord, thy Church is still thy dwelling,
  Still is precious in thy sight;
Judah's temple far excelling,
  Beaming with the gospel's light.

3 On the Rock of Ages founded,
  What can shake her sure repose?
With salvation's wall surrounded,
  She can smile at all her foes.

4 Glorious things of thee are spoken,
  Zion, city of our God ;
He whose word can ne'er be broken,
  Chose thee for his own abode.
                                    NEWTON.

724. Cant. 2: 4.

1 JESUS spreads his banner o'er us,
  Cheers our famished souls with food ;
He the banquet spreads before us,
  Of his mystic flesh and blood.

2 Precious banquet, bread of heaven,
  Wine of gladness, flowing free ;
May we taste it, kindly given,
  In remembrance, Lord, of thee !

3 In thy trial and rejection,
  In thy sufferings on the tree,
In thy glorious resurrection,
  May we, Lord, remember thee.

725. Psalm 127.

1 VAINLY through night's weary hours,
  Keep we watch, lest foes alarm ;
Vain our bulwarks and our towers,
  But for God's protecting arm.

2 Vain were all our toil and labor,
  Did not God that labor bless ;
Vain, without his grace and favor,
  Every talent we possess.

3 Vainer still the hope of heaven,
  That on human strength relies ;
But to him shall help be given,
  Who in humble faith applies.

4 Seek we, then, the Lord's Anointed ;
  He shall grant us peace and rest :
Ne'er was suppliant disappointed,
  Who to Christ his prayer addressed.
                                    LYTE.

726. Communion.

1 WHILE in sweet communion feeding
  On this earthly bread and wine,
Saviour, may we see thee bleeding
  On the cross, to make us thine.

2 Though unseen, now be thou near us,
  With the still small voice of love ;
Whispering words of peace to cheer us,
  Every doubt and fear remove.

3 Bring before us all the story
  Of thy life and death of woe ;
And, with hopes of endless glory,
  Wean our hearts from all below.

The Lord's Supper.

ROSEFIELD. 7s. 6l.   DR. MALAN.

727.   1 Cor. 11: 26.
1 MANY centuries have fled
Since our Saviour broke the bread,
And this sacred feast ordained,
Ever by his Church retained :
Those his body who discern
Thus shall meet till his return.

2 Through the Church's long eclipse,
When, from priest or pastor's lips,
Truth divine was never heard, —
'Mid the famine of the word,
Still these symbols witness gave
To his love who died to save.

3 All who bear the Saviour's name
Here their common faith proclaim;
Though diverse in tongue or rite,
Here, one body to unite;
Breaking thus one mystic bread,
Members of one common Head.

4 Come, the blessed emblems share,
Which the Saviour's death declare;
Come, on truth immortal feed;
For his flesh is meat indeed :
Saviour! witness with the sign
That our ransomed souls are thine.
                      CONDER.

728.   Psalm 67.
1 GOD of mercy, God of grace!
Show the brightness of thy face :
Shine upon us, Saviour! shine,
Fill thy Church with light divine,
And thy saving health extend
To the earth's remotest end.

2 Let the people praise thee, Lord!
Be by all that live adored :
Let the nations shout and sing,
Glory to their Saviour King;
At thy feet their tribute pay,
And thy holy will obey.

3 Let the people praise thee, Lord!
Earth shall then her fruits afford ;
God to man his blessing give;
Man to God devoted live ;
All below, and all above,
One in joy and light and love.
                      LYTE.

729.   Gethsemane.
1 Go to dark Gethsemane,
   Ye that feel the tempter's power,
Your Redeemer's conflict see,
   Watch with him one bitter hour:
Turn not from his griefs away,
Learn of Jesus Christ to pray.

2 Follow to the judgment-hall,
   View the Lord of life arraigned:
Oh, the wormwood and the gall !
   Oh, the pangs his soul sustained !
Shun not suffering, shame, or loss ;
Learn of him to bear the cross.

3 Calv'ry's mournful mountain climb ;
   There, adoring at his feet,
Mark that miracle of time,
   God's own sacrifice complete !
"It is finished," hear him cry ;
Learn of Jesus Christ to die.
                      MONTGOMERY.

ARLINGTON. C. M.   DR. ARNE.

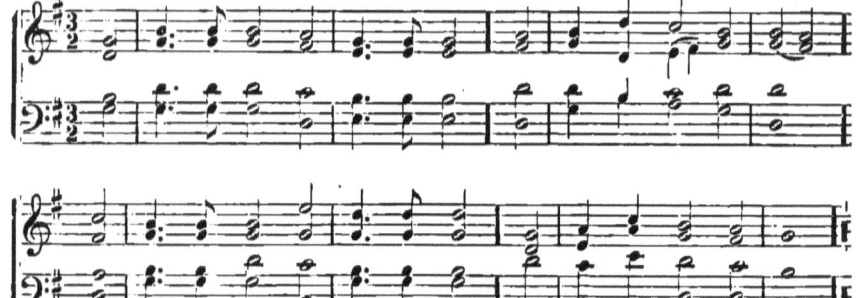

730. *Meet, and remember Me!*—Luke 22: 19.

1 If human kindness meets return,
   And owns the grateful tie;
   If tender thoughts within us burn,
   To feel a friend is nigh; —

2 Oh, shall not warmer accents tell
   The gratitude we owe
   To Him who died our fears to quell —
   Our more than orphan's woe?

3 While yet in anguish he surveyed
   Those pangs he would not flee,
   What love his latest words displayed:
   "Meet and remember me!"

4 Remember thee — thy death, thy shame!
   Our sinful hearts to share!
   O memory! leave no other name
   But his recorded there.
                          NOEL.

731.   Luke 22: 19.

1 According to thy gracious word,
   In meek humility,
   This will I do, my dying Lord,
   I will remember thee.

2 Thy body, broken for my sake,
   My bread from heaven shall be;
   Thy testamental cup I take,
   And thus remember thee.

3 Gethsemane can I forget?
   Or there thy conflict see,
   Thine agony and bloody sweat,
   And not remember thee?

4 When to the cross I turn mine eyes,
   And rest on Calvary,
   O Lamb of God, my sacrifice!
   I must remember thee; —

5 Remember thee, and all thy pains,
   And all thy love to me;
   Yea, while a breath, a pulse remains,
   Will I remember thee.

6 And when these failing lips grow dumb,
   And mind and memory flee,
   When thou shalt in thy kingdom come,
   Then, Lord, remember me!
                          MONTGOMERY.

732.   Jer. 31: 3.

1 How sweet and awful is the place,
   With Christ within the doors;
   While everlasting love displays
   The choicest of her stores!

2 While all our hearts, and all our songs,
   Join to admire the feast,
   Each of us cries, with thankful tongues,
   "Lord, why was I a guest?"

3 "Why was I made to hear thy voice,
   And enter while there's room,
   When thousands make a wretched choice,
   And rather starve than come?"

4 'Twas the same love that spread the feast
   That sweetly drew us in;
   Else we had still refused to taste,
   And perished in our sin.
                          WATTS.

733. *Lord's Table.*

1 LORD! at thy table I behold
  The wonders of thy grace;
  But most of all admire that I
  Should find a welcome place.

2 What strange, surprising grace is this,
  That such a soul has room!
  My Saviour takes me by the hand,
  My Jesus bids me come.

3 Ye saints below and hosts of heaven,
  Join all your praising powers;
  No theme is like redeeming love,
  No Saviour is like ours.

4 Had I ten thousand hearts, dear Lord,
  I'd give them all to thee;
  Had I ten thousand tongues, they all
  Should join the harmony.
  STENNETT.

734. *"A Good Profession before many Witnesses."*
1 Tim. 6: 12.

1 WITNESS, ye men and angels, now
  Before the Lord we speak;
  To him we make our solemn vow, —
  A vow we dare not break : —

2 That, long as life itself shall last,
  Ourselves to Christ we yield;
  Nor from his cause will we depart,
  Or ever quit the field.

3 We trust not in our native strength,
  But on his grace rely,
  That with returning wants the Lord
  Will all our need supply.

4 Oh, guide our doubtful feet aright,
  And keep us in thy ways;
  And while we turn our vows to prayers,
  Turn thou our prayers to praise!
  BEDDOME.

735. *Preparation for Communion.*

1 PREPARE us, Lord, to view thy cross,
  Who all our griefs hast borne;
  To look on thee whom we have pierced,
  To look on thee, and mourn.

2 While thus we mourn, we would rejoice,
  And, as thy cross we see,
  Let each exclaim in faith and hope, —
  "The Saviour died for me!"

736. *Communion.*

1 O GOD, unseen yet ever near,
  Thy presence may we feel;
  And, thus inspired with holy fear,
  Before thine altar kneel!

2 We come, obedient to thy word,
  To feast on heavenly food;
  Our meat, the body of the Lord,
  Our drink, his precious blood.

3 Thus may we all thy words obey,
  For we, O God, are thine;
  And go rejoicing on our way,
  Renewed with strength divine.

737. Isaiah 49: 15.

1 A MOTHER may forgetful be,
  For human love is frail;
  But thy Creator's love to thee,
  O Zion, cannot fail.

2 No, thy dear name engraven stands,
  In characters of love,
  On thy almighty Father's hands,
  And never shall remove.

3 Before his ever-watchful eye
  Thy mournful state appears,
  And every groan, and every sigh,
  Divine compassion hears.

4 O Zion, learn to doubt no more,
  Be every fear suppressed;
  Unchanging truth and love and power
  Dwell in thy Saviour's breast.
  MRS. STEELE.

738. Psalm 103: 17, 18.

1 O LORD, thy covenant is sure
  To all who fear thy name;
  Thy mercies age on age endure,
  Eternally the same.

2 In thee our fathers put their trust;
  Thy ways they humbly trod;
  Honored and sacred is their dust,
  And still they live to God.

3 Heirs in their faith, their hope, their prayer,
  We the same path pursue;
  Entail the blessing to our heirs;
  Lord, show thy promise true.
  CONDER.

CASSEL. 7s. 6l.

739. *"Joy in the Atonement."*

1 Sion's daughter, weep no more,
  Though thy troubled heart be sore;
  He of whom the Psalmist sung,
  He who woke the Prophet's tongue, —
  Christ, the Mediator blest, —
  Brings thee everlasting rest.

2 In a garden man became
  Heir of sin and death and shame;
  Jesus in a garden wins
  Life and pardon for our sins;
  Through his hour of agony,
  Praying in Gethsemane.

3 There for us he intercedes;
  There with God the Father pleads;
  Willing there for us to drain
  To the dregs the cup of pain,
  That, in everlasting day,
  He may wipe our tears away.

4 Therefore to his name be given
  Glory, both in earth and heaven;
  To the Father, and the Son,
  And the Spirit, three in One,
  Honor, praise, and glory be,
  Now, and through eternity.
  Monks' Coll.

740. *Love to Christ.*

1 Resting from his work to-day
  In the tomb the Saviour lay;
  Still he slept, from head to feet,
  Shrouded in the winding-sheet,
  Lying in the rock alone,
  Hidden by the sealèd stone.

2 Late at evening there was seen,
  Watching long, the Magdalene!
  Early, ere the break of day,
  Sorrowful she took her way
  To the holy garden glade
  Where her buried Lord was laid.

3 So, with thee, till life shall end,
  I would solemn vigil spend:
  Let me hew thee, Lord, a shrine
  In this rocky heart of mine,
  Where, in pure, embalmèd cell,
  Thou and thou alone shall dwell.

4 Myrrh and spices will I bring,
  True affection's offering;
  Close the door from sight and sound
  Of the busy world around;
  And in patient watch remain
  Till my Lord appear again.
  Monks' Coll.

NUREMBURG. 7s.   GERMAN.

741. *Bread of Heaven.*

1 BREAD of heaven! on thee we feed,
  For thy flesh is meat indeed:
  Ever let our souls be fed
  With this true and living bread!

2 Vine of heaven! thy blood supplies
  This blest cup of sacrifice:
  Lord! thy wounds our healing give,
  To thy cross we look and live.

3 Day by day with strength supplied,
  Through the life of him who died,
  Lord of life! oh, let us be
  Rooted, grafted, built on thee!
                              CONDER.

742.   Ruth 1: 16.

1 PEOPLE of the living God,
    I have sought the world around,
  Paths of sin and sorrow trod,
    Peace and comfort nowhere found.

2 Now to you my spirit turns,—
    Turns, a fugitive unblest;
  Brethren! where your altar burns,
    Oh, receive me into rest!

3 Lonely I no longer roam,
    Like the cloud, the wind, the wave:
  Where you dwell shall be my home,
    Where you die shall be my grave.

4 Mine the God whom you adore,
    Your Redeemer shall be mine;
  Earth can fill my soul no more,
    Every idol I resign.
                        MONTGOMERY.

743.   *Joy in Praise.*

1 JOYFUL be the hours to-day;
    Joyful let the season be;
  Let us sing, for well we may:
    Jesus! we will sing of thee.

2 Should thy people silent be,
    Then the very stones would sing:
  What a debt we owe to thee,
    Thee, our Saviour, thee our King!

3 Joyful are we now to own,
    Rapture thrills us as we trace
  All the deeds thy love hath done,
    All the riches of thy grace.

4 'Tis thy grace alone can save;
    Every blessing comes from thee,
  All we have and hope to have,
    All we are and hope to be.

5 Thine the name to sinners dear!
    Thine the name all names before!
  Blessed here and everywhere;
    Blessed now and evermore!
                              KELLY.

744.   Matt. 5: 3.

1 WHEN, my Saviour, shall I be
  Perfectly resigned to thee?
  Poor and vile in mine own eyes,
  Only in thy wisdom wise?

2 Fully in my life express
  All the heights of holiness?
  Sweetly let my spirit prove
  All the depths of humble love.
                              C. WESLEY.

DORMAN. 7s.

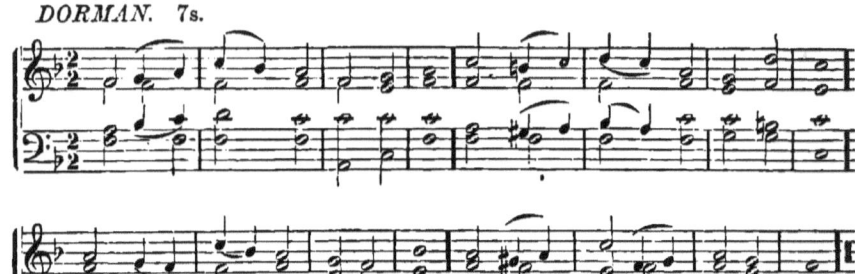

745. *2 Cor. 4: 10.*
1 O my Saviour crucified,
    Near thy cross may I abide,
    There to gaze with steadfast eye
    On thy dying agony.

2 Jesus bruised and put to shame,
    Tells me all the Father's name;
    God is love, I surely know
    By my Saviour's depths of woe.

3 In his sinless soul's distress,
    I behold my guiltiness;
    Oh, how vile my low estate,
    Since my ransom was so great!

4 Dwelling on Mount Calvary,
    Contrite shall my spirit be;
    Rest and holiness shall find,
    Fashioned like my Saviour's mind.

746. *Acts 2: 16.*
1 Fount of everlasting love!
    Rich thy streams of mercy are;
    Flowing purely from above,
    Beauty marks their course afar.

2 Lo! thy Church, athirst and faint,
    Drinks the full, refreshing tide;
    Thou hast heard her sad complaint,
    Floods of grace are sweeping wide!

3 God of mercy, to thy throne
    Now our fervent thanks we bring;
    Thine the glory, thine alone,
    Joyous praise to thee we sing.

4 While we lift our grateful song,
    Let thy Spirit still descend;
    Roll the tide of grace along,
    Widening, deepening, to the end!
                                     RAY PALMER.

747. *"Hear my Cry."*
1 Thou who didst on Calvary bleed,
    Thou who dost for sinners plead,
    Help me in my time of need,
    Jesus, Saviour, hear my cry!

2 In my darkness and my grief,
    With my heart of unbelief,
    I, who am of sinners chief,
    Jesus, lift to thee mine eye!

3 Foes without and fears within,
    With no plea thy grace to win,
    But that thou canst save from sin,
    Jesus, to thy cross I fly!

4 There, on thee I cast my care,
    There, to thee I raise my prayer,
    Jesus, save me from despair,
    Save me, save me, or I die!

5 When the storms of trial lower,
    When I feel temptation's power,
    In the last and darkest hour,
    Jesus, Saviour, be thou nigh!

NOTE.—By simply separating the tied notes in the first measure of each line, this beautiful tune may be used as a Long Metre, with the hymns on the opposite page.

Showing forth the Lord's Death. 303

LOUVAN. L. M.   V. C. TAYLOR.

748. *Communion.*

1 O Jesus, bruised and wounded more
    Than bursted grape, or bread of wheat,
  The Life of life within our souls,
    The cup of our salvation sweet!

2 We come to show thy dying hour,
    Thy streaming vein, thy broken flesh ;
  And still that blood is warm to save,
    And still thy fragrant wounds are fresh.

3 Let nevermore our sinful souls
    The anguish of thy cross renew ;
  Nor forge again the cruel nails
    That pierced thy victim body through.

4 Come, Bread of heaven, to feed our souls,
    And with thee, Jesus, enter in !
  Come, Wine of God ! and as we drink
    His precious blood, wash out our sin !

749. *Communion.*

1 Jesus, thou everlasting King!
    Accept the tribute which we bring ;
  Accept the well-deserved renown,
    And wear our praises as thy crown.

2 Let every act of worship be
    Like our espousals, Lord, to thee ;
  Like the dear hour when from above
    We first received thy pledge of love.

3 The gladness of that happy day,
    Our hearts would wish it long to stay ;
  Nor let our faith forsake its hold,
    Nor comfort sink, nor love grow cold.

4 Each following minute, as it flies,
    Increase thy praise, improve our joys,
  Till we are raised to sing thy name,
    At the great supper of the Lamb.
                WATTS.

750. *" This do in Remembrance of Me."*

1 At thy command, our dearest Lord,
    Here we attend thy dying feast ;
  Thy blood, like wine, adorns thy board,
    And thine own flesh feeds every guest.

2 Our faith adores thy bleeding love,
    And trusts for life in One that died ;
  We hope for heavenly crowns above,
    From a Redeemer crucified.

3 Let the vain world pronounce it shame,
    And fling their scandals on the cause ;
  We come to boast our Saviour's name,
    And make our triumphs in his cross.

4 With joy we tell the scoffing age,
    He that was dead has left his tomb ;
  He lives above their utmost rage,
    And we are waiting till he come.
                WATTS.

751. *Prayer for Purification.*

1 We pray thee, wounded Lamb of God,
    Cleanse us in thine atoning blood ;
  Grant us, by faith, to view thy cross,
    Then life or death is gain to us.

2 Take our poor hearts, and let them be
    Forever closed to all but thee ;
  Seal thou our breasts, and let us wear
    That pledge of love forever there.

The Church of Christ.

ERNAN. 10s.   DR. MASON.

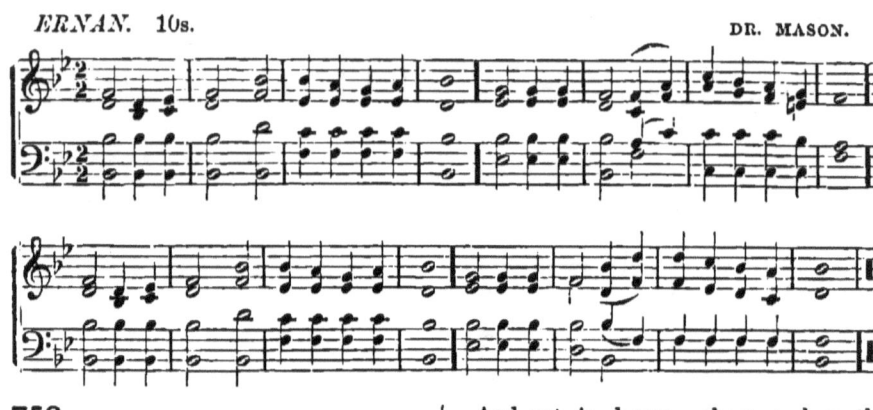

752.   *Matt. 26: 29.*

1 Here, O my Lord, I see thee face to face;
   Here would I touch and handle things unseen;
   Here grasp with firmer hand the eternal grace,
   And all my weariness upon thee lean.

2 Here would I feed upon the bread of God;
   Here drink with thee the royal wine of heaven;
   Here would I lay aside each earthly load;
   Here taste afresh the calm of sin forgiven.

3 Too soon we rise; the symbols disappear;
   The feast, though not the love, is passed and gone;
   The bread and wine remove, but thou art here, —
   Nearer than ever, — still my Shield and Sun.

4 Feast after feast thus comes and passes by;
   Yet, passing, points to the glad feast above,
   Giving sweet foretaste of the festal joy,
   The Lamb's great bridal feast of bliss and love.
                                         BONAR.

753.   *The Holy Catholic Church.*

1 The Church of Christ, which he hath hallowed here
   To be his house, is scattered far and near;
   And yet in heaven above and earth abroad,
   The church is one in Jesus Christ her Lord.

2 O Spirit of the Lord! all life is thine!
   Come, fill thy Church with life and power divine!
   Let all the sons of men be born of thee,
   And spread thy knowledge like the boundless sea!
                         A. G. SPANGENBURG, 1747.

754.   *Death of a Minister.*

1 Go to the grave in all thy glorious prime,
   In full activity of zeal and power;
   Thou art not called away before thy time;
   The Lord's appointment is the servant's hour.

2 Go to the grave; at noon from labor cease;
   Rest on thy sheaves, thy harvest-task is done;
   Come from the heat of battle, and in peace,
   Soldier, go home; with thee the fight is won.

3 Go to the grave; for there the Saviour lay
   In death's embraces ere he rose on high;
   And all the ransomed, by that narrow way,
   Pass to eternal life beyond the sky.
                                      MONTGOMERY.

Consecration and Welcome.

WARD. L. M.   SCOTTISH.

755. *Hymn of Consecration.*

1 OH, happy day, that fixed my choice
  On thee, my Saviour, and my God!
Well may this glowing heart rejoice,
  And tell its raptures all abroad.

2 Oh, happy bond, that seals my vows
  To him who merits all my love!
Let cheerful anthems fill his house,
  While to that sacred shrine I move.

3 'Tis done, the great transaction's done;
  I am my Lord's and he is mine:
He drew me, and I followed on,
  Charmed to confess the voice divine.

4 Now, rest, my long-divided heart!
  Fixed on this blissful centre, rest;
With ashes who would grudge to part,
  When called on angel's bread to feast.

5 High heaven, that heard the solemn vow,
  That vow renewed shall daily hear;
Till in life's latest hour I bow,
  And bless in death a bond so dear.
                DODDRIDGE.

756. *The Lord's Supper.*

1 'TWAS on that dark, that doleful night,
  When powers of earth and hell arose
Against the Son of God's delight,
  And friends betrayed him to his foes.

2 Before the mournful scene began,
  He took the bread, and blessed and brake;
What love through all his actions ran!
  What wondrous words of grace he spake!

3 "This is my body broke for sin;
  Receive and eat the living food;"
Then took the cup and blessed the wine;
  "'Tis the new cov'nant in my blood."

4 "Do this," he cried, "till time shall end,
  In mem'ry of your dying Friend;
Meet at my table and record
  The love of your departed Lord."

5 Jesus! thy feast we celebrate;
  We show thy death, we sing thy name,
Till thou return, and we shall eat
  The marriage-supper of the Lamb.
                WATTS.

757. *Welcome to Christian Fellowship.*

1 COME in, thou blessèd of our God,
  In Jesus' name we bid thee come;
No more thy feet shall roam abroad,
  Henceforth a brother, — welcome home.

2 Those joys which earth cannot afford,
  We'll seek in fellowship to prove,
Joined in one spirit to our Lord,
  Together bound by mutual love.

3 And while we pass this vale of tears,
  We'll make our joys and sorrows known;
We'll share each other's hopes and fears,
  And count a brother's cares our own.

4 Once more our welcome we repeat;
  Receive assurance of our love;
Oh, may we all together meet
  Around the throne of God above.
                MONTGOMERY.

BOYLSTON. S. M.   DR. MASON.

758.   *Communion.* — Mark 14: 24.
1   Blest feast of love divine!
     'Tis grace that makes us free
   To feed upon this bread and wine,
     In memory, Lord, of thee!

2   That blood which flowed for sin,
     In symbol here we see,
   And feel the blessèd pledge within,
     That we are loved of thee.

3   Oh, if this glimpse of love
     Be so divinely sweet,
   What will it be, O Lord, above,
     Thy gladdening smile to meet?

4   To see thee face to face,
     Thy perfect likeness wear,
   And all thy ways of wondrous grace
     Through endless years declare!

759.   *Baptism.*
1   Great God, now condescend
     To bless our rising race;
   Soon may their willing spirits bend,
     The subjects of thy grace.

2   Oh, what a pure delight
     Their happiness to see;
   Our warmest wishes all unite
     To lead their souls to thee.

3   Now bless, thou God of love,
     This ordinance divine;
   Send thy good Spirit from above,
     And make these children thine.
                        FELLOWS.

760.   Acts 2: 39.
1   Our children thou dost claim,
     O Lord, our God, as thine:
   Ten thousand blessings to thy name
     For goodness so divine!

2   Thee let the fathers own,
     Thee let the sons adore;
   Joined to the Lord in solemn vows,
     To be forgot no more.

3   How great thy mercies, Lord!
     How plenteous is thy grace,
   Which, in the promise of thy love,
     Includes our rising race!

4   Our offspring, still thy care,
     Shall own their fathers' God!
   To latest times thy blessings share,
     And sound thy praise abroad.

761.   Matt. 19: 14.
1   The Saviour kindly calls
     Our children to his breast;
   He folds them in his gracious arms,
     Himself declares them blest.

2   "Let them approach," he cries,
     "Nor scorn their humble claim;
   The heirs of heaven are such as these;
     For such as these I came."

3   With joy we bring them, Lord,
     Devoting them to thee,
   Imploring that, as we are thine,
     Thine may our offspring be.

Baptism of Children.

762. C. M. *Beauty of Early Piety.*

1 By cool Siloam's shady rill
 How sweet the lily grows;
 How sweet the breath beneath the hill
 Of Sharon's dewy rose!

2 Lo! such the child whose early feet
 The paths of peace have trod,
 Whose secret heart, with influence sweet,
 Is upward drawn to God.

3 By cool Siloam's shady rill
 The lily must decay;
 The rose that blooms beneath the hill
 Must shortly fade away.

4 And soon, too soon, the wintry hour
 Of man's maturer age
 Will shake the soul with sorrow's power,
 And stormy passions rage.

5 O thou who givest life and breath,
 We seek thy grace alone,
 In childhood, manhood, age, and death,
 To keep us still thine own.
  HEBER.

763. C. M. Matt. 19: 14.

1 See Israel's gentle Shepherd stand
 With all-engaging charms;
 Hark, how he calls the tender lambs,
 And folds them in his arms!

2 "Permit them to approach," he cries,
 "Nor scorn their humble name;
 For 'twas to bless such souls as these,
 The Lord of angels came."

3 We bring them, Lord, in thankful hands,
 And yield them up to thee;
 Joyful that we ourselves are thine, —
 Thine let our offspring be.
  DODDRIDGE.

764. L. M. *Prayer for Pastor.*

1 With heavenly power, O Lord, defend
 Him whom we now to thee commend;
 Thy faithful messenger secure,
 And make him to the end endure.

2 Gird him with all-sufficient grace;
 Direct his feet in paths of peace;
 Thy truth and faithfulness fulfil,
 And arm him to obey thy will.

765. C. M. Gen. 17 : 7. Rom. 15: 8.

1 How large the promise, how divine,
 To Abra'm and his seed! —
 "I'll be a God to thee and thine,
 Supplying all their need."

2 The words of his extensive love
 From age to age endure;
 The angel of the cov'nant proves,
 And seals the blessing sure.

3 Jesus the ancient faith confirms,
 To our great fathers given;
 He takes young children to his arms,
 And calls them heirs of heaven.

4 Our God, how faithful are his ways!
 His love endures the same;
 Nor from the promise of his grace,
 Blots out the children's name.
  WATTS.

766. C. M. *Consecration of Children.*

1 Our children, Lord! in faith and prayer,
 We now devote to thee;
 Let them thy cov'nant mercies share,
 And thy salvation see.

2 In early days their hearts secure
 From worldly snares, we pray;
 And let them to the end endure
 In every righteous way.

3 Grant us before them, Lord, to live
 In holy faith and fear;
 And then to heaven our souls remove,
 And bring our children there.
  BICKERSTETH'S COLL.

767. C. M. *Covenant Hymn.*

1 Come, let us join our souls to God,
 In everlasting bands;
 And seize the blessings he bestows,
 With eager hearts and hands.

2 Come, let us seal without delay
 The cov'nant of his grace;
 Nor shall the years of distant life
 Its memory efface.

3 Thus may our rising offspring haste
 To seek their fathers' God;
 Nor e'er forsake the happy path
 Their youthful feet have trod.
  DODDRIDGE.

Note. — The hymns on this page, with one exception, are in *Common Metre*, and suitable tunes for them may be found on pages 208, 191, and 142.

PILGRIM SONG. S. M.   MENDELSSOHN.

768.   Matt. 9: 38.

1 LORD of the harvest! hear
   Thy needy servants cry;
Answer our faith's effectual prayer,
   And all our wants supply.
On thee we humbly wait;
   Our wants are in thy view;
The harvest truly, Lord, is great,
   The laborers are few.

2 Convert and send forth more
   Into thy Church abroad;
And let them speak thy word of power,
   As workers with their God.
Give the pure Gospel-word,
   The word of general grace;
Thee let them preach, the common Lord,
   The Saviour of our race.

3 Oh, let them spread thy name;
   Their mission fully prove;
Thy universal grace proclaim,
   Thy all-redeeming love.
On all mankind, forgiven,
   Empower them still to call,
And tell each creature under heaven
   That thou hast died for all.
                    C. WESLEY.

769.   Isaiah 52: 7.

1 How beauteous are their feet
   Who stand on Zion's hill!
Who bring salvation on their tongues,
   And words of peace reveal!
How charming is their voice!
   How sweet the tidings are!
"Zion, behold thy Saviour, King;
   He reigns and triumphs here."

2 How happy are our ears
   That hear this joyful sound!
Which kings and prophets waited for,
   And sought, but never found.
How blessed are our eyes
   That see this heavenly light!
Prophets and kings desired it long,
   But died without the sight.

3 The watchmen join their voice,
   And tuneful notes employ;
Jerusalem breaks forth in songs,
   And deserts learn the joy.
The Lord makes bare his arm
   Through all the earth abroad;
Let every nation now behold
   Their Saviour and their God.
                    WATTS.

770. L. M. *Dedication.*

1 Oh, bow thine ear, Eternal One!
  On thee our heart adoring calls;
  To thee the followers of thy Son
  Have raised, and now devote these [walls.

2 Here let thy holy days be kept;
  And be this place to worship given,
  Like that bright spot where Jacob slept,
  The house of God, the gate of heaven.

3 Here may thine honor dwell; and here,
  As incense, let thy children's prayer,
  From contrite hearts and lips sincere,
  Rise on the still and holy air.

4 Here be thy praise devoutly sung;
  Here let thy truth beam forth to save,
  As when, of old, thy Spirit hung,
  On wings of light, o'er Jordan's wave.

5 And when the lips, that with thy name
  Are vocal now, to dust shall turn,
  On others may devotion's flame
  Be kindled here, and purely burn!

771. L. M. *Ordination.*

1 Here, Lord of life and light, to thee
  Our pilgrim fathers bowed the knee;
  Thou heard'st their prayer, and in this place
  They reared the temple of thy grace.

2 Here thy own servants preached thy word,
  Safe from the prison and the sword;
  Nor preached in vain, each rolling year
  Gave witness that the Lord was here.

3 Here still thy word is preached, and still,
  As once on Zion's sacred hill,
  Thy grace descends like timely showers,
  For still our fathers' God is ours.

4 Amid our fathers' graves, to-day,
  To thee, our fathers' God, we pray:
  Here on thy Church, till time shall end,
  Let showers of heavenly grace descend.
                    L. BACON.

772. C. M. *Dedication.*

1 God of the universe, to thee
  This sacred fane we rear,
  And now, with songs and bended knee,
  Invoke thy presence here.

2 Long may this echoing dome resound
  The praises of thy name,
  These hallowed walls to all around
  The triune God proclaim.

3 Here let thy love, thy presence dwell;
  Thy glory here make known;
  Thy people's home, oh, come and fill,
  And seal it as thine own.

4 And when the last long Sabbath morn
  Upon the just shall rise,
  May all who own thee here be borne
  To mansions in the skies.

773. C. M. *Dedication.*

1 O thou, whose own vast temple stands,
  Built over earth and sea,
  Accept the walls that human hands
  Have raised to worship thee!

2 Lord, from thine inmost glory send,
  Within these courts to bide,
  The peace that dwelleth without end
  Serenely by thy side!

3 May erring minds that worship here
  Be taught the better way;
  And they who mourn, and they who fear,
  Be strengthened as they pray.

4 May faith grow firm, and love grow warm,
  And pure devotion rise,
  While round these hallowed walls the storm
  Of earth-born passion dies.
                    BRYANT.

774. L. M. *Dedication.*

1 And will the great eternal God,
  On earth establish his abode?
  And will he from his radiant throne
  Accept our temples for his own?

2 These walls we to thy honor raise;
  Long may they echo with thy praise!
  And thou, descending, fill the place
  With choicest tokens of thy grace.

3 Here let the great Redeemer reign,
  With all the graces of his train;
  While power divine his word attends,
  To conquer foes, and cheer his friends.

4 And in the great decisive day,
  When God the nations shall survey,
  May it before the world appear,
  That crowds were born to glory here.
                    DODDRIDGE.

The Church: Spread of the Gospel.

ST. MICHAEL'S. S. M.   JOHN DAY'S PSALTER.

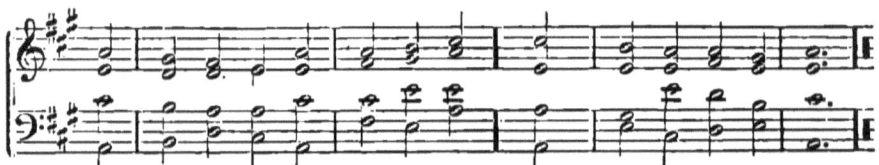

775.   *Matt. 6: 10.*
1 Come, kingdom of our God,
 Sweet reign of light and love!
 Shed peace and hope and joy abroad,
 And wisdom from above.

2 Over our spirits first
 Extend thy healing reign;
 There raise and quench the sacred thirst
 That never pains again.

3 Come, kingdom of our God!
 And make the broad earth thine;
 Stretch o'er her lands and isles the rod
 That flowers with grace divine.

4 Soon may all tribes be blest
 With fruit from life's glad tree;
 And in its shade like brothers rest,
 Sons of one family.
                    JOHNS.

776.   *Isaiah 60: 2.*
1 O Lord our God! arise,
 The cause of truth maintain;
 And wide o'er all the peopled world
 Extend her blessed reign.

2 Thou Prince of life! arise,
 Nor let thy glory cease;
 Far spread the conquests of thy grace,
 And bless the earth with peace.

3 Thou Holy Ghost! arise,
 Extend thy healing wing,
 And, o'er a dark and ruined world,
 Let light and order spring.

777.   *Phil. 2: 10, 11.*
1 O thou whom we adore!
 To bless our earth again,
 Assume thine own almighty power,
 And o'er the nations reign.

2 The world's desire and hope,
 All power to thee is given;
 Now set the last great empire up,
 Eternal Lord of heaven!

3 According to thy word,
 Now be thy grace revealed;
 And with the knowledge of the Lord,
 Let all the earth be filled.
                    C. WESLEY.

778.   *Prayer for Revival.*
1 O Lord, thy work revive,
 In Zion's gloomy hour;
 And make her dying graces live
 By thy restoring power.

2 Awake thy chosen few
 To fervent, earnest prayer;
 Again their sacred vows renew;
 Thy blessed presence share.

3 Thy Spirit then will speak
 Through lips of feeble clay,
 And hearts of adamant will break,
 And rebels will obey.

4 Lord! lend thy gracious ear;
 Oh, listen to our cry!
 Oh, come and bring salvation here!
 Our hopes on thee rely.
                    BROWNE.

Ordination. Installation. Death of a Pastor.

779. L. M. *Convocation of Ministers.*

1 Pour out thy Spirit from on high;
  Lord! thine assembled servants bless;
  Graces and gifts to each supply,
  And clothe thy priests with righteous- [ness.

2 Within thy temple where we stand,
  To teach the truth as taught by thee,
  Saviour! like stars in thy right hand,
  The angels of the churches be!

3 Wisdom and zeal and faith impart,
  Firmness with meekness from above,
  To bear thy people on our hearts,
  And love the souls whom thou dost love:—

4 To watch and pray, and never faint;
  By day and night strict guard to keep;
  To warn the sinner, cheer the saint,
  Nourish thy lambs, and feed thy sheep.

5 Then, when our work is finished here,
  In humble hope our charge resign:
  When the chief Shepherd shall appear,
  O God! may they and we be thine.
  MONTGOMERY.

780. S. M. *Death of a Pastor.*

1 Rest from thy labor, rest,
   Soul of the just, set free!
  Blest be thy memory, and blest
   Thy bright example be.

2 Now, toil and conflict o'er,
   Go, take with saints thy place;
  But go as each has gone before,
   A sinner saved by grace.

3 Saviour! into thy hands
   Our pastor we resign,
  And now we wait thine own commands;
   We were not his, but thine.

4 Thou art thy Church's Head;
   And when the members die,
  Thou raisest others in their stead;
   To thee we lift our eye.

5 On thee our hopes depend,
   We gather round our Rock;
  Send whom thou wilt, but condescend
   Thyself to feed thy flock.
  MONTGOMERY.

781. L. M. *Installation or Ordination.*

1 Draw near, O Son of God! draw near;
  Us with thy flaming eye behold;
  Still in thy Church do thou appear,
  And let our candlestick be gold.

2 Oh, clothe their words with power divine,
  And let those words be ever thine;
  To them thy sacred truth reveal;
  Suppress their fear, inflame their zeal.

3 Teach them to sow the precious seed;
  Teach them thy chosen flock to feed;
  Teach them immortal souls to gain;—
  And thus reward their toil and pain.

4 Let thronging multitudes around
  Hear from their lips the joyful sound,
  In humble strains thy grace implore,
  And feel thy Spirit's living power.
  C. WESLEY.

782. C. M. *Ministry.*

1 'Tis not a cause of small import,
   The pastor's care demands;
  But what might fill an angel's heart,
   And filled a Saviour's hands.

2 They watch for those for whom the Lord
   Did heavenly bliss forego;
  For souls, that must forever live
   In rapture, or in woe.

3 All to the great tribunal haste,
   Th' account to render there; [faults,
  And shouldst thou strictly mark our
   Lord, how should we appear!

4 May they that Jesus, whom they preach,
   Their own Redeemer see;
  And watch thou daily o'er their souls,
   That they may watch for thee.
  DODDRIDGE.

783. C. M. *Ordination.*

1 Father of mercies! condescend
   To hear our fervent prayer,
  While this our brother we commend
   To thy paternal care.

2 Before him set an open door;
   His various efforts bless;
  On him thy Holy Spirit pour,
   And crown him with success.

3 In every tempting, trying hour,
   Uphold him by thy grace;
  And guard him by thy mighty power
   Till he shall end his race.
  MORELL.

MISSIONARY CHANT. L. M.   CHAS. ZEUNER.

784. *Proclamation of the Gospel.*
1 YE Christian heralds! go, proclaim
Salvation through Immanuel's name;
To distant climes the tidings bear,
And plant the Rose of Sharon there.

2 He'll shield you with a wall of fire,
With flaming zeal your hearts inspire,
Bid raging winds their fury cease,
And hush the tempest into peace.

3 And when our labors all are o'er,
Then we shall meet to part no more,—
Meet with the blood-bought throng to fall,
And crown our Jesus—Lord of all!

785. Phil. 2: 10, 11.
1 O SPIRIT of the living God,
In all thy plenitude of grace,
Where'er the foot of man hath trod,
Descend on our apostate race.

2 Give tongues of fire and hearts of love,
To preach the reconciling word;
Give power and unction from above,
Where'er the joyful sound is heard.

3 Be darkness, at thy coming, light;
Confusion — order, in thy path;
Souls without strength inspire with might;
Bid mercy triumph over wrath.

4 Baptize the nations far and nigh;
The triumphs of the cross record;
The name of Jesus glorify,
Till every kindred call him Lord.
                    MONTGOMERY.

786. Psalm 72.
1 JESUS shall reign where'er the sun
Does his successive journeys run;
His kingdom stretch from shore to shore,
Till moons shall wax and wane no more.

2 People and realms of every tongue
Dwell on his love with sweetest song;
And infant voices shall proclaim
Their early blessings on his name.

3 Blessings abound where'er he reigns;
The prisoner leaps to loose his chains;
The weary find eternal rest,
And all the sons of want are blest.

4 Let every creature rise and bring
Peculiar honors to our King;
Angels descend with songs again,
And earth repeat the loud Amen!
                    WATTS.

787. Rev. 11: 15.
1 Soon may the last glad song arise
Through all the millions of the skies,—
That song of triumph which records
That all the earth is now the Lord's!

2 Let thrones and powers and kingdoms be
Obedient, mighty God, to thee!
And, over land and stream and main,
Wave thou the sceptre of thy reign!

3 Oh, let that glorious anthem swell,
Let host to host the triumph tell
That not one rebel heart remains,
But over all the Saviour reigns!

788. *"Jesus, thine own Messiah reigns."*

1 Why, on the bending willows hung,
   Israel! still sleeps thy tuneful string?
   Still mute remains thy sullen tongue,
   And Zion's song denies to sing?

2 Awake! thy sweetest raptures raise;
   Let harp and voice unite their strains;
   Thy promised King his sceptre sways;
   Jesus, thine own Messiah, reigns!

3 No taunting foes the song require;
   No strangers mock thy captive chain;
   But friends provoke the silent lyre,
   And brethren ask the holy strain.

4 Nor fear thy Salem's hills to wrong,
   If other lands thy triumph share:
   A heavenly city claims thy song;
   A brighter Salem rises there.

5 By foreign streams no longer roam;
   Nor, weeping, think of Jordan's flood;
   In every clime behold a home,
   In every temple see thy God.

789. *Day of Promise.*

1 Behold the way to Zion's hill,
   Where Israel's God delights to dwell;
   He fixes there his lofty throne,
   And calls the sacred place his own.

2 "Behold the way!" ye heralds! cry,
   Spare not, but lift your voices high,
   Convey the sound from shore to shore,
   And bid the captive sigh no more.

3 Auspicious dawn! thy rising ray
   With joy we view, and hail the day:
   Thou Sun! arise, supremely bright,
   And fill the world with purest light.
   KELLY.

790. *Mal. 4: 2.*

1 O Sun of righteousness, arise,
   With gentle beams on Zion shine;
   Dispel the darkness from our eyes,
   And souls awake to life divine.

2 On all around let grace descend,
   Like heavenly dew or copious showers;
   That we may call our God our friend;
   That we may hail salvation ours.

791. *"All nations shall praise Thee."*

1 Though now the nations sit beneath
   The darkness of o'erspreading death;
   God will arise with light divine,
   On Zion's holy towers to shine.

2 That light shall shine on distant lands,
   And wandering tribes, in joyful bands,
   Shall come, thy glory, Lord, to see,
   And in thy courts to worship thee.

3 O light of Zion, now arise!
   Let the glad morning bless our eyes!
   Ye nations, catch the kindling ray,
   And hail the splendors of the day.
   L. BACON.

792. *God entreated for Zion.*

1 Indulgent Sovereign of the skies!
   And wilt thou bow thy gracious ear?
   While feeble mortals raise their cries,
   Wilt thou, the great Jehovah, hear?

2 How shall thy servants give thee rest,
   Till Zion's mouldering walls thou raise?
   Till thy own power shall stand confessed,
   And make Jerusalem a praise!

3 Look down, O God! with pitying eye,
   And view the desolation round;
   See what wide realms in darkness lie,
   And cast their idols to the ground.

4 Loud let the gospel trumpet blow,
   And call the nations from afar;
   Let all the isles their Saviour know,
   And earth's remotest ends draw near.
   DODDRIDGE.

793. *Missionary Hymn.*

1 Sovereign of worlds! display thy power,
   Be this thy Zion's favored hour,
   Bid the bright morning star arise,
   And point the nations to the skies.

2 Set up thy throne where Satan reigns,
   On Afric's shore, on India's plains,
   On lonely isles and lands unknown;
   And make the nations all thine own.

3 Speak! and the world shall hear thy voice;
   Speak! and the desert shall rejoice;
   Scatter the gloom of heathen night,
   And bid all nations hail the light.
   PRATT'S COLL.

PETERBORO'. C. M.

794. *Matt. 13: 17.*

1 O God! our God! thou shinest here,
Thine own this latter day;
To us thy radiant steps appear;
Here beams thy glorious way!

2 The fathers had not all of thee!
New births are in thy grace;
All open to our souls shall be
Thy glory's hiding-place.

3 On us thy Spirit hast thou poured,
To us thy Word has come;
We feel, we bless thee, quickening Lord,
Thou shalt not find us dumb.

4 Thou comest near; thou standest by;
Our work begins to shine;
Thou dwellest with us mightily;
On speed the years divine!
GILL.

795. *The Times of Promise.*

1 The Lord will come, and not be slow;
His footsteps cannot err;
Before him righteousness shall go,
His royal harbinger.

2 Mercy and Truth, that long were missed,
Now joyfully are met;
Sweet Peace and Righteousness have kissed,
And hand in hand are set.

3 The nations all whom thou hast made
Shall come, and all shall frame
To bow them low before thee, Lord!
And glorify thy name.

4 Truth from the earth, like to a flower,
Shall bud and blossom then,
And Justice, from her heavenly bower,
Look down on mortal men.

5 Thee will I praise, O Lord, my God!
Thee honor and adore
With my whole heart, and blaze abroad
Thy name for evermore!
MILTON.

796. *Rev. 21: 1-5.*

1 Lo! what a glorious sight appears
To our believing eyes!
The earth and seas are passed away,
And the old rolling skies.

2 From the third heaven, where God resides,
That holy, happy place,
The New Jerusalem comes down
Adorned with shining grace.

3 The God of glory down to men
Removes his blest abode, —
Men, the dear objects of his grace,
And he, the loving God.

4 His own soft hands shall wipe the tears
From every weeping eye;
And pains and groans and griefs and fears
And death itself shall die.

5 How long, dear Saviour! oh, how long
Shall this bright hour delay?
Fly swifter round, ye wheels of time,
And bring the welcome day.
WATTS.

ST. MARTIN'S. C. M.   TANSUR.

797.   Gen. 1: 2.
1 SPIRIT of power and might, behold
   A world by sin destroyed!
   Creator Spirit, as of old,
   Move on the formless void.

2 Give thou the word: that healing sound
   Shall quell the deadly strife,
   And earth again, like Eden, crowned,
   Produce the tree of life.

3 If sang the morning stars for joy
   When nature rose to view,
   What strains will angel harps employ
   When thou shalt all renew!

4 And if the sons of God rejoice
   To hear a Saviour's name,
   How will the ransomed raise their voice,
   To whom that Saviour came!

5 Lo! every kindred, tongue, and tribe,
   Assembling round the throne,
   The new creation shall ascribe
   To sovereign love alone.
                     MONTGOMERY.

798.   *Latter-day Glory.*
1 IN latter days the mount of God
   O'er mountain tops shall rise;
   Shall be exalted o'er the hills,
   And draw the wondering eyes.

2 The beams that shine on Zion's hill
   Shall lighten every land;
   The King who reigns in Zion's towers
   Shall all the world command.

3 The nations, by his justice blest,
   Shall give their battles o'er;
   To ploughshares they shall beat their swords,
   And learn to war no more.

4 Come, then, — oh, come from every land,
   To worship at his shrine;
   And, walking in the light of God,
   With holy beauty shine.
                     LOGAN.

799.   Isaiah 52: 1, 2.
1 DAUGHTER of Zion, from the dust
   Exalt thy fallen head;
   Again in thy Redeemer trust, —
   He calls thee from the dead.

2 Awake, awake, put on thy strength, —
   Thy beautiful array;
   Thy day of freedom dawns at length, —
   The Lord's appointed day.

3 Rebuild thy walls, thy bounds enlarge,
   And send thy heralds forth;
   Say to the south, "Give up thy charge,
   And keep not back, O north!"

4 They come! they come! thine exiled bands,
   Where'er they rest or roam,
   Have heard thy voice in distant lands,
   And hasten to their home.

5 Thus, though the universe shall burn,
   And God his works destroy,
   With songs thy ransomed shall return,
   And everlasting joy.
                     MONTGOMERY.

WATCHMAN, TELL US OF THE NIGHT. 7s.   H. KNECHT, 1793.

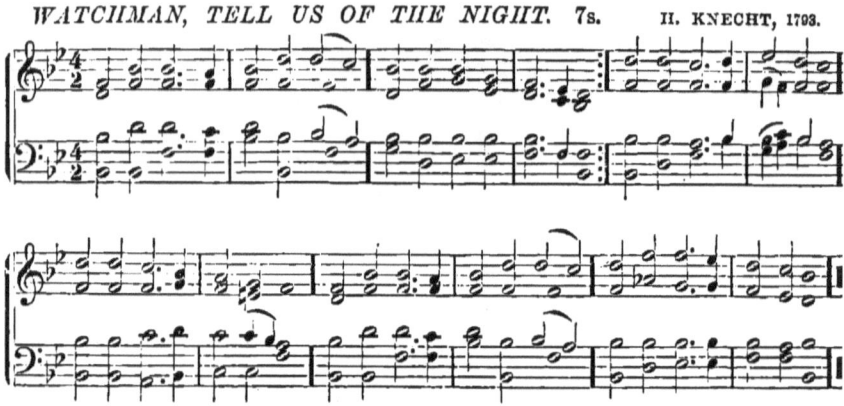

800.   Isaiah 21: 11.
1 WATCHMAN! tell us of the night,
    What its signs of promise are.
  Traveller! o'er yon mountain's height,
    See that glory beaming star!
  Watchman! does its beauteous ray
    Aught of hope or joy foretell?
  Traveller! yes, it brings the day,
    Promised day of Israel.

2 Watchman! tell us of the night,
    Higher yet that star ascends.
  Traveller! blessedness and light,
    Peace and truth its course portends.
  Watchman! will its beams alone
    Gild the spot that gave them birth?
  Traveller! ages are its own,
    See, it bursts o'er all the earth.

3 Watchman! tell us of the night,
    For the morning seems to dawn.
  Traveller! darkness takes its flight,
    Doubt and terror are withdrawn.
  Watchman! let thy wandering cease;
    Hie thee to thy quiet home.
  Traveller! lo! the Prince of peace,
    Lo! the Son of God is come!
                            BOWRING.

801.   Rev. 11: 15.
1 HARK! the song of jubilee,
    Loud as mighty thunders roar,
  Or the fulness of the sea,
    When it breaks upon the shore!
  Hallelujah! for the Lord
    God omnipotent shall reign!
  Hallelujah! let the word
    Echo round the earth and main.

2 Hallelujah! hark, the sound,
    From the depths unto the skies,
  Wakes above, beneath, around,
    All creation's harmonies!
  See Jehovah's banner furled,   [done
  Sheathed his sword, he speaks — 'tis
  And the kingdoms of this world
    Are the kingdoms of his Son!

3 He shall reign from pole to pole,
    With illimitable sway;
  He shall reign when, like a scroll,
    Yonder heavens are passed away.
  Then the end: beneath his rod
    Man's last enemy shall fall:
  Hallelujah! Christ in God,
    God in Christ, is all in all!
                          MONTGOMERY.

NOTE.—A slightly different arrangement of this noble choral is given on page 130 ("Veni, Sancte Spiritus".) It should be remembered that a tune is not necessarily of a slow movement because it is written in minims. If sung in a slow, heavy style, most of the chorals will be robbed of much of their true power.—EDITORS.

Triumph of the Gospel.

TELEMANN'S CHANT. 7s.   ZEUNER.

802.   *The Gospel's Triumph.*

1 HASTEN, Lord! the glorious time,
   When, beneath Messiah's sway,
Every nation, every clime,
   Shall the gospel call obey.

2 Mightiest kings his power shall own,
   Heathen tribes his name adore;
Satan and his host, o'erthrown,
   Bound in chains shall hurt no more.

3 Then shall wars and tumults cease,
   Then be banished grief and pain;
Righteousness and joy and peace,
   Undisturbed shall ever reign.

4 Bless we, then, our gracious Lord!
   Ever praise his glorious name;
All his mighty acts record,
   All his wondrous love proclaim
                           LYTE

803.   1 Tim. 6: 15.

1 WAKE the song of jubilee,
   Let it echo o'er the sea!
Now is come the promised hour;
   Jesus reigns with sov'reign power!

2 All ye nations, join and sing,
   Praise your Saviour, praise your King;
Let it sound from shore to shore,—
   "Jesus reigns for evermore!"

3 Hark! the desert lands rejoice,
   And the islands join their voice;
Joy! the whole creation sings,
   "Jesus is the King of kings!"
                           L. BACON.

804.   1 Kings 18: 44.

1 SAW ye not the cloud arise,
   Little as the human hand?
Now it spreads along the skies,
   Hangs o'er all the thirsty land.

2 Lo, the promise of a shower
   Drops already from above;
But the Lord will shortly pour
   All the blessings of his love.

3 More and more it spreads and grows,
   Ever mighty to prevail;
Sin's strongholds it now o'erthrows,
   Shakes the trembling gates of hell.

4 Sons of God! your Saviour praise;
   He the door hath opened wide;
He hath given the word of grace;
   Jesus' word is glorified!
                          C. WESLEY.

805.   Luke 1: 78.

1 SONS of men, behold from far,
   Hail the long-expected Star!
Star of truth that gilds the night,
   Guides bewildered men aright.

2 Nations all, remote and near,
   Haste to see your Lord appear;
Haste, for him your hearts prepare,
   Meet him manifested there!

3 There behold the Day-spring rise,
   Pouring light on mortal eyes;
See it chase the shades away,
   Shining to the perfect day!
                          C. WESLEY.

The Church of Christ.

OAKSVILLE. C. M.   ZEUNER.

806.   *" The Age of Gold."*

1 Lord! send thy word, and let it fly,
    Armed with thy Spirit's power;
Ten thousands shall confess its sway,
    And bless the saving hour.

2 Beneath the influence of thy grace,
    The barren wastes shall rise
With sudden greens and fruits arrayed,
    A blooming paradise.

3 Peace, with her olives crowned, shall stretch
    Her wings from shore to shore;
No trump shall rouse the rage of war,
    Nor murderous cannon roar.

4 Lord! for those days we wait; those days
    Are in thy word foretold;
Fly swifter, sun and stars! and bring
    This promised age of gold.
                        GIBBONS.

807.   *Prayer for the Heathen.*

1 Great God, the nations of the earth
    Are by creation thine;
And in thy works, by all beheld,
    Thy radiant glories shine.

2 But, Lord, thy greater love has sent
    Thy gospel to mankind,
Unveiling what rich stores of grace
    Are treasured in thy mind.

3 Lord, when shall these glad tidings spread
    The spacious earth around,
Till every tribe, and every soul,
    Shall hear the joyful sound?
                        GIBBONS.

808.   *" Send forth Thy Word."*

1 Jesus, immortal King! arise,
    Assert thy rightful sway,
Till earth, subdued, its tribute brings,
    And distant lands obey.

2 Ride forth, victorious Conqueror! ride,
    Till all thy foes submit,
And all the powers of hell resign
    Their trophies at thy feet.

3 Send forth thy word, and let it fly
    The spacious earth around,
Till every soul beneath the sun
    Shall hear the joyful sound.
                        BURDER.

809.   *Christ Triumphing.*

1 Hail, mighty Jesus! how divine
    Is thy victorious sword!
The stoutest rebel must resign
    At thy commanding word.

2 Still gird thy sword upon thy thigh,
    Ride with majestic sway;
Go forth, great Prince! triumphantly,
    And make thy foes obey.

3 And when thy victories are complete,
    And all the chosen race
Shall round the throne of mercy meet,
    To sing thy conquering grace;—

4 Oh, may my humble soul be found
    Among that favored band;
And I with them thy praise will sound
    Throughout Immanuel's land.
                        WALLIN.

Good Soldiers of Christ. Missionaries.

STAND UP FOR JESUS. 7s. & 6s.   JOHN CRÜGER, 1653.

310. *"Stand up for Jesus."*

1 STAND up! — stand up for Jesus!
  Ye soldiers of the cross;
  Lift high his royal banner,
  It must not suffer loss:
  From vict'ry unto vict'ry
  His army shall he lead,
  Till every foe is vanquished,
  And Christ is Lord indeed.

2 Stand up! — stand up for Jesus!
  Stand in his strength alone;
  The arm of flesh will fail you, —
  Ye dare not trust your own:
  Put on the gospel armor,
  And, watching unto prayer,
  Where duty calls, or danger;
  Be never wanting there!

3 Stand up! — stand up for Jesus!
  The strife will not be long;
  This day the noise of battle,
  The next the victor's song:
  To him that overcometh,
  A crown of life shall be;
  He with the King of glory
  Shall reign eternally!

DUFFIELD.

811. *For Missionaries.*

1 ROLL on, thou mighty ocean!
  And as thy billows flow,
  Bear messengers of mercy
  To every land below.
  Arise, ye gales! and waft them
  Safe to the destined shore,
  That man may sit in darkness
  And death's black shade no more.

2 O thou eternal Ruler!
  Who holdest in thine arm
  The tempests of the ocean,
  Protect them from all harm.
  Thy presence e'er be with them,
  Wherever they may be;
  Though far from us who love them,
  Still let them be with thee.

PRATT'S COLL.

812. *Final Reign of Christ.*

1 WHEN shall the voice of singing
  Flow joyfully along?
  When hill and valley, ringing
  With one triumphant song,
  Proclaim the contest ended,
  And Him who once was slain
  Again to earth descended,
  In righteousness to reign.

PRATT'S COLL.

ZION. 8s., 7s., & 4s.   DR. HASTINGS.

813. *Isaiah 52: 7.*
1 On the mountain's top appearing,
  Lo! the sacred herald stands,
  Welcome news to Zion bearing, —
    Zion, long in hostile lands:
      Mourning captive!
  God himself shall loose thy bands.

2 Has thy night been long and mournful?
  Have thy friends unfaithful proved?
  Have thy foes been proud and scornful,
    By thy sighs and tears unmoved?
      Cease thy mourning;
  Zion still is well beloved.

3 God, thy God, will now restore thee;
  He himself appears thy friend;
  All thy foes shall flee before thee;
    Here their boasts and triumphs end:
      Great deliverance
  Zion's King will surely send.

4 Peace and joy shall now attend thee;
  All thy warfare now is past;
  God thy Saviour will defend thee;
    Victory is thine at last;
      All thy conflicts
  End in everlasting rest.
                                    KELLY.

814. *Psalm 125: 2.*
1 Zion stands with hills surrounded, —
    Zion kept by power divine;
  All her foes shall be confounded,
    Though the world in arms combine;
      Happy Zion,
  What a favored lot is thine!

2 Every human tie may perish;
  Friend to friend unfaithful prove;
  Mothers cease their own to cherish;
    Heaven and earth at last remove:
      But no changes
  Can attend Jehovah's love.

3 In the furnace God may prove thee,
  Thence to bring thee forth more bright,
  But can never cease to love thee;
    Thou art precious in his sight;
      God is with thee, —
  God, thine everlasting light.
                                    KELLY.

815. *The Fountain of Salvation.*
1 See, from Zion's sacred mountain,
    Streams of living water flow;
  God has opened there a fountain
    That supplies the world below!
      They are blessèd
  Who its sovereign virtues know.

2 Through ten thousand channels flowing,
    Streams of mercy find their way;
  Life and health and joy bestowing,
    Waking beauty from decay:
      O ye nations,
  Hail the long-expected day.

3 Gladdened by the flowing treasure,
    All-enriching as it goes,
  Lo! the desert smiles with pleasure,
    Buds and blossoms as the rose:
      Lo, the desert
  Sings for joy where'er it flows.
                                    KELLY.

Spread of the Gospel.

HAMDEN. 8s., 7s., & 4s.　　DR. MASON.

816.　　*Luke 2: 32.*
1 O'er the gloomy hills of darkness,
　Cheered by no celestial ray,
　Sun of righteousness! arising,
　　Bring the bright, the glorious day;
　　　Send the gospel
　To the earth's remotest bound.

2 Kingdoms wide that sit in darkness, —
　Grant them, Lord! the glorious light:
　And, from eastern coast to western,
　　May the morning chase the night;
　　　And redemption,
　Freely purchased, win the day.

3 Fly abroad, thou mighty gospel!
　Win and conquer, never cease;
　May thy lasting, wide dominion
　　Multiply and still increase;
　　　Sway thy sceptre,
　Saviour! all the world around.
　　　　　　　　　　WILLIAMS.

817.　　*Christ's Messengers.*
1 Men of God, go take your stations;
　Darkness reigns o'er all the earth;
　Go, proclaim among the nations
　　Joyful news of heavenly birth:
　　　Bear the tidings,
　Tell the Saviour's matchless worth.

2 Go, — and when exposed to dangers,
　Jesus will your souls defend;
　Go, and when 'mid foes and strangers,
　　He will still appear your friend:
　　　His kind presence
　Shall be with you to the end.
　　　　　　　　　　KELLY.

818.　　*Luke 2: 32.*
1 O'er the realms of pagan darkness
　Let the eye of pity gaze;
　See the kindreds of the people
　　Lost in sin's bewildering maze;
　　　Darkness brooding
　On the face of all the earth.

2 Light of them who sit in darkness!
　Rise and shine, thy blessings bring;
　Light to lighten all the Gentiles!
　　Rise with healing in thy wing.
　　　To thy brightness
　Let all kings and nations come.

3 May the heathen, now adoring
　Idol-gods of wood and stone,
　Come, and worshipping before him,
　　Serve the living God alone.
　　　Let thy glory
　Fill the earth, as floods the sea.
　　　　　　　　　　COTTERELL.

819.　　*The Day breaking.*
1 Yes! we trust the day is breaking,
　Joyful times are near at hand:
　God, the mighty God, is speaking
　　By his word in every land:
　　　God is speaking, —
　Darkness flies at his command.

2 With the voice of joy and singing
　Let us hail the dawning ray;
　Lo! the blessed day-star, bringing
　　O'er the earth a glorious day:
　　　At his rising,
　Gloom and darkness flee away.
　　　　　　　　　　KELLY.

The Church of Christ.

MISSIONARY HYMN. 7s. & 6s. — DR. MASON.

820. *Proclamation of the Gospel.*

1 FROM Greenland's icy mountains,
 From India's coral strand,
Where Afric's sunny fountains
 Roll down their golden sand:
From many an ancient river,
 From many a palmy plain,
They call us to deliver
 Their land from error's chain.

2 What though the spicy breezes
 Blow soft o'er Ceylon's isle;
Though every prospect pleases,
 And only man is vile?
In vain with lavish kindness
 The gifts of God are strown;
The heathen, in his blindness,
 Bows down to wood and stone!

3 Shall we, whose souls are lighted
 With wisdom from on high, —
Shall we, to men benighted,
 The lamp of life deny?
Salvation, oh, salvation!
 The joyful sound proclaim,
Till each remotest nation
 Has learned Messiah's name.

4 Waft, waft, ye winds, his story,
 And you, ye waters, roll,
Till, like a sea of glory,
 It spreads from pole to pole;
Till o'er our ransomed nature,
 The Lamb for sinners slain,
Redeemer, King, Creator,
 In bliss returns to reign!
HEBER.

821. Matt. 25: 6.

1 REJOICE, rejoice, believers!
 And let your lights appear;
The shades of eve are thickening,
 And darker night is near;
The watchers on the mountains
 Proclaim the Bridegroom near,
Go, meet him, as he cometh,
 With hallelujahs clear.

2 The saints, who here in patience
 Their cross and sufferings bore,
With him shall reign forever,
 When sorrow is no more:
Around the throne of glory
 The Lamb shall they behold,
Adoring cast before him
 Their diadems of gold.

3 Our hope and expectation,
 O Jesus, now appear!
Arise, thou Sun, so looked-for,
 O'er this benighted sphere!
With hearts and hands uplifted,
 We plead, O Lord, to see
The day of our redemption,
 And ever be with thee.
LAURENTI.

WEBB. 7s. & 6s.   GEO. J. WEBB.

822.   *Isaiah 66: 8.*

1 THE morning light is breaking;
   The darkness disappears;
The sons of earth are waking
   To penitential tears;
Each breeze that sweeps the ocean
   Brings tidings from afar,
Of nations in commotion,
   Prepared for Zion's war.

2 Rich dews of grace come o'er us
   In many a gentle shower;
And brighter scenes before us
   Are opening every hour:
Each cry to heaven going
   Abundant answer brings;
And heavenly gales are blowing,
   With peace upon their wings.

3 See heathen nations bending
   Before the God we love,
And thousand hearts ascending
   In gratitude above;
While sinners, now confessing,
   The gospel call obey,
And seek the Saviour's blessing,—
   A nation in a day.

4 Blest river of salvation,
   Pursue thine onward way;
Flow thou to every nation,
   Nor in thy richness stay:
Stay not till all the lowly
   Triumphant reach their home;
Stay not till all the holy
   Proclaim, "The Lord is come."
                   S. F. SMITH.

823.   *Psalm 72.*

1 HAIL to the Lord's Anointed,
   Great David's greater Son!
Hail, in the time appointed,
   His reign on earth begun!
He comes to break oppression,
   To set the captive free,
To take away transgression,
   And rule in equity.

2 He comes with succor speedy,
   To those who suffer wrong;
To help the poor and needy,
   And bid the weak be strong;
To give them songs for sighing,
   Their darkness turn to light,
Whose souls, condemned and dying,
   Were precious in his sight.

3 He shall come down like showers
   Upon the fruitful earth,
And love and joy, like flowers,
   Spring in his path to birth:
Before him on the mountains,
   Shall peace, the herald, go;
And righteousness, in fountains,
   From hill to valley flow.

4 For him shall prayer unceasing,
   And daily vows ascend;
His kingdom still increasing,—
   A kingdom without end:
The tide of time shall never
   His covenant remove;
His name shall stand forever,—
   That name to us is — Love.
                   MONTGOMERY.

Section VIII.

MORTALITY AND IMMORTALITY.

(*a.*) *Brevity of Life. Contemplation of Death. Prayers for Grace and Deliverance. The Gain of Death. Burial of the Dead. Hymns of Consolation.*

(*b.*) *The Resurrection of the Dead.*

(*c.*) *The Judgment. Christ our only Stay and Hope. The Righteous justified, and the Wicked condemned. Prayers for Mercy.*

(*d.*) *Heaven. Joys and Glories of Heaven. Rest and Home. The Father's House. The Saints in White Robes and with Palms in their Hands. No Night there, nor Sin, nor Sorrow, nor Death. The Native Country of our Souls.*

"THERE REMAINETH, THEREFORE, A REST FOR THE PEOPLE OF GOD." — *Hebrews* 4: 9.

MORTALITY AND IMMORTALITY.

BERA. L. M.   ROOT & SWEETSER'S COLL.

824.   *Psalm 127: 2.*
1 WHY should we start, and fear to die!
   What timorous worms we mortals are!
Death is the gate of endless joy,
   And yet we dread to enter there.

2 Oh, if my Lord would come and meet,
   My soul should stretch her wings in haste,
Fly fearless through death's iron gate,
   Nor feel the terrors as she passed!

3 Jesus can make a dying bed
   Feel soft as downy pillows are,
While on his breast I lean my head,
   And breathe my life out sweetly there!
                       WATTS.

825.   *Psalm 39.*
1 ALMIGHTY Maker of my frame,
   Teach me the measure of my days;
Teach me to know how frail I am,
   And spend the remnant to thy praise.

2 My days are shorter than a span,
   A little point my life appears;
How frail at best is dying man!
   How vain are all his hopes and fears!

3 Oh, spare me, and my strength restore,
   Ere my few hasty minutes flee!
And when my days on earth are o'er,
   Let me forever dwell with thee.
                       MRS. STEELE.

826.   *Psalm 103: 15.*
1 How vain is all beneath the skies!
   How transient every earthly bliss!
How slender all the fondest ties,
   That bind us to a world like this!

2 The evening cloud, the morning dew,
   The withering grass, the fading flower,
Of earthly hopes are emblems true,—
   The glory of a passing hour!

3 But though earth's fairest blossoms die,
   And all beneath the skies is vain,
There is a land, whose confines lie
   Beyond the reach of care and pain.

4 Then let the hope of joys to come
   Dispel our cares, and chase our fears:
If God be ours, we're travelling home,
   Though passing through a vale of tears.

827.
1 WHEN from my sight all fades away,
   And when my tongue no more can say,
Then come, Lord Jesus, come with speed,
   And help me in my hour of need.

2 When all my mind is darkened o'er,
   And human help can do no more,
Then let me, resting on thy word,
   Securely sleep in thee, my Lord.

Death of the Righteous.

FEDERAL ST. L. M. — H. K. OLIVER.

828. 1 Thess. 4: 14–18.

1 Asleep in Jesus! blessed sleep!
From which none ever wake to weep;
A calm and undisturbed repose,
Unbroken by the last of foes.

2 Asleep in Jesus! oh, how sweet
To be for such a slumber meet!
With holy confidence to sing
That death hath lost its venomed sting!

3 Asleep in Jesus! peaceful rest!
Whose waking is supremely blest;
No fear, no woe, shall dim that hour
Which manifests the Saviour's power.

4 Asleep in Jesus! oh, for me
May such a blissful refuge be!
Securely shall my ashes lie,
And wait the summons from on high.
Mrs. Mackay.

829. Rev. 14: 13.

1 How blest the righteous when he dies,
When sinks a weary soul to rest!
How mildly beam the closing eyes!
How gently heaves th' expiring breast!

2 So fades a summer cloud away;
So sinks the gale when storms are o'er;
So gently shuts the eye of day;
So dies a wave along the shore.

3 Triumphant smiles the victor's brow,
Fanned by some guardian angel's wing;
O grave, where is thy victory now?
And where, O death! where is thy sting?
Letitia Barbauld.

830. Eccl. 12: 7.

1 Unveil thy bosom, faithful tomb!
Take this new treasure to thy trust;
And give these sacred relics room
To slumber in the silent dust.

2 Nor pain, nor grief, nor anxious fear,
Invade thy bounds; no mortal woes
Can reach the peaceful sleeper here,
While angels watch the soft repose.

3 So Jesus slept; God's dying Son
Passed thro' the grave and blessed the bed:
Rest here, blest saint, till from his throne
The morning break, and pierce the shade.

4 Break from his throne, illustrious morn!
Attend, O earth! his sovereign word!
Restore thy trust: a glorious form
Shall then ascend to meet the Lord!
Watts.

831. Psalm 103: 16.

1 So fades the lovely blooming flower,
Frail, smiling solace of an hour!
So soon our transient comforts fly,
And pleasure only blooms to die.

2 Is there no kind, no lenient art
To heal the anguish of the heart?
Divine Redeemer, be thou nigh:
Thy comforts were not made to die!

3 Then gentle patience smiles on pain,
And dying hope revives again;
Hope wipes the tear from sorrow's eye,
And faith points upward to the sky.
Mrs. Steele.

Hope of the Resurrection.

LINWOOD. L. M. (QUARTETTE.)   Theme from BEETHOVEN.

832.   *Psalm 17.*

1 WHAT sinners value I resign;
  Lord, 'tis enough that thou art mine;
  I shall behold thy blissful face,
  And stand complete in righteousness.

2 This life's a dream, an empty show;
  But the bright world to which I go
  Hath joys substantial and sincere;
  When shall I wake and find me there?

3 O glorious hour! O blest abode!
  I shall be near and like my God!
  And flesh and sin no more control
  The sacred pleasures of the soul.

4 My flesh shall slumber in the ground
  Till the last trumpet's joyful sound;
  Then burst the chains with sweet surprise,
  And in my Saviour's image rise.
                      WATTS.

833.   *The Resurrection.*

1 CEASE, cease, ye vain, desponding fears;
  When Christ, our Lord, from darkness sprang,
  Death, the last foe, was captive led,
  And heaven with praise and wonder rang.

2 Faith sees the bright, eternal doors
  Unfold to make his children way;
  They shall be clothed with endless life,
  And shine in everlasting day.

3 The trump shall sound, the dust awake,
  From the cold tomb the slumberers spring;
  Through heaven with joy their myriads rise, [King.
  And hail their Saviour and their
                      DWIGHT.

834.   *Hope of the Resurrection.*

1 WHEN God is nigh, my faith is strong,
  His arm is my almighty prop:
  Be glad, my heart, rejoice, my tongue;
  My dying flesh shall rest in hope.

2 Though in the dust I lay my head,
  Yet, gracious God, thou wilt not leave
  My soul forever with the dead,
  Nor lose thy children in the grave.

3 My flesh shall thy first call obey,
  Shake off the dust, and rise on high;
  Then shalt thou lead the wondrous way
  Up to thy throne above the sky.

4 There streams of endless pleasure flow;
  And full discoveries of thy grace,
  Which we but tasted here below, [place.
  Spread heavenly joys through all the
                      WATTS.

835.   *The Resurrection.*

1 AWHILE they rest within the tomb
  In sweet repose till morning come!
  Then rise with joy to meet their God,
  And ever dwell in his abode.

2 Celestial dawn! triumphant hour!
  How glorious that awakening power,
  Which bids the sleeping dust arise,
  And join the anthems of the skies.

3 This weary life will soon be past,
  The lingering morn will come at last,
  And gloomy mists will roll away
  Before that bright, unfading day.

Home and Rest in Heaven.

ELYRIA. L. M.   From CHERUBINI.

836.   *Isaiah 57: 2.*
1 Gently, my Saviour, let me down,
   To slumber in the arms of death;
   I rest my soul on thee alone,
   E'en till my last expiring breath.

2 Soon will the storm of life be o'er,
   And I shall enter endless rest;
   There I shall live to sin no more,
   And bless thy name, forever blest.

3 Bid me possess sweet peace within;
   Let childlike patience keep my heart;
   Then shall I feel my heaven begin,
   Before my spirit hence depart.

4 Oh, speed thy chariot, God of love!
   And take me from this world of woe;
   I long to reach those joys above,
   And bid farewell to all below.
                                HILL.

837.   *"Gone Before."*
1 Dear is the spot where Christians sleep,
   And sweet the strains their spirits pour;
   Oh, why should we in anguish weep?—
   They are not lost, but gone before.

2 Secure from every mortal care,
   By sin and sorrow vexed no more,
   Eternal happiness they share
   Who are not lost, but gone before.

3 To Zion's peaceful courts above,
   In faith triumphant may we soar,
   Embracing, in the arms of love,
   The friends not lost, but gone before.

4 To Jordan's bank whene'er we come,
   And hear the swelling waters roar,
   Jesus! convey us safely home,
   To friends not lost, but gone before.

838.   *Heb. 13: 14.*
1 "We've no abiding city here:"
   Sad truth, were this to be our home;
   But let this thought our spirits cheer,
   "We seek a city yet to come."

2 "We've no abiding city here;"
   We seek a city out of sight;
   Zion its name, the Lord is there,
   It shines with everlasting light.

3 Oh, sweet abode of peace and love,
   Where pilgrims freed from toil are blest!
   Had I the pinions of the dove,
   I'd fly to thee, and be at rest.

4 But hush, my soul! nor dare repine;
   The time my God appoints is best:
   While here, to do his will be mine,
   And his to fix my time of rest.
                                KELLY.

839.   *A Well-spent Life.*
1 How blest is he whose tranquil mind,
   When life declines, recalls again
   The years that time has cast behind,
   And reaps delight from toil and pain.

2 So, when the transient storm is past,
   The sudden gloom and driving shower,
   The sweetest sunshine is the last;
   The loveliest is the evening hour.

Nearer Home. Death of the Righteous.

DAWN. S. M.   E. P. PARKER.

840.   *Nearer Home.*

1 ONE sweetly solemn thought
   Comes to me o'er and o'er, —
Nearer my home, to-day, am I
   Than e'er I've been before;

2 Nearer my Father's house,
   Where many mansions be;
Nearer my Saviour's glorious throne;
   Nearer the crystal sea;

3 Nearer the bound of life,
   Where burdens are laid down;
Nearer to leave the heavy cross;
   Nearer to gain the crown.

4 But, lying dark between,
   Winding down through the night,
There rolls the deep and unknown stream
   That leads at last to light.

5 E'en now, perchance, my feet
   Are slipping on the brink,
And I, to-day, am nearer home, —
   Nearer than now I think.

6 Father, perfect my trust!
   Strengthen my power of faith!
Nor let me stand, at last, alone
   Upon the shore of death.
                PHŒBE CAREY.

841.   Num. 23: 10.

1 OH for the death of those
   Who slumber in the Lord!
Oh, be like theirs my last repose,
   Like theirs my last reward!

2 Their bodies in the ground,
   In silent hope may lie,
Till the last trumpet's joyful sound
   Shall call them to the sky.

3 Their ransomed spirits soar,
   On wings of faith and love,
To meet the Saviour they adore,
   And reign with him above.

4 With us their names shall live
   Through long, succeeding years,
Embalmed with all our hearts can give,
   Our praises and our tears.

5 Oh for the death of those
   Who slumber in the Lord!
Oh, be like theirs my last repose,
   Like theirs my last reward!

842.   Zech. 1: 5.

1 How swift the torrent rolls,
   That bears us to the sea!
The tide which hurries thoughtless souls
   To vast eternity!

2 Our fathers, where are they,
   With all they called their own?
Their joys and griefs and hopes and cares
   And wealth and honor gone!

3 God of our fathers, hear,
   Thou everlasting Friend!
While we, as on life's utmost verge,
   Our souls to thee commend.

4 Of all the pious dead
   May we the footsteps trace,
Till with them in the land of light,
   We dwell before thy face.
                DODDRIDGE.

The Death of Friends.

CORINTH. C. M. — DR. MASON.

843. *Phil. 1: 21.*

1 Why should our tears in sorrow flow,
When God recalls his own;
And bids them leave a world of woe
For an immortal crown?

2 Is not e'en death a gain to those
Whose life to God was given?
Gladly to earth their eyes they close,
To open them in heaven.

3 Their toils are past, their work is done,
And they are fully blest:
They fought the fight, the victory won,
And entered into rest.

4 Then let our sorrows cease to flow,—
God has recalled his own;
And let our hearts in every woe,
Still say, "Thy will be done!"

844. *2 Cor. 5: 8.*

1 Why do we mourn departing friends,
Or shake at death's alarms?
'Tis but the voice that Jesus sends,
To call them to his arms.

2 Are we not tending upward, too,
As fast as time can move?
Nor would we wish the hours more slow,
To keep us from our love.

3 Why should we tremble to convey
Their bodies to the tomb?
There the dear flesh of Jesus lay,
And scattered all the gloom.

4 The graves of all the saints he blessed;
And softened every bed;
Where should the dying members rest,
But with the dying Head?

5 Thence he arose, ascending high,
And showed our feet the way;
Up to the Lord we, too, shall fly,
At the great rising day.

6 Then let the last loud trumpet sound,
And bid our kindred rise;
Awake! ye nations under ground;
Ye saints! ascend the skies.
WATTS.

845. *"They rest from their Labors."*

1 Not for the pious dead we weep;
Their sorrows now are o'er;
The sea is calm, the tempest past,
On that eternal shore.

2 Their peace is sealed, their rest is sure,
Within that better home;
Awhile we weep and linger here,
Then follow to the tomb.

3 Oh, might some dream of visioned bliss,
Some trance of rapture, show
Where, on the bosom of their God,
They rest from human woe!

4 Jesus! our shadowy path illume,
And teach the chastened mind
To welcome all that's left of good,
To all that's lost resigned.
BARBAULD.

Here and Hereafter.

846. *"Treasures in Heaven."*

1 ANOTHER hand is beckoning us,
  Another call is given,
And glows once more with angel steps
  The path that leads to heaven.

2 Unto our Father's will alone
  One thought hath reconciled:
That He whose love exceedeth ours
  Hath taken home his child.

3 Fold her, O Father, in thine arms,
  And let her henceforth be
A messenger of love between
  Our human hearts and thee.

4 Still let her mild rebuking stand
  Between us and the wrong,
And her dear memory serve to make
  Our faith in goodness strong.
                    WHITTIER.

847. *The Undiscovered Country.*

1 THERE is a state unknown, unseen,
  Where parted souls must be;
And but a step doth lie between
  That world of souls and me.

2 I see no light, I hear no sound,
  When midnight shades are spread;
Yet angels pitch their tents around
  And guard my quiet bed.

3 The things unseen, O God, reveal;
  My spirit's vision clear,
Till I shall feel and see and know
  That those I love are near.

4 Impart the faith that soars on high,
  Beyond this earthly strife;
That holds sweet converse with the sky,
  And lives eternal life.
                    J. TAYLOR.

848.   2 Sam. 12: 23.

1 THRO' sorrow's night and danger's path,
  Amid the deepening gloom,
We, followers of our suffering Lord,
  Are marching to the tomb.

2 There, when the turmoil is no more,
  And all our powers decay,
Our cold remains in solitude
  Shall sleep the years away.

3 Our labors done, securely laid
  In this our last retreat,
Unheeded o'er our silent dust,
  The storms of earth shall beat.

4 Yet not thus buried or extinct
  The vital spark shall lie;
For o'er life's wreck that spark shall rise
  To seek its kindred sky.

5 These ashes, too, this little dust,
  Our Father's care shall keep,
Till the last angel rise and break
  The long and dreary sleep.

6 Then love's soft dew o'er every eye
  Shall shed its mildest rays,
And the long-silent voice awake
  With shouts of endless praise.
                    H. K. WHITE.

849.   *"To die is Gain."*

1 DEAR as thou wert, and justly dear,
  We will not weep for thee;   [tear;
  One thought shall check the starting
  It is, that thou art free.

2 And thus shall faith's consoling power
  The tears of love restrain:
Oh, who that saw thy parting hour
  Could wish thee back again.

3 Triumphant in thy closing eye
  The hope of glory shone;
Joy breathed in thine expiring sigh,
  To think the fight was won.

4 Gently the passing spirit fled,
  Sustained by grace divine:
Oh, may such grace on me be shed,
  And make my end like thine!
                    DALE.

850. *"As a Flower of the Field, so he flourisheth."*

1 LET others boast how strong they be,
  Nor death nor danger fear;
But we confess, O Lord! to thee,
  What feeble things we are.

2 Fresh as the grass our bodies stand,
  And flourish bright and gay:
A blasting wind sweeps o'er the land,
  And fades the grass away.

3 Our life contains a thousand springs,
  And dies if one be gone;
Strange that a harp of thousand strings
  Should keep in tune so long!

4 But 'tis our God supports our frame,—
  The God who made us first;
Salvation to th' almighty name
  That reared us from the dust.
                    WATTS.

Time and Eternity.

DENNIS. S. M. From NAGELI.

851. *James 4: 13-15.*
1 To-morrow, Lord, is thine,
   Lodged in thy sovereign hand,
And if its sun arise and shine,
   It shines by thy command.

2 The present moment flies
   And bears our life away;
Oh, make thy servants truly wise,
   That they may live to-day.

3 Since on this wingèd hour
   Eternity is hung,
Waken, by thine almighty power,
   The aged and the young.

4 One thing demands our care,
   Oh, be it still pursued!
Lest, slighted once, the season fair
   Should never be renewed.

5 To Jesus may we fly,
   Swift as the morning light,
Lest life's young golden beams should die,
   In sudden, endless night.
                            DODDRIDGE.

852. *Job 10: 25.*
1 And must this body die?
   This mortal frame decay?
And must these active limbs of mine
   Lie mouldering in the clay?

2 God, my Redeemer, lives,
   And ever from the skies
Looks down and watches all my dust,
   Till he shall bid it rise.

3 Arrayed in glorious grace
   Shall these vile bodies shine,
And every shape, and every face
   Look heavenly and divine.

4 These lively hopes we owe
   To Jesus' dying love;
We would adore his grace below,
   And sing his power above.

5 Dear Lord! accept the praise
   Of these our humble songs,
Till tunes of nobler sound we raise
   With our immortal tongues.
                            WATTS.

853. *1 Thess. 4: 17.*
1 Forever with the Lord!
   Amen, so let it be;
Life from the dead is in that word,
   'Tis immortality.

2 Here, in the body pent,
   Absent from thee I roam;
Yet nightly pitch my moving tent
   A day's march nearer home.

3 My Father's house on high,
   Home of my soul! how near
At times to faith's foreseeing eye
   Thy golden gates appear.

4 Ah! then my spirit faints
   To reach the land I love,
The bright inheritance of saints,
   Jerusalem above.
                            MONTGOMERY.

The Rewards of Faithful Service.

GORTON. S. M.   BEETHOVEN.

854.   *"The Recompense of Reward."*

1 Oh, what if we are Christ's,
 Is earthly shame or loss?
Bright shall the crown of glory be,
 When we have borne the cross.

2 Keen was the trial once,
 Bitter the cup of woe,
When martyred saints, baptized in blood,
 Christ's sufferings shared below.

3 Bright is their glory now,
 Boundless their joy above,
Where, on the bosom of their God,
 They rest in perfect love.

4 Lord, may that grace be ours,
 Like them in faith to bear
All that of sorrow, grief, or pain
 May be our portion here.

5 Enough if thou at last
 The word of blessing give,
And let us rest beneath thy feet,
 Where saints and angels live.

855. *"Well done, Good and Faithful Servant."*

1 Servant of God, well done!
 Rest from thy loved employ:
The battle fought, the victory won,
 Enter thy Master's joy.

2 The voice at midnight came;
 He started up to hear:
A mortal arrow pierced his frame;
 He fell, but felt no fear.

3 At midnight came the cry,
 "To meet thy God prepare!"
He woke, and caught his Captain's eye;
 Then, strong in faith and prayer,

4 His spirit, with a bound,
 Left its encumbering clay:
His tent, at sunrise, on the ground
 A darkened ruin lay.

5 The pains of death are past;
 Labor and sorrow cease;
And life's long warfare closed at last,
 His soul is found in peace.

6 Soldier of Christ, well done!
 Praise be thy new employ;
And, while eternal ages run,
 Rest in thy Saviour's joy.
                         MONTGOMERY.

856.   Jer. 13: 16.

1 The swift declining day,
 How fast its moments fly!
While evening's broad and gloomy shade
 Gains on the western sky.

2 Ye mortals, mark its pace,
 And use the hours of light;
And know its Maker can command
 At once eternal night.

3 Give glory to the Lord,
 Who rules the whirling sphere;
Submissive at his footstool bow,
 And seek salvation there.

4 Then shall new lustre break
 Through death's impending gloom,
And lead you to unchanging light,
 In your celestial home.
                         DODDRIDGE.

336 — The Transient and the Eternal.

BLOOM. 8s. & 7s. — Arranged from FRANZ.

857. *"Mother Earth."*

1 Shall I fear, O Earth! thy bosom,
  Shrink and faint to lay me there,
Whence the fragrant, lovely blossom
  Springs to gladden earth and air?

2 Whence the tree, the brook, the river,
  Soft clouds floating in the sky,
All fair things come, whispering ever
  Of the love divine on high?

3 Yea, whence One arose victorious
  O'er the darkness of the grave,
His strong arm revealing, glorious
  In its might Divine to save?

4 No, fair Earth! a tender mother
  Thou hast been, and yet canst be:
And through him, my Lord and Brother,
  Sweet shall be my rest in thee!
  — Thomas Davis.

858. Isa. 64: 6.

1 See the leaves around us falling,
  Dry and withered to the ground;
Thus to thoughtless mortals calling,
  In a sad and solemn sound: —

2 "Sons of Adam, once in Eden,
  When, like him, ye blighted fell,
Hear the lesson we are reading,
  'Tis alas! the truth we tell.

3 "Youth, on length of days presuming,
  Who the paths of pleasure tread,
View us, late in beauty blooming,
  Numbered now among the dead.

4 "Though as yet no losses grieve you,
  Gay with health and many a grace,
Let no cloudless skies deceive you,
  Summer gives to autumn place.

5 "Yearly in our course appearing,
  Messengers of shortest stay,
Thus we preach in mortal hearing —
  Ye, like us, shall pass away."

6 On the tree of life eternal,
  Oh, let all our hopes be laid!
This alone, forever vernal,
  Bears a leaf that shall not fade.
  — Horne.

859. *"And there shall be no more Death."*

1 Cease, ye mourners, cease to languish
  O'er the grave of those you love;
Pain and death and night and anguish
  Enter not the world above.

2 While our silent steps are straying,
  Lonely, through night's deepening shade,
Glory's brightest beams are playing
  Round the happy Christian's head.

3 Light and peace at once deriving
  From the hand of God most high,
In his glorious presence living,
  They shall never, never die.

4 Now, ye mourners, cease to languish
  O'er the grave of those you love;
Far removed from pain and anguish,
  They are chanting hymns above.
  — Collyer.

To Die is Gain. Sweet Home.

FREDERICK. 11s. GEO. KINGSLEY.

860. Job 7: 16.

1 I would not live alway: I ask not to stay
Where storm after storm rises dark o'er the way;
The few lurid mornings that dawn on us here
Are enough for life's woes, full enough for its cheer.

2 I would not live alway; no, welcome the tomb;
Since Jesus hath lain there, I dread not its gloom;
There sweet be my rest, till he bid me arise
To hail him in triumph descending the skies.

3 Who, who would live alway, away from his God,
Away from yon heaven, that blissful abode,
Where the rivers of pleasure flow o'er the bright plains,
And the noontide of glory eternally reigns?

4 Where the saints of all ages in harmony meet,
Their Saviour and brethren transported to greet;
While the anthems of rapture unceasingly roll,
And the smile of the Lord is the feast of the soul.
MUHLENBURG.

861. "Sweet Home."

1 'Mid scenes of confusion and creature complaints,
How sweet to my soul is communion with saints;
To find at the banquet of mercy there's room,
And feel in the presence of Jesus at home.

2 I sigh from this body of sin to be free,
Which hinders my joy and communion with thee;
Though now my temptation like billows may foam,
All, all will be peace when I'm with thee at home.

3 While here in the valley of conflict I stay,
Oh, give me submission and strength as my day;
In all my afflictions to thee would I come,
Rejoicing in hope of my glorious home.

4 Whate'er thou deniest, oh, give me thy grace,
The Spirit's sure witness, and smiles of thy face;
Endue me with patience to wait at thy throne,
And find, even now, a sweet foretaste of home.

Translation of the Righteous. Burial of the Dead.

MONTGOMERY. S. H. M.

862.   1 Cor. 15: 19.

1 Friend after friend departs;
  Who has not lost a friend?
There is no union here of hearts
  That finds not here an end:
Were this frail world our only rest,
Living or dying, none were blest.

2 Beyond the flight of time,
  Beyond this vale of death,
There surely is some blessed clime
  Where life is not a breath,
Nor life's affections transient fire,
Whose sparks fly upward and expire.

3 There is a world above
  Where parting is unknown;
A whole eternity of love
  Formed for the good alone;
And faith beholds the dying here
Translated to that happier sphere.

4 Thus star by star declines
  Till all are passed away,
As morning high and higher shines
  To pure and perfect day:
Nor sink those stars in empty night;.
They hide themselves in heaven's own
    light.
              MONTGOMERY.

863.   1 Cor. 15: 36.

1 This place is holy ground!
  World, with its cares, away!
A holy, solemn stillness, round
  This lifeless, mouldering clay:
Nor pain, nor grief, nor anxious fear,
Can reach the peaceful sleeper here.

2 Behold the bed of death,
  The pale and mortal clay!
Heard ye the sob of parting breath?
  Marked ye the eye's last ray?
No! life so sweetly ceased to be,
It lapsed in immortality.

3 Why mourn the pious dead?
  Why sorrows swell our eyes?
Can sighs recall the spirit fled?
  Shall vain regrets arise?
Though death has caused this altered
    mien,
In heaven the ransomed soul is seen.

4 Bury the dead, and weep
  In stillness o'er the loss:
Bury the dead! in Christ they sleep
  Who bore on earth his cross;
And from the grave their dust shall rise.
In his own image to the skies.
              MONTGOMERY.

Blessedness of Such as die in the Lord.

HATTON. 7s.

864. Rev. 14: 13.
1 HARK! a voice divides the sky!
  Happy are the faithful dead
In the Lord who sweetly die!
  They from all their toils are freed.

2 Ready for their glorious crown,
  Sorrows past and sins forgiven, —
Here they lay their burden down,
  Hallowed and made meet for heaven.

3 Yes, the Christian's course is run!
  Ended is the glorious strife ;
Fought the fight, the work is done;
  Death is swallowed up in life!

4 Lo! the pris'ner is released, —
  Lightened of his heavy load ;
Where the weary are at rest,
  He is gathered in to God!

5 When from flesh the spirit freed,
  Hastens homeward to return,
Mortals cry, "A man is dead!"
  Angels sing, "A child is born!"
  C. WESLEY.

865. *Gathered Home.*
1 CHRIST will gather in his own
  To the place where he is gone,
Where their heart and treasure lie,
Where our life is hid on high.

2 Day by day the voice saith, "Come,
  Enter thine eternal home ;"
Asking not if we can spare
This dear soul it summons there.

3 Did he ask us, well we know,
  We should say, "Oh, spare this blow!"
Yes, with streaming eyes should pray,
"Lord, we love him, let him stay!"

4 Many a heart no longer here,
  Ah! was all too inly dear:
Yet, O Love, 'tis thou dost call,
Thou who art our all in all.
  MORAVIAN.

866. John 11: 23.
1 BROTHER, though from yonder sky
  Cometh neither voice nor cry,
Yet we know from thee, to-day,
Every pain hath passed away.

2 Not for thee shall tears be given,
  Child of God, and heir of heaven ;
For he gave thee sweet release ;
Thine the Christian's death of peace.

3 Well we know thy living faith
  Had the power to conquer death ;
As a living rose may bloom
By the border of the tomb.

4 Brother, in that solemn trust
  We commend thee, dust to dust!
In that faith we wait, till, risen,
Thou shalt meet us all in heaven.

5 While we weep as Jesus wept,
  Thou shalt sleep as Jesus slept;
With thy Saviour thou shalt rest,
Crowned and glorified and blest.
  BANCROFT.

Death, Judgment, Eternity.

DOWNS. C. M.   DR. MASON.

867.   Matt. 24: 44.

1 THERE is an hour when I must part
   With all I hold most dear;
And life, with its best hopes, will then
   As nothingness appear.

2 There is an hour when I must sink
   Beneath the stroke of death;
And yield to Him who gave it first,
   My struggling vital breath.

3 There is an hour when I must stand
   Before the judgment-seat;
And all my sins, and all my foes,
   In awful vision meet.

4 There is an hour when I must look
   On one eternity;
And nameless woe, or blissful life,
   My endless portion be.

5 O Saviour, then, in all my need
   Be near, be near to me:
And let my soul, by steadfast faith,
   Find life and heaven in thee.

868.   Matt. 25: 41.

1 THAT awful day will surely come,
   The appointed hour makes haste,
When I must stand before my Judge,
   And pass the solemn test.

2 Thou lovely Chief of all my joys,
   Thou Sovereign of my heart!
How could I bear to hear thy voice
   Pronounce the sound, "Depart!"

3 Jesus, I throw my arms around,
   And hang upon thy breast:
Without a gracious smile from thee,
   My spirit cannot rest.

4 Oh, tell me that my worthless name
   Is graven on thy hands!
Show me some promise in thy book,
   Where my salvation stands.

5 Give me one kind, assuring word,
   To sink my fears again;
And cheerfully my soul shall wait
   Her threescore years and ten.
                           WATTS.

869.   *Eternity.* — Psalm 90.

1 O GOD, our help in ages past,
   Our hope for years to come,
Our shelter from the stormy blast,
   And our eternal home!

2 Before the hills in order stood,
   Or earth received her frame,
From everlasting thou art God,
   To endless years the same.

3 Thy word commands our flesh to dust;
   "Return, ye sons of men;"
All nations rose from earth at first,
   And turn to earth again.

4 Time, like an ever-rolling stream,
   Bears all its sons away;
They fly, forgotten, as a dream
   Dies at the opening day.

5 O God, our help in ages past,
   Our hope for years to come,
Be thou our guard while troubles last,
   And our eternal home!
                           WATTS.

Resurrection and Judgment.

HAVERHILL. S. M. — DR. MASON.

870. *Matt. 25: 13.*

1 Thou Judge of quick and dead,
  Before whose bar severe,
With holy joy, or guilty dread,
  We all shall soon appear ; —

2 Our cautioned souls prepare
  For that tremendous day ;
Oh, fill us now with watchful care,
  And stir us up to pray ; —

3 To pray, and wait the hour,
  That awful hour unknown,
When robed in majesty and power,
  Thou shalt from heaven come down !

4 Oh, may we all be found
  Obedient to thy word, —
Attentive to the trumpet's sound,
  And looking for our Lord !

5 Oh, may we all insure
  A home among the blest ;
And watch a moment to secure
  An everlasting rest !
                        C. WESLEY.

871. *Resurrection and Judgment.*

1 And am I born to die ?
  To lay this body down ?
And must my trembling spirit fly
  Into a world unknown ?

2 Waked by the trumpet's sound,
  I from the grave must rise,
And see the Judge with glory crowned,
  And see the flaming skies.

3 I must from God be driven,
  Or with my Saviour dwell :
Must come at his command to heaven,
  Or else depart — to hell.

4 O thou, that wouldst not have
  One wretched sinner die,
Who died'st thyself, my soul to save
  From endless misery ; —

5 Show me the way to shun
  Thy dreadful wrath severe ;
That, when thou comest on thy throne,
  I may with joy appear.
                        LUTHERAN COLL.

872. *The Judgment.*

1 And will the Judge descend,
  And must the dead arise,
And not a single soul escape
  His all-discerning eyes ?

2 How will my heart endure
  The terrors of that day,
When earth and heaven before his face
  Astonished shrink away ?

3 But ere the trumpet shakes
  The mansions of the dead,
Hark, from the gospel's cheering sound
  What joyful tidings spread !

4 Ye sinners, seek his grace
  Whose wrath ye cannot bear ;
Fly to the shelter of his cross,
  And find salvation there.
                        DODDRIDGE.

The Judgment. Falling Asleep in Jesus.

JUDGMENT HYMN. — M. LUTHER.

873.   Rev. 20: 6.

1 Great God, what do I see and hear!
   The end of things created!
The Judge of man I see appear,
   On clouds of glory seated;
The trumpet sounds; the graves restore
The dead which they contained before;
   Prepare, my soul, to meet him.

2 The dead in Christ shall first arise,
   At the last trumpet's sounding,
Caught up to meet him in the skies,
   With joy their Lord surrounding,
No gloomy fears their souls dismay,
His presence sheds eternal day
   On those prepared to meet him.

3 But sinners, filled with guilty fears,
   Behold his wrath prevailing;
For they shall rise, and find their tears
   And sighs are unavailing:
The day of grace is past and gone;
Trembling they stand before the throne,
   All unprepared to meet him.

4 Great God! what do I see and hear!
   The end of things created!
The Judge of man I see appear,
   On clouds of glory seated:
Beneath his cross I view the day
When heaven and earth shall pass away,
   And thus prepare to meet him.
                  MARTIN LUTHER.

874.   Psalm 31: 5.

1 When my last hour is close at hand,
   My last sad journey taken,
Do thou, Lord Jesus! by me stand;
   Let me not be forsaken:
O Lord! my spirit I resign
Into thy loving hands divine:
   'Tis safe within thy keeping.

2 Countless as sands upon the shore
   My sins may then appall me;
Yet, though my conscience vex me sore,
   Despair shall not enthrall me;
For as I draw my latest breath,
I'll think, Lord Christ! upon thy death,
   And there find consolation.

3 I shall not in the grave remain,
   Since thou death's bonds hast severed;
By hope with thee to rise again
   From fear of death delivered,
I'll come to thee, where'er thou art,
Live with thee, from thee never part;
   Therefore I die in rapture.

4 And so to Jesus Christ I'll go,
   My longing arms extending;
So fall asleep in slumber deep, —
   Slumber that knows no waking,
Till Jesus Christ, God's only Son,
Opens the gates of bliss, leads on
   To heaven, to life eternal.
       FROM THE GERMAN, BY BOWRING.

Death a Sleep. The Coming of Christ.

SANFORD. L. M.   From DONIZETTI.

875.   *Death conquered.*

1 DEATH is no more among our foes,
Since Christ, the mighty Conqu'ror rose;
Both power and sting the Saviour broke;
He died, and gave the finished stroke.

2 Saints die, and we should gently weep;
Sweetly in Jesus' arms they sleep;
Far from this world of sin and woe,
Nor sin, nor pain, nor grief they know.

3 Death is a sleep; and oh, how sweet
To souls prepared its stroke to meet!
Their dying beds, their graves are blest,
For all to them is peace and rest.

4 Soon shall the earth's remotest bound
Feel the archangel's trumpet sound;
Then shall the grave's dark caverns shake,
And joyful all the saints shall wake.
            MEDLEY.

876.   2 Thess. 1: 7.

1 THE Lord shall come! the earth shall quake;
The mountains to their centre shake;
And withering from the vault of night,
The stars withdraw their feeble light.

2 The Lord shall come! but not the same
As once in lowly form he came, —
A silent Lamb before his foes,
A weary man, and full of woes.

3 The Lord shall come! a dreadful form,
With wreath of flame, and robe of storm,
On cherub-wings and wings of wind,
Anointed Judge of human kind!

4 While sinners in despair shall call,
"Rocks, hide us! mountains, on us fall!"
The saints, ascending from the tomb,
Shall sing for joy, "The Lord is come!"
            HEBER.

877.   2 Peter 3: 10.

1 THAT day of wrath! that dreadful day,
When heaven and earth shall pass away!
What power shall be the sinner's stay?
How shall he meet that dreadful day?

2 When, shrivelling like a parched scroll,
The flaming heavens together roll;
When louder yet, and yet more dread,
Swells the high trump that wakes the dead!

3 Oh! on that day, that wrathful day,
When man to judgment wakes from clay,
Be thou the trembling sinner's stay,
Though heaven and earth shall pass away!
       WALTER SCOTT FROM CELANO.

878.   *Fear of God's Wrath.*

1 FATHER! — if I may call thee so, —
I tremble with my one desire:
Lift up this heavy load of woe,
Nor let me in my sins expire!

2 I tremble lest the wrath divine,
Which bruises now my sinful soul,
Should bruise and break this soul of mine,
Long as eternal ages roll.

3 Thy wrath, I fear, thy wrath alone,
This endless exile, Lord, from thee!
Oh, save! oh, give me to thy Son,
Who trembled, wept, and bled for me!

The Day of Wrath.

DIES IRAE. 7s. Arranged from an OLD PROVENCAL MELODY. E. P. P.

879. Matt. 24: 30.

1 Day of anger! that dread day
Shall the sign in heaven display,
And the earth in ashes lay.
Oh, what trembling shall appear,
When his coming shall be near,
Who shall all things strictly clear!

2 When the trumpet shall command,
Through the tombs of every land,
All before the throne to stand!
Death shall shrink and nature quake,
When all creatures shall awake,
Answer to their Judge to make!

3 What shall I before him say?
How shall I be safe that day,
When the righteous scarcely may?
King of awful majesty!
Saving sinners graciously,
Fount of mercy! save thou me!

4 Leave me not, my Saviour! — one
For whose soul thy course was run, —
Lest I be that day undone!
Thou didst toil my soul to gain,
Didst redeem me with thy pain, —
Be such labor not in vain!

5 Thou didst heal the sinner's grief,
Thou didst hear the dying thief,
Even I may hope relief!
Low thine ear in mercy bow,
Broken is my heart, and low!
Guard of my last end be thou!

6 When thy voice in wrath shall say,
"Cursed ones, depart away!"
Call me with the blest, I pray!
In that day, that mournful day,
When to judgment wakes our clay,
Show me mercy, Lord, I pray!

CELANO, BY ALFORD.

NOTE. — From the great number and variety of translations of this incomparable hymn, the version of Dean Alford has been selected for this book, not as in all respects the best, but as, on the whole, the most suitable for the purposes of public worship.

Prayer for Acceptance at the Judgment.

MERIBAH. C. P. M.   DR. MASON.

880.   Matt. 25: 46.

1 WHEN thou, my righteous Judge, shalt come
To take thy ransomed people home,
Shall I among them stand?
Shall such a worthless worm as I,
Who sometimes am afraid to die,
Be found at thy right hand?

2 I love to meet thy people now,
Before thy feet with them to bow,
Though vilest of them all;
But, can I bear the piercing thought,
What if my name should be left out,
When thou for them shalt call?

3 O Lord, prevent it by thy grace,
Be thou my only hiding-place,
In this the accepted day;
Thy pardoning voice, oh, let me hear,
To still my unbelieving fear,
Nor let me fall, I pray.

4 Among thy saints let me be found,
Whene'er the archangel's trump shall sound,
To see thy smiling face;
Then, loudest of the throng, I'll sing,
While heaven's resounding mansions ring
With shouts of sovereign grace.

881.   *The Two Worlds.*

1 Lo! on a narrow neck of land,
'Twixt two unbounded seas I stand,
Secure! insensible!
A point of time, a moment's space,
Removes me to yon heavenly place,
Or shuts me up in hell.

2 O God! my inmost soul convert,
And deeply on my thoughtful heart
Eternal things impress:
Give me to feel their solemn weight,
And save me ere it be too late;—
Wake me to righteousness.

3 Before me place in dread array,
The pomp of that tremendous day,
When thou with clouds shalt come
To judge the nations at thy bar;
And tell me, Lord! shall I be there
To meet a joyful doom?

4 Be this my one great business here,—
With holy trembling, holy fear,
To make my calling sure!
Thine utmost counsel to fulfil,
And suffer all thy righteous will,
And to the end endure!

5 Then, Saviour, then my soul receive,
Then bid me in thy presence live,
And reign with thee above;
Where faith is sweetly lost in sight,
And hope in full, supreme delight,
And everlasting love.

C. WESLEY.

Christ coming to Judgment.

BREST. 8s., 7s., & 4s.   DR. MASON.

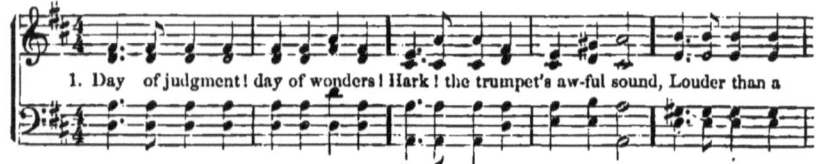

1. Day of judgment! day of wonders! Hark! the trumpet's aw-ful sound, Louder than a

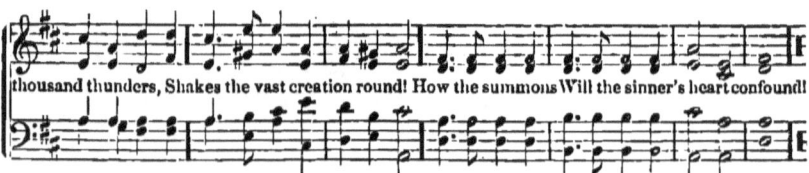

thousand thunders, Shakes the vast creation round! How the summons Will the sinner's heart confound!

882.   Matt. 25 : 34.

2 See the Judge, our nature wearing,
   Clothed in majesty divine!
You, who long for his appearing,
   Then shall say, "This God is mine!"
      Gracious Saviour!
   Own me in that day for thine.

3 At his call the dead awaken,
   Rise to life from earth and sea;
All the powers of nature, shaken
   By his looks, prepare to flee:
      Careless sinner!
   What will then become of thee?

4 But to those who have confessed,
   Loved and served the Lord below,
He will say, "Come near, ye blessèd!
   See the kingdom I bestow!
      You forever
Shall my love and glory know."
              NEWTON.

883.   The Judgment.

1 Lo! He comes, with clouds descending,
   Once for favored sinners slain;
Thousand thousand saints attending,
   Swell the triumph of his train.
      Hallelujah!
   God appears, on earth to reign.

2 Every eye shall now behold Him
   Robed in dreadful majesty;
Those that set at naught and sold Him,
   Pierced and nailed Him to the tree,
      Deeply wailing,
   Shall the true Messiah see!

3 Yea, Amen! let all adore thee,
   High on thine eternal throne;
Saviour! take the power and glory,
   Claim the kingdom for thine own.
      Oh, come quickly!
   Everlasting God! come down.
              OLIVER.

884.   Matt. 24 : 27.

1 Lo! the mighty God appearing —
   From on high Jehovah speaks!
Eastern lands the summons hearing,
   O'er the west his thunder breaks:
      Earth beholds him:
   Universal nature shakes.

2 Zion all its light unfolding,
   God in glory shall display:
Lo! he comes, — nor silence holding,
   Fire and clouds prepare his way:
      Tempests round him
   Hasten on the dreadful day.

3 Now the heavens on high adore him,
   And his righteousness declare:
Sinners perish from before him,
   But his saints his mercies share:
      Just his judgment!
   God, himself the Judge, is there.
              W. GOODE.

The Joys and Glories of Heaven.

BRUNSWICK. L. M. — HENRY CAREY.

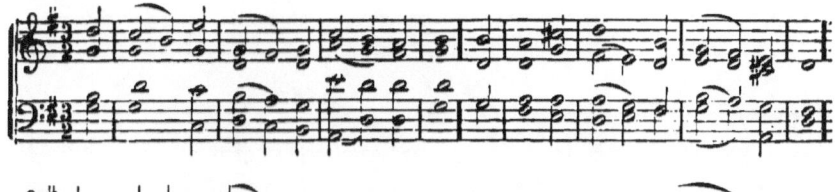

885. Rev. 21: 23.

1 Oh for a sweet, inspiring ray,
To animate our feeble strains,
From the bright realms of endless day,—
The blissful realms where Jesus reigns!

2 There, low before his glorious throne,
Adoring saints and angels fall;
And, with delightful worship, own
His smile their bliss, their heaven, their all.

3 Immortal glories crown his head,
While tuneful hallelujahs rise,
And love and joy and triumph spread
Through all th' assemblies of the skies.

4 He smiles, and seraphs tune their songs
To boundless rapture, while they gaze;
Ten thousand thousand joyful tongues
Resound his everlasting praise.

5 There all the followers of the Lamb
Shall join at last the heavenly choir:
Oh, may the joy-inspiring theme
Awake our faith and warm desire!
Mrs. Steele.

886. 1 Cor. 2: 9.

1 Now let our souls, on wings sublime,
Rise from the vanities of time,
Draw back the parting veil, and see
The glories of eternity.

2 Born by a new celestial birth,
Why should we grovel here on earth?
Why grasp at transitory toys,
So near to heaven's eternal joys?

3 Should aught beguile us on the road,
When we are walking back to God?
For strangers into life we come,
And dying is but going home.

4 Welcome, sweet hour of full discharge!
That sets our longing souls at large,
Unbinds our chains, breaks up our cell,
And gives us with our God to dwell.

5 To dwell with God, to feel his love,
Is the full heaven enjoyed above;
And the sweet expectation now
Is the young dawn of heaven below.
Gibbons.

887. The Glories and Joys of Heaven.

1 Oh for a sight, a pleasing sight,
Of our almighty Father's throne!
There sits our Saviour, crowned with light,
Clothed in a body like our own.

2 Adoring saints around him stand, [fall;
And thrones and powers before him
The God shines gracious thro' the Man,
And sheds sweet glories on them all.

3 Oh, what amazing joys they feel,
While to their golden harps they sing,
And sit on every heavenly hill, [King!
And spread the triumphs of their

4 When shall the day, dear Lord, appear,
That I shall mount, to dwell above;
And stand and bow and worship there,
And view thy face, and sing and love?
Watts.

Happiness of the Saints in Heaven.

ALFORD. L. M. — WHITTAKER.

888. *The Happiness of Heaven.*

1 O happy saints, that dwell in light,
   And walk with Jesus clothed in white,
   Safe landed on that peaceful shore,
   Where pilgrims meet to part no more.

2 Released from sorrow, sin, and strife,
   Death was the gate to endless life,
   And now they range the heavenly plains,
   And sing his love in melting strains.

3 They gaze upon his beauteous face,
   And tell the wonders of his grace;
   Or, overwhelmed with raptures sweet,
   Sink down, adoring at his feet.

4 Ah, Lord! with faltering steps I creep,
   And sometimes sing, and sometimes weep.
   When shall I wake in heaven to prove
   The heights and depths of Jesus' love?

889. Rev. 5: 9.

1 Hark! how the choral song of heaven
   Swells full of peace and joy above;
   Hark! how they strike their golden harps,
   And raise the tuneful notes of love.

2 No anxious care nor thrilling grief,
   No deep despair, nor gloomy woe
   They feel, when high their lofty strains
   In noblest, sweetest concord flow.

3 When shall we join the heavenly host,
   Who sing Immanuel's praise on high,
   And leave behind our doubts and fears,
   To swell the chorus of the sky?

890. Rev. 22: 4.

1 Lo! round the throne, a glorious band,
   The saints in countless myriads stand:
   Of every tongue redeemed to God,
   Arrayed in garments washed in blood.

2 Through tribulation great they came;
   They bore the cross, despised the shame;
   But now from all their labors rest,
   In God's eternal glory blest.

3 They see the Saviour face to face;
   They sing the triumph of his grace;
   And day and night, with ceaseless praise,
   To him their loud hosannas raise.

891. *Heaven.*

1 There is a land mine eye hath seen
   In visions of enraptured thought,
   So bright, that all which spreads between
   Is with its radiant glories fraught.

2 A land, upon whose blissful shore
   There rests no shadow, falls no stain:
   There those who meet shall part no more,
   And those long parted meet again.

3 Its skies are not like earthly skies,
   With varying hues of shade and light;
   It hath no need of suns to rise
   To dissipate the gloom of night.

4 There sweeps no desolating wind
   Across that calm, serene abode;
   The wanderer there a home may find
   Within the paradise of God.

Home and Rest in Heaven.

NAUMANN. C. M.   J. A. NAUMANN.

892.   *Rest in Heaven.*

1 THERE is an hour of peaceful rest,
    To mourning wanderers given;
There is a joy for souls distressed,
    A balm for every wounded breast:
        'Tis found above — in heaven.

2 There is a home for weary souls,
    By sin and sorrow driven, —
When tossed on life's tempestuous shoals,
Where storms arise and ocean rolls,
        And all is drear — but heaven.

3 There faith lifts up her cheerful eye,
    To brighter prospects given;
And views the tempest passing by,
The evening shadows quickly fly,
        And all serene — in heaven.

4 There fragrant flowers immortal bloom,
    And joys supreme are given;
There rays divine disperse the gloom;
Beyond the confines of the tomb
        Appears the dawn of heaven.
                      WM. B. TAPPAN.

893.   *" Home of Sweet Repose."*

1 THERE is an hour of hallowed peace,
    For those with cares oppressed,
When sighs and sorrowing tears shall cease,
    And all be hushed to rest.

2 'Tis then the soul is freed from fears
    And doubts which here annoy;
Then they who oft have sown in tears
    Shall reap again in joy.

3 There is a home of sweet repose,
    Where storms assail no more;
The stream of endless pleasure flows
    On that celestial shore.

4 There purity with love appears,
    And bliss without alloy;
There they who oft had sown in tears
    Shall reap again in joy.
                      TAPPAN.

894.   *Longing for Heaven.*

1 THE roseate hues of early dawn,
    The brightness of the day,
The crimson of the sunset sky,
    How fast they fade away!

2 Oh for the pearly gates of heaven,
    Oh for the golden floor,
Oh for the Sun of righteousness,
    That setteth nevermore!

3 Oh for a heart that never sins,
    Oh for a soul washed white,
Oh for a voice to praise our King,
    Nor weary day nor night!

4 Here faith is ours, and heavenly hope,
    And grace to lead us higher;
But there are perfectness and peace,
    Beyond our best desire.

5 Oh, by thy love and anguish, Lord,
    And by thy life laid down,
Grant that we fall not from thy grace,
    Nor cast away our crown.

WOODSTOCK. C. M. R. DUTTON.

895. *2 Cor. 5: 1.*

1 There is a house not made with hands,
  Eternal, and on high:
  And here my spirit waiting stands,
  Till God shall bid it fly.

2 Shortly this prison of my clay
  Must be dissolved and fall;
  Then, O my soul, with joy obey
  Thy heavenly Father's call.

3 We walk by faith of joys to come;
  Faith lives upon his word;
  But while the body is our home,
  We're absent from the Lord.

4 'Tis pleasant to believe thy grace,
  But we had rather see;
  We would be absent from the flesh,
  And present, Lord, with thee.
  WATTS.

896. *Joys of Heaven.*

1 Oh, could our thoughts and wishes fly
  Above these gloomy shades,
  To those bright worlds beyond the sky,
  Which sorrow ne'er invades!

2 There joys unseen by mortal eyes,
  Or reason's feeble ray,
  In ever-blooming prospect rise,
  Unconscious of decay.

3 Lord! send a beam of light divine
  To guide our upward aim;
  With one reviving touch of thine
  Our languid hearts inflame.

4 Then shall, on faith's sublimest wing,
  Our ardent wishes rise
  To those bright scenes where pleasures spring
  Immortal in the skies.
  MRS. STEELE.

897. *1 Cor. 2: 9, 10.*

1 Nor eye hath seen, nor ear hath heard,
  Nor sense nor reason known,
  What joys the Father has prepared
  For those that love his Son.

2 But the good Spirit of the Lord
  Reveals a heaven to come;
  The beams of glory in his word
  Allure and guide us home.

3 Pure are the joys above the sky,
  And all the region peace;
  No wanton lips nor envious eye
  Can see or taste the bliss.

4 Those holy gates forever bar
  Pollution, sin, and shame;
  None shall obtain admittance there,
  But followers of the Lamb.
  WATTS.

898. *Aspiration.*

1 My soul, amid this stormy world,
  Is like some fluttered dove,
  And fain would be as swift of wing
  To flee to Him I love.

2 Ah! leave me not in this dark world
  A stranger still to roam;
  Come, Lord! and take me to thyself;
  Come, Jesus! quickly come.
  R. C. CHAPMAN.

HAWES. C. M.

899. *Heb. 6: 12.*

1 GIVE me the wings of faith to rise
Within the veil, and see
The saints above, how great their joys,
How bright their glories be!

2 Once they were mourning here below,
And wet their couch with tears;
They wrestled hard, as we do now,
With sins and doubts and fears.

3 I ask them whence their victory came:
They, with united breath,
Ascribe their conquest to the Lamb,
Their triumph to his death.

4 They marked the footsteps that he trod;
His zeal inspired their breast;
And, following their incarnate God,
Possess the promised rest.

5 Our glorious Leader claims our praise
For his own pattern given,
While the long cloud of witnesses
Show the same path to heaven.
WATTS.

900. *Deut. 34: 1.*

1 THERE is a land of pure delight,
Where saints immortal reign,
Infinite day excludes the night,
And pleasures banish pain.

2 There everlasting spring abides,
And never-withering flowers:
Death, like a narrow sea, divides
This heavenly land from ours.

3 Sweet fields beyond the swelling flood
Stand dressed in living green;
So to the Jews old Canaan stood,
While Jordan rolled between.

4 Oh, could we make our doubts remove,—
These gloomy doubts that rise,—
And see the Canaan that we love,
With unbeclouded eyes:—

5 Could we but climb where Moses stood,
And view the landscape o'er,—
Not Jordan's stream, nor death's cold
flood,
Should fright us from the shore.
WATTS.

901. *Heb. 11.*

1 RISE, O my soul, pursue the path
By ancient worthies trod;
Aspiring, view those holy men
Who lived and walked with God.

2 Though dead, they speak in reason's ear,
And in example live;
Their faith and hope and mighty deeds
Still fresh instruction give.

3 'Twas through the Lamb's most precious
blood
They conquered every foe;
And to his power and matchless grace
Their crowns of life they owe.

4 Lord! may I ever keep in view
The patterns thou hast given,
And ne'er forsake the blessed road
That led them safe to heaven.
NEEDHAM.

The City of God. Death is Gain.

RHINE. C. M.   GERMAN.

902.   *Rev. 21: 10.*
1 O MOTHER dear, Jerusalem,
   When shall I come to thee?
  When shall my sorrows have an end?
   Thy joys when shall I see?

2 O happy harbor of God's saints!
   O sweet and pleasant soil!
  In thee no sorrow can be found,
   Nor grief, nor care, nor toil.

3 No dimly cloud o'ershadows thee,
   Nor gloom, nor darksome night;
  But every soul shines as the sun,
   For God himself gives light.

4 Thy walls are made of precious stone,
   Thy bulwarks diamond-square,
  Thy gates are all of orient pearl,—
   O God! if I were there!

903.   *Rev. 21.*
1 JERUSALEM! my happy home!
   Name ever dear to me!
  When shall my labors have an end,
   In joy and peace in thee?

2 Oh, when, thou city of my God,
   Shall I thy courts ascend,
  Where congregations ne'er break up,
   And Sabbaths have no end?

3 There happier bowers than Eden's bloom,
   Nor sin nor sorrow know;   [scenes
  Blest seats! through rude and stormy
   I onward press to you.

4 Why should I shrink at pain and woe?
   Or feel, at death, dismay?
  I've Canaan's goodly land in view,
   And realms of endless day.

5 Apostles, martyrs, prophets, there,
   Around my Saviour stand;
  And soon my friends in Christ below
   Will join the glorious band.

6 Jerusalem! my happy home!
   My soul still pants for thee!
  Then shall my labors have an end,
   When I thy joys shall see.

904.   *Death is Gain.*
1 WHEN musing sorrow weeps the past,
   And mourns the present pain,
  'Tis sweet to think of peace at last,
   And feel that death is gain.

2 'Tis not that murmuring thoughts arise,
   And dread a Father's will;
  'Tis not that meek submission flies,
   And would not suffer still:

3 It is that heaven-born faith surveys
   The path that leads to light,
  And longs her eagle plumes to raise,
   And lose herself in sight.

4 Oh, let me wing my hallowed flight
   From earth-born woe and care,
  And soar above these clouds of night,
   My Saviour's bliss to share!

                                        NOEL.

IN MEMORIAM.

905.

1 They are all gone into the | *world of light,*
And I alone sit | *lingering here!*
Their very memory is | *fair and bright,*
And my sad | *thoughts doth clear.*

2 I see them walking in an | *air of glory,*
Whose light doth trample | *on my days;*
My days, which are at best but | *dull and hoary,*
Mere glimmerings | *and decays.*

3 Dear, beauteous death, the jewel | *of the just,*
Shining nowhere but | *in the dark;*
What mysteries do lie be- | *yond thy dust,*
Could man out- | *look that mark!*

4 He that hath found some fledged bird's | *nest may know*
At first sight if the | *bird be flown;*
But what fair dell or grove he | *sings in now,*
That is to | *him unknown.*

5 And yet, as angels in some | *brighter dreams* [*sleep;*
Call to the soul when | *man doth*
So some strange thoughts transcend our | *wonted themes,*
And into | *glory peep.*

6 If a star were confined in- | *to a tomb,*
Her captive flame must | *needs burn there;*
But when the hand that locked her | *up gives room,*
She'll shine through | *all the sphere!*

7 O Father of eternal | *life, and all*
Created glories | *under thee!*
Resume my spirit from this | *world of thrall*
Into true | *liberty!*

8 Either disperse these mists, which | *blot and fill*
My perspective still | *as they pass;*
Or else remove me hence un- | *to that hill*
Where I shall | *need no glass.*
AMEN.
VAUGHAN.

906. *Ancient Burial Hymn.*

1 In the midst of life we | *are in death:*
Of whom may we | *seek for succor*
But of | *thee, O Lord?*
Who for our sins art | *justly displeas - ed.*

2 Yet, O Lord | *God most holy,*
O | *Lord most mighty,*
O holy and most | *merciful Saviour,*
Deliver us not into the bitter pains of e- | *ternal death.*

3 Thou knowest, Lord, the secrets | *of our hearts;*
Shut not thy merciful ears | *to our prayer;*
But spare us, | *Lord most holy,*
Spare us, | *Lord most holy.*

4 O God most mighty, O holy and | *merciful Saviour,*
Thou most worthy | *Judge eternal,*
Suffer us not at | *our last hour,*
For any pains of death, to | *fall from thee.* AMEN.

NOTKER.

The Saints in Glory; their Joys and Songs.

BEULAH. 7s.   E. IVES.

907. *"God shall wipe away all tears from their eyes."*

1 High in yonder realms of light,
   Dwell the raptured saints above ;
Far beyond our feeble sight,
   Happy in Immanuel's love :
Pilgrims in this vale of tears,
   Once they knew, like us below,
Gloomy doubts, distressing fears,
   Torturing pain, and heavy woe.

2 But these days of weeping o'er,
   Passed this scene of toil and pain,
They shall feel distress no more, —
   Never, never weep again :
'Mid the chorus of the skies,
   'Mid th' angelic lyres above,
Hark, their songs melodious rise, —
   Songs of praise to Jesus' love !

3 All is tranquil and serene,
   Calm and undisturbed repose ;
There no cloud can intervene,
   There no angry tempest blows ;
Every tear is wiped away,
   Sighs no more shall heave the breast,
Night is lost in endless day,
   Sorrow, in eternal rest.
                             RAFFLES.

908.   Rev 7: 13.

1 Who are these in bright array,
   This innumerable throng,
Round the altar night and day
   Hymning one triumphant song ? —
"Worthy is the Lamb, once slain,
   Blessing, honor, glory, power,
Wisdom, riches, to obtain,
   New dominion every hour."

2 These through fiery trials trod ;
   These from great affliction came :
Now, before the throne of God,
   Sealed with his almighty name,
Clad in raiment pure and white,
   Victor-palms in every hand,
Through their dear Redeemer's might,
   More than conquerors they stand.

3 Hunger, thirst, disease unknown,
   On immortal fruits they feed ;
Them the Lamb, amid the throne,
   Shall to living fountains lead :
Joy and gladness banish sighs ;
   Perfect love dispels all fears ;
And forever from their eyes
   God shall wipe away the tears.
                          MONTGOMERY.

Our Heavenly Home: Beautiful and Blessed.

REST. 6s. *(8s. with the small notes and without the ties.)* ARRANGED.

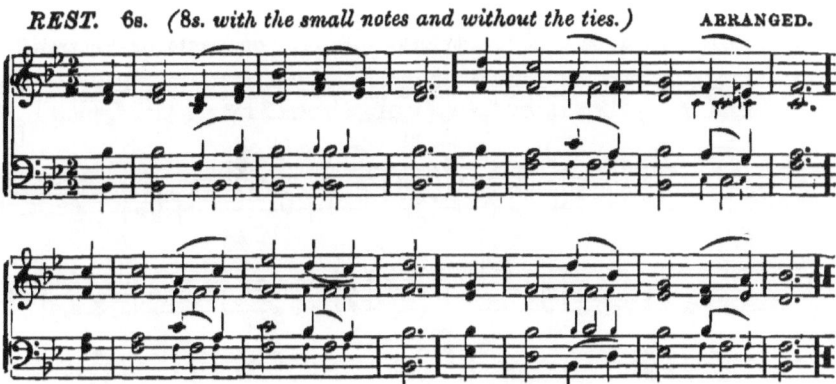

909. *Home in Heaven.*

1 THERE is a blessèd home
  Beyond this land of woe,
  Where trials never come,
  Nor tears of sorrow flow;

2 Where faith is lost in sight,
  And patient hope is crowned,
  And everlasting light
  Its glory throws around.

3 There is a land of peace;
  Good angels know it well;
  Glad songs that never cease
  Within its portals swell.

4 Look up, ye saints of God!
  Nor fear to tread below
  The path your Saviour trod
  Of daily toil and woe.

5 Wait but a little while
  In uncomplaining love;
  His own most gracious smile
  Shall welcome you above.
                       BAKER.

910. *"What must it be to be there!"*

1 WE speak of the realms of the blest,
  That country so bright and so fair,
  And oft are its glories confessed;
  But what must it be to be there!

2 We speak of its freedom from sin,
  From sorrow, temptation, and care,
  From trials without and within;
  But what must it be to be there!

3 We speak of its service of love,
  The robes which the glorified wear,
  The Church of the first-born above;
  But what must it be to be there!

4 Do thou, Lord, 'mid sorrow and woe,
  Still for heaven my spirit prepare,
  And shortly I also shall know,
  And feel, what it is to be there.

911. *Longing to be with Jesus.*

1 To Jesus, the crown of my hope,
  My soul is in haste to be gone;
  Oh, bear me, ye cherubim, up,
  And waft me away to his throne.

2 My Saviour, whom, absent, I love;
  Whom, not having seen, I adore;
  Whose name is exalted above
  All glory, dominion, and power; —

3 When that happy era begins,
  When arrayed in thy glories I shine,
  Nor grieve any more, by my sins,
  The bosom on which I recline, —

4 Oh, then shall the veil be removed!
  And round me thy brightness be poured;
  I shall meet him whom absent I loved,
  I shall see whom unseen I adored.

5 And then, never more shall the fears,
  The trials, temptations, and woes,
  Which darken this valley of tears,
  Intrude on my blissful repose.
                       COWPER.

The Native Country of our Souls.

MUNICH. 7s. & 6s. "Cast thy burden on the Lord:" ORATORIO OF "ELIJAH."

Ancient Hymns of Zion.

912.

1 For thee, O dear, dear country,
  Mine eyes their vigils keep:
For very love, beholding
  Thy happy name, they weep.
Thou hast no shore, fair ocean!
  Thou hast no time, bright day!
Dear fountain of refreshment
  To pilgrims far away.

2 There is the throne of David;
  And there, from care released,
The shout of them that triumph,
  The song of them that feast.
And they who with their Leader
  Have conquered in the fight,
Forever and forever
  Are clad in robes of white.

3 They stand, those halls of Sion,
  All jubilant with song;
And bright with many an angel,
  And all the martyr throng.
O sweet and blessed country,
  Shall I e'er see thy face?
O sweet and blessed country,
  Shall I e'er win thy grace?

4 E'en now, by faith, I see thee!
  E'en now thy walls discern!
To thee my thoughts are kindled,
  And strive and pant and yearn.
Jerusalem! exulting
  On that securest shore,
I hope thee, wish thee, sing thee,
  And love thee evermore!
      BERNARD, BY DR. NEALE.

913.

1 Brief life is here our portion,
  Brief sorrow, short-lived care!
The life that knows no ending,
  The tearless life is there!
And now we watch and struggle,
  And now we live in hope,
And Sion, in her anguish,
  With Babylon must cope.

2 But He whom now we trust in
  Shall then be seen and known;
And they that know and see him
  Shall have him for their own.
The morning shall awaken,
  The shadow shall decay,
And each true-hearted servant
  Shall shine as doth the day.

3 There God, our King and portion,
  In fulness of his grace,
Shall we behold forever,
  And worship face to face.
Then all the halls of Sion
  For aye shall be complete,
And in the land of beauty,
  All things of beauty meet.
      BERNARD, BY DR. NEALE.

The Transient and Eternal.

AMSTERDAM. 7s. & 6s.   NARES.

914. *Aspiration.*

1 Rise, my soul! and stretch thy wings,
  Thy better portion trace;
Rise from transitory things,
  Toward heaven, thy native place.
Sun and moon and stars decay;
Time shall soon this earth remove;
Rise, my soul! and haste away
  To seats prepared above.

2 Rivers to the ocean run,
  Nor stay in all their course;
Fire, ascending, seeks the sun;
  Both speed them to their source;
So a soul, that's born of God,
Pants to view his glorious face,
Upward tends to his abode,
  To rest in his embrace.

3 Fly me, riches! fly me, cares!
  While I that coast explore;
Flattering world! with all thy snares,
  Solicit me no more:
Pilgrims fix not here their home;
Strangers tarry but a night;
When the last dear morn is come,
  They'll rise to joyful light.

4 Cease, ye pilgrims! cease to mourn,—
  Press onward to the prize!
Soon your Saviour will return
  Triumphant in the skies;
Yet a season, and you know
Happy entrance will be given,
All your sorrows left below,
  And earth exchanged for heaven.
                      CENNICK.

915. *" The Transient and Eternal."*

1 Time is winging us away
  To our eternal home;
Life is but a winter's day—
  A journey to the tomb;
Youth and vigor soon will flee,
Blooming beauty lose its charms;
All that's mortal soon shall be
  Enclosed in death's cold arms.

2 Time is winging us away
  To our eternal home;
Life is but a winter's day—
  A journey to the tomb;
But the Christian shall enjoy
Health and beauty, soon, above,
Far beyond the world's alloy,
  Secure in Jesus' love.
                      J. BURTON.

Section IX.

MISCELLANEOUS HYMNS.

(*a.*) *Times and Occasions. The Seasons. The Close of the Year. The New Year. Days of Fasting. Days of Thanksgiving. Harvest. Temperance. Prayers for those in Peril on the Sea. Historic and National Hymns.*

(*b.*) *Hymns pertaining to the Family. The Happy Home. Early Piety. The Nurture of Children. Family Worship.*

"BOTH YOUNG MEN, AND MAIDENS; OLD MEN, AND CHILDREN; LET THEM PRAISE THE NAME OF THE LORD."—Psalm 147: 12.

New Year. Close of the Year.

BENEVENTO. 7s. (DOUBLE.)   S. WEBBE.

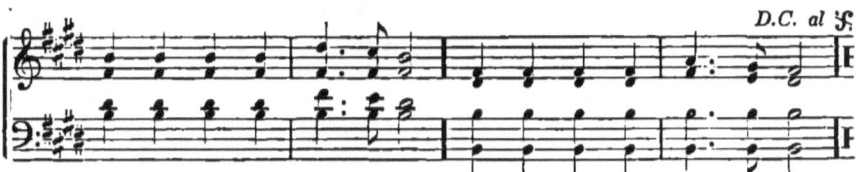

916. *New Year.*

1 WHILE, with ceaseless course, the sun
  Hasted through the former year,
Many souls their race have run,
  Nevermore to meet us here:
Fixed in an eternal state,
  They have done with all below;
We a little longer wait;
  But how little none can know.

2 As the wingèd arrow flies
  Speedily the mark to find;
As the lightning from the skies
  Darts, and leaves no trace behind, —
Swiftly thus our fleeting days
  Bear us down life's rapid stream;
Upward, Lord, our spirits raise,
  All below is but a dream.

3 Thanks for mercies past receive;
  Pardon of our sins renew;
Teach us henceforth how to live,
  With eternity in view:
Bless thy word to old and young;
  Fill us with a Saviour's love;
When our life's short race is run,
  May we dwell with thee above.
            NEWTON.

917. *Close of the Year.*

1 THOU who roll'st the year around,
  Crowned with mercies large and free,
Rich thy gifts to us abound,
  Warm our praise shall rise to thee.
Kindly to our worship bow,
  While our grateful thanks we tell,
That, sustained by thee, we now
  Bid the parting year farewell!

2 All its numbered days are sped,
  All its busy scenes are o'er,
All its joys forever fled,
  All its sorrows felt no more.
Mingled with the eternal past,
  Its remembrance shall decay;
Yet to be revived at last,
  At the solemn judgment-day.

3 All our follies, Lord, forgive!
  Cleanse us from each guilty stain;
Let thy grace within us live,
  That we spend not years in vain.
Then, when life's last eve shall come,
  Happy spirits, may we fly
To our everlasting home,
  To our Father's house on high!
            RAY PALMER.

BOWDOIN SQUARE. C. M.   VOGLER.

918.   *New Year.*

1 Our Father! through the coming year
   We know not what shall be;
But we would leave, without a fear,
   Its ordering all to thee.

2 It may be we shall toil in vain
   For what the world holds fair;
And all the good we thought to gain,
   Deceive, and prove but care.

3 It may be it shall darkly blend
   Our love with anxious fears,
And snatch away the valued friend,
   The tried of many years.

4 It may be it shall bring us days
   And nights of lingering pain;
And bid us take a farewell gaze
   Of these loved haunts of men.

5 But calmly, Lord, on thee we rest;
   No fears our trust shall move;
Thou knowest what for each is best,
   And thou art Perfect Love.

919.   *The Old Year.*

1 The year is gone beyond recall,
   With all its hopes and fears,
With all its bright and gladdening smiles,
   With all its mourner's tears.

2 To thee we come, O gracious Lord!
   The new-born year to bless;
Defend our land from pestilence;
   Give peace and plenteousness.

3 From evil deeds that stain the past
   We now desire to flee;
And pray that future years may all
   Be spent, good Lord! for thee.

4 O Father! let thy watchful eye
   Still look on us in love,
That we may praise thee year by year,
   As angels do above.

5 All glory to the Father be;
   All glory to the Son;
All glory, Holy Ghost! to thee,
   While endless ages run.

920.   *Psalm 65.*

1 'Tis by thy strength the mountains stand,
   God of eternal power!
The sea grows calm at thy command,
   And tempests cease to roar.

2 Thy morning light and evening shade
   Successive comforts bring;
Thy plenteous fruits make harvest glad;
   Thy flowers adorn the spring.

3 Seasons and times and moons and hours,
   Heaven, earth, and air are thine;
When clouds distil in fruitful showers,
   The author is divine!

4 Thy showers the thirsty furrows fill;
   And ranks of corn appear;
Thy ways abound with blessings still,—
   Thy goodness crowns the year.
                               WATTS.

The Seasons crowned with Goodness.

921. *Psalm 147.*

1 With songs and honors sounding loud,
  Address the Lord on high;
Over the heavens he spreads his cloud,
  And waters veil the sky.

2 He sends his showers of blessings down,
  To cheer the plains below;   [crown,
He makes the grass the mountains
  And corn in valleys grow.

3 His steady counsels change the face
  Of the declining year;
He bids the sun cut short his race,
  And wintry days appear.

4 His hoary frost, his fleecy snow,
  Descend and clothe the ground;
The liquid streams forbear to flow,
  In icy fetters bound.

5 He sends his word, and melts the snow,
  The fields no longer mourn;
He calls the warmer gales to blow,
  And bids the spring return.

6 The changing wind, the flying cloud,
  Obey his mighty word;
With songs and honors sounding loud,
  Praise ye the sovereign Lord.
  WATTS.

922. *The Opening Year.*

1 When brighter suns and milder skies
  Proclaim the opening year,
What various sounds of joy arise!
  What prospects bright appear!

2 Earth and her thousand voices give
  Their thousand notes of praise;
And all that by his mercy live
  To God their offering raise.

3 Thus, like the morning, calm and clear,
  That saw the Saviour rise,
The spring of heaven's eternal year
  Shall dawn on earth and skies.

4 No winter there, no shades of night,
  Obscure those mansions blest,
Where, in the happy fields of light,
  The weary are at rest.
  W. B. O. PEABODY.

923. *The Flight of Time.*

1 Thee we adore, Eternal Name!
  And humbly own to thee
How feeble is our mortal frame,
  What dying worms are we!

2 The year rolls round, and steals away
  The breath that first it gave;
Whate'er we do, whate'er we be,
  We're travelling to the grave.

3 Great God! on what a slender thread
  Hang everlasting things!
Th' eternal state of all the dead
  Upon life's feeble strings!

4 Infinite joy or endless woe
  Attends on every breath;
And yet, how unconcerned we go
  Upon the brink of death!

5 Waken, O Lord, our drowsy sense,
  To walk this dangerous road!
And if our souls are hurried hence,
  May they be found with God.
  WATTS.

924. *Goodness of Providence.*

1 God of our lives! thy various praise
  Our voices shall resound;
Thy hand revolves our fleeting days,
  And brings the seasons round.

2 To thee shall daily incense rise,
  Our Father and our Friend;
While daily mercies from the skies
  In genial streams descend.

3 In every scene of life, thy care,
  In every age we see:
And constant as thy favors are,
  So let our praises be.

4 Still may thy love, in every scene,
  In every age appear;
And let the same compassion deign
  To bless the opening year.

5 If mercy smile, let mercy bring
  Our wandering souls to God:
And in affliction we shall sing,
  If thou wilt bless the rod.
  HEGINBOTHAM.

Goodness of God seen in the Seasons.

DUKE ST. L. M.   HATTON.

925.   *The New Year.*

1 GREAT God! we sing that mighty hand
By which supported still we stand;
The opening year thy mercy shows;
Let mercy crown it till it close.

2 By day, by night, at home, abroad,
Still we are guarded by our God;
By his incessant bounty fed,
By his unerring counsel led.

3 With grateful hearts the past we own;
The future, all to us unknown,
We to thy guardian care commit,
And peaceful leave before thy feet.

4 In scenes exalted or depressed,
Be thou our joy, and thou our rest;
Thy goodness all our hopes shall raise,
Adored through all our changing days.

5 When death shall interrupt our songs,
And seal in silence mortal tongues,
Our Helper, God, in whom we trust,
In better worlds our souls shall boast.
DODDRIDGE.

926.   *Thanksgiving.*

1 ETERNAL Source of every joy!
Well may thy praise our lips employ,
While in thy temple we appear,
Whose goodness crowns the circling year.

2 Wide as the wheels of nature roll,
Thy hand supports and guides the whole;
The sun is taught by thee to rise,
And darkness when to veil the skies.

3 The flowery spring, at thy command,
Embalms the air, and paints the land;
The summer rays with vigor shine,
To raise the corn and cheer the vine.

4 Thy hand in autumn richly pours
Through all our coasts redundant stores;
And winters, softened by thy care,
No more a face of horror wear.

5 Seasons and months and weeks and days
Demand successive songs of praise;
Still be the cheerful homage paid,
With opening light and evening shade.
DODDRIDGE.

927.   *Thanksgiving.*

1 OUR Helper, God! we bless thy name,
The same thy power, thy grace the same;
The tokens of thy loving care
Open and crown and close the year.

2 Amid ten thousand snares we stand,
Supported by thy guardian hand;
And see, when we survey our ways,
Ten thousand monuments of praise.

3 Thus far thine arm hath led us on;
Thus far we make thy mercy known;
And while we tread this desert land,
New mercies shall new songs demand.

4 Our grateful souls on Jordan's shore
Shall raise one sacred pillar more;
Then bear, in thy bright courts above,
Inscriptions of immortal love.
DODDRIDGE.

NUREMBURG. 7s.   GERMAN.

928. *Thanksgiving.*

1 Praise to God, immortal praise,
   For the love that crowns our days!
   Bounteous source of every joy,
   Let thy praise our tongues employ!

2 For the blessings of the field,
   For the stores the gardens yield,
   For the joy which harvests bring,
   Grateful praises now we sing.

3 Clouds that drop refreshing dews;
   Suns that genial heat diffuse;
   Flocks that whiten all the plain;
   Yellow sheaves of ripened grain;

4 All that Spring, with bounteous hand,
   Scatters o'er the smiling land;
   All that liberal Autumn pours
   From her overflowing stores;

5 These, great God, to thee we owe,
   Source whence all our blessings flow;
   And, for these, our souls shall raise
   Grateful vows and solemn praise.
                      BARBAULD.

929. *New Year. Thanksgiving.*

1 For thy mercy and thy grace,
    Constant through another year,
   Hear our song of thankfulness;
    Jesus, our Redeemer! hear.

2 In our weakness and distress,
    Rock of Strength! be thou our stay;
   In the pathless wilderness,
    Be our true and living way.

3 Who of us death's awful road
    In the coming year shall tread, —
   With thy rod and staff, O Lord!
    Comfort thou his dying-bed.

4 Make us faithful, make us pure;
   Keep us evermore thine own;
   Help thy servants to endure;
   Fit us for the promised crown.

5 So within thy palace-gate
    We shall praise, on golden strings,
   Thee, the only Potentate!
    Lord of lords! and King of kings!

930. *Fast.*—Psalm 60.

1 Why, O God! thy people spurn?
   Why permit thy wrath to burn?
   God of mercy! turn once more,
   All our broken hearts restore.

2 Thou hast made our land to quake,
   Heal the sorrows thou dost make;
   Bitter is the cup we drink,
   Suffer not our souls to sink.

3 Be thy banner now unfurled,
   Show thy truth to all the world;
   Save us, Lord, we cry to thee,
   Lift thine arm, thy chosen free.

4 Give us now relief from pain, —
   Human aid is all in vain:
   We, through God, shall yet prevail,
   He will help, when foes assail.
                      HATFIELD.

HARVEST-HOME. 7s. (DOUBLE.)

931. *Harvest-Hymn.*

1 Come, ye thankful people ! come,
Raise the song of Harvest-Home !
All is safely gathered in
Ere the winter storms begin ;
God our Maker doth provide
For our wants to be supplied ;
Come to God's own temple, come !
Raise the song of Harvest-Home !

2 We ourselves are God's own field,
Fruit unto his praise we yield ;
Wheat and tares together sown,
Unto joy or sorrow grown,
First the blade and then the ear,
Then the full corn shall appear :
Grant, O Harvest Lord, that we
Wholesome grain and pure may be.

3 For the Lord our God shall come
And shall take his harvest home ;
From his field shall, in that day,
All offences purge away ;
Give his angels charge, at last,
In the fire the tares to cast ;
But the fruitful ears to store
In his garner evermore.

4 Then, thou Church triumphant ! come,
Raise the song of Harvest-Home !
All are safely gathered in,
Free from sorrow, free from sin,
There forever, purified,
In God's garner to abide :
Come, ten thousand angels, come,
Raise the glorious Harvest-Home !

ALFORD.

ST. PETERSBURGH. L. M. 6l. RUSSIAN.

932. *The Holy Nation.*

1 O HAPPY nation! where the Lord
Reveals the treasures of his word,
   And builds his Church, his earthly
     throne:
His eye the heathen world surveys,
He formed their hearts, he knows their
     ways;
But God, their Maker, is unknown.

2 The eye of thy compassion, Lord,
Does most secure defence afford
   When death or dangers threatening
     stand;
Thy watchful eye preserves the just
Who make thy name their fear and trust,
   When wars or famine waste the land.

3 In sickness, or the bloody field,
Thou our physician, thou our shield,
   Send us salvation from thy throne:
We wait to see thy goodness shine;
Let us rejoice in help divine,
   For all our hope is God alone.
                      WATTS.

933. *Thanksgiving.*

1 WITH grateful hearts, with joyful
     tongues,
To God we raise united songs;
   His power and mercy we proclaim.
Our Union bless, and make us own
Jehovah here has fixed his throne,
   And triumph in his mighty name.

2 Long as the moon her course shall run,
Or men behold the circling sun,
   Within our borders hold thy reign;
Crown our just counsels with success,
With truth and peace our nation bless,
   And all thy sacred rights maintain.

934. *For Those in Perils of Waters.*

1 ETERNAL Father! strong to save,
Whose arm hath bound the restless
     wave,
Who bidd'st the mighty ocean deep
   Its own appointed limits keep;
Oh, hear us when we cry to thee
For those in peril on the sea!

2 O Christ! whose voice the waters heard,
And hushed their raging at thy word,
Who walkedst on the foaming deep,
   And calm amidst its rage didst sleep;
Oh, hear us when we cry to thee
For those in peril on the sea!

3 Most Holy Spirit! who didst brood
Upon the chaos dark and rude,
And bid its angry tumult cease,
   And give, for wild confusion, peace;
Oh, hear us when we cry to thee
For those in peril on the sea!

4 O Trinity of love and power!
Our brethren shield in danger's hour;
From rock and tempest, fire and foe,
   Protect them wheresoe'er they go.
Thus evermore shall rise to thee
Glad hymns of praise from land and sea.

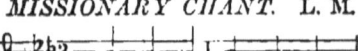

MISSIONARY CHANT. L. M.   CHAS. ZEUNER.

935.   *Our Pilgrim Fathers.*

1 O God, beneath thy guiding hand,
   Our exiled fathers crossed the sea;
And when they trod the wintry strand,
   With prayer and psalm they worshipped thee.

2 Thou heard'st, well-pleased, the song, the prayer,—
   Thy blessing came; and still its power
Shall onward, through all ages, bear
   The memory of that holy hour.

3 Laws, freedom, truth, and faith in God
   Came with those exiles o'er the waves,
And where their pilgrim feet have trod,
   The God they trusted guards their graves.

4 And here thy name, O God of love,
   Their children's children shall adore,
Till these eternal hills remove,
   And spring adorns the earth no more.
                          L. BACON.

936.   *Slavery and Oppression.*

1 O holy Father! just and true
   Are all thy works and words and ways,
And unto thee alone are due
   Thanksgiving and eternal praise!

2 As children of thy gracious care,
   We veil the eye, we bend the knee,
With broken words of praise and prayer,
   Father and God, we come to thee.

3 For thou hast heard, O God of right!
   The sighing of the hapless slave;
And stretched for him the arm of might,
   Not shortened that it could not save.

4 Speed on thy work, Lord God of hosts!
   And when the bondsman's chain is riven,
And swells from all our country's coasts
   The anthem of the free to heaven,

5 Oh, not to those whom thou hast led,
   As with thy cloud and fire before,
But unto thee in fear and dread,
   Be praise and glory evermore.
                          WHITTIER.

937.   *Thanksgiving.*

1 Great God of nations! now to thee
   Our hymn of gratitude we raise;
With humble heart and bending knee,
   We offer thee our song of praise.

2 Thy name we bless, Almighty God!
   For all the kindness thou hast shown
To this fair land the pilgrims trod,—
   This land we fondly call our own.

3 Here Freedom spreads her banner wide,
   And casts her soft and hallowed ray:
Here, thou our fathers' steps didst guide
   In safety, through their dangerous way.

4 We praise thee, that the gospel's light,
   Through all our land, its radiance sheds,
Dispels the shades of error's night,
   And heavenly blessings round us spreads.

938. *The Providence of God over Nations.*

1 GREAT God! beneath whose piercing eye
 The earth's extended kingdoms lie;
 Whose favoring smile upholds them all,
 Whose anger smites them, and they fall; —

2 Thy kindness to our fathers shown,
 Their children's children long shall own;
 To thee, with grateful hearts, shall raise
 The tribute of exulting praise.

3 Upheld by thine unfailing aid,
 Secure, the paths of life we tread;
 And, freely as the vital air,
 Thy first and noblest bounties share.

4 Great God, our guardian, guide, and friend!
 Oh, still thy sheltering arm extend;
 Preserved by thee for ages past,
 For ages let thy kindness last!
 ROSCOE.

939. *Fasting and Prayer.*

1 WHILE o'er our guilty land, O Lord,
 We view the terrors of thy sword;
 Oh, whither shall the hopeless fly?
 To whom but thee direct their cry?

2 On thee, our guardian God, we call,
 Before thy throne of grace we fall;
 And is there no deliverance there?
 And must we perish in despair?

3 See, we repent, we weep, we mourn,
 To our forsaken God we turn;
 Oh, spare our guilty country, spare
 The church, which thou hast planted here!
 DAVIES.

940. *A Prayer against Public Enemies.*

1 O THOU preserver of mankind, [God!
 Our hope, our shield, our strength, our
 Thou hast an ear to prayer inclined;
 Our cries have reached thy dread abode.

2 Our cause thy justice will maintain,
 Avenge th' oppressed and guard the poor:
 Ne'er shall thy children ask in vain,
 And our proud foes shall boast no more.

3 Their banded hosts shall fly, or fall;
 A shaking leaf their thousands chase;
 Our God shall hear our nation's call;
 We shall be saved, and sing his praise.
 DWIGHT.

941. *Prayer for Peace.*

1 THY footsteps, Lord, with joy we trace,
 And mark the conquests of thy grace;
 Complete the work thou hast begun,
 And let thy will on earth be done.

2 Oh, show thyself the Prince of peace;
 Command the din of war to cease:
 Oh, bid contending nations rest,
 And let thy love rule every breast!

3 Then peace returns with balmy wing;
 Glad plenty laughs, the valleys sing;
 Reviving commerce lifts her head,
 And want and woe and hate have fled.

4 Thou good and wise and righteous Lord,
 All move subservient to thy word;
 Oh, soon let every nation prove
 The perfect joy of Christian love!
 WARDLAW'S COLL.

942. *Peace.*

1 GREAT God, whom heaven and earth and sea,
 With all their countless hosts obey,
 Upheld by thee the nations stand,
 And empires fall at thy command.

2 Oh, show thyself the Prince of peace,
 Command the din of war to cease;
 With sacred love the world inspire,
 And burn its chariots in the fire.

3 In sunder break each warlike spear;
 Let all the Saviour's ensigns wear;
 The universal Sabbath prove,
 The perfect rest of Christian love!
 PRATT'S COLL.

943. *Prayer for Seamen.*

1 WHILE o'er the deep thy servants sail,
 Send thou, O Lord, the prosperous gale;
 And on their hearts, where'er they go,
 Oh, let thy heavenly breezes blow.

2 If on the morning's wings they fly,
 They will not pass beyond thine eye;
 The wanderer's prayer thou bend'st to hear,
 And faith exults to know thee near.

3 When tempests rock the groaning bark,
 Oh, hide them safe in Jesus' ark!
 When in the tempting port they ride,
 Oh, keep them safe at Jesus' side!
 G. BURGESS.

Our Native Land. Confession of Sin.

BARBY. C. M.   TANSUR.

944. *Prayer for our Native Land.*

1 Lord! while for all mankind we pray,
Of every clime and coast,
Oh, hear us for our native land,—
The land we love the most.

2 Our fathers' sepulchres are here,
And here our kindred dwell;
Our children, too; how should we love
Another land so well?

3 Oh, guard our shores from every foe,
With peace our borders bless;
With prosperous times our cities crown,
Our fields with plenteousness.

4 Unite us in the sacred love
Of knowledge, truth, and Thee;
And let our hills and valleys shout
The songs of liberty.

5 Lord of the nations! thus to thee
Our country we commend;
Be thou her Refuge and her Trust,
Her everlasting Friend!
                        WELFORD.

945. *Our Country.*

1 In thee, Great God! with songs of praise,
Our favored States rejoice;
And, blest with thy salvation, raise
To heaven their cheerful voice.

2 Thy sure defence through nations round
Hath spread our rising name,
And hath our weak beginnings crowned
With freedom and with fame.

3 In deep distress our injured land
Implored thy power to save;
For life we prayed; thy bounteous hand
The timely blessing gave.

4 On thee, when perils rise again
Our hearts alone rely;
Our rights thy mercy will maintain,
And all our wants supply.

5 Thus, Lord! thy wondrous power declare,
And still exalt thy fame;
While we glad songs of praise prepare
For thine almighty name.
                        BARLOW.

946. *Fasting and Prayer.*

1 See, gracious God! before thy throne
Thy mourning people bend;
'Tis on thy sovereign grace alone
Our humble hopes depend.

2 Dark, frowning judgments from thy hand
Thy dreadful power display;
Yet mercy spares this guilty land,
And still we live to pray.

3 How changed, alas! are truths divine,
For error, guilt, and shame!
What impious numbers, bold in sin,
Disgrace the Christian name!

4 Oh, turn us, turn us, mighty Lord,
By thy resistless grace;
Then shall our hearts obey thy word,
And humbly seek thy face.

947. *"Our Fathers have told us."* — Psalm 44.

1 O LORD, our fathers oft have told,
  In our attentive ears,
Thy wonders in their days performed,
  And elder times than theirs.

2 For not their courage, nor their sword
  To them salvation gave;
Nor strength that from unequal force
  Their fainting troops could save.

3 But thy right hand and powerful arm,
  Whose succor they implored;
Thy presence with the chosen race,
  Who thy great name adored.

4 As thee, their God, our fathers owned,
  Thou art our sovereign King;
Oh, therefore, as thou didst to them,
  To us deliverance bring!

5 To thee the triumph we ascribe,
  From whom the conquest came;
In God we will rejoice all day,
  And ever bless thy name.
            TATE AND BRADY.

948. Psalm 114.

1 WHEN forth from Egypt's trembling
    strand
  The tribes of Israel sped,
And Jacob, in the stranger's land,
  Departing banners spread; —

2 Then One, amid their thick array,
  His kingly dwelling made,
And all along the desert way
  Their guiding sceptre swayed.

3 The sea beheld, and struck with dread,
  Rolled all its billows back:
And Jordan through his deepest bed,
  Revealed their destined track.

4 What ailed thee, O thou mighty sea,
  And rolled thy waves in dread?
What bade thy tide, O Jordan, flee,
  And bare its deepest bed?

5 O earth, before the Lord, the God
  Of Jacob, tremble still;
Who makes the waste a watered sod,
  The flint a gushing rill.
            G. BURGESS.

949. *God of our Fathers.*

1 GOD of our fathers, to thy throne
  Our grateful songs we raise,
Thou art our God, and thou alone, —
  Accept our humble praise.

2 Unnumbered benefits from thee
  Are showered upon our land;
Behold! through all our coasts we see
  The bounties of thy hand.

3 Here thou wert once the pilgrims' guide;
  Thou gav'st them here a place,
Where freedom spreads its blessings
    wide
  O'er all their favored race.

4 Here, Lord, thy gospel's holy light
  Is shed on all our hills;
And, like the rains and dews of night,
  Celestial grace distils.

5 Still teach us, Lord, thy name to fear,
  And still our guardian be;
Oh, let our children's children here
  Forever worship thee.
            L. BACON.

950. S. M. ("OLMUTZ.")
        Temperance.

1 MOURN for the thousands slain,
  The youthful and the strong;
Mourn for the wine-cup's fearful reign,
  And the deluded throng.

2 Mourn for the tarnished gem,
  For reason's light divine,
Quenched from the soul's bright diadem,
  Where God had bid it shine.

3 Mourn for the ruined soul, —
  Eternal life and light
Lost by the fiery, maddening bowl,
  And turned to helpless night.

4 Mourn for the lost, — but call,
  Call to the strong, the free;
Rouse them to shun that dreadful fall,
  And to the refuge flee.

5 Mourn for the lost, — but pray,
  Pray to our God above,
To break the fell destroyer's sway,
  And show his saving love.

Our Country.

AMERICA. 6s. & 4s.

951. *"God Save the State!"*

1 God bless our native land!
 Firm may she ever stand,
  Through storm and night;
 When the wild tempests rave,
 Ruler of winds and wave,
 Do thou our country save
  By thy great might.

2 For her our prayer shall rise
 To God above the skies;
  On him we wait;
 Thou who art ever nigh,
 Guarding with watchful eye,
 To thee aloud we cry,
  God save the State!
  J. S. Dwight.

952. *The Voice of National Joy.*

1 My country, 'tis of thee,
 Sweet land of liberty,
  Of thee I sing:
 Land where my fathers died,
 Land of the pilgrim's pride,
 From every mountain side
  Let freedom ring!

2 My native country, thee, —
 Land of the noble free, —
  Thy name I love:
 I love thy rocks and rills,
 Thy woods and templed hills;
 My heart with rapture thrills
  Like that above.

3 Let music swell the breeze,
 And ring from all the trees
  Sweet freedom's song!
 Let mortal tongues awake;
 Let all that breathe partake;
 Let rocks their silence break, —
  The sound prolong!

4 Our fathers' God! to thee,
 Author of liberty,
  To thee we sing!
 Long may our land be bright
 With freedom's holy light;
 Protect us by thy might,
  Great God, our King!
  S. F. Smith.

Doxology.

To the great One in Three,
The highest praises be,
 Hence evermore;
His sovereign majesty
May we in glory see,
And to eternity
 Love and adore.

ROCKINGHAM. L. M.   DR. MASON.

953. *Family Worship.*

1 FATHER of men! thy care we bless,
  Which crowns our families with peace.
  From thee they sprung, and by thy hand
  Their root and branches are sustained.

2 To God, most worthy to be praised,
  Be our domestic altars raised,
  Who, Lord of heaven, scorns not to dwell
  With saints in their obscurest cell.

3 To thee may each united house,
  Morning and night, present its vows;
  Our servants here and rising race
  Be taught thy precepts and thy grace.

4 Oh, may each future age proclaim
  The honors of thy glorious name;
  While, pleased and thankful, we remove
  To join the family above.
                                DODDRIDGE.

954. *An Evening Hymn.*

1 GREAT God! to thee my evening song
  With humble gratitude I raise;
  Oh, let thy mercy tune my tongue,
  And fill my heart with lively praise.

2 My days unclouded as they pass,
  And every gentle, rolling hour,
  Are monuments of wondrous grace,
  And witness to thy love and power.

3 And yet this thoughtless, wretched heart,
  Too oft regardless of thy love,
  Ungrateful, can from thee depart,
  And, fond of trifles, vainly rove.

4 Seal my forgiveness in the blood
  Of Jesus; his dear name alone
  I plead for pardon, gracious God!
  And kind acceptance at thy throne.

5 Let this blest hope mine eyelids close,
  With sleep refresh my feeble frame;
  Safe in thy care may I repose,
  And wake with praises to thy name.
                                MRS. STEELE.

955. *Prayer for Children.*

1 DEAR Saviour, if these lambs should stray
  From thy secure enclosure's bound,
  And, lured by worldly joys away,
  Among the thoughtless crowd be found,—

2 Remember still that they are thine,
  That thy dear sacred name they bear;
  Think that the seal of love divine,
  The sign of cov'nant grace they wear.

3 In all their erring, sinful years,
  Oh, let them ne'er forgotten be!
  Remember all the prayers and tears
  Which made them consecrate to thee.

4 And when these lips no more can pray,
  These eyes can weep for them no more,
  Turn thou their feet from folly's way;
  The wanderers to thy fold restore.

Doxology.

PRAISE God, from whom all blessings flow,
Praise him, all creatures here below,
Praise him above, ye heavenly host,
Praise Father, Son, and Holy Ghost.

The Christian Home.

MEAR. C. M.

956. *The Happy Home.*

1 HAPPY the home, when God is there,
    And love fills every breast;
  Where one their wish, and one their prayer,
    And one their heavenly rest.

2 Happy the home where Jesus' name
    Is sweet to every ear;
  Where children early lisp his fame,
    And parents hold him dear.

3 Happy the home where prayer is heard,
    And praise is wont to rise;
  Where parents love the sacred word,
    And live but for the skies.

4 Lord! let us in our homes agree
    This blessed peace to gain;
  Unite our hearts in love to thee,
    And love to all will reign.

957. Psalm 78.

1 LET children hear the mighty deeds
    Which God performed of old, —
  Which in our younger years we saw,
    And which our fathers told.

2 He bids us make his glories known,
    His works of power and grace;
  And we'll convey his wonders down
    Through every rising race.

3 Our lips shall tell them to our sons,
    And they again to theirs,
  That generations yet unborn
    May teach them to their heirs.

4 Thus they shall learn, in God alone
    Their hope securely stands,
  That they may ne'er forget his works,
    But practise his commands.
                              WATTS.

958. *Early Piety.*

1 GRACE is a plant, where'er it grows,
    Of pure and heavenly root;
  But fairest in the youngest shows,
    And yields the sweetest fruit.

2 Ye careless ones, betimes obey
    The voice of sovereign love!
  Ye rove in folly's dangerous way,
    But mercy reigns above.

3 For you the public prayer is made,
    Oh, join the public prayer!
  For you the secret tear is shed,
    Oh, shed yourselves a tear!
                              COWPER.

959. *Family Worship.*

1 LORD of all families below,
    To thee our prayers we send;
  Do thou from danger, and from woe,
    Our dwelling-place defend.

2 Here let thy peace, O Father, rest,
    Here let thy love abide!
  Our every joy in thee more blest,
    Each sorrow sanctified.

3 Teach us, with hearts made one in love,
    To do thy pure commands;
  And give us, in thy time, above,
    A house not made with hands.

ARDEN. C. M. E. P. PARKER.

960. *"Suffer little Children."*

1 AROUND the throne of God in heaven
    Thousands of children stand,—
Children, whose sins are all forgiven,
    A holy, happy band.

2 What brought them to that world above,
    That heaven so bright and fair,
Where all is peace and joy and love?
    How came those children there?

3 Because the Saviour shed his blood
    To wash away their sin:
Bathed in that pure and precious flood,
    Behold them white and clean.

4 On earth they sought their Saviour's grace,
    On earth they loved his name:
So now they see his blessèd face,
    And stand before the Lamb.

961. *Family Evening Hymn.*

1 LORD of the world, who hast preserved
    Us safely through this day,
Now guard us in the silent night,
    And in all time, we pray!

2 Be present, in thy peace, to those
    Who as thy suppliants wait;
Blot out the record of our sin;
    Our gloom illuminate!

3 Let not, amid our hours of sleep,
    Life's enemy steal in;
Let not a vision of the night
    Have power to whisper sin.

4 Guard every avenue from guile,
    When slumber seals our eyes;
And guiltless as we laid us down,
    So guiltless let us rise.
                            BREVIARY.

962. S. M. *Marriage.*

1 YES, welcome was the call,
    And sweet the festal lay,
When Jesus deigned in Cana's hall
    To bless the marriage day.

2 And happy was the bride,
    And glad the bridegroom's heart,
For He who tarried at their side
    Bade grief and ill depart.

3 O Lord of life and love,
    Come thou again to-day;
And bring a blessing from above
    That ne'er shall pass away.

4 Oh, bless, as erst of old,
    The bridegroom and the bride;
Bless with the holier stream that flowed
    Forth from thy piercèd side.

5 Before thine altar-throne
    This mercy we implore;
As thou dost knit them, Lord, in one,
    So bless them evermore.

GREAT SHEPHERD OF THE SHEEP.

963.

1 GREAT Shepherd of the sheep,
Who all thy flock dost keep,
: | Leading by waters calm ; | :
Do thou my footsteps guide,
To follow by thy side : —
Make me thy little Lamb.

2 I fear I may be torn
By many a sharp-set thorn,
: | As far from thee I stray ; | :
My weary feet may bleed,
For rough are paths which lead
Out of thy pleasant way.

3 But when the road is long,
Thy tender arm, and strong,
: | The weary one will bear ; | :
And thou wilt wash me clean,
And lead to pastures green,
Where all the flowers are fair.

4 Till, from the soil of sin
Cleansed and made pure within,
: | Dear Saviour, whose I am, | :
Thou bringest me in love,
To thy sweet fold above,
A little snow-white lamb.

GENTLE SHEPHERD. GERMAN.

964.

1 GENTLE Shepherd, grant thy blessing
On us now,
While before thy throne we bow.

2 Gentle Shepherd, we thy children
Seek thy face :
Give us now thy heavenly grace.

3 Gentle Shepherd, bless the children
Of this fold :
Cleanse the hearts of young and old.

4 Gentle Shepherd, when life's ended,
Take us home,
Never from thy side to roam.

GLORY TO JESUS.

Glo-ry to Je-sus, Our gra-cious King: Glo-ry to Je-sus! We will ev-er sing.

965.

1 ALL glory, laud, and honor,
  To thee, Redeemer, King!
  To whom the lips of children
  Made sweet hosannas ring.
    Chorus:

2 The company of angels
  Are praising thee on high,
  And mortal men, and all things
  Created make reply.
    Chorus:

3 The people of the Hebrews,
  With psalms before thee went;
  Our praise and prayer and anthems
  Before thee we present.
    Chorus:

4 Thou didst accept their praises:
  Accept the prayers we bring,
  Who in all good delightest,
  Thou good and gracious King.
    Chorus:

JESUS, TENDER SAVIOUR.

1. Je-sus, ten-der Sa-viour! Hast thou died for me? Make me ver-y thank-ful, In my heart, to thee.

966.

2 When the sad, sad story
  Of thy grief I read,
  For my sins, oh, make me
  Penitent indeed.

3 Soon I hope, in glory,
  At thy side to stand;
  Make me fit to meet thee,
  In that happy land.

POND. 7s.

967.

1 Children's voices high in heaven
　　Make sweet music round the throne;
　Them the King of kings hath given
　　Glory lasting as his own.
　Lord! it was thy mercy free
　Suffered them to come to thee.

2 We would think of them to-day,
　　And their everlasting song;
　We would sing as blest as they,
　　In the spirit-land, erelong;
　Lord! let us thy children be;
　Suffer us to come to thee.

3 Now to come, with loving mind,
　　Simple faith, and earnest prayer,
　Seeking thy dear cross, to find
　　Full and free salvation there.
　Lamb of God! our Saviour be;
　Suffer us to come to thee.

4 Lord, we come! be thou our guide
　　Through life's dark and troubled way;
　And, when trained and sanctified,
　　Raise us to the perfect day;
　Then in heaven thy words shall be,
　"Suffer them to come to me."

968.

1 Once was heard the song of children
　　By the Saviour when on earth;
　Joyful in the sacred temple
　　Shouts of youthful praise had birth,
　　　And hosannas
　Loud to David's Son broke forth.

2 Palms of victory strewn around him,
　　Garments spread beneath his feet,
　Prophet of the Lord they crowned him,
　　In fair Salem's crowded street,
　　　While hosannas
　From the lips of children greet.

3 Blessed Saviour, now triumphant,
　　Glorified and throned on high,
　Mortal lays, from man or infant,
　　Vain to tell thy praise essay;
　　　But hosannas
　Swell the chorus of the sky.

4 God o'er all in heaven reigning,
　　We this day thy glory sing;
　Not with palms thy pathway strewing,
　　We would loftier tribute bring,—
　　　Glad hosannas
　To our Prophet, Priest and King.

Shall we Gather at the River.

BEAUTIFUL RIVER. From "HAPPY VOICES," by permission.

969.

1 SHALL we gather at the river,
  Where bright angel feet have trod,
  With its crystal tide forever
  Flowing by the throne of God?
  Chorus:

2 On the margin of the river,
  Washing up its silver spray,
  We will walk and worship ever,
  All the happy golden day.
  Chorus:

3 Ere we reach the shining river,
  Lay we every burden down;
  Grace our spirits will deliver,
  And provide a harp and crown.
  Chorus:

THROUGH THE VALLEY.

We're al-most down to the riv-er-side, Soon shall our wand'rings cease; If Jesus himself will be our guide, We shall walk thro' the valley in peace.

970. *The Dark Valley before us.*

1 BEFORE us lies a valley dim,
  Which soon our feet may tread;
 And through it rolls a sullen stream,
  The river of the dead.
    Chorus:

2 Though dark the vale and cold the stream,
  It cannot us affright;
 For Christ hath passed through the valley dim,
  To the home of joy and light.
    Chorus:

3 Though death's dark shades around may be,
  My Shepherd still is near;
 His rod and staff shall comfort me,
  No evil shall I fear.
    Chorus:

4 Baptized beneath death's chilling flood,
  In glory shall we rise,
 To meet the conquering Son of God,
  Descending from the skies.
    Chorus:

The Invitation of Jesus.

COME TO ME.
E. P. PARKER.

We come, we come, to taste thy grace, So full, so rich, so free; O Thou, the way, the truth, the life! Be-hold, we come to Thee.

971.

1 Come to me! come to me!
All for sin oppressed;
All ye that toil, all ye that mourn,
And I will give you rest.
Chorus:

2 Come to me! come to me!
Seek my sheltering breast;
My yoke is sweet, my burden light,
And I will give you rest.
Chorus:

3 Come to me! come to me!
And ye shall be blest;
For full of grace and truth am I,
And I will give you rest.
Chorus:

4 Come to me! come to me!
Jesus cries to me!
O Saviour dear, thy voice I hear,
And gladly come to thee.
Chorus:

O SAVIOUR DEAR.

Chorus: O Saviour dear, remember me, And never cease thy care, Till in the realms above the sky, Thy love and bliss I share.

972.

1 O HOLY Saviour, pray for me,
　While far from heaven and thee;
　I wander in a fragile bark,
　　O'er life's tempestuous sea.
　Then, holy Saviour, from thy throne,
　　So bright in bliss above,
　Protect thy child in virtue's path,
　　With thy bright smile of love.
　　　Chorus:

2 When rude temptations try my heart,
　And pleasure spreads a snare;
　Thy loving aid shall heal the smart,
　　And show a Shepherd's care.
　Vain should each earthly prospect prove,
　　Still will I ne'er despair;
　But trust me to a Saviour's love,
　　And feel a Saviour's care.
　　　Chorus:

973.

1 DEAR Jesus, ever at my side,
　　How loving thou must be,
　To leave thy home in heaven, to guard
　　A little child like me.
Thy beautiful and shining face
　I see not, though so near;
The sweetness of thy soft low voice
　I am too deaf to hear.
　　Chorus: [Same as in preceding hymn.]

2 I cannot feel thee touch my hand
　　With pressure light and mild,
　To check me, as my mother did,
　　When I was but a child.
　But I have felt thee in my thoughts,
　　Fighting with sin for me;
　And when my heart loves God, I know
　　The sweetness is from thee.
　　　Chorus:

3 And when, dear Saviour, I kneel down,
　　Morning and night, to prayer,
　Something there is within my heart
　　Which tells me thou art there.
　Yes! when I pray, thou prayest too—
　　Thy prayer is all for me;
　But when I sleep, thou sleepest not,
　　But watchest patiently.
　　　Chorus:
　　　　　　　　　FABER (ALTERED).

Christ the Sinner's Refuge and Rest.

FLEE AS A BIRD. E. P. PARKER.

974.

1 FLEE as a bird to your mountain,
  Thou who art weary of sin;
Go to the clear flowing fountain,
  Where you may wash and be clean.
Fly, for th' avenger is near thee;
Call, and the Saviour will hear thee;
He on his bosom will bear thee,—
O thou who art weary of sin.

2 He will protect thee forever,
  Wipe every sad falling tear,
He will forsake thee, oh, never,
  Cherished so tenderly there;
Haste, then, the hours now are flying;
Spend not the moments in sighing;
Cease from your sorrow and crying,
The Saviour will wipe every tear.

3 Come, then, to Jesus thy Saviour,
  He will redeem thee from sin;
Bless with a sense of his favor,
  Make thee all glorious within:
Call, for the Saviour is near thee,
Waiting in mercy to hear thee,
And by his presence to cheer thee,
O thou, who art weary of sin.

ALPHABETICAL INDEX OF HYMNS.

[Figures refer to the numbers of the hymns.]

A broken heart, my God, my King,	*Watts.*	334
A charge to keep I have,	*Wesley.*	574
A few more years shall roll,	*Bonar.*	604
A glory gilds the sacred page,	*Cowper.*	93
A mighty fortress is our God,	*Luther.*	302
A mother may forgetful be,	*Mrs. Steele.*	737
A stranger in a barren land,	*E. P. Parker.*	345
Abide with me; fast falls the eventide,	*Lyte.*	77
According to thy gracious word,	*Montgomery.*	731
Again our earthly cares we leave,	*Anon.*	28
Ah! how shall fallen man,	*Watts.*	256
Alas, and did my Saviour bleed,	*Watts.*	353
Alas, what hourly dangers rise,	*Mrs. Steele.*	460
All glory, laud, and honor,	*Anon.*	905
All hail the power of Jesus' name,	*Duncan.*	207
All is dying, hearts are breaking,	*Anon.*	570
All praise to thee, eternal Lord,	*Luther.*	156
Almighty God, thy word is cast,	*Anon.*	97
Almighty Maker of my frame,	*Mrs. Steele.*	825
Along my earthly way,	*Edmeston.*	562
Always with us, always with us,	*Nevin.*	535
Am I a soldier of the cross,	*Watts.*	626
Amazing grace, how sweet the sound,	*Newton.*	269
Amid the splendors of thy state,	*Pratt's Coll.*	118
Amidst thy wrath remember love,	*Watts.*	462
And am I born to die,	*Luth. Coll.*	871
And dost thou say, ask what thou wilt,	*Anon.*	684
And must this body die,	*Watts.*	852
And will the great eternal God,	*Doddridge.*	774
And will the Judge descend,	*Doddridge.*	872
And wilt thou now forsake me, Lord,	*Anon.*	470
Another hand is beckoning us,	*Whittier.*	846
Another six days' work is done,	*Stennett.*	42
Approach, my soul, the mercy seat,	*Newton.*	687
Arise, my soul, arise,	*Wesley.*	276
Arise, my soul, my joyful powers,	*Watts.*	418
Arise, O King of grace, arise,	*Watts.*	716
Arise, ye saints, arise,	*Anon.*	616
Around the Saviour's lofty throne,	*Kelly.*	217
Around the throne of God in heaven,	*Anon.*	960
As pants the hart for cooling streams,	*Anon.*	451
As the hart with eager looks,	*Montgomery.*	521
As when the weary traveller gains,	*Newton.*	630
As with gladness men of old,	*Anon.*	168
Asleep in Jesus, blessed sleep,	*Mrs. Mackay.*	828
At thy command, our dearest Lord,	*Watts.*	750
Awake, and sing the song,	*Hammond.*	203
Awake, my soul, stretch every nerve,	*Doddridge.*	625
Awake, our souls, away our fears,	*Watts.*	624
Awaked by Sinai's awful sound,	*Occum.*	380
Awhile they rest within the tomb,	*Anon.*	835
Be thou exalted, O my God!	*Watts.*	100
Before Jehovah's awful throne,	*Watts.*	127
Before us lies a valley dim,	*H. L. Hastings.*	970
Behold a Stranger at the door,	*Gregg.*	283
Behold the glories of the Lamb,	*Watts.*	261
Behold the Lamb of God,	*Monk's Coll.*	178
Behold the throne of grace,	*Newton.*	694
Behold the way to Zion's hill,	*Kelly.*	789
Behold, what wondrous grace,	*Watts.*	397
Bless, O my soul, the living God,	*Watts.*	151
Blessed are the sons of God,	*Humphries.*	490
Blessed fountain, full of grace,	*Kelly.*	521
Blessed Saviour, thee I love,	*Duffield.*	488
Blest are the pure in heart,	*Anon.*	567
Blest are the sons of peace,	*Watts.*	660
Blest are the souls that hear and know,	*Watts.*	94
Blest be the tie that binds,	*Fawcett.*	661
Blest Comforter divine,	*Anon.*	232
Blest feast of love divine,	*Anon.*	758
Blest hour when mortal man retires,	*Raffles.*	686
Blest is the man whose softening,	*L. Barbauld.*	666
Blest morning whose young dawning rays,	*Watts.*	35
Blow ye the trumpet, blow,	*Toplady.*	274
Bread of heaven, on thee we feed,	*Conder.*	741
Brief life is here our portion,	*Dr. Neale.*	913
Bright King of glory, dreadful God,	*Watts.*	216
Bright source of everlasting love,	*Anon.*	663
Brightest and best of the sons of the,	*Heber.*	164
Broad is the road that leads to death,	*Watts.*	245
Brother, though from yonder sky,	*Bancroft.*	866
Burdened with guilt wouldest thou be blest,	*Anon.*	323
By cool Siloam's shady rill,	*Heber.*	762
Call Jehovah thy salvation,	*Montgomery.*	508
Calm on the listening ear of night,	*Sears.*	160
Can sinners hope for heaven,	*Anon.*	252
Cast thy burden on the Lord,	*Anon.*	575
Cease, cease, ye vain desponding fears,	*Dwight.*	833
Cease, ye mourners, cease to languish,	*Collyer.*	859
Child of sin and sorrow,	*Hastings.*	330
Children of God, who, faint and slow,	*Bowdler.*	502
Children of the heavenly King,	*Cennick.*	611
Children's voices high in heaven,	*Anon.*	967
Christ and his cross are all our theme,	*Watts.*	271
Christ is made the sure foundation,	*Anon.*	708
Christ, of all my hopes the ground,	*Windham.*	551
Christ the Lord is risen to-day,	*Cutworth.*	191
Christ, whose glory fills the skies,	*Toplady.*	489
Christ will gather in his own,	*Moravian.*	865
Christian brethren, ere we part,	*Anon.*	55

(385)

Alphabetical Index of Hymns.

Come at the morning hour,	*Briggs' Coll.*	689
Come, dearest Lord, descend and dwell,	*Watts.*	711
Come, divine and peaceful guest,	*Anon.*	147
Come, every pious heart,	*Stennett.*	272
Come, gracious Spirit, heavenly Dove,	*Browne.*	224
Come, happy souls, approach your God,	*Watts.*	287
Come hither, all ye weary souls,	*Watts.*	284
Come, Holy Spirit, calm my mind,	*Burder.*	227
Come, Holy Spirit, come,	*Hart.*	234
Come, Holy Spirit, heavenly Dove,	*Watts.*	221
Come in, thou blessed of our God,	*Montgomery.*	757
Come, Jesus, Redeemer, abide thou,	*Ray Palmer.*	600
Come, kingdom of our God,	*Johns.*	775
Come, let us join our cheerful songs,	*Watts.*	209
Come, let us join our souls to God,	*Doddridge.*	767
Come, let us lift our joyful eyes,	*Watts.*	263
Come, let us sing the song of songs,	*Montgomery.*	218
Come, my soul, thy suit prepare,	*Newton.*	701
Come, O my soul, in sacred lays,	*Blacklock.*	104
Come, O thou traveller unknown,	*Wesley.*	513
Come, said Jesus' sacred voice,	*L. Barbauld.*	309
Come, sinner, to the gospel feast,	*Huntingdon.*	296
Come, sound his praise abroad,	*Watts.*	131
Come, thou Almighty King,	*Madan.*	239
Come, thou desire of all thy saints,	*Mrs. Steele.*	46
Come, thou fount of every blessing,	*Robinson.*	507
Come to me, come to me,	*E. P. Parker.*	971
Come to the house of prayer,	*Taylor.*	691
Come to the land of peace,	*Anon.*	306
Come, trembling sinner, in whose breast,	*Jones.*	291
Come unto me when shadows darkly,	*Anon.*	584
Come, wandering sheep, O come,	*Anon.*	384
Come, weary souls, with sin distressed,	*Mrs. Steele.*	281
Come, ye disconsolate,	*Moore.*	326
Come, ye souls by sin afflicted,	*Swain.*	320
Come, ye thankful people, come,	*Alford.*	931
Come, ye that love the Lord,	*Watts.*	494
Come, ye that love the Saviour's,	*Mrs. Steele.*	478
Come, ye weary souls oppressed,	*Anon.*	310
Creator, Spirit, by whose aid,	*Dryden's Trans.*	226
Crown his head with endless blessing,	*Anon.*	211
Daughter of Zion, from the dust,	*Montgomery.*	799
Day of anger, that dread day,	*Celano, by Alford.*	879
Day of judgment, day of wonders,	*Newton.*	882
Dear as thou wert, and justly dear,	*Dale.*	849
Dear Father, to thy mercy seat,	*Mrs. Steele.*	678
Dear Jesus, ever at my side,	*Faber.*	973
Dear is the spot where Christians sleep,	*Anon.*	837
Dear Lord, amid the throng that pressed,	*Anon.*	539
Dear Refuge of my weary soul,	*Mrs. Steele.*	674
Dear Saviour, if these Lambs should stray,	*Anon.*	955
Dear Saviour, we are thine,	*Doddridge.*	492
Dear Saviour, when my thoughts,	*Mrs. Steele.*	354
Dearest of all the names above,	*Watts.*	516
Death is no more among our foes,	*Medley.*	875
Deep are the wounds which sin has,	*Mrs. Steele.*	247
Depth of mercy, can there be,	*Wesley.*	363
Did Christ o'er sinners weep,	*Beddome.*	485
Didst thou, dear Jesus, suffer shame,	*Kirkham.*	477
Dismiss us with thy blessing, Lord,	*Hart.*	72
Do not I love thee, O my Lord,	*Doddridge.*	479
Does the Gospel word proclaim,	*Newton.*	576
Draw near, O Son of God, draw near,	*Wesley.*	781
Early, my God, without delay,	*Watts.*	13
Ere to the world again we go,	*Anon.*	70
Eternal Father, strong to save,	*Anon.*	934
Eternal Source of every joy,	*Doddridge.*	926
Eternal Spirit, we confess,	*Watts.*	225
Eternal Sun of righteousness,	*Wesley.*	430
Everlasting arms of love,	*Macduff.*	578
Faith adds new charms to earthly bliss,	*Watts.*	638
Faith is a living power from heaven,	*Anon.*	639
Far as thy name is known,	*Watts.*	51
Far down the ages now,	*Bonar.*	721
Far from my heavenly home,	*Lyte.*	504
Far from my thoughts, vain world, be gone,	*Watts.*	6
Far from the world, O Lord, I flee,	*Cowper.*	464
Father, beneath thy sheltering wing,	*Anon.*	437
Father, bless thy word to all,	*Kelly.*	149
Father, hear our humble claim,	*Wesleyan.*	657
Father, how wide thy glory shines,	*Watts.*	242
Father, I know that all my life,	*Mrs. Waring.*	460
Father, if I may call thee so,	*Anon.*	878
Father of eternal grace,	*Montgomery.*	531
Father of men, thy care we bless,	*Doddridge.*	953
Father of mercies, bow thine ear,	*Beddome.*	713
Father of mercies, condescend,	*Morell.*	783
Father of mercies, in thy word,	*Mrs. Steele.*	98
Father of mercies, send thy grace,	*Doddridge.*	668
Father, whate'er of earthly bliss,	*Mrs. Steele.*	592
Flee as a bird to your mountain,	*Anon.*	974
For a season called to part,	*Newton.*	659
For all thy saints, O God,	*Anon.*	645
For me to live is Christ,	*Anon.*	605
For the mercies of the day,	*Montgomery.*	41
For thee, O dear man,	*Bernard, by Dr. Neale.*	912
For thy mercy and thy grace,	*Anon.*	929
Forever here my rest shall be,	*Wesley.*	343
Forever with the Lord,	*Montgomery.*	853
Fount of everlasting love,	*Ray Palmer.*	746
Fountain of grace, rich, full, and free,	*Anon.*	544
Frequent the day of God returns,	*Browne.*	36
Friend after friend departs,	*Montgomery.*	862
From all that dwell below the skies,	*Watts.*	103
From every earthly pleasure,	*Davis.*	609
From every stormy wind that blows,	*Stowell.*	685
From Greenland's icy mountains,	*Heber.*	820
From the cross uplifted high,	*Hawes.*	299
From the recesses of a lowly spirit,	See Page	40
Gentle Shepherd, grant thy blessing,	*Anon.*	964
Gently, gently lay the rod,	*Lyte.*	366
Gently, Lord, O gently lead us,	*Hastings.*	537
Gently, my Saviour, let me down,	*Hill.*	836
Give me the wings of faith to rise,	*Watts.*	899
Give to the winds thy fears,	*Gerhardt.*	398
Glorious city! Heavenly Salem,	*Anon.*	700
Glorious things of thee are spoken,	*Newton.*	723
Glory to God on high,	*Anon.*	240
Glory to God whose witness train,	*Moravian.*	648

Alphabetical Index of Hymns. 387

Glory to thee, my God, this night,	*Ken*.	71
Go, labor on, while it is day,	*Bonar*.	622
Go to dark Gethsemane,	*Montgomery*.	729
Go to the grave, in all thy glorious,	*Montgomery*.	754
God bless our native land,	*J. S. Dwight*.	951
God in the gospel of his Son,	*Beddome*.	84
God is a spirit, just and wise,	*Watts*.	117
God is love, his mercy brightens,	*Bowring*.	143
God is the refuge of his saints,	*Watts*.	122
God moves in a mysterious way,	*Cowper*.	153
God, my supporter and my hope,	*Watts*.	405
God of mercy, God of grace,	*Lyte*.	728
God of my life, through all my days,	*Doddridge*.	386
God of my life, to thee I call,	*Cowper*.	589
God of my salvation, hear,	*Wesley*.	362
God of our fathers, to thy throne,	*L. Bacon*.	949
God of our lives, thy various praise,	*Heginbotham*.	924
God of our salvation, hear us,	*Anon*.	80
God of the sunlight hours, how sad,	*Anon*.	59
God of the universe, to thee,	*Anon*.	772
God's glory is a wondrous thing,	*Faber*.	468
Grace is a plant where'er it grows,	*Cowper*.	953
Grace, 'tis a charming sound,	*Doddridge*.	253
Gracious spirit, love divine,	*Stocker*.	229
Great God, attend, while Zion sings,	*Watts*.	31
Great God, beneath whose piercing eye,	*Roscoe*.	938
Great God, how infinite art thou,	*Watts*.	155
Great God, in vain man's narrow view,	*Kippis*.	106
Great God, now condescend,	*Fellows*.	750
Great God of nations, now to thee,	*Anon*.	937
Great God, the nations of the earth,	*Gibbons*.	807
Great God, to thee my evening song,	*Mrs. Steele*.	954
Great God, we sing that mighty hand,	*Doddridge*.	923
Great God, what do I see and hear,	*Luther*.	873
Great God, when I approach thy throne,	*Anon*.	260
Great God, whom heaven and earth,	*Anon*.	942
Great is the Lord our God,	*Watts*.	26
Great Shepherd of the sheep,	*Anon*.	963
Great Shepherd of thine Israel,	*Watts*.	710
Great Sun of righteousness, arise,	*Watts*.	83
Guide me, O thou great Jehovah,	*Oliver*.	606
Had I the tongues of Greeks and Jews,	*Watts*.	650
Hail, mighty Jesus, how divine,	*Wallin*.	809
Hail the night, all hail the morn,	*Anon*.	171
Hail to the Lord's anointed,	*Montgomery*.	823
Hail to the Prince of life and peace,	*Doddridge*.	189
Hallelujah! best and sweetest,	*Breviary*.	608
Happy the heart where graces reign,	*Watts*.	654
Happy the home when God is there,	*Anon*.	956
Happy the man whose cautious feet,	*Watts*.	631
Happy the meek whose gentle breast,	*J. Scott*.	642
Happy the souls to Jesus joined,	*Wesley*.	656
Hark! a voice divides the sky,	*Wesley*.	864
Hark, hark! the notes of joy,	*Anon*.	278
Hark! how the choral song of heaven,	*Anon*.	889
Hark! my soul, it is the Lord,	*Cowper*.	577
Hark! ten thousand harps and voices,	*Kelly*.	212
Hark! the glad sound, the Saviour,	*Doddridge*.	161
Hark! the herald angels sing,	*Wesley*.	167
Hark! the song of Jubilee,	*Montgomery*.	801

Hark! the voice of love and mercy,	*Francis*.	210
Hark! what celestial sounds,	*Anon*.	165
Hark! what mean those holy voices,	*Cawood*.	164
Hasten, Lord, the glorious time,	*Lyte*.	802
Hasten, sinner, to be wise,	*T. Scott*.	315
Have we no tears to shed for him,	*Lyra Cath*.	280
He dies, the Friend of sinners dies,	*Watts*.	190
He kneIt, the Saviour knelt,	*Mrs. Hemans*.	206
He lives, the great Redeemer lives,	*Mrs. Steele*.	186
He reigns, the Lord the Saviour reigns,	*Watts*.	214
He that goeth forth with weeping,	*Hastings*.	569
He, who on earth as man was known,	*Newton*.	200
He who once in righteous vengeance,	*Anon*.	180
Hear, O sinner, mercy hails you,	*Reed*.	319
Hear the heralds of the gospel,	*Allen's Coll*.	321
Hear what God the Lord hath spoken,	*Cowper*.	534
Hearken, Lord, to my complaints,	*Montgomery*.	491
Heavenly Father, sovereign Lord,	*Montgomery*.	696
Heavenly Spirit, may each heart,	*Edmeston*.	702
Here, Lord of life and light to thee,	*L. Bacon*.	774
Here, O my Lord, I see thee face to face,	*Bonar*.	752
High in the heavens, eternal God,	*Watts*.	124
High in yonder realms of light,	*Raffles*.	907
Holy Father, hear my cry,	*Bonar*.	375
Holy Ghost! thou source of light,	*Anon*.	230
Holy Ghost! with light divine,	*Reed*.	231
Holy Lord, our hearts prepare,	*Anon*.	699
Holy Spirit! Lord of,	*King Robert of France*.	228
Hosanna to the Prince of light,	*Watts*.	162
How beauteous are their feet,	*Watts*.	769
How blest is he whose tranquil mind,	*Anon*.	839
How blest the righteous when he,	*L. Barbauld*.	829
How calm and beautiful the morn,	*Hastings*.	205
How charming is the place,	*Stennett*.	22
How deep and tranquil is the joy,	*Reed*.	465
How do thy mercies close me round,	*Wesley*.	424
How firm a foundation, ye saints,	*Kirkham*.	599
How gentle God's commands,	*Doddridge*.	302
How heavy is the night,	*Watts*.	251
How helpless guilty nature lies,	*Mrs. Steele*.	273
How honored is the place,	*Watts*.	722
How large the promise, how divine,	*Watts*.	705
How lovely are thy dwellings, Lord,	*Milton*.	30
How oft, alas, this wretched heart,	*Mrs. Steele*.	344
How pleasant, how divinely fair,	*Watts*.	3
How pleased and blest was I,	*Watts*.	18
How precious is the book divine,	*Fawcett*.	96
How sad our state by nature is,	*Watts*.	241
How shall the young secure their hearts,	*Watts*.	91
How sweet and awful is the place,	*Watts*.	732
How sweet, how calm, this Sabbath morn,	*Anon*.	47
How sweet, how heavenly is the sight,	*Swain*.	664
How sweet the name of Jesus sounds,	*Newton*.	510
How sweet to be allowed to pray,	*Follett*.	704
How sweet to bless the Lord,	*Anon*.	690
How sweet to leave the world awhile,	*Kelly*.	7
How sweetly flowed the gospel's sound,	*Bowring*.	688
How swift the torrent rolls,	*Doddridge*.	842
How vain is all beneath the skies,	*Anon*.	826
I ask not now for gold to gild,	*Whittier*.	646

Alphabetical Index of Hymns.

Hymn	Author	No.
I bow my forehead to the dust,	Whittier.	406
I cannot always trace the way,	Anon.	441
I cannot call affliction sweet,	Montgomery.	504
I come to thee once more, my God,	Faber.	705
I hear thy word with love,	Watts.	571
I heard the voice of Jesus say,	Bonar.	346
I know thy thoughts are peace toward me,	Anon.	409
I lay my sins on Jesus,	Bonar.	376
I love the Lord, he heard my cries,	Watts.	404
I love the sacred book of God,	Kelly.	85
I love the volume of thy word,	Watts.	88
I love the windows of thy grace,	Watts.	457
I love thy kingdom, Lord,	Dwight.	720
I love to steal awhile away,	Mrs. Brown.	58
I send the joys of earth away,	Watts.	390
I sing th' almighty power of God,	Watts.	137
I thirst, but not as once I did,	Cowper.	454
I was a wandering sheep,	Bonar.	356
I would not live alway, I ask not,	Muhlenburg.	860
If God is mine, then present things,	Anon.	410
If human kindness meets return,	Noel.	730
If through unruffled seas,	Anon.	559
I'll praise my Maker with my breath,	Watts.	89
I'm but a stranger here,	T. R. Taylor.	556
I'm not ashamed to own my Lord,	Watts.	490
Immortal power, eternal One,	Mrs. Collins.	400
In all my vast concerns with thee,	Watts.	120
In deep distress our Saviour prayed,	Watts.	177
In heavenly love abiding,	Mrs. Waring.	610
In latter days the mount of God,	Logan.	798
In the cross of Christ I glory,	Bowring.	506
In the dark and cloudy day,	Anon.	582
In the midst of life we are in death,	Notker.	906
In thee, great God, with songs of praise,	Barlow.	945
In thy name, O Lord, assembling,	Kelly.	79
In vain we seek for peace with God,	Watts.	243
Indulgent Sovereign of the skies,	Doddridge.	792
Is not the way to heavenly gain,	Lyte.	433
Is this the kind return,	Watts.	359
It came upon the midnight clear,	E. H. Sears.	159
Jehovah God! thy gracious power,	Thomson.	121
Jehovah reigns, his throne is high,	Watts.	111
Jerusalem, my happy home,	Anon.	903
Jesus, all atoning Lamb,	Wesley.	634
Jesus, and didst thou leave the sky,	Mrs. Steele.	270
Jesus, and shall it ever be,	Gregg.	542
Jesus, calls us o'er the tumult,	Anon.	318
Jesus, cast a look on me,	Berridge.	635
Jesus Christ is risen to-day,	Latin.	194
Jesus gently calls,	E. P. Parker.	331
Jesus, I love thy charming name,	Doddridge.	496
Jesus, I my cross have taken,	Lyte.	368
Jesus, Immortal King! arise,	Burder.	808
Jesus, let thy pitying eye,	Wesley.	361
Jesus, Lord, we look to thee,	Wesley.	658
Jesus, Lover of my soul,	Wesley.	550
Jesus, most holy, pray I to thee,	Anon.	381
Jesus, only when the morning,	Nason.	373
Jesus, our Lord, how rich thy grace,	Doddridge.	672
Jesus, save my dying soul,	Hastings.	364
Jesus shall reign where'er the sun,	Watts.	786
Jesus, Shepherd of the sheep,	Anon.	522
Jesus spreads his banner o'er us,	Anon.	724
Jesus, still lead on,	Zinzendorff.	545
Jesus, take me for thine own,	Anon.	632
Jesus, tender Saviour,	Anon.	906
Jesus, the very thought of thee,	Bernard.	486
Jesus, these eyes have never seen,	Ray Palmer.	509
Jesus, thou art the sinner's friend,	Parkinson.	476
Jesus, thou everlasting King,	Watts.	749
Jesus, thou joy of loving,	Bernard, by Palmer.	543
Jesus, thy blood and,	Wesley's Trans.	340
Jesus, thy boundless love to me,	Anon.	519
Jesus, thy love shall we forget,	Anon.	511
Jesus, we look to thee,	Wesley.	695
Jesus, where'er thy people meet,	Cowper.	45
Jesus, who knows full well,	Newton.	693
Jesus, who on Calvary's mountain,	Anon.	372
Jesus, whom angel hosts adore,	Bonar.	183
Join all the glorious names,	Watts.	275
Joy to the world, the Lord is come,	Watts.	163
Joyful be the hours to-day,	Kelly.	743
Just as I am without one plea,	Charlotte Elliot.	333
Keep silence, all created things,	Watts.	116
Keep us, Lord, oh, keep us ever,	Anon.	607
Kingdoms and thrones to God belong,	Watts.	101
Laboring and heavy laden,	Rankin.	371
Lamp of our feet, whereby we trace,	Barton.	90
Lead, kindly light, amid,	Newman, see page	41
Lead us, heavenly Father, lead us,	Anon.	528
Let children hear the mighty deeds,	Watts.	957
Let everlasting glories crown,	Watts.	87
Let me be with thee where thou art,	Anon.	540
Let not your heart be faint,	Anon.	572
Let others boast how strong they be,	Watts.	850
Let our songs of praise ascending,	Anon.	170
Let saints below in concert sing,	Wesley.	655
Let sinners take their course,	Watts.	399
Let us keep steadfast guard,	Breviary.	506
Let us with a joyful mind,	Milton.	144
Let worldly minds the world pursue,	Newton.	414
Light of those whose dreary dwelling,	Wesley.	533
Like sheep we went astray,	Watts.	255
Lo! God is here, let us adore,	J. Wesley.	34
Lo! he comes with clouds descending,	Oliver.	883
Lo! on a narrow neck of land,	Wesley.	881
Lo! round the throne, a glorious band,	Anon.	890
Lo! the day of rest declineth,	Robbins.	76
Lo! the mighty God appearing,	W. Goode.	884
Lo! what a glorious Corner-stone,	Watts.	8
Lo! what a glorious sight appears,	Watts.	796
Look up, my soul, with cheerful eye,	Anon.	248
Lord, as to thy dear cross we flee,	Anon.	607
Lord, at thy table I behold,	Stennett.	733
Lord, dismiss us with thy blessing,	Burder.	78
Lord, how delightful 'tis to see,	Watts.	4
Lord, how secure my conscience was,	Watts.	257
Lord, I am vile, conceived in sin,	Watts.	244
Lord, I believe, thy power I own,	Wreford.	423
Lord, I have made thy word my choice,	Watts.	95

Alphabetical Index of Hymns. 389

Lord, I hear that showers of blessing,	Anon.	367	My only Saviour, when I feel,	Anon.	541
Lord, in the morning thou shalt hear,	Watts.	11	My Saviour bids me come,	Wesley.	357
Lord, in the temples of thy grace,	Anon.	43	My Saviour, let me hear thy voice,	Doddridge.	498
Lord, in this, thy mercy's day,	Anon.	382	My Saviour, my almighty Friend,	Watts.	481
Lord, in thy great, thy glorious name,	Mrs. Steele.	388	My soul, amid this stormy world,	Chapman.	898
Lord, it belongs not to my care,	Baxter.	431	My soul, be on thy guard,	Heath.	619
Lord, lead the way the Saviour went,	Croswell.	665	My soul, how lovely is the place,	Watts.	15
Lord, my weak thought in vain,	Ray Palmer.	114	My spirit looks to God alone,	Anon.	427
Lord of all being, throned afar,	O. W. Holmes.	159	My spirit on thy care,	Lyte.	557
Lord of all families below,	Anon.	959			
Lord of earth, thy forming hand,	Grant.	143	Nearer, my God, to thee,	S. F. Adams.	555
Lord of the harvest, hear,	Wesley.	768	New every morning is the love,	Keble.	33
Lord of the world, who hast preserved,	Breviary.	961	No more, my God, I boast no more,	Watts.	339
Lord of the worlds above,	Watts.	16	No, never shall my heart despond,	Anon.	679
Lord, send thy word, and let it fly,	Gibbons.	806	Nor eye hath seen, nor ear hath heard,	Watts.	897
Lord, teach us how to pray aright,	Montgomery.	681	Not all the blood of beasts,	Watts.	254
Lord, thou hast searched, and seen me,	Watts.	152	Not all the outward forms on earth,	Watts.	259
Lord, thou on earth didst love thine,	Ray Palmer.	671	Not by the martyr's death alone,	Anon.	641
Lord, thou wilt hear me when I pray,	Watts.	63	Not for the pious dead we weep,	L. Barbauld.	845
Lord, we come before thee now,	Hammond.	39	Not with our mortal eyes,	Watts.	483
Lord, we confess our numerous faults,	Watts.	432	Now be my heart inspired to sing,	Watts.	173
Lord, we have wandered forth through,	Anon.	585	Now begin the heavenly theme,	Langford.	613
Lord, what a thoughtless wretch was I,	Watts.	246	Now for a tune of lofty praise,	Watts.	158
Lord, when my thoughts delighted,	Mrs. Steele.	185	Now is th' accepted time,	Dobell.	305
Lord, where shall guilty souls retire,	Watts.	110	Now let our cheerful eyes survey,	Doddridge.	515
Lord, while for all mankind we pray,	Welford.	944	Now let our souls on wings sublime,	Gibbons.	886
Lord, with glowing heart I'd praise thee,	S. F. Key.	142	Now let our voices join,	Doddridge.	621
Love divine, all love excelling,	Wesley.	532	Now may he who from the dead,	Newton.	57
			Now, my soul, thy voice upraising,	Anon.	179
Majestic sweetness sits enthroned,	Stennett.	487	Now to the Lord, a noble song,	Watts.	473
Man's wisdom is to seek,	Cowper.	692	Now to the Lord who makes us know,	Watts.	220
Many centuries have fled,	Conder.	727			
May he, by whose kind care we meet,	Newton.	632	O bless the Lord, my soul, His,	Montgomery.	129
May the grace of Christ our Saviour,	Newton.	81	O bless the Lord, my soul, Let,	Watts.	130
Men of God, go take your stations,	Kelly.	817	O blessed souls are they,	Watts.	258
'Mid scenes of confusion and,	Anon.	861	O bow thine ear, eternal One!	Anon.	770
Mighty one! before whose face,	Bryant.	148	O cease, my wandering soul,	Muhlenburg.	304
Millions within thy courts have met,	Montgomery.	67	O Christ! I long to know thee,	Ray Palmer.	548
Mine eyes and my desire,	Watts.	561	O Christ! our ever-blessed Lord,	Anon.	206
Morning breaks upon the tomb,	Collyer.	102	O Christ! with each returning morn,	Latin.	44
Mourn for the thousand slain,	Anon.	950	O could I find from day to day,	Anon.	458
Must Jesus bear the cross alone,	Allen.	637	O could I speak the matchless worth,	Medley.	504
My country, 'tis of thee,	S. F. Smith.	952	O could our thoughts and wishes fly,	Mrs. Steele.	896
My dear Redeemer, and my Lord,	Watts.	172	O day of rest and gladness,	Wordsworth.	1
My faith looks up to thee,	Ray Palmer.	546	O deem not they are blest alone,	Bryant.	453
My Father God! how sweet the sound,	Doddridge.	415	O eyes that are weary, and hearts that are,	Anon.	597
My God, accept my early vows,	Watts.	651	O for a closer walk with God,	Cowper.	449
My God, accept my heart this day,	Lyra Cath.	349	O for a heart to praise my God,	Wesley.	455
My God, how endless is thy love,	Watts.	65	O for a shout of sacred joy,	Watts.	175
My God, how wonderful thou art,	Anon.	420	O for a sight, a pleasing sight,	Watts.	887
My God, is any hour so sweet,	See page	42	O for a sweet, inspiring ray,	Mrs. Steele.	845
My God, my Father, blissful name,	Mrs. Steele.	422	O for a thousand tongues to sing,	Wesley.	501
My God, my Father, while I stray,	Charlotte Elliot.	440	O for the death of those,	Anon.	841
My God, my King, thy various praise,	Watts.	123	O God! beneath thy guiding hand,	L. Bacon.	935
My God, my portion, and my love,	Watts.	417	O God! by whom the seed is given,	Heber.	49
My God, oh, could I make the claim,	Mrs. Steele.	456	O God of Bethel by whose hand,	Doddridge.	411
My God, permit me not to be,	Watts.	452	O God! our God, thou shinest here,	Gill.	794
My God, the covenant of thy love,	Doddridge.	434	O God! our help in ages past,	Watts.	869
My God, the spring of all my joys,	Watts.	495	O God! thou art my God alone,	Montgomery.	445
My hope is built on nothing less,	Anon.	512	O God! unseen, yet ever near,	Anon.	756
My Jesus, as thou wilt,	Schmolk.	590	O happy day, that fixed my choice,	Doddridge.	755
My Maker, and my King,	Mrs. Steele.	133	O happy nation, where the Lord,	Watts.	932
			O happy saints, that dwell in light,	Anon.	888

390 Alphabetical Index of Hymns.

O happy soul, that lives on high,	Watts.	403	Once was heard the song of children,	Anon.	968
O help us, Lord, each hour of need,	Milman.	450	One prayer I have, all prayers in one,	Montgomery.	706
O holy Father! just and true,	Whittier.	936	One sweetly solemn thought,	Phœbe Carey.	840
O holy Saviour! Friend unseen,	Anon.	324	One there is above all others,	Newton.	316
O holy Saviour! pray for me,	Anon.	972	Our blest Redeemer, ere he breathed,	Lyte.	222
O how divine, how sweet the joy,	Needham.	351	Our children, Lord, in faith and prayer,	Anon.	766
O how I love thy holy law,	Watts.	92	Our children, thou dost claim,	Anon.	700
O Jesus! bruised and wounded more,	Anon.	748	Our Christ hath reached his,	Frothingham.	715
O Lamb of God, still keep me,	Anon.	549	Our country is Immanuel's ground,	L. Barbauld.	649
O Lord and Master of us all,	Whittier.	474	Our Father, God! who art in heaven,	Judson.	676
O Lord, how full of sweet content,	Mad. Guion.	444	Our Father, through the coming year,	Anon.	918
O Lord, how infinite thy love,	Lyte.	262	Our heavenly Father calls,	Doddridge.	307
O Lord, I would delight in thee,	Ryland.	428	Our helper God, we bless thy name,	Doddridge.	927
O Lord, our carnal mind control,	Anon.	647	Our Lord is risen from the dead,	Wesley.	188
O Lord, our fathers oft have told,	Tate and Brady.	947			
O Lord, our God, arise,	Anon.	776	People of the living God!	Montgomery.	742
O Lord, our heavenly King,	Watts.	132	Pilgrims in this vale of sorrow,	Hastings.	568
O Lord, thy covenant is sure,	Conder.	738	Pity, Lord, the child of clay,	Anon.	553
O Lord, thy work revive,	Browne.	778	Pleasant are thy courts above,	Lyte.	10
O love divine, how sweet thou art,	Wesley.	505	Plunged in a gulf of dark despair,	Watts.	267
O love divine, that stooped to share,	O. W. Holmes.	430	Pour out thy Spirit from on high,	Montgomery.	779
O love, who o'er life's earliest dawn,	Anon.	503	Praise to God, immortal praise,	L. Barbauld.	926
O mother dear, Jerusalem,	Quarles.	902	Praise to thee, thou great Creator,	Fawcett.	141
O my Saviour! crucified,	Anon.	745	Praise waits in Zion, Lord, for thee,	Watts.	29
O my Saviour, guardian true,	Anon.	54	Praise ye the Lord, my heart shall join,	Watts.	108
O my soul, what means this sadness,	Fawcett.	527	Prayer is the breath of God in man,	Anon.	677
O praise the Lord, for he is good,	Wrangham.	435	Prayer is the soul's sincere desire,	Montgomery.	675
O sacred Head, now wounded,	Gerhardt.	547	Prepare us, Lord, to view thy cross,	Anon.	735
O Saviour, who didst come,	Anon.	560	Prince of peace, control my will,	Anon.	583
O say to all men far and near,	Novalis.	196			
O sinner, lift the eye of faith,	Anon.	385	Quiet, Lord, my froward heart,	Newton.	525
O sinners, come, and taste his love,	Watts.	288	Raise your triumphant songs,	Watts.	204
O Spirit of the living God,	Montgomery.	785	Rejoice in God alway,	Moultrie.	620
O Sun of righteousness, arise,	Anon.	790	Rejoice, rejoice, believers,	Laurenti.	821
O sweetly breathe the lyres above,	Ray Palmer.	438	Rejoice, the Lord is King,	Wesley.	484
O that I could forever dwell,	Reed.	588	Rejoice to-day, with one accord,	Anon.	393
O that I knew the secret place,	Watts.	446	Rejoice, ye saints, rejoice and praise,	Anon.	471
O that my load of sin were gone,	Wesley.	335	Remember thy Creator now,	Anon.	292
O that the Lord would guide my ways,	Watts.	99	Rest from thy labor, rest,	Montgomery.	780
O the sweet wonders of that cross,	Watts.	187	Resting from his work to-day,	Anon.	740
O thou, from whom all goodness flows,	Anon.	447	Return, my roving heart, return,	Doddridge.	436
O thou Preserver of mankind,	Dwight.	940	Return, my soul, and sweetly rest,	Latrobe.	425
O thou that hearest prayer,	Anon.	236	Return, O wanderer, now return,	Collyer.	297
O thou, the contrite sinner's Friend,	C. Elliott.	325	Return, O wanderer, to thy home,	Hastings.	290
O thou to whom in ancient time,	Ware.	32	Ride on, ride on, in majesty,	Milman.	213
O thou who driest the mourner's tear,	Moore.	448	Rise, my soul, and stretch thy wings,	Cennick.	914
O thou who hear'st the prayer of faith,	Toplady.	379	Rise, O my soul, pursue the path,	Needham.	901
O thou whom we adore,	Wesley.	777	Rock of Ages! cleft for me,	Toplady.	552
O thou whose own vast temple stands,	Bryant.	773	Roll on, thou mighty ocean,	Pratt's Coll.	811
O thou whose tender mercy hears,	Mrs. Steele.	350			
O what a lonely path were ours,	Anon.	421	Safely through another week,	Newton.	9
O what amazing words of grace,	Medley.	280	Salvation! O the joyful sound,	Watts.	261
O what if we are Christ's,	Anon.	854	Saviour, breathe an evening blessing,	Edmeston.	74
O where are kings and empires now,	A. C. Coxe.	718	Saviour, like a Shepherd lead us,	Anon.	526
O where shall rest be found,	Montgomery.	308	Saviour, teach me day by day,	Anon.	530
O worship the king, all glorious above,	Grant.	140	Saviour, what gracious words,	Anon.	662
O Zion! afflicted with wave upon wave,	Anon.	508	Saviour, when in dust to thee,	Grant.	374
O'er the gloomy hills of darkness,	Williams.	816	Saw ye not the cloud arise,	Wesley.	804
O'er the realms of pagan darkness,	Cotterell.	818	Say, sinner, hath a voice within,	Hyde.	285
Oft in sorrow, oft in woe,	H. K. White.	612	See, from Zion's sacred mountain,	Kelly.	815
On the mountain's top appearing,	Kelly.	813	See, gracious God, before thy throne,	Mrs. Steele.	946
Once I thought my mountain strong,	Newton.	554	See Israel's gentle Shepherd stand,	D'd bridge.	763

Alphabetical Index of Hymns.

See the leaves around us falling,	Horne.	858
See what a living stone,	Watts.	25
Servant of God, well done,	Montgomery.	835
Shall I fear, O earth, thy bosom,	Davis.	857
Shall we gather at the river,	R. Lowry.	969
Shepherd, with thy tenderest love,	Anon.	523
Show pity, Lord, O Lord, forgive,	Watts.	336
Silently the shades of evening,	Anon.	73
Since all the varying scenes of time,	Hervey.	412
Sing, ye redeemed of the Lord,	Doddridge.	627
Sinner, rouse thee from thy sleep,	Anon.	313
Sinners, turn, why will ye die,	Wesley.	312
Sion's daughter, weep no more,	Anon.	730
So fades the lovely blooming flower,	Mrs. Steele.	831
So let our lips and lives express,	Watts.	629
Soft and holy is the place,	Hastings.	697
Softly fades the twilight ray,	S. F. Smith.	56
Softly now the light of day,	Doane.	53
Soldiers of Christ, arise,	Wesley.	617
Songs of praise the angels sang,	Montgomery.	193
Sons of men, behold from far,	Wesley.	805
Soon as I heard my Father say,	Watts.	348
Soon may the last glad song arise,	Anon.	787
Soul, then know thy full salvation,	Lyte.	369
Sovereign of worlds, display thy power,	Anon.	793
Sow in the morn thy seed,	Montgomery.	573
Spirit of peace! celestial Dove,	Lyte.	707
Spirit of power and might, behold,	Montgomery.	797
Spirit of truth, on this thy day,	Heber.	37
Stand up, and bless the Lord,	Montgomery.	24
Stand up, my soul, shake off thy fears,	Watts.	623
Stand up, stand up for Jesus,	Duffield.	810
Stay, thou insulted Spirit, stay,	Wesley.	342
Stealing from the world away,	Ray Palmer.	698
Sun of my soul, thou Saviour dear,	Keble.	64
Sweet is the light of Sabbath eve,	Edmeston.	66
Sweet is the memory of thy grace,	Watts.	407
Sweet is the prayer whose holy,	H. Martineau.	680
Sweet is the work, my God, my King,	Watts.	2
Sweet is the work, O Lord,	Lyte.	23
Sweet peace of conscience, heavenly,	Heginbotham.	443
Sweet Saviour, bless us ere we go,	Monk's Coll.	68
Sweet the moments, rich in blessing,	Anon.	536
Sweet the time, exceeding sweet,	Burder.	146
Sweet was the time when first I felt,	Newton.	459
Sweeter sounds than music knows,	Newton.	520
Sweeter to Jesus when on earth,	H. Kimball.	538
Take me, O my Father, take me,	Ray Palmer.	317
Take my heart, O Father, take it,	Anon.	370
Tarry with me, O my Saviour,	Anon.	73
Teach me, my God and King,	Herbert.	395
The Almighty reigns, exalted high,	Watts.	110
That awful day will surely come,	Watts.	864
That day of wrath, that,	Celano, by W. Scott.	877
The billows swell, the winds are high,	Cowper.	587
The bird let loose in eastern skies,	Moore.	636
The Church of Christ, which he hath,	Spangenberg.	753
The Comforter has come,	Anon.	233
The day is past and gone,	Leland.	50
The festal morn, my God, has come,	Merrick.	29
The floods, O Lord, lift up their voice,	Burgess.	113
The golden gates are lifted up,	Anon.	195
The harvest dawn is near,	Burgess.	565
The Head that once was crowned with,	Kelly.	208
The heavens declare thy glory, Lord,	Watts.	82
The King of heaven his table spreads,	Doddridge.	294
The Lord in trouble hear thee,	Lyte.	378
The Lord is Judge, before his throne,	W. Goode.	126
The Lord is my Shepherd, no want,	Montgomery.	601
The Lord is our refuge, the Lord is our guide,	Lyte.	603
The Lord is risen, indeed,	Kelly.	202
The Lord Jehovah reigns, And,	Watts.	19
The Lord Jehovah reigns, His,	Watts.	238
The Lord my pasture shall prepare,	Addison.	134
The Lord my Shepherd is,	Watts.	396
The Lord of glory is my light,	Watts.	714
The Lord our God is full of might,	H. K. White.	138
The Lord shall come, the earth shall quake,	Heber.	876
The Lord will come, and not be slow,	Milton.	795
The lovely form of God's own Church,	Alford.	717
The morning light is breaking,	S. F. Smith.	822
The people of the Lord,	Anon.	644
The pity of the Lord,	Watts.	128
The roseate hues of early dawn,	Anon.	894
The Saviour calls, let every ear,	Mrs. Steele.	268
The Saviour kindly calls,	Anon.	761
The Saviour! O what endless charms,	Mrs. Steele.	265
The Saviour! what a noble flame,	Cowper.	176
The Son of God goes forth to war,	Anon.	401
The spacious firmament on high,	Addison.	125
The Spirit in our hearts,	Anon.	303
The Spirit like a peaceful Dove,	Watts.	653
The sun is sinking in the west,	Anon.	61
The swift declining day,	Doddridge.	856
The twilight falls, the night is near,	Anon.	52
The voice of free grace cries,	Thornby.	328
The year has gone beyond recall,	Anon.	919
Thee we adore, Eternal Name,	Watts.	923
There is a blessed home,	Baker.	909
There is a book who runs may read,	Keble.	431
There is a fountain filled with blood,	Cowper.	264
There is a house not made with hands,	Watts.	895
There is a land mine eye hath seen,	Anon.	891
There is a land of pure delight,	Watts.	900
There is a state, unknown, unseen,	Jane Taylor.	847
There is an hour of hallowed,	Wm. B. Tappan.	893
There is an hour of peaceful rest,	Tappan.	892
There is an hour when I must part,	Anon.	867
There is none other name than thine,	Anon.	250
There's nothing bright above, below,	Moore.	112
They are all gone into the world of light,	Vaughan.	905
They who seek the throne of grace,	Anon.	700
Thine earthly Sabbaths, Lord, we love,	Doddridge.	5
Thine forever, God of love,	Anon.	703
Think gently of the erring one,	Fletcher.	670
This is the day the Lord hath made,	Watts.	12
This place is holy ground,	Montgomery.	663
Thou art gone to the grave, but we,	Heber.	329
Thou art gone up on high,	Anon.	355
Thou art, O God, the life and light,	Moore.	135
Thou art the way, to thee alone,	Doane.	268
Thou dear Redeemer, dying Lamb,	Cennick.	475
Thou gracious God, and kind,	Pratt's Coll.	360

Alphabetical Index of Hymns.

Hymn	Author	No.
Thou Holy Spirit, Lord of grace,	Anon.	38
Thou Judge of quick and dead,	Wesley.	870
Thou, Lord, of all the parent art,	Martineau's Coll.	113
Thou lovely source of true delight,	Mrs. Steele.	500
Thou Maker of my vital frame,	Watts. See page	39
Thou only Sovereign of my heart,	Mrs. Steele.	391
Thou Prince of glory, slain for me,	Collyer.	337
Thou Saviour, from thy throne on,	Ray Palmer.	682
Thou very present aid,	Wesley.	643
Thou who didst on Calvary bleed,	Anon.	747
Thou who roll'st the year around,	Ray Palmer.	917
Though all the world my choice deride,	Terstegan.	341
Though faint, yet pursuing,	Anon.	602
Though now the nations sit beneath,	L. Bacon.	791
Through all the changing scenes,	Tate and Brady.	429
Through sorrow's night and danger's,	H. K. White.	848
Thus far the Lord has led me on,	Watts.	69
Thy footsteps, Lord, with joy we trace,	Anon.	941
Thy goodness, Lord, our souls confess,	Gibbons.	408
Thy holy will, my God. be mine,	Ray Palmer.	595
Thy mighty working, mighty God,	Anon.	21
Thy way is in the sea,	Fawcett.	482
Thy way, not mine, O Lord,	Bonar.	501
Thy will be done! in devious,	Bowring. See page	41
Thy works, not mine, O Christ,	Bonar.	273
Time is winging us away,	J. Burton.	915
'Tis by the faith of joys to come,	Watts.	640
'Tis by thy strength the mountains stand,	Watts.	920
'Tis finished! so the Saviour cried,	Stennett.	184
'Tis God, the Spirit, leads,	Anon.	235
'Tis midnight, and on Olive's brow,	Tappan.	182
'Tis my happiness below,	Cowper.	579
'Tis not a cause of small import,	Doddridge.	782
To-day the Saviour calls,	Anon.	327
To God, the only wise,	Watts.	493
To heaven I lift my waiting eyes,	Watts.	154
To Him that chose us first,	Watts.	237
To Jesus, the crown of my hope,	Cowper.	911
To our Redeemer's glorious name,	Mrs. Steele.	480
To thee all angels cry aloud,	Anon.	102
To thy pastures fair and large,	Merrick.	520
To thy temple, we repair,	Montgomery.	40
To whom, my Saviour, shall I go,	Anon.	463
To-morrow, Lord, is thine,	Doddridge.	851
Trembling before thine awful throne,	Hillhouse.	338
Triumphant Christ ascends on high,	Mrs. Steele.	199
Triumphant Zion, lift thine head,	Doddridge.	712
Try us, O God, and search the ground,	Wesley.	673
Turn not thy face away, O Lord,	Anon.	347
'Twas on that dark, that doleful night,	Watts.	756
Unshaken as the sacred hill,	Watts.	413
Unveil thy bosom, faithful tomb,	Watts.	830
Up to the hills, I lift mine eyes,	Watts.	387
Up to the Lord who reigns on high,	Watts.	100
Upon the Gospel's sacred page,	Bowring.	86
Upward I lift mine eyes,	Watts.	166
Vainly through night's weary hours,	Lyte.	725
Wait, O my soul, thy Maker's will,	Beddome.	105
Wake the song of jubilee,	L. Bacon.	603
Watchman, tell us of the night,	Bowring.	800
We are on our journey home,	Charles Beecher.	615
We bless thee for thy peace, O God,	Anon.	467
We love the place, O God,	Anon.	52
We love the venerable house,	Emerson.	719
We praise thee oft for hours of bliss,	J. P. Hopps.	596
We pray thee, wounded Lamb of God,	Anon.	751
We sinners, Lord, with earnest heart,	Bernard.	352
We speak of the realms of the blest,	Anon.	910
We stand in deep repentance,	Ray Palmer.	377
We would see Jesus, for the shadows,	Anon.	586
Weary of wandering from my God,	Wesley.	518
Weary sinner, keep thine eyes,	Anon.	311
Weary souls that wander wide,	Wesley.	300
Welcome, delightful morn,	Hayward.	17
Welcome, sweet day of rest,	Watts.	27
Welcome, welcome, dear Redeemer,	Anon.	322
We've no abiding city here,	Kelly.	838
What equal honors shall we bring,	Watts.	215
What grace, O Lord, and beauty,	Anon.	669
What shall I render to my God,	Watts.	419
What shall the dying sinner do,	Watts.	249
What sinners value, I resign,	Watts.	832
What various hindrances we meet,	Cowper.	683
When all thy mercies, O my God,	Addison.	402
When along life's thorny road,	Anon.	580
When brighter suns and milder skies,	Peabody.	922
When forth from Egypt's trembling,	Burgess.	943
When from my sight all fades away,	Anon.	827
When gathering clouds around I view,	Grant.	517
When God is nigh, my faith is strong,	Watts.	834
When God revealed his gracious name,	Watts.	406
When I can read my title clear,	Watts.	416
When I survey the wondrous cross,	Watts.	181
When Jordan hushed his waters still,	T. Campbell.	157
When languor and disease invade,	Toplady.	593
When, like a stranger on our sphere,	Montgomery.	174
When marshalled on the nightly,	H. K. White.	472
When musing sorrow weeps the past,	Noel.	904
When my last hour is close at,	Trans. by Bowring.	874
When, my Saviour, shall I be,	Wesley.	744
When on Sinai's top I see,	Montgomery.	365
When our heads are bowed with woe,	Heber.	561
When overwhelmed with grief,	Watts.	563
When shall the voice of singing,	Pratt's Coll.	812
When sins and fears prevailing rise,	Mrs. Steele.	442
When the harvest is past and the,	S. F. Smith.	383
When the worn spirit wants repose,	Edmeston.	60
When thou, my righteous Judge, shall come,	Anon.	880
When thy mortal life is fled,	S. F. Smith.	314
When winds are raging,	Mrs. Stowe. See page	42
While in sweet communion feeding,	Anon.	726
While life prolongs its precious light,	Dwight.	282
While my Redeemer's near,	Mrs. Steele.	558
While o'er our guilty land, O Lord,	Davies.	939
While o'er the deep thy servants sail,	Burgess.	943
While thee I seek, protecting.	Miss Williams.	14
While with ceaseless course the sun,	Newton.	916
Whither, O whither should I fly,	Wesley.	426
Who are these in bright array,	Montgomery.	908
Who, O Lord, when life is o'er,	Lyte.	633
Who shall ascend thy heavenly,	Watts.	628

Alphabetical Index of Hymns.

Whom have we, Lord, in heaven but thee,	*Lyte.*	497	Witness, ye men and angels, now,	*Beddome.*	734
Why do we mourn departing friends,	*Watts.*	844	Worthy the Lamb of boundless sway,	*Shirley.*	219
Why, O God, thy people spurn,	*Hatfield.*	930			
Why on the bending willows hung,	*Anon.*	788	Ye Christian heralds, go proclaim,	*Anon.*	784
Why should our tears in sorrow flow,	*Anon.*	843	Ye hearts with youthful vigor warm,	*Doddridge.*	205
Why should the children of a king,	*Watts.*	223	Ye humble souls, approach your God,	*Mrs. Steele.*	198
Why should we start and fear to die,	*Watts.*	824	Ye humble souls that seek the Lord,	*Doddridge.*	197
Why will ye waste on trifling cares,	*Doddridge.*	286	Ye nations, round the earth rejoice,	*Watts.*	107
Will not that joyful be,.	*Schwienitz.*	614	Ye saints, your music bring,	*Reed.*	277
With all my powers of heart and tongue,	*Watts.*	380	Ye servants of God, your Master proclaim,	*Anon.*	139
With broken heart and contrite sigh,	*Anon.*	332	Ye servants of the Lord,	*Doddridge.*	618
With grateful hearts, with joyful tongues,	*Anon.*	933	Ye who in these courts are found,	*Anon.*	301
With heavenly power, O Lord, defend,	*Anon.*	764	Ye wretched, hungry, starving poor,	*Mrs. Steele.*	293
With joy we hail the sacred day,	*Lyte.*	48	Yes, we trust the day is breaking,	*Kelly.*	819
With joy we meditate the grace,	*Watts.*	514	Yes, welcome was the call,	*Anon.*	962
With reverence let the saints appear,	*Watts.*	136	Your harps, ye trembling saints,	*Toplady.*	304
With songs and honors sounding loud,	*Watts.*	921			
With tearful eyes I look around,	*Anon.*	279	Zion stands with hills surrounded.	*Kelly.*	814

INDEX OF SUBJECTS.

[Figures refer to numbers of hymns.]

Abiding,—
  in Christ, 509, 549, 597, 740.
  Christ in us, 73, 543, 600, 607.
Absence from God, 446, 449, 491, 561.
Accepted time, 305, 327.
Access to God, 263, 307, 693, 694.
Activity, 573, 622, 626.
Adoption, 397, 415, 422.
Advent of Christ,
  at birth. (See Christ.)
  to judgment, 214, 220, 876, 880–884.
Adoration,—
  of God. (See God.)
  of Christ. (See Christ.)
  of Holy Ghost. (See Holy Ghost.)
  of Trinity. (See Trinity.)
Afflictions, 433, 453, 517, 575, 579, 580–584, 589, 590, 594, 596.
Always with us, 196, 535.
Ashamed of Jesus, 499, 542.
Asleep in Jesus, 828, 864, 865, 874, 875.
Aspiration,—
  after God, 3, 417, 452, 458, 491, 495, 553, 561, 646.
  after heaven. (See heaven.)
  after higher life, 221, 449, 455, 459, 505, 555, 585, 588.
Assurance, 223, 369, 397, 409, 415, 416, 424, 442, 479, 515, 599.
Atonement,—
  effect of, on men, 181, 185, 337, 343, 504, 511.
  faith in, 254, 276, 536, 552. (See Trust.)
  glory of God in, 242, 365, 408, 745.
  ground of pardon and hope, 179, 180, 183, 243, 256, 260, 273, 512, 520, 521, 536, 552.
  necessity of, 87, 244, 255, 385, 516.
  origin of, in God's love, 151, 198, 204, 253, 490.
  praise for, 87, 142, 201, 203, 204, 242, 254, 262, 263, 266, 267, 272, 507, 530, 743.
  sufficient and complete, 179, 210, 275, 328, 476, 512, 739.
  universal, 184, 247, 328.

Baptism (children), 759, 760, 763, 765, 766.
Benevolence, 663, 665, 666, 669, 672.
Bible. (See Holy Scriptures.)
Brotherly kindness, 653, 654, 661, 664, 667, 668, 671.
Burial hymns, 329, 830, 862, 863, 865, 906. (See, also, Death.)
Calvary, 179, 180, 183, 266, 365, 503, 546, 739, 745, 747. (See Christ.)
Cares,—
  casting on God, 339, 432, 439, 461, 575, 580, 682, 693, 747.
Charity. (See Love.)
Children and youth, 91, 292, 762, 955, 958, 964.
Childlikeness, 525, 635, 646.
Christ,—
  adoration of, 156, 158, 161, 162, 165, 167, 171, 173, 187, 190, 191, 193, 194, 202, 203, 209, 210, 211, 212, 216–220, 240, 272, 478, 480, 493, 497, 504, 520, 536, 603, 613, 743.
  ascension of, 190, 195.
  birth of, 156, 157, 159, 160, 163–165, 167, 169, 171.
  character of, 172, 176, 665, 669, 671, 682.
  conflict and sufferings, 177–182, 206, 385, 511, 547, 603, 687, 747.
  crucifixion of, 181, 184, 190, 385, 745. (See Calvary and Gethsemane.)
  exaltation and glory, 158, 162, 163, 188, 189, 195, 197, 200, 201, 207, 208, 494, 500, 821.
  intercession of, 186, 276, 325.
  resurrection of, 35, 175, 188, 191, 192, 194, 196, 199, 202, 205.
Christ, names of,—
  Advocate, 248, 276, 307, 476, 589.
  "All in All," 463, 519, 521, 543, 550, 586, 643.
  "Day-Star," 489.
  Fountain, 264, 521, 543, 544, 551.
  "Friend of Sinners," 316, 513, 536, 542.
  High Priest, 514, 515.

Christ, names of,—
  Immanuel, 516, 520.
  Judge, 484, 880, 882–884.
  King, 195, 478, 484, 821.
  "Lamb of God," 254, 546, 549.
  "Light," 489, 533, 543.
  "Refuge," 550, 580, 599, 674, 679.
  "Rock," 512, 582, 586.
  Shepherd, 522, 523, 526, 529, 553, 601.
  Son of God, 158, 485.
  Son of Man, 182, 374, 514, 581.
  "Way, Truth, and Life," 268, 474.
  "Unseen but Precious," 483, 509.
Christians, 490, 534, 631, 633, 671, 703.
Church,—
  divinely founded, 708–710, 718, 723.
  catholic, 657, 717, 753.
  glory of, 534, 716, 720, 722, 723.
  God's care of, 51, 598, 711, 713, 813, 814.
  institutions of. (See Ministry.)
  love to, 714, 719, 720, 723.
  ordinances of. (See Baptism and Lord's Supper.)
Close of worship, 36, 38, 41, 52, 55, 57, 60, 66, 67, 68, 70, 72, 78, 80.
Close of year, 920, 927, 929.
Comforter. (See Holy Ghost.)
Coming to Christ, 291, 332–334, 346, 361, 362, 371, 381, 438, 463, 541, 543, 567, 687, 688, 701.
Coming to God, 436, 578, 681, 700, 705.
Communion,—
  of saints, 51, 652, 655, 656.
  with God and Christ, 58, 307, 452, 464, 465, 536, 593, 686.
  at Lord's table. (See Lord's Supper.)
Confession, 244, 254, 332, 333, 334, 336, 347, 352, 358, 362, 363, 364, 372.
Confidence, 387, 396, 413, 466, 493, 499, 529, 544, 545, 557, 558, 578, 593, 597, 601, 602, 610.
Conflict, 554, 587, 612, 610, 644, 721.
Conscience,—
  peace of, 243, 250, 254, 443, 638, 639, 640.

(394)

Index of Subjects. 395

Consecration, —
  of self, 185, 419, 449, 477, 488, 492, 546, 503, 583, 634, 703, 734, 742, 755.
  of children, 661, 759, 763, 766.
Consolations and comfort, 279, 309, 326, 439, 440, 441, 448, 453, 517, 534, 535, 537, 538, 541, 562, 568, 582, 584, 585, 593, 745, 747, 843–846, 849, 859, 866, 892, 693, 904.
Constancy, 463, 602, 636.
  inconstancy lamented, 492, 518, 695.
Contentment, 444, 525, 559, 591, 601.
Conversion. (See Regeneration, Repentance.)
Conviction. (See Repentance, Heart.)
Corner-stone, 709.
Courage, 387, 573, 612, 616, 622–626, 971.
Covenant, 409, 434, 509, 734, 738, 760, 765, 767.
Cross, at the, 180, 536, 745, 747. (See Lord's Supper.)
  bearing the, 208, 368, 539, 605, 637.
  glorying in, 161, 187, 271, 277, 339, 508, 539, 542.
  salvation by, 179, 180, 187, 243, 277, 438, 488, 516, 520, 547, 552, 739.
Death, 329, 824, 830, 831, 836, 867.
  a sleep, 830, 832, 835, 837, 848, 857, 875.
  blessedness of the dead in Christ, 828, 829, 837, 843–845, 859, 862–865.
  conquered, 875.
  is gain, 841, 904.
  of dear ones, 849.
Decrees, 104, 105, 114, 412.
Dedication, 708, 709, 770, 772, 773, 774.
Delight in God, 405, 417, 428, 445, 461, 495.
Delay, 312–315, 383, 960. (See Repentance and Exhortations.)
Dependence, 121, 271, 405, 461, 528, 599, 600, 601, 606, 624, 628, 648.
Depravity, 241, 244, 251, 258, 265, 266, 267.
Election, 116, 237, 490, 732.
Encouragements, 309, 535, 565, 569, 572, 597, 599, 602, 610, 611, 612, 614, 621, 624, 627, 630, 737.
Eternity, 135, 308, 869, 878, 891, 886.
Evening hymns, 50, 53, 54, 56, 58, 59, 61–66 69, 71, 73–76.
Excellence of Christ, 487, 500, 501, 504.
Exhortations, —
  to activity, etc., 573, 616, 617, 623–626.

Exhortations, —
  to repentance, 274, 281, 283, 285, 286, 292, 297, 300, 301, 305, 310–315, 319, 321, 327, 330, 331, 851, 960.
Faith. (See Confidence and Trust.)
  a grace, 639, 640.
  power of, 638, 639.
  living by, 559, 560, 895.
Faithfulness, 409, 431.
  of God, 578, 599, 641.
Family, 660, 953, 956, 957, 959, 961.
Fasting, 930, 939, 946.
Father, —
  "Our Father," 422, 440, 531, 562, 676.
Fellowship, 657, 658, 660, 685, 753, 757.
Forgiveness, —
  atonement, the ground of, 179, 254, 515, 552, 653.
  joys of, 338, 351, 358, 498, 697.
  prayers for, 310, 332, 335, 336, 337, 402, 518, 528, 546, 552, 684, 687, 701.
Friend of sinners, 390, 461, 476, 481, 513, 536, 542.
Future punishment, 246, 308, 631, 854, 871, 873, 878, 882, 883, 884.
Gentleness, 653, 669, 670.
  of God's commands, 302.
Gethsemane, 180, 182, 729.
God, —
  adoration of, 100–104, 107, 108, 109, 111, 113, 123, 127, 131, 132, 136–142, 151, 201, 387, 388, 391, 425, 493, 608, 696.
  compassions of, 108, 122, 128–130.
  condescension of, 109, 132, 204, 238, 420.
  Creator, 125, 137.
  eternal and self-existent, 19, 103, 155, 869.
  goodness, 107, 124, 143, 408, 429, 437, 441, 466, 595, 601.
  grace and mercy, 107, 118, 142, 143, 151, 389, 397, 402, 407, 418, 425, 441, 473.
  holiness and justice, 117, 124, 143, 251, 256, 257.
  incomprehensibleness, 105, 106, 114, 123, 153.
  love of, 118, 143, 420, 441. (See Love.)
  majesty and glory, 19, 100, 101, 104, 138, 140, 258, 242, 468.
  omnipotence, 101, 111, 115, 138.
  omnipresence, 119, 121, 150, 444, 700.
  omniscience, 119, 120, 152.
  providence. (See Providence.)
  sovereignty, 102, 105, 109–111, 116, 131.

God, —
  spirituality, 117.
  wisdom, 105, 114, 116, 143, 153, 398, 412, 426, 437, 493, 501.
  works of nature and grace, 21, 106, 125, 132, 135, 242, 431.
Gospel. (See Holy Scriptures.)
Grace, —
  growth in, 224, 231, 449, 458, 531, 532, 555, 673, 774.
  salvation by, 178–180, 241, 251–255, 260, 261, 269, 273, 344, 356, 473, 899.
Grieving the Spirit, 283, 315, 330, 342, 382, 539.
Guidance, 37, 224, 411, 522, 526, 528, 537, 545, 558, 564, 591, 606, 696.
Happiness, 145, 431, 444, 531, 588, 631.
Harvest, 928, 931.
Heart, —
  broken and contrite, 334, 361, 455.
  change of, 354, 357, 359, 361, 370, 438.
  hardness of, 354, 357, 359.
  surrender of, 317; 333, 349, 370, 507, 583, 634, 684, 701.
Heaven, —
  aspiration for, 540, 564, 604, 615, 630, 836, 853, 860, 861, 894, 898, 902, 903, 912, 914.
  blessedness of, 584, 614, 860, 864, 907, 910, 912, 913.
  home in, 556, 564, 602, 605, 649, 861, 892, 893, 895, 900, 914.
  rest in, 616, 644, 836, 838, 892, 893, 911.
  joys of saints in, 832, 837, 845, 864, 885–890, 891, 894, 897, 899, 900–905, 907, 908, 912.
Hell, 108, 256, 286, 308, 854, 871.
High Priest, 514, 515.
Holiness, 343, 403, 531, 567, 628, 629, 631, 633, 645.
Holy Ghost, —
  adoration, 225, 457, 797.
  Comforter, 222, 223, 232, 233, 785.
  divine, 147, 226, 231, 235.
  fruits and gifts of, 226, 228–231, 707.
  office of, 222, 224, 225, 234.
  prayers for, 147, 221–224, 226, 228–236, 449, 528, 652, 702, 785.
  strivings of, 222, 285, 303, 312, 359.
Holy Scriptures, 82–100.
Hope, 451, 491, 524, 558, 601, 616, 824, 874.
Humility, 455, 469, 530, 567, 632, 744.
Imitation of Christ, 172, 180, 531, 665–669.
Immanuel, 171, 264, 516, 520.

Immortality, 688, 848, 852.
Incarnation. (See Christ.)
Indwelling, —
　of Christ, 480, 532, 567, 600.
　of Spirit, 222, 223, 228, 229, 234.
Ingratitude, 354, 359, 363.
Installation. (See Ministry.)
Intercession of Christ, 186, 263, 325, 518.
Invitations of the Gospel, 270, 281, 282, 284, 287-299, 302-310, 318, 320, 323, 326-328, 331, 346, 384, 584, 971.
Jews, 786.
Joy, —
　in Christ, 373, 471, 495, 527, 536, 542, 543, 588, 597, 600.
　in God, 393, 401, 417, 422, 428, 484, 613, 620, 740.
　in hope of glory, 369, 494, 611, 614, 615, 740.
　in pardoned sin, 338, 351.
Judgment, 126, 214, 220, 854, 867, 868, 870, 871, 872, 876, 877, 879, 882, 883, 884.
Justification by faith, 256, 273, 339, 340, 379, 512, 516, 874.
Kindness, 663, 665, 666, 667.
Kingdom of Christ, 173, 484, 720, 740, 775, 786, 787, 798, 799, 801-803, 812, 823.
Lamb of God, 254, 264, 274, 362, 546, 549, 731, 751, 994.
Law of God, 92, 243, 257, 494. (See Holy Scriptures.)
Life, —
　brevity of, 825, 826, 842, 850, 856, 858, 859, 913, 915, 926.
　object of, 531, 551, 851, 881.
　uncertainty of, 826, 850, 851, 858, 924.
Likeness to Christ, 44, 172, 456, 531, 567, 667-669. (See Imitation.)
Litany, 374.
Long suffering of God, 283, 344, 356, 363.
Looking to Jesus, 447, 450, 476, 527, 546, 550, 551, 580-582, 597, 600.
Lord's day, 1, 2, 9, 20, 24, 25, 27, 35-37, 42, 47, 48, 60, 66.
Lord's house. (See Sanctuary.)
Lord's Prayer, 676.
Lord's Supper, 724, 726, 727, 729, 730-736, 739, 741, 743, 748-752, 756, 758.
Love, —
　a grace, 530, 650, 654, 664, 669, 707.
　of Christ, 267, 280, 316, 486, 503, 511, 513, 516, 519, 530, 532, 577, 600, 668.

Love, —
　of God, 118, 143, 151, 198, 204, 287, 420, 473, 737.
　to the brethren, 671-673.
　to Christ, 479, 488, 496, 509, 520, 543, 544, 546.
　to the church, 719, 720.
　to God, 404, 428, 445, 497.
Marriage, 962.
Meekness, 172, 525, 642, 667, 669.
Mercy and grace of God, 144, 146, 151, 204, 242, 263, 287, 293, 299, 328, 381, 402, 404, 407, 425, 429, 473.
Mercy-seat, 679, 685, 687, 694.
Ministry, 754, 768, 769, 771, 779-783, 855.
Miracles, 174.
Missions, 775, 778, 784-806, 809, 811, 815-823.
Morning hymns, 11, 13, 17, 27, 33, 35, 44, 46, 47, 65.
Nation. (See Our Country.)
Nature, 21, 112, 431.
Nearing home, 840, 844, 853.
New Year, 916, 918, 922, 923, 925, 926.
Old age, 435, 470, 590, 839.
Omnipotence, Omnipresence, etc. (See God.)
Opening of worship, 1-4, 9, 10, 20-30, 35, 37, 39-46, 79.
Ordination. (See Ministry.)
Our country, 932-940, 944-949, 951, 952.
Pardon. (See Forgiveness.)
Parting hymns, 52, 55-57, 68, 72-81, 659, 702.
Patience, —
　a grace, 595, 596.
　of God, 344, 356, 359, 537.
Peace, 229, 230, 467, 572, 583, 653.
　of conscience. (See Conscience.)
Perseverance, 402, 568, 599, 602, 605, 610, 616, 623, 624, 626.
Pilgrim-fathers, 935, 947, 949.
Pilgrimage, 604-606, 609, 611, 621, 630, 649, 721, 914.
Prayer, 62, 63, 675-707.
Prayers for various objects, —
　all believers, 522.
　acceptance at the judgment, 867, 868, 871, 873, 874, 877, 879-881, 906.
　assurance, 223, 415.
　blessing in worship, 9, 14, 15, 36, 37, 39, 40, 43, 44, 46, 52, 57, 72, 78-80.
　blessing on the church, 710, 711, 728.
　calm and thankful heart, 585, 592.
　childlike spirit, 525, 530, 632, 635.

Prayers for various objects, —
　children, 955.
　Christ's intercession, 325.
　Christ's remembrance, 447, 476, 711.
　Christian unity, etc., 657, 658.
　cleansing grace, 229, 336, 550, 757.
　country, 938-942, 944, 946, 951.
　delivering grace, 257, 532, 561, 587.
　evening blessing, 69, 71, 73-77.
　extension of Christ's kingdom, 746, 775-777, 785, 790, 792, 793, 797, 802, 806-810.
　fruitfulness of the word, 49, 70, 97, 149, 768.
　forgiveness and acceptance, 335, 336, 349, 350, 361, 362, 304, 306, 370, 372, 381, 402, 518, 528, 546.
　gifts of the Spirit, 224, 226, 228, 229, 234.
　grace in the hour of death, 73, 517, 836, 837, 840, 842, 647, 906.
　guidance, 411, 426, 523, 526, 528, 529, 537, 545, 553, 564, 606.
　help in trouble, 563, 580, 674, 678, 745, 747.
　help in sorrow, 517, 546, 581, 582, 589, 594.
　Holy Spirit, 221, 226, 230, 231, 234.
　increase of faith, 423.
　indwelling of Christ, 222, 489, 711, 736.
　indwelling of the Holy Ghost, 234.
　justification and adoption, 379.
　likeness to Christ, 531, 668, 684.
　mercy, 332, 342, 347, 357, 360, 363, 382.
　ministers, 146, 713, 764, 768, 779, 781, 783.
　peace, 38, 467, 583, 600, 711.
　purification, 436, 647, 751.
　rest in Christ, 227, 540, 541.
　reviving, 367, 449, 450, 491, 554.
　sanctification, 230, 231, 532, 533, 546, 552, 604.
　spiritual quickening, 221, 455, 456, 458, 477, 711.
　submission, 440, 442, 595, 596, 644, 716.
　sustaining grace, 585, 825, 827, 860.
Preciousness of Christ, 62, 64, 475, 486, 495, 496, 503, 510, 516, 519, 520, 739, 740.
Pressing onward, 602, 609, 612, 619, 623-625, 636, 644, 649.
Probation, 282, 285, 286, 314, 315, 383.

Index of Subjects. 397

Procrastination. (See Delay.)
Profession of religion, 734, 742, 755, 757.
Promises, 409, 442, 499, 534, 535, 561, 599.
Prophet, Priest, and King. 169, 275.
Providence of God, 392, 402, 407, 469, 925.
  delight in, 14, 421, 429, 469, 525, 601.
  deliverances of. 388, 406, 667.
  trust in, 14, 129, 130, 134, 396. 400, 411, 426, 429, 469, 537, 539, 596, 601, 692.
  wisdom of, 288, 412, 422, 469.
Purity, 567, 647, 965.
Punishment. (See Future Punishment.)
Redemption. (See Atonement.)
Refuge, 122, 387, 390, 471, 550, 552, 599, 602, 674, 869.
Regeneration, —
  God's work, 234, 252, 258, 259.
  necessity of, 241, 244, 247, 251, 252, 258, 359, 380.
  prayers for, 244, 245, 258, 357, 359.
Renunciation, —
  of self, 339, 368, 438, 503, 541.
  of the world, 389, 414, 452, 454, 825, 832.
Repentance, 244, 254, 257, 332-337, 342-347, 350, 354, 356, 361-364, 370, 372, 377, 381, 385, 436, 438, 462, 518, 553, 554, 576, 687, 695.
Resignation. (See Submission.)
Rest, —
  in Christ. 249, 343, 376, 424, 540, 541, 544, 576, 597, 643, 679.
  in God, 154, 304, 308, 425, 426, 437, 508, 595, 678, 705.
  in heaven. (See Heaven.)
Resurrection, 740, 832-835, 841, 848, 852, 854, 856, 873-875.

Retirement, 464, 465, 588, 682, 686, 698.
Revivals, 367, 449, 450, 491, 554, 804.
Righteousness, —
  Lord our, 273, 340, 379, 504, 512.
  of faith, 339, 340, 379.
  robe of, 340, 379.
Rock of Ages, 689.
Sabbath. (See Lord's Day.)
Sacraments. (See Baptism and Lord's Supper.)
Salvation by Christ, 158, 179, 201, 243, 247, 249, 250, 251, 254, 260, 274, 362, 376, 507, 512, 516, 521, 526, 536, 542, 547, 899, 901.
Sanctification, 224, 523, 526, 531-533, 546, 549, 552, 571, 604, 673.
Sanctuary, 2-4, 9, 10, 15, 22, 23, 28-31, 34, 40, 43, 46, 67.
Seamen, 934, 943.
Seasons, 917-924.
Secret prayer, 464, 465, 680, 682.
Self-denial, 245, 629, 641. (See Consecration.)
Self-examination, 117, 119, 120, 152, 436, 479.
Shepherd, —
  Christ a, 522, 523, 526, 529.
  God a, 134, 396, 601, 610.
Sickness, 593.
Sin. (See, also, Depravity.)
  conviction of, 244, 247, 251, 256, 257, 380.
  man's condition in, 241, 244, 251, 256, 258.
  punishment of, 108, 246, 334, 336, 631.
Simplicity, 525, 632, 635.
Social worship, 652, 690, 697, 698.
Sovereignty of God, —
  in government, 105, 109, 110, 398.
  in providence, 153, 422, 482, 595, 596.
  in redemption, 116, 250, 482.
Steadfastness, 602, 617.

Submission, 440, 531, 590-595, 616.
Sufficiency of Christ, 264, 266, 474 512, 519, 523, 535, 543, 544, 546.
Sun of righteousness, 489, 698.
Surrender of self, 317, 322, 333, 353, 370, 438, 476, 507, 554.
Sympathy, —
  of Christ, 439, 514, 515, 517, 538, 580.
  of Christians, 661, 666-669.
Temperance, 950.
Thanksgiving, 920-927.
Throne of grace. (See Mercy-seat.)
Time. (See Life.)
Trials, 430, 460, 537, 562, 563, 579, 587, 594-597.
Trinity, 1, 216, 237, 239, 375.
Trust, —
  in Christ, 241, 250, 341, 362, 364, 376, 423, 442, 470, 474, 516, 536, 546, 547, 549, 550, 552, 557, 590, 591, 602, 745, 747, 840.
  in God, 166, 348, 390, 393, 394, 427, 439-441, 505, 597, 643, 674, 704, 706.
Union, —
  among Christians, 657, 660, 661, 671.
  with Christ, 492.
  with saints in glory, 655, 656.
Waiting on God, 88, 348, 394, 427, 433, 558.
Watchfulness, 566, 571, 574, 618, 619, 651.
Way, Truth, and Life, 268, 474.
Way of salvation. (See Salvation by Christ.)
Well-spent life, 830.
Worship, —
  delight in, 1-4, 10, 23, 30-33, 40-48, 690, 714, 716.
Wrath of God. 877-879.
Wrestling with God, 513.
Zion. (See Church.)

INDEX OF TEXTS.

[Figures refer to numbers of hymns.]

GENESIS.
1: 2	797
5: 24	444, 449, 458
6: 3	285
8: 9	304
17: 7	765
17: 19	765
19: 7	328
24: 31	757
24: 63	464
26: 24	509
28: 10-22	411, 555
28: 16	34
28: 17	7
32: 24	513
45: 5, 7	153

EXODUS.
15: 2	24
15: 11	482
15: 17	791
15: 18	111
16: 23	12, 17
19: 18	365
25: 22	685
33: 14	444
33: 22	552
34: 6	408

LEVITICUS.
25: 8, 13	274

NUMBERS.
10: 29	757
23: 10	841
24: 17	472

DEUTERONOMY.
11: 19	956, 957
12: 9	308
26: 17, 18	734, 755
31: 6	409
32: 3	101
34: 1	900
34: 1	630

JOSHUA.
1: 5	977

4: 21, 22	957
10: 12, 13	138

JUDGES.
8: 4	602

RUTH.
1: 16, 17	742

1st SAMUEL.
1: 22, 28	763
2: 6-9	109, 392
3: 18	105, 590
7: 12	507
1: 12, 13	677

2d SAMUEL.
12: 23	848
22: 9-12	140
22: 47	100

1st KINGS.
8: 39	120
18: 44	804

1st CHRONICLES.
4: 10	78
16: 12	151
29: 11-13	19, 136

2d CHRONICLES.
1: 10, 11	646
6: 2	716
6: 41	773, 782, 779
14: 11	450

NEHEMIAH.
9: 5	24
13: 19	9, 17, 27, 42
13: 14-24	447

ESTHER.
4: 16	291, 687

JOB.
1: 21	706

5: 9	50
7: 16	86
7: 18	13
9: 1-10	25
11: 7	10
13: 15	153, 67
19: 25, 26	186, 442, 85
23: 3	44
29: 2	449, 459, 55
33: 13	105, 114, 11
33: 15	6
38: 7	193, 79
38: 11	13

PSALMS.
1	63
2: 6	48
3	6
4	6
4: 4	43
5	1
5: 3	4
6: 1, 2	36
7	12
8	13
8: 3, 4	137, 42
10: 14	10
11	67
11: 4	119, 12
15: 698	63
16: 11	444, 85
17	83
17: 8	7
17: 15	54
18: 35	53
19	82, 88, 125, 57
19: 8-11	9
20	37
22	177, 45
23	134, 306, 529, 558, 6C
24	188, 19
25	56
26: 8	3, 7, 16, 3
27	348, 71
27: 4, 5	3, 7, 16, 3
27: 9	47
27: 14	39
30	338, 45

(398)

67: 3, 5	24, 103	131	479, 632	55: 6	282, 286, 315	**AMOS.**	
68	101	133	660, 707	55: 7, 8	282, 297, 312	4: 12	314, 870
68: 19, 123, 129, 130, 402, 928		134	107, 131	56: 7	697	**MICAH.**	
69	335	136	144, 433	57: 15	109, 334	2: 10	644, 838
70	430	137	564, 720	57: 21	246, 257	4: 1-7	791
71	433, 481	138	389, 621	58: 6, 7	628, 683	6: 6-8	628, 633, 666, 667
71: 15, 16	340, 379	139	119, 120, 121, 152	58: 13, 14	2, 3, 27, 30, 42	**NAHUM.**	
72	786, 823	141	651	59: 1, 2	459, 462		
73	246, 405, 497	143: 2	256	60: 2	776	1: 15	769, 813
73: 25	145, 417	144: 12	955, 960	60: 18	534	**HABAKKUK.**	
74: 16	135	145	123, 407	61: 10	340		
77: 11-14	137	146	89, 108, 386	64: 6	858	2: 14	812, 823
78	857	147	921	66: 8	822	3: 2	462
79	13, 134, 396	148	141	**JEREMIAH.**		3: 4	104
80	710	149: 1	193	1: 5	767	3: 17-19	324, 400, 559
80: 14-16	221	**PROVERBS.**		1: 29	333	**ZECHARIAH.**	
84	10, 15, 16, 30, 31,	1: 24, 32	282	2: 13	244, 344, 459	1: 5	842
84: 11	150, 386, 429	3: 6	591	3: 22	344, 350	4: 6	725
85: 6	221, 354, 711	4: 18	555, 986	8: 20	302, 363	9: 9	207
87	723	8: 17	205	8: 22	247	9: 12	241
88	282	18: 24	316	10: 10	155	13: 1	264, 328
89	94, 136	23: 26	317, 370	10: 23	153, 426	13: 6	342, 363
89: 18	198, 386	**ECCLESIASTES.**		12: 5	383	14: 8	778
90	155, 869	9: 10	282, 621	13: 16	856	14: 9	655, 715, 786, 803
91	165, 392, 506	11: 1, 2	665	14: 7, 8	43, 350, 456	**MALACHI.**	
92	2, 23	11: 6	573	17: 7, 8	3, 108, 413	1: 11	786, 823
92: 12-14	628, 633	12: 1	292	22: 10	844, 850	3: 2	668, 860
93	115, 238	12: 7	830	23: 6	344	3: 7	297, 314
94: 12	453	**CANTICLES.**		29: 13	291, 331, 346	3: 16	652
95	131	2: 4	724	31: 3	732	3: 18	246
96: 4	101, 238	2: 16	495	**LAMENTATIONS.**		4: 2	816
96: 13	873, 877, 882	5: 10-15	487	1: 4	778	**MATTHEW.**	
97	110, 111, 214	**ISAIAH.**		3: 23	65	1: 21	406
98	163	1: 2	359	3: 24	445	2: 2	164, 800
100	107, 127	1: 11	117, 629	3: 26	348, 525, 583, 674	2: 9	472
100: 4	8, 51, 720	7: 14	438, 520	3: 33	466	2: 10	104
101: 2	390	9: 6, 7	165, 167, 169	**EZEKIEL.**		4: 19	318
102	710	21: 11	800	2: 6, 7	784	4: 22	545
103	128, 129, 130, 151	25: 4	166, 392, 550	3: 18-27	618, 782, 784	5: 3	744
103: 15	826	26: 3	392, 413	18: 31	286, 312, 381	5: 5	642
103: 16	831	28: 16	25, 496, 772	22: 14	314, 383	5: 6	428, 443, 451
103: 17, 18	738	29: 19	403, 602	33: 11	286, 312	5: 8	567
104	21	32: 2	552	**DANIEL.**		5: 14-16	629
104: 13-15	135, 921, 922	33: 17	630	2: 44	718	6: 10	440, 770, 775
107: 43	118, 392, 402, 493	35: 8-10	611, 627	7: 13, 14	786, 803	6: 10-13	676
108	123, 419	40: 9	813	9: 3-19	946	6: 19-21	389
109: 3, 4	669	40: 11	526	9: 7	342	6: 25-34	470
110: 3	259, 359	40: 28	624	**HOSEA.**		6: 33	432
113: 5	109	43: 1, 2,	281, 599	5: 15	440, 453, 594	7: 7	694, 701
114	948	45: 7	65	6: 1	344	7: 13, 14	245, 628, 633
116	404, 419, 425	49: 15	737	10: 12	436	8: 24-26	547
117	103	50: 10	304, 398, 559	14: 1	350	9: 24	423
118	8, 12, 25	51: 12, 13	453, 542	**JOEL.**		9: 38	768
119	91, 92, 95, 99	52: 1, 2	712 790	2: 12	344	10: 24	477
119: 51	439	52: 7	769	2: 13	117	10: 25	477, 539, 677
119: 105	96	53	255, 273	2: 17	711, 946	11: 19	316, 362
121	154, 166, 387	53: 4-6	163, 311			11: 28	279, 284, 309, 310
122	18, 20	54: 8	502				371, 584, 686
125	413, 814	55: 1, 2	293			12: 19	669
126	406, 565, 569						
127	824, 827						
128	956						

Ref	Pages	Ref	Pages	Ref	Pages	Ref	Pages
12: 46-50	316	5: 8	244	4: 24	117	5: 41	477, 542, 637
13: 8	49, 97	5: 11	545	5: 39	82, 83, 88, 95	7: 38	721
15: 25	450	5: 31-32	333, 362	6: 37	328, 333	7: 60	528
16: 24	245, 477	6: 21	453	6: 39	409, 599	10: 33	696
16: 26	246, 2~6, 399	6: 36	668	6: 44	258, 259	11: 23	324
17: 8	373, 486	6: 38	666, 667	6: 68	377, 391, 463, 634	14: 17	408, 921
18: 1-5	525, 635	7: 34	316	7: 37	323, 543	14: 25	315, 319
18: 20	695	8: 5-15	49	8: 12	489, 533	15	746
19: 14	761, 763	8: 23-25	943	9: 4	622	16: 9	820
20: 28	211	9: 23	368, 369, 637	9: 5	489, 533	16: 13	702
21: 22	684, 694	9: 46-48	525, 635	10	955	16: 28	245
22: 4	293	9: 57	634	10: 11	255	17: 25, 26	124, 133
24: 27	884	10: 29-37	668	10: 14	497	17: 28	121, 133, 152, 198
24: 30	879	10: 39	588	10: 11-16	134, 396, 522	17: 31	868, 877
24: 44	867, 868	10: 42	286, 505, 634		526, 529, 537, 558	20: 28	618
25: 6	740, 821	11: 2-4	676	11: 23	866	20: 35	665
25: 13	618, 870	12: 22-31	470	11: 25	329	21: 14	440, 591
25: 34	882	12: 32	610	12: 12-15	213	24: 16	403, 443
25: 40	672, 868	12: 35-38	618, 619, 870	12: 21	586	24: 25	305, 327
25: 46	880	14: 17	290	12: 32	185, 299	26: 22	916
26: 29	752	14: 22	203, 204, 296	12: 35, 36	489		
26: 36-42	179, 180, 206	14: 26-33	245, 389, 832	13: 1	671	1: 16	ROMANS. 240, 341, 477
26: 41	619	15: 7	351	13: 7	562		499, 542
26: 42	440, 591, 704	15: 11-32	281, 297, 333, 344	13: 9	343	1: 20	112, 132, 431
26: 64	876		363, 518	14: 2	195, 909	1: 21	359
26: 75	361	15: 17-21	290, 345	14: 3	195, 540	1: 22-32	241, 244
27: 30	536	18: 1	693	14: 6	268, 543	2: 1	670
27: 45	353	18: 13	332, 333, 336	14: 18	600	2: 4	250
28: 6	180, 191, 192, 197, 202	18: 16	763	14: 19	442	2: 7	612
28: 20	533, 616	19: 10	161, 267	14: 27	572, 583	3: 10-20	241, 243, 244
		19: 41	485	15: 2	594	3: 21, 22	242, 251, 254
MARK.		21: 1-5	665	15: 4	570	3: 23	241, 244
2: 17	333, 362	21: 36	460, 619, 682	15: 5	324, 492	3: 25	204, 263, 367
3: 35	316	22: 19	730, 731	15: 7	684, 694	4: 5	254, 340
4: 37-41	587, 598, 943	23: 33	365	15: 9	316	4: 15	243, 257
6: 46	14, 158, 464	22: 42	178, 179, 440, 591	15: 16	259, 273	5: 1	204, 263, 337
7: 37	412		646	16: 7	222	5: 3-5	433, 453
8: 34	477, 626, 637	22: 43	182	16: 8-13	221, 224, 225, 234	5: 5	221, 222, 224, 225
8: 38	477, 499, 542	22: 62	485	16: 16	604	5: 8	270, 440
9: 24	423	23: 34	361	17: 9	703	5: 10	516, 694
10: 14, 15	464, 469, 525	23: 42	447, 476	17: 16	556, 644	5: 12	241, 244
	635, 736, 765	24: 1-7	35, 191, 202	17: 17-19	83, 88, 91	7: 9	257, 554
10: 28-30	368, 369, 832	24: 5	205	17: 21, 22	654, 655, 715	7: 24	205
10: 32	176	24: 26	190	17: 23, 24	492, 540, 887	8: 8	252, 256, 258
11: 8-70	213	24: 29	64, 77	19	180, 547	8: 14	221, 223, 224, 307
11: 33-37	574, 619	24: 32	98, 652	19: 25	539	8: 15	415
14: 7-9	665	24: 34	202	19: 30	180, 184, 210, 536	8: 28	153, 410
14: 24	758	24: 50	78	20: 1-18	192, 197	8: 31-37	368, 369
14: 26	603	24: 53	30	20: 19, 7, 22, 28, 45, 64, 652		8: 35-39	392, 495
14: 32-42	179, 182, 440, 591			20: 21	572	9: 5	173, 211
15	180, 547	JOHN.		20: 24-29	28, 423, 732	9: 15-18	114, 116
15: 46	830	1: 9	251, 533	21: 15-17	436, 479, 577	10: 3	243, 259
16	12, 191, 192, 197	1: 12	397, 442, 490			10: 4	340, 572
16: 15-20	784	1: 13	258, 259	ACTS.		10: 5-10	333
		1: 14	156, 267	1: 7	114, 116, 153	10: 14	782, 783
LUKE.		1: 29	254, 264, 274, 362	1: 11	272	10: 15	769
1: 46	108		546, 549, 731, 751	2: 16	746	11: 33	114
1: 47	520	3: 3	250, 380	2: 39	760	12: 4, 5	655, 715
1: 78	533, 805	3: 14, 15	311, 546	2: 44-46	664	12: 10	664
2: 8-14	157, 159, 160, 161,	3: 17	204, 287	4: 12	243, 250	12: 12	494, 593
	164, 165, 167, 169, 171,	4: 16	523	4: 32	664	12: 15	663, 668
	272, 278						
4: 18	161, 174, 662	4: 21	32, 45	5: 30	782, 784	13: 11, 12	204, 617, 630, 840

13: 14 . . . 172, 340	6: 10 . . . 493, 410	4: 11 444	TITUS.
14: 7, 8 395	6: 18 . . . 397, 422	4: 13 560	2: 6 292
15: 4 . . . 88, 93, 96	7: 1 647	COLOSSIANS.	2: 10-13 . . . 629
15: 8 765	8: 9 183		2: 14 477
15: 30 . . 714, 779	9: 6 . . 666, 667, 668	1: 14 . 181, 254, 264, 512	3: 5-7 . 273, 356, 743
16: 25-27 . . 52, 220	9: 15 . 187, 204, 242, 272 287, 480	1: 15-17 . . 211, 216 1: 18 753	HEBREWS.
1st CORINTHIANS.	13: 5 . . . 436, 577	1: 19 544	1: 3 156, 173, 175, 207, 493
1: 8, 9 . . . 400, 500	13: 14 81	1: 20 . . . 277, 904	1: 6 212
1: 10 . . . 660, 664	GALATIANS.	1: 21 . . . 338, 356	1: 8, 9 173, 189, 199, 211
1: 22-24 . . 271, 516		2: 9 . . 265, 275, 520	1: 8, 9 173, 189, 199, 211
1: 30 . . . 251, 340	1: 4 . . . 267, 272	2: 10 275	2: 3 . . . 252, 315
2: 2 . . 264, 277, 536	2: 16 . . . 243, 273	3: 1-4 . 389, 403, 551	2: 6, 7 . . . 132
2: 4 149	2: 20 187, 260, 339, 492, 546	3: 12 . 666, 668, 744	2: 9 208
2: 9, 10 . . 886, 897	3: 13 . . 254, 379, 552	3: 14 . . . 650, 654	2: 17 514
2: 11-14 . . 224, 234	3: 28 . . . 656, 661	3: 15 . 443, 467, 572, 583	2: 18 . . . 514, 517
3: 6, 7 . . . 259, 271	4: 4, 5 . 156, 204, 287, 397	3: 17 . . . 395, 551	3: 13-15 . 305, 315, 327
3: 16, 17 . 147, 532, 567	4: 6 397	4: 2 . 619, 675, 677, 696	330, 383
3: 21-23 . . 410, 557	5: 14 . . . 650, 654	4: 3 . . 714, 764, 779	4: 1 . . . 207, 426
6: 11 . 261, 269, 553, 732	6: 1 670		4: 7 . . . 282, 327
6: 19 . . . 532, 567	6: 9 . . . . 573, 622	1st THESSALONIANS.	4: 9 5, 42, 864, 892, 893,
9: 24 624	6: 14 . 181, 339, 414, 506	4: 3 . . . 222, 531	4: 14-16 128, 514, 517, 561
9: 25-27 . . . 626	542, 551	4: 14-18 . 828, 833, 873	4: 16 . . 665, 667, 664
10: 4 552	6: 15 259	876, 877, 879, 882	5: 7 514
10: 31 395	EPHESIANS.	4: 17 853	6: 12 . . 645, 699, 901
11: 26 727		5: 2 979	6: 18 . . . 442, 599
11: 28 436	1: 3-5 . 116, 204, 287	5: 6 . . . 460, 619	6: 19 . . . 398, 630
12: 27 492	1: 7 . . . 201, 218	5: 8 . . . 616, 617	6: 20 . . . 195, 201
13: 1-3 . . 650, 664	1: 10 . . 655, 786, 821	5: 10 339	7: 25 . 254, 264, 325, 376
13: 4 670	1: 11 . . . 114, 116	5: 16 . 471, 484, 620, 740	7: 26 475
13: 12 . . . 457, 482	1: 19-23 . 175, 189, 200	5: 17 663	9: 12-14 . . 254, 475
13: 13 . 653, 654, 707	2: 4-8 . 251, 253, 269	5: 19 342	9: 24 . . . 186, 325
14: 20 . . . 525, 635	2: 12-14 . 362, 385, 549	5: 23, 24 . 38, 409, 673	9: 27 852, 868, 872, 879
15: 3 353	3: 15 655	5: 25 . . . 764, 779	9: 28 . . . 376, 796
15: 10 . 253, 269, 507, 521	4: 4-8 . . . 162, 657		10: 19-22 . . 687, 694
15: 19 562	4: 30-32 . 315, 342, 653	2d THESSALONIANS.	11 . . 638, 630, 756, 901
15: 20 191	5: 14-16 . . 313, 574	1: 7-10 214, 873, 876, 877	11: 8 640
15: 24, 25 . . 173, 200	6: 4 956	879, 882	11: 13 648
15: 36 863	6: 11-14 . . 617, 623	3: 13 . 573, 616, 622	11: 16 696
15: 55-57 . . 190, 829	6: 18 700		11: 25 . . . 389, 632
15: 58 . . . 573, 622	6: 18-20 . . . 779	1st TIMOTHY.	12: 1 . . . 625, 899
16: 2 . . . 661, 665	PHILIPPIANS.	1: 15 . 267, 333, 363, 376	12: 2 . . 311, 546, 597
16: 13. 612, 617, 619, 623, 626		987	12: 3 . . 172, 539, 669
	1: 6 . . . 409, 470, 577	1: 17 . . . 100, 103	12: 6-11 422, 442, 579. 640
2d CORINTHIANS.	1: 21 . 551, 605, 843, 904	2: 5, 6 . . 183, 372, 511	12: 18-25 . . 655, 656
1: 2 443	1: 23 . . . 853, 860	2: 8 45	13: 5 599
1: 5 582	1: 29 369	3: 16 155	13: 8 538
1: 11 . . . 714, 779	2: 6-8 . 156, 216, 547	4: 16 . . . 618, 782	13: 14 . . . 556, 838
1: 12 443	2: 9 . . . 200, 250	6: 17-19 . 623, 624, 626, 734	13: 20, 21 . 38, 57, 434
1: 20 . . . 599, 657	2: 10 . 173, 207, 209, 218	6: 17-19 . . 666, 667	JAMES.
1: 22 . . 222, 223, 229	777, 785	2d TIMOTHY.	
2: 15, 16 . . . 271	2: 12 . . . 286, 315		1: 5 . 99, 236, 646, 654
3: 18 510	2: 13 . 225, 230, 231, 235	1: 8 . . 477, 499, 542	1: 6 423
4: 10 745	258, 259	1: 12 . . . 470, 499	1: 17 . . . 133, 400
4: 14 . . . 818, 832	3: 7-9 181, 339, 454, 488,	2: 3 . 616, 617, 619	1: 27 . . 666, 667, 668
5: 1 . . 195, 895, 904	506	2: 19 . . . 413, 599	2: 14-26 . 117, 629, 659
5: 7 559	3: 13, 14 . . 616, 625	2: 22 91	4: 13, 14 128, 826, 851, 869
5: 8 . 416, 844, 860, 887	3: 21 . . . 848, 852	3: 15 91	915, 924
5: 10 . . 868, 872, 679	4: 4 387, 471, 484, 620, 740	3: 15-17 . 83, 88, 93, 96	5: 8 849
5: 14 . . 187, 241, 480	4: 7 . . . . 38, 572	4: 8 . . . 614, 630	5: 13 589
6: 2 . . . 305, 327	4: 6 629	4: 18 . 409, 413, 493	5: 19-20 . . . 670

402 Index of Texts.

1st PETER.

Ref	Pages
1: 5	409, 418, 470
1: 7	594
1: 8	483, 486, 504, 509
1: 19	243, 254, 385
1: 24	128, 825, 826
2: 6	25, 599
2: 7	275, 486, 487, 496, 504, 510, 570
2: 9	201, 218
2: 24	183, 254, 255, 273, 376, 385, 547
2: 25	255, 356, 526
3: 16	443
3: 18	183, 254, 385, 994
4: 17, 18	314, 383, 868, 870, 880
5: 4	779, 784
5: 7	14, 58, 62, 575, 674

2d PETER.

Ref	Pages
1: 10	416
1: 19	489
3: 3, 4	399
3: 7-12	877
3: 10	873, 877, 879
3: 13	796

1st JOHN.

Ref	Pages
1: 7	254, 264
2: 1	186, 518
2: 2	294, 552, 994
2: 6	172, 669
2: 8	489, 533
2: 17	825, 826
3: 1, 2	397, 422, 490
3: 2	540, 832, 897
3: 14	490
3: 16	185, 353
3: 17	663, 668
4: 7	259, 650
4: 8	118, 143, 441
4: 9	204, 242, 287
4: 10	242
4: 16	118, 143, 441
4: 19	530
4: 21	604
5: 4	495, 639
5: 10	222, 223

JUDE.

Ref	Pages
14, 15	877, 879, 882
24,	413
24, 25	493

REVELATION.

Ref	Pages
1: 5-8	220, 876
1: 18	186, 189
2: 4	449, 459
3: 2, 3	460, 619
3: 20	6, 283, 307
4: 8-11	201, 209, 218, 696
5	201, 209, 215, 218, 240
5: 9	209, 218, 889
5: 12	240
6: 14-17	876
7: 9-12	139, 209, 218
7: 11-17	899, 907, 908
11: 15	484, 786, 787, 801
14: 3	201, 218
14: 13	829, 864
15: 3, 4	203. 209
19: 3	608
19: 6	111, 801
20: 6	873
20: 12-15	868, 877, 879, 882
21: 1-5	21, 615, 644, 796, 843, 859, 862, 903, 906
21: 10	902
21: 23	885, 887
21: 27	252, 897
22: 3, 4	885, 887, 910
22: 17	296, 303, 306, 323, 331
22: 20	836, 876, 890

ALPHABETICAL INDEX OF TUNES.

[*Figures in this Index refer to the pages of the book.*]

Adrian, ... 284	Dalston, ... 56	Hamden, . . . 259, 321
Alford, ... 105, 348	Dana, ... 243	Hardy, ... 280
Alsace, ... 51	Darwin, ... 82	Harmony, ... 139
Altar, ... 178	Dawn, ... 154, 331	Hartford, ... 194
Ambrose, ... 157	Dedham, . . . 150, 218	Harvest-Home, . . . 366
America, ... 372	Deliverance, ... 91	Hatton, . . . 248, 339
Amsterdam, ... 357	Denfield, ... 191	Haverhill, ... 341
Arden, ... 167, 375	Dennis, ... 334	Hawes, ... 351
Ariel, ... 57, 221	Denton, ... 276	Haydn, ... 140, 214
Arlington, . . . 144, 298	Dies Irae, ... 344	Heber, . . . 192, 206
Aspiration, ... 132	Dorman, . . . 292, 302	Hebron, ... 72, 273
Atwater, ... 106, 215	Downs, ... 340	Herbert, ... 166
Autumn, ... 231	Duke St., ... 118, 364	Herschel, ... 185
Ava, ... 163	Dundee, ... 142	Holland, ... 202
		Holley, ... 67
Balerma, ... 194	Eastland, ... 143	Holmes, ... 61
Barby, ... 198, 370	Easton, . . . 282, 348	Horton, . . . 150, 247
Beautiful River, . . . 379	Eckhardstein, . . . 170	How Calm and Beautiful, . 123
Beulah, ... 354	Ein' Feste Burg, . . . 187	Hullah, ... 226
Behold the Lamb of God, . 114	Elijah, ... 277	Hummel, ... 266
Bemerton, . . . 203, 223	Elparan, ... 64	Huntington, . . . 60, 209
Benevento, ... 361	Elyria, ... 131, 330	Hymn, ... 65, 212
Bera, ... 233, 327	Ernan, . . . 129, 234, 304	
Bethany, ... 240	Eventide, ... 74	In Memoriam (chant), . . 353
Bloom, ... 336	Ever Thine, Only Thine, . 220	Inverness, ... 245
Bonar, ... 168		Invitation, . . . 68, 132
Bond, ... 137, 272	Federal St., . . . 148, 201, 328	Italian Hymn, . . . 134
Bowdoin Square, . . . 169, 362	Frederick, ... 337	
Boylston, ... 285, 306	Flee as a Bird, . . . 383	Jesus, Most Holy, . . 160
Brandt, ... 186		Jesus, still lead on, . . 235
Brastow, ... 160	Galena, . . . 190, 210	Jesus, Tender Saviour, . . 377
Brattle Street, . . . 54	Gardner, ... 100	Judgment Hymn, . . 126, 342
Brest, ... 346	Geer, ... 208, 294	
Brownell, ... 97	Gentle Call, ... 163	Keble, ... 70
Brunswick, ... 347	Gentle Shepherd, . . . 376	
Burlington, ... 274	Germania, ... 237	Laban, ... 264
Burton, ... 172	Germany, ... 197	Leighton, ... 58
	Gilead, ... 265	Lent, ... 160
Calm, ... 241, 271	Glory to Jesus, . . . 377	Linwood, ... 329
Calvary, ... 182	Goodman, . . . 102, 275	Lisbon, ... 59
Carver Street, . . . 261	Gorton, ... 335	Litany, . . . 177, 238
Cassel, ... 300	Grace, ... 228	Looking Off, ... 254
Christmas, ... 98	Great Shepherd of the Sheep, . 376	Louvan, . . . 90, 303
Come to Me, ... 381	Greenfield, ... 250	Lucy, ... 196
Come, ye Disconsolate, . 161	Greenport, ... 253	Luton, ... 88
Comfort, ... 249	Greenville, ... 159	Lyons, ... 99
Corinth, ... 332	Greenwood, ... 263	
Corner Stone, ... 224	Grostete, ... 211	Manoah, . . . 128, 269
Coronation, ... 124		Marlow, ... 84
	Hagar, ... 195	Mary, ... 116
Dallas, ... 268	Hamburg, . . . 138, 164	

(403)

Alphabetical Index of Tunes.

Mear,	374	Pond,	229, 378	St. Thomas,
Medfield,	113	Portuguese Hymn,	253	Stephens, ... 83,
Mendon,	112			Still-Waters,
Mercy,	174	Rathbun,	222, 296	Stockwell, . . . 158,
Meribah,	179, 345	Reo,	225	Stonefield,
Michael,	55, 109	Rest,	355	Sweetland,
Migdol,	80	Retreat,	283	Telemann's Chant,
Milton,	101, 110	Rhine,	352	Thatcher,
Missionary Chant,	127, 312, 368	Robinson,	256	The Saviour's Call,
Missionary Hymn,	322	Rock of Ages,	239	Thompson,
Montgomery,	338	Rockingham,	117, 373	Though Faint, yet Pursuing,
Mt. Blanc,	262	Rodman,	108	Through the Valley,
Munich,	356	Rome,	267	Underwood,
		Rosehill,	205	Uxbridge, ... 50,
Naomi,	252	Rosefield,	153, 297	Veni Sancte Spiritus,
Nashville,	81			Vesper,
Naumann,	349	Salem,	291	Waldo,
Nazareth,	79	Sanford,	343	Ward, ... 93,
Newman,	133	Scotland,	162	Warsaw,
Newton,	52	Sebastian,	171	Warwick, ... 53,
Nuremburg,	119, 301, 365	Serene,	155	Watchman,
		Seymour,	246	Watchman, tell us,
O Sacred Head,	236	Sheldon,	60	Webb, ... 49,
O Saviour Dear,	382	Shepherd-call,	181	Weber,
Oaksville,	318	Sicily,	75, 125	Weberton,
Old Hundred,	87	Silver St.,	96	Webster,
Olivet,	235	Sojourner's Song,	260	When the Harvest is Past,
Olmutz,	188, 295	South Church,	175	Will not that joyful be,
		Spanish Hymn,	216	Williams, ... 92,
Park St.,	94	Stand up for Jesus,	319	Wilmot,
Parting Song,	71	St. Ann's,	62	Wilson,
Penitence,	173	St. Bride's,	242	Woodstock, . . . 204,
Pentonville,	95	St. Denys,	115	Zamora,
Peterboro',	314	St. Martin's,	107, 315	Zion,
Pilgrim Song,	258, 366	St. Michael's,	310	
Pleyel's Hymn,	63, 287	St. Petersburg,	367	

METRICAL INDEX OF TUNES.

[Figures refer to the pages of the book.]

L. M.

Alford,	105, 348
Alsace,	51
Bera,	233, 327
Brandt,	186
Brownell (six lines),	97
Brunswick,	347
Corner-stone (six lines),	224
Dorman,	292
Duke St.,	118, 364
Easton,	282, 348
Elparan,	64
Elyria,	330
Ernan,	129, 234
Ever thine (Pec.),	220
Federal St.,	148, 201, 328
Germany,	197
Gilead,	265
Greenfield,	250
Grostete,	211
Harmony,	130
Hebron,	72, 273
Hamburg,	138, 164
Herbert,	166
Herschel,	185
Holland,	202
Holmes,	61
Hullah (six lines),	226
Judgment Hymn,	126, 342
Keble,	70
Linwood,	329
Louvan,	90, 303
Luton,	88
Mary,	116
Mendon,	112
Migdol,	80
Missionary Chant,	127, 312, 368
Nazareth,	79
Old Hundred,	87
Park St.,	94
Parting Song,	71
Retreat,	283
Rockingham,	117, 373
Rome,	267
Rose Hill,	205
Sanford,	343
St. Petersburgh (six lines),	367
Stonefield,	103
Uxbridge,	50, 270
Ward,	93, 305
Weberton,	200

C. M.

Arden,	107, 375
Arlington,	144, 298
Atwater,	106, 215
Balerma,	194
Barby,	198, 370
Bemerton,	203, 223
Bonar,	168
Bond,	137, 272
Bowdoin Square,	109, 362
Brattle St.,	54
Burlington,	274
Christmas,	98
Corinth,	332
Coronation,	124
Darwin,	82
Dedham,	150, 218
Deliverance,	91
Denfield,	181
Downs,	340
Dundee,	142
Eastland,	143
Eckhardsheim,	170
Elijah,	277
Galena,	100, 210
Geer,	208, 294
Greenport,	263
Hagar,	195
Hardy,	280
Hartford,	104
Hawes,	351
Heber,	192, 206
Hummel,	266
Huntington,	69, 209
Hymn,	65, 212
Invitation,	68, 152
Lucy,	196
Manoah,	128, 260
Marlow,	84
Mear,	374
Medfield,	113
Naomi,	252
Naumann,	349

O Saviour Dear,	382
Oakville,	318
Peterboro',	314
Reo,	225
Rhine,	352
Sheldon,	60
St. Ann's,	62
St. Martin's,	107, 315
Stephens,	83, 278
Sweetland,	288
Through the Valley,	380
Warwick,	53, 293
Williams,	92, 120
Woodstock,	204, 350

S. M.

Adrian,	284
Aspiration,	132
Boylston,	285, 306
Burton,	172
Calm,	241, 271
Dana,	243
Dawn,	154, 331
Denton,	276
Dennis,	334
Gorton,	335
Greenwood,	263
Haverhill,	341
Haydn,	140, 214
Inverness,	215
Laban,	264
Leighton,	58
Lisbon,	59
Olmutz,	188, 295
Pentonville,	95
Pilgrim Song,	258, 308
Sebastian,	171
Serene,	155
Silver St.,	96
St. Bride's,	242
St. Michael's,	310
St. Thomas,	217
Thatcher,	122
Thompson,	141
Underwood,	66
Watchman,	159

Metrical Index of Tunes.

7s.

Beulah,	354
Ambrose,	157
Benevento,	361
Carver St.,	261
Cassel,	300
Dallas,	268
Dies Irae,	344
Dorman,	302
Elyria,	131
Goodman,	102, 275
Grace (six lines),	228
Harvest Home,	308
Hatton,	248, 339
Holley,	67
Horton,	156, 247
Lent,	180
Litany,	177, 238
Mercy,	174
Milton,	101, 110
Newton (six lines),	52
Nuremburg,	119, 301, 365
Pleyel's Hymn,	63, 287
Rock of Ages (six lines),	239
Rosefield (six lines),	153, 297
Seymour,	246
Spanish Hymn,	216
Still-Waters,	230
Telemann's Chant,	317
Veni Sancte Spiritus (six lines),	130
Waldo,	227
Watchman, tell us,	316
Weber,	286

8s. & 7s.

Autumn,	231
Beautiful River,	379
Bloom,	336
Gardner,	100
Pond,	378
Rathbun,	222, 296
Salem,	291
South Church,	175
St. Denys,	115
Stockwell,	158, 232
Vesper,	73
Wilmot,	111
Wilson,	176
Zamora,	244

8s., 7s., & 4s.

Brest,	346
Greenville,	159
Hamden,	259, 321
Pond,	229
Sicily,	75, 125
Zion,	320

H. M.

Michael,	55, 109
Newman,	133
Warsaw,	146

C. L. M.

How Calm and Beautiful,	123

C. P. M.

Ariel,	57, 221
Meribah,	179, 345

L. P. M.

Nashville,	81
Hullah,	226

S. H. M.

Montgomery,	338

S. P. M.

Dalston,	56

6s.

Great Shepherd of the,	376
Shepherd Call,	181
Webster,	251

6s. & 4s.

America,	372
Ava,	163
Bethany,	240
Italian Hymn,	134
Olivet,	235
The Saviour's Call,	161

6s. & 5s.

Come to Me,	381
Jesus, Tender Saviour,	377

7s. & 6s.

Altar,	178
Amsterdam,	357
Germania,	237
Missionary Hymn,	322
Munich,	356
O Sacred Head,	236
Stand up for Jesus,	319
Sojourner's Song,	260
Webb,	49, 323

8s. & 5s.

Brastow,	160

10s.

Ernan,	304
Eventide,	74

11s.

Frederick,	337
Looking Off,	254
Portuguese Hymn,	255
Robinson,	256
Though Faint yet Pursuing,	257

11s. & 10s.

Comfort,	249
Lyons,	99
Rodman,	108

12s.

Scotland,	162

12s. & 8s.

When the Harvest is past,	181

P. M.

Beautiful River,	379
Behold the Lamb of God,	114
Calvary,	182
Come to Me,	361
Come, ye Disconsolate,	161
Ever Thine, Only Thine,	220
Flee as a Bird,	363
Gentle Call,	163
Gentle Shepherd,	376
Glory to Jesus,	377
Great Shepherd of the Sheep,	376
In Memoriam,	353
Jesus Most Holy,	180
Jesus Tender Saviour,	377
Luther's Tune,	187
Mt. Blanc,	262
Penitence,	173
Parting Song,	71
Through the Valley,	380
Will not that Joyful be,	262

www.ingramcontent.com/pod-product-compliance
Lightning Source LLC
Chambersburg PA
CBHW050846300426
44111CB00010B/1154